Modern Marketing Thought

SECOND EDITION

J. Howard Westing
Professor of Business
University of Wisconsin

Gerald Albaum
Associate Professor of Marketing
University of Oregon

THE MACMILLAN COMPANY
COLLIER-MACMILLAN LIMITED, LONDON

To Margaret and Carol

Third Printing, 1970

Earlier edition © copyright 1964 by The Macmillan Company.

Library of Congress catalog card number: 69–17106

THE MACMILLAN COMPANY
COLLIER-MACMILLAN CANADA, LTD., TORONTO, ONTARIO

Printed in the United States of America

Preface

Books of readings in the field of marketing continue to be published in great variety and with increasing frequency. Therefore, one should have a clearly defined purpose if he adds to this proliferating list.

If the reader will review recent volumes, he will find that most of them have a specialized and limited objective. For example, one may be designed to reflect the most recent theory in the field; another may be planned to demonstrate how mathematical and statistical techniques can be applied to marketing; a third may emphasize the managerial aspects of marketing; and still another may relate the behavioral sciences to marketing. These are all appropriate objectives, but such anthologies are not books of readings in the sense in which that term was used originally —excerpts from the literature intended to illustrate and illuminate textbook material. We believe that there still is a need for such a book for marketing instructors who desire to expose their students to a variety of points of view on everyday marketing subjects in a convenient and economical form. *Modern Marketing Thought* has that purpose as its objective.

As in the first edition, the organization of this book reflects the concept that marketing managers are involved continually in adapting their firms to the economic, social, and political environment within which they operate. The divisions of the book, however, have been made intentionally broad enough to be readily adaptable to any approach the instructor may take to the subject. An introductory paragraph has been added to each article to give the reader some background against which to evaluate the article, and at this point we may have been guilty of injecting our own prejudices and ideas. Even so, we hope these comments will be useful in stimulating discussion and in pointing out controversial material, of which there is much in the readings.

There are countless articles available from a myriad of sources. In selecting the limited number of readings to be included in this second edition, we have had to be somewhat arbitrary, and many good articles had to be omitted for lack of space. Over three fourths of the articles did not appear in the first edition. The present selection can be defended only on the grounds that these were the articles that appealed most to us, from the point of view of reader interest. Some articles have been overlooked, and certainly more good articles will appear in the future. We shall appreciate having these called to our attention in order that, in subsequent editions, this collection may represent more points of view.

We wish to express our sincere thanks to the many authors without whom, obviously, this book would have been impossible.

J. H. W.

G. A.

Contents

III

The Structure of Distribution

IV

Environmental Forces

A. Competition

B. The Government

V

The Marketing Mix

D. Marketing Communications

E. Price Determination and Administration

F. Channels of Distribution

VI

Special Areas

A. Industrial Marketing

B. Risk Management

C. Marketing of Services

VII

International Marketing

VIII

Management Science in Marketing

IX

Postscript

I

Introduction

1

Make Your Company Marketing Conscious

John E. Wakefield

This article deals with an approach to marketing often called the marketing concept. This concept represents a radically new approach to marketing which has evolved during the past twenty years as business has discovered that it cannot succeed by selling customers products and services that are not well designed to serve them. There have come to be so many things competing for the customer's money and time that a successful marketer today must plan his entire business to please the increasingly jaded taste of the customer.

"What is marketing?

"How should we go about using it—and why?"

These questions were recently put to me by the president of a medium-sized manufacturing company. I hear them frequently these days. Apparently, many chief executives have become interested in marketing, done a bit of investigating and found themselves thoroughly confused.

One of the major sources of confusion is the number and variety of definitions of marketing. For example, Peter Drucker, the well-known business writer, defines it as "the entire business as seen from the point of view of the customer." Theodore Levitt, professor of marketing at the Harvard Business School, says, "Marketing focuses on the need of the buyer. Selling focuses on the need of the seller."

Reprinted by permission from *Business Management*, October 1965, pp. 82–84. Copyright 1965 by Management Magazines, Inc.

The American Management Association defines marketing as "the identification or creation of customer needs, and then the motivation and coordinated use of all functions within a business that can fill those needs with benefit to buyer and seller." And the American Marketing Association calls it "the performance of business activities that direct the flow of goods and services from producer to consumer or user."

In just these four definitions of marketing, which represent only a few of those current, there are obviously wide differences of meaning and, therefore, plenty of room for confusion. More important than the differences, however, are the similarities.

A State of Mind

Almost all of the definitions contain such phrases as "the point of view of the customer," "the need of the buyer," and "customer needs." In other words, marketing is a state of mind that recognizes the importance of: *defining the customers a company wants to serve and the needs it wants to satisfy; knowing all that can reasonably be learned about those customers; and using this knowledge in the conduct of the business.*

Before examining this state of mind, let's look at all the functions marketing encompasses. Then, we'll see what top management must do to keep its company conscious of its customers.

Marketing's subfunctions are nine in number. They include:

Market research. This activity is concerned primarily with getting to know the customer—his habits and methods of doing business, his needs and wants, and his capacity to pay for the satisfaction of these needs and wants. In short, it seeks to supply top management with knowledge of its customers that it could otherwise obtain only through intimate personal association.

Product management. It is marketing's responsibility to initiate ideas for new products or services and to suggest changes in or arrange for elimination of obsolete and unprofitable products. The marketing department must make its recommendations on the basis of information it has obtained through market research and all other possible sources.

Pricing. Market research finds out what customers are willing to pay for satisfaction of their needs or solutions to their problems. So the person who has over-all responsibility for marketing should have considerable influence on the prices of his company's products or services. These prices must be set not only in terms of the company's costs and profit objectives, but even more in terms of what the market and competition will permit.

Sales planning and policy. Determining how to reach and persuade customers is an important part of marketing. Thus, whoever holds the top marketing post

in a company should have a major voice in top management councils.

Sales forecasts, quotas, budgets and controls. This is the control and record-keeping side of the marketing function. What is the company going to sell—in volume, in product mix, in types of customers? What should be the goals of its salesmen and sales units? What expense is permissible in light of the desired sales volume? What can be done to improve the efforts of the sales force?

Sales organization, training and compensation. How should the company's sales power be organized to take advantage of what market research has learned about the company's customers? How many salesmen should there be? Where located? How supported? Answers to these questions will help determine how the salesmen are trained and paid.

Advertising and sales promotion. Advertising and sales promotion communicate with the customer, stating what has been done to satisfy his needs and how it is proposed to satisfy them further.

Selling. All other marketing subfunctions are performed mainly to increase the effectiveness of this one. In most businesses it is the personal communication of one person to another that accomplishes the desired result.

Customer service. This subfunction embraces a variety of activities—processing the customer's orders, answering his questions and, in general, making sure that he is served in a satisfactory fashion.

What the President Must Do

To ensure that a fully effective marketing job is done, the chief executive must take the lead. This is vital to success. Many companies fail to get the most out of marketing because their presidents give it only lip service. Here's what the chief executive must do to put marketing to work in his company:

1. Adopt a Marketing State of Mind. Marketing can be delegated to a subordinate, but a marketing state of mind cannot. You have to acquire it yourself before it will be reflected in your subordinates.

What is this state of mind? It does not involve an assumption that the customer is always right. He isn't. In fact, he often doesn't fully understand his own real needs. But it does involve the assumption that the customer is always important.

2. Define Your Business. Determine the customers you wish to serve and the needs you intend to satisfy. This isn't as easy as it sounds. It may take a lot of time, effort and conversation before you and your subordinates fully realize what business you are in and what kind of customers you should have.

For example, there's quite a difference between manufacturing batteries and producing portable packaged power. Similarly, providing surface finishes is substantially different from paint manufacturing.

3. Allocate Responsibilities. Determine how the many subfunctions of marketing should be carried out in your company and how they can be coordinated. This will depend on the nature of your business and its size and diversity.

If your company is small, you may want to manage the marketing function yourself. But don't do this unless you can keep in close touch with your customers and closely supervise the various marketing subfunctions described earlier.

If your company is of moderate size and centralized, marketing may be delegated to a competent marketing executive. Be sure you include him in top

management councils, and be guided by the information he passes along from customers.

If the company is large and widely diversified, you'll probably need line marketing executives in each division, plus a staff marketing coordinator in the corporate group.

Whatever your situation, make certain that all the marketing subfunctions are clearly defined and that someone is directly responsible for their fulfillment.

4. Develop a Marketing Plan. Your marketing plan should include a statement of your over-all objectives, policies and plans. It should go into considerable detail on the following matters:

- Background information on your markets—number and types of accounts, their location, economic factors, competition, market trends and the like.
- Identification of major problem areas and obstacles to be overcome, plus opportunities to be exploited.
- Specific objectives for a predetermined period.
- Detailed plans for each major product or service.
- Strategies and techniques to be employed in carrying out the program.

5. Indoctrinate Key People. If your company is to be really marketing oriented, a marketing state of mind must permeate the entire organization. This means your financial, manufacturing and other executives must be indoctrinated, too.

Your marketing executive can be most helpful in acquainting others in the company with marketing and its subfunctions. But he cannot do the job successfully without the backing and help of the chief executive officer. It takes a president's authority, knowledge and enthusiasm to get the job done properly. There are several other ways to indoctrinate key people in marketing. One of the best is through seminars and courses at the American Management Association, the National Industrial Conference Board and similar groups. For example, the A.M.A. holds seminars on marketing for nonmarketing executives.

Why It's Important

Why should your company adopt a marketing state of mind?

The main reason is that you will lose ground to competitors if you don't. Isn't it apparent that the company that selects its customers carefully and knows the most about their needs, desires and habits is going to be the most successful? Isn't it also apparent that the company that fails to adopt a marketing state of mind and follow its dictates, is going to lose out to companies that do?

Take this case in point. A manufacturer of electric motors had consistently failed to obtain business from a manufacturer of electrical appliances. Finally, in an effort to get to the bottom of the matter, the motor manufacturer's vice president-marketing went to see the appliance manufacturer's vice president-purchasing. It didn't take long to find the trouble.

"Your salesman," said the vice president-purchasing, "talks only about quality. But that's not what we need. The motors you're talking about must go into a moderately priced line of record players, and our customers just won't pay a higher price than we've established. What we need is adequate quality at an acceptable price."

The failure of this company to design motors to meet its customer's need is a typical example of why industrial concerns need modern marketing. Once the need was fully understood, the company was able to modify its motors and get the business.

This story illustrates the main point. Marketing is a customer consciousness that permeates the thinking of all key people in the company. Without it, no company can adequately coordinate marketing's various subfunctions. And if these are not properly handled, the company will neither grow nor prosper.

2

Marketing's Role in Company Growth

Alfred C. Viebranz

The "marketing concept" has not received easy and widespread acceptance in business. Historically, business has been oriented toward production rather than marketing. Production orientation was the proper way to maximize profits when demand exceeded supply, and it has been difficult for many managers to shift orientation when supply exceeded demand.

This article is an attempt by one businessman to explain the new environment and its significance to other businessmen.

Since the turn of the century, businessmen have proclaimed the customer as the reason for their existence. Posters were, and still are, printed to remind employees of this fact. But in the past, much of management's thinking was introspective. The concern was, "What is right for the factory in terms of cost and production efficiency?" The customer was usually a distributor, agent, or dealer, but rarely the actual end user. The technique was to plan a long economic production run and load up the middleman.

The monumental work of Frederick Taylor, acknowledged as the "Father of Scientific Management," directed the attention of management to the financial and manufacturing considerations of running a business. There was nothing wrong with this thinking, but little consideration was directed to the needs of the end user. Planning based on a competitive edge derived from the end user's interpretation of value, both economic and psychological, was in short supply. The typical channels of distribution were regarded as the end of the line—they *were* the market. Redistribution was the exclusive problem of the wholesaler or dealer and of little concern to the manufacturer.

The elements of more effective marketing have existed for a long time. We see evidence of the concept, as we know it today, throughout our industrial history. Although Henry Ford was a mechanical genius, the core of his achievement was the conviction that the American public

From *Business Topics*, Winter 1967, pp. 45–49. Reprinted by permission of the publisher, the Bureau of Business and Economic Research, Division of Research, Graduate School of Business Administration, Michigan State University.

needed a serviceable low-priced car. Up until that time, the automobile was the toy of the more affluent element of our society. His conviction became reality and revolutionized the American economy and our way of life.

During the past twenty years, we have witnessed a reversal of conditions that existed during the prior quarter of a century. Our technological advances during World War II put a renewed velocity on research, which made old ways of doing things obsolete; as worker income rose, manufacturers continued their drive to greater and more efficient production. New products started to pour forth to satisfy increases in consumer spending power. Investment money was available so that young aggressive businessmen could jump into the competitive swim.

Within this outpouring of capability, increasing attention was directed to the consumer. The companies that embraced this consumer-oriented viewpoint became so impressed with the results that the familiar phrase "the marketing concept" was coined.

Establishing the Marketing Department

It is an American business phenomenon that every time a new management function is recognized, progressive companies tend to "climb on the bandwagon." New organizational units are created and charged with the responsibility for developing the function. In the early fifties it was the marketing department. Books and articles like Ted Levitt's "Marketing Myopia" appeared to reassure management on their decision, and from within the sales organization the marketing function was born. As evidence of this, 86 percent of the men in marketing management have come up through sales. But establishing a department or juggling titles is little assurance that significant change will take place.

The problem remained, and to some extent still remains, of giving marketing the recognition and authority that top management accords the functions of manufacturing and accounting. Long experience in manufacturing and accounting had established standard practices that proved workable in the past. There was an aura of tangibility in existing procedure. To induce change within an organization was and continues to be difficult.

Although the organization charts were neatly drawn, internal resistance to operational change existed. The sales manager cast in his new role was burning the midnight oil trying to refine his approach. He had difficulty grasping the magnitude of his decisions and the necessity of integrating his planning with the other more established functions within the company. To his associates in management, his image remained that of the fellow concerned only with achieving a sales quota.

Lack of Precision

Adding to the resistance to change is marketing's lack of precision as compared to the physical and mathematical sciences. The engineering-trained manager is accustomed to the established laws of mathematics or physics. He can refer to tables that define structural strength of metal or the electrical properties of matter. He can utilize formulas that can predict a solution with high accuracy.

Marketing decisions are based of necessity on such abstractions as population growth, share of market, discretionary spending power, and the subtleties of social, legislative, or cultural change.

Information may be only 75 percent correct even if the best marketing research is used. Yet the 75 percent figure may be all that is needed to get the job done.

From Art to Science

Until we started to refine the responsibility and authority of the marketing function, it was regarded as an art form. The decision-maker was viewed as a man with a gift of prophecy. When he was right, he was made a vice president; when he was wrong, he started to get his résumé together.

The complex and intricate elements involved challenged the most astute of marketing minds. Let us consider a few of the major elements involved in marketing decisions:

1. To a major corporation, the consumers are so varied and out of direct control of the seller that he must rely on a variety of persuasive techniques to get the action he seeks. Yet persuasion can never be 100 percent applicable to all people at all times.
2. Within the marketing mix, the seller has at his command and must use a combination of devices and methods to affect the end user he is trying to persuade.
3. As I have indicated, economic and social conditions are continually changing both at the national and local levels.
4. In addition, the position of the Justice Department in Washington is to make certain that a competitive business environment is maintained. Our free economy gives the consumer a choice of the product or company he desires to deal with. Within this framework, competition's goal is to outmaneuver you at both the technological and marketing levels. This may cause you to scrap months of planning and in-

vestment before it comes to fruition.

5. For the most part, the American consumer lives comfortably above his physical need. Now we must contend not only with rival products but compete for consumer discretionary spending power —(buy a new Color TV or a new bedroom set).

6. The profusion of "me too" products puts a premium on market penetration and persuasiveness in selling. Technological duplication also has an inhibiting effect on a company's efforts to grow as planned.

7. The scramble for channels of distribution using a composite of wholesalers, original equipment manufacturers, direct dealers, or national accounts can start pyramiding to an extent that you may wind up competing with your own customer.

8. Multidivisional corporations, under decentralization, can duplicate market effort by having four or five salesmen selling in compatible markets, and often to the same customer.

9. Heavy capital investment coupled with high fixed cost provides more opportunity for small business to find a market dissatisfied with traditional product lines or services. This is the large company's Achilles' Heel.

These are just a few of the complex variables that keep marketing men awake at night. Furthermore, if we consider the degree a company is locked in on long-term commitments required by automated plants, labor contracts, basic research, and multimillion dollar advertising campaigns, we are compelled to embrace a more scientific approach that affords us the measurement and controls necessary. The magnitude of a major marketing mistake in today's environment can impose such a serious financial burden that a business may go under or, at best, take several years to recover.

Today's market planning has taken on a new meaning. We, at Sylvania, are constantly updating marketing information methods. We are improving the measurement and control systems that analyze past experience and appraise present facts in order to sharpen future decisions. . . .

Technological Change

It is obvious that any company with growth aspirations must have a strong R & D or technological base. New product development has given rise to the cry, "innovate or perish." This expression is valid, but the task facing a growth company is the integration, exploitation, and control of this capability within the marketing function. I have seen more than one alleged engineering breakthrough where the throttle was full open before anyone bothered to ask where, to whom, and how are we going to sell this product? By the same token, companies spin their wheels in product redesign which attempts to produce obsolescence without adding to the value or function performed by the product. In the latter case, sales and advertising are left with the frustrating problem of trying to make like products seem unalike.

In addition, we see evidence of companies that resist change to a new technology or product concept introduced by a competitor. On many occasions these companies could have gotten in on the ground floor but preferred to fight a losing battle before the verdict in the market place compelled them to make a change.

A review of the ranking changes of the leading 100 manufacturing companies over the past twenty years can prove some of these points. The ones that have dropped down can be seen as digging in for a defensive battle against more vigorous competitors. Many of these situations can be traced back to businesses that conceived their obligation to the market place too narrowly.

One marketing objective is not only to increase sales by depriving historic competitors of market position that is already firmly established, but to direct the application of research and insight to the task of creating new markets—indeed, new businesses. When this occurs, management has fully embraced the marketing concept.

Innovation

A good example of technological innovation geared to market needs can be found in the photographic industry. Much of the average camera fan's buying motivation is based on the pride or nostalgia that's reflected in the end result—the finished photograph. Major advertising campaigns have been based on the theme "memories fade but pictures live forever."

The threat to the photographic manufacturer is the discouragement a camera owner feels from poor results. If he decides that photography is too complex or poor pictures are an expensive investment, he will put his camera on a shelf and forget it. In the past, cameras, films, and flash equipment presented a mishmash of inconvenience and confusion. Flash equipment was bulky, exposure settings were complicated, the average housewife couldn't load the film. These were but a few of the consumers' irritations.

Innovations introduced in the latest cameras have eliminated most of these problems. We now have simplified methods that provide foolproof film loading and automatic camera operation.

Originally, flash was the tool of the professional. The equipment was cumbersome, and the typical flash bulb was the size of a 100 watt light bulb. We long recognized that photography could become a 24-hour, 12-month-a-year hobby for a mass market of amateur camera owners. At the outset, design modifications were made, but the inconvenience of bulk remained. The flash unit's not being an integral part of the camera added to the problem. Often it was more convenient to carry the camera and leave flash unit and bulbs behind.

Today we see the results of the consumer-oriented product design approach. The flash unit is built into the camera with no additional bulk. Wherever the camera goes, the flash unit goes also. This past year Sylvania introduced with frightening sales success the "Flashcube," a multiple flash bulb not much larger than a lump of sugar. Now the camera fan can take four flash pictures in sequence, eliminating the inconvenience of changing bulbs. The consumer can now carry a complete supply of "Flashcubes" in his pocket, when at the outset he needed an overnight bag. I cite this as a marketing approach in expanding an established market.

Now growth through product development is essential, but we must consider other objectives. Profit is not a dirty word when weighed against survival. Profit takes on a different shading within an aggressively oriented marketing company. Considerable investment is plowed back into the business in the form of R & D, plant, equipment and training. This commitment is designed for *future* profit based on the marketing plan.

But industry's fervor to add new products and markets can take on the semblance of the California gold rush. As new products are introduced, new categories of customers come forth, new applications compete with the old, and the product lines multiply like a hutch of rabbits. Under these conditions the motto seems to be "Forfeit Nothing." I can appreciate the sales advantage of a complete product line, but this must be assessed against sales potential and competitive market entrenchment. In addition, a company must weigh its present and future capabilities from a technological, production, and manpower viewpoint. Through this approach we can avoid the profit erosion caused by "product line clutter" and "organizational clutter."

Profit contribution of product lines must be viewed against the backdrop of future profit and market potential. Some hard nosed thinking must be directed against an attitude of trying to be all things to all people. More times than not, a sharp pruning knife can be a most profitable long-range instrument. Peter Drucker in his book, *The Practice of Management,* hit this point right on the head by saying, "Management has to manage and managing isn't just passive, adoptive behavior; it means taking action to make the desired results come to pass."

If companies were more objective in admitting their mistakes or analyzing some of the losing battles they are fighting, a great deal of needless investment could be directed into more profitable channels.

Marketing Leadership

With students of marketing, I don't expect much argument with the concepts I have presented, but the marketing function has one final dimension. This is the catalytic action supplied in the chemistry of leadership. There are many organizational departments within a business that are essential to growth, but marketing remains the sole revenue producing activity. In accepting this responsibility, marketing management cannot forfeit its leadership role. Although titles can confer authority, respect for marketing's role must come through leadership, and marketing management must earn this respect.

We have all seen, especially in the sports world, an organization that looked great on paper but was never able to play together well enough to win the top award. What was lacking was the leadership cohesiveness and momentum found in the desire to achieve a common goal.

Marketing management faces the challenge of setting the leadership pace for the entire organization. It must supply direction and inspiration to R & D in its product function; it must intelligently assess marketing risk and recommend future financial commitments for the controller's function; and manufacturing looks to marketing management for guidance and advice in production activities. In effect, marketing is charged with charting the future course a company must take. If this course is vague, devious, or indecisive, there will be few followers.

We recognize that calculated risk is an integral part of marketing management's leadership function. I question if marketing will ever become an exact "science." There remains a vital need for sound judgment and intellectual courage. Marketing management must have the guts to take action when scientific planning has led it as far as it can and, in effect, says, "Now you know how much you don't know." This judgment is where a marketing manager earns his salary.

Leadership must be self-generating. Often getting a plan off the ground is more important than making certain everything is accurate to the fifth decimal point. But marketing leadership must steer a wary course between emotional drive and sound thinking. At this point we must also consider the importance of an accurate sense of timing. The difference between good leadership and poor may be that the latter makes its move at the wrong time, sometimes too early, but more often too late.

The essence of the marketing function is creativity. Marketing management must supply the vision of what the company might be, the role it will play, and the results the company seeks. This type of leader cannot languish in the euphoria of complacency or become so preoccupied with administrative trivia that the operation is functioning on a day-to-day basis. The kind of leadership I have in mind isn't content merely to wait for new trends. It must, rather, keep its imagination vividly alive so as to originate ideas and start trends. If the marketing leaders within a company can't get aroused, if they don't recognize problems and chafe in the anticipation of their solution, then the infectious spirit that fuels desire and creativity within an organization will be dissipated.

Effective leadership is the most nebulous commodity of human endeavor—there will always be a place in marketing for men who can supply it.

3

Marketing Myopia

Theodore Levitt

Contrary to superficial appearances, there is no such thing as a growth industry. There are only companies that capitalize on growth opportunities. Many companies, and even entire industries, presently are in a state in which their growth is threatened, slowed, or stopped. The reason is not market saturation, but management stagnation. As Levitt points out, companies must be willing and able to adapt themselves to the requirements of the market. This will be facilitated if management thinks of itself as a buyer of customers rather than a producer of goods and services.

Every major industry was once a growth industry. But some that are now riding a wave of growth enthusiasm are very much in the shadow of decline. Others which are thought of as seasoned growth industries have actually stopped growing. In every case the reason growth is threatened, slowed, or stopped is *not* because the market is saturated. It is because there has been a failure of management.

Abridged from *Harvard Business Review*, July-August, 1960, Vol. 38, no. 4, pp. 45 ff., by special permission.

Fateful Purposes

The failure is at the top. The executives responsible for it, in the last analysis, are those who deal with broad aims and policies. Thus:

The railroads did not stop growing because the need for passenger and freight transportation declined. That grew. The railroads are in trouble today not because the need was filled by others (cars, trucks, airplanes, even telephones), but because it was *not* filled by the railroads themselves. They let others take customers away from them because they assumed themselves to be in the railroad business rather than in the transportation business. The reason they defined their industry wrong was because they were railroad-oriented instead of transportation-oriented; they were product-oriented instead of customer-oriented.

Hollywood barely escaped being totally ravished by television. Actually, all the established film companies went through drastic reorganizations. Some simply disappeared. All of them got into trouble not because of TV's inroads but because of their own myopia. As with the railroads, Hollywood defined its business incorrectly. It thought it was in the movie business when it was actually in the entertainment business. "Movies" implied a specific, limited product. This produced a fatuous contentment which from the beginning led producers to view TV as a threat. Hollywood scorned and rejected TV when it should have welcomed it as an opportunity—an opportunity to expand the entertainment business.

Today TV is a bigger business than the old narrowly defined movie business ever was. Had Hollywood been customer-oriented (providing entertainment), rather than product-oriented (making movies), would it have gone through the fiscal purgatory that it did? I doubt it. What ultimately saved Hollywood and accounted for its recent resurgence was the wave of new young writers, producers, and directors whose previous successes in television had decimated the old movie companies and toppled the big movie moguls.

There are other less obvious examples of industries that have been and are now endangering their futures by improperly defining their purposes. I shall discuss some in detail later and analyze the kind of policies that lead to trouble. Right now it may help to show what a thoroughly customer-oriented management *can* do to keep a growth industry growing, even after the obvious opportunities have been exhausted; and here there are two examples that have been around for a long time. They are nylon and glass—specifically, E. I. duPont de Nemours & Company and Corning Glass Works:

Both companies have great technical competence. Their product orientation is unquestioned. But this alone does not explain their success. After all, who was more pridefully product-oriented and product-conscious than the erstwhile New England textile companies that have been so thoroughly massacred? The DuPonts and the Cornings have succeeded not primarily because of their product or research orientation but because they have been thoroughly customer-oriented also. It is constant watchfulness for opportunities to apply their technical know-how to the creation of customer-satisfying uses which accounts for their prodigious output of successful new products. Without a very sophisticated eye on the customer, most of their new products might have been wrong, their sales methods useless.

Aluminum has also continued to be a growth industry, thanks to the efforts of two wartime-created companies which deliberately set about creating new customer-satisfying uses. Without Kaiser Aluminum & Chemical Corporation and Reynolds Metals Company, the total demand for aluminum today would be vastly less than it is.

Error of Analysis

Some may argue that it is foolish to set the railroads off against aluminum or the movies off against glass. Are not aluminum and glass naturally so versatile that the industries are bound to have more growth opportunities than the railroads and movies? This view commits precisely the error I have been talking about. It defines an industry, or a product, or a cluster of know-how so narrowly as to guarantee its premature senescence. When we mention "railroads," we should make sure we mean "transportation." As transporters, the railroads still have a good chance for very considerable growth. They are not limited to the railroad business as such (though in my opinion rail transportation is potentially a much stronger transportation medium than is generally believed).

What the railroads lack is not opportunity, but some of the same managerial imaginativeness and audacity that made them great. Even an amateur like Jacques Barzun can see what is lacking when he says:

> I grieve to see the most advanced physical and social organization of the last century go down in shabby disgrace for lack of the same comprehensive imagination that built it up. [What is lacking is] the will of the companies to survive and to satisfy the public by inventiveness and skill.[1]

Shadow of Obsolescence

It is impossible to mention a single major industry that did not at one time qualify for the magic appellation of "growth industry." In each case its assumed strength lay in the apparently unchallenged superiority of its product. There appeared to be no effective substitute for it. It was itself a runaway substitute for the product it so triumphantly replaced. Yet one after another of these celebrated industries has come under a shadow. Let us look briefly at a few more of them, this time taking

[1] Jacques Barzun, "Trains and the Mind of Man," *Holiday*, February, 1960, p. 21.

examples that have so far received a little less attention:

DRY CLEANING . . . This was once a growth industry with lavish prospects. In an age of wool garments, imagine being finally able to get them safely and easily clean. The boom was on.

Yet here we are 30 years after the boom started and the industry is in trouble. Where has the competition come from? From a better way of cleaning? No. It has come from synthetic fibers and chemical additives that have cut the need for dry cleaning. But this is only the beginning. Lurking in the wings and ready to make chemical dry cleaning totally obsolescent is that powerful magician, ultrasonics.

ELECTRIC UTILITIES . . . This is another one of those supposedly "no-substitute" products that has been enthroned on a pedestal of invincible growth. When the incandescent lamp came along, kerosene lights were finished. Later the water wheel and the steam engine were cut to ribbons by the flexibility, reliability, simplicity, and just plain easy availability of electric motors. The prosperity of electric utilities continues to wax extravagant as the home is converted into a museum of electric gadgetry. How can anybody miss by investing in utilities, with no competition, nothing but growth ahead?

But a second look is not quite so comforting. A score of nonutility companies are well advanced toward developing a powerful chemical fuel cell which could sit in some hidden closet of every home silently ticking off electric power. The electric lines that vulgarize so many neighborhoods will be eliminated. So will the endless demolition of streets and service interruptions during storms. Also on the horizon is solar energy, again pioneered by nonutility companies.

Who says that the utilities have no competition? They may be natural monopolies now, but tomorrow they may be natural deaths. To avoid this prospect, they too will have to develop fuel cells, solar energy, and other power sources. To survive, they themselves will have to plot the obsolescence of what now produces their livelihood.

GROCERY STORES . . . Many people find it hard to realize that there ever was a thriving establishment known as the "corner grocery store." The supermarket has taken over with a powerful effectiveness. Yet the big food chains of the 1930's narrowly escaped being completely wiped out by the aggressive expansion of independent supermarkets. The first genuine supermarket was opened in 1930, in Jamaica, Long Island. By 1933 supermarkets were thriving in California, Ohio, Pennsylvania, and elsewhere. Yet the established chains pompously ignored them. When they chose to notice them, it was with such derisive descriptions as "cheapy," "horse-and-buggy," "cracker-barrel storekeeping," and "unethical opportunists."

The executive of one big chain announced at the time that he found it "hard to believe that people will drive for miles to shop for foods and sacrifice the personal service chains have perfected and to which Mrs. Consumer is accustomed."[2] As late as 1936, the National Wholesale Grocers convention and the New Jersey Retail Grocers Association said there was nothing to fear. They said that the supers' narrow appeal to the price buyer limited the size of their market. They had to draw from miles around. When imitators came, there would be wholesale liquidations as volume fell. The current high sales of the supers was said to be partly due to their novelty. Basically people wanted convenient neighborhood gro-

[2] For more details see M. M. Zimmerman, *The Super Market: A Revolution in Distribution.* New York: McGraw-Hill Book Company, Inc., 1955, p. 48.

cers. If the neighborhood stores "cooperate with their suppliers, pay attention to their costs, and improve their service," they would be able to weather the competition until it blew over.[3]

It never blew over. The chains discovered that survival required going into the supermarket business. This meant the wholesale destruction of their huge investments in corner store sites and in established distribution and merchandising methods. The companies with "the courage of their convictions" resolutely stuck to the corner store philosophy. They kept their pride but lost their shirts.

Self-deceiving Cycle

But memories are short. For example, it is hard for people who today confidently hail the twin messiahs of electronics and chemicals to see how things could possibly go wrong with these galloping industries. They probably also cannot see how a reasonably sensible businessman could be as myopic as the famous Boston millionaire who 50 years ago unintentionally sentenced his heirs to poverty by stipulating that his entire estate be forever invested exclusively in electric streetcar securities. His posthumous declaration, "There will always be a big demand for efficient urban transportation," is no consolation to his heirs who sustain life by pumping gasoline at automobile filling stations.

Yet, in a casual survey I recently took among a group of intelligent business executives, nearly half agreed that it would be hard to hurt their heirs by tying their estates forever to the electronics industry. When I then confronted them with the Boston streetcar example, they chorused unanimously, "That's different!" But is it? Is not the basic situation identical?

[3] *Ibid.,* pp. 45–47.

In truth, *there is no such thing* as a growth industry, I believe. There are only companies organized and operated to create and capitalize on growth opportunities. Industries that assume themselves to be riding some automatic growth escalator invariably descend into stagnation. The history of every dead and dying "growth" industry shows a self-deceiving cycle of bountiful expansion and undetected decay. There are four conditions which usually guarantee this cycle:

1. The belief that growth is assured by an expanding and more affluent population.
2. The belief that there is no competitive substitute for the industry's major product.
3. Too much faith in mass production and in the advantages of rapidly declining unit costs as output rises.
4. Preoccupation with a product that lends itself to carefully controlled scientific experimentation, improvement, and manufacturing cost reduction.

Population Myth

The belief that profits are assured by an expanding and more affluent population is dear to the heart of every industry. It takes the edge off the apprehensions everybody understandably feels about the future. If consumers are multiplying and also buying more of your product or service, you can face the future with considerably more comfort than if the market is shrinking. An expanding market keeps the manufacturer from having to think very hard or imaginatively. If thinking is an intellectual response to a problem, then the absence of a problem leads to the absence of thinking. If your product has an automatically expanding market, then you will not give much thought to how to expand it.

Production Pressures

Mass-production industries are impelled by a great drive to produce all they can. The prospect of steeply declining unit costs as output rises is more than most companies can usually resist. The profit possibilities look spectacular. All effort focuses on production. The result is that marketing gets neglected.

John Kenneth Galbraith contends that just the opposite occurs.[4] Output is so prodigious that all effort concentrates on trying to get rid of it. He says this accounts for singing commercials, desecration of the countryside with advertising signs, and other wasteful and vulgar practices. Galbraith has a finger on something real, but he misses the strategic point. Mass production does indeed generate great pressure to "move" the product. But what usually gets emphasized is selling, not marketing. Marketing, being a more sophisticated and complex process, gets ignored.

The difference between marketing and selling is more than semantic. Selling focuses on the needs of the seller, marketing on the needs of the buyer. Selling is preoccupied with the seller's need to convert his product into cash; marketing with the idea of satisfying the needs of the customer by means of the product and the whole cluster of things associated with creating, delivering, and finally consuming it.

In some industries the enticements of full mass production have been so powerful that for many years top management in effect has told the sales departments, "You get rid of it; we'll worry about profits." By contrast, a

[4] *The Affluent Society*. Boston: Houghton Mifflin Company, 1958, pp. 152–160.

truly marketing-minded firm tries to create value-satisfying goods and services that consumers will want to buy. What it offers for sale includes not only the generic product or service, but also how it is made available to the customer, in what form, when, under what conditions, and at what terms of trade. Most important, what it offers for sale is determined not by the seller but by the buyer. The seller takes his cues from the buyer in such a way that the product becomes a consequence of the marketing effort, not vice versa.

Product Provincialism

The tantalizing profit possibilities of low unit production costs may be the most seriously self-deceiving attitude that can afflict a company, particularly a "growth" company where an apparently assured expansion of demand already tends to undermine a proper concern for the importance of marketing and the customer.

The usual result of this narrow preoccupation with so-called concrete matters is that instead of growing, the industry declines. It usually means that the product fails to adapt to the constantly changing patterns of consumer needs and tastes, to new and modified marketing institutions and practices, or to product developments in competing or complementary industries. The industry has its eyes so firmly on its own specific product that it does not see how it is being made obsolete.

The classical example of this is the buggy whip industry. No amount of product improvement could stave off its death sentence. But had the industry defined itself as being in the transportation business rather than the buggy whip business, it might have survived. It would have done what survival always entails, that is, changing. Even if it had only

defined its business as providing a stimulant or catalyst to an energy source, it might have survived by becoming a manufacturer of, say, fanbelts or air cleaners.

Beginning and End

The view that an industry is a customer-satisfying process, not a goods-producing process, is vital for all businessmen to understand. An industry begins with the customer and his needs, not with a patent, a raw material, or a selling skill. Given the customer's needs, the industry develops backwards, first concerning itself with the physical *delivery* of customer satisfactions. Then it moves back further to *creating* the things by which these satisfactions are in part achieved. How these materials are created is a matter of indifference to the customer, hence the particular form of manufacturing, processing, or what-have-you cannot be considered as a vital aspect of the industry. Finally, the industry moves back still further to *finding* the raw materials necessary for making its products.

The irony of some industries oriented toward technical research and development is that the scientists who occupy the high executive positions are totally unscientific when it comes to defining their companies' over-all needs and purposes. They violate the first two rules of the scientific methods—being aware of and defining their companies' problems, and then developing testable hypotheses about solving them. They are scientific only about the convenient things, such as laboratory and product experiments. The reason that the customer (and the satisfaction of his deepest needs) is not considered as being "the problem" is not because there is any certain belief that no such problem exists, but because an organizational lifetime has conditioned management to look in the opposite direction. Marketing is a stepchild.

I do not mean that selling is ignored. Far from it. But selling, again, is not marketing. As already pointed out, selling concerns itself with the tricks and techniques of getting people to exchange their cash for your product. It is not concerned with the values that the exchange is all about. And it does not, as marketing invariably does, view the entire business process as consisting of a tightly integrated effort to discover, create, arouse, and satisfy customer needs. The customer is somebody "out there" who, with proper cunning, can be separated from his loose change.

Actually, not even selling gets much attention in some technologically minded firms. Because there is a virtually guaranteed market for the abundant flow of their new product, they do not actually know what a real market is. It is as if they lived in a planned economy, moving their products routinely from factory to retail outlet. Their successful concentration on products tends to convince them of the soundness of what they have been doing, and they fail to see the gathering clouds over the market.

Conclusion

Less than 75 years ago American railroads enjoyed a fierce loyalty among astute Wall Streeters. European monarchs invested in them heavily. Eternal wealth was thought to be the benediction for anybody who could scrape a few thousand dollars together to put into rail stocks. No other form of transportation could compete with the railroads in speed, flexibility, durability, economy, and growth potentials. As Jacques Barzun put it, "By the turn of the century it was an institution, an image of man,

a tradition, a code of honor, a source of poetry, a nursery of boyhood desires, a sublimest of toys, and the most solemn machine—next to the funeral hearse—that marks the epochs in man's life."[5]

Even after the advent of automobiles, trucks, and airplanes, the railroad tycoons remained imperturbably self-confident. If you had told them 60 years ago that in 30 years they would be flat on their backs, broke, and pleading for government subsidies, they would have thought you totally demented. Such a future was simply not considered possible. It was not even a discussable subject, or an askable question, or a matter which any sane person would consider worth speculating about. The very thought was insane. Yet a lot of insane notions now have matter-of-fact acceptance—for example, the idea of 100-ton tubes of metal moving smoothly through the air 20,000 feet above the earth, loaded with 100 sane and solid citizens casually drinking martinis—and they have dealt cruel blows to the railroads.

What specifically must other companies do to avoid this fate? What does customer orientation involve? These questions have in part been answered by the preceding examples and analysis. It would take another article to show in detail what is required for specific industries. In any case, it should be obvious that building an effective customer-oriented company involves far more than good intentions or promotional tricks; it involves profound matters of human organization and leadership. For the present, let me merely suggest what appear to be some general requirements.

Visceral Feel of Greatness

Obviously the company has to do what survival demands. It has to adapt

[5] *Op. cit.*, p. 20.

to the requirements of the market, and it has to do it sooner rather than later. But mere survival is a so-so aspiration. Anybody can survive in some way or other, even the skid-row bum. The trick is to survive gallantly, to feel the surging impulse of commercial mastery; not just to experience the sweet smell of success, but to have the visceral feel of entrepreneurial greatness.

No organization can achieve greatness without a vigorous leader who is driven onward by his own pulsating *will to succeed*. He has to have a vision of grandeur, a vision that can produce eager followers in vast numbers. In business, the followers are the customers. To produce these customers, the entire corporation must be viewed as a customer-creating and customer-satisfying organism. Management must think of itself not as producing products but as providing customer-creating value satisfactions. It must push this idea (and everything it means and requires) into every nook and cranny of the organization. It has to do this continuously and with the kind of flair that excites and stimulates the people in it. Otherwise, the company will be merely a series of pigeonholed parts, with no consolidating sense of purpose or direction.

In short, the organization must learn to think of itself not as producing goods or services but as *buying customers*, as doing the things that will make people *want* to do business with it. And the chief executive himself has the inescapable responsibility for creating this environment, this viewpoint, this attitude, this aspiration. He himself must set the company's style, its direction, and its goals. This means he has to know precisely where he himself wants to go, and to make sure the whole organization is enthusiastically aware of where that is. This is a first requisite of leadership, for *unless he knows where he is going, any road will take him there.*

If any road is okay, the chief executive might as well pack his attaché case and go fishing. If an organization does not know or care where it is going, it does not need to advertise that fact with a ceremonial figurehead. Everybody will notice it soon enough.

The Consumer

4

Welcome to the Consumption Community

Daniel J. Boorstin

From the beginning of time man has struggled to achieve the bare necessities of life. For the first time, through technology and effective organization, the United States (and other countries with varying degrees of lag) has reached the point where its standard of living is restricted less by the production of goods than it is by such things as the distribution of income, the knowledge of what to make to please the consumer, the ability to educate the consumer to new ways of doing things and a growing uncertainty on the part of the consumer concerning the desirability of more material things. This situation makes for a new kind of economic environment—one to which business has not yet adjusted. The following article deals with some of these points.

People tell us we are a *rich* nation. And that what distinguishes us is our *high* standard of living. But an Old World vocabulary conceals what is most radically distinctive about our material well-being. It is not that we are well off; there have been rich nations before us. It is not that we have a *high* standard of living. What is different is our very notion of a standard of living, and our New World way of thinking about and consuming material goods.

The movement from the Old World to the New was a movement from an ancient and traditional view of wealth to

Condensed from *Fortune*, Sept. 1967. Copyright 1967 Daniel J. Boorstin. This essay originally appeared in *Fortune*, September 1967, and will be developed in the 3rd vol. of the author's interpretive history of American civilization entitled *The Americans: The World Experience*, to be published by Random House, Inc.

the new view that goes by the name of the standard of living. "Wealth," which was at the center of English mercantilist economic thinking before the American Revolution, was a static notion. The wealth of the world, which was measured primarily in gold and silver, was supposed to be a fixed quantity. It was a pie that could be sliced one way or another. But the size of the pie could not be substantially increased. A bigger slice for Great Britain meant a smaller slice for France or Spain or somebody else, and one nation's gain was another's loss.

The New World changed that way of thinking. People who came to live here came to better their lot in the world, to improve their "way of life." They sought opportunities to rise, to get better land, to think and speak freely, to move, to worship, to secure more education, to grow. By contrast with that of the Old World,

America bred a vaguer and much more expansive view of the material world.

The American Revolution itself was among other things a struggle between two different concepts of wealth. Britain stood for the older, more rigid view of wealth. Autarky—economic self-sufficiency—was the ideal of national power. But this way of thinking was uncongenial to the New World. The indefinite expanse of a half-known and temperate continent opened unimagined possibilities for nearly everybody. "Strangers are welcome," Franklin explained in his *Information to Those Who Would Remove to America* (published in 1782), "because there is room enough for them all, and therefore the old inhabitants are not jealous of them."

Americans were not merely struggling for their slice of the pie, every day they were actually making the pie bigger. The indefinite expansibility of material wealth was an American axiom, never abandoned. The Old World's notions about what was material well-being, what was worth fighting about were becoming obsolete.

In the Old World poverty was one of the inescapable facts of life. Those who wished to justify God's design even said that poverty was not without its social benefits, since it made charity possible. The American view was different. The advantages of poverty, Andrew Carnegie explained in 1891, were mainly to provide the conditions for young men to rise in the world and become wealthy. The ideal self-made man was the man who rose, not at the expense of others, but while building new communities where others would flourish. The slogans of "The New Freedom," "The New Deal," "The New Frontier," and "The Great Society" have carried these hopes forward into the twentieth century.

With this novel, vague, and expansive view of material well-being came a new way of talking about the wealth of the society. This new view was *communitarian*. Its focus was not on riches but on the way of life, not on the individual but on the community. Or, rather, on many novel kinds of communities. One of these, which came to dominate the twentieth century, was the byproduct of innovation in manufacturing and distributing things. To it I give the name "Consumption Community." A Consumption Community is held together by much thinner, more temporary ties than those that bound earlier Americans. It does not replace earlier kinds of communities. But it draws together in novel ways people who would not otherwise have been drawn together—people who do not share ideology, who are not voyaging together on the prairie or building new towns. It is a hallmark of American life today.

A Consumption Community consists of people who have a feeling of shared well-being, shared risks, common interests, and common concerns that come from consuming the same kinds of objects. It can be the community of Scotch drinkers who rally to the J & B brand, of three-button-suit wearers, of Chevrolet sports-car drivers, of super-king-sized cigarette smokers, or of Doublemint gum chewers. As the advertisers of nationally branded and nationally advertised products we are joining a special group—the Dodge Rebellion, the Pepsi Generation, those who throw in their lot with Avis because it is only No. 2. And each of us eagerly joins many such groups. Yet we are slow to admit that buying these products and services actually puts us into novel—extremely attenuated, yet characteristically American—communities.

We remain imprisoned in an old-fashioned vocabulary. We still talk as if we were back in the world of the gunsmith who made his gun to suit a particular customer, in the days when nearly everybody wore home-made clothing and the few who wore store-boughten suits patronized a custom tailor. The world of the consumer and the experience of the consumer have not yet been given the dignity of "community." We readily speak of religious communities and political communities, but we have not yet learned to think of the consumer as belonging to communities or to speak of Consumption Communities.

The Man in the Store-Boughten Suit

Consumption Communities could not come into being until there were large numbers of objects being made that were, from the consumer's point of view, indistinguishable from one another. So long as a man purchased his gun from his own gunsmith, who had made the object for him alone, his use and enjoyment of his gun could not tie him to very many other people. Every gun—like other custom-made objects, such as suits or shoes—was designed partly by the buyer, and then made by the craftsman to the buyer's specifications. But when Whitney or Colt or a large manufacturing concern in Springfield began making guns, and making them in standard models by the thousands, every buyer of a Whitney or a Colt or a Springfield was risking his money (and sometimes, too, his life) with many others. American industry prospered on more and more ways of making precisely similar objects.

The needs of a large army in the Civil War produced masses of similar items, and after the war the new way of making things created the early Consumption Communities. The great development of factory-made shoes and clothing was partly a result of that war. Before the Civil War it was widely assumed that well-fitting clothes could not be manufactured in large quantities since

everybody was supposed to be a different size. But makers of uniforms found that, among large numbers of men, certain sizes recurred in a regular way; this laid the foundation for a science of "anthropometry." By the time of the publication in 1880 of Daniel Edward Ryan's *Human Proportions in Growth: Being the Complete Measurement of the Human Body for Every Age and Size During the Years of Juvenile Growth,* the factory-made clothing industry was on its way. For the first time in modern history it became possible for thousands of men of all social classes to wear clothing of the same design, cut, and manufacture, coming from a central factory. Before the end of the nineteenth century all but a small proportion of American men were wearing store-boughten clothing.

The making of large numbers of similar objects gradually extended to all items of consumption. Cigarettes, which until the later nineteenth century had been mostly hand-made, were now rolling off speedy new machines that, by the 1930's, were producing about 150 billion per year. Foods, soft drinks, and gadgets of all kinds were soon available in identical forms and in quantities that by the early twentieth century had dominated the lives of most Americans. And the supreme achievement of precise mass production was, of course, the automobile, which soon became the omnipresent symbol of American Consumption Communities. By the third decade of the century, the house that a man lived in, together with antiques and certain art works (and the land that he lived on), was almost the only object that had not become fungible—readily replaced in the market by others that were indistinguishable.

This capacity to produce millions of similar objects was necessary to the creation of Consumption Communities. But it was not enough. Community requires a *consciousness* of community. And at the same time, in the century after the Civil War, there grew in America new institutions that made men and women aware of their membership in Consumption Communities. Two large developments brought the new consciousness into being.

First came the retailing revolution. Its two principal novel agents were the department store and the mail-order house. Before the middle of the nineteenth century, city dwellers bought their goods from numerous specialized shops, each offering a relatively small stock of one kind of commodity—drygoods, hardware, groceries, crockery, or tableware. Then, in 1846, A. T. Stewart in New York City pioneered with his Marble Dry-Goods Palace at Broadway and Chambers Street. He gave a hint of the vastness and grandeur of the new retailing enterprises with his new eight-story building in 1862, which became famous as Stewart's Cast Iron Palace. Others, too— R. H. Macy in New York, John Wanamaker in Philadelphia and New York, Marshall Field and Carson Pirie Scott in Chicago, and many more —combined their pioneering in large-scale retailing with pioneering in architecture. They opened new perspectives to the entering customer—long vistas of appealing merchandise, and numerous clusters of buyers, shoppers, and just lookers. These were displayed not in the motley disorder of a country fair, but as the common offering of a single great enterprise. A buyer at Stewart's or Macy's or Wanamaker's was not simply putting his confidence in the integrity of a particular shopkeeper. He was joining a large community of consumers, all of whom put their confidence (and their cash) in the same large firm. When the one-price system, popularized by R. H. Macy, took the place of the ancient custom of haggling, buyers more than ever were sharing their confidence in the merchant.

A Common Iconography in the Catalogue

What the department store was to the city dweller, the mail-order house was to the farmer. Montgomery Ward, which had begun only in 1872, issued a catalogue for 1884 that numbered 240 pages and listed over 10,000 items. Sears, Roebuck & Co., which had started as a one-man mail-order watch business in 1886, was grossing over $50 million by 1907, selling every shape and size of merchandise. In that year catalogue circulation already exceeded three million. The Ward and Sears catalogues, full of vivid illustrations (soon printed in color, in the development of which the mail-order houses were pioneers), opened the outside world to many lonely farm families. Thousands wrote in for personal advice. Buyers from the catalogue were putting their confidence in a firm located in a far-off city. It was no accident that the catalogue came to be called "the farmer's Bible." Men remote from one another found in their Sears catalogue a common iconography. They were tied together somehow by their common involvement in the large community of Sears customers.

At the same time there grew nationwide chains of poor man's department stores, 5-and-10-cent stores selling thousands of standardized small items. The customers of F. W. Woolworth shared the belief that these items could nowhere be bought more cheaply, and that they were good value for the money. This expanding confidence of the growing community of 5-and-10 customers within a few decades built what was at that time the highest building in the U.S.

People who shopped at Stewart's, Macy's, Wanamaker's, or Marshall Field's or who mailed in their orders to Ward or Sears, could see and feel that they had entered a new community of consumers. But another new force was reaching out into the city and the country, tying other groups of consumers together. It used the pages of newspapers and magazines, the painted sides of barns, signs along the road, trolley cars and buses and commuter trains, and ultimately smoke writing in the sky, and words and music and images on the airwaves of radio and television. Before the middle of the twentieth century empty spaces everywhere were being filled with words and pictures, and the channels were crammed with words and music and pictures—designed to enlist new consumers into new Consumption Communities, and to keep old customers loyal to the Consumption Communities they had joined. This new force was, of course, advertising.

Nothing can be more misleading than to describe advertising as "salesmanship in words." True enough, advertising aims to sell. But salesmanship is aimed at the individual consumer, advertising at *groups* of consumers. Since the nineteenth century these groups have become larger and larger.

Salesmanship and Advertising Differ

There are crucial differences between selling a single buyer and creating a community of buyers. Different arguments become effective and different satisfactions are received by everyone concerned. The primary argument of the salesman is personal and private: this hat is perfect for *you* (singular). The primary argument of the advertisement is public and general: this hat is perfect for *you* (plural). The salesman is effective when he persuades the customer that the item is peculiarly suited to his unique needs. The advertisement is effective when it persuades groups of buyers that the item is well suited to the needs of all persons in the group. The salesman's focus is on the individual; he succeeds when he manages, cajoles, flatters, and overwhelms the ego. The advertisement's focus is on some group; it succeeds when it discovers, defines, and persuades persons who can be brought into that community of consumers.

A buyer who gives in to a salesman has satisfied his ego. But a consumer who is persuaded by an advertisement is also yielding to his desire or willingness to be counted in a group—a community of consumers. An advertisement is, in fact, a form of insurance to the consumer that by buying this commodity, by smoking this brand of cigarette, or driving this make of car he will not find himself alone. The larger the advertising campaign, the more widespread and the more effective, the more the campaign itself offers a kind of communitarian seal of approval. Surely a million customers can't be wrong! An advertisement, then, is a kind of announcement that, in the well-informed judgment of experts, some kind of Consumption Community probably exists. Won't you join?

Too much of the discussion of advertising has treated it as simply another form of salesmanship. Estimates of its social value have centered around its cost as a selling device, its relation to planned obsolescence and to other aspects of production. We must begin to realize that Consumption Communities actually offer many of the satisfactions that were once associated only with other kinds of groups.

A Bond for Americans

In its primary sense, a "community" was a group of people living together, under all the same conditions of life. In origin it appears to have come from the Latin *com* (together) plus the Latin *munus* (service, office, function, or duty)—hence meaning persons who paid taxes together or worked together. By extension it came to mean persons held together by some one common interest or concern, generally political or religious. In its primary sense, as in the New England community, or the New York community, or the plantation community, it meant persons who lived in geographic proximity. But it has also come to mean any group (the business community, the Catholic community, the Negro community, the Jewish community, the teen-age community, the suburban community) aware of its common characteristic, and somehow held together, even though its members do not necessarily live close to one another. Those groups, which we commonly call "communities," show the following characteristics: (1) people are aware of their membership in the group and are aware that the membership gives them some common interests or concerns. (2) people are more or less free to enter or leave the community (if only by emigration), (3) people show more or less loyalty to some common object.

The peculiar importance of Consumption Communities in recent America helps us to understand how it has been possible here to assimilate—to "Americanize"—the many millions who have come within the last century and a half. Consumption Communities helped hold together as Americans people who in the older world would have been bound mainly by distinction of class, ideology, or ancestry.

Here are some of the peculiarities of Consumption Communities—by contrast with other kinds of communities.

Consumption Community is quick. It takes generations to become an Englishman, one can never become a Frenchman. But, through joining Consumption Communities, it has been easy for immigrants to become Americans. In his *Rise of David Levinsky,* Abraham Cahan recounts how Jewish immigrants who arrived in New York City in the 1880's, feeling uneasily foreign, became quickly Americanized by buying ready-made clothes, by getting an American haircut, and by purchasing all kinds of small commodities, which were the signs of being a genuine American. The shrewd F. W. Woolworth, expanding his chain of 5-and-10-cent stores in the 1890's, consciously directed them toward this market of the newly arrived who wanted to buy like Americans.

Consumption Community is non-ideological. No profession of faith, no credo or orthodoxy, no ritual is required to join a Consumption Community. With only a few exceptions (now mostly having to do with housing), people of all races, beliefs, and religious and political creeds can join. And therefore:

Consumption Community is democratic. This is the great American democracy of cash, which so exasperates the aristocrats of all older worlds. Consumption Communities generally welcome people of all races, ancestry, occupations, and income levels, provided they have the price of admission. The boss and the worker both own a Westinghouse washer and both drive a Mustang.

The Consumption Community is even more democratic than many a "democratic" political community. English law reformers used to say, "British justice, like the Ritz Hotel, is open to Rich and Poor alike." To secure a room in the Ritz, or in other de luxe London accommodations, though, you needed not only to have enough money but also to be a "gentleman" and to be a member of the right race. The struggle for "civil rights" in the U.S. has been in large part a struggle for the right to consume—a struggle to enlarge and complete the democracy of consumption. The purpose of the public-accommodation provisions of the Civil Rights Acts is to ensure that the Ritz Hotel and all other hotels, motels, and restaurants are open to whoever has the money.

People who want to protest against this peculiarly indiscriminate American democracy can do so only by underconsumption. It is possible, although increasingly inconvenient, to stay out of even the largest Consumption Communities. Latter-day Boston Brahmins must strain for exclusiveness by refusing to own an automobile or a television set. I have one such acquaintance who has the hardiness not to have a telephone—on the pretext that he is waiting for it to be perfected! The democracy of cash, even with all its present limitations in America, is probably one of the most real and present and unadulterated democracies in history.

Consumption Communities tend to become the model of all other communities. All experience tends to be treated more and more like the experience of consuming. It becomes the right of all citizens not merely to consume whatever they can afford to buy, but to consume it in the presence of (and in community with) all others who can afford to buy it. And of course we use advertising to create and strengthen old-style communities—communities of believers, religious and political.

The growth of Consumption Communities has signaled a transformation of the attitude to all material goods. By contrast with the rigid, Old World notion of wealth, the New World idea of standard of living has had certain obvious characteristics. I will mention only two.

Standard of living is public. It is possible to be rich in secret. A man can hide his treasure in a vault, in his garden, in a mattress. "If rich, it is easy enough to conceal your wealth," an Englishman wrote in 1820; "it is less difficult to hide a thousand guineas than a hole in your coat." It is not possible to have a high standard of living in secret.

Well-being Goes on Display

The word "standard" (which comes into English from the Old French *estandard*, "banner") means a symbol that is displayed for all to see. Its very function is to be seen, to inform as much as to affirm. A standard of living, then, is a publicly seen and known measure of how people do live, and of how they should live.

The willingness of Americans to display their material well-being is rooted deep in our history. The fact that our homes front upon the street (and not inward to a court as did the middle-class homes of French and Spanish colonists), and that the symbols of urban residential comfort here are not the wall or the fence but the broad, open front lawn and the front porch—these are clues from small-town America of the last century. In mid-twentieth century, the Oldsmobile, Cadillac, or Continental conspicuously parked in front of the house offers new opportunities to display the well-being of the residents. But the Americans' willingness to display their prosperity on the façades of their homes, in their picture windows, on their lawns, and in the parking places in front of their houses is by no means universal. Americans who travel the Continent of Europe are sometimes shocked at the shabby exterior of the dwellings of well-to-do families of the middle class. The ancient institution of the tax farmer, who could estimate his exactions by the wealth displayed, put a premium on the ability to seem impecunious.

Because a high standard of living is a public fact, it becomes a public benefit. You can become rich without my becoming richer. But it is hard for *you* to have a high standard of living without incidentally raising mine. The rich classes of India, protected by their eight-foot stone walls, can enjoy luxury. They do not really have a high standard of living in the American sense so long as the squalor outside their walls threatens them with crime and disease. If, in addition to your material goods, your standard of living includes your freedom from threat of crime or disease, your education, the education of your children, the air you breathe, the water you drink, the roads you drive on, the public transportation system you use, your peace of mind—then does it not inevitably include *my* opportunities and the opportunities of my children for education (in the institutions you support), the air *I* breathe, the water *I* drink, the roads *I* drive on, the public transportation *I* use, and *my* freedom from threat of crime or disease?

Standard of living is pervasive, reciprocal, and communal. This plainly follows. Wealth is by definition what a man *possesses*. Property is what is "proper" to a person, peculiar or special to him. How obvious, then, that the wealth of some should explain the poverty of others. "The pleasures of the rich," wrote the Englishman Thomas Fuller in 1732, "are bought with the tears of the poor."

But standard of living is what a man *shares*. One man's standard of living cannot be sharply separated from that of others. Each person is part of everyone else's standard of living. *You* are my environment. And my environment is my standard of living. In a society that lives by a standard of living, no man is an island, for every man is part of every

other man's standard of living. In a wealth society your gain is my loss; in a standard-of-living society your gain is my gain. If you live healthily I am less likely to catch a disease. If you and others are educated and content, the crime rate declines, and that improves my standard of living. By the wealth idea, one man is poor because another man is rich; by a standard of living, one man is poor because another is poor.

It is no wonder, then, that in the mid-twentieth century, when, as never before, we are dominated by concern for our standard of living, we should give a central place to education. For the education of my neighbors, we assume, improves my human environment, and hence raises my standard of living. To build a public school may not increase my wealth; it is likely to affect my standard of living. The 1954 integration decision of the Supreme Court was based on the assumption that a standard of living is pervasive, reciprocal, and communal. It was not enough that Negroes should have access to similar instruction, or to private instruction. Equality in a standard-of-living society meant the right to be educated together with and in the presence of other Americans. The opportunities that had historically been given to white Americans could themselves benefit the Negro—but only if he received his education along with them, and in their presence.

Although standard of living is somehow a measure, and a public measure, it is necessarily vague. Wealth can be specifically and precisely defined and weighed, but standard of living has no boundaries. It includes everything in our experience—the production and distribution systems that help us acquire material goods, the climate, the air we breathe, the water we drink, our access to the woods, the richness of our thoughts, the sensitivity of our feelings, and our peace of mind.

The very notion of standard of living is cosmopolitan and universalizing. Just as the Old World mercantilist idea of wealth (essentially treasure) drove toward autarky and competition among nations, so the American idea of standard of living drive us toward cooperation and world community. In the long run, our ability to raise our American standard of living will depend on our ability to remove the menaces to our health and peace of body and mind, which come from the dissatisfactions and lack of satisfactions of men anywhere.

The Sharing Experience

In the eighteenth century, nations believing the mercantilist dogma organized their laws and commerce to prevent other nations from acquiring their knowhow. Jefferson had to smuggle rice seeds out of France and Italy. The plans for the first weaving machines had to be illegally exported from England; it was unlawful for a skilled workman to leave the country. By contrast, in the twentieth century the Marshall plan, Point IV, and other aid programs express our belief that peace and prosperity may depend on our ability to raise the standard of living of others. What could more dramatically express our belief in the communal character of material wellbeing?

It is misleading, then, to think of "conspicuous consumption" as a pathological expression of the oddities of the rich or the perverse. In the U.S. in the mid-twentieth century nearly all consumption has become conspicuous. Private consumption is the phenomenon of wealth societies. Ours is a standard-of-living society. How otherwise than by public consumption can one signal his membership in Consumption Communities? We learn how to consume, how to join these communities, by seeing how others consume. Advertisers seek to inform us of Consumption Communities and to persuade us to join them. Each of us informs other consumers of our loyalty to these Consumption Communities simply by showing how we consume. The sharing experience that comes to groups of us because we consume the same brands, comes to all of us because we share a standard of living.

To speak of American "materialism" is, then, both an understatement and a misstatement. The material goods that historically have been the symbols which elsewhere separated men from one another have become, under American conditions, symbols which hold men together. From the moment of our rising in the morning, the breakfast food we eat, the coffee we drink, the automobile we drive to work—all these and nearly everything we consume becomes a thin, but not negligible, bond with thousands of other Americans.

When the impoverished cannot afford to consume like others they are not merely deprived—they are excluded. They become outsiders because they are not linked by bonds that unite other Americans.

Consumption Communities, both by their strengths and by their weaknesses, reveal to us peculiar features of American life in our time. Older forms of community—of nation and of religion—of course still continue to bind men together. But the distinctive twentieth-century form of community evolved in modern America is the Consumption Community—measured and displayed in a standard of living.

The New Fellowships

Modern American life, if we count Consumption Communities among its permanent features, is characterized by new communities far more numerous and far less intense than those of earlier ages. Many—even most—are communities of men and women not in one another's presence. They are diffused and dispersed over the country. Of course these communities are milder, less exclusive and less intense than those that held men together in an early New England Puritan village, in a westward-moving wagon train, in the Chicago of 1840.

But the communities of Winston smokers and Mustang drivers—or, more broadly, of cigarette smokers and sportscar owners—are nonetheless communities. Their members recognize one another, and share their illusions, hopes, and disappointments. These illusions, hopes, and disappointments are, to be sure, trivial beside those of the Visible

Saints of the Massachusetts Bay Colony. But while the seventeenth-century New Englanders were members of only a few communities, the twentieth-century American is a member of countless communities.

The modern American is tied—by the thinnest of threads, perhaps, and by the most volatile, switchable loyalties—to thousands of other Americans by nearly everything he eats or drinks, or wears, or reads, or uses. Old-fashioned political communities and religious communities themselves now become only two among many new, but once unimagined, fellowships. We are held to other men, not only by a few iron bonds, but by countless gossamer webs tying together the trivia of our lives every day.

Consumer Protection Via Increased Information

Louis L. Stern

Economic theory assumes that the buyer and seller meet in the marketplace on roughly equal terms and that, as a result of a balanced bargaining process, they arrive at an equitable conclusion. With the growing complexity of goods and sophisticated communications devices the advantage in the bargaining process has shifted toward the seller. A satisfactory balance must be restored if the public is to retain its faith in the marketplace mechanism. It may well take some measure of government intervention to achieve this end. The question is whether the government should make decisions for the consumer or merely make sure that the consumer has enough information to make an intelligent decision for himself. This article argues for the latter approach.

Reprinted from the *Journal of Marketing*, national quarterly publication of the American Marketing Association, Vol. 31, No. 2, April 1967, pp. 48–52.

What about consumer protection?

The great concern of businessmen about recent demands for consumer protection is indicated by the establishment of: (1) a consumer-information service by the National Association of Manufacturers, known as Techniques in Product Selection (TIPS); and (2) a program of cooperation between the Association of Better Business Bureaus and federal departments and agencies that affect consumer-business relationships.

Although the NAM and ABBB programs may be public-relations efforts to mollify demands for consumer protection, nevertheless their creation reflects businessmen's concern that, "Unless business moves to organize some communication apparatus, it will soon be confronted with a benevolent, bureaucratic structure that will take over such functions."[1]

Nor is such concern unfounded. Consider recent proposals to establish an Office or Department of Consumers, and for the federal government to engage in "Consumers Union" types of product-evaluation and reporting. Is it madness to speculate that the precedents set by the Drug Amendments of 1962 (1962) and the "fair labeling and packaging" bill might lead to proposals for a "fair advertising" law?

Probably no other Congress ever faced as many consumer-protection proposals as the 89th. Even the U.S. Supreme Court showed an interest in consumer protection, as evidenced by its handling of the Rapid Shave case.[2]

Other signs of increasing government interest in consumer protection include:

1. Completion by Congress, the Food and Drug Administration, the National Commission on Food Marketing, and the Consumer Advisory Council of voluminous reports relating to consumer protection

2. Establishment of a special division within the U.S. Department of Agriculture to handle the Department's labeling programs

3. Establishment by the Office of Economic Opportunity of an experimental program of consumer education

4. Within the Federal Trade Commission, setting up of a new office of federal-state cooperation; new studies of consumer-goods marketing practices; and new trade-regulation guides and rules pertaining to the marketing of consumer goods.

But perhaps the best indication of the great amount of government interest in consumer protection is the statement of Charles Sweeny, Chief of the FTC's Bureau of Deceptive Practices: "The present Commission is more deeply determined to combat consumer deception than any Commission I have known in my 30 years of service."[3]

Why is there so much interest in consumer protection?

One reason is that rising incomes and a cornucopia of new products has multiplied the number, value, and variety of consumers' market transactions. Therefore, there are far more opportunities for consumer deception than ever before. Furthermore, the mounting variety of consumer products is increasing the competitiveness of our economic system. In turn, this may be leading to a deterioration of business ethics, thus giving rise to added interest in consumer protection.

Yet it is not at all clear that deception in the marketplace has, in fact, increased. What is clear is that the history of the

---

[1] "GF's Cleaves Calls for Food Industry Consumer Information Unit," *Advertising Age*, Vol. 36 (April 19, 1965), p. 16.

[2] Colgate Palmolive Co. v. FTC, 85 S. Ct. 1035.

[3] "Druggist May Be Liable for Brand Copy in His Ads," *Advertising Age*, Vol. 36 (June 7, 1965), pp. 1 and 135, at p. 1.

United States is a record of accumulated social and technological efforts to protect the individual from adversity of every sort. The drive for consumer protection may be viewed as simply a continuation of those efforts.

The Need for Product Information

Do consumers have a right to be informed, as distinct from a right not to be deceived?

Our economic system is based on the belief that free and intelligent decisions in the marketplace, rather than by government fiat, will produce the most efficient allocation of resources toward the achievement of private and social goals. To exercise free and intelligent choices in the marketplace, consumers must have access to terms of sale and product information.

However, it is likely that the loss of personal relationships in the marketplace has reduced both the availability and the reliability of product information.

A second factor contributing to the problem is the rising level of technology. New materials, new operating principles, new functions, new designs, and new packaging have increased the difficulty of choosing one product or brand over another. The growing number of synthetic textiles and textile mixtures with varying prices and performance characteristics amply illustrates this situation.

Because of their usually greater complexity, durable products may reflect more advances in technology than non-durable products. Hence, the problem of adequacy and comprehension of product-performance information may be compounded in the case of durable goods. Furthermore, consumers are less capable of personally evaluating durable products because the long life and varied conditions under which these products are used cloud post-purchase brand comparisons. To make matters even more difficult, the reports of such organizations as *Consumers Union* are quickly rendered obsolete by model changes or model number changes.

A third factor contributing to the problem of adequacy of product information is the language of advertising. From Martineau to Weir, many advertisers and copywriters have preached the sermon of *image*.

In the words of Pierre Martineau, "It is generally insufficient to convince a person on intellectual grounds. His feelings must be involved. And this we achieve by affective or esthetic suggestion and imagery, by the meanings behind the words and pictures."[4]

Consider also the "heretical" words of William D. Tyler, *Advertising Age* columnist: "Most advertising down the years has done little more than say sweet nothings about a product. . . . It has contained the least information, the fewest facts, of almost anything ever written. We have relied mainly on adjectives, on charm, on manner of presentation, coupled with unspecific, unsupported claims of superiority."[5]

The question is how greater disclosure of product and terms-of-sale information can be achieved. The difficulties of attempting to provide greater information to consumers are substantial. The problem of communicating technical information to a non-technical audience, the time and space limitations of the vehicle of communication, and the cost of the time and space used must all be taken into account.

On the other hand, there is the question of *methods*. Will the methods of

[4] Pierre Martineau, *Motivation in Advertising* (New York: McGraw-Hill Book Co., 1957), p. 187.

[5] William D. Tyler, "Is Competitive Comparison Really Bad in Advertising? Reform With Care," *Advertising Age*, Vol. 37 (March 14, 1966), pp. 61–62, at p. 61.

information be voluntary or compulsory? Will they involve standards, labeling requirements, consumer-advisory services, consumer-education programs, or some combination of these?

Voluntary Disclosure

Private industry has made great strides in attempting to provide information to consumers and to forestall government activity. Consider the following:

1. Formation over the years of codes of ethics by various associations in the packaging field.
2. Adoption by the 50th National Conference on Weights and Measures (June, 1965) of a standard for conspicuous labeling, as an amendment to the Model State Regulation Pertaining to Packages. (The new standard defines officially and nationally for the first time what constitutes a "clear and conspicuous" statement of net contents on package labels.)
3. Adoption by the American Standards Association, the National Bureau of Standards, and many other groups of standards for the size, shape, or performance ratings (such as BTU output) of innumerable products and containers.

Government Intervention

Of course, government regulations are sometimes unduly rigid, and create legal hazards for even the conscientious corporate citizen. (For example, the present standard of identity for butter was formulated at the turn of the century and does not permit the addition of emulsifiers or preservatives to butter, an unconscionable shackle to the butter industry's competition with margarine.

Neither does it provide for the addition of vitamins to butter or the continuous-process method of manufacturing butter, both of which are common today.) Nevertheless, even more regulations probably are in prospect.

Terms of Sale

Aside from regulations pertaining to safety or gross misrepresentation, the greatest need for consumer protection is in regard to clarity of terms of sale. The least restrictive measure would require merely a statement of net contents on the package. However, mere knowledge of the weight or quantity of a product is an inadequate basis for intelligent choice; and if the statement of net contents is inconspicuous or the shopper unobservant, not even that much information will be known.

A further level of protection would be to provide for standardization of weights and quantities in which a consumer product may be distributed for retail sale. State laws already provide for standard package sizes for a few stable food products such as bread, butter, margarine, milk, cream, and flour.

Standardization of weights and quantities would provide informational gains to consumers. It would enable many shoppers to compare the price of equivalent amounts of alternative brands. In contrast, indications of price per ounce carried out to several decimal places would be no real improvement, and actually might distract consumers from making price comparisons of total amounts.

Standardization of weights and quantities would also call attention to price increases, which are otherwise hidden from some consumers in the form of a reduction in quantity.

It would be desirable, therefore, to

establish standard weights or quantities in which selected consumer goods might be distributed. Provision for variations from these standards in multiples of 25% of the standard amounts would probably satisfy most consumer preferences for size of unit of purchase.

Establishment of standard weights and quantities might reduce the number of opportunities for using one size and style of container for packaging a variety of products as soup, cracker, and cereal companies now do. Considerable expense would also be involved in adjusting packaging machinery to the new weight or quantity standards. Nevertheless, the long-run advantages to consumers probably would exceed these disadvantages.

A still higher level of restriction, to regulate container sizes and shapes, is not only unnecessary but contrary to consumers' interests. It would severely inhibit package innovation. However, the International Organization for Standardization, whose standards may acquire the effect of law in over 50 member nations, has launched a program to develop retail package size standards that would affect *all* consumer products. Its program could, within a few years, force U.S. manufacturers to adopt similar standards for export purposes.

Standards and Grade-labeling

Compulsory standards of minimum quality or performance can be a useful form of consumer protection where health or safety is involved. Minimum standards can also serve to prevent consumers from being sold grossly inferior products.

Product standards usually impose minimum product requirements. On the other hand, grade-labeling involves an attempt to communicate in one or more symbols the relative quality of a product

as influenced by a variety of characteristics.

Because grade-labeling requires a high degree of agreement as to what constitutes the best combination of product characteristics, its utility is limited to simple products having few attributes. Yet these products tend to be those which consumers are most capable of evaluating themselves. And even for these products, the whirlwind pace of product and package innovation occurring today would present an enormous grade-labeling task.

Furthermore, the effects of grade-labeling upon product research and innovation must also be considered. Grade-labeling would reduce product differentiation and thereby tend to promote price competition. As a result, smaller marketing margins would yield less research-and-development revenues.

Consumer Advisory Services

As proposed by Donald Turner, Chief of the U.S. Justice Department's Antitrust Division, another means of communicating more information to consumers would be for the federal government to evaluate products and publish its evaluations, or to subsidize organizations such as *Consumers Union*.[6] Such publications as *Consumers Bulletin* or *Consumer Reports* provide a source of clear and continuing product information; and their evaluations can be both capsulized and detailed.

On the other hand, their value is limited by their remoteness from the point of purchase. A more serious disadvantage, were they to achieve wide-

[6] "Anti-Trust Chief Urges Alternative to Advertising," *Advertising Age*, Vol. 37 (June 6, 1966), pp. 1 and 147–148, at p. 147.

spread consumer influence, would be the power they would come to possess over the economic fate of individual companies. If the majority of consumers followed their brand recommendations, producers of lower-rated brands would be strongly induced to imitate the preferred brand as closely as possible.

Accordingly, product differentiation might be expected to decrease, and this would be to consumers' disadvantage. Simultaneously, a loss of product differentiation might lead to a reduction in the number of producers, another undesirable effect.

Full Disclosure

"Full disclosure" has a variety of implications. Most commonly, it is assumed to imply disclosure of the dangerous nature of a product. Such laws as the Flammable Fabrics Act (1953), the Hazardous Substances Labeling Act (1960) the Drug Amendments of 1962 (1962), and the Cigarette Labeling Act (1965) already impose this level of meaning.

A second level of meaning would compel disclosure of component ingredients, net contents, and other terms-of sale information, such as interest and related charges. Laws such as the Food, Drug and Cosmetics Act (1938), the Wool Products Labeling Act (1939), the Fur Products Labeling Act (1951), the Textile Fiber Products Identification Act (1958), and the Automobile Information Disclosure Act (1958) are intended to provide legislative mandate for this type of disclosure. Disclosure of component ingredients is primarily useful in relation to determining the healthfulness, safety, value, or performance of a product. Over and above this, compulsion of such disclosure might be interpreted as protection for and responsiveness to

the existence of individual preferences for certain products.

The next higher level of disclosure is the revelation of a product's performance characteristics. To some extent this level of disclosure is implemented voluntarily by manufacturers of above-average quality products who employ rational selling appeals. Horsepower ratings, BTU ratings, and lumber ratings are familiar voluntary disclosures by manufacturers and distributors of performance characteristics. But unfortunately, many voluntary performance descriptions are meaningless or unreliable and sometimes refer to inputs rather than outputs.

Most manufacturers prefer to avoid direct performance statements in favor of evocative expressions or episodes. This is especially likely to be the case where no substantial differences in performance exist among rival brands, because for these products disclosure of meaningful performance information would tend to reduce the apparent differentiation among brands.

The Drug Amendments of 1962 (1962), although passed in the wake of the thalidomide scare and applying to a narrow and emotionally-charged area of consumption, provide a legislative precedent for regulatory agency concern with product performance *even where health or safety are not involved.* Witness the FDA's attempt to require vitamins to be labeled with the statement: ". . . Except for persons with special medical needs, there is no scientific basis for recommending routine use of dietary supplements." A likely outcome of regulations pertaining to *nonperformance* would be regulations pertaining to *degrees* of performance.

As to the question of consumers' abilities to understand performance information, this problem will diminish over time in response to rising levels of education, the enormous capacity of consumers to learn informally, the effectiveness of media in informing consumers, and, most importantly, the challenge to learn presented by the availability of such information.

A still higher level of disclosure pertains to potentially derogatory information unrelated to health, safety, terms of sale, or performance of a product—illustrated by the FTC requirement of disclosure, where applicable, of the foreign origin of a product or component part. Conceivably, the FTC requirement could be extended to include disclosure, where applicable, of ratings by such groups as *Consumers Union,* production by companies not subscribing to voluntary codes of advertising practice, or production by nonunionized labor, etc.

The U.S. Supreme Court decision pertaining to disclosure of use of television mockups falls within this category of compulsory disclosure.[7] The Court took the extreme position that not only misrepresentations, but also deceptive presentations of valid claims, even if necessary to compensate for the technical deficiencies of communications media, are illegal.

Implementation

Note especially that the FTC may be capable of expanding its disclosure requirements without the aid of new legislation. FTC Commissioner Everette MacIntyre has been quite explicit on this matter.[8]

Furthermore, the position taken by the Commissioner is this: "The question . . . is not whether the Commission may declare substantive standards and principles, for it plainly may and must. The

question is whether the Commission may . . . promulgate them only in the course of adjudication."[9]

In the Commission's opinion, it is also free to promulgate them in formal rule-making proceedings.

The issue is whether consumers have expectations of receiving some standard of product performance, say, average for that industry's product. If they do, then failure to disclose the fact that a particular brand is below that standard of expectation would appear to be deceptive. If, in addition, the performance factor in question is material to the consumer's purchase decision, its nondisclosure violates the FTC Act.

The principle that nondisclosure of material information constitutes a misrepresentation is well established in law.[10] Moreover, the U.S. Supreme Court made abundantly clear in the Rapid Shave case that reviewing courts should ordinarily accept the Commission's judgment as to what constitutes deception.[11] ". . . When the Commission finds deception it is also authorized, within the bounds of reason, to infer that the deception will constitute a material factor in a purchaser's decision to buy."[12] Accordingly, the opportunity for the FTC to widen its requirements for full disclosure is clear.

The selection of what additional disclosures should be required is admittedly a difficult administrative decision, particularly so the more complex the product involved.

Nevertheless, a reasonable compromise could be reached whereby certain information would have to be provided with the product, and whereby other,

[7] Same reference as footnote 2.
[8] *The Packaging-Labeling Controls Bill* (Washington, D.C.: Chamber of Commerce of the United States, 1965), p. 14.

[9] Same reference as footnote 8, at p. 18.
[10] P. Lorillard Co. v. FTC, 186 F2d 52; Raladam Co. v. FTC, 283 U.S. 643. But see also Alberty v. FTC, 182 F2d 36, Certiorari denied, 340 U.S. 818.
[11] Same reference as footnote 2 at p. 1043.
[12] Same reference as footnote 2 at p. 1046.

more extensive, information would have to be made readily available on request. Nothing in this proposal would prevent a manufacturer from extolling additional characteristics of his products. Nor does this proposal imply that compulsory disclosures should be included in advertising or in promotion.

In short, this proposal would improve the functioning of the marketplace by increasing the amount of information therein. It would enable consumers to choose products rationally *if* they wished to do so.

In Conclusion

The consumer-protection movement is definitely in the ascendancy. The issue is not whether consumers will be better protected, but what form the protection will take.

Better and more relable product and terms-of-sale information on package labels is perhaps the most economical and least restrictive type of consumer protection. Moreover, *full disclosure* might help to dissuade current demands for additional restrictions on advertising.

The Image of the Consumer in the Year 2000

Nelson N. Foote

Some popular critics of our economy charge it with having surfeited consumers with goods and services. This is a curious criticism because the purpose of an economy is to supply the consumer with goods and services. Although the charge against the economy may be superficial and misdirected, it should not be disregarded because it is based on a developing set of circumstances that is certain to alter drastically the nature of our society and economy. If the success of our economy leads consumers to elect to enjoy higher productivity in the form of leisure rather than physical consumption, we shall face a new challenge in trying to run an economy at half throttle, with the attendant problems of spreading employment and income. In the accompanying article a sociologist looks forward to the time when the constraints upon consumption may be time and learning. He does not deal with the economic problems that this will create.

From the 1963 Report of the Boston Conference on Distribution, pp. 13–18, edited by Stuart L. Mandell, International Marketing Institute, Cambridge, Mass. Reprinted by permission.

. . .Our thesis will be that the propensity to increase consumption is becoming obsolete as a fundamental motive attributed to consumers by people engaged in the distribution of goods.

A person acts toward others not as they are, but as he imagines they are. This image may or may not closely resemble reality; an image once valid may cease to be valid. Whenever a manufacturer or a merchant takes an action toward a consumer, it is premised on his image of what that consumer is like, in particular, his expectation regarding the consumer's wants. The term *image* has many cloudy meanings; here it will mean only the assumption that the consumer who earns more will buy more. Will he, always?

We are about as far from the year 2000 now as we are from the onset of the great depression of the Thirties. During the period since the Twenties, there has been a rapid obsolescence of erstwhile images of the consumer. It is therefore intriguing to wonder what assumptions will oust those on which present practices in distribution are based. Before proceeding either to look critically at assumptions about consumer wants which now prevail, or speculatively at those which might take their place, let us establish the scale of our perspective by looking backward at several which were common in the Twenties.

In the Twenties, the effective majority of citizens felt that the appetite for alcohol should and could be curbed by legal prohibition of its sale. Similarly, in states like Massachusetts, the effective majority still seems to believe that the desire to control family size should and can be foiled by forbidding the sale of contraceptives. Despite the persistenece of these efforts to make the state a censor of taste and morals, few here would deny that change has occurred in the image of human adults which underlies censorship of the kind for which Boston has been known. Citizens in general are nowadays regarded as more capable of exercising their own critical ability in these matters than they used to be. The arguments that persist over what is decent in literature, drama and beachwear revolve mainly around what children should be exposed to, not adults. The image of the consumer of entertainment, in other words, has been upgraded in judgment, independence, and adulthood.

Prior to the depression, it was common sense to suppose that—except for a few invalids—every man possessed the capacity to provide for himself economically; hence, who did not work should not eat. It took a major economic disaster to qualify the assumption that everyone is the author of his own good or bad fortune, and substitute the recognition that everyone participates in an economic system which itself can be judged to work well or badly. The view that the actions of the federal government strongly influence the economic system has been a staple plank in the platforms of politicians of all parties ever since.

The great depression, which terminated a similar long season of prosperity, had the effect of strongly reinforcing the traditional notion of economic activity as the overcoming of scarcity. The ancient image of the consumer has lingered —that of a person permanently in want. According to this image, consumer need is never in doubt, whereas means for satisfying need are always scant and precarious. Whence the classic definition of economics as the study of the allocation of scarce means to unlimited wants. Whence also the very terms *consumer* and *consumption,* suggesting a hungry mouth ingesting food.

Yet the one law on which economists seem to agree is Engel's law—that as household income rises, the proportion expended on food diminishes. This law describes and predicts what actually happens, but for the mass of consumers it does not explain what else they might spend their extra income on. What we see around us as a result of our recent run of prosperity is a society suffering from obesity, in the literal as well as in countless figurative forms. It is a society which has largely emerged from a state of chronic scarcity—in which the given physiological wants were hard to satisfy—into a state in which the satisfaction of these wants could be largely taken for granted.

For lack of a realistically contemporary image of the consumer, both manufacturers and merchants go on re-enacting their old roles toward him—trying to stuff more goods and services into already-satiated stomachs and closets and houses—congesting the stores, congesting the highways, congesting the media of advertising. Fantastically, the staff economist of the largest advertising agency keeps recommending that the only relief possible for this age of stuffing is higher appropriations for advertising to increase the rate of stuffing. It is obviously time to turn to a new image of the consumer.

Professor Galbraith of Harvard, in his attempted diagnosis of the present situation, deplores the advertising agencies on the weakest of all possible grounds, that they are in fact effective in creating new wants. He recommends that the government play a bigger role in stimulating other kinds of consumption, through enhancing socially-supported services such as health, education, research and recreation. Insofar as Professor Galbraith is really interested in the relative capabilities of corporations and government to stimulate higher standards of health, education, research and recreation, I think he underestimates the influence of corporations. Much of the upgrading of household standards of living in these respects has come about because the husband of the family

has first experienced higher standards at work. I am not referring merely to appetites developed through expense accounts. Starting first with managerial ranks but extending rapidly downward to other ranks, the corporation has been teaching its personnel how to use their added income to elevate their standard of living beyond just enrichment of diet and décor—for example, regular physical examinations, refresher courses, conferences, travel. These fringe benefits are becoming each year a larger fraction of total personnel cost. As corporations become increasingly dependent for competitive success on attracting highly qualified technical and professional employees, they enhance the non-salary rewards they offer. Improvements of consumption on the job, however, lose their efficacy as competitors match them, and may be curbed before they begin to pall. The corporation's success in fostering increased consumption of goods —whether as purveyor or employer— thus may still be insufficient to keep up with its success in fostering productivity. By contrast, no ultimate ceiling can be foreseen to raising the intrinsic satisfactions of the work itself. Thus a new image of the consumer-on-the-job would be as timely as a new image of the consumer-off-the-job.

Last year the Chairman of General Electric compared the situation of manufacturing industry with that of agriculture in the United States. Through tremendous infusions of chemical and biological research, the productivity of agriculture has been raised so rapidly that one farmer now supplies almost twenty other people in the labor force with all their food and fiber requirements; even so, agriculture could manage very well with several million fewer people employed on the nation's farms. Over-production, unemployment, excess capacity, price deterioration— these terms seem to characterize agriculture and industry about equally well. For federal farm subsidies, substitute defense contracts for distressed areas, and the analogy becomes almost complete.

Thus our national passion for productivity runs through the primary industries like agriculture and mining and the secondary industries like manufacturing and construction. If we look then beyond the secondary industries to the tertiary industries like transportation and distribution, we see productivity outpacing demand in the very same way. The airlines—our newest form of travel—already worry lest they share the plight of the railroads, any sign of returning health in which brings shudders to the truckers. . . . Merchandising is becoming massively more efficient, through automatic vending, leasing, discounting and a variety of other strategies and tactics.

Each saving in the costs of distribution, like each saving in the costs of production, passed on to the consumer in lower prices, produces some increment in demand as long as some price elasticity remains. In the history of any particular product, however, we observe that price elasticity of demand diminishes with each successive year it is on the market until its curve is almost flat. Faced with this fact, and anxious to keep their output from descending to the status of agricultural commodities, both manufacturers and distributors have tried to combat the entropic trend of price and profit by introducing new products. Despite the shaking out of many individual firms, the inputs of new products have more or less sufficed in the aggregate to keep up with the decline of old products. Already it is evident, however, that the slowness of customers to adopt new products looms as a severe constraint on the expansion of overall demand through innovation. There is a widening

segment of customers whose financial means to acquire new products runs ahead of their readiness to acquire the corollary new habits. Even among customers with a strong appetite for innovation, there is strong resistance to mere gadgets that do not contribute real utility and to devices they fear will make them soft. The widening of their repertoire of wants, moreover, inevitably diminishes their demand for the average item they use. From the standpoint of the manufacturer, even when he has been successful in introducing successive new products, there is real difficulty in collecting the intended benefits of innovation through added sales and profits. Once a new product begins to show market potential, it usually attracts a swarm of imitative competitors seeking to employ their abounding productive capacity. This phenomenon has become so customary—saturation occurs so swiftly —that in the durables field we no longer think of industry sales of a new product as following the classic growth curve. Sales go up steeply to a peak far above the plateau of replacement demand to which they all too quickly descend, and prices come tumbling down with demand, followed in a vicious circle by liquidations and further deterioration.

Just as the armor makers used to try to counter every move of the cannon makers, people in marketing have responded to these assaults on the gains made through introducing new products by efforts to strengthen their franchises with the customers gained. The technology of market defense is becoming as resourceful as the technology of market capture. It is imaginable that, in time, as much effort will be devoted in marketing and merchandising to building permanent relations with old customers as to recruiting new customers. Closer adaptation of manufacturers and merchants to their particular clienteles can prove mutually satisfying. For the seller, the advantage of such loyal relationship may be received in price premiums or in stable repeat demand and consequent savings in distribution costs. For the buyer, such a relationship would let him take consumption even more for granted than now and turn his attention to other activities.

It has been commonplace since the great depression to complain of hunger in the midst of agricultural surplus. Surplus agricultural commodities are still being distributed in vast quantities by the government to the poor both in the United States and abroad. So far this lot has not befallen industrial commodities, although vast quantities are purchased by the government for defense, foreign aid and what is called stockpiling. Great ingenuity is being exerted by businessmen to find foreign markets for their goods independently of government purchases and donation, but how successful the growth of foreign markets will be in absorbing the continuous rise in productivity is uncertain. Exports must be compensated for by imports of goods to the American market unless we are either unilaterally to subsidize consumption abroad, or in effect to pay increased prices for whatever we do import through devaluation of the dollar. Meanwhile manufacturing abroad is so rapidly emulating our productivity that before the end of the century it may leapfrog us in one country after another. Japanese and Germans may be the first, but others will follow.

Hearing this statement of the problem of the consumer who does not consume enough, or whose consumption does not rise fast enough, the listener may anticipate that some solution will finally be recommended. Instead the conclusion that seems to emerge is that there is no solution. Indeed, we might summarize the meaning of these massive trends by amplifying Engel's Nineteenth-Century

law to cover all categories of consumption. We might bring Engel up to date by declaring that, as incomes rise further, not only will the proportion of household expenditure devoted to food fall, but the proportion devoted to consumption of all kinds will fall. The consumer in the year 2000 may devote his attention mainly to the satisfaction of wants that do not require consumption, or production, or distribution, like stimulating conversation.

In achieving satisfaction of these wants, the customer of 2000 will experience as his first constraint not income but time; as his second constraint, learning. For example, even now, my main problem in acquiring phonograph records from those who have made them so cheaply available is to widen my time for listening and my taste for enjoying them. My children, however, are less inclined to listen to music than to make it. The chief constraint on their enjoyment in the future may be the problem of finding an audience willing to listen, since the ultimate joy in performance is the response of our audience. Hence we can add a corollary to our image of the consumer in the year 2000. Instead of conceiving manufacturers as producers of goods, distributors as sellers of goods and customers as consumers of goods, the millennium may find all these relationships defined in terms of performers of services and of audiences who enjoy and respond to these performances.

Children ask nowadays when their parents tell them they are doing something they were not supposed to do, "Is that bad?" I do not know where the phrase came from, but I find it highly descriptive of the change that goes on between generations. Is it bad that the consumer should outgrow consumption for its own sake? Is he violating an obligation to others if he gets fed up with too much? Would he not be violating a greater obligation to himself if he stopped learning to discriminate ever more critically among the alternatives he is offered?

From the standpoint of the consumer, as a consumer, it is hard to see how any problem arises from this prospect, other than finding time and learning how to enjoy its use in other ways than in getting and spending. These are the problems everyone should be delighted to suffer. As consumers ourselves, may we not hope that no one will ever take these problems out of our hands.

Behavioral Models for Analyzing Buyers

Philip Kotler

In economic theory and in business it has been customary to assume that consumers behave as purely economic men, that is, that value is largely a function of the physical use to which a product may be put and that, therefore, consumers respond almost solely and quite predictably to price changes for the product. Of course, it has always been tacitly recognized that social and psychological factors were also present, but little attempt was made to deal with them in an explicit fashion, as had been done with economic factors. Recently attempts have been made to view the consumer as the complex and subtle individual that he really is. The following article outlines the several models by which one may begin this difficult process of analyzing consumers.

In times past, management could arrive at a fair understanding of its buyers through the daily experience of selling to them. But the growth in the size of firms and markets has removed many decision-makers from direct contact with buyers. Increasingly, decision-makers have had to turn to summary statistics and to behavioral theory, and

Reprinted from the *Journal of Marketing*, national quarterly publication of the American Marketing Association, Vol. 29, No. 4, October 1965, pp. 37–45.

are spending more money today than ever before to try to understand their buyers.

Who buys? How do they buy? And why? The first two questions relate to relatively overt aspects of buyer behavior, and can be learned about through direct observation and interviewing.

But uncovering *why* people buy is an extremely difficult task. The answer will tend to vary with the investigator's behavioral frame of reference.

The buyer is subject to many influences which trace a complex course

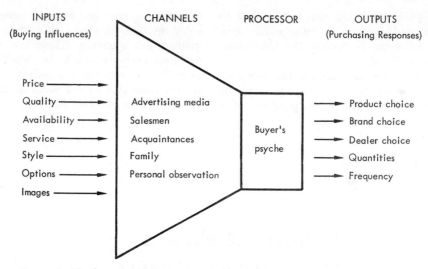

Figure 1. The buying process conceived as a system of inputs and outputs.

through his psyche and lead eventually to overt purchasing responses. This conception of the buying process is illustrated in Figure 1. Various influences and their modes of transmission are shown at the left. At the right are the buyer's responses in choice of product, brand, dealer, quantities, and frequency. In the center stands the buyer and his mysterious psychological processes. The buyer's psyche is a "black box" whose workings can be only partially deduced. The marketing strategist's challenge to the behavioral scientist is to construct a more specific model of the mechanism in the black box.

Unfortunately no generally accepted model of the mechanism exists. The human mind, the only entity in nature with deep powers of understanding, still remains the least understood. Scientists can explain planetary motion, genetic determination, and molecular behavior. Yet they have only partial, and often partisan, models of *human* behavior.

Nevertheless, the marketing strategist should recognize the potential interpretative contributions of different partial models for explaining buyer behavior. Depending upon the product, different variables and behavioral mechanisms may assume particular importance. A psychoanalytic behavioral model might throw much light on the factors operating in cigarette demand, while an economic behavioral model might be useful in explaining machine-tool purchasing. Sometimes alternative models may shed light on different demand aspects of the same product.

What are the most useful behavioral models for interpreting the transformation of buying influences into purchasing responses? Five different models of the buyer's "black box" are presented in the present article, along with their respective marketing applications: (1) the Marshallian model, stressing economic motivations; (2) the Pavlovian model, learning; (3) the Freudian model, psychoanalytic motivations; (4) the Veblenian model, social-psychological factors; and (5) the Hobbesian model, organizational factors. These models represent radically different conceptions of the mainsprings of human behavior.

The Marshallian Economic Model

Economists were the first professional group to construct a specific theory of buyer behavior. The theory holds that purchasing decisions are the result of largely "rational" and conscious economic calculations. The individual buyer seeks to spend his income on those goods that will deliver the most utility (satisfaction) according to his tastes and relative prices.

The antecedents for this view trace back to the writings of Adam Smith and Jeremy Bentham. Smith set the tone by developing a doctrine of economic growth based on the principle that man is motivated by self-interest in all his actions.[1] Bentham refined this view and saw man as finely calculating and weighing the expected pleasures and pains of every contemplated action.[2]

Bentham's "felicific calculus" was not applied to consumer behavior (as opposed to entrepreneurial behavior) until the late 19th century. Then, the "marginal-utility" theory of value was formulated independently and almost simultaneously by Jevons[3] and Marshall[4] in England, Menger[5] in Austria, and Walras[6] in Switzerland.

Alfred Marshall was the great consolidator of the classical and neoclassical tradition in economics; and his synthesis in the form of demand-supply analysis constitutes the main source of modern micro-economic thought in the English-speaking world. His theoretical work aimed at realism, but his method was to start with simplifying assumptions and to examine the effect of a change in a single variable (say, price) when all other variables were held constant.

He would "reason out" the consequences of the provisional assumptions and in subsequent steps modify his assumptions in the direction of more realism. He employed the "measuring rod of money" as an indicator of the intensity of human psychological desires. Over the years his methods and assumptions have been refined into what is now known as *modern utility theory:* economic man is bent on maximizing his utility, and does this by carefully calculating the "felicific" consequences of any purchase.

As an example, suppose on a particular evening that John is considering whether to prepare his own dinner or dine out. He estimates that a restaurant meal would cost $2.00 and a home-cooked meal 50 cents. According to the Marshallian model, if John expects less than four times as much satisfaction from the restaurant meal as the home-cooked meal, he will eat at home. The economist typically is not concerned with how these relative preferences are formed by John, or how they may be psychologically modified by new stimuli.

Yet John will not always cook at home. The principle of diminishing marginal utility operates. Within a given time interval—say, a week—

---

[1] Adam Smith, *An Inquiry into the Nature and Causes of the Wealth of Nations,* 1776 (New York: The Modern Library, 1937).

[2] Jeremy Bentham, *An Introduction to the Principles of Morals and Legislation,* 1780 (Oxford, England: Clarendon Press, 1907).

[3] William S. Jevons, *The Theory of Political Economy* (New York: The Macmillan Company, 1871).

[4] Alfred Marshall, *Principles of Economics,* 1890 (London: The Macmillan Company, 1927).

[5] Karl Menger, *Principles of Economics,* 1871 (Glencoe, Illinois: Free Press, 1950).

[6] Leon Walras, *Elements of Pure Economics,* 1874 (Homewood, Illinois: Richard D. Irwin, Inc., 1954).

the utility of each additional home-cooked meal diminishes. John gets tired of home meals and other products become relatively more attractive.

John's *efficiency* in maximizing his utility depends on the adequacy of his information and his freedom of choice. If he is not perfectly aware of costs, if he misestimates the relative delectability of the two meals, or if he is barred from entering the restaurant, he will not maximize his potential utility. His choice processes are rational, but the results are inefficient.

Marketing Applications of Marshallian Model

Marketers usually have dismissed the Marshallian model as an absurd figment of ivory-tower imagination. Certainly the behavioral essence of the situation is omitted, in viewing man as calculating the marginal utility of a restaurant meal over a home-cooked meal.

Eva Mueller has reported a study where only one-fourth of the consumers in her sample bought with any substantial degree of deliberation.[7] Yet there are a number of ways to view the model.

From one point of view the Marshallian model is tautological and therefore neither true nor false. The model holds that the buyer acts in the light of his best "interest." But this is not very informative.

A second view is that this is a *normative* rather than a *descriptive* model of behavior. The model provides logical norms for buyers who want to be "rational." Although the consumer is not likely to employ economic analysis

[7] Eva Mueller, "A Study of Purchase Decisions," Part 2, *Consumer Behavior, The Dynamics of Consumer Reaction,* edited by Lincoln H. Clark (New York: New York University Press, 1954), pp. 36–87.

to decide between a box of Kleenex and Scotties, he may apply economic analysis in deciding whether to buy a new car. Industrial buyers even more clearly would want an economic calculus for making good decisions.

A third view is that economic factors operate to a greater or lesser extent in all markets, and, therefore, must be included in any comprehensive description of buyer behavior.

Furthermore, the model suggests useful behavioral hypotheses such as: (a) The lower the price of the product, the higher the sales. (b) The lower the price of substitute products, the lower the sales of this product; and the lower the price of complementary products, the higher the sales of this product. (c) The higher the real income, the higher the sales of this product, provided that it is not an "inferior" good. (d) The higher the promotional expenditures, the higher the sales.

The validity of these hypotheses does not rest on whether *all* individuals act as economic calculating machines in making their purchasing decisions. For example, some individuals may buy *less* of a product when its price is reduced. They may think that the quality has gone down, or that ownership has less status value. If a majority of buyers view price reductions negatively, then sales may fall, contrary to the first hypothesis.

But for most goods a price reduction increases the relative value of the goods in many buyers' minds and leads to increased sales. This and the other hypotheses are intended to describe average effects.

The impact of economic factors in actual buying situations is studied through experimental design or statistical analyses of past data. Demand equations have been fitted to a wide variety of products—including beer, refrigerators, and chemical fertilizers.[8] More recently, the impact of economic variables on the fortunes of different brands has been pursued with significant results, particularly in the case of coffee, frozen orange juice, and margarine.[9]

But economic factors alone cannot explain all the variations in sales. The Marshallian model ignores the fundamental question of how product and brand preferences are formed. It represents a useful frame of reference for analyzing only one small corner of the "black box."

The Pavlovian Learning Model

The designation of a Pavlovian learning model has its origin in the experiments of the Russian psychologist Pavlov, who rang a bell each time before feeding a dog. Soon he was able to induce the dog to salivate by ringing the bell whether or not food was supplied. Pavlov concluded that learning was largely an associative process and that a large component of behavior was conditioned in this way.

Experimental psychologists have continued this mode of research with rats and other animals, including people. Laboratory experiments have been designed to explore such phenomena as learning, forgetting, and the ability to discriminate. The results have been integrated into a stimulus-response model of human behavior, or as someone has

"wisecracked," the substitution of a rat psychology for a rational psychology.

The model has been refined over the years, and today is based on four central concepts—those of *drive, cue, response,* and *reinforcement.*[10]

Drive. Also called needs or motives, drive refers to strong stimuli internal to the individual which impels action. Psychologists draw a distinction between primary physiological drives—such as hunger, thirst, cold, pain, and sex—and learned drives which are derived socially —such as cooperation, fear, and acquisitiveness.

Cue. A drive is very general and impels a particular response only in relation to a particular configuration of cues. Cues are weaker stimuli in the environment and/or in the individual which determine when, where, and how the subject responds. Thus, a coffee advertisement can serve as a cue which stimulates the thirst drive in a housewife. Her response will depend upon this cue and other cues, such as the time of day, the availability of other thirst-quenchers, and the cue's intensity. Often a relative change in a cue's intensity can be more impelling than its absolute level. The housewife may be more motivated by a 2-cents-off sale on a brand of coffee than the fact that this brand's price was low in the first place.

Response. The response is the organism's reaction to the configuration of cues. Yet the same configuration of cues will not necessarily produce the same response in the individual. This depends on the degree to which the experience was rewarding, that is, drive-reducing.

[8] See Erwin E. Nemmers, *Managerial Economics* (New York: John Wiley & Sons, Inc., 1962), Part II.

[9] See Lester G. Telser, "The Demand for Branded Goods as Estimated from Consumer Panel Data," *Review of Economics and Statistics,* Vol. 44 (August, 1962), pp. 300–324; and William F. Massey and Ronald E. Frank, "Short Term Price and Dealing Effects in Selected Market Segments," *Journal of Marketing Research,* Vol. 2 (May, 1965), pp. 171–185.

[10] See John Dollard and Neal E. Miller, *Personality and Psychotherapy* (New York: McGraw-Hill Book Company, Inc., 1950), Chapter III.

Reinforcement. If the experience is rewarding, a particular response is reinforced; that is, it is strengthened and there is a tendency for it to be repeated when the same configuration of cues appears again. The housewife, for example, will tend to purchase the same brand of coffee each time she goes to her supermarket so long as it is rewarding and the cue configuration does not change. But if a learned response or habit is not reinforced, the strength of the habit diminishes and may be extinguished eventually. Thus, a housewife's preference for a certain coffee may become extinct if she finds the brand out of stock for a number of weeks.

Forgetting, in contrast to extinction, is the tendency for learned associations to weaken, not because of the lack of reinforcement but because of nonuse.

Cue configurations are constantly changing. The housewife sees a new brand of coffee next to her habitual brand, or notes a special price deal on a rival brand. Experimental psychologists have found that the same learned response will be elicited by similar patterns of cues; that is, learned responses are *generalized*. The housewife shifts to a similar brand when her favorite brand is out of stock. This tendency toward generalization over less similar cue configurations is increased in proportion to the strength of the drive. A housewife may buy an inferior coffee if it is the only brand left and if her drive is sufficiently strong.

A counter-tendency to generalization is *discrimination*. When a housewife tries two similar brands and finds one more rewarding, her ability to discriminate between similar cue configurations improves. Discrimination increases the specificity of the cue-response connection, while generalization decreases the specificity.

Marketing Applications of Pavlovian Model

The modern version of the Pavlovian model makes no claim to provide a complete theory of behavior—indeed, such important phenomena as perception, the subconscious, and interpersonal influence are inadequately treated. Yet the model does offer a substantial number of insights about some aspects of behavior of considerable interest to marketers.[11]

An example would be in the problem of introducing a new brand into a highly competitive market. The company's goal is to extinguish existing brand habits and form new habits among consumers for its brand. But the company must first get customers to try its brand; and it has to decide between using weak and strong cues.

Light introductory advertising is a weak cue compared with distributing free samples. Strong cues, although costing more, may be necessary in markets characterized by strong brand loyalties. For example, Folger went into the coffee market by distributing over a million pounds of free coffee.

To build a brand habit, it helps to provide for an extended period of introductory dealing. Furthermore, sufficient quality must be built into the brand so that the experience is reinforcing. Since buyers are more likely to transfer allegiance to similar brands than dissimilar brands (generalization), the company should also investigate what cues in the leading brands have been most effective. Although outright imitation would not necessarily effect the most transference, the question of providing enough similarity should be considered.

[11] The most consistent application of learning-theory concepts to marketing situations is found in John A. Howard, *Marketing Management: Analysis and Planning* (Homewood, Illinois: Richard D. Irwin, Inc., revised edition, 1963).

The Pavlovian model also provides guide lines in the area of advertising strategy. The American behaviorist, John B. Watson, was a great exponent of repetitive stimuli; in his writings man is viewed as a creature who can be conditioned through repetition and reinforcement to respond in particular ways.[12] The Pavlovian model emphasizes the desirability of repetition in advertising. A single exposure is likely to be a very weak cue, hardly able to penetrate the individual's consciousness sufficiently to excite his drives above the threshold level.

Repetition in advertising has two desirable effects. It "fights" forgetting, the tendency for learned responses to weaken in the absence of practice. It provides reinforcement, because after the purchase the consumer becomes selectively exposed to advertisements of the product.

The model also provides guide lines for copy strategy. To be effective as a cue, an advertisement must arouse strong drives in the person. The strongest product-related drives must be identified. For candy bars, it may be hunger; for safety belts, fear; for hair tonics, sex; for automobiles, status. The advertising practitioner must dip into his cue box—words, colors, pictures—and select that configuration of cues that provides the strongest stimulus to these drives.

The Freudian Psychoanalytic Model

The Freudian model of man is well known, so profound has been its impact on 20th century thought. It is the latest of a series of philosophical "blows" to which man has been exposed in the last 500 years. Copernicus destroyed the idea

[12] John B. Watson, *Behaviorism* (New York: The People's Institute Publishing Company, 1925).

that man stood at the center of the universe; Darwin tried to refute the idea that man was a special creation; and Freud attacked the idea that man even reigned over his own psyche.

According to Freud, the child enters the world driven by instinctual needs which he cannot gratify by himself. Very quickly and painfully he realizes his separateness from the rest of the world and yet his dependence on it.

He tries to get others to gratify his needs through a variety of blatant means, including intimidation and supplication. Continual frustration leads him to perfect more subtle mechanisms for gratifying his instincts.

As he grows, his psyche becomes increasingly complex. A part of his psyche —the id—remains the reservoir of his strong drives and urges. Another part— the ego—becomes his conscious planning center for finding outlets for his drives. And a third part—his super-ego —channels his instinctive drives into socially approved outlets to avoid the pain of guilt or shame.

The guilt or shame which man feels toward some of his urges—especially his sexual urges—causes him to repress them from his consciousness. Through such defense mechanisms as rationalization and sublimation, these urges are denied or become transmuted into socially approved expressions. Yet these urges are never eliminated or under perfect control; and they emerge, sometimes with a vengeance, in dreams, in slips-of-the-tongue, in neurotic and obsessional behavior, or ultimately in mental breakdown where the ego can no longer maintain the delicate balance between the impulsive power of the id and the oppressive power of the super-ego.

The individual's behavior, therefore, is never simple. His motivational wellsprings are not obvious to a casual observer nor deeply understood by the individual himself. If he is asked why he purchased an expensive foreign sports-car, he may reply that he likes its maneuverability and its looks. At a deeper level he may have purchased the car to impress others, or to feel young again. At a still deeper level, he may be purchasing the sports-car to achieve substitute gratification for unsatisfied sexual strivings.

Many refinements and changes in emphasis have occurred in this model since the time of Freud. The instinct concept has been replaced by a more careful delineation of basic drives; the three parts of the psyche are regarded now as theoretical concepts rather than actual entities; and the behavioral perspective has been extended to include cultural as well as biological mechanisms.

Instead of the role of the sexual urge in psychic development—Freud's discussion of oral, anal, and genital stages and possible fixations and traumas—Adler[13] emphasized the urge for power and how its thwarting manifests itself in superiority and inferiority complexes; Horney[14] emphasized cultural mechanisms; and Fromm[15] and Erickson[16] emphasized the role of existential crises in personality development. These philosophical divergencies, rather than debilitating the model, have enriched and extended its interpretative value to a wider range of behavioral phenomena.

Marketing Applications of Freudian Model

Perhaps the most important marketing implication of this model is that buyers

[13] Alfred Adler, *The Science of Living* (New York: Greenberg, 1929).

[14] Karen Horney, *The Neurotic Personality of Our Time* (New York: W. W. Norton & Co., 1937).

[15] Erich Fromm, *Man For Himself* (New York: Holt, Rinehart & Winston, Inc., 1947).

[16] Erik Erikson, *Childhood and Society* (New York: W. W. Norton & Co., 1949).

are motivated by *symbolic* as well as *economic-functional* product concerns. The change of a bar of soap from a square to a round shape may be more important in its sexual than its functional connotations. A cake mix that is advertised as involving practically no labor may alienate housewives because the easy life may evoke a sense of guilt.

Motivational research has produced some interesting and occasionally some bizarre hypotheses about what may be in the buyer's mind regarding certain purchases. Thus, it has been suggested at one time or another that

- Many a businessman doesn't fly because of a fear of posthumous guilt—if he crashed, his wife would think of him as stupid for not taking a train.
- Men want their cigars to be odoriferous, in order to prove that they (the men) are masculine.
- A woman is very serious when she bakes a cake because unconsciously she is going through the symbolic act of giving birth.
- A man buys a convertible as a substitute "mistress."
- Consumers prefer vegetable shortening because animal fats stimulate a sense of sin.
- Men who wear suspenders are reacting to an unresolved castration complex.

There are admitted difficulties of proving these assertions. Two prominent motivational researchers, Ernest Dichter and James Vicary, were employed independently by two separate groups in the prune industry to determine why so many people dislike prunes. Dichter found, among other things, that the prune aroused feelings of old age and insecurity in people, whereas Vicary's main finding was that Americans had an emotional block about prunes' laxative qualities.[17] Which is the more valid interpretation? Or if they are both operative, which motive is found with greater statistical frequency in the population?

Unfortunately the usual survey techniques—direct observation and interviewing—can be used to establish the representativeness of more superficial characteristics—age and family size, for example—but are not feasible for establishing the frequency of mental states which are presumed to be deeply "buried" within each individual.

Motivational researchers have to employ time-consuming projective techniques in the hope of throwing individual "egos" off guard. When carefully administered and interpreted, techniques such as word association, sentence completion, picture interpretation, and role-playing can provide some insights into the minds of the small group of examined individuals; but a "leap of faith" is sometimes necessary to generalize these findings to the population.

Nevertheless, motivation research can lead to useful insights and provide inspiration to creative men in the advertising and packaging world. Appeals aimed at the buyer's private world of hopes, dreams, and fears can often be as effective in stimulating purchase as more rationally-directed appeals.

The Veblenian Social-Psychological Model

While most economists have been content to interpret buyer behavior in Marshallian terms, Thorstein Veblen struck out in different directions.

Veblen was trained as an orthodox economist, but evolved into a social thinker greatly influenced by the new science of social anthropology. He saw man as primarily a *social animal*—conforming to the general forms and norms of his larger culture and to the more specific standards of the subcultures and face-to-face groupings to which his life is bound. His wants and behavior are largely molded by his present group-memberships and his aspired group-memberships.

Veblen's best-known example of this is in his description of the leisure class.[18] His hypothesis is that much of economic consumption is motivated not by intrinsic needs or satisfaction so much as by prestige-seeking. He emphasized the strong emulative factors operating in the choice of conspicuous goods like clothes, cars, and houses.

Some of his points, however, seem overstated by today's perspective. The leisure class does not serve as everyone's reference group; many persons aspire to the social patterns of the class immediately above it. And important segments of the affluent class practice conspicuous underconsumption rather than overconsumption. There are many people in all classes who are more anxious to "fit in" than to "stand out." As an example, William H. Whyte found that many families avoided buying air conditioners and other appliances before their neighbors did.[19]

Veblen was not the first nor the only investigator to comment on social influences in behavior; but the incisive quality of his observations did much to stimulate further investigations. Another stimulus came from Karl Marx, who held that each man's world-view was deter-

[17] L. Edward Scriven, "Rationality and Irrationality in Motivation Research," in Robert Ferber and Hugh G. Wales, editors, *Motivation and Marketing Behavior* (Homewood, Illinois: Richard D. Irwin, Inc., 1958), pp. 69–70.

[18] Thorstein Veblen, *The Theory of the Leisure Class* (New York: The Macmillan Company, 1899).

[19] William H. Whyte, Jr., "The Web of Word of Mouth," *Fortune*, Vol. 50 (November, 1954), pp. 140 ff.

mined largely by his relationship to the "means of production."[20] The early field-work in primitive societies by social anthropologists like Boas[21] and Malinowski[22] and the later field-work in urban societies by men like Park[23] and Thomas[24] contributed much to understanding the influence of society and culture. The research of early Gestalt psychologists—men like Wertheimer,[25] Köhler,[26] and Koffka[27]—into the mechanisms of perception led eventually to investigations of small-group influence on perception.

Marketing Applications of Veblenian Model

The various streams of thought crystallized into the modern social sciences of sociology, cultural anthropology, and social psychology. Basic to them is the view that man's attitudes and behavior are influenced by several levels of society—culture, subcultures, social classes, reference groups, and face-to-face groups. The challenge to the marketer is to determine which of these

[20] Karl Marx, *The Communist Manifesto*, 1848 (London: Martin Lawrence, Ltd., 1934).

[21] Franz Boas, *The Mind of Primitive Man* (New York: The Macmillan Company, 1922).

[22] Bronislaw Malinowski, *Sex and Repression in Savage Society* (New York: Meridian Books, 1955).

[23] Robert E. Park, *Human Communities* (Glencoe, Illinois: Free Press, 1952).

[24] William I. Thomas, *The Unadjusted Girl* (Boston: Little, Brown and Company, 1928).

[25] Max Wertheimer, *Productive Thinking* (New York: Harper & Brothers, 1945).

[26] Wolfgang Köhler, *Gestalt Psychology* (New York: Liveright Publishing Co., 1947).

[27] Kurt Koffka, *Principles of Gestalt Psychology* (New York: Harcourt, Brace and Co., 1935).

social levels are the most important in influencing the demand for his product.

Culture

The most enduring influences are from culture. Man tends to assimilate his culture's mores and folkways, and to believe in their absolute rightness until deviants appear within his culture or until he confronts members of another culture.

Subcultures

A culture tends to lose its homogeneity as its population increases. When people no longer are able to maintain face-to-face relationships with more than a small proportion of other members of a culture, smaller units or subcultures develop, which help to satisfy the individual's needs for more specific identity.

The subcultures are often regional entities, because the people of a region, as a result of more frequent interactions, tend to think and act alike. But subcultures also take the form of religions, nationalities, fraternal orders, and other institutional complexes which provide a broad identification for people who may otherwise be strangers. The subcultures of a person play a large role in his attitude formation and become another important predictor of certain values he is likely to hold.

Social Class

People become differentiated not only horizontally but also vertically through a division of labor. The society becomes stratified socially on the basis of wealth, skill, and power. Sometimes castes develop in which the members are reared for certain roles, or social classes develop in which the members feel empathy with others sharing similar values and economic circumstances.

Because social class involves different attitudinal configurations, it becomes a useful independent variable for segmenting markets and predicting reactions. Significant differences have been found among different social classes with respect to magazine readership, leisure activities, food imagery, fashion interests, and acceptance of innovations. A sampling of attitudinal differences in class is the following:

Members of the *upper-middle* class place an emphasis on professional competence; indulge in expensive status symbols; and more often than not show a taste, real or otherwise, for theater and the arts. They want their children to show high achievement and precocity and develop into physicists, vice-presidents, and judges. This class likes to deal in ideas and symbols.

Members of the *lower-middle* class cherish respectability, savings, a college education, and good housekeeping. They want their children to show self-control and prepare for *careers* as accountants, lawyers, and engineers.

Members of the *upper-lower* class try to keep up with the times, if not with the Joneses. They stay in older neighborhoods but buy new kitchen appliances. They spend proportionately less than the middle class on major clothing articles, buying a new suit mainly for an important ceremonial occasion. They also spend proportionately less on services, preferring to do their own plumbing and other work around the house. They tend to raise large families and their children generally enter manual occupations. This class also supplies many local businessmen, politicians, sports stars, and labor-union leaders.

Reference Groups

There are groups in which the individual has no membership but with which he identifies and may aspire to—reference groups. Many young boys identify with big-league baseball players or astronauts, and many young girls identify with Hollywood stars. The activities of these popular heroes are carefully watched and frequently imitated. These reference figures become important transmitters of influence, although more along lines of taste and hobby than basic attitudes.

Face-to-Face Groups

Groups that have the most immediate influence on a person's tastes and opinions are face-to-face groups. This includes all the small "societies" with which he comes into frequent contact: his family, close friends, neighbors, fellow workers, fraternal associates, and so forth. His informal group memberships are influenced largely by his occupation, residence, and stage in the life cycle.

The powerful influence of small groups on individual attitudes has been demonstrated in a number of social psychological experiments.[28] There is also evidence that this influence may be growing. David Riesman and his co-authors have pointed to signs which indicate a growing amount of *other-direction*, that is, a tendency for

[28] See, for example, Solomon E. Asch, "Effects of Group Pressure Upon the Modification & Distortion of Judgments," in Dorwin Cartwright and Alvin Zander, *Group Dynamics* (Evanston, Illinois: Row, Peterson & Co., 1953), pp. 151–162; and Kurt Lewin, "Group Decision and Social Change," in Theodore M. Newcomb and Eugene L. Hartley, editors, *Readings in Social Psychology* (New York: Henry Holt Co., 1952).

individuals to be increasingly influenced by their peers in the definition of their values rather than by their parents and elders.[29]

For the marketer, this means that brand choice may increasingly be influenced by one's peers. For such products as cigarettes and automobiles, the influence of peers is unmistakable.

The role of face-to-face groups has been recognized in recent industry campaigns attempting to change basic product attitudes. For years the milk industry has been trying to overcome the image of milk as a "sissified" drink by portraying its use in social and active situations. The men's-wear-industry is trying to increase male interest in clothes by advertisements indicating that business associates judge a man by how well he dresses.

Of all face-to-face groups, the person's family undoubtedly plays the largest and most enduring role in basic attitude formation. From them he acquires a mental set not only toward religion and politics, but also toward thrift, chastity, food, human relations, and so forth. Although he often rebels against parental values in his teens, he often accepts these values eventually. Their formative influence on his eventual attitudes is undeniably great.

Family members differ in the types of product messages they carry to other family members. Most of what parents know about cereals, candy, and toys comes from their children. The wife stimulates family consideration of household appliances, furniture, and vacations. The husband tends to stimulate the fewest purchase ideas, with the exception of the automobile and perhaps the home.

The marketer must be alert to what attitudinal configurations dominate in different types of families, and also to how these change over time. For example, the parent's conception of the child's rights and privileges has undergone a radical shift in the last 30 years. The child has become the center of attention and orientation in a great number of households, leading some writers to label the modern family a "filiarchy." This has important implications not only for how to market to today's family, but also on how to market to tomorrow's family when the indulged child of today becomes the parent.

The Person

Social influences determine much but not all of the behavioral variations in people. Two individuals subject to the same influences are not likely to have identical attitudes, although these attitudes will probably converge at more points than those of two strangers selected at random. Attitudes are really the product of social forces interacting with the individual's unique temperament and abilities.

Furthermore, attitudes do not automatically guarantee certain types of behavior. Attitudes are predispositions felt by buyers before they enter the buying process. The buying process itself is a learning experience and can lead to a change in attitudes.

Alfred Politz noted at one time that women stated a clear preference for G.E. refrigerators over Frigidaire, but that Frigidaire continued to outsell G.E.[30] The answer to this paradox was

[29] David Riesman, Reuel Denney, and Nathan Glazer, *The Lonely Crowd* (New Haven, Connecticut: Yale University Press, 1950).

[30] Alfred Politz, "Motivation Research —Opportunity or Dilemma?", in Ferber and Wales, same reference as footnote 17, at pp. 57–58.

that preference was only one factor entering into behavior. When the consumer preferring G.E. actually undertook to purchase a new refrigerator, her curiosity led her to examine the other brands. Her perception was sensitized to refrigerator advertisements, sales arguments, and different product features. This led to learning and a change in attitudes.

The Hobbesian Organizational-Factors Model

The foregoing models throw light mainly on the behavior of family buyers.

But what of the large number of people who are organizational buyers? They are engaged in the purchase of goods not for the sake of consumption, but for further production or distribution. Their common denominator is the fact that they (1) are paid to make purchases for others and (2) operate within an organizational environment.

How do organizational buyers make their decisions? There seem to be two competing views. Many markeing writers have emphasized the predominance of rational motives in organizational buying.[31] Organizational buyers are represented as being most impressed by cost, quality, dependability, and service factors. They are portrayed as dedicated servants of the organization, seeking to secure the best terms. This view has led to an emphasis on performance and use characteristics in much industrial advertising.

Other writers have emphasized personal motives in organizational buyer behavior. The purchasing agent's interest to do the best for his company is tem-

pered by his interest to do the best for himself. He may be tempted to choose among salesmen according to the extent they entertain or offer gifts. He may choose a particular vendor because this will ingratiate him with certain company officers. He may shortcut his study of alternative suppliers to make his work day easier.

In truth, the buyer is guided by both personal and group goals; and this is the essential point. The political model of Thomas Hobbes comes closest of any model to suggesting the relationship between the two goals.[32] Hobbes held that man is "instinctively" oriented toward preserving and enhancing his own well-being. But this would produce a "war of every man against every man." This fear leads men to unite with others in a corporate body. The corporate man tries to steer a careful course between satisfying his own needs and those of the organization.

Marketing Applications of Hobbesian Model

The import of the Hobbesian model is that organizational buyers can be appealed to on both personal and organizational grounds. The buyer has his private aims, and yet he tries to do a satisfactory job for his corporation. He will respond to persuasive salesmen and he will respond to rational product arguments. However, the best "mix" of the two is not a fixed quantity; it varies with the nature of the product, the type of organization, and the relative strength of the two drives in the particular buyer.

Where there is substantial similarity in what suppliers offer in the way of products, price, and service, the pur-

[31] See Melvin T. Copeland, *Principles of Merchandising* (New York: McGraw-Hill Book Co., Inc., 1924).

[32] Thomas Hobbes, *Leviathan*, 1651 (London: G. Routledge and Sons, 1887).

chasing agent has less basis for rational choice. Since he can satisfy his organizational obligations with any one of a number of suppliers, he can be swayed by personal motives. On the other hand, where there are pronounced differences among the competing vendors' products, the purchasing agent is held more accountable for his choice and probably pays more attention to rational factors. Short-run personal gain becomes less motivating than the long-run gain which comes from serving the organization with distinction.

The marketing strategist must appreciate these goal conflicts of the organizational buyer. Behind all the ferment of purchasing agents to develop standards and employ value analysis lies their desire to avoid being thought of as order-clerks, and to develop better skills in reconciling personal and organizational objectives.[33]

Summary

Think back over the five different behavioral models of how the buyer translates buying influences into purchasing responses.

- Marshallian man is concerned chiefly with economic cues—prices and income—and makes a fresh utility calculation before each purchase.
- Pavlovian man behaves in a largely habitual rather than thoughtful way; certain configurations of cues will set off the same behavior because of rewarded learning in the past.
- Freudian man's choice are influenced strongly by motives and fantasies which take place deep within his private world.
- Veblenian man acts in a way which is shaped largely by past and present social groups.
- And finally, Hobbesian man seeks to reconcile individual gain with organizational gain.

Thus, it turns out that the "black box" of the buyer is not so black after all. Light is thrown in various corners by these models. Yet no one has succeeded in putting all these pieces of truth together into one coherent instrument for behavioral analysis. This, of course, is the goal of behavioral science.

---

[33] For an insightful account, see George Strauss, "Tactics of Lateral Relationship: The Purchasing Agent," *Administrative Science Quarterly*, Vol. 7 (September, 1962), pp. 161–186.

8

Probabilistic Models of Consumer Buying Behavior

Alfred A. Kuehn and Ralph L. Day

While some marketing scholars are attempting more realistic theories of consumer behavior by supplementing the economic model of the consumer with behavioral counterparts, other scholars are seeking to learn more about him and predict his behavior more accurately by applying quantitative methods to the evidence that can be secured about his past actions. This might be described as the inductive approach to consumer behavior, in contrast to the economic-behavioral approach, which is largely deductive. The accompanying article is a good example of this inductive approach.

The probabilistic approach to developing complex marketing models has strong parallels with the methods of nuclear physicists. In estimating shielding requirements for nuclear reactors, physicists utilize probabilistic models of the behavior of nuclear particles. Through the use of Monte Carlo techniques, they develop predictions of the levels of escaping particles with various levels of shielding. This permits the design of efficient shielding systems for proposed reactors.

In much the same way the builder of a marketing model can develop models which will reflect marketing influences and yield predictions of marketing results. The major differences are: the marketing scientist traces the purchasing

Reprinted from the *Journal of Marketing*, national quarterly publication of the American Marketing Association, Vol. 28, No. 4, October 1964, pp. 27–31.

behavior of individuals or households rather than nuclear particles; the relevant occurrences are exposures to merchandising influences and purchases, rather than collisions among particles; and the aggregate results are measured in the number of purchases (sales), rather than in the number of particles passing through shielding materials.

Probabilistic models of consumer behavior are still in an early stage of development relative to the progress made in nuclear physics. Emphasis so far has been on understanding the influence of marketing variables such as advertising, price changes, product variation, and special promotions rather than on forecasting sales. If a particular probabilistic model gives good predictions of market behavior, the reasons the model works are of more importance at the present stage of marketing science than the fact that it does work.

The Uncertain Consumer

The starting point in the probabilistic analysis of consumer behavior is the simple static model of the consuming unit (household or individual). The consumer is described by a set of probabilities reflecting the likelihood of his choosing any particular brand of a product class on his next purchase.

At a given time the particular brand an individual will choose is neither wholly predetermined nor a matter of pure chance. Most consumers are predisposed to prefer some brand or brands over others. These predispositions can be influenced by a great variety of factors: recent experiences, custom or habit, reference group influences, or exposures to advertising. The likelihood of purchase of particular brands will also be influenced by external factors such as the availability of favored products in stores the consumer patronizes.

Suppose there are four brands of a particular product, designated A, B, C, and D. As a result of his basic preferences, experiences, and market influences, a particular consumer might have the following probabilities of purchasing each brand: $P_A = .70$, $P_B = .20$; $P_C = .05$, and $P_D = .05$. In other words, chances are 7 in 10 he will buy brand A, 1 in 5 he will buy B, 1 in 20 he will buy C, and 1 in 20 he will buy D.

The Dynamic Consumer

Purchase probabilities for an individual consumer can be expected to change over time. Even if no specific events directly affect the consumer's purchase probabilities, the mere passage of time will modify them as circumstances change and memories of previous experiences fade. The probability of purchasing a favored brand tends to decrease with the passage of time unless

some event—such as a new purchase of the brand or an advertising message—reinforces the consumer's predisposition to buy the brand. Other events—such as purchases of competing brands or exposures to competing advertisements —tend to weaken the probability of purchase of the brand.[1]

Figure 1 illustrates how the probability of the consumer's purchase of brand A might decrease with time, in the absence of any significant events. As the probability of purchase of a favored brand declines with time, the likelihood of purchasing a competing brand increases. Pleasant associations with the favored brands and unpleasant associations with the less favored brands tend to be forgotten with time.

The Effects of Experience

The consumer's experience can be expected to have greater effect on his purchase probabilities than the mere passage of time, especially when he purchases the product often or when some or all of the brands are frequently advertised. Each new purchase of the product, whether or not the most favored brand is chosen, will almost certainly modify the individual's purchase probabilities. In general, the purchase of a brand increases the probability of that brand's being chosen on the next buying occasion and decreases the purchase probabilities of other brands.

If a purchase is made under "normal" circumstances without special inducements, the expected influence of the purchase will be greater than if the purchase was made as the result of a temporary manufacturer's "deal" or retailer's "special."

[1] Alfred A. Kuehn, "Consumer Brand Choice as a Learning Process," *Journal of Advertising Research*, Vol. 2 (December, 1962), pp. 10–17, at p. 14.

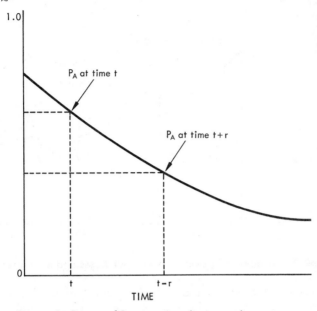

Figure 1. Decay of P_A over time (no events).

Occurrences not directly related to a previous purchase, such as exposures to advertising, might also significantly alter the consumer's purchase probabilities. Figure 2 illustrates how a series of events could affect purchase probabilities and modify the time decay pattern shown in Figure 1.

The probability level which existed in time period t declined when no significant events occured at t + 1. A repeat purchase of A in t + 2 reinforced P_A. No purchase occurred at t + 3 but an exposure to an advertisement for brand C raised P_C and lowered P_A slightly. A purchase of brand B at t + 4 caused a further reduction in P_A. Purchases of brand A in period t + 5 and t + 6 caused increases in the level of P_A. Thus Figure 2 graphically illustrates how an individual's probability of purchasing a particular brand might change with the passage of time and the occurrence of significant events.

Implications for Analysis

The rest of this article is devoted to dynamic models, but the value of the simple probability model as a static analytical concept should not be overlooked. Bothersome analytical difficulties in interpreting the results of product tests can frequently be cleared up when the housewife's behavior is viewed in probabilistic terms.[2] When a substantial number of housewives say that they prefer one of two brands in blind pair comparison tests and then say they prefer the other when the test is repeated, some researchers have concluded that housewives are inconsistent and

[2] For a more complete discussion, see Alfred A. Kuehn and Ralph L. Day, "A Probabilistic Approach to Consumer Behavior," in Reavis Cox, Wroe Alderson, and Stanley J. Shapiro, editors, *Theory in Marketing: Second Series* (Homewood, Illinois: Richard D. Irwin, Inc., 1964), pp. 380–390.

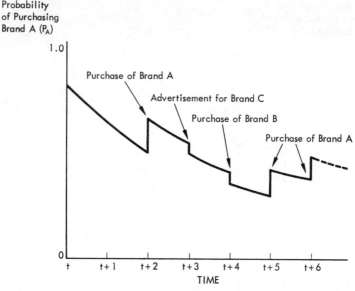

Probability
of Purchasing
Brand A (P_A)

Figure 2. Changes in P_A over time with purchases and exposures to advertising.

unpredictable. Yet researchers would agree that it is unreasonable to think that housewives are absolutely infallible in making product evaluations.

In probabilistic terms, the lack of infallibility means that there is some probability on any particular trial that a housewife may choose the sample she does *not* prefer. A reversal on a repeat test merely means that she failed to choose the one she preferred on *one* of the two trials. If preferences are weak and the probability of recognizing the preferred sample is little greater than chance, then the expected number of reversals in a test panel could approach 50%. Since differences between the brands being tested are often slight, one should expect frequent . reversals on repeat tests.

A Dynamic Model of Buying Behavior

A useful dynamic model of consumer brand choice behavior must provide a

method of revising the individual's set of purchase probabilities to show changes induced by the passage of time, new purchase experiences, and exposures to merchandising influences. No simple structure can adequately reflect these complex changes.

Although they have gained considerable attention and are conceptually appealing, simple Markov chain models are of limited value as the basis of a brand choice model. Ronald A. Howard has classified the major problems in using Markovian analysis in three categories: irregular patterns of purchase (random interpurchase time), difficulties of aggregation, and difficulties in revising transition matrices to reflect new information.[3]

A model which has proven useful as a means of revising purchase probabilities in extensive empirical work is equivalent to a generalized form of a stochastic

[3] Ronald A. Howard, "Stochastic Process Models of Consumer Behavior," *Journal of Advertising Research,* Vol. 3 (September, 1963), pp. 35–42.

Probability
of Purchasing
Brand A on
Trial t + 1

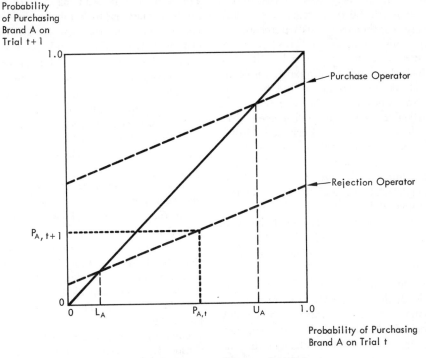

Figure 3. Revising purchase probabilities.

learning model (associative learning under conditions of reward).[4] When the learning model is applied to the brand choice situation, the relevant "trials" are purchases of the product class. After each trial, the probability of the purchase of a particular brand on the next trial is revised in view of the choice made on that trial. If the brand in question was purchased, the probability of its purchase on the subsequent trial will normally be increased. If a brand is rejected (another brand is purchased), its probability of purchase on the next

[4] William K. Estes, "Individual Behavior in Uncertain Situations: An Interpretation in Terms of Statistical Association Theory," in R. M. Thrall, C. H. Coombs, and R. L. Davis, editors, *Decision Processes* (New York: John Wiley & Sons, Inc., 1954); and Robert R. Bush and Frederick Mosteller, *Stochastic Models for Learning* (New York: John Wiley & Sons, Inc., 1955).

purchase occasion will normally be reduced.

The major components of the model are two functions or "operators" which determine the new probability level for a brand after each purchase. These are illustrated in Figure 3. The probability of purchasing brand A on trial t $(P_{A, t})$ is shown at the bottom scale of the diagram. The revised probability $(P_{A, t+1})$ after a purchase is made is read from the vertical scale of the diagram. The value of $P_{A, t+1}$ when another brand is purchased is read from the "rejection operator" as shown by the dotted line in Figure 3. The value of $P_{A, t+1}$ when A is purchased would be read from the "purchase operator" in a similar manner, yielding a higher value of $P_{A, t+1}$ than when another brand was purchased.

The model contains upper and lower limits on the probability of purchasing a brand on the next trial so that it can never reach 1.0 or 0, regardless of how many continuous repeat purchases or rejections might occur. This recognizes that a consumer never reaches the state where the purchase of a particular brand is absolutely certain on the next purchase. Conversely, the rejection of a particular brand never becomes absolutely certain. Using Bush and Mosteller's terminology, this is an incomplete learning, incomplete extinction model.[5] In Figure 3, the lower limit on P_A is designated as L_A and the upper limit is designated U_A.

The increment of change induced in the purchase probability for a brand by either a purchase or a rejection depends on the position and slope of the two operators. If the lines in Figure 3 were moved closer together, the amount of change in the purchase probability would be less than if the lines remained as shown. Similarly, changes in the slopes of the lines would change the degree of influence of the results of a particular trial.

The value of the purchase probability for trial $t + 1$ depends on the purchase probability for trial t, the actual outcome of trial t, and the intercepts and slopes of the lines. To incorporate the effects of the passage of time and of merchandising influences, the four parameters defining the Purchase and Rejection operators are made functions of time and merchandising influences.

Using the Model

At present, the primary use of the model is in studying patterns of consumer behavior and evaluating the effects of merchandising activity by studying recent purchase records of consumers.

[5] Same reference as footnote 4.

The first step in studying a particular product class is to estimate the four parameters as a function of the time elapsed between the tth and $t + 1^{st}$ purchases. The importance of differences in the frequency of purchase seems to vary considerably from product class to product class; but, in general, the influence of the most recent purchase on an individual's purchase probabilities is greater for consumers who purchase the product frequently.

In terms of the lines in Figure 3, as the time between purchases becomes small, the slopes of the lines tend to approach the diagonal and the upper limit becomes close to 1.0 and the lower limit close to 0. As the time between purchases becomes very large, the upper and lower limits come close together and the slopes of the lines approach the horizontal.

Once the effect of time between purchases is generally understood for a product class, the model can be used to study the effects of competitive marketing activity. The parameters of the model are estimated from data covering relatively short periods of time. Changes in the parameters can then be examined in relationship to the activities and policies pursued by the various brands during the period studied. Methods have been developed to estimate the parameters from consumer panel data on the basis of purchase sequences of three and four purchases. Procedures for estimating the parameters for short periods of time are necessary since merchandising conditions in the marketplace change frequently.

In Conclusion

The probabilistic approach provides a useful conceptual framework for considering the expected purchase behavior of consumers. When the expected behavior of an individual is viewed as a set of probabilities related to the available brands, a richer and more flexible concept of "brand loyalty" is provided. When expected behavior in a product test is viewed in probabilistic terms, bothersome analytical difficulties are frequently cleared up. As useful as the simple probability model of individual consumers might be in static analysis, its use as a building block in the construction of dynamic, aggregative models of consumer brand choice behavior has been stressed in this article.

A model equivalent to a generalized form of a stochastic learning model was presented as the basis of a dynamic model of brand choice behavior. The model provides revised estimates of the purchase probability for a particular brand after each purchase occasion. The extent to which a purchase of the brand reinforces the probability of its purchase on the next purchase occasion, or the extent to which a rejection in favor of a competing brand reduces the probability, depends on the values of four parameters. These parameters are treated as functions of time and of merchandising variables.

The parameters are estimated from sequences of purchases recorded by members of consumer panels. While the effect of time tends to vary among product classes, it is relatively stable for each product class. Once the effect of time is established for a product class, the parameters can be estimated from data covering reasonably short periods of time, and changes in purchase probabilities not attributed to the passage of time can be related to merchandising activity during the period under study.

Much remains to be done before a model can be developed which can adequately treat concomitant variation in all major marketing variables; but the probabilistic approach offers an encouraging start.

Riesman Revisited

Harold H. Kassarjian

During recent years marketing scholars, in their urgent desire to explain complex consumer behavior, have borrowed liberally from the theories of behavioral scientists and attempted to apply these theories to the marketing environment. One popular source of applied theory has been the David Riesman book The Lonely Crowd. *In the process of adapting theory to new uses it is easy to misconstrue or misapply the theory. In the accompanying article the author gives his version of Riesman's conceptualization of social character and points out what he considers to be some misinterpretations of his theories.*

In recent years models, theories, and information from the behavioral sciences —especially psychology and sociology— have permeated the field of marketing. Authors of current texts in marketing are devoting more space to materials from the behavioral sciences than previous authors, but some authors of texts are making serious errors in interpretation.

The concept of social character, as presented by David Riesman (and his colleagues) in *The Lonely Crowd*,[1] is one of the concepts or theories from the behavioral sciences that has attracted considerable attention. References to Riesman and the terms, *tradition-direction, inner-direction,* and *other-direction* have become part of the vocabulary of many people in the field of marketing as well as authors of some of the recent textbooks.[2]

In brief, the Riesman thesis is that human beings in general can be grouped into three major types of social character, and that each society or culture manifests predominantly one or other types according to its particular phase of development. By social character Riesman means the "ways of behavior" or "modes of conformity to the culture and society" in which the individual is locomoting.

Reprinted from the *Journal of Marketing*, national quarterly publication of the American Marketing Association, Vol. 29, No. 2, April 1965, pp. 54–56.

[1] David Riesman, Nathan Glazer, and Reuel Denney, *The Lonely Crowd* (New Haven: Yale University Press, 1961, abridged edition).

[2] John A. Howard, *Marketing Management* (Homewood, Ill.: Richard D. Irwin, Inc., rev. ed., 1963); E. Jerome McCarthy, *Basic Marketing: A Managerial Approach* (Homewood, Ill.: Richard D. Irwin, Inc., rev. ed., 1964); Edward W. Cundiff and Richard R. Still, *Basic Marketing: Concepts, Environments and Decisions* (Englewood Cliffs, N.J.: Prentice-Hall, Inc., 1964).

Tradition-Direction

Tradition-direction is prevalent in societies characterized by general slowness of change, dependence on family and kin organization, low social mobility, and a tight web of values.

This phase characterizes more than half the world's population: India, Egypt, China, Central Africa, and parts of Central and South America. These societies are found in areas almost untouched by industrialization; and children are taught to succeed the parents rather than *to succeed* by rising in the social system. The culture provides ritual, routine, and religion to occupy and orient everyone.

Little energy is directed toward finding new solutions of the age-old problems, let us say, of agricultural technique or medicine. The important relationships of life are controlled by careful and rigid etiquette, learned by the young during intensive socialization within the extended family that end with initiation into full adult membership.[3]

Inner-Direction

The *inner-directed* society, found in western society emerging from the Renaissance and Reformation until today, is fostered by industrialization, greater social mobility, and less security for the individual.

Such a society is characterized by a rapid accumulation of capital (teamed with devastating technological shifts), and by an almost constant expansion: intensive expansion in the production of goods and people and extensive expansion in exploration, colonization, and imperialism.[4] The greater choice this

[3] Riesman, same reference as footnote 1, p. 11.

[4] Riesman, same reference as footnote 1, p. 14.

society gives—and the greater initiatives it demands in order to cope with its novel problems, combined with increasing population and increasing opportunity—leads to sharp competition in the job market as well as in private life. The "source of direction for the individual is 'inner' in the sense that it is implanted early in life by the elders and directed toward generalized but nonetheless inescapably destined goals."[5]

Parents in such a society face the problem of preparing their children for life in fast changing and therefore unpredictable surroundings. Individuals have to learn to be able to meet and handle novel situations. Thus, no particular pattern of behavior is any longer as sufficient as in the tradition-directed society. The emphasis must be on character training, and the child has to incorporate principles or values rather than details of behavior.

An inner-directed person gains a feeling of control over his own life, and sees himself as an individual with a career to make. However, he goes through life less independent than he seems, for he is obeying and conforming to an internal piloting based on the values and principles he has incorporated. Education, training, child-rearing practices, occupational opportunities, recreation and economics are so closely correlated in the inner-directed society that the inner-directed person is prepared to live in a rather unstable, unreliable world by finding stability within himself.

Riesman states that such a person prefers individual sports, hobbies, and task-oriented occupations, rather than jobs concerned with human frailty. The educational sphere is formal and concerned with impersonal matters, with an emphasis on intellectual content. In the economic field one finds a "free market"

and a stress on production. Riches are accumulated, and consumption is ostensible.

The inner-directed man does not consume for the sake of consumption but because of status and prestige, as a pathway to success, and has a passionate desire to make things *his*. He may lavish money and energy on a house to the point where it may resemble a department store; or go in for diamonds, libraries, or treasures of Europe, engrossed in showing off his possessions, to fit into a role demanded of him by his station or hoped-for station in life.[6]

Other-Direction

The *other-directed* person lives in a different world, one in which there is social mobility, but also a world of servomechanisms, electronic computers, and mechanized gadgetry in which production is no longer a problem.

It is a world of abundance, in which the individual must learn to live not as a producer but must be carefully taught to live as a consumer. His path to success is not by way of producing a more competitive product but by merchandising a pleasing personality. Getting along with others is the magic key to accomplishment, depending less on what he is and what he does than on what others think of him and how competent he is in the art of being manipulated as well as manipulating others.

"What is common to all other-directed people is that their contemporaries are the source of direction for the individual —either those known to him or those with whom he is indirectly acquainted, through friends and through the mass media. This source is of course 'internalized' in the sense that dependence on

---

[5] Riesman, same reference as footnote 1, p. 15.

[6] Riesman, same reference as footnote 1, pp. 117–118.

it for guidance in life is implanted early. The goals toward which the other-directed person strives shift with that guidance: it is only the process of striving itself and the process of paying close attention to the signals from others that remain unaltered throughout life."[7]

The home is no longer the agent of greatest influence in implanting the social values in a child; instead, the peer group becomes all important. The character of the other-directed person is such that the peer groups are looked to for guidance by both the children themselves and by the parents. The group the other-directed person belongs to and whose goals and values he internalizes is made up of his contemporaries.

In education, cooperation and "getting along" is stressed rather than academic matters. In the occupational and economic sphere, the free market is replaced by cooperation and fair trade. Amassing wealth is no longer important. Spending is now stressed; and the art of proper consumption must be carefully learned, for it must not be conspicuous.

The other-directed person "is kept within his consumption limits not by goal-directed but by other-directed guidance, kept from splurging too much by others' envy and from consuming too little by his own envy of the other."[8]

Above all, the other-directed man needs the approval of others and hence must not be overly competitive. Riesman holds that in the United States one can no longer find tradition-direction, but a population largely made up of inner- and other-directed individuals. In the metropolitan areas other-direction is gradually overtaking inner-direction. However, he clearly makes the point that the majority of the population of this country would

still have to be counted as being closer to inner-direction than other-direction.[9]

Errors in Interpretation

In the revised edition of his basic marketing text, McCarthy exemplifies the type of interpretations Riesman seems to evoke.[10] He says: "The 'inner-directed' man has his own value system and directs his own activities, whereas the 'outer-directed' [he means other-directed] person is the one whose character is formed chiefly by those around him. Those 'outer-directed' [other-directed] people—the vast majority of our society, according to Riesman—are led by each other, and consequently there is a strong tendency to conform."[11]

This statement is quoted only because it typifies some of the types of errors made by other marketing men. What are some of these erroneous assumptions made by people in marketing?

First, other-direction does not encompass the vast majority of our society. At best, Riesman claims that in the metropolitan areas other-direction is overtaking inner-direction.[12]

Second, it is erroneous to imply that the inner-directed man is completely free to behave as he wishes in directing his activities. Riesman states that the inner-directed man is much less free than he seems for his source of direction is implanted early in life by the elders and

[7] Riesman, same reference as footnote 1, p. 21.

[8] Riesman, same reference as footnote 1, p. 79.

[9] Also see Waltraud M. Kassarjian, A Study of Riesman's Theory of Social Character, unpublished doctoral dissertation, University of California, Los Angeles, 1960, pp. 75–92; and Richard Centers, "An Examination of the Riesman Social Character Typology: A Metropolitan Survey," Sociometry, Vol. 25 (September, 1962), pp. 231–240.

[10] McCarthy, same reference as footnote 2.

[11] Same reference, p. 256.

[12] See references, footnote 9.

directed toward generalized but none-theless inescapably destined goals.[13] Once implanted, his value system determines to a great extent the decisions he will make the rest of his life, and clearly he is not free to direct his own activities.

Third, it is often believed that the other-directed person is one whose character is formed chiefly by his peers. The Riesman thesis is that the character is formed to be sensitive to the peer group, and is prepared to accept change, not that the peers form the character of the adult individual.

Fourth, many people in marketing seem to believe that the other-directed person, as compared with the inner-directed, is more of a conformist. True, in his attempts to get along in the group and to gain their approval and acceptance, the other-directed person does conform to the expectations and influences of his peers. But the inner-directed man may be just as much a conformist,

if not more so.[14] Riesman points out that the reasons for which he conforms may be different and the manner of conformity may differ, but he conforms almost rigidly to the established standards and values he has incorporated.

Finally, an error of interpretation sometimes made (but usually not discussed by marketing people) is that the concepts of inner- and other-direction are somehow related to introversion-extroversion or other personality variables. Riesman claims that social character is not personality but that which is ". . . shared among significant social groups and which . . . is the product of the experience of these groups. [Unlike personality] the notion of social character permits us to speak . . . of the character of classes, groups, regions and nations."[15]

[13] Riesman, same reference as footnote 1, p. 15.

[14] Waltraud M. Kassarjian, "A Study of Riesman's Theory of Social Character," *Sociometry*, Vol. 25 (September, 1962), pp. 213–230.

[15] Riesman, same reference as footnote 1, p. 4; also Kassarjian, same reference as footnote 14.

10

Limits of Persuasion: The Hidden Persuaders Are Made of Straw

Raymond A. Bauer

In recent years the public has developed an exaggerated fear of the possibility of being controlled and manipulated by others. Some of this fear probably traces back to the "technique of the big lie," which seemed to delude the masses in dictator countries, as well as to the "brainwashing" stories that came out of the Korean War. These fears have been played upon by popular writers until half-truths are accepted as verified facts. In this article a psychologist takes a sober look at many of these unreasoned fears and puts them in better perspective.

Man seems to live in perpetual hope and horror that infallible means have been developed whereby one man can control another's behavior. As usual, the hope and the horror are opposite sides of the same coin:

On the hopeful side, some selfishly see the possibility of advantage for themselves in gaining control over their fellow men. Others, more idealistically, look to a "science of man" as the basis for establishing a Utopia which will be optimally efficient in the production of both material goods and human happiness.

On the side of horror, some fear that they themselves will be "manipulated" to the advantage of someone else. Others fear the motives for their own relations to their fellow men. The image of a potential Utopia gets turned inside out and we see that the reverse image is that of 1984—the totalitarian state of George Orwell's novel—in which the best qualities of man are lost.

Recent developments in the science of psychology, and the publicity given to some of its more sensational applications —such as "subliminal advertising" or "brainwashing"—have strengthened our anxiety. The significance of these developments is of particular concern to businessmen, for they, along with politicians, will be responsible for the use of the new techniques. But there is no reason for panic. Anxiety stems, in part, from ignorance of the causal relations between the "persuaders" and the "persuaded." To show this relationship, and the limi-

Reprinted by permission from *Harvard Business Review,* Vol. 36, No. 5, September-October, 1958, pp. 105–110.

tations it imposes on the techniques, we must consider three broad areas of application:

Propaganda and human relations.
Appeals to "noneconomic" motives.
Appeals to "unconscious" motives.

With a better understanding of the functioning of these techniques, we will be in a stronger position to evaluate them realistically.

New Fear or Old Scare?

The specter of "manipulation" and "hidden persuasion" has stalked all the lands that man has ever inhabited. The most primitive manifestation of the deep anxiety which we feel on this issue is represented by Nightmare Alice, the witch of Li'l Abner Land. From time to time, Nightmare Alice makes an effigy of one of the "good people" of Dogpatch and places this person under her hidden control. Black magic is found among most nonliterate peoples, and the fear of it persists. In the Middle Ages, people were "possessed by the devil"; in our own colonial times we went back to "witches."

In recent decades, to be sure, we have done away with such superstitions and become more "scientific." Or have we simply dressed up our old fears in modern fashions? Remember how during the 1920's and 1930's we worried about the mysterious powers of the mass media, particularly as manipulated by such practitioners as George Creel and Ivy L. Lee? My point is that although this century has led to tremendous progress in our knowledge of the human mind, our fear that this knowledge will be misused is as old as the history of man.

But what are the facts? Does modern psychology give us the tools to control each other? The full range of considerations is, of course, beyond our purview here. Moreover, any discussion of psychological techniques of persuasion and manipulation must, of course, be done without knowing what new knowledge may be developed. It is my belief, however, that what I have to say must hold in principle for almost any conceivable situation that may develop.

Ratio of Resistance

Let me begin my positive assertions with what may seem like a paradoxical statement. Without doubt we have, largely on the basis of improved social science knowledge in the fields of psychology, sociology, and anthropology, developed increasingly refined and effective means of persuasion. It does not follow, however, that even in the field of advertising we are able to effect more persuasion. How can this be? Simply because the increased knowledge benefits not only the persuader but also the target of persuasion. As the persuaders become more sophisticated, so do the people to be persuaded.

One way of reading the history of the development of techniques of persuasion is that the persuaders have been in a race to keep abreast of the developing resistance of the people to be persuaded. Thus:

In the decades following World War I, we were very excited about the power of propaganda. We came close to saying that if it were possible to get a story in the newspapers or on the radio, people would automatically believe it and act on it. But what happened? Many people became so suspicious of propaganda that

they would scarcely believe the news on the sports page.

As a result, World War II propaganda in the Western countries was markedly different from that of World War I. Propagandists—that is, "persuaders"—were scrupulously careful not to test the credulity of their readers and listeners; they also avoided more blatant emotional appeals.

Why? People had become more sophisticated, and more resistant to "persuasion." Social science research on the effects of communications, by the beginning of World War II, had pretty well destroyed the myth of propaganda's omnipotence.

We see today similar developments in advertising. There is still some advertising that is reminiscent of the oldfashioned pitchman selling snake oil. However, the development of the "soft sell" seems to me a tacit acknowledgment of the developing resistance of the potential consumer.

Manipulation More Difficult

Within business and industry we have witnessed the evolving concern with human relations and communication. These events also have been viewed with horror as evidence of the growth of manipulation. But the viewers-with-horror naively assume that the knowledge on which this presumed manipulation is based is limited to the manipulators. Without in any way deprecating the desirability of the human relations approach—I not only favor it but even try to practice it—I doubt if it has produced any increase in manipulation.

As a matter of fact, all this new concern must have made the process of interpersonal communications more complicated. It is traditional that, as people become more diplomatic, their communications become more subtle. Perhaps we are all reaching the point of the diplomat who, on being informed of the death of his opposite number, queried: "I wonder what he meant by that." So in the absence of any long-run trend statistics on the number of effective persuasive and manipulative acts in business and industry, I shall remain content with pointing to the obvious mechanisms of resistance to persuasion; noting that manipulation has become more difficult; and suggesting there is no more reason to believe that the actual practice of manipulation has increased than that it has lessened. The data to prove me wrong are unobtainable.

Hidden Persuaders?

Our main fear, however, is not that we will be taken in by the persuasive logic of a Madison Avenue salesman but that, through appeals to deep, unconscious motives, we can be manipulated without even knowing it.

A book such as Vance Packard's *Hidden Persuaders*[1] generates a good deal of soul searching, both among the general public and within professional circles. This book, for the benefit of the fortunate few who are not familiar with it, tells a story, though certainly not *the* story, of how psychology has been applied in market research. By determining people's unconscious motives "via the principles of modern dynamic psychology," researchers are able to devise methods whereby mysterious and miraculous marketing results are produced. The consumer is powerless to resist these techniques, and he just buys and buys without knowing why. From this it is, of course, only one step to applying these techniques in politics, and 1984 will arrive at least twenty years

[1] New York, David McKay Company, Inc., 1957.

ahead of schedule. Packard's picture, needless to say, is a trifle stylized.

Packard wrote his book to warn the public. The net impact of the volume is that there has been a complete revolution in market research in the form of motivation research, the term for the intensive exploration of the psychological factors involved in consumer behavior and product usage. But it is only the *intensity of concern* that is new. So far as I can see, the major practical result has been—as one might expect—an increased and unrealistic demand for motivation research. Packard succeeded in painting the picture of psychological demonology so persuasively that motivation researchers are now concerned with giving their clients a more realistic notion of what they can do.

But Packard also succeeded in creating again the primitive anxiety that we are on the verge of being able to establish complete control over human behavior to the extent that the victims of this control will not have a chance to resist it because they do not realize it is there.

Noneconomic Motives

In the first place, people *do* have some chance to resist the motives associated with the new techniques. People buy many things for *noneconomic* reasons, but such motives are not necessarily *unconscious*. It is a serious mistake to equate the two; and the use of the term *irrational* makes the confusion even worse. Once you label noneconomic motives irrational, you imply they are unreasonable, and you are well on the way to assuming they are unconscious.

When I say that people do things for noneconomic reasons (what others might call "irrational"), I am talking about the fact that people may buy a particular automobile because they desire status, the esteem of themselves and others;

because they like products which fit their own self-image; or even because a man likes the feeling of potency which comes from driving an overhorsepowered vehicle. But I can see no reason to say a man is more "rational" to want transportation than to want self-respect and the esteem of others—though if it helps you to understand why he is doing what he is doing, you can say he is being less economic.

It is true that most of the motives I have just mentioned are not usually cited in response to the direct question: "Why did you buy that product?" In our culture, the accepted reasons for buying a product bear on its primary economic function: for instance, the cost of transportation provided by the car, the cleaning effectiveness of a soap, and so on. Accordingly, we are not as likely to think of the noneconomic motives as reasons for buying, bearing as they do on the secondary functions (or "added value") of products. Or, if we do, perhaps we feel a little ashamed and so are reticent about them. But in no meaningful sense are these motives unconscious. With a little stimulation almost every one of us recognizes their existence.

Practical Consequences

This is no mere quibble. The fact that people can and do acknowledge the existence of these motives has considerable practical consequence. The use of appeals directed to such motives—as well as the widespread discussion, which we have already witnessed, of the them into the center of consciousness as concern given such motives in product design and merchandising—is bringing buying motives even if they were not there before. Some people will come to accept these as proper buying motives, and will probably learn to shop as

astutely for the product that gives them the most prestige as for the product that has the lowest price, best mechanical qualities, and so on. Other people will resist these appeals, not accepting the secondary functions as a legitimate reason for buying.

Appeals to such motives may still serve, as in the past, to win the merchandiser a temporary advantage. However, as such appeals become customary and the public becomes generally aware of them, they will leave the merchandiser just about where he was to start with as far as his "persuasive advantage" is concerned.

Just because marketing and product design are based increasingly on psychologically oriented market research, it does not follow that products will continue to be sold increasingly on the basis of their secondary functions or "added value." At this time merchandisers are becoming more and more alert to the power of the secondary characteristics of products to satisfy consumer wants. As a psychologist I can have no conceivable objection in principle to people's noneconomic wants being satisfied. But we must look seriously at the possibility that this trend may reach the point of saturation.

Even now, the "irrationality"—a word I detest—of the consumer may be grossly overestimated. In few, if any, of the discussions of consumer motivation is there any mention of the growth of such consumer information services as Consumer's Research and Consumer's Union. The notion that people are not concerned with and do not understand the technical aspects of the products they buy may have to be tempered in the future. Today's consumers are almost certainly more interested and better informed on the technical features of products than they have been in the past.

There is something ironical in depicting the housewife shopping in the supermart as being indifferent to economy, being cozened by hidden persuaders into spending 15% more for her market basket than some stringent criterion says is necessary. Remember, the corner grocery store offers the housewife psychological rewards that the supermart does not. Yet in the interests of economy housewives have deserted the corner grocery store for the more impersonal, but more economical, supermart. This very same group of housewives has patronized discount houses, which scarcely give them the same psychological satisfaction as do department and high-class specialty stores.

One of the established arguments for stressing the secondary functions of a product is that all products in a given line are virtually identical with respect to their primary economic function. But suppose all automobiles in a given price range became virtually identical with regard to their symbolic value: this might drive the manufacturers to strive again for differentiation on the basis of the primary function of transportation. This notion is far from facetious. While Chrysler may indeed have gotten into difficulty a few years ago by de-emphasizing styling, today it is the small economical car—American Rambler or a foreign make—that is making inroads into the market, not the cars with "sex appeal."

This is not to brush aside the importance of the motives that the motivation researchers have stressed. I am merely suggesting that we keep our image of the consumer in somewhat clearer perspective. The merchandiser who concentrates too much on the secondary characteristics of products will find himself in as much difficulty as the one who ignores them completely. Motivation research may indeed become indispensable *because* of the very trends in the population I have been describing. The merchandiser will probably need increasingly detailed psychological knowledge of consumers as the years go on, if only to know what difficulties he is up against and how far he must stay away from noneconomic appeals.

Unconscious Motives

This is not the whole picture. All that I have said to this point is that many of the motives with which motivation research deals are not unconscious *in any meaningful sense;* and that, as these particular motives are appealed to, the consumer recognizes them more explicitly as motives linked to consumer behavior, and develops the capacity for a critical appraisal of appeals to such motives.

But there *are* some truly unconscious motives—that is, motives which the individual would not acknowledge consciously to *himself* even if, or especially if, they are called explicitly to his attention. To illustrate:

One of the most spectacular of the claims for the exploitation of unconscious motives is the development of the hardtop convertible. The hardtop is labeled as a compromise between the male buyer's dual attachment to the stable, reliable wife, symbolized by the sedan, and the flashy, unreliable mistress, symbolized by the convertible.

Certainly, in psychoanalytic thinking, it is accepted that the male child has conflict over thinking of his mother as a sexual object, and develops a split image of women. But I cannot conceivably take a stand on whether or not this is the complete story of the hardtop, or what substantial portion of the story it may comprise. I use it only as an example of appealing to a motive that is meaningfully referred to as unconscious.

There is something very plausible in the notion that if we understand another person's unconscious motivation, then we can appeal to his motives and get him to do something without his knowing why he did it. Certainly, he ought to be powerless to resist. To some extent this is true. But the entire picture is more complicated. Remember that there is a reason for certain motives remaining unconscious; in general, conscious acknowledgment of these motives would produce intolerable anxiety. Hence, appeal to such motives may backfire, and backfire violently. Thus, on an *a priori* basis, combining the "mistress and the wife" in the form of the hardtop convertible *could* have aroused anxiety and caused people to stay away from this model in droves.

Power to Resist

I am not arguing for or against the effectiveness of any of these techniques of persuasion. I have merely indicated that individuals have the capacity to resist even on the unconscious level. I *am* arguing that the individual's resistance to persuasion probably increases in proportion to the efforts made to persuade him against his own perceived interest. We may even go further than that. Our primitive anxiety concerning the possibility of being manipulated leads us to resist persuasion by others, even in some instances where it may be *in our own interest*. Thus we have the automatic response, "Nobody's going to tell me what's good for me."

My guess is that over the years the American people have developed resistance to manipulation at about the same rate that our techniques of persuasion have become more sophisticated and effective. I mean, of course, that *if the audience had remained the same*, our new techniques would be more effective than our old ones. But the audience has not remained the same. The pace of the

race has grown swifter, but it is difficult to say who has gained on whom.

Another point to remember is that merchandising is a competitive activity, and any technique of research or persuasion is about equally available to anyone who wants to make use of it. Even the vaunted subliminal advertisements would tend to cancel out each other if all refrigerator manufacturers, for example, were to use them on television. Competition among persuaders, indeed, is very much like that between the persuader and the object of his persuasion. Adoption of a new technique may well give a momentary competitive advantage, but this advantage lasts only until competitors have also adopted that technique. As long as there is a multiplicity of advertisers, it is difficult to see how the public at large can become the passive puppets of "hidden persuaders."

Omnipotent Control?

But there is still one other dread possibility to dispose of, if we can. Let us consider what might happen if there were *no* competition—if the tools of manipulation were in one group's hands. This would be 1984, the society in which an elite group will direct the behavior of everyone else in so subtle a way that no one is aware that it is happening. Perhaps it has already happened? How could we tell when it began?

I would not say for a moment that there are no situations in which one person can exercise absolute control over another. Give one man a gun (known in the vernacular as a "persuader"), and he can do a pretty good job of directing the activities of an unarmed man. True, some people in such a situation have escaped, taken the gun from the man, or got themselves shot. But I would not like to quibble about such a small minority, particularly in view of the fact that the effectiveness of this persuader depends on its presence being known, not hidden.

Accounts of brainwashing and similar phenomena indicate that—with a considerable expenditure of effort, careful control of a man's environment (which includes isolating him and getting him in a state of fatigue), good intuitive psychological insight, and a great deal of patience—it *is* possible to change the beliefs of a large proportion of one's victims. There is even some threat in the offing that the use of drugs and of electrodes implanted in the brain may make such procedures more effective.

Although I have some modicum of competence on such subjects, I frankly do not know exactly how far one can go now or in the immediate future with such procedures of influencing people. But look at how remote this is from the notion of controlling *a large society* via psychological techniques. Not only is it doubtful if strictly psychological practices would effect a considerable amount of brainwashing in the absence of all the other factors of control over the individual's environment, but there is the very practical matter that the amount of time and energy expended on each individual must be at least equal to his own time and energy. In short, the influencing of a single individual in a confined situation and by a large number of people is an entirely different case from that of a small number of people influencing a large number of people on a societal level. The Soviet Union is the closest approximation to this latter circumstance that we have seen, and I can say from my own studies of that society that the persuasion was far from hidden, far from total, and, possibly, far from desirable for the efficient functioning of the society.[2]

[2] See, for example, Raymond A. Bauer, "Brainwashing, Psychology or Demonology," *Journal of Social Issues,* Vol. 13, No. 3, 1957, p. 41.

To be quite realistic, I do not see how anyone who has observed or operated any large-scale organization can take seriously the notion of complete control of behavior. In particular, social science has taught us at least as much about the *necessity* of permitting initiative—which a 1984 society by definition cannot do —as it has taught us about directing behavior.

Conclusion

In sum, I am skeptical about the extreme pictures of "hidden persuasion" that have been drawn for either the present or future of business or politics. This does not mean I am indifferent to the prospects of individual instances of the unscrupulous use of psychological or other social science knowledge. What I have been attacking is the notion of the possibility of omnipotent control over the behavior of large numbers of human beings. That such a notion rears its head repeatedly comes, I believe, from our primitive anxiety over manipulation. This anxiety is caused, on the one hand, by our fear that other people may be doing it to *us,* and therefore that we have lost control over our own destiny. It comes, on the other hand from the notion that *we* may be doing it to others; and here we have a sense of guilt concerning our own motives and behavior toward those others.

I may be fighting a straw man in the sense that this particular *object* of people's fears is not real. But the *fears* exist; they are real. To date most people have not recognized that the threat of omnipotent control over man's behavior *is* a straw man. It may be that my contribution here is that of pointing out that the "hidden persuaders" in their exaggerated form are, in fact, made of straw.

11

A New Approach to Consumer Motivation

Jon G. Udell

Almost all marketing textbooks, and most people who have anything to do with advertising, categorize buying motives as rational or emotional. Although this distinction has a long and honorable history, it is not soundly based in fact or logic. The author of the next article effectively points out the deficiencies of the present classification and proposes a better alternative.

The importance of customer buying motives in the marketing success of a product was emphasized forty years ago in the pioneering work of Melvin T. Copeland.[1] In an attempt to present a classification of motives useful to business management, Copeland proposed separating them into two categories, rational and emotional:

Rational buying motives are those which are aroused by appeals to reason. The group includes such motives as dependability in use, durability, and economy in purchase.[2]

Emotional buying motives include emulation, satisfaction of the appetite, pride of personal appearance, cleanliness, pleasure of recreation, securing home comfort, and analogous motives.

These motives have their origin in human instincts and emotions and represent impulse or unreasoning promptings to action.[3]

Copeland's approach is still widely used in the literature of marketing and advertising. Each year thousands of college men and women preparing to take their place in the world of business, learn that buying motives fall into these two categories, and that the type of motive should determine the nature of the appeal to be used in merchandising the product.

Ironically, the current definitions of consumer buying motives, while retaining Copeland's original distinction, vary considerably from author to author. Charles Phillips and Delbert Duncan, co-authors of a widely-used marketing textbook, emphasize the importance of reasoning—its presence or its absence —in the motivation to purchase:

Emotional product motives are those which lead the consumer to buy a

Reprinted from the *Journal of Retailing,* Vol. 40, No. 1, Winter, 1964–65, p. 6 10.

[1] Melvin T. Copeland, *Principles of Merchandising,* New York: A. W. Shaw Company, 1924, pp. 155–167.

[2] *Ibid.,* p. 162.

[3] *Ibid.*

certain product without considering the reasons for or against the action.[4] In contrast, rational product motives for buying are usually described as those which involve conscious reasoning about a course of action.[5]

In a recent book by Richard H. Buskirk, a rational buying motive is defined as "any consideration affecting the full, long-run cost of the article to the purchaser."[6] Still another author, Jerome McCarthy, distinguishes between the motives by stating that, "So-called 'rational' motives can be appealed to directly without offending consumers, whereas 'emotional' motives must be appealed to more subtly."[7]

A New Classification Needed

Copeland's basic classification has weathered many years of criticism and redefinition, probably because of its simplicity and because of its identification with the type of advertising appeals to be used in merchandising a product. Many alternative classifications, most of them more detailed and psychologically more sophisticated, have been proposed; but none has been widely adopted.

Despite the appeal and continued use of Copeland's rational-emotional distinction, the classification is not adequate to meet today's needs. It is, at best, confusing and may be very damaging in the

implications it conveys to marketing management.

Many objections can be raised to its continued use, three of which are covered by the following remarks:

1. The choice of expressions to describe the two types of motives is very unfortunate. By labeling one set of motives rational, the other group is assumed to be not rational or irrational. However, it is not irrational to seek emotional satisfaction. Vast numbers of American consumers are far beyond satisfying their basic physical needs for survival, and consequently are also striving to satisfy their emotional and psychological desires. Such satisfaction often constitutes very real utility for both individuals and society as a whole. In short, *emotionally-based purchases are often very rational purchases.*

2. The definitions used to differentiate between emotional and rational motives are meaningless and contradictory. Emotional buying motives, according to Copeland, have their origins in human instincts and emotions and, as such, represent impulse buying and unreasoned purchasing. However, many goods are purchased for emotional and psychological reasons after considerable deliberation and thought. Surely this is the application of the process of reasoning to the purchasing decision (which contradicts the original definition). A similar criticism can be leveled at Copeland's assertion that rational buying motives are those which are aroused by appeals to reason. Most buying motives can be aroused by appeals to reason. Many advertising campaigns have hit pay dirt by using reason to help the customer rationalize his emotional desire for a product. In addition, it is often effective to appeal directly to the

[4] Charles F. Phillips and Delbert J. Duncan, *Marketing Principles and Methods,* Homewood, Illinois: Richard D. Irwin, Inc., Fourth Ed., 1960, p. 51.

[5] *Ibid.*

[6] Richard H. Buskirk, *Principles of Marketing—The Management View,* New York: Holt, Rinehart, and Winston, Inc., 1961, p. 174.

[7] E. Jerome McCarthy, *Basic Marketing, A Managerial Approach,* Homewood, Illinois: Richard D. Irwin, Inc., 1960, p. 85.

customer's judgment by emphasizing the emotional satisfaction to be gained from a particular product or service. In brief, there may be a continuous interplay of emotion and reason in all types of consumer buying motives.

3. In the light of the above comments, it follows that the rational-emotional classification is of little value to management in designing a marketing program. Should the vendors of sailboats use a rational or an emotional appeal? If an emotional appeal is used, should it appeal directly to the desires for creation and prestige, or should it appeal indirectly by attempting to rationalize these desires for the consumer? The classification gives little guidance in answering these and other important questions.

What Are Buying Motives?

Motives are the drives, impulses, wishes, or desires which initiate the sequence of activities known as behavior. Some psychologists do not consider the words "motives," "drives," "impulses," "wishes," and "desires" as synonymous, whereas others use them interchangeably. From the marketing executive's point of view, there is little to be gained by drawing hairline distinctions among these terms; therefore the author, taking a management point of view, concurs with the latter school of thought.

Unfortunately, buying motives are not identified with precision in the literature of marketing. The following definition is typical: "Buying motives are those influences or considerations which impel and produce the purchase of certain goods from particular firms."[8] The student or reader may well ask what influences and considerations are being referred to by the authors. Again, others

define product buying motives as "those influences which lead a consumer to choose one product in preference to another" including "all the influences and reasons that cause a consumer to purchase a given product."[9] These definitions are vague and superficial. There are many influences other than motives that enter into the purchasing decision. The billions of dollars spent on advertising and promotion certainly have some influence on the purchasing behavior of both industrial buyers and ultimate consumers. To define buying motives as the influences or considerations which impel the purchase of a product is to include all the inducements, incentives, and stimuli that prompt purchasing behavior, and not just the motives for the behavior. Therefore, product buying, motives can be defined more adequately as all those impulses, desires, and considerations of the customer which induce the purchase of certain goods and services.[10] In short, buying motives encompass the underlying conscious and unconscious reasons why people buy what they buy.

A Reclassification of Product Buying Motives

The objective of this reclassification is to identify buying motives in a way that will guide managerial decision making towards the development of effective marketing programs. The buyer's needs and desires must be appealed to and satisfied, and this satisfaction can be derived from the following sources:

[9] Rayburn D. Tousley, Eugene Clark, and Fred E. Clark, *Principles of Marketing*, New York: The Macmillan Co., 1962, pp. 112, 113.

[10] Patronage motives would be defined as the impulses, desires, and considerations within the customer which induce the purchase of goods and services from particular firms.

[8] Phillips and Duncan, *op. cit.*, p. 52.

1. The product's physical performance, or
2. The consumer's social and psychological interpretation of the product and its performance, or
3. A combination of the product's physical performance and the consumer's social and psychological interpretation of the product.

Given the two basic sources of satisfaction, physical performance and socio-psychological interpretation, product buying motives may be classified according to two extremes, those which are *operational* and those which are *socio-psychological.*

Operational buying motives include those reasons for the purchase which are directly related to the anticipated performance of the product. In other words, their satisfaction is derived from the product's physical performance. The majority of product buying motives for industrial goods falls within this class. For example, a road construction company purchases a new dump truck because it will serve the firm by hauling construction materials. A consumer's operational buying motive may be illustrated by a Michigan homeowner's desire to have an efficient oil burner to heat his home.

Socio-psychological buying motives comprise those reasons for the purchase which are only indirectly related to the anticipated performance of the product but directly related to the consumer's social and psychological interpretation of the product. The utility which the consumer receives is only indirectly derived from the product's physical performance. The direct source of utility is the psychological satisfaction which the consumer receives through the ownership, use, and social prestige of the product. This psychological satisfaction may be received at the buyer's conscious or subconscious level of thought. If a young lady receives psychological satisfaction from a bottle of expensive French perfume because she associates it with an advertisement picturing a heavy romance, she is probably receiving psychological satisfaction at a subconscious level. However, if the satisfaction is primarily derived from her belief in the social prestige of the perfume, the psychological satisfaction is received at a more conscious level.

The potential source of satisfaction is the controlling factor in distinguishing between the two types of buying motives. However, it is important to recognize that a product is rarely purchased on the basis of one motive, and that the motives inducing a purchase can seldom be classified as entirely socio-psychological or entirely operational. Therefore, the motives inducing the purchase of a product should be visualized as existing on the continuum

The Buying Motive Continuum

Operational Buying Motives	Socio-Psychological Buying Motives
Satisfaction to be derived from physical performance of product	Satisfaction to be derived from consumer's social and psychological interpretation of the product and its performance

between the two extreme types of buying motives.

The suggested classification takes on a fuller meaning when it is applied to the marketing strategy of the business firm. Although all aspects of the marketing program may relate to both the socio-psychological and operational buying motives, advertising and sales efforts are more closely related to the socio-psychological buying motives, whereas the quality of the product and product service are more closely related to the operational buying motives.

It is suggested that this set of relationships can be used in allocating marketing efforts between product and sales efforts. Suppose a cosmetics manufacturer were to analyze the buying motives and purchasing behavior involved in the purchase of cosmetics. The manufacturer finds that some minimum quality level is important, but that many major factors in the consumer's purchase relate to the individual's psychological interpretation of the product and the social prestige of the product. Assuming that the minimum quality level is met, the manufacturer will find it most profitable to invest his marketing efforts in advertising and sales promotion. These efforts should be designed to create a favorable product image, an image which would appeal to the consumer's socio-psychological buying motives. An example of this approach is provided by the success of Revlon with its promotion of the "Tiger Lady" image.

On the other hand, one would expect manufacturers of major installations to emphasize the quality of their products and services in their marketing programs because the majority of the buying motives for major installations are operational in nature. Motives such as productivity of the equipment, durability, efficiency, and profitability are predominant. The sellers of major installations do, in fact, emphasize product and service more than sales efforts. In a sample study, twelve producers of major installations were asked to select the five most important areas in their marketing program and they unanimously selected "product research and development" and "product service."[11] No other facet of marketing strategy received a 100 per cent selection ratio. In fact, advertising and sales promotion was selected by only 33 per cent of the respondents.

Conclusion

Copeland's rational-emotional distinction was a significant contribution to marketing thought and practice in 1924. Today, this classification is obsolete and even misleading in its implications for management. The socio-psychological and operational continuum offers a more useful approach to buying motives. This classification emphasizes the importance of customer buying motives in the development of the *entire* marketing program. In addition, it provides management with a general guide for the allocation of marketing strategy between product efforts and sales efforts.

[11] Jon G. Udell, *A Model of Non-Price Competitive Strategy*, Madison, Wisconsin: Wisconsin Selected Papers, Vol. I, No. 1, Bureau of Business Research and Service, University of Wisconsin, 1963, p. 15.

12

Shopping, Specialty, or Convenience Goods?

Arno K. Kleimenhagen

In recent years there has been a tendency for marketing scholars to question the time-honored classification of consumer goods into convenience, shopping, and specialty goods. Since the original classification was not based on significant research there was good reason to question its validity. However, much of the more recent theorizing has been almost equally based on subjective judgment. The author of the following article has made an interesting study by the observational method of research. The research method itself is interesting in that it illustrates the extent to which it is possible to observe the behavior of people minutely without their knowledge—or objection after they are told they have been observed. The conclusions also throw some interesting light on the traditional classification of consumer goods.

The traditional consumer goods classification system defines goods in terms of patterns of shopping behavior. Melvin T. Copeland, from casual observation of consumers in the market place, divided merchandise sold in retail stores into the three well-known classes of: (1) convenience goods, (2) shopping goods, and (3) specialty goods.[1] His purpose was to demonstrate how the relationship between consumer behavior and the purchase of goods could be used as a

guide for manufacturers to follow in distributing their wares.

This system, although long subject to criticism, has endured and can be found in one form or another in both past and current marketing textbooks. In fact this classification system and its progeny,[2] all based on hypotheses of buying habits,

Reprinted from the *Journal of Retailing,* Winter 1966–1967, Vol. 42, pp. 32–39.

[1] Melvin T. Copeland, "Relation of Consumers' Buying Habits to Marketing Methods," *Harvard Business Review,* I (April 1923), 282–89.

[2] Definitions Committee, American Marketing Association, "Report of the Definitions Committee," *Journal of Marketing,* XIII (October 1948), 202–17, at p. 206, p. 215. Richard H. Holton, "The Distinction Between Convenience Goods, Shopping Goods, and Specialty Goods," *Journal of Marketing,* XXIII (July 1958), 53–56. Louis P. Bucklin, "Retail Strategy and the Classification of Consumer Goods," *Journal of Marketing,* XXVII (January 1963), 51–56.

have become the basis for various forms of marketing strategy and practice for both manufacturers and retailers. Despite its importance as a marketing concept, the literature contains little evidence of testing the theory inherent in the system. This leads one to suggest that if the consumer goods classification system is to serve as a helpful concept for businessmen to follow, then frequent and varied testing of the hypotheses of behavior implied in the definitions should be conducted.

The study reported here deals with some of the observable behavior of consumers in purchasing goods—more specifically with their shopping effort when attempting purchase. Its purpose was to ascertain the extent to which actual behavior in the market place matches the behavior of the classification system. One aspect of behavior the author considered to be readily observable is the shopping effort the consumer makes while attempting a purchase.

As a starting point it will be useful to examine the shopping effort suggested in each definition:[3]

Convenience Goods: Those goods that the consumer usually desires to purchase frequently, immediately, and with a minimum of effort.

The effort hypotheses: It is usually assumed from this definition that the consumer would not travel a great distance from his place of residence to place of purchase, not visit more than one outlet, and not devote much time negotiating purchase. Certainly these measures of shopping effort should be noticeably less than for shopping goods or specialty goods.

Shopping Goods: Those goods that the consumer usually wishes to pur-

chase only after comparing quality, price, and style in a number of stores.

The effort hypotheses: In this instance the expectation is that the consumer would travel a considerable distance to avail himself of an adequate and proper clustering of store types to allow making the desired comparisons; that he would visit more than one store before purchase; and that considerable time would be involved in accomplishing purchase. Without doubt the task of search should be a readily observable feature of the customer's behavior inasmuch as he must discover which items he wants to buy and from which store.

Specialty Goods: Those goods that have a particular attraction for the consumer so that he is willing to make a special purchasing effort.

The effort hypotheses: In this case, as in the case of convenience goods, it is assumed that the consumer has full knowledge of the product he wishes to purchase before he begins his shopping trip. But in the case of the specialty goods he is willing to expend considerable effort in order to obtain the desired item. His behavior should reveal that he would travel a great distance and that he is likely to visit only one store at a center in attempting purchase. For in the case of the specialty goods the consumer will not accept a substitute and would postpone purchase until the particular item can be found.

This study will attempt to measure these aspects of behavior once the consumer has embarked on a buying expedition. The author would suggest that if these behavior traits are observed, then the basis for classifying goods in the present manner is supported and any

[3] Definitions Committee, American Marketing Association, *ibid.*

strategy based on this concept, whether for a manufacturer or retailer, would rest on an empirically firmer foundation.

Methodology

In order to determine the extent to which this theoretical shopping behavior manifests itself in actual shopping expeditions, data were obtained from the observation of 248 consumers in 10 regional shopping centers in 4 metropolitan areas. Controlled regional centers were selected because (1) all three classes of consumers' goods could be purchased there, (2) each center comprised a well-defined area within which the behavior of a shopper could be observed from time of arrival until departure, and (3) center design, layout, and store composition duplicate traditional shopping locations which have evolved in response to consumer behavior patterns.

The operational field technique used direct observation combined with interview. This combination: (1) permitted the recording of the behavior as it occurred; (2) did not depend on either the willingness or ability of the subject observed to report; and (3) did not require that the subject be conscious of his behavior. In addition the interview at the termination of the visit augmented and clarified the observed actions. For example, the consumer was asked to identify the item or items in which he was most interested and to estimate the distance he lived from the center he visited.

All the items a customer purchased or looked at while at the center were placed into classical consumer goods classes. The standard marketing texts supplemented by Copeland's contribution provided the guidance necessary for the task of classifying. If a clear class could not be found for an item or a task it was placed in an "other" category. The "other" category consisted primarily of services, e.g., exchanges, paying of bills, professional services, repairs, and the patronizing of eating and drinking places. In addition to classifying goods into their traditional classes, the item or items the customer identified as being those in which he was most interested were classified as the main item that generated the shopping trip. All other items he either purchased or "looked at" while at the center were classed as "incidental" items. Without knowledge of the item or items that originated the trip the behavior observed would have little meaning. Accordingly, the data were analyzed according to the respondent's identified main item.

The Matching of Actual Behavior with the Behavior of the Consumer's Goods Definitions

The association of items with overt shopping behavior was observed in terms of the shopping effort implied in the consumer's goods definitions. Thus measures were made in terms of: (1) time spent at the center, (2) distance traveled to the center, and (3) number of stores visited.

Time Spent at Center

The consumer's goods definitions imply that time spent in negotiating a purchase should vary with the class of item. The convenience good purchase requires the least time. Shopping and specialty goods require more time, with shopping goods requiring the greatest expenditure of time because the task of search in this instance is the most complicated.

The data contained in Table I indicates that the time generalizations of the definitions are supported. Those persons identifying a shopping good as their main item spent on the average 44.4 minutes at the center. This was more than twice the average time spent by persons identifying convenience goods and more time than those identifying specialty goods.

Table I. Main Item: Average Time Spent at Center

Class of Main Item	Average Time in Minutes
Shopping Good	44.4
Specialty Good	32.7
Other	26.6
Convenience Good	19.6

Distance Traveled

One would expect from reading the definitions that the trading area for convenience goods would be small compared with the trading areas for shopping and specialty goods. The data in Table II shows that individuals who identified convenience goods as their main item tended to travel lesser distances than those identifying shopping or specialty goods, while those individuals who identified specialty goods tended to travel the greatest distances of all. This would appear to be the behavior implied in the definitions.

Number of Stores Visited

Further, the definitions would indicate that those individuals seeking shopping goods will visit more than one store before accomplishing a purchase. This is expected because the exact nature of the merchandise is not known until after some interstore inspection has been done. In the case of the convenience good, inspection is not important and

in the case of the specialty good the nature of the merchandise is known so that interstore inspection is unnecessary.

Examination of the data in Table III indicates that the proportion of persons seeking a shopping good and visiting more than one store is greater than twice that of persons seeking a convenience good. This finding would tend to support the behavior implied in the definitions.

However, it was noted that almost 75 percent of the persons identifying a shopping good visited only one store for that item. The number of stores visited for the main item is summarized in Table IV.

This evidence would seem to support the argument of some scholars who, in analyzing the basic causes of retail decentralization, have suggested that buying habits have significantly changed. They have stated that "through the instruments of television, newsreels, more widespread circulation of magazines, and improved techniques of illustration in newspaper advertising, most shoppers are reasonably well-informed regarding fashion trends and the characteristics of available merchandise. They (the consumers) seem to be more content to make purchases in nearby stores without the benefit of time-consuming store comparisons than was the case in former years."[4]

However, if this is the case, then one would expect the other measures of effort (time and distance) to be similar to the effort expended in purchasing specialty goods or convenience goods, but the evidence does not reveal this to be so. Rather, the evidence supports the behavior contentions of the definitions regarding time and distance. One could of course argue that the narrow-

[4] William R. Davidson and Paul L. Brown, *Retailing Management,* 2d ed. (New York: Ronald Press Company, 1960), pp. 53–54.

Table II. Main Item: Distance Lived from Center

| Distance from Center | Class of Main Item | | | | | | | |
| | Shopping Good | | Convenience Good | | Specialty Good | | Other | |
	Percent	Cumulative Percent	Percent	Cumulative Percent	Percent	Cumulative Percent	Percent	Cumulative Percent
Up to 1 Mile	13.0	13.0	36.9	36.9	9.5	9.5	26.7	26.7
Over 1 to 2 Miles	20.3	33.3	22.6	59.5	23.8	33.3	13.3	40.0
Over 2 to 3 Miles	13.8	47.1	17.9	77.4	19.1	52.4	6.7	46.7
Over 3 to 4 Miles	10.6	57.7	1.2	78.6	4.7	57.1	13.3	60.0
Over 4 to 5 Miles	14.6	72.3	10.7	89.3		57.1	20.0	80.0
Over 5 to 10 Miles	17.1	89.4	7.1	96.4	14.3	71.4	13.3	93.3
Over 10 Miles	10.6	100.0	3.6	100.0	28.6	100.0	6.7	100.0

ness of the market would account for the variations in time and distance.

The author would argue, however, that the resolution of the seeming contradiction lay not with behavior associated with the main item of the shopping trip but with the "incidental" items in which customers expressed interest. The shopper's "incidental" items were also classed into convenience, shopping, and specialty goods. In respect to these "incidental" items of the shopping trip, it was found that the behavior of the definitions is more strongly supported. Table V shows the types of "incidental" items looked at and the percentage of these items that were purchased.

Table III. Classified Main Item: Number of Stores Visited at Center

| Number of Stores Visited | Class of Main Item | | | |
	Shopping Good Percent	Specialty Good Percent	Other Percent	Convenience Good Percent
1	34.5	57.1	68.8	72.7
2	24.8	23.8	25.0	14.3
3	20.8	9.5	6.2	8.3
4	11.2			3.6
5	4.0	4.8		1.2
6	2.4			
7	.8	4.8		
8	.8			
9	.8			

Table IV.   Classified Main Item: Number of Stores Visited for Main Item

| Number of Stores Visited | Class of Main Item | | | |
	Shopping Good Percent	Specialty Good Percent	Convenience Good Percent	Other Percent
1	74.4	76.5	91.6	100.0
2	16.8	14.0	3.6	
3	5.6	4.8	4.8	
4	2.4	4.8		
5	.8			
6	.8			

The largest percentage of "incidental" items purchased were those classed as convenience goods. Shopping goods, although they comprised the largest number of "incidental" items looked at, were not purchased often. It appeared from the observed behavior of the shoppers examining these "incidental" shopping goods that they were primarily seeking information. The same could be said for specialty goods when they were the class of "incidental" items looked at. It is also interesting to note that when these items were purchased they tended to be lower priced shopping or specialty goods of the variety now carried in what would be termed convenience outlets, e.g., supermarkets, variety, drug, and hardware stores. This finding tended to give weight to Lockley's principle of drift.[5] However, it did not support the hypothesis that consumers are content to make purchases without benefit of store comparisons. Rather the behavior observed relating to "incidental" items appears to support the behavior of the definitions.

It appears from the data that the customer desires to accomplish two tasks while on a purchase expedition:

(1) he wishes to engage in the task of search and (2) he wishes to complete the task of exchange.[6] The data seems to make clear that the task of search for an item is not always conducted on the same shopping trip as the task of exchange for the same item. This is especially important to note in the case of shopping goods.

Conclusion

The shopping behavior generalizations associated with the consumer goods definitions is supported by the data of this research. However, it is important to emphasize to those who desire to evaluate the existing classification system that the two tasks associated with the purchase of goods—the task of search (particularly time-consuming activity in the case of a shopping good) and the task of exchange for an item are not always conducted during the same expedition. This of course in no way implies that the consumer does not wish for a convenient grouping of stores to facilitate making his desired comparisons. Indeed the data idicates that once the consumer has embarked on an

[5] Lawrence C. Lockley, "An Approach to Marketing Theory," in Reavis Cox, Wroe Alderson, and Stanley Shapiro, editors, *Theory in Marketing* (Homewood, Ill.: Richard D. Irwin, Inc., 1964), pp. 44–46.

[6] Louis P. Bucklin, "Retail Strategy and the Classification of Consumer Goods," *Journal of Marketing*, XXVII (January 1963), 51.

Table V.   Types of Incidental Items Looked at and Purchased

	Class of Item		
	Convenience Good	Shopping Good	Specialty Good
Number of Incidental Items Looked at	113	213	29
Percent Purchased	59.3	31.4	20.6

exchange expedition he appreciates the convenience that controlled centers provided for the task of making comparisons.

The observed behavior showed that the consumer uses exchange expeditions for the task of searching for items he will purchase on some later shopping trip. This fact is particularly evident when the main item of the purchase expedition is a shopping or specialty good. Although at the controlled shopping center, where a large variety of all the classes are present in a convenient store clustering, shoppers whose main item is a convenience good will also use the opportunity to search for what may eventually result in future purchases of shopping or specialty goods.

There is little doubt that the consumer is more mobile than ever before,[7] but such mobility does not necessarily indicate that the isolated store location (based on the concept of convenience) is superior to a conventional clustering. Evidence is beginning to come in to indicate that stores selling goods classed as shopping goods in an isolated location do not fare particularly well when a controlled center appears on the scene to compete.[8] The controlling factor would seem to be the existence of a class of goods that consumers wish to compare before purchase in the most convenient way possible. This is a particularly important fact for small retailers of shopping goods to consider in their location decisions. The controlled center meets this need by providing for the consumer a conventional clustering of stores whose evolution is based on the concept of goods first developed for the literature by Melvin Copeland.

The present study did not resolve what happens in the case of specific items. Specific goods may well move between classes or drift as suggested by Lockley. A manufacturer or retailer may want to check this from time to time. But the study does show that consumers look upon goods as shopping, convenience, or specialty items and thus it supports the concept of the definition system.

[7] *Chicago Tribune, How Chicago Shops: The Changing Retail Market*, a publication of the Research Department of the *Chicago Tribune* (Chicago, Ill.: The Tribune Company, 1964) p. 30.

[8] *Retail Memo* (November 6, 1964), Retail Department Bureau of Advertising, ANPA, New York, N.Y.

III

The
Structure
of
Distribution

13

Dual Distribution vs. the Small Retailer

Thomas J. Murray

The field of retailing seems to be peculiarly susceptible to institutional change and turnover. This is so true that in marketing we speak of the "wheel of retailing" to suggest the speed of institutional change in retailing. At present, established retailers see a new threat in the tendency of manufacturers to establish their own retail outlets as a means of augmenting, and sometimes replacing, retailers owned independently. The term dual distribution has become the descriptive designation of this practice. Independently owned retailers quite naturally are fighting dual distribution, but instead of battling it out in terms of economic efficiency, they are turning to the legislature for regulatory help. If history has any precedent value it strongly suggests that a legislative solution provides a truce at best. Any true solution will have to come through economic channels.

Since he first set up shop in 1948, hard-working August G. Huchting has built up his Ontario, California paint store into a tidy, profitable business. Year by year customers of the small store on a pleasant, tree-lined street in this town of 30,000 grew in number; year by year the sales ledgers steadily grew fatter.

Then, suddenly not so long ago Huchting's business suffered a setback: his major supplier, a top-ranking manufacturer, opened its own retail-store outlet close by and began selling identical lines of paint. Worse, it sold

Reprinted by special permission from *Dun's Review and Modern Industry*, August, 1964. Copyright 1968, Dun & Bradstreet Publications Corp.

them at a price with which Huchting could not possibly compete. "Out of this new store," says the soft spoken Huchting bitterly, "they have been selling the larger paint contractors the same materials we handle, at our cost, thus making it impossible for us to compete for the contractors' business."

August Huchting's predicament is no isolated piece of bad luck; it is just one symptom of a fast-moving marketing method—called dual distribution—that has already hurt numerous independent businessmen and menaces thousands more. This dry, unevocative term is the marketing industry's label for any form of sales competition between an independent businessman and his own suppliers.

Right now, dual distribution is hurting the small marketer at every level: manufacturing, wholesaling and retailing. For instance, an independent fabricator of structural steel fights a severe price squeeze forced by his own major raw-material suppliers, the metal mills, which are also selling the same products to the same customers; a candy wholesaler loses business when a big supplier begins to sell its chocolate bars directly to many of his largest retail customers.

But it is the independent retailer who is hardest hit. For in the past few years the number of big manufacturers who are setting up or expanding their own strings of company-owned retail outlets has reached alarming proportions. Not only that, small merchants point to the damaging volume of direct factory-to-customer selling: mail-order sales of books and records, bulk selling of office machines to corporations, big orders of appliances sold directly to builders of large-scale projects, and the like.

To make matters worse, the small merchant finds that competition from the manufacturer is frequently far more damaging than that from a rival independent. For the manufacturer can squeeze the small retailer badly by keeping the wholesale price of his goods inflexible while he himself sells through the company outlet at a retail price equal to, only fractionally above or sometimes even below the independent's cost price.

Dual distribution, of course, is nothing new in itself. For several decades now oil companies and tire manufacturers have owned substantial numbers of their outlets. And for many years paint manufacturers have retailed a large proportion of their own goods. What *is* new, however, is the recent surge in the growth of dual distribution and the spreading of the practice to completely new industries.

There is no single reason behind this surge. Rather, there are several underlying causes that together form a major threat to independent retailing:

- Intensifying competition in many industries has spurred manufacturers to open their own stores in markets where no suitable outlet already exists.
- Manufacturers are learning the value of running a number of their own retail stores for testing both products and new merchandising techniques. President Michael Daroff of Botany Industries, for instance, claims that the firm's 75 retail outlets serve as a "retail laboratory" and that they have aided the company immeasurably in learning about style trends, costs and merchandising. "This information," he says, "makes us better manufacturers because it has put us in a position to know what retailers need and to act quickly on those needs."
- The hardening of the Justice Department's attitude towards external expansion through merger has left many giant manufacturers with vertical integration—such as a move into retailing—as the only major expansion route.
- In recent years large companies have been piling up internally generated cash—frequently more than they know what to do with. Consequently, the financing of their own retail chains is no problem today.
- The massive shift of retailing from city to suburb has dealt a blow at the would-be small retailer, who often cannot raise sufficient capital for a stake in the new shopping centers. Consequently, many big manufacturers are opening their own stores to provide an outlet for their goods.

■ Finally, and increasingly attractive as competition gets rougher, there is the old lure of extra profits that can be made through cutting out the middleman and selling directly to the final customer.

Under the spur of such incentives, then, it is not surprising that company outlets are increasing at a brisk pace and that several new industries are turning to dual distribution. A major new entry, for example, are the appliance makers, some of whom are bypassing their dealers with millions of dollars worth of refrigerators, washing machines and cooking equipment sold directly to home builders. Too, plumbing fixtures are being sold for the first time through manufacturers' retail outlets; microfilm manufacturers are selling in volume directly to large corporations; and within the last ten years dual distribution has spread to the marketing of numerous other goods, ranging from plywood to records and photographic equipment.

One of the areas where dual distribution is currently threatening to hurt badly is in the men's clothing field. To be sure, it is no newcomer there, but in the past few years it has spread rapidly. Only recently, for example, such leading makers of men's wear as Genesco, Louis Roth Co. and Hat Corp. of America have expanded their own retail chains, and all the signs point to further converts to dual distribution.

A typical victim of this trend is proprietor J. Gerald Saul, whose Long Island store has become a profitable local market for several lines of quality clothes. Only recently, Saul declares, a leading supplier took over a store less than one block from his own and began to sell the same lines. "I can't accurately measure the injury we suffered." Saul laments, "but it sure didn't do us any good. And the real harm is still to come."

Chorus of Complaints

Indeed, the complaints of independent businessmen are heard on all sides. R. E. Eubanks of B & E Paint Co. in Shreveport, Louisiana states flatly that competition from suppliers (including Sherwin-Williams Co., Glidden Co. and Pittsburgh Paint Supply), both through company outlets and direct sales from factory locations, forced him to sell out his business. Morris F. Hoffman of Hoffman Glass Service in Joliet, Illinois asserts that after 22 years of operating at the same location, one of his major suppliers, Pittsburgh Plate Glass Co., opened a retail outlet in the same marketing area and approached long-standing customers of his with prices equal to his costs. Says Hoffman: "They make it impossible for me to compete."

Moreover, worse may be yet to come. J. Gerald Saul speaks for many when he declares that he and others like him face risks ranging from the retailer's supply line being dropped off to total manufacturer domination and even, perhaps, eventual extinction as independents. Says Benjamin L. Finn, executive director of Independent Shoemen, largest dealer organization in the shoe industry: "This trend has accelerated to the point where it has now become a move to dominate the industry and control distribution."

And Federal Trade Commission Chairman Paul Rand Dixon himself acknowledges that dual distribution has placed many smaller concerns at a distinct competitive disadvantage. As an independent, says Dixon, "you are subject at all times to being cut off by your supplier."

The small retailers' fears of dual distribution are scarcely allayed by the manufacturers themselves. "We envision a steady growth of both the number and sales volume of our retail leased departments in department stores," says Executive Vice President James C. Taylor of Brown Shoe's Wohl division. And from other giants of this industry, International Shoe Co., Genesco and Endicott Johnson Corp., come similar reports of expansion in their own retail activities.

The story is the same in the tire, paint and gasoline industries. And in the men's wear field, Hart Schaffner & Marx, Botany Industries, Hat Corp. of America, Louis Roth and others have all been adding to their chains of retail outlets. Says Cluett, Peabody & Co. retail stores division President Thomas Macleod: "This aspect of our operations will continue to grow at a normal rate. In the past couple of years our retail outlets have gone up from 30 to 44."

In brief, while there is no way of measuring dual-distribution sales in terms of dollars, the evidence is overwhelming that it is forcing significant changes in the structure of retailing. Many independent retailers are feeling its effects only marginally, but many others are being seriously damaged, and a number have actually been put out of business.

The independent businessman has few weapons to fight back with. Dual distribution is, of course, an entirely legal practice, and a manufacturer is at liberty to compete with the retailer to whom he also sells his goods—and at any price he wishes. Neither is it illegal for the manufacturer to refuse to sell to whomever he wishes. The Federal Trade Commission has no mandate to protect independents from such competition where "unfair methods" are not involved, and the Justice Department is not currently attacking dual distribution as a specific antitrust problem.

Be that as it may, the independent merchant has a number of important factors working for him. In the first place, a large proportion of small retailers are simply not threatened by dual distribution at all. "Manufacturer-owned stores," explains marketing expert Professor Leonard W. Prestwich, "are feasible only for companies that produce full lines of related products or products that are of a relatively high unit value. Otherwise, adequate sales volume cannot be realized in a single retail store without buying products from other manufacturers to round out the line." Consequently, such retailers as the local tobacconist, newspaper vendor, florist, dry-goods store and small variety shop would appear to be free of the potential threat of added competition from the opening of retail outlets by their own suppliers.

In addition, a number of leading manufacturers hold that dual distribution is purely and simply bad business. Good managers, they feel, are hard eonugh to come by without spreading them even more thinly through a venture into retailing. Even more compelling is the desire of such firms to retain the goodwill of the independent retailing force that is already working for them. Such a concern is The Maytag Co., which flatly condemns dual distribution. "I'm enough of a businessman," declares Maytag Marketing Vice President Claire G. Ely, "to know that my future is wrapped up in the sale of my products through normal distributive channels— by sales through dealers to the ultimate consumer. I know that I can't serve two causes at the same time. I can't forever work both sides of the street."

Occasionally a manufacturer will even move in the opposite direction— away from dual distribution. "I know of one company," relates Prestwich, "that, after a study lasting for several years, decided to distribute *entirely* through industrial distributors rather than directly to large customers and through industrial distributors to small customers as they had been doing. Management felt that the dual policy jeopardized their entire distributive system."

Moreover, dealers in the appliance industry have been making headway against one damaging form of dual distribution. Direct sales of appliances by General Electric, Westinghouse and others to builders for installation in large housing projects and apartment buildings have been infuriating the independents for the past few years. In defense of the practice, Edward L. Stehle, general manager of GE's major appliance division's distribution sales operation, recently asserted: "It is simply a hard fact of economic life that many of these customers . . . buy little, if any, of their material requirements in the retail market."

Nevertheless, a number of manufacturers have been pressed into making some adjustments to their sales programs. Philco Corp., for instance, recently eliminated direct sales to builders from its distributors in three cities. Then, too, some of the companies have taken steps to correct an abuse whereby builders have been reselling these appliances at retail in direct competition with the independents.

Help Coming?

Above all, however, small retailers have been looking to Washington for help—not, to be sure, against dual distribution per se, but at least against such practices as below-cost sales by manufacturers, or the ploy whereby manufacturers encourage an independent to go into business selling their goods and then, when the market is fully developed, cut off supplies and launch a company outlet instead. And, stirred by mounting protests, Congress finally moved to investigate.

Last year hearings were held by a subcommittee of the House Select Committee on Small Business, chaired by Representative James Roosevelt (Dem.,

Calif.), a long-time campaigner on behalf of small business. Into these sessions paraded representatives from over 35 industries to give testimony of abuses of dual distribution by suppliers. The subcommittee's report is expected to stress the pervasiveness of dual distribution, and its adverse effects on small business. . . .

The report has excellent credentials. Last March [1964] highly placed staff members of the Small Business Administration, the Federal Trade Commission and the Justice Department's Antitrust Division met together. Their goal: to correlate the findings of the House hearings and a number of other investigations and to coordinate the approach to be used in the final report and recommendations of the subcommittee. To most retailer organizations, this concentration of governmental forces in their interests seems to bode well for the future.

Clearly, Congressman Roosevelt hopes that this report will improve the chances for passage of a bill proposing that firms practicing dual distribution disclose each outlet's operating data; and, even more significant, provide the impetus for an FTC drive against the abuses in dual distribution.

Meanwhile, a group of independent businessmen have started their own drive against dual distribution. Just last June [1964] President Lawrence Schacht of Schacht Steel Construction joined with some 150 independent businessmen to form the Conference on Dual Distribution, a body that has the blessing of Congressman Roosevelt. Its immediate aim: to attract a membership of around 40,000 firms in a drive to help the bills now pending onto the floor for action and, ultimately, to bring about some Government control over manufacturer-supplier competition.

Schacht, an independent fabricator of structural steel, is himself fighting a severe price squeeze caused by his own suppliers, the major metal mills. They generate this pressure, he explains, by keeping his raw-material costs high and simultaneously selling the same finished products at his prices or below them. "Dual distribution," he likes to say, "is nothing less than domestic dumping."

But in spite of all this activity, independent merchants are not optimistic about the future. To them it seems inevitable that dual distribution must spread.

And the spread, they believe, will be explosive, because when big manufacturers turn to retailing they use no half measures. As Congressman Roosevelt puts it: "When a large manufacturer makes a decision to go into distribution, it is improbable that he will open one retail outlet. He is more apt to arrive on the scene with a great number of outlets or to rapidly build up a distribution network over a short period of time."

14

The Resurgence of the Small Retailer Through Franchising

Grey Matter

One of the surprising aspects of retailing has been the hardiness of the small independent operator. With each new institutional development in the field of retailing there is a wave of predictions of the death of the small operator. To say the least, these predictions have been premature. Today the organizational device of franchising is the vehicle through which the small merchant is seeking, and securing, his survival. Although the franchisee may give up some of his independence in the process of accepting a franchise, he does secure survival and often a good living as well. The accompanying article contains a good description of franchising as well as its potentialities and prospects.

A favorite shibboleth of these times, particularly in food retailing, is that the little grocery stores, affectionately called "mom and pop" stores, went the way of the harness shops, the village black-

Reprinted from *Grey Matter*, June, 1964, Vol. 35, No. 6, a Bulletin on Thoughts and Ideas on Advertising and Marketing issued by Grey Advertising, Inc.

smith and the buggy whip maker. And they *did*, at the rate of 10,000 a year in the past 10 years. Yet those of us who peer *beyond* the obvious and keep a sharp eye on *trends* in distribution are aware of a *resurgence* of the small owner-operated store, not only in the food field, but in a wide variety of merchandise and service categories.

What's more, it's reasonable to expect that the small retailer, *franchised by a large advertiser,* may well prove a countervailing force to the growing power of store-controlled brands. Beset by retailers' *demands* for *more* margin, advertising allowances, display allowances, store-opening contributions and direct-to-consumer shipments, it should not be surprising if giant advertisers seek channels of distribution where they can have *better control* of their distributive dollar. The *franchised operation* may be the answer in many more merchandise categories than it is today.

An Energizing Force

Let us therefore examine the small retailer's place in the burgeoning "franchise" system, which offers not merely a means of survival, but an *energizing* force in his comeback:

1. What *forms* is the retail franchise system taking?
2. What are the *social* and *economic* forces favorable to this type of retailing?
3. What *progress* is franchising making in the marketing world?
4. What will its growth mean to brand advertisers?

Many Forms of Franchising

Franchising is hardly new. Certainly, in the automotive industry it is one of the oldest examples of distribution. But today franchising is assuming many new *shapes.* A company may confine a specific product or even a line of products to a *selected* number of dealers. This is "selective distribution," but not really "franchising" as we use the term here. We are concerned here with the type of franchising in which the franchiser gives the franchisee the right to conduct a business only in an *established* pattern under conditions like the following:

1. The store must be identified by name and appearance as a member of the group. Example: Howard Johnson, Ben Franklin, etc.
2. Standardized merchandise, form of service, policies and procedure promotion based on a *contractural* relationship.
3. The franchisee *invests* in the enterprise and is its sole owner or a partner with the franchiser.

Franchising in Ferment

Since the 1890's franchising was given further *impetus* by such companies as Ben Franklin Stores, Liggett Drug Stores, gasoline and oil stations. Franchising really commenced to grow at the end of World War II and its progress began to accelerate only *recently.* It is estimated that the franchising business adds up to about $60 billion, embracing almost every conceivable kind of merchandise and service. There are close to 350,000 *individuals* engaged in franchise-type operations, including 16,000 grocery stores. It is estimated that *this year* (1964) franchising companies will open about 30,000 units. Today there are about *1100* companies engaged in franchising, compared to about 200 in 1945. The rental rampage, which we described in a recent issue of Grey Matter, gave franchising a *thrust* by the establishment of franchised shops where anything could be *rented* from tools to trailers. In addition, a considerable share of the total market in food, drugs, hardware, and general merchandise, is *sold* through *completely* franchised or *partially* franchised outlets.

Market Pressures Favor Franchising

Many forces in the marketplace are giving franchising a boost. Some of the more important ones are:

1. The growing power of giant retailers is forcing manufacturers to seek forms of distribution in which they will have greater *control, supervision,* and *direction* over the prices and sale of their products. Owning their own stores is one way. But owning stores in *partnership* with the man who runs the store offers new possibilities, for there is a difference in *dedication* between a hired store manager and a partner who also has an investment in the enterprise. Since investment under franchising is *shared,* more outlets can be acquired more rapidly with less investment by the franchiser.

2. The attrition of the small retailer by giant chains has been forcing the individual small entrepreneur to seek the *protection* of strong wholesale groups. A *franchise* is another umbrella.

3. Despite the unceasing trend toward mergers and concentration, the small store is keeping its niche in the retail picture. Example: *Convenience or bantam food stores.* It is expected that by 1965 there will be more than 5,000 drive-in bantam or convenience food stores in operation.

4. Add to this the growing number of department store "twigs," neighborhood *hardware stores,* "midget" *discount* stores and others. It doesn't require much imagination to visualize the opportunities which exist for the *company* which wants to go into franchising or the *man* who wants to become a franchisee.

5. The unquenchable desire of so many Americans to own a "business of their own," held in check by the proliferation of giants, finds an *outlet* in franchise distribution.

6. A spur to franchising is coming from an unexpected source: the *shorter work week.* Operating a franchise will replace moonlighting as a source of additional income and as a use for spare time. Many an ad for franchisees spells out "opportunities for husband and wife full or part time."

7. Earlier retirement and increase in proportion of our older population will result in more people seeking franchises to *supplement* retirement income.

The Coming Franchising Battle

As we interpret the signs, franchising is sure to multiply in the years ahead. This does not mean a let-up in the trend toward giant stores by giant companies in giant shopping centers. But as we have said so often, there are countervailing forces to one-stop distribution.

In these pages we've tried to throw the spotlight on the *unnoticed* and often *pooh-poohed* burgeoning little store, combining the convenience of location, the friendliness and local know-how of its owner. His dedication to his business can rarely be matched by a *hired manager,* taking his orders from an impersonal corporate headquarters. He was falling by the wayside because he couldn't match the skill, resources, and the merchandising and promotion knowledge of the corporate chain. *The franchiser can supply both.* It's conceivable that more manufacturers will go into *franchised* distribution.

As fewer sites become available, as population density in urban areas increases, in suburban fringes as well as in "renewed" downstown, the *small* store will play a more *prominent* part in our distribution picture than it does today. That's significant to both *suppliers* and to retail giants. Yes, "Mom and Pop" are coming back, but they will look so different. You'll never recognize them. It will be no surprise if the battle for this market between manufacturers and giant retailers gets hotter.

15

Competitive Dynamics Behind Retailing Trends

Malcolm P. McNair

From the beginning of the twentieth century to the present, the retailing segment of our economy has been characterized by institutional change. New types of retailing institutions have appeared and gained prominence at the expense of established institutions. Have these changes been random, or is there some logical explanation? The author of this article, a long-time student of retailing, observes that the major institutional changes appear to conform to a definite cycle, which he calls the "Wheel of Retailing."

What are the dynamics of the institutional changes [in retail distribution] we can see taking place? It seems to me that there is a more or less definite cycle in American distribution. The wheel always revolves, sometimes slowly, sometimes more rapidly, but it does not stand still. The cycle frequently begins with the bold new concept, the innovation. Somebody gets a bright new idea. There is a John Wanamaker, a George Hartford, a Frank Woolworth, a W. T.

Abridged by special permission from Malcolm P. McNair, "Significant Trends and Developments in the Postwar Period," in Albert B. Smith, ed., *Competitive Distribution in a Free High-Level Economy and Its Implications for the University*. Pittsburgh: University of Pittsburgh Press, 1958.

Grant, a General Wood, a Michael Cullen, a Eugene Ferkauf. Such an innovator has an idea for a new kind of distributive enterprise. At the outset he is in bad odor, ridiculed, scorned, condemned as "illegitimate." Bankers and investors are leery of him. But he attracts the public on the basis of the price appeal made possible by the low operating costs inherent in his innovation. As he goes along he trades up, improves the quality of his merchandise, improves the appearance and standing of his store, attains greater respectability. Then, if he is successful, comes the period of growth, the period when he is taking business away from the established distribution channels that have clung to the old methods. Repeatedly something like this has happened in American distribution. The department stores took it away from the smaller merchants in the cities in the late 19th and early 20th century; the original grocery chains took it away from the old wholesaler-small-retailer combination; the supermarkets then began taking it away from the original grocery chains to the extent that the latter had to climb on the supermarket band wagon. And today the discount houses and the supermarkets are taking it away from the department stores and variety chains.

During this process of growth the institution rapidly becomes respectable in the eyes of both consumers and investors, but at the same time its capital investment increases and its operating costs tend to rise. Then the institution enters the stage of maturity. It has a larger physical plant, more elaborate store fixtures and displays, and it undertakes greater promotional efforts. At this stage the institution finds itself competing primarily with other similar institutions rather than with old-line competitors. The maturity phase soon tends to be followed by topheaviness, too great conservatism, a decline in the rate of return on investment and eventual vulnerability. Vulnerability to what? Vulnerability to the next revolution of the wheel, to the next fellow who has a bright idea and who starts his business on a low-cost basis, slipping in under the umbrella that the old-line institutions have hoisted.

Sometimes the wheel turns slowly and at other times it turns faster. In the department store field the revolution has been very slow, but in the food distribution field the wheel has been turning rapidly. The point is that sooner or later marketing institutions seem to arrive at the point of vulnerability, and then they face the dilemma that they must either innovate and evolve or be content with fighting a rearguard action and dropping into positions of secondary importance. For instance, the strictly service type of retail grocery store, with emphasis on credit, telephone, and delivery service, has all but vanished from the scene. Likewise the old-time service wholesale grocer who failed to innovate in the direction of supermarket or voluntary chain operation is today almost extinct.

To my mind, this position of maturity and potential vulnerability is occupied today by some of the high-cost retail distributors such as the drug store, the variety chain and the department store.

Retail Capacity and the Expense Rate

It is clear that competition between the older and the newer forms of distribution hinges in considerable part on the expense rate, which is substantially twice as great for department stores and variety chains as for supermarkets and discount houses. Difference in services offered and differences in speed of stockturn are among the obvious causes of the expense differential, stockturn, for instance, being 13 or 14 times a year for supermarkets against approximately 4 times a year for both department stores and variety chains. Most of this turnover difference, of course, is inherent in the nature of the goods sold, and presumably the spread will narrow in some degree as supermarkets move farther into the nonfood categories.

But there are also other factors which affect the expense differential. The market disparity in sales per square foot (influencing the rental cost percentage) among these types of retail distribution may reflect in part some differences in the inherent stockturn potential of the goods, but both this ratio and the stockturn ratio are greatly influenced by the density of consumer traffic and the size of the average sales transaction. Annual sales per square foot in discount houses are reported to run as high as $300 in some instances,[1] though no definitive study has been made; in supermarkets an average of more than $150 is indicated,[2] whereas in department stores the average usually will not exceed $100 a square foot of selling space.[3]

Thus the extent of utilization of capacity appears to be a critical factor in the expense rate. In other words, the high volume of traffic drawn by the supermarkets, originally because of the marked price appeal and perhaps subsequently by the effectiveness of merchandise assortments, presentation, and display, helps to explain their relatively low expense rate. And of course foodstuffs by their very nature have a relatively high degree of both frequency and regularity of purchase. In the case of discount houses, this latter factor of normal frequency and regularity of purchase is not present to so great a degree, and hence the reported high sales per square foot seem to reflect a combination of highly effective price appeal, high value of sales transaction, a policy of carrying small selections of high-turnover items, and the practice of selling from sample.

Perhaps, then, the generalization is warranted that the innovating forms of retail distribution, once they have caught on, tend to have higher utilization of plant capacity during the period of their early growth. The gradual erosion of this advantage through the growing competition of others of their own kind is part of the "revolution of the wheel" referred to earlier. For instance, among members of the Super Market Institute the rate of new supermarket additions rose from

14 per cent in 1954 to 17 per cent in 1955.[4] In 1955, new supermarkets were opened by 31 per cent of the companies in the Institute, and 22 per cent carried out major remodeling jobs.[5] The new supermarkets included in the Super Market Institute study for 1955 averaged 18,000 square feet in size; and in 1956, new supermarkets included in the study averaged 21,000 square feet of space.[6] Although a considerable number of food stores were closed during these years, there were also many modernizations and enlargements. It is perhaps significant that 87 per cent of the new supermarkets opened by members of the Super Market Institute in 1956 were reported to be in immediate competition with one or more other supermarkets in the same trading area.[7] Just possibly these facts may be taken as an indication that the future trend of the supermarket expense ratio will be up. As for discount houses, no statistics on the rate of growth in total capacity are available; but there is every evidence that it is high.

From all this fragmentary evidence there seems to be a fair presumption that retail plant capacity in the United States is growing at least as fast as population and purchasing power, and in some lines probably faster. If this is the case, then the inference is warranted that in a free high-level competitive economy a condition of under-utilization of capacity in retailing is likely to be chronic, and that any advantages in superior utilization that may be enjoyed by particular forms of enterprise at various times are not likely to be permanent. By way of broadening the gen-

---

[1] *Fortune*, November, 1956, p. 124.

[2] Various studies of the Super Market Institute.

[3] Various studies of the Harvard Bureau of Business Research.

[4] Super Market Institute, Inc., *The Super Market Industry Speaks*. The Eighth Annual Report by the Members of the Super Market Institute (Chicago, 1956), p. 4.

[5] *Ibid.*, p. 14.

[6] Curt Kornblau, op. cit., p. 1.

[7] *Ibid.*, p. 3.

eralization we may venture the further inference that competition among retail distributors tends generally in the direction of higher costs (barring cyclical factors) except for the vital influence of continuing innovation.

16

The Market Place of the Future

Joseph L. Hudson, Jr.

A retailing institution that recently has been subjected to heavy competitive assaults by a new form of retailing, the discount house, has been the department store. To some extent it may have invited attack because it seemed to assume at the outset that it was invulnerable. However, when the discount competition became intense the department store showed a remarkable ability to adapt and to counterattack. At the present time this battle seems to have reached a stalemate in which each of the institutions has borrowed so freely from the other that it is hard to tell them apart. In this article an executive of one of the largest department stores in the country discusses the future of the department store in the central business district and in shopping centers.

I suppose one reason why I was invited to participate in this conference is that a retailer is constantly living in the future—he is planning for business next month, next quarter, next year. But I must confess that trying to look ahead 50 years is an exercise to which I am not accustomed.

Of course, my associates and I must do a considerable amount of forward planning as our company continues to expand. We plan to open a new Hudson branch store in Oakland Mall next summer to serve the Troy and Birmingham

Reprinted by permission from the March, 1968, issue of the *Michigan Business Review*, published by the Graduate School of Business Administration, The University of Michigan.

area. We expect to have two complete shopping centers ready for opening in 1970—Southland Center in the Detroit area and Genessee Valley Center just outside of Flint. We continue to look for additional outstate locations and will probably be busy building more stores well into 1975. . . .

We have projected our company's future needs for warehouse and delivery facilities as far ahead as 1980. And in 1981 our company will be 100 years old! That's about as far ahead as we have tried to look.

Personally, I am very much interested in what developments may occur over the next 50 years, because I have a good chance of being alive over that span of time. In the year 2017 I will be 86 years old—if all goes well. Probably at that point no one will be so unkind as to tell an old man that some of his forecasts were wrong in 1967, so I feel reasonably safe today in venturing to discuss the market place of the future.

Frankly, I can't pretend to see 50 years ahead. One can barely do more than guess, at this time, where technological change will lead us. Changes in transportation and communication may well be as great or greater than those of the last 50 years. Therefore, I can only attempt to develop a few points about current trends in retailing, and then discuss some developments that I foresee in future years—principally the next 10 to 15 years.

At the outset, I am making a number of broad assumptions. I expect in future years:

- Continued growth in our economy.
- Continued rising consumer income.
- A rising price level.
- Continued increases in discretionary spending.
- And continued use of the automobile, or something closely resembling it.

Where Will People Live?

Before the end of this year, the population of the United States will total 200 million people. A half century from now, the population of the United States will be nearly twice as large as it is today. Further, we will find 80 per cent of America's population living in urban areas.

Today in Michigan, more than 75 per cent of our population lives in 10 metropolitan areas of the state. As time goes on, it is entirely possible that the principal population growth will occur in our central cities, with the heaviest concentration of people in large apartment proj-

ects; but I think it is more likely that the principal growth will be in new suburbs—with continuing outward expansion. It is reasonable to assume that we have seen only the beginning of suburbanization.

This means that there will undoubtedly be a continued expansion of shopping facilities in order to meet the needs of our growing population. To anyone connected with retailing, this should present a bright picture for the future. But to me, this prospect of increasing urban concentration is not altogether a pleasant one, because it brings to mind immediately many of the serious problems that are confronting America today.

Some Serious Problems

We are going to have to find jobs for more and more people. Particularly, we are going to have to develop jobs for the many unemployed people living in the poor sections—the so-called "hard core" areas of our big cities today.

The principal problem of the unemployed is lack of education. This means that we are going to have to train people to prepare them for jobs, as well as providing education for them in many other areas of living. In this connection private business leadership and private funds will be required.

We are going to have to do a massive job of providing housing to replace the slums in which millions of Americans live today, plus the building that will be necessary to provide for our growing population.

We must find better ways of providing opportunities for those who continue to migrate from rural areas in the South to our cities in the North. We shall need to make substantial revisions in our social fabric of today, if the next 50 years are to be free from the disorders and the bitter frustration we saw last summer in Detroit and other cities. This is a problem that deserves the highest priority in our thinking and our forward planning today. And again, private sector leadership will be an important element.

In addition to the urgent needs that I have indicated for employment, education, and housing to provide greater opportunities for Negroes, we must, as businessmen, be concerned with a range of other problems which are closely linked to urban concentration and suburban expansion. I am thinking now of measures to control air and water pollution in our metropolitan areas. I am thinking of measures needed to control crime in our suburbs as well as in our central cities. I am thinking of the need for adequate health and medical services and, finally, the need to provide sufficient open space, recreational and cultural facilities for an expanding urban population.

All of these environmental factors will need increasing attention if we expect our businesses to be successful in the years ahead. It is not enough to say that these are problems for government. We need to become personally involved in helping to shape the solutions.

The best way I know to avoid being apprehensive about the future is to take an active part in the planning efforts that are so necessary today.

Where Will People Stop?

During the past quarter century we have seen an explosive growth of population in the suburbs, accompanied by increased demand for conveniently located shopping facilities.

We can remember when a single great department store in a single location covered an entire metropolitan area. But that day is over. Increasingly, the department store of the future will be a multiple unit operation. It will have units not only in the suburban areas, which are close to the parent store, but also it will have outlying stores in cities within a radius of 100 or even 200 miles. These new branch stores will be located in planned regional shopping centers, because customers have demonstrated that they like the one-stop shopping convenience that modern shopping centers provide.

With the growth of shopping centers, you have seen department stores in the forefront of shopping center development. Department stores in many large cities have found that they must establish branches in the suburbs to retain their sales volume and their market share. In the future, this decentralization of retail trade will undoubtedly continue.

Two years ago, a study of the 100 top department stores in the United States showed that these top stores account for some 60 per cent of total department store volume. It is estimated that by 1970 most of these 100 top stores will do over 65 per cent of their annual volume in branch stores, and by 1975 branch stores may account for 80 per cent of their total volume.

What we are seeing in the growth of shopping centers is the creation of concentrated shopping facilities similar to the downtown shopping areas that have attracted customers in the past. These suburban shopping areas have been most successful where they have combined a department store with a variety of specialty stores and services, for comparison shopping. I expect to see new centers built in the future as they are needed to serve a growing population and generally they will be built in locations readily accessible to suburban customers.

Let me give you some quick facts about shopping centers:

- Today, more than 10,000 shopping centers are operating in the United States and Canada.
- Regional centers, such as Northland,

Eastland, and Westland, enjoy 43 per cent of all shopping center volume.

- Community centers, ranging from 100,000 to 200,000 square feet of leasable area, do 30 per cent of the business.
- The remaining 26 per cent is done in neighborhood shopping centers with less than 100,000 square feet of leasable area.
- Nationally, about 37 per cent of retail trade is done in shopping centers now. By 1970, shopping centers are expected to be doing about 45 per cent of general merchandise sales.

Generally, I do not expect to see the building of shopping centers in the future as large as Northland or Eastland; but I expect that more centers in the future will have two or more department stores. This will be the case at Oakland Mall where Hudson's and Sears will be in direct competition. Also, I expect to see increased use of the enclosed mall concept, as at Westland Center.

Central Business District

As retailers have followed their customers into the suburbs by building branch stores, the importance of the central business district as a retailing center has been steadily decreasing over the past 20 years. Fortunately, new strength is developing in the downtown picture today.

The central business district is the logical hub of business and commerce, with financial institutions centered there as well as governmental offices. The concentration of offices in our large cities will increase, in my opinion, adding more jobs downtown. This will also mean that more business visitors will have reason to come downtown, adding to the number of available customers.

We have talked to people who work in the downtown area. To them, the outstanding advantage of downtown shopping is the convenience of stores located near where they work. They like the selections and wide variety of merchandise. They would like stores to be open more evenings for shopping after work.

Of great importance is the potential of downtown for residential areas and new apartments. As we get rid of blighted and obsolete buildings, downtown is becoming an increasingly attractive place for living. In addition to people who work downtown and live in the downtown area, there are those who come into the city for conventions and exhibits, and visitors generally. So we can look to several kinds of customers to provide continuing future traffic for downtown stores.

Other Customers Are Needed

But we should not delude ourselves. These customers, important as they are, cannot provide the amount of business needed to support large stores in the central business area. There must be a continuing flow of people from other parts of the city and from suburban areas to sustain downtown store operation on a profitable basis. This, I believe, presents one of the greatest challenges for large retailers in the future. Indeed, the challenge is here today.

Our Research Department has conducted interviews with customers who regularly shop in our branch stores but sometimes shop downtown. We asked them what advantages they found in shopping downtown, and 50 per cent said they liked the broader selection of merchandise they found, as compared with suburban shopping. Other advantages cited were more variety of merchandise, pleasant shopping atmosphere, and more stores in the central shopping area.

The principal disadvantages mentioned were parking problems, traffic confusion, and the length of driving time. Customers told us they would shop downtown more frequently if more parking were provided closer to downtown stores; if a decent system of rapid transit were developed so you could travel downtown in 15 or 20 minutes; if downtown stores stayed open every evening; and if downtown restaurants, exhibits, and special events were improved to make downtown a more attractive area for a leisurely day of shopping and entertainment.

Goods Carried in the Stores

The Sunday magazine of the Detroit Free Press a few months ago carried a feature article about the experiences of a lady reporter as she tried to spend a million dollars in one day by making a comprehensive shopping tour of Hudson's Downtown Store. She didn't actually buy anything; but by the end of the day, she had made a long list of items that she would have liked to buy, and it totaled only $342,000. Now the interesting thing is that many of the items on her list could have been bought in our large branch stores—including wines, gourmet foods, cosmetics, luggage, sheets, pillow cases, table linen, electric appliances, and a broad range of wearing apparel.

But there were many items that could be found only in our Downtown Store— such as expensive jewelry, antique silverware, expensive sculpture and paintings, a $6,000 chinchilla coat, a $775 evening gown, several custom-designed hats, handmade wigs from France, a $400 teddy bear, a quilted velvet bedspread, and a long list of furniture items, including complete new furnishings and decor for the living room and bedroom.

Let me be sure that the point is clear. I am not saying that everything in our Downtown Store is expensive; that you need to be loaded with money in order to shop there. Rather, it is that we can afford to carry in our Downtown Store many items of merchandise which are not practical to stock in our branch stores from the standpoint of inventory investment and turnover. Further, there are space limitations in branch stores which do not permit the breadth of assortments and the variety of merchandise offerings and customer services which are available in our Downtown departments.

We know that outlying shopping centers will stress the value of their location convenience. Downtown shopping areas must offer definite advantages if they are to attract customers from the suburbs. I am confident that downtown stores can do this. For example, there is growing interest in imported merchandise, and we carry a wide range of this year-around in the Downtown Store. This is being featured currently in our "Shops of Europe" displays. Suburban customers will continue to find the Downtown Store a unique merchandise mart for their major purchases, especially when these involve home furnishings coordination and decorating services. Distinctive offerings of high-quality merchandise and unusual items for special gifts will continue to be strong attractions of downtown stores as they compete in the future with suburban stores.

Much has been done in Detroit over recent years to provide convenient parking for suburban shoppers, and more will be done in the future. More basically, Detroit needs improved rapid transit for people to get downtown more easily, whether to work or to shop. Improved transportation is a key ingredient needed for revitalization and future growth of the Central Business District in Detroit.

New Competition

Thus far I have been discussing the conveniences and the inconveniences, of store location—on the premise that customers will continue to get out of their homes and travel to stores for most of their shopping needs.

I think the modern woman is saying to retailers today: "Make shopping faster for me and make it easier. Simplify my life." Probably this is one reason why catalog selling is making gains in America's metropolitan areas. Direct-mail advertising sells a lot of phonograph records and books. Credit card holders are receiving special offers to buy power tools, typewriters, luggage, and many other merchandise items traditionally sold in department stores. Many people living in urban areas are now buying by mail because they find it more convenient than going out to shop. If picture telephones become generally available in the future at a reasonable cost, telephone shopping will undoubtedly become a much more important operation for large retailers than it is today.

A few months ago, an article in the *Harvard Business Review* entitled "Next Revolution in Retailing" described a new method of shopping from the customer's home so she will no longer need to go out to the store. The article suggested, rather persuasively, that "convenience" goods—such as staple groceries, toiletries, drug sundries, and many household supply items—can be adapted to highly centralized, mechanized, and computerized distribution techniques. Such items could be marketed in the future through a few large distribution centers in each major market area. Retail transactions would be made by electronic telecommunications and push-button devices installed in private homes.

The authors of this article visualize that to do her shopping in the future, a housewife will sit at her planning desk in the kitchen where a closed circuit color television screen is mounted on the wall. A Direct-Shop console is on her desk, and she will press a set of buttons to connect her with the distribution center to which she subscribes by paying a monthly fee. As she pushes various product-code buttons, images of merchandise appear on the screen. She punches keys to register the items and quantities she wants. When she pushes a tally button, a recap of her order appears on the screen, itemized and totaled. She pushes another button to confirm the order, authorizing the warehouse to begin processing it and at the same time clearing payment from her bank account. In less than 10 minutes, she could complete her shopping. At the warehouse end, everything is handled by an elaborate computer system which receives, interprets, and processes her order and schedules it for delivery.

Is Electronic Shopping Coming?

Is all of this fanciful? Perhaps. But if we are taking a long look into the future, we must recognize the possibility of such an order-taking, packing and delivery system being developed. Its first application would undoubtedly be in the supermarket field, and its proponents even contemplate special low temperature containers for delivery of frozen foods and perishables.

I happen to believe that it will be a long time before customers will be ready to switch to push-button buying. From my observation, most people like to see and handle the merchandise they are buying. Someday we will have a pill which is equal to a full meal, but I think most people will prefer eating real food rather than taking pills!

An automated warehouse-to-consumer system would not be appropriate for "big ticket" items, nor would it be suitable for any merchandise that requires personal fitting or direct inspection to determine its quality. Customers often need product information which can only be supplied by salespeople.

For these reasons, I do not look for the early demise of department stores, variety stores, drugstores, nor specialty shops which we have today; and I expect the modern supermarket to be popular for a long time. As I look ahead, I believe that active shopping by customers going to stores will continue at a high level. But the question is this: Which stores will get the greatest share of business?

The Customer of Tomorrow

When we ask the question, "Which stores will get the greatest share of future business?", I think we must first consider some new characteristics of today's customers.

I am sure that the function of merchandising in the future must be more fully consumer-directed. We must have a greater understanding of how our customers think and act. We must be more sensitive to what they like and dislike. Particularly is this true as we look toward a market of potential new customers who, for the most part, have not developed loyalty to any particular retailer.

We are rapidly approaching the time when a majority of the United States population will be made up of people who are 25 years of age, or younger. Today there is a bulge in the 18 to 34 age group, which represents a great market for general merchandise retailers as these people marry, have children, and build homes. Today, many conventional department stores are still catering to the mothers rather than the daughters, and special efforts must be made to

attract these younger customers. This new generation represents youth in body and dress, mind and spirit. This generation knows nothing about depressions. It has discarded the old concepts of thrift and saving. It enjoys spending and makes the fullest use of credit. It is the mood of this generation to go for fun, fashions, and fads.

At the same time, it is a generation of great sophistication. It represents a high level of education and culture. It is interested in self-development, self-expression, and individuality. Automobiles and air transportation make it a highly mobile generation. These customers—men as well as women—are looking for fashion. They are seeking the new, the original, and the forward-looking trends.

Take new products, for example. Retailers are finding increasing evidence today that many new products sell well just because they are new. Younger customers, sophisticated, modern customers are new-product minded. In fact, some retailers today make a special point of urging their buyers to hunt for new items. These are the stores that have established a reputation for being first with the new.

Fashion obsolescence will increasingly motivate future buying of all types of merchandise, and people will no longer keep things until they wear out. The big job that merchandising people will have to do will be to keep themselves customer-oriented in a rapidly moving world of new developments. They will need to give increased attention to the merchandise preferences, the style and price preferences of tomorrow's customers.

Innovations and Improvements

Moreover, the stores that hope to cater to these customers will need to be forward-looking in every aspect of their business. They will need to give special attention to store layout and design, to merchandise presentation and to sales promotion. They will need to emphasize ease of shopping and speed in handling transactions. Customers with heightened appreciation of taste and quality may spend time and thought in making their selections, but they will not tolerate delay, confusion, or ineptness in the clerical aspects of completing a sale. I think the stores that are most likely to get an increasing share of tomorrow's business are the retail giants of today; and I think the smaller independent stores will find it increasingly difficult to survive. One of the reasons for this is what we call "scrambled retailing." Supermarkets are tending to become general merchandise stores. Mail order firms are operating large department stores. Apparel and variety chains are becoming junior department stores and, sometimes, full-line stores. The result is that we now have, and we will have more, intensified competition throughout retailing creating serious problems for the smaller stores.

On the other side of the coin, there will definitely be a place for small specialty stores and shops which can offer the combination of unique merchandise, imaginative presentation, and personal attention to customers. Customers will continue to expect individual interest and attention. The satisfactions they seek will be more psychological than functional. But satisfying customers is really the key to successful retailing. This is something every retailer knows;

and with all the competition there will be in future years, it will be interesting to see who can do the best job.

In my opinion—and this will be my final prediction for today—you may expect to see department stores occupying an important position in the future of American marketing. In fact, I believe they may well take a more active and lively part on the retail scene as they continue to expand into suburban shopping centers. They have learned how to innovate, and today they are introducing both merchandising and technological changes at a rapid rate.

The well-managed department stores of today know who their competition is, and where it is; and they realize full well that in the fast-moving world of retailing there is no guarantee of survival. You must compete to survive, and you must constantly adjust to new conditions. I am confident that the forward-looking department stores of today will compete with strength and effectiveness in the market place of tomorrow.

In closing, I would like to leave you a simple motto that was cherished by the founder of our company, Joseph L. Hudson. To him it spoke these inspiring words each day:

> If there is a way, I'll find it;
> If none exists, I'll make one.

That thought, I feel, can serve all of us well as we look ahead to a future which is new and unknown—but one which will surely be filled with great interest and challenge.

17

The High Cost of the Supermarket Revolution

Colston E. Warne

The following article, by a well-known critic of modern marketing practices, implies that supermarkets are engaged in a nefarious scheme to mislead the public into believing that they are providing efficient grocery distribution by deceptive pricing which uses leader pricing to suggest an overall low price level. The basic fact—that margins of supermarkets today are not substantially lower than were the margins of small independents thirty years ago—is correct, but the author's interpretation is only one possible explanation. The reader will find the article a good vehicle through which to consider the complex matter of costs and margins in a high-level economy.

Few marketing revolutions have been accomplished with as little social comment as the transfer of the nation's allegiance from the neighborhood store to the supermarket and the shopping center. Our cities and towns have become encircled with vast structures, beckoning the buyer with neon signs and a bewildering display of competitive brands and sanitized packages.

As the revolution has proceeded, lines between types of merchandising outlets have become blurred. Grocery stores encroach upon the high-margin lines of drugstores, clothing stores and variety stores. Discount houses add groceries. Everywhere there are supermarkets, each seeking to outdo their rivals in the

Reprinted from *Challenge*, The Magazine of Economic Affairs, a publication of Challenge Communications, Inc., Vol. 15, No. 2 (November–December, 1966), pp. 8–11.

proliferation of brands and the number of promotion gimmicks.

Yet the problems posed by the supermarket of today do not seem so dissimilar from those suggested more than a century ago by John Stuart Mill in his *Principles of Political Economy* (1848). Mill wrote:

"But retail price, the price paid by the actual consumer, seems to feel very slowly and imperfectly the effect of competition; and when competition does exist, it often, instead of lowering prices, merely divides the gains of the high price among a greater number of dealers. Hence it is that, of the price paid by the consumer, so large a proportion is absorbed by the gains of retailers; and anyone who inquires into the amount which reaches the hands of those who made the things he buys, will often be astonished at its smallness."

The question plaguing consumers today, however, is not the mounting gains of retailers; it is, rather, that the advancing efficiency of our basic industries seems ever to be absorbed by higher marketing costs. The political reaction to the growing discrepancy between what the farmer gets for his wheat and what the consumer pays for his bread was well reflected in the recent report of the National Commission on Food Marketing. The report also raised many doubts as to whether the supermarket, as now operated, fulfills the promise which it initially held out to consumers.

The sad truth seems to be emerging that, as a nation, we have moved full range from a small-scale, inefficient food distribution system to a large-scale and highly costly one. The supermarket of today has not brought a decrease in total distribution costs. Moreover, it has transferred many of the costs of retailing squarely onto the shoulders of the consumer who now pays an ever mounting retail margin for only a fragment of the service he used to get.

Fifty years ago the genial neighborhood grocer of American folklore solicited orders from customers either at their homes or by telephone. He packaged and assembled his merchandise. He extended credit for a week, a month, and sometimes in rural areas until the harvest was in. In most communities he delivered the goods. He kept long hours. His store was unquestionably inefficient, often unsanitary and limited in selection.

Yet for all its defects the local grocery was a highly competitive and vigorous segment of our enterprise economy. Its profits were a meager portion of the typical markup of about 25 per cent.

Battered remnants of this American heritage still survive. Today, however, no eager driver comes to the door to solicit orders. Little, if any, credit is extended by grocers. Store hours are circumscribed by custom, by legislation and by unions. (In some areas, however, hours are being lengthened to meet consumer needs.) The retailer receives few telephone orders.

The packaging function at the retail level has so shrunk that a typical grocery clerk needs little or no competence other than that of stamping prices on prepackaged merchandise and carting it to a spot along the counter. He knows nothing about the goods on sale save their shelf location.

A significant share of the cost of marketing has been transferred to the consumer. Upon him falls the laborious chore of navigating a shopping cart through the seemingly endless supermarket aisles and assuming the full burden of selecting, assembling and transporting groceries, meat and vegetables from store to home—often even grinding his own coffee. In essence, the consumer has become an uncompensated store clerk, assuming many marketing functions that were traditionally those of the seller.

Stimulated by soft music and fortified by "cents off" unstipulated prices and by double trading stamps, the shopper of today has accepted his role as a second-class member of the distributive team. But consumers are slowly awakening to the fact that they are now paying almost as high a percentage in distribution costs for food as they did 50 years ago when they received home delivery, credit and service.

Those who eulogize our burgeoning supermarkets are prone to accent the convenience of prepackaging. Yet this very prepackaging is decidedly a mixed blessing. Modern packaging has clearly netted sanitary gains which the "mom and pop" stores did not possess. It is also time saving.

Yet, as Senator Philip Hart (D.-

Mich.) has pointed out, in today's supermarket, prepackaging practices have led to endless deception as declining weights have been employed to offset price decreases or to create confusion for the shopper. All of this makes valid price comparisons well nigh impossible.

Moreover, prepackaging may commonly be employed to conceal the scrawny sweet potato at the bottom of the cellophane container or the odd detached leaves of spinach. It may also allow the seller to tuck in odd scraps of meat or hide the end of the bone—in a word, to prevent the close inspection that was traditional in the corner grocery.

A recent study by Paul E. Nelson, Jr. and Lee E. Preston (published by the Institute of Business and Economic Research of the University of California, Berkeley) has surveyed for a typical city, Greensboro, North Carolina, the price fabric of modern retail stores with their off-street parking, air conditioning, automatic doors, carry-out service, shopping carts, trading stamps, check cashing facilities, coffee grinders, music and highly promoted specials.

Wide differences were found in the individual store prices and in the pricing practices of retail food stores. A central observation was "variable price merchandising." Retailers were, through their advertised specials, seeking to attract consumers by creating the impression of being low-price stores.

This sort of manipulation, as the authors suggest, was based upon the fact that "only a small number of prices within the total price mix of a retail establishment can be known or evaluated by any individual consumer." What the alert manager then does is to establish a suitable "price mix" of high prices and low prices. He accents his constantly shifting roster of specials so as to entice purchasers, oftentimes without regard to the market. "By raising and lowering different prices relatively often, the large stores may be able to maintain a reputation for price reductions sufficient to assure their continued patronage without actually bringing about a permanent change in the level of prices in the market."

Because of the chaos of current merchandising tactics, our retail food markets seem increasingly to be segmented into a mass market of large stores and a variety of small isolated ones catering to specialized consumer contingents. "Variable price merchandising thus creates a kind of price discrimination against the customer who is limited by taste, knowledge, income or location to one store or group of items, and in favor of the customer with the time, equipment and information required for careful shopping."

In summary, it would appear that modern variable price merchandising is a euphemistic description of consumer deception based upon the rapid juggling of certain prices so as to insure higher profit margins on other lines.

In the early days of the supermarket, sites for shopping centers were relatively cheap. Farmers could be induced to part with land at low prices with little realization that new traffic arteries and urbanization would skyrocket land values. Today a new type of real estate speculator has emerged to make careful studies of suburban shopping sites and to estimate statistically the pulling power of each. This often involves difficult calculations.

Major arteries have come to be lined with competitive shopping centers, each established under the impression that it would draw patronage from a given radius when, in fact, another similarly motivated enterprise emerged on a nearby corner. Mounting land costs, higher mortgage costs and the splintering of business between competing shopping centers have conspired to pyramid overhead costs.

One of the spectacular cost advantages of the early chain supermarkets was rapid turnover. Each unit had a small inventory of cash-and-carry items that could be sold with a markup of 15 per cent or less. Today the old-fashioned, prewar chain store has, for the most part, been abandoned. In its place is the supermarket with 6,000 to 8,000 items stacked on its burgeoning shelves.

Some of these items represent a real benefit or convenience to the consumer in precooking or prepreparation and in other innovations such as frozen foods. The supermarket can truly be said to have adapted itself to a different type of shopper, to the employed woman, or at least to the woman who no longer bakes and is glad to have the food manufacturer provide relief from the more arduous kitchen chores.

Yet the vast majority of items on the overburdened shelves of supermarkets emerge from competitive inventiveness —the proliferation of cereals in a variety of shapes and sizes of packaging and sugar coating, the host of novel soaps and sprays, the wide range of seasonings and sauces.

The packaging explosion has been characterized by colorful containers in which the package has become the principal salesman. The buyer is seldom offered a simple, unbranded generic item —sugar, salt, popcorn, green tea. Instead, he is presented with shelfloads of similar but differentiated goods, each with a unique container, each fortified by special advertising plans, some with "cents off," some even with lotteries for trips to Bermuda.

Merchandising is no longer a simple transaction of buying beans, bread and butter. It is surrounded by the siren voices of radio and television that seek to imbue a brand consciousness in listeners, young and old. At the checkout counter the buyer presents a miscellany of coupons and receives a miscellany of stamps, bingo cards and pictures to match. The modern supermarket presents itself as a virtual treasure trove with specials around hidden corners.

Coupons addressed to "the occupant" come through the mail offering products, new and old, at "cents off" prices. Dealers are offered extra enticements to handle these coupons. Favorable shelf space is often leased to the highest bidders—a modern kind of merchandising payola. The very arrangement of the merchandise accents high markup items.

In the constant effort to increase profits, the private brand has come to play a significant role. National brands have been laboring under two serious handicaps—first, they must employ extensive and costly national advertising to secure and maintain their following. Not infrequently, the manufacturer may indeed help cover the cost of the retailer's promotion of a national brand. Second, once entrenched in the community, the national brand can fairly readily be associated with a certain, well-remembered price.

Given these two attributes, the national brand becomes a logical football for competitive retailers, each wishing to create a vivid (though false) impression of low prices by advertising as specials the nationally advertised article. Such specials may, in the short run, entrench the national brand in the market.

Yet the ascendancy of the national brand has, by no means, been complete, nor is its dominance apt to be permanent. The countervailing power of large retail chains has increasingly been demonstrated in the emergence of private brands of detergents, canned goods, bread, and a host of other items. These private brands are indeed often packed by the very manufacturers who market competing products.

In setting its prices, the supermarket

chain can exact from the consumer a considerably higher profit margin and yet sell considerably below the price of the nationally advertised article. Thus national advertising has created an umbrella under which private labeling has come to flourish. Yet consumer prices have risen with the higher inventory costs resulting from duplication.

The rising birthrate of supermarkets in the last decade or so has created for each a skein of high overhead costs. The net effect is, to repeat, that retailing exacts in margins an even larger percentage from the consumer's pocketbook.

One item that should not be neglected in this analysis is the cost of labor. Formerly, retailing was essentially a non-union trade, heavily subsidized by the underpayment of clerks as well as of proprietors. Not a little of this type of hidden subsidy still persists, although most supermarkets have been compelled to draw on an ever more costly labor force and, in metropolitan areas, have been confronted with the necessity of bargaining with white-collar unions, which have demanded wages commensurate with those prevailing elsewhere.

In this setting, supermarket retailing has lost some of the cost advantage it once possessed. Its economy in the use of labor has by now been measurably dissipated by the extra gimmicks provided, by the extra stamps and coupons handled, by extra brands and by the extra inventories.

Now, however, a new type of "stripped-down" supermarket seems to be emerging, a supermarket that limits its brands and noisily accents price competition. Whether such an effort will make serious inroads upon American supermarketing would appear to depend largely upon whether consumers can be attracted to such new cut-price undertakings. As a phase of this surge toward lower cost merchandising, periodically some of the larger chains strip themselves of the cost of stamps and proclaim their immunity from some of the cost-pyramiding practices. Such efforts thus far have been short-lived.

Looked at in perspective, it does not appear that in the years immediately ahead the consumer will gain great advantage from the new merchandising trends. While the Food Marketing Commission has urged the employment of A, B, C labels to delineate the quality of an increasing range of foodstuffs, it seems unlikely that for some time legislation requiring such labels will be readily accepted either at the manufacturing level or at the retail level. The status quo seems to offer better profit prospects. And the House Commerce Committee has cut the heart out of Senator Hart's "truth-in-packaging" bill—the most comprehensive piece of legislation in this area in years.

There was a day when, here and abroad, the cooperative movement possessed a dynamism which promised the consumer some respite from rising marketing costs. Through this movement, consumers owned and controlled retail enterprises. Consumer-owners would bear the risks and secure the gains of efficiency. By owning the retail store they could increase the turnover, assure quality products and secure a respite from exaggerated advertising.

Such cooperative enterprises are still of great significance in Scandinavia and persist in a number of American cities. The probability, however, that the cooperative solution will be widely adopted in the United States seems increasingly remote. The stores of our supermarket era are large anonymous units patronized by a mobile populace possessed of little loyalty toward any particular enterprise.

For good or ill, the consumer seems destined, for some time to come, to push his shopping cart, rejoice in his packaged miracles, sing in harmony with the canned music and pay the mounting bill. Some will seek buying guidance and will search out bargains. For most, however, the pressures of time are great, so great that the supermarket will continue to be tailored to the hasty plucking of the impulse buyer.

18

Has Discounting Run Out of Gas?

Grey Matter

The discount house is a retail phenomenon of the 1950–1960 decades. It arose suddenly, grew spectacularly, and to some is apparently fading out through a process of merging with other types of retail institutions. This naturally gives rise to the question of whether it ever was truly a distinct retailing institution. Or to phrase the question differently, what characteristics must a retailing development have in order to constitute a distinct institution? The following article contends that, contrary to appearances, the discount house is still an innovating factor in retailing. If this is true, it still leaves the intriguing question: When is an institution not an institution?

There is a smugness in many marketing circles about the discount retailer which would seem to indicate that *this type of retailing* is no longer considered a *factor* in distribution. You hear it on all sides:

> The discount retailer has *lost his identity*. He has traded up until his price lines overlap those of the conventional store.

> His *margins* have also gone *so high* that they offer very little competition to the supermarket.

Reprinted from *Grey Matter*, May, 1967, Vol. 38, No. 5, a Bulletin on Thoughts and Ideas on Advertising and Marketing, issued by Grey Advertising, Inc.

Many of them even *shun* the word "discount" in favor of the appellation "low margin retailer."

These notions about discount retailing prevail because in recent years the fanfare about this category of store has *subsided* and is no longer headline news.

Discounters' Progress and Power Going Up

Marketers of consumer goods who dismiss the discount store with a wave of the hand are in for some *surprises* if they take a closer look at the *progress* this comparative tyro is making in the competitive retail arena. Marketers who look beyond the obvious and delve more deeply into the potentials of the market place are aware that *discount stores* are steadily *getting a larger share of total retail volume* in most consumer goods categories. *Take food:* Despite predictions of their early demise, "discount" supermarkets are eating into conventional supermarkets' volume.

So widely used is price appeal in supermarket advertising that an experiment recently conducted by home economists of the U.S. Department of Agriculture revealed that they were able to cut 25% of their total grocery bill by choosing from the specials in advertisements of stores in a *single neighborhood.* Says the Department study: "Discounters had the highest average sale per customer—some 10% above sales per customer of conventional supermarkets and nearly 20% above sales per customer in the independent food stores." The report estimated that food discounting can no longer be viewed as a fad or solely as a promotional device for general merchandise stores." In 1965 food discounting accounted for 11% of grocery store sales. Food giants everywhere are expanding their *discount* operations.

Expanding discount operations of *health-and-beauty aids* in supermarkets under consideration or under way as the result of sharp competition from discount stores and drug stores. Marketers of products sold through drug stores should pay close attention to the accelerated pace at which *bantam discount drug stores* are being opened across the country.

Number One in General Merchandise, Too

According to Barron's, discount stores (counting food volume) are slightly ahead of conventional department stores in total volume. The business and financial weekly points out that discount retailers "have survived a period in which growth came only at the price of intensive competition, a number of financial failures and a few important consolidations. For most the worst is over—but now and then a big discounter continues to bite the dust." The article also emphasizes that many sections of this country are far from well served and that "millions of Americans find it difficult even to find a discount store today."

What's the consumer's attitude toward food discount stores? A study done by Burgoyne Index, Inc., in nine cities indicates that 62% *of the women queried* say that they shop in discount stores and that food is part of the attraction.

Giant *general merchandise* retailers are expanding their discount operations. When it opened its new Woolco store in Dallas recently, Woolworth's counted its *53rd discount unit.* J. C. Penney Co. is expanding their "Treasure Island" discount chain to Atlanta. In hitting the billion dollar mark in 1966, S. S. Kresge doubled its volume in the past 3½ years and went up 28% in the last year. This chain expects to open at least 50 new K-Mart discount stores, a rise of 40 over last year. *Significant to marketers* is Kresge's apparent strategy of saturating key market areas, i.e., Chicago and Kansas City.

Smaller Chains Edging In

But giants of retaildom are not the only ones who are pushing a deeper wedge into low margin retailing. *Smaller chains* edging into discount retailing are legion. Example: M. H. Fishman Company. Their "Mason's" discount stores now make 80% of chain's profit.

Chains such as Grant, Woolworth, Kresge and Penney have proven that sound basic merchandising principles can *succeed* in the *low margin field.* In fact, Woolworth is aspiring to leadership in the "promotional department store" arena, just as it achieved domination among variety stores.

The plain facts are that the so-called "discount industry" keeps on *moving ahead* and is reported to have chalked up a record of more than $13 billion in 1965, a gain of over 25% over 1964. The way the industry is going, it is projected that discount retailing will *reach $20 billion by 1970.* As time goes on, more and more of the billion dollar retail giants are doffing their hats to their *discount operations.*

Shift in Consumers' Attitude

The reason for this renewed vigor of the discounter's thrust in distribution is a shift in consumer attitude. The trade-up boom has slowed down.

While ours is still a status-seeking society, and more and more families are climbing to higher rungs on the ladder of affluence, can we marketers overlook the fact that stretching the family income to cover expanding family desires is becoming more and more *difficult?* What's more, housewives are advised by "consumer protectors" to avoid high-priced foods, watch for sales, shun out-of-season items. In fact, studies by the National Commission on Food Marketing revealed that 50% of food shoppers *look for the lowest price.*

Current consumer research, too, reveals that more families are talking more about keeping their cars longer. The price of *services* is taking a growing chunk of family income. Homeowning families and those enjoying the comforts and pleasures of our electronic and mechanical age are experiencing added drains on their incomes from the cost of *maintaining* the hardware which supplies these conveniences.

All this means that a mounting number of families are compelled to shop around for price advantages and often choose the *lower price* as against the *better quality.*

Meaning to Marketers

The continued surge of the discount retailer is bringing new challenges to marketers of consumer goods. One challenge is the direct result of the increasing growth and power of discount chains: *proliferation of strong store brands.* Originally discount retailing was founded on the concept of cutting prices of manufacturers' advertised brands. Today more and more "underselling" stores are promoting *their own brands.* This intensifies the "Battle of the Brands," which we have discussed frequently in *Grey Matter.* But as heretofore, marketers will meet this challenge by strengthening the *value image* of their product with continued product improvement and differentiation, superior packaging and stepped up advertising power. Greater efficiency and productivity via automation will also help bridge *the price gap* between manufacturers brands and the rising volume of labels being developed by discount chains.

The spread of discount retailing also demands a re-evaluation of *sales and distribution* policies by many manufacturers of consumer goods. It means wiping away the *cobwebs* which may have accumulated in the past few years when so many manufacturers thought that the progress of this type of retailing had been halted by the wave of mergers and failures. This does not mean that *all* present policies of dealing with discount chains must be abandoned. But it does mean that since discounting is bringing so many new and often larger

opportunities, as well as challenges, *policies* may have to be *modified* to meet new situations.

19

Shopping at Home

Kenneth G. Slocum

For years, as mail-order sales declined steadily, marketing scholars and marketing textbooks predicted that mail-order selling would atrophy until it was only a vestigial retailing institution. No doubt the scholars were right in their predictions on the basis of the role that mail-order selling fulfilled in the kind of economy they visualized. However, they failed to reckon with growing congestion, traffic difficulties, and the consumer's increasing desire for leisure time. Today the mail-order institution is staging a comeback, in somewhat different guise but with very similar results. This development neatly illustrates the danger inherent in predictions which concern the ever-changing consumer. It also highlights the fascination of the field of marketing which in a sense is always changing but in another sense remains much the same.

A merchandising tool of horse and buggy vintage—the general catalog—is proving surprisingly popular with jet-age shoppers.

Just a few days ago, for example, suburban Chicago housewife Dolly Sellman disposed of her normally arduous Christmas shopping chores in a matter of minutes. With a Montgomery Ward catalog in her lap and a phone in her hand, the young mother of five sat in her living room and casually ordered 23 Christmas items.

Though Mrs. Sellman's $109 purchase is larger than most, it's hardly unique for the catalog business these days.

Reprinted from the *Wall Street Journal*, December 20, 1963.

Complete national figures are hard to come by because many of the department stores and specialty shops using catalogs do not report such sales separately. However, there is general agreement catalog volume is climbing and this is confirmed by Goverment estimates.

Penney's Enters Field

. . . J. C. Penney Co., Inc., after 61 years in the retail store field, this fall [1963] issued its first major catalog, an impressive 1,254-page book. "We entered the catalog business because we're convinced of its great future importance," says Lester Naylor, vice president of catalog sales and operation.

Equally convinced, Montgomery Ward & Co. this year doubled the size of its catalog sales and promotion staff. "Catalogs have greater potential now than ever before in history," exclaims M. L. Erickson, manager of Ward's big mail order center in Chicago. "Whenever we go into a new area with a catalog order store, we see astounding growth."

The giant of the mail-order field, Sears, Roebuck & Co., is enjoying a similar experience. "For more than a year, Sears catalog sales gains have been outstripping our retail sales increases," comments Crowdus Baker, Sears president. Sears catalog sales are running 10% ahead of the year-ago pace and company officials estimate mail-order volume in the current fiscal year ending January 31 [1964] will hit $1.3 billion, or about 25% of total predicted sales. In its last fiscal year, Sears catalog volume accounted for 22% of total sales.

Once Written Off

This is an impressive showing for an industry written off years ago by many retailers and customers as obsolete because of the advent of center-of-the-city expressways and suburban shopping centers. Just what's behind this catalog boom?

"In one word—convenience," declares Modie Spiegel, chairman of Spiegel, Inc., which in recent years has closed up its retail stores to concentrate exclusively on catalog selling. "There's a consumer revolt taking place. Highways are cluttered and many stores don't give adequate service. So, many shoppers are swearing off self-service shopping and turning to the catalog for the ultimate in shopping convenience."

A San Francisco office worker agrees, "I did every bit of my Christmas shopping by mail this year," he declares. "Why should I go downtown and get a

parking ticket and maybe my pocket picked, too?"

But some retailers see convenience as only part of the answer. Generally lower prices offered in catalogs is an equally potent factor in mail-order growth, they maintain.

Help from Discounters

"The increased emphasis on discount selling in recent years has made the public more price conscious than ever," says Lawrence Gabrini, president of National Bellas Hess, Inc., Kansas City catalog house. "The net result has been to call the public's attention again to the bargains offered by catalogs."

Store executives generally agree that prices in their catalogs are 5% to 10% lower than identical merchandise on their retail shelves. Specifically, Gamble-Skogmo, Inc., Minneapolis, estimates its customers save about 7% after transportation costs on items bought through its catalog rather than over its store counters.

Whether it's price or convenience, catalog firms are exploiting the trend by appealing to more consumers, increasing personal services for catalog shoppers, speeding up deliveries and sprucing up the decor of the once colorless catalog office.

The service accorded Chicago's Mrs. Sellman is a case in point. Just before Thanksgiving, she was contacted on the phone by a Ward catalog promotion girl from the Wheaton, Ill., office and asked if she would like to place her Christmas order. Busy at the time, Mrs. Sellman made an appointment for a later call.

Keeping Close Tab

The promotion girl is one of the new devices Ward uses to give customers more personal attention. Each girl has a list of catalog customers she calls personally, to inform them of weekly sales specials, take Christmas lists or remind them of special occasions such as Father's Day. The girls keep a personal card file on each customer with assorted information gleaned from conversations, such as the number of children, special likes and coming occasions when gifts are in order. They even note when a child is sick, so they remember to ask about it the next time they call.

Such service is apparently effective. "I shop by catalog because I got tired of fighting highway traffic and being pushed around in stores," explains Mrs. Sellman. "I particularly like being called when there are special sales. Not only do I get bargains I otherwise might miss, but this personal attention makes me feel Ward's is interested in keeping me as a customer."

Ward's is also adding a staff of outside salesmen to catalog offices. When the catalog office staff learns that a customer is interested in a sizeable item such as floor coverings, a salesman calls on the customer in her home, toting hundreds of samples of material so the housewife can match draperies and furniture. Potential appliance buyers are transported to catalog offices, where salesmen demonstrate various models.

Looking to "Picture Phones"

Catalog houses are aggressively exploiting modern communications and transportation to whittle away the traditional advantages of retail store shopping, principally the time involved in getting merchandise. More than 80% of catalog orders now come in speedily by telephone, while 50 years ago some 95% moved slowly by mail. And catalog men already are planning for the day, which they estimate to be only 10 to 15 years away, when "picture phones"—telephones with screens showing the speaker —are in common use. Through these, they plan to demonstrate fashions and operation of appliances to housewives at home.

Jet planes also are providing the catalog houses an assist in their efforts to trim delivery times. For instance, California customers of Spiegel, Inc., for 58 years received their merchandise by parcel post, requiring a delivery time of at least 4½ days after the order was received at the firm's Chicago warehouse. But last month Spiegel began trucking parcel-post-size merchandise to the airport, where it is loaded in surplus baggage space of California-bound jet passenger planes. Customers, who pay nothing extra for the air service, now get merchandise in about two days.

Shortly after Christmas, Ward's will initiate next-day delivery to catalog offices in the Chicago area, enabling customers to receive goods a full day sooner. The faster time will be accomplished mainly by establishing a car pick-up service to collect from the catalog offices the orders customers have placed for goods, instead of relying on mail service as it does now. Picked up one day, the orders will be processed the following morning and then delivered by Ward's truck fleet to catalog offices the same day. Ward's already has next-day delivery in a few metropolitan areas.

Penney's which this fall [1963] distributed some 2 million general catalogs and 1,500,000 toy catalogs in the Midwest, plans to have nation-wide service with 48-to-72-hour delivery within six years, officials say. The company, which entered the business by acquiring General Merchandise Co. of Milwaukee, maintains that this now-doubled catalog facility "has a highly integrated computer and materials handling system considered well ahead of the industry in its ability to handle most functions involved in catalog sales distribution."

More and Brighter Offices

To cash in on the sales surge, the major companies are speeding up the openings of new catalog offices. . . . Not only are the offices growing more numerous but they are growing larger and fancier. In contrast with the dreary catalog counter offices common in the period right after World War II, many of the new offices are bright and cheery and resemble small stores. Customers often can browse among samples of gleaming appliances, television sets and toys, while background music sets an atmosphere of unhurried friendliness.

The 46 million big general catalogs distributed this year [1963], which is about 15% more than were sent out five years ago, boast larger selections than any except the biggest department stores. Sears' big books stock some 135,000 items, compared with about 80,000 for their largest stores.

20

The Role of Rentals in Demand Stimulation

Francis A. Babione

People have tended to think of goods and services as unique, distinctly different categories of consumption items. With the growing popularity of renting goods it is becoming increasingly apparent that products are only a form of congealed service—physical embodiments of services that can be released over time. It was pointed out in an earlier article that eventually time may become the element that the consumer finds to be in shortest supply. As we approach this state of affairs the probability is that the practice of renting goods will increase dramatically, because this permits the individual consumer to match more neatly the maximum of goods and services with his limited available time. The article below describes the growth in the practice of renting goods.

Enactment of he new federal tax law brings to the fore the problem of stimulating consumption. If the multiplier effect functions as hoped for, the $11 billion of additional purchasing power will generate more than double that amount of production and spending. Implicit in this expectation is the assumption that most recipients of income are willing to spend it forthwith.

The need for stimulating demand is made clear by projecting the per-capita growth of the economy over a ten-year period at, say a 4 per cent rate. Ignoring

Reprinted by permission from the May 1964, issue of *Michigan Business Review*, published by the Graduate School of Business Administration, The University of Michigan.

price changes, this indicates that ten years hence the American people will have nearly 50 per cent more goods and services than at present if this growth objective is to be achieved.

This propensity to consume has been questioned (among others) by Professor Ferdinand Mauser of Wayne State University, especially as it applies to the more affluent segments of our society[1] As the supply of goods grows apace over the coming decades, Mauser suggests that busy people will not want to bother with owning more goods; that they will be more concerned with "buying time rather than product."

A greater use of equipment rentals can provide a partial solution to this problem by making it easy for consumers to use a growing variety of appliances, cars, and other appurtenances to pleasant living. There will be less consumer resistance to trying new products because of the trial-use aspect of rentals. Concern for service will be a smaller deterrent to purchase because it is commonly provided by the rental firm. Replacement with new models will be almost automatic at the end of the contract period. As a further factor in stimulating demand, families with lower incomes will be able to rent costly equipment which otherwise would be beyond their financial reach for years.[2]

In the following discussion rentals are first considered as a method of marketing services which a durable good can render. The ease with which plans can be varied to meet the needs of different consumer groups is pointed out next.

Similarities between rentals and installment sales are stressed to indicate that a rental economy" may be viewed as a furher step in a trend toward use without ownership. Current applications by retailers are described to suggest various merchandising missions which rentals can support. Finally, the role of rentals in the planning of manufacturers is outlined.

The Growth of Services

Growing outlays for services is a striking postwar trend. By 1963 these outlays accounted for more than 40 per cent of consumers' spending—$154.5 billion out of $373.2 billion personal consumption expenditures.[3] As the economy has grown more prosperous, producers of food, clothing, and durable goods have lost ground relative to gains by a variety of service establishments, professional services, repair services, travel, education, and so on.

Rental services account for a small but growing part of this service sector. More important, however, the trend to greater spending for service supports the proposition that affluent consumers may become satiated with goods as such, and will increasingly prefer to buy the services of goods, free from the cares and responsibilities of owning them. As expressed in a time-worn quip: "I wouldn't want to *be* a millionaire, but I'd like to *live* like one."

Professors Eiteman and Davisson developed the concept that one buys a durable good because "it is capable of rendering a series of services."[4] Viewing

---

[1] Ferdinand F. Mauser, "The Future Challenges Marketing," *Harvard Business Review*, November–December 1963, p. 172.

[2] The term *rental* is broadly used to cover both short-term and long-term contracts to use a product owned by another. The term *lease* is preferred for contracts running for a year or more. The latter term is widely used in the industrial field.

[3] "National Income and Product in 1963," *Survey of Current Business,* January 1964, p. 6.

[4] Wilford J. Eiteman and Charles N. Davisson, *The Lease as a Financing and Selling Device,* (Ann Arbor, Bureau of Business Research, University of Michigan, 1951), p. 8.

goods as a "bundle of services" leads to the conclusion that it is often wiser to buy the services as needed, and let others assume the risks and cares of ownership.

This emphasis on buying services when needed is especially logical for goods which are used intermittently or for only short periods. If the product is costly, or hard to store because of size, a number of consumers may prefer to rent it for short periods, with gains in cost and convenience for all users. A case at point is the rental of cars by apartment dwellers in a large city.

Use Without Ownership

Prosperous consumers like rentals because of the convenience and time-saving features. Avoiding large cash outlays is a smaller concern. For the less affluent, however, financial restraints loom large, and rentals make possible immediate use of durable goods which otherwise might be impossible. The same plan can meet the needs of both groups, as follows:

Visualize a family of modest means on a week-long vacation trip to the sea shore. According to a New York Times advertisement, they can rent a 26-foot "sea skiff" (with Chrysler power) from Monday through Friday for $30; or $35 for the weekend. Rental plans such as this make it possible for consumers over a wide income range to enjoy boating. Noteworthy, too, the services are priced according to their time utility to the consumer. Thus, the daily charge for use of the boat on Saturday and Sunday is almost three times the per-day cost during the week ($17.50 as against $6). Conceivably, prosperous families spend a number of weekends at the shore, and view the rental plan primarily as a great convenience. Furthermore, twenty or more families may use the same boat

during a season, thus drastically reducing the cost to any one user.

Much the same flexibility and accommodation to different needs is present in car leasing. In New York City one can rent a car by the hour, day, week, month; or for the vacation season in Florida. If one needs the car only during the business day, a lower rate is quoted than for a 24-hour period. Another driver may then rent the car for overnight use. Too, the leasing company may move a number of cars from one city to another to accommodate special peak demands.

It may be asked whether consumers get the same satisfaction from using rented goods as from goods they own. A feeling of security and pride of ownership are gratifying aspects of ownership. However, assuming an "economy of abundance" in the future, security will be a lesser concern. As for pride of ownership, proponents of rentals suggest that accumulation and evidence of wealth are becoming less of a status symbol. Individuals will be increasingly judged by their taste in things they enjoy rather than by how much they own. For example, quality paintings may be rented by the month. Friends presumably will be more impressed with one's esthetic discrimination in enjoying a succession of good paintings than by the fact that one or two are owned. Too, as a "conversation piece" a series of rented art objects offer more than a single item which is owned through the years.

Installment Sales as Quasi-Rentals

The rental economy is currently just beyond an embryonic stage. Relative to its long-run potential it may be about as advanced as was installment selling in the early 1920's. There are pronounced similarities in rentals and installment selling, and the rapid growth of the latter indicates that we are well on the way toward an economy in which use of goods without ownership will be common.

A recent article on private debt reported that total annual consumer-debt payments in 1963 amounted to $59 billion.[5] On the average, consumers pay 20 per cent of spendable income on ordinary private debt plus mortgage payments. Considering only those who make substantial use of credit buying, their share of income spent on debt payments must be much larger.

The manner in which much private debt resembles rentals is apparent in the cases where new cars are purchased before the old ones are paid for. Similarly, houses may be bought on 30-year mortgage plans with no expectation of living in them until they are paid for.

The close parallel between installment selling and rentals is illustrated in 1964 finance plans of car dealers in New York City. One dealer sells a "standard" Chevrolet for $189 down and $61 per month. Another dealer leases the same model under a 24-month lease for $66 per month. This is a "net lease," which means that the driver pays all maintenance and insurance costs. It probably requires an initial payment of the first and last months' lease charges—or $132, as compared with $189 down payment in the installment plan.

Technically, a major difference between installment selling and rentals is that the former places ownership risks on the user. However, in certain car leasing plans the user contracts to reimburse the rental firm at the expiration of the contract if the resale value of the car is below the value anticipated when

the lease was signed. If the value is greater, the user is paid the difference. With this arrangement the net over-all cost should be much the same under either plan.

Current Uses by Retailers

Retailers are the logical outlets for rental goods. Consideration of rental plans now in use sheds light on the various roles of rentals in marketing. The following, with one exception, are illustrative applications in retailing:

1. **Trial-Use Rentals.** This plan allows the consumer to rent the equipment for a few months, with part or all rentals subsequently applied to the purchase, if he decides to buy. It is reported that 80 per cent of all band instruments are sold under this plan, permitting the parent to be sure of the child's aptitude or interest before making a purchase commitment. This plan will speed the acceptance of any new products which are revolutionary in design or use.

This plan could be useful in selling the growing amounts of used equipment, which will increase as replacement rates are accelerated. For example, a television dealer rents used sets for an eight-week period for $29.90. If the user finds the set satisfactory, he may apply half the rental toward the purchase price.

2. **Intermittent or Emergency Rentals.** This is the plan used exclusively by rental dealers such as United Rent-Alls (over 400 affiliated dealers) and Hertz Rent-All stores. Sears Roebuck experimentally opened several rental stores in 1962, but evidently found the volume insufficient to make them profitable.

This is a natural for a variety of regular retailers, either to build goodwill and store traffic, or to function as a profitable department in its own right. It has much in common with the prior plan because a consumer who rents,

[5] "Is Private Debt Too Big?" U.S. News and World Report, February 17, 1964, pp. 50–52.

say, a hedge trimmer for an afternoon may decide that he would find it more convenient to own it. A drug chain which promoted the rental of convalescent aids found that 75 per cent of the users converted to purchase (with all rentals applied to the purchase price). Retailers have an advantage over rental firms in using this plan because rental firms commonly do not make outright sales.

3. Service Equipment in Stores. In certain circumstances it may be best to provide use of equipment at a central point. For example, a dealer in office supplies maintains a demonstration copying machine in his store. For a nominal charge customers may bring material to be copied. This is helpful to smaller firms which cannot justify buying the machine, and also provides a measure of trial use.

The potential in this kind of service is illustrated by a copying service available in libraries on the Penn State campus. Xerox copying machines are leased from the manufacturer, and in addition to use by librarians students may have material copied for ten cents a page. On one peak-volume day, 2,000 pages were processed through the machines. Important for this discussion, students are provided with a helpful service; and as a byproduct hundreds of possible future Xerox customers learn about the merits of the equipment.

4. Adjunct to Supply Sales. The rental of equipment required for using certain products, such as ladders with paint or spreaders with fertilizer, is a type of rental for intermittent use. The purpose, however, is to build sales of a product, and the rental is primarily an accommodation. Thus, there may be no charge for rental of a spreader if fertilizer is purchased. Hardware stores charge only one dollar for a day's use of an electric carpet brush if Glamorene is purchased. Subject to a refundable

$20 deposit, Sears Roebuck loans fairly costly tools to customers who buy floor tile.

Parallels can be drawn from the industrial field, where such plans have been used for decades to promote a variety of products. For example, a rivet manufacturer might lease a $10,000 rivet-setting machine for only $500 per year if the customer agreed to purchase rivets exclusively from his firm. Antitrust action against these plans, however, has largely forced manufacturers to drop the restrictive agreements.

5. Alternative to Installment Selling. As previously noted, many rental plans contain purchase options, some of which permit the user to apply all, or nearly all of the rentals toward outright purchase. After the equivalent of the selling price and finance charge has been paid, the option price may be as low as one or two per cent of the list price; or purely nominal, as one dollar.

These plans can be construed as conditional sales; and the courts regard them as such when tax considerations are at issue. The rental (or lease) designation stems in part from the growing popularity of leasing. Evidently many prospective buyers (including business firms) are hesitant to incur further debt but find it "smart" or prudent to substitute leasing for installment purchase.

6. True Long-Term Leasing. The word "true" is used to suggest that the user has no intention or likelihood of ever owning the equipment currently used. It implies that he has a continuing need for the equipment; he does not want responsibility for maintenance and risks of ownership; and he expects to replace it with new equipment at the expiration of the lease contract.

Except for car leasing, most of which is done by business firms, ultimate consumers have been offered few such leases. However, it is this type of leasing which is contemplated by those who nvisage a rental economy. The challenge for retailers and manufacturers will be one of having such plans ready when the time is opportune.

The creative planning needed for embarking on a rental economy is illustrated n a research study made by the Nationwide Mutual Insurance Company. A poll of representative policyholders led to the conclusion that a majority of car owners would like to make monthly "package" payments to the company covering cost of car leasing, insurance, gasoline, and all other operating costs. The plan would e sold by the thousands of Nationwide gents. Local car dealers and finance ompanies would lose a great volume f business if such a plan proved successul.

7. Service "Rentals." Soft goods, too, may be rented, as evidenced by linen nd diaper services. Here, the emphasis s on service, and secondarily on the osts and risks of ownership. For a $1.75 weekly charge a linen supply company provides an inventory of eleven shirts, nd launders five of them each week. he original shirts are replaced with new nes when requested by the customer. Significant for local clothing stores, the hirts are manufactured by a private-brand producer, and traditional channels re bypassed.

If a rental economy should embrace wide range of soft goods, retailers would have to offer such services themelves. Illustrative of the penalty of delay s the belated rental of cars by franhised dealers—long after rental firms nade great strides in this field.

8. Contract Selling. This is not a ental plan, but it offers an important eature of rentals—a predetermined cost or using equipment for a specified period. The key feature of the plan is he advance stipulation of the subsequent trade-in value of the equipment. For example, several decades ago a car lealer offered to trade cars at 10,000-

mile intervals. The "depreciation charge" was 3 cents per mile, or $300 for the period the car was used. Some years later, in the 1930's, Ford dealers were featuring annual trades for a trade-in cost of $175 (approximately one fourth of the current list price).

Contract selling has merit for the retailer who may be confronted with competition from rental firms. He avoids ownership risks, and selling costs should be greatly reduced. Repeat business is largely assured at predetermined intervals. The chief problem is that of making sure the equipment will be given reasonable care, but this is a concern in rental plans as well.

Retailers have much to gain from the promotional features of leasing, and they should benefit greatly from their use. As compared with rental firms, retailers are located close to prospective customers, know their needs, and can offer a choice between outright or conditional sales, short-term rentals, purchase-option plans, and long-term rentals in which ownership is not contemplated.

If they do not develop their own plans, a parallel distribution system through rental firms may emerge, to the detriment of franchised dealers. Illustrative of this threat, in 1962 it was reported that 70–85 per cent of the TV sets marketed in Britain were placed by rental firms. In any event, smaller retailers will find the going rough because they lack the resources and aggressiveness requisite to engaging in this kind of service and competition. As noted subsequently, the extent to which they will benefit from rental programs depends largely on the support they may receive from manufacturers.

Manufacturers' Interest in Rentals

Decisions of manufacturers will determine the relative importance of retailers vs. other rental agencies in the expanded use of rental programs. More important than the choice between rental outlets is the manufacturer's interest in any plans which stimulate demand. Collectively, all manufacturers favor plans which encourage spending of "discretionary income." As members of an industry group, the challenge is to divert spending to one product (power boats as against color television, and travel trailers vs. foreign travel). As individual firms there is both an immediate and long-run concern with sales volume and share of market.

Marketing tasks for which rentals may prove helpful in stimulating sales are: (a) introduction of new products; (b) promoting new uses for old products; (c) enlarging the use of present products by current users (car rentals on vacation trips); (d) promoting consumption at lower income levels; and (e) acquainting oncoming generations with the merits of either old or new products (the four million youths who reach adulthood each year).

Inherent in most of these goals of rental programs is an element of sampling. This role of rentals is much the same as the trial-use feature cited in the prior discussion. However, it takes on an added dimension when viewed from the manufacturer's standpoint. He can incorporate rentals in his promotional plans as an alternative to other advertising and sales efforts; and has the resources to do it on a major scale.

Assume, for example, that a certain manufacturer has budgeted $3 million for advertising and sales promotion. The mission of this promotional effort is to inform and persuade "target" prospec groups to give favorable consideratio to his product. It may well be that mone spent on one of these rental plans, o some combination of them, will offe more effective impact on a given pros pect group than an equivalent expendi ture on, say, advertising. Using hypo thetical figures, this manufacturer coulc allocate $100,000 ($200 for each o 5,000 dealers) for subsidizing and im plementing a dealer-level rental plan Assuming records could attribute specifi sales to the rental plan, he might find i to be one of his best promotional tools

As a case in point, Datsun cars—: fairly recent Japanese import—can be rented in New York City for $2.49 pe day, plus 4 cents a mile. These rental: may not prove profitable, but as method of demonstrating the cars th plan may be far less costly than usinɡ sales demonstrations or other method: of making contact with car owners.

All of these suggested types of renta programs and missions in promotiona strategy fall short of the extent of us assumed in a full-blown rental economy A large measure of imaginative thinkinɡ will have to characterize managemen planning if widespread rental of durable goods by consumers is to come to pass Meanwhile, there is ample room fo experimentation with a variety of renta programs well within the reach of manu facturers and retailers, large and small In light of the evident need for main taining a flow of spending commensurate with our growing capacity to produce, rentals should loom larger in busines: planning.

IV

Environmental Forces

A

Competition

21

Competition? Yes, But. . . .

Charles F. Phillips

The preservation of competition has long been a tradition or philosophy of behavior in our society. However, people differ in the way they define competition. Using illustrations from various segments of our society, the author of the following article points out that many people feel that if they are hurt by the actions of their competitors, these actions constitute "unfair competition." He sums up this attitude as follows: "We all like competition, but. . . ."

To ask an American businessman—whether he be grocer, baker, or candlestick maker—if he believes in competition is almost like asking for a sock on the nose. *Of course,* he believes in competition—and he raises his voice to add emphasis to his answer.

But after he has cooled off a bit from your question, you may find that he has his own definition of competition. For example, let's walk with him down the street toward the grocery store of which he is the proprietor. Across the way in a window of one of his competitors is a large sign: "Sugar, X cents per pound." You call it to his attention and at once his brow knits. "That's unfair competition," he says. "That so-and-so

Reprinted by permission of The Foundation for Economic Education, Inc.

has cut his price again to attract my customers." I remind him that he believes in competition. "Why, yes," he replies, "but not unfair and ruthless competition." And, if you then ask him, "but why is it unfair for a competitor to cut his price" he will explode, "Why, any darn fool knows that it is unfair to sell sugar for X cents. You can't make any money at that price. There ought to be a law in this state against such practices."

We Are for Freedom, But

I wonder if the reaction of our friend, the grocer, does not illustrate a simple truth which can be expressed in the short but incomplete sentence: "We all like competition, but. . . ."

We all like competition since we know
is essential for our type of economy,
id we like the freedoms which our
onomy gives to each of us—the free-
)m to enter or withdraw from any
)ecific field or career; freedom to set
ir own prices; yes, even freedom to
idersell somebody else and take busi-
:ss away from him.

But . . . all too often when a com-
ititor really acts like a competitor and
)es something which hurts us—cuts a
·ice, sells harder, improves quality—
becomes "unfair competition" and we
in to our trade association, our re-
)urces, or the government for protec-
)n.

Of course, you think I am exaggerat-
g the situation, and to a degree I
n; but perhaps less than you think.
et's take a little look around this dis-
ibution world of ours.

We might begin by a little historical
ccursion in the retail field. If we go
ick to the turn of the present century,
e find that small country merchants
ere going through the mail-order scare.
ollowing the lead of Montgomery Ward
ompany and Sears, Roebuck & Com-
iny, mail-order firms were springing
) in many parts of our country. To the
nall country retailer, this newer form
: retailing was unfair. It did not em-
loy salespeople. It did not involve
ie operation of a retail store. It could
urchase in huge quantities. For these
id other reasons, the local merchant
as undersold and he objected to this
:sult. Obviously, such competition was
nfair! In a number of communities,
rade at home" clubs were organized
·hile some local retailers organized mail-
rder catalogue burning parties.

Jnfair, They Say

Along about the same time, the "un-
iir" competition of the department

store was also growing. As a matter of
fact, by 1895 the department store had
developed to such an extent that a
group of retailers meeting in convention, "after an exciting debate," passed
a resolution condemning this form of retailing, as it would "result in oppression
of the public by suppressing competition
(note that word 'suppressing') and causing the consumer in the end to pay
higher prices and ultimately create a
monopoly . . . and, further, that it
(would) close to thousands of energetic
young men who lack great capital the
avenue of business which they should
find open to them."[1] Once again, the
bogey of unfair competition had reared
its ugly head. Yet, it is probably not
being cynical to remark that what these
retailers really were opposed to was the
fact that the department store was a
formidable competitor.

What happened in the late Twenties
and the early Thirties in the chain store
field is known from personal experience
to practically all of us attending this
Conference today. Based on charges
that the chains were monopolistic; that
they used such unfair practices as loss
leaders; that they were a detriment to
community life because of their absen-
tee ownership, unfairness to local bankers, failure to pay their fair proportion
of taxes; and that they were unfair to
their employees through long hours, low
wages, and offering little chance of
advancement, smaller retailers spent
much time, effort, and money in attacking this new method of unfair competition. Customers were urged to curtail
their purchases at chains. The Robinson-
Patman Act was sponsored, the mis-
named Fair Trade laws were encouraged,
and in over twenty states special taxes

[1] Quoted in C. F. Phillips, *Marketing.*
Boston: Houghton Mifflin Company, 1938,
p. 308.

discriminating against the chains were enacted.

We all like competition, but. . . .

Of course, this excursion into retail history belongs to the past, and you may ask: Is anything like this going on at the present time? The answer is "yes"— and in practically every area of business. Let's note a few illustrations.

Pick up the trade paper of today, and you will discover that discount houses are a form of unfair competition. All over the country, they are rapidly springing up on the basis of underselling the so-called established retailer, which means, and I now quote the executive secretary of the National Association of Retail Druggists, that they are trying to destroy "every established retailer in the United States . . . by unfair competition . . . ."[2] And he goes on with two sentences which might well have been lifted verbatim from dozens of speeches made against the chain store twenty-five years ago.

> Unless the discount house is effectively curbed . . . there will inevitably be anarchy in the market place. The American public must ask itself whether it wishes to sacrifice the legitimate retailers who make outstanding contributions to our economic and community life and who are the backbone of our mass distribution system.

Discount houses are even pointed to as being unfair to the consumer because, after all, they do not offer him all the services of the established retailer. Incidentally, whether the customer wants those services or not is rarely considered when this argument is advanced.

[2] Quoted by Cameron Day, "More discount houses everywhere—is this a threat to advertising?" *Printers' Ink,* April 30, 1954, p. 33.

Solution by Elimination

And, what do the established retailers offer as a solution to the discount house? Is it an honest effort on their part to meet this new competitive factor by reducing their own margins and prices—which, if history proves anything, *must* be the way to meet it in the long run? In a few instances, the answer is yes. To illustrate, here is a refreshing statement from the chairman of the board of Sears, Roebuck & Company, Theodore Houser, who says:

> I have no patience with people who say that there ought to be some way to stop the discount house. The important thing is to bring down the price to the consumer. If the discount house can do that, good. It's Sears job to get in there and pitch.[3]

But Houser's statement is really the exception which proves the rule. The majority of established retailers act as if they think the answer is *more* Fair Trade—despite the fact that it is the wide margins set by Fair Trade which are playing a important role in encouraging the growth of the discount house. Consequently, they clamor for the manufacturer to cut off the flow of merchandise to the price cutter and to enforce his Fair Trade contracts. In brief, they say: Let's not meet competition; let's have someone eliminate it for us.

Another form of what some of today's retailers refer to as unfair competition can be discovered by talking with a downtown merchant in any city where one or more major outlying shopping centers have been developed. "Here am, a well-established retailer," he will tell you. "I have been in this location for

[3] "For Sears: A New Era and a New Problem," *Business Week,* May 1, 1954, p. 44.

thirty years, and I have always given good service to the public. Now, some real estate operator has come along and developed a shopping center five miles outside of this community, and *my* customers are driving out there where they have ample room to park and where they can shop during the evening. In view of all I've done for this community, don't think it is fair."

Or, again, talk with the president of one of today's drug chains. Twenty-five years ago *his* organization was the culprit. At that time, *he* was the unfair competitor—the price cutter—but, to-day, he finds that the supermarket has added a drug section and is underselling him.[4] Whereas he opposed resale price maintenance laws twenty-five years ago, today he is one of their strongest advocates. His own definition of unfair competition has shifted rapidly, depending upon who is being undersold. Incidentally, this same shift in opinion is becoming evident among the executives of the older and well-established food chains, and the leading trade paper in his area is now an advocate of Fair Trade.[5]

Make Competition Illegal

We see another aspect of the Fair Trade fight in New Jersey. Here—as elsewhere—the supermarkets began to sell packaged medicines at reduced prices. The regular druggists' reaction was not to meet competition in the market place, but to try for a court ruling to prevent sales of packaged medicines in stores not having registered pharmacists.[6] This method of fighting competition is catching: It has also appeared in Minnesota, California, and other states.[7]

We all like competition, but . . .

Or again, consider the so-called plight of the automobile dealer during these past several months. For a number of years now, he has been riding the gravy train. Cars were hard to get; he was in a sellers' market and he made money. But, late in 1953, it became apparent that a shift was occurring; and by last spring, it was clear that the tide was out. The sellers' market turned into a buyers' market.

Many dealers who had grown up in the industry during its easy selling days and had never been trained for the "hard sell" suddenly found themselves in trouble. Their profit margin disappeared; they went into the "red." Some of them began to appear in Dun & Bradstreet's failure statistics. Of course, said the dealers, it was all the manufacturer's fault. As the dealers put it: "The real trouble is that auto-makers are producing more cars than dealers can sell,"[8] and they urged their resources to reduce their production. Oh, the dealers would admit that they might have had some part to play in the situation, since some of them were bootlegging cars— selling them to so-called illegitimate dealers who in turn would sell them at reduced prices. To check such so-called unfair competition, the National Automobile Dealers Association even asked the United States Justice Department to come to the dealers' rescue and prohibit bootlegging!

But, we do not have to limit ourselves

[4] For a study of this trend, cf. "Grocer Horns in on Druggists," *Business Week,* February 16, 1952, p. 158 ff.

[5] Cf. Godfrey M. Lebhar's editorial on "Is Fair Trade in Jeopardy?" in *Chain Store Age* (Grocery edition), June, 1954, p. 51.

[6] "New Jersey Supers Resist Druggists' Smears," *Super Market Merchandising,* May, 1954, pp. 191–5.

[7] *Printers' Ink,* September 12, 1952, p. 7.

[8] *Time,* June 7, 1954, p. 104.

to illustrations from what we normally consider the retail field. Did you follow the ten-month strike of Local 15 of the United Hatters and Millinery Workers International Union against the Hat Corporation of America? The strike started in July of 1953, brought on basically by the Union's demand that the company sign a contract containing a clause that would prohibit it from opening new plants outside of the Norwalk area and from transferring work now done in Norwalk to any outside plant.

What the Union wanted was a limit on competition. It did not want its members to compete with workers in some other area where Hat Corporation might establish a factory. Fortunately, after ten months, the Union lost its fight. It is worth contemplating, however, what would have happened had a similar strike been won when the United States was still located on he East Coast only. Obviously, it would still be located on the East Coast only; and equally obviously, its standard of living today would be far below what it now is.

Agriculture and Exports

Then, of course, there is the farmer—the so-called individualist, the man who stands on his own feet, and, as the politician puts it, "is the backbone of the nation." Here, of course, is someone who believes in competition. Yes, he does, but again there comes that but —and the but in his case is a big one, so big that through powerful lobbies he has forced through Congress price support laws which give him protection far in excess of even that provided for the retailer through Fair Trade.

In the foreign trade area, we can find this same attitude. A Randall Commission was appointed; and last January it came up with a program which could be described by the phrase, "more trade,

less aid." For a time, it seemed as practically everyone in the country w: in agreement that this slogan would a good one to put into practice. looked as if we were going to mal progress in minimizing some of o tariff barriers which limit competitic and result in lower standards of livir both here and abroad. Yet, when a sp cific program to accomplish these en was proposed last March, many of tho who, at their trade association meeting are warm advocates of competition, su denly found that there were certa wage cost differentials which led the to oppose lower tariffs "as posing grave threat to the domestic economy. As they warmed up to their subject, th pointed out that lower tariffs wou throw American workers out of jol curtail purchasing power, and send into a depression. The fact that dom tic difficulties in specific areas would far more than offset by benefits in oth areas is something with which th were not concerned.

We all believe in competition, but. .

I can even illustrate this attitude the field of education—college educ tion at that. Throughout the Unit States, colleges use scholarships to ca ture students—and I use the wo "capture" deliberately. Sometimes want them for their I.Q., sometimes their A.P. (athletic prowess) and son times for both. At my college, of cour (or president Jones' college if he is t one doing the talking) we limit the scholarships to students who are in se ous financial need; but, unfortunate (that is the word used by college pre dents when several of them gat together in a room to discuss the sit tion), there are a few colleges whi

[9] For more details on these arguments, "U.S. Foreign Economic Policy," in Natio *City Monthly Letter on Business a Economic Conditions*, May, 1954, pp. 55–

use scholarships as an unfair method of price-cutting. Don't you think, their conversation continues, our regional association can do something about this?

Even educators like competition, but. . .

Anti-Competitive Attitude

By no means is this anti-competitive attitude confined to the United States. As a matter of fact, we are probably less prone to accept this attitude than businessmen throughout the world. In Guy le Carmony's excellent little article on "What's Wrong with France?" he suggests that:

In great part the French crisis is moral. Too many Frenchmen have developed the habit of seeking government protection. Industrialists, already protected against domestic competition by cartels, want the government to shield them against foreign competition by high tariffs and restrictive quotas. The peasants want government subsidies to enable them to buy the highly priced French manufactured goods. The workers want the government to supplement their inadequate wages with generous family allowances and other social benefits, while demanding at the same time the closing of borders to foreign labor, even when it is needed for expansion of the French economy.[10]

He then adds, that, while "the French believe that they still have a free economy . . . (what) they actually have . . . is the competition for subsidies of innumerable groups, each of which presses the state to protect its acquired position by artificial means." To underline his

[10] de Carmony, Guy, "What's Wrong with France?" *Reader's Digest*, May 1954, pp. 17–122.

point, he adds that currently 35 per cent of the national budget of France goes for direct and indirect subsidies to business, industry, and agriculture.

Apparently, France believes in competition, but. . . .

Now, as I conclude, let me be sure that I am not misunderstood as to the point I am trying to make. Please do not think I am saying there is no such thing as unfair competition. When a competitor resorts to false and misleading advertising, engages in misbranding, and makes false and disparaging statements against competitors or their products, he is engaging in practices which all of us would denounce.

What I am saying is this: Much of what we daily refer to as unfair competition is really just keen competition. It is the kind of competition that is essential to our type of economic system. If we want to maintain the freedoms which our system gives us—to enter businesses of our choice, to produce the merchandise we please, to set our own prices—then we must accept the competition which is essential to that kind of an economy. We must not always look to our trade association or our government to protect us from the actions of our competitors.

Do We Want Another System?

Of course, there are other kinds of economic systems. I studied one at first hand last winter when I spent several months in India. There I discovered that if you want to make a substantial capital investment in your plant, you must get the approval of the government licensing committee and this is not easy to do. To illustrate, during 1953, the textile industry in India—as in the United States—was not having a very happy time. A number of companies decided to install automatic looms to reduce their cost and, hence, to compete better both in the domestic and in the world markets. During the year, ten applications for such installations came before the government licensing committee. All ten applications were refused: The committee felt that the automatic looms would create unfair competition for the firms not installing similar equipment. As a result, India's textile industry finds itself increasingly unable to compete in today's market and, what is even more important, Indian customers were continuing to pay the higher prices required by the older, less efficient and, hence, more costly looms. Perhaps it is this kind of reasoning—perhaps it is this limitation on competition—which plays a part in explaining why the average per capita income in today's India is about $39.00 per year.

I would make this positive suggestion. Let us spend more time—in our offices, stores, conferences, and trade association meetings—improving our operations and less time trying to curb our competitors. Not only will individual companies be better off, but so will society. If America wants to continue its long-time development toward a rising standard of living, we need to encourage more, not less, competition.

When Stuyvesant Fish was president of the Illinois Central Railroad, there walked into his office one morning an Irishman, hat on and pipe in mouth, who said:

"I want a pass to St. Louis."

"Who are you?" asked president Fish, somewhat startled.

"I'm Pat Casey, one of your switchmen."

Mr. Fish, thinking it was a good chance to impart a lesson in etiquette, said, "Now, Pat, I'm not going to say that I will refuse your request, but there are certain forms a man should observe in asking a favor. You should knock at the door; and when I say 'Come in' you

should enter and, taking off your hat and removing your pipe from your mouth, you should say, 'Are you president Fish?' I would say, 'I am. Who are you?' Then you should say, 'I am Pat Casey, one of your switchmen.' Then I would say, 'What can I do for you?' Then you would tell me, and the matter would be settled. Now you go out and come in again and see if you can't do better."

So the switchman went out. About two hours later there was a knock on the door and president Fish said, "Come in." In came Pat Casey with his hat off and pipe out of his mouth.

"Good morning," he said, "are you president Fish of the Illinois Central Railroad?"

"I am. Who are you?"

"I am Pat Casey, one of your switchmen."

"Well, Mr. Casey, what can I do for you?"

"You can go to hell. I got a job and a pass on the Wabash."[11]

Pat Casey might have spent the rest of his life cursing president Fish and voting for congressmen who pledged themselves to work for the removal of Fish as the president of the Illinois Central Railroad. Instead, he exercised his ingenuity and got a job and a pass on the Wabash. Rather than spending our time cursing our competitors and making efforts to limit their competitive activities, some of us need to get a job and a pass on the Wabash.

[11] Botkin, B. A., and Harlow, A. F., *Treasury of Railroad Folklore.* Crown, 1953.

B

The Government

22

How Much Freedom Does Business *Really* Want?

Joseph W. McGuire

Anyone who has observed the behavior of businessmen in their relationships with government over the issue of the regulation of business will have noted a strange ambivalence on the part of the businessmen. They are firmly—and vehemently—opposed to all forms of government regulation except those particular regulations which they happen to favor. The author of the present article deals with this somewhat paradoxical behavior of businessmen.

A popular recent motion picture possessed the unlikely title, *Dr. Strange-love, or: How I Learned to Stop Worrying and Love the Bomb.* To me this title is remarkable for the glimpse it affords of the psychotic interests in our modern society. And I believe I can understand the strange subtitle. After all, the bomb has been with us but a relatively brief time and nuclear oblivion seems to be so final (a once-and-for-all sort of event) that it would not seem too surprising if people would stop worrying about the bomb, for apparently we can do little about it.

Reprinted from *Business Horizons,* Summer 1965, Vol. 8, No. 2, pp. 73–78, by special permission.

On the other hand, I would be most surprised to see a movie entitled, say, *Mr. Businessman, or: How I Learned to Stop Worrying and Love the Government.* Such a motion picture would immediately suggest that we were losing a cherished neurosis of long standing, one that has cheered us in depression years and given us comfort in our alternating periods of high economic spirits. For, indeed, it is an accepted truism of our times that business and government must be incompatible. The public pronouncements by business leaders inform us with considerable vigor that these men are worried, and that they are intensely discontented with government activities.

In fact, it seems that the federal

government can do little that meets with business approval. For example, it is commonplace for executives to complain about high taxes, but in recent months I have heard several also object to tax reduction. The small businessman— often called the backbone of our free enterprise system—has again stated that government is not protective enough, and has actively lobbied for new retail price-fixing legislation under the catchy slogan of "quality stabilization." One of President Johnson's major decisions has involved the proper location of a $170 million atom smasher, with vehement Midwestern legislators, industrialists, and even university presidents vying with their counterparts on both coasts to place pressure upon the AEC and the President.

These illustrations are meant to convey more than a vague impression of the confused relationships that exist between business and government. More deeply and significantly, these and similar examples are symptomatic of a widespread quest by business for new rules and orderly procedures in an altered although affluent environment.

In a society of ever-mounting complexity, a reconstructed framework that guides and limits business activities is required. Beneath the superficial vestiges of business-government antipathy lies a not too well-hidden reliance by business upon government, for businessmen are well aware that the federal government is the one institution that can establish the rules and procedures which bring order to our modern business world. Businessmen are aware of the great necessity for order in their affairs, for business is future oriented, and only through order and rules can environmental uncertainty be reduced in a rapidly changing society. In their search for order businessmen have recognized—discretely to be sure—the limitations of our traditional system and are groping toward new parameters and a fresh perspective for business behavior. Our subject, then, is the necessity for order in modern business affairs and the altered nature of the ordering mechanism.

Traditional Business Freedoms

The question of freedom in American business has been discussed for decades. Terms such as free enterprise, free competition, and our free economic system have been bandied about so often and so loosely that they have become meaningless slogans. It is said that increased order achieved through government intervention must inhibit freedom in business. Yet freedom in business is, and always has been, a relative term. Business still enjoys freedom, and let us hope that it always will. However, it should be clearly recognized that this freedom is never absolute or perfect, and that it must be, as it always has been, held prudently and wisely by prudent and wise men.

Freedom—or order, for that matter— accrues only to persons. Of course, order prevails in the universe and in nature, but for our purposes this is significant only as it affects people. Freedom and order also exist in a business system that is described traditionally, and it is these attributes of a traditional system, as they relate to people, that we will examine briefly first.

A business system described by traditional economics contains various participants, such as consumers, suppliers of goods and services, and entrepreneurs. All of these persons have participative freedom; they are free to participate or not in the business process. Needless to add, in the real world participative freedom for most individuals is a bogus freedom; they must participate or face consequences that are most unpleasant

rsons who choose not to participate
ay be confronted with alternatives such
unemployment, starvation, or bank-
ptcy.

A second area of freedom can be
peled freedom of mobility. The partic-
ants can move from one alternative
thin the system to another, and these
ovements are based upon a personal
eference scale, and, in some cases,
on performance. Thus, consumers in
aditional economics are free to buy
and X over Brand Y if they so desire,
to change about among products as
ey wish. Entrepreneurs, likewise, are
e to produce what they want.

ontrols and Business

These two areas—participation and
obility—include the principal free-
oms available to persons in a traditional
onomic system. However, even such a
stem maintains control mechanisms
tablished to bring about order. *First,*
is always assumed, at least tacitly, that
dividuals act in their self-interest and
lf-interest in turn is always quantifiable
monetary terms. Because of this per-
nal control people perform in a predict-
le manner. *Second,* it is assumed that
siness behavior is controlled by the
personal forces of the market. Thus,
mpetition, and supply and demand
rces regulate the activities of the en-
e system and of each person in it.
onomists conventionally pay special
tention to these controls. *Third,* it is
sumed that the firm is autocratic, that
that subordinates within the enter-
ise follow the dictates of entrepreneurs
r their own welfare. Just as the first of
ese assumptions is properly in the field
psychology, the third is closely re-
ted to sociology.

These, then, are the devices for control
the traditional business model: the
rsonal, impersonal, and internal regu-

lating mechanisms. It could be argued
that the second and third of these
controls stem from the first. It could
also be argued that, because of the
personal element, it has been necessary
to seek new methods of control to preserve order.

In our twentieth century world it is
evident that personal controls still operate. Man does pursue his self-interest. It
is not quite so clear today, however, that
this pursuit is as straightforward as it
appeared in traditional economics. *First,*
men are never as rational in real life as
they are in theory. They did not, and do
not, pursue higher profits or wages, or
lower prices with the single-minded
devotion depicted by tradition. *Second,*
even if men would rationally select and
consistently adhere to that one alternative which would bring them, let us say,
higher profits, it is possible to do so
in our business society because of uncertainty. In a business world as complex as ours, it is often true that the
business executive simply does not know
all the courses of action open to him, and
does not know how to choose that "best"
alternative from those that he does
perceive.

Third, we imperfect humans have
multiple goals that are conditioned by
personality as well as by cultural forces.
Thus, an individual not only wants to be
successful in business, but he also is
confronted by pressures that insist that
he be a good citizen, a fine family man,
a deeply religious man, and a faithful
friend and generous employer. Caught
at the center of a host of societal forces,
modern man becomes a creature far
removed from the economic man of
traditional economic theory.

Illusion and Reality

The modern real business world, therefore, is filled to the brim with confusion

and trauma. This confusion, furthermore, is heightened by the fact that the only explanations of this world that are widespread and generally acceptable are those which stem from traditional economic theory. Today, when one-third of the professional and technical men, and every eighth factory worker is employed by the government it is difficult for sensible men to maintain this theoretical façade; consequently, a number of signs indicate that it is crumbling. Just to give one example, a 1963 survey of 1,588 businessmen revealed that 61 per cent believed that the federal government should establish a target rate of long-term economic growth. Since the setting of a rate would be meaningless in itself, it is implied that these businessmen also believed that government should act to maintain growth at the desired rate. However, the same survey revealed that 68 per cent of the respondents blamed government policies for their inhibiting effects on economic growth, evidence of the considerable ambivalence that still remains in the attitudes of businessmen toward government.

Senator Fulbright of Arkansas began a recent controversial speech on foreign policy with the words (reflective of a Kantian philosophy): "There is an inevitable divergence, attributable to the imperfections of the human mind, between the world as it is and the world as men perceive it." This is the sort of divergence that has existed between the traditional economic concept of our business system and the real world of business. Nevertheless, it is difficult to believe that it is healthy for modern businessmen to cling to outdated perceptions of the actual business system, to speak of this system as though we were still a nation of small businesses with no government intervention. More and more, I believe, men are recognizing that change has occurred and is still

taking place. Businessmen are increa ingly turning to government for orde and control. As they do this, howeve they are naturally uneasy, for they a moving into a conventionally unpopul and unchartered relationship.

Change, Freedom, and Order

What has happened to freedom i business during the decades of trans tion? Men still must participate, for th most part, or face dire consequence For employees, however, the alternative are less severe with the advent of u employment insurance. The most dr matic changes have occurred in th freedom to move. For consumers, ce tainly, the range of choice has bee enlarged. The market offers more prod ucts than ever before, and the gover ment has ensured that many of these a sold honestly and are of satisfacto quality. Labor is not as mobile as it onc was, perhaps, but this lack of mobili results more from incentives such pension plans, other fringe benefits, an union activities than from any gover mental schemes. On the other hand, th public employment service has undoub edly abetted labor mobility. Entrepr neurs and capitalists probably have, balance, about the same freedom undertake alternatives in their expecte self-interest. There do not seem to any clear indications that governme activities over-all have decreased interfered with these sorts of freedom business.

The principal change in busine operations has occurred because of th altered ordering mechanism—from co petition to government regulation. Co petition still exists in our busine system, of course, but the trend for th past eighty years has been towa regulation by government rather th through market forces. The substitutio of government for market has, furthermore, been largely in response to demands by the public and by businessmen that government intervene because of the feeling that the market mechanism has failed in some areas.

Thus, the Interstate Commerce Commission in 1887 was "demanded" by the Granger movement, by the farmer, and by the small businessman. The Sherman Act, Clayton Act, and Robinson-Patman Acts were passed in response to similar pressures. In fact, all of the regulatory legislation of the 1930's emerged because of the deep-seated public attitudes toward what were believed to be the abuses of businessmen in the 1920's, and these laws were designed to prevent the recurrence of such abuses and to aid the economy in its efforts to recover from the Great Depression.

Without government intervention—without government rules and regulations—our economy today would be substantially altered. If we did not have a set of antitrust laws, it is probable that monopoly would be rampant in many industries. The lack of patent protection would probably retard innovation. Abuses in the securities markets would undoubtedly occur even more regularly and flagrantly than now. Chaos would most likely result in the banking industry in the absence of the Federal Reserve System and the Federal Deposit Insurance Corporation. Strikes would probably be much more common without the order produced by labor legislation. Our foods and drugs would be suspect more often, and consumers would be subject, even more than now, to the blandishments of unscrupulous advertisers and promoters. Small enterprises would have disappeared in many industries where they now exist. The structure of agriculture, transportation, and communications would now—for better or for worse—be entirely different.

Today's Close Bonds

The obvious conclusion that government has acted as a druggist filling prescriptions for its business patients is scarcely debatable. Many businessmen, however, would disagree with the statement that business was a willing patient. Yet it is a fact that the business community is not a cohesive entity, and often large segments of this community have insisted upon government assistance and protection. As we noted earlier, more and more frequently businessmen have come to rely upon the government as the source of prosperity, welfare, and order.

This reliance, by the way, is not without detrimental side effects, effects that accompany most health-giving drugs. There is no such thing as perfect order, just as there is no perfect mechanism for granting order. The difficulties that beset the government as an order-giving body for business are many: it is often inflexible, it is bureaucratic, it is wasteful, and it is bound up in red tape. Government is not quick to act, but, when it does, the agency established or the law passed to rectify some business evil often becomes permanent. Thus, when conditions change and the governmental action or body subsequently becomes a hindrance rather than a help, the law or body seems to have a life of its own that defies attempts to dislodge it.

Nevertheless, for better or for worse, government and business are tied closely together by the closest of bonds. At this time divorce is unthinkable, for chaos would surely result. The advice for nuptial bliss is perhaps not as simple as one might wish, but I believe it goes something like this. *First,* both parties should recognize the permanency of the arrangement and forget their dreams of single status. *Second,* each should recognize that the other has a life apart, a private world, into which its partner should not intrude without good reason. This region of privacy should not be violated except in emergency, for each violation is costly to both sides. *Third,* each partner should have separate primary tasks apart from the other. Thus, government must intervene only when all other orderly procedures have failed or when the demand for reform is so strong that it cannot be denied.

This, then, is the state of our present business system, that it is inextricably tied to government. For most persons, this union has produced little diminution in freedom. On the other hand, orderly procedures have developed. The great objective of a strictly designed free enterprise system is not freedom but material prosperity—the most efficient allocation of resources for the public welfare. This dream, however, contemplates a perfectly competitive economy, and if there is one fact that stands out it is that the real world is imperfect.

For decades businessmen have adamantly tried to regain a competitive utopia, and their thoughts and state-ments have been directed toward this end. Many, if not most, businessmen still adhere to this ambition. Nevertheless, more and more of these men are recognizing that the dream of a business utopia without government intervention, as described in traditional economics is, after all, only a dream. They are moving from the shadows of this dream world toward the acceptance of modern realities wherein government is an active participant producing order in their affairs. Indeed, this is the only conclusion for the sensible realist.

This conclusion does not assume that businessmen can stop worrying and learn to love the government. Quite the contrary, businessmen should continue to be worried, for only through disenchantment can we continue to progress in an orderly fashion. Nor is it necessary for businessmen to love the government. It is essential, however, that they recognize the strange alliance that has brought some degree of order into our economy, and from this point continue to strive for ever-increasing improvement—not destruction—of the business-government relationship.

23

The Influence of Government on Decision Making in Marketing

Corwin D. Edwards

One often assumes that the regulatory activity of government is the only activity importantly affecting marketing. However, as this article so clearly points out, marketing decisions are also importantly influenced by the behavior of government as a provider of basic information and as a purchaser of goods and services. An interesting sidelight is that the effect of the government's purchasing activity often seems to be contrary to its regulatory philosophy.

Among the many types of government activities that affect marketing decisions, three seem to me to be of greatest importance. These are government purchase of commodities and services, government provision of basic information, and government regulation of the marketing process.

Government Purchase of Goods and Services

Within the last generation, government, particularly the Federal government, has become such a large buyer of goods and services that its purchases play a predominant part in determining the amount and character of the demand

Abridged from *Changing Structure and Strategy in Marketing,* edited by Robert V. Mitchell, 1957 Marketing Symposium, University of Illinois, Bureau of Economic and Business Research, Urbana, 1958, by special permission.

for the products of considerable segments of American industry. Changes in the government budget affect the level of business activity and the climate in which private business is done. Choice as to the types of goods bought by government may induce the rapid expansion of some industries and the rapid contraction of others. Decisions on stockpiling modify the demand for particular commodities and determine the size of the reserve supplies that overhang the market. Government policies as to placement of orders—for example, the size of the contracts upon which the government invites bids and the division of orders between large and small enterprises—may significantly affect the relative chances of concerns that are different in size or structure. Where negotiated contracts have replaced competitive bidding, government decisions may make or break particular enterprises. Specifications adopted for government purchase may have a substantial influence upon the technology of production and upon the standards of quality accepted by concerns that do business with the government. Government-financed research may go far toward determining the channels of industrial progress and the companies that lead this progress.

In the industries from which the government is a substantial purchaser, the effects of government buying are likely to extend over market decisions that are concerned with private as well as with governmental customers. So far as government decisions affect the size of the concern, the extent of its research, the nature of its technology, and similar aspects of its structure and performance, they give the company a character that is not lost in its contact with the private market. Moreover, commodity specifications, ways of doing business, and price policies that are appropriate in selling to the government are likely to be adopted for general use, partly because they become habitual and partly because there are advantages in using uniform producing and marketing methods. Government has so recently become important as a major buyer of a wide range of commodities that its impact in this respect has not been carefully studied and its significance in changing marketing decisions is largely unknown.

With respect to the size of business enterprise, however, public controversy has highlighted the significance of the government's role. A buyer for the government can do his job more quickly and conveniently by making a few large purchases than by making many small ones, can more readily find out whether a few large companies are reliable than explore the reliability of large numbers of concerns that are not well known, and can more easily make contact with big companies that have Washington representatives than with smaller ones that do not. Therefore, government buy-

ing tends to be concentrated with big suppliers, who thus enhance their places in their various industries. Alarmed by this tendency, Congress has enacted in recent years legislation establishing a series of small business agencies, equipped to various degrees with power to assure that small enterprises shall obtain some of the government business. A preferential status has thus been accorded to small concerns, and policies toward government purchases have thus become significant parts of the forces affecting the degree of industrial concentration in the United States.

Government Provision of Basic Information

The second aspect of government that has great significance for marketing is the role of the government in supplying large amounts of basic information. The population census, the census of manufactures, the census of distribution, the wholesale price and cost of living indexes, the studies of consumer purchases and of business trends—these and other similar bodies of statistical information constitute large parts of the basic data used in marketing decisions and large parts of the materials which are manipulated and supplemented by private agencies engaged in market research. In addition to collecting and publishing basic data, the government makes available to the public a considerable amount of formal and informal advice and evaluation. A vice-president of a large American enterprise asked the department [Department of State] for information that would help his company decide how far to go in proposing investment programs in a foreign country. The department made available to him a roomful of experts concerned with various aspects of political and economic affairs. For two hours he questioned them about matters as various as the policies of the central bank, the likelihood of exchange rate fluctuations, standards of living, the stability of the various political parties, the prospects of the labor movement, the availability of private capital, and diplomatic relations with neighboring countries. The answers he received provided an evaluation unique in range and competence. Similar aid is available to anyone with an economic problem.

Nevertheless, the government fails to supply a considerable part of the basic information that could be supplied without significant increase in expenditure. I have no idea how numerous and important the lost opportunities may be in the aggregate.

A difficult gap to fill, but a very important one, has to do with statistics of consumption. The census of manufactures provides information about shipments. It can be used for a breakdown of the origin of goods. However, it does not furnish information about the destination of the shipments and consequently cannot be used to show how much of a product was consumed within a given area. For many purposes, government and private, the total consumed in a region is more important than the total produced there. A major marketing need is the provision of basic data as to the places to which important commodities are shipped or in which they are consumed.

Though some of the gaps in government statistics are due to the failure to provide funds with which existing information services can be slightly expanded, one important gap is due to exaggerated emphasis upon the secrecy of information with reference to particular business enterprises. The most conspicuous example of this overemphasis on secrecy is the disclosure rule of the Bureau of the Census, which prevents publication of census totals for any category so small that the figures for

any enterprise included in the category can be reliably computed or estimated by the public or by a competitor. In highly concentrated industries, totals for the industry cannot be published because one competitor may be able to deduct its own figures from the totals and thus determine the figures for a rival. Geographical breakdowns of the manufacturing census must be limited, so that similar identified data do not become available in any geographic area. Doubtless the disclosure rule was justified when it was formulated, for at that time statistical inquiries were suspect, business enterprises had fewer uses for statistics, and the publication of the facts about particular operations was relatively uncommon. Today, however, the statistical climate has changed. Relatively few concerns would be troubled about the disclosure of the broad characteristics of their operations with a time lag equivalent to that which prevails for the census of manufactures. Indeed, a growing number of companies publish some of the same information voluntarily.

Government Regulation of the Marketing Process

The third aspect of government consists in government control of the marketing process. The scope of this control has grown substantially within the last generation.

One important type of control appears in the antitrust laws. Although the prohibitions of the Sherman Act have not been changed in wording since 1890, judicial interpretation has broadened the application of the act to business conduct. Conspiracy to restrain trade has been detected in the meeting of minds through informal agreement and through mutual adherence to pricing formulas, as well as in the more overt types of agreement that were formerly recognized. Circumstantial evidence from price identities and price movements has been considered sufficient to prove conspiracy. In consequence the law of conspiracy has a more pervasive application to pricing policy than it had in the 1920's.

Similarly, the application of the law of monopoly has been extended. Since the aluminum case, a concern that has power to control prices in the market has been legally a monopolist if it could have avoided having such power but did not do so. Early decisions had stressed unconscionable conduct or monopolistic purpose and had contained dicta such as that mere size is no offense and that the possession of unexercised power is no offense. Under the new doctrine, a large concern must not only watch its conduct and refrain from deliberately attempting to destroy its rivals but must also take affirmative steps to avoid control attained through accretions of power if it is to escape the condemnation of the law.

The scope of the Clayton Act has been extended, partly by interpretation and partly by amendment. The law as to exclusive dealing arrangements has been broadened by interpretation, so that now tying and exclusive contracts may be adjudged illegal if they affect a significant fraction of commerce, without specific inquiry as to their economic effect. The law of price discrimination has been broadly extended through the Robinson-Patman Act, so that discriminations are unlawful not only when they tend to create a monopoly or to reduce the vigor of the competitive protection enjoyed by the consumer but also when they tend to injure one class of intermediate buyers for the benefit of another. Supplementary portions of this statute forbid brokerage payments by a seller to a buyer or a buyer's representative, regardless of their effect, and forbid sellers to provide or pay for selling service unless the service is available to all on proportionately equal terms, also regardless of effect. Under the Robinson-Patman Act the details of price policies and of collaboration with distributors in sales policies have become pervasively subject to legal scrutiny.

Other laws of general application have supplemented the antitrust laws in extending the controls over marketing. Under the Wheeler-Lee Act, false advertising and other forms of unfair practice have been forbidden, not only when they injure competitors but also when they injure consumers. The conception of falsehood has been broadened to the point at which a seller must not only avoid false statements but must also assume, to a considerable extent, the duty of providing information that will offset false impressions the buyer would otherwise obtain.

State legislation has also limited the marketer's freedom of action. Nearly all of our states have enacted laws authorizing owners of trademarks to fix the resale prices that shall be observed by persons selling the trademarked goods, whether or not the reseller consents to such control; and although such laws have suffered legal vicissitudes they are still in effect in 33 states. About half the states have passed laws forbidding sale below cost and providing some method of defining cost for purposes of establishing a cost floor under prices. Through these two sets of statutes, explicit price control has been enacted in a large part of the country, the control being exercised either by state governments or by private persons with government sanction.

These are the principal laws that have general application to the marketing process. They have been supplemented, however, by many other statutes which apply to particular industries or to types of transactions that take place only in particular segments of industry. To find and list all of these special-purpose laws would be a forbidding task. I shall limit myself to mention of a few of the more important ones.

The Federal agricultural program includes important controls over marketing—controls designed to give the farmer stated percentages of parity prices, controls over production designed to set quotas for the amounts of agricultural products to be marketed, nonrecourse loans designed to help farmers keep their products off the market when prices are thought to be low, and programs for the diversion of agricultural surpluses from the ordinary commercial uses of the products diverted.

Closely related are Federal, state, and local programs for the marketing of milk. These include price controls at successive market levels; quality standards and programs of inspection designed to fix the butterfat content and to assure sanitation; and the fixation of limits upon the market areas covered by urban milk markets, sometimes through direct regulation but more commonly through limitation of the territory within which the necessary inspections will be provided.

Another body of laws applies to the sale of food, drugs, and curative devices. It imposes controls upon the quality of such products and regulates the identification of them and the disclosures that must be made as to their ingredients.

Sellers of textile products are subject to other special-purpose laws. Wool and fur fabrics sold in interstate commerce must be labeled in a way that identifies the fiber content and the source of the fur. Through the interpretation of the Federal Trade Commission Act in its bearing upon the misrepresentation of fabrics containing artificial fibers, the producers of rayon products are, in practice, subject to a similar requirement as to fiber identification.

Producers of petroleum are subject to proration laws enacted by the principal petroleum-producing states and supported by Federal "hot oil" legislation. Although the avowed purpose of proration is to conserve the petroleum supply, the authority of the most important state avowedly thinks of conservation as including so-called "economic" conservation, designed to assure a reasonable price for the petroleum that is marketed.

There is also a miscellany of so-called trade barrier laws, through which various states subject goods from other states (1) to inspections at the border, designed for such purposes as pest control; (2) to use taxes collected at ports of entry; and (3) to uncoordinated regulations concerned with such matters as the weight of the load in truck shipments. So important are these controls in the aggregate that for a time in the late 1930's and early 1940's the Department of Commerce maintained an office concerned wholly with the impact of trade barrier laws upon the national economy. This office was one of the casualties of the second World War.

Superimposed upon such formal legislative controls are various informal controls exercised by public officials through advice, publicity, and implied threat of formal action. How extensive these may be it is impossible to say.

These increases in the scope of public control over the marketing process have reflected two sharply different types of influence. In part, controls have been extended because lawmaking bodies believed that the general public needed increased protection from various kinds of evils. Two recurrent elements have appeared in the situations that were thought to necessitate public safeguards. One is the power of large enterprises. The laws concerning monopoly, conspiracy, and price discrimination were tightened primarily because of concern about this problem. The plight of small business in competition with big business was offered as one of the principal reasons for the laws against price discrimination and sale below cost and as a part of the justification for control over agricultural marketing. The second recurrent reason for the extension of public safeguards has been the belief that the complexity of products and processes has become so great that the ordinary citizen can no longer protect himself. This view has underlain the legislation of false advertising and on the identification or control of elements of quality in food, milk, drugs, and textile fibers.

But alongside the belief that the public needs more protection there has been a second influence toward the extension of controls that has probably been equally important. This is the insistent demand by businessmen (including farmers) that they or their competitors be more tightly regulated. Business groups have urged the government to protect their prices and profits and enhance their security by various types of public control. Some groups have sought to obtain an advantageous position over their competitors by preferential legislation. The two purposes, protection from impersonal market forces and advantage over particular competitors, have been so commingled that in some instances, for example in the demand for laws permitting maintenance of resale prices, they could scarcely be distinguished from one another. In general, one can say, however, that the agricultural legislation, the laws as to resale-price maintenance and sale below cost, the controls over brokerage payments, and the proration of petroleum were sponsored primarily by the groups that these laws were designed to regulate rather than by others desiring protection from these groups. The laws as to milk and as to wool fibers were at least partly due to similar demands to be regulated.

Thus competition in the market has been supplemented, and in some segments of industry partly replaced, by competition in legislative lobbies and government offices. Lawmaking and litigation have become part of competitive tactics. The lobbyist and the house counsel have acquired marketing functions. During the last generation businessmen probably have been more responsible than their critics for the extension of government controls over the marketing process.

As government controls have become more pervasive, the process of decision making in marketing has been increasingly affected by legal considerations. Some legal requirements merely establish well-defined boundaries beyond which the marketer goes at his peril. Others, however, confront the marketing executive with complex requirements that he finds difficult to evaluate. A part of the difficulty is due to the diversity of legislative requirements where these have been imposed by states and localities rather than by a uniform Federal law. Building codes, for example, are generally local and differ greatly from one place to another. To ascertain the geographical and substantive limitations that these codes will impose upon the sale of a particular component of a building is a formidable task. Similarly, standards of freshness for such a food product as the oyster are so different in different places that small oystermen testified in the Federal Trade Commission's case against the Atlantic and Pacific Tea Company that they were able to keep track of the requirements only by consulting A & P's oyster buyer.

Apart from the diversity of the laws, there are inherent ambiguities in the standards of legality that are applied in some of the most important statutes. Advertising is unlawful if it is deceptive; but there is a range of uncertainty as to whether or not particular language will deceive particular groups to whom it is addressed. Under the price discrimination law, sale services are illegal unless they are available on proportionately equal terms, but the proportionality of some kinds of service is not a self-evident matter. Under the same law, price differences can be justified if they merely reflect differences in cost; but there are major accounting problems in allocating costs to show the differences properly attributable to particular transactions with particular customers.

Moreover, in some cases legality must be determined not merely by present conduct or the present consequences of it, but also by a forecast of its probable future consequences. The Clayton Act forbids certain courses of action "where the effect may be" to reduce competition substantially, and the courts have held that under this standard the specified course of action is illegal if there is a reasonable probability of the specified effect. Thus inference as to the future becomes necessary in considering the lawfulness of a price discrimination or an exclusive contract.[1]

The extension of legal controls over marketing has affected not only the processes of managerial decision but also the quality thereof. Statutes such as the Robinson-Patman Act and the Wheeler-Lee Act have undoubtedly brought about a widespread re-evalua-

tion of pricing and advertising policies by business management. Changes intended to avoid legal trouble have undoubtedly been frequent. Moreover, in some cases the close examination of facts necessary in setting the company's legal house in order has thrown new light upon the business considerations underlying a policy. For example, business enterprises which, after the Robinson-Patman Act was passed, analyzed their costs in an effort to determine which discounts could be cost-justified found sometimes that existing discount structures were not good business, whether or not they were lawful. One such company decided that a large fraction of its total sales volume was being marketed in transactions so small that the costs of making the sale exceeded the gross margin over labor and material costs. Though it had examined its costs for legal reasons, it revised its prices for business reasons.

Although detailed information with which one can measure the impact of government control is not available, I think most informed observers would agree that law has brought about significant changes in business conduct in the following respects.

First, price fixing and similar collective restrictions have become less frequent than in most other private-enterprise societies; and because such agreements must be secret, the ones that still operate are weaker than they would otherwise be.

Second, powerful business enterprises have become more circumspect in their conduct toward their competitors than such enterprises were in this country at the turn of the century. If weak concerns are coerced or excluded from the market, the techniques are more subtle and less drastic. On balance, there has been a substantial reduction in the risks faced by a small concern confronted with a powerful rival.

---

[1] A related problem of uncertainty probably arises in the application of the rule of reason under the Sherman Act. The rule of reason has been variously defined, but the best authority seems to hold that in conspiracy cases its function is to distinguish between restrictions that are central to a course of conduct and those that are peripheral, and that in monopoly cases its function is to evaluate evidence that purports to show that the defendant has a degree of control of the market which he could have avoided. Obviously there are situations in which reasonable men could disagree on such matters.

Third, false advertising and advertising that seeks to mislead through indirection have become less common than they used to be.

Fourth, most concerns that do an interstate business have substituted some form of relatively orderly price structure for catch-as-catch-can pricing in which a new price is made for every significant customer. In general, the quantity and volume discounts available to large buyers are probably smaller than before and the advertising services and allowances offered by sellers are probably more widely available than before.

Fifth, phantom freight has generally disappeared from delivered price systems, and buyers located near a producer have a better chance than before to benefit pricewise from their location.

Sixth, where loss leaders are used, price reductions upon these leaders are smaller than they used to be.

In these ways and probably in others, the laws applied to marketing have helped bring about appreciable changes in American business conduct. There is, of course, room for dispute as to the relative importance of these laws and other factors in evoking many of the changes. For example, wartime shortages and postwar booms have obviously changed the economic climate so far as price reductions are concerned.

Alongside the changes that reflect acceptance of legal standards and conformity to them, there have been other changes designed to evade these standards. In using the word "evade," I do not mean to imply that the conduct of the companies to which the term is applied has been either unlawful or unethical. I mean merely that these concerns have sought to accomplish the same business purposes in ways consistent with the new legal standards and that they have been alert to take advantage of exemptions and limitations contained in the statutes.

Faced with the problem of remaining within the fences of legality in spite of the fact that the exact location of some of the fences is uncertain, many executives tend to avoid trouble by playing safe. Instead of skirting the edge of legality they leave a substantial margin. In advertising they avoid misrepresentation by substituting meaningless statements for statements that have meaning. Thus we get the pseudo-technical term, coined by the advertiser and having no content except what he chooses to put into it; the open-end comparison, which says that goods are better without saying better than what; and the bare assertion of merit without particulars. Since people are distressingly capable of being persuaded by plausible nonsense, the reduction of the informative content of advertising is often possible without impairment of the buyer's loyalty.

Similarly, partly because of the various controls over prices and over competition that is monopolistically destructive, there appears to be a tendency for large buyers not to push vigorously for the best terms and for large competitors not to compete vigorously against small rivals. Such tactics have sometimes been described as soft competition.

Again, sellers apparently seek to avoid trouble with the price discrimination law by making sure that the savings they realized from the methods or quantities in which some customers buy are decidedly greater than the discounts they give to those customers for buying in that way. From an economist's point of view, prices may be unduly uniform as well as unduly different, and refusal to recognize cost reductions by price concessions must be regarded as a diminution of the incentives for the buyer to use the most efficient buying methods.

A similar reduction of efficiency appears to attach to the play-safe policy that some buyers and sellers use with regard to the employment of brokers. Since it is unlawful for any seller to pay any buyer an allowance in lieu of brokerage and since any allowance given to a direct-buying customer may be interpreted as a substitute for brokerage if the seller employs brokers in transactions with other customers, some sellers play safe by selling wholly through brokers and some buyers play safe by buying through brokers when a direct approach to the seller would be simpler.

I do not suggest, of course, that businessmen should always skirt the edge of legality nor that failures to do so are always wasteful. Where the type of conduct that is forbidden is clearly objectionable, a margin of safety in avoiding it is likely to be desirable. But in some fields, of which the law of price discrimination is a good instance, what is needed is well-balanced conduct that deviates neither toward rigidity and uniformity nor toward unequal treatment. In these cases the effect of playing safe is likely to be a systematic distortion of business conduct from the desirable standard.

Moreover, the desire to play safe and the desire to evade statutes both provide strong incentives to cling to a course of conduct that can withstand legal attack. Thus they discourage experiment with new methods of pricing and new marketing tactics and thereby tend to reduce the flexibility of business response to economic forces.

To list these matters is not, of course, to state their absolute or relative importance. The most I can say is that the influences that shape economic decisions include considerations, such as I have mentioned, that grow out of the pervasiveness of legal controls. It is often hard to determine the impact of the law amid the changes that accompany the transition from depression to boom, from peace to war and back to peace, from one kind of technology to another, and from one stage to another of an evolving standard of living. When I have sought to ascertain the effects of a particular judicial decree or Federal Trade Commission order, I have often found that the environment was changing so fast that the situation prevailing in the market had little relation to that to which the decree was addressed. Similarly, the adjustments made by businessmen for the sake of avoiding lawsuits may be lost among greater changes. How important legal influences are can be only a guess. My own guess is that they are relatively unimportant as compared with other forces affecting business decisions and inducing change in them. If this is true, I do not regret it. The proper functions of government in the field of marketing are to prevent misconduct and to preserve competition, not to dominate the economy. In a healthy private-enterprise system, private forces can be expected to be more important than government forces.

24

Antitrust Laws with Amendments

U.S. Government

Most marketing textbooks discuss the subject of federal antitrust legislation without stating the text of the laws or relevant sections of the laws. Because of this, the student may not fully comprehend the meaning of the court and regulatory-agency interpretations of these acts. The following extracts from the major antitrust laws should aid in evaluating the regulatory activities of the federal government.

Sherman Antitrust Act (1890)[1]

Section 1. Every contract, combination in the form of trust or otherwise, or conspiracy, in restraint of trade or commerce among the several States, or with foreign nations, is hereby declared to be illegal. Every person who shall make any such contract or engage in any such combination or conspiracy, shall be deemed guilty of a misdemeanor, and, on conviction thereof, shall be punished by fine not exceeding fifty thousand dollars, or by imprisonment not exceeding one year, or by both said punishments, in the discretion of the court.

Section 2. Every person who shall monopolize, or attempt to monopolize, or combine or conspire with any other person or persons, to monopolize any part of the trade or commerce among

Abridged from *Antitrust Laws with Amendments 1890–1966*, United States Government Printing Office, 1966.

[1] As amended by Public 135 of the 84th Congress, approved July 7, 1955.

the several States, or with foreign nations, shall be deemed guilty of a misdemeanor, and, on conviction thereof, shall be punished by fine not exceeding fifty thousand dollars, or by imprisonment not exceeding one year, or by both said punishments, in the discretion of the court.

Section 3. Every contract, combination in form of trust or otherwise, or conspiracy, in restraint of trade or commerce in any Territory of the United States or of the District of Columbia, or in restraint of trade or commerce between any such Territory and another, or between any such Territory or Territories and any State or States or the District of Columbia, or with foreign nations, or between the District of Columbia and any State or States or foreign nations, is hereby declared illegal. Every person who shall make any such contract or engage in any such combination or conspiracy, shall be deemed guilty of a misdemeanor, and, on conviction thereof, shall be punished by fine not exceeding fifty thousand dollars, or by imprisonment not exceeding one year, or by both said punishments, in the discretion of the court.

Section 7. Any person who shall be injured in his business or property by any other person or corporation by reason of anything forbidden or declared to be unlawful by this act, may sue therefor in any circuit court of the United States in the district in which the defendant resides or is found, without respect to the amount in controversy, and shall recover threefold the damages by him sustained, and the costs of suit, including a reasonable attorney's fee.

Clayton Act (1914)[2]

Section 2. That is shall be unlawful for any person engaged in commerce, in the course of such commerce, either directly or indirectly, to discriminate in price between different purchasers of commodities, which commodities are sold for use, consumption, or resale within the United States or any Territory thereof or the District of Columbia or any insular possession or other place under the jurisdiction of the United States, where the effect of such discrimination may be to substantially lessen competition to tend to create a monopoly in any line of commerce: *Provided,* That nothing herein contained shall prevent discrimination in price between purchasers of commodities on account of differences in the grade, quality, or quantity of the commodity sold, or that makes only due allowance for differences in the cost of selling or transportation, or discrimination in price in the same or different communities made in

[2] As amended by Public 899 of the 81st Congress, approved December 29, 1950; and Public 137 of the 84th Congress, approved July 7, 1955.

good faith to meet competition: *And provided further,* That nothing herein contained shall prevent persons engaged in selling goods, wares, or merchandise in commerce from selecting their own customers in bona fide transactions and not restraint of trade.

Section 3. That it shall be unlawful for any person engaged in commerce, in the course of such commerce, to lease or make a sale or contract for sale of goods, wares, merchandise, machinery, supplies, or other commodities, whether patented or unpatented, for use, consumption, or resale within the United States or any Territory thereof or the District of Columbia or any insular possession or other place under the jurisdiction of the United States, or fix a price charged therefor, or discount from, or rebate upon, such price, or the condition, agreement, or understanding that the lessee or purchaser thereof shall not use or deal in the goods, wares, merchandise, machinery, supplies, or other commodity of a competitor or competitors of the lessor or seller, where the effect of such lease, sale, or contract for sale or such condition, agreement, or understanding may be to substantially lessen competition or tend to create a monopoly in any line of commerce.

Section 4. That any person who shall be injured in his business or property by reason of anything forbidden in the antitrust laws may sue therefor in any district court of the United States in the district in which the defendant resides or is found or has an agent, without respect to the amount in controversy, and shall recover threefold the damages by him sustained, and the cost of suit, including a reasonable attorney's fee.

Section 4A. Whenever the United States is hereafter injured in its business or property by reason of anything forbidden in the antitrust laws it may sue therefor in the United States district court for the district in which the defendant resides or is found or has an agent, without respect to the amount in controversy, and shall recover actual damages by it sustained and the cost of suit.

Section 6. That the labor of a human being is not a commodity or article of commerce. Nothing contained in the antitrust laws shall be construed to forbid the existence and operation of labor, agricultural, or horticultural organizations, instituted for the purpose of mutual help, and not having capital stock or conducted for profits, or to forbid or restrain individual members of such organizations from lawfully carrying out the legitimate objects thereof; nor shall such organizations, or the members thereof, be held or construed to be illegal combinations or conspiracies in restraint of trade under the antitrust laws.

Section 7. That no corporation engaged in commerce shall acquire, directly or indirectly, the whole or any part of the stock or other share capital and no corporation subject to the jurisdiction of the Federal Trade Commission shall acquire the whole or any part of the assets of another corporation engaged also in commerce, where in any line of commerce in any section of the country, the effect of such acquisition may be substantially to lessen competition, or to tend to create a monopoly.

No corporation shall acquire, directly or indirectly, the whole or any part of the stock or other share capital and no corporation subject to the jurisdiction of the Federal Trade Commission shall acquire the whole or any part of the assets of one or more corporations engaged in commerce, where in any line of commerce in any section of the country, the effect of such acquisition, of such stocks or assets, or of the use of such stock by the voting or granting of proxies or otherwise, may be substantially to lessen competition, or to tend to create a monopoly.

This section shall not apply to corporations purchasing such stock solely for investment and not using the same by voting or otherwise to bring about, or in attempting to bring about, the substantial lessening of competition. Nor shall anything contained in this section prevent a corporation engaged in commerce from causing the formation of subsidiary corporations for the actual carrying on of their immediate business, or the natural and legitimate branches or extensions thereof, or from owning and holding all or a part of the stock of such subsidiary corporations, when the effect of such formation is not to substantially lessen competition.

Section 14. That whenever a corporation shall violate any of the penal provisions of the antitrust laws, such violation shall be deemed to be also that of the individual directors, officers, or agents of such corporation who shall have authorized, ordered, or done any of the acts constituting in whole or in part such violation, and such violation shall be deemed a misdemeanor, and upon conviction therefor of any such director, officer, or agent he shall be punished by a fine of not exceeding $5,000 or by imprisonment for not exceeding one year, or by both, in the discretion of the court.

Federal Trade Commission Act (1914)[3]

Be it enacted by the Senate and House of Representatives of the United States of America in Congress assembled, That a commission is hereby created and established, to be known as the

[3] As amended by Public Law No. 447 of the 75th Congress (Wheeler-Lea Amendment), 1938.

Federal Trade Commission (hereinafter referred to as the commission), which shall be composed of five commissioners, who shall be appointed by the President, by and with the advice and consent of the Senate.

Section 5. (A) Unfair methods of competition in commerce, and unfair or deceptive acts or practices in commerce, are hereby declared unlawful.

The commission is hereby empowered and directed to prevent persons, partnerships, or corporations, except banks, common carriers subject to the Acts to regulate commerce, and persons, partnerships, or corporations subject to the Packers and Stockyards Act, 1921, except as provided in section 406 (b) of said Act, from using unfair methods of competition in commerce and unfair or deceptive acts or practices in commerce.

Section 6. That the commission shall also have power—

(a) To gather and compile information concerning, and to investigate from time to time the organization, business, conduct, practices, and management of any corporation engaged in commerce, excepting banks and common carriers subject to the Act to regulate commerce, and its relation to other corporations and to individuals, associations, and partnerships.

(b) To require, by general or special orders, corporations engaged in commerce, excepting banks, and common carriers subject to the Act to regulate commerce, or any class of them, or any of them, respectively, to file with the commission in such form as the commission may prescribe annual or special, or both annual and special, reports or answers in writing to specific questions, furnishing to the commission such information as it may require as to the organizations, business, conduct, practices, management, and relation to other corporations, partnerships, and individuals of the respective corporations filing such reports or answers in writing. Such reports and answers shall be made under oath, or otherwise, as the commission may prescribe, and shall be filed with the commission within such reasonable period as the commission may prescribe, unless additional time be granted in any case by the commission.

Section 9. That for the purposes of this Act the commission, or its duly authorized agent or agents, shall at all reasonable times have access to, for the purpose of examination, and the right to copy any documentary evidence of any corporation being investigated or proceeded against; and the commission shall have power to require by subpoena the attendance and testimony of witnesses and the production of all such documentary evidence relating to any matter under investigation. Any member of the commission may sign subpoenas, and members and examiners of the commission may administer oaths and affirmations, examine witnesses, and receive evidence.

Such attendance of witnesses, and the production of such documentary evidence, may be required from any place in the United States, at any designated place of hearing. And in case of disobedience to a subpoena the commission may invoke the aid of any court of the United States in requiring the attendance and testimony of witnesses and the production of documentary evidence.

Any of the district courts of the United States within the jurisdiction of which such inquiry is carried on may, in case of contumacy or refusal to obey a subpoena issued to any corporation or other person, issue an order requiring such corporation or other person to appear before the commission, or to produce documentary evidence if so ordered, or to give evidence touching the matter in question; and any failure to obey such order of the court may be punished by such court as a contempt thereof.

Section 12. (a) It shall be unlawful for any person, partnership, or corporation to disseminate, or cause to be disseminated, any false advertisement—

1. By United States mails, or in commerce by any means, for the purpose of inducing, or which is likely to induce, directly or indirectly, the purchase of food, drugs, devices, or cosmetics; or

2. By any means, for the purpose of inducing, or which is likely to induce, directly or indirectly, the purchase in commerce of food, drugs, devices, or cosmetics.

(b) The dissemination or the causing to be disseminated of any false advertisement within the provisions of subsection (a) of this section shall be an unfair or deceptive act or practice in commerce within the meaning of section 5.

Robinson-Patman Act (1936)[4]

Be it enacted by the Senate and House of Representatives of the United States of America in Congress assembled, That section 2 of the Act entitled "An Act to supplement existing laws against unlawful restraints and monopolies, and for other purposes," approved October 15, 1914, as amended (U.S.C., title 15, sec. 13), is amended to read as follows:

Section 2. (a) That it shall be unlawful for any person engaged in commerce, in the course of such commerce, either directly or indirectly, to discriminate in price between different purchasers of commodities of like grade and quality, where either or any of the purchases involved in such discrimination are in commerce, where such commodities are sold for use, consumption,

or resale within the United States or any Territory thereof or the District of Columbia or any insular possession or other place under the jurisdiction of the United States, and where the effect of such discrimination may be substantially to lessen competition or tend to create a monopoly in any line of commerce, or to injure, destroy, or prevent competition with any person who either grants or knowingly receives the benefit of such discrimination, or with customers of either of them: *Provided,* That nothing herein contained shall prevent differentials which make only due allowance for differences in the cost of manufacture, sale, or delivery resulting from the differing methods or quantities in which such commodities are to such purchasers sold or delivered: *Provided, however,* That the Federal Trade Commission may, after due investigation and hearing to all interested parties, fix and establish quantity limits, and revise the same as it finds necessary, as to particular commodities or classes of commodities, where it finds that available purchasers in greater quantities are so few as to render differentials on account thereof unjustly discriminatory or promotive of monopoly in any line of commerce; and the foregoing shall then not be construed to permit differentials based on differences in quantities greater than those so fixed and established: *And provided further,* That nothing herein contained shall prevent persons engaged in selling goods, wares, or merchandise in commerce from selecting their own customers in bona fide transactions and not in restraint of trade: *And provided further,* That nothing herein contained shall prevent price changes from time to time where in response to changing conditions affecting the market for or the marketability of the goods concerned, such as but not limited to actual or imminent deterioration of perishable goods, obsolescence of seasonal goods,

---

[4] Amendment to the Clayton Act (1914).

distress sales under court process, or sales in good faith in discontinuance of business in the goods concerned.

(b) Upon proof being made, at any hearing on a complaint under this section, that there has been discrimination in price or services or facilities furnished, the burden of rebutting the prima-facie case thus made by showing justification shall be upon the person charged with a violation of this section, and unless justification shall be affirmatively shown, the Commission is authorized to issue an order terminating the discrimination: *Provided, however,* That nothing herein contained shall prevent a seller rebutting the prima-facie case thus made by showing that his lower price or the furnishing of services or facilities to any purchaser or purchasers was made in good faith to meet an equally low price of a competitor, or the services or facilities furnished by a competitor.

(c) That it shall be unlawful for any person engaged in commerce, in the course of such commerce, to pay or grant, or to receive or accept, anything of value as a commission, brokerage, or other compensation, or any allowance or discount in lieu thereof, except for services rendered in connection with the sale or purchase of goods, wares, or merchandise, either to the other party to such transaction or to an agent, representative, or other intermediary therein where such intermediary is acting in fact for or in behalf, or is subject to the direct or indirect control, of any party to such transaction other than the person by whom such compensation is so granted or paid.

(d) That it shall be unlawful for any person engaged in commerce to pay or contract for the payment of anything of value to or for the benefit of a customer of such person in the course of such commerce as compensation or in consideration for any services or facilities furnished by or through such customer in connection with the processing, handling, sale, or offering for sale of any products or commodities manufactured, sold, or offered for sale by such person, unless such payment or consideration is available on proportionally equal terms to all other customers competing in the distribution of such products or commodities.

(e) That it shall be unlawful for any person to discriminate in favor of one purchaser against another purchaser or purchasers of a commodity bought for resale, with or without processing, by contracting to furnish or furnishing, or by contributing to the furnishing of, any services or facilities connected with the processing, handling, sale, or offering for sale of such commodity so purchased upon terms not accorded to all purchasers on proportionally equal terms.

(f) That it shall be unlawful for any person engaged in commerce, in the course of such commerce, knowingly to induce or receive a discrimination in price which is prohibited by this section.

Section 3. It shall be unlawful for any person engaged in commerce, in the course of such commerce, to be a party to, or assist in, any transaction of sale, or contract to sell, which discriminates to his knowledge against competitors of the purchaser, in that, any discount, rebate, allowance, or advertising service charge is granted to the purchaser over and above any discount, rebate, allowance, or advertising service charge available at the time of such transaction to said competitors in respect of a sale of goods of like grade, quality, and quantity; to sell, or contract to sell, goods in any part of the United States at prices lower than those exacted by said person elsewhere in the United States for the purpose of destroying competition, or eliminating a competitor in such part of the United States; or, to sell, or contract to sell, goods at unreasonably low prices for the purpose of destroying competition or eliminating a competitor.

Any person violating any of the provisions of this section shall, upon conviction thereof, be fined not more than $5,000 or imprisoned not more than one year, or both.

Section 4. Nothing in this Act shall prevent a cooperative association from returning to its members, producers, or consumers the whole, or any part of, the net earnings or surplus resulting from its trading operations, in proportion to their purchases or sales from, to, or through the association.

Miller-Tydings Resale Price Maintenance (1937)[5]

Section 1 of the act entitled "An act to protect trade and commerce against unlawful restraints and monopolies," approved July 2, 1890, is amended to read as follows:

Section 1. Every contract, combination in the form of trust or otherwise, or conspiracy, in restraint of trade or commerce among the several States, or with foreign nations, is hereby declared to be illegal: *Provided,* That nothing herein contained shall render illegal, contracts or agreements prescribing minimum prices for the resale of a commodity which bears, or the label or container of which bears, the trade mark, brand, or name of the producer or distributor of such commodity and which is in free and open competition with commodities of the same general class produced or distributed by others, when contracts or agreements of that description are lawful as applied to intrastate transactions, under any

statue, law, or public policy now or hereafter in effect in any State, Territory, or the District of Columbia in which such resale is to be made, or to which the commodity is to be transported for such resale, and the making of such contracts or agreements shall not be an unfair method of competition under section 5, as amended and supplemented, of the act entitled 'An act to create a Federal Trade Commission, to define its powers and duties, and for other purposes,' approved September 26, 1914: *Provided further,* That the preceding provisio shall not make lawful any contract or agreement, providing for the establishment or maintenance of minimum resale prices on any commodity herein involved, between manufacturers, or between producers or between wholesalers, or between brokers, or between factors, or between retailers, or between persons, firms, or corporations in competition with each other. Every person who shall make any contract or engage in any combination or conspiracy hereby declared to be illegal shall be deemed guilty of a misdemeanor and, on conviction thereof, shall be punished by fine not exceeding $5,000, or by imprisonment not exceeding one year, or by both said punishments, in the discretion of the court.

McGuire Amendment (1952)[6]

Be it enacted by the Senate and House of Representatives of the United States of America in Congress assembled, That it is the purpose of this Act to protect the rights of States under the United States Constitution to regulate

---

[5] Amendment to the Sherman Antitrust Act (1890).

[6] Amendment to Federal Trade Commission Act (1914).

ieir internal affairs and more par-
cularly to enact statutes and laws, and
► adopt policies, which authorize con-
acts and agreements prescribing mini-
ıum or stipulated prices for the resale
ŕ commodities and to extend the mini-
ıum or stipulated prices prescribed by
ıch contracts and agreements to per-
ɔns who are not parties thereto. It is
ıe further purpose of this Act to permit
ıch statutes, laws, and public policies
► apply to commodities, contracts,
ʒreements, and activities in or affecting
ıterstate or foreign commerce.

Section 2. Section 5 (a) of the Fed-
·al Trade Commission Act, as amended,
hereby amended to read as follows:

Section 5. (a) (1) Unfair methods of competition in commerce,
and unfair or deceptive acts or
practices in commerce, are hereby
declared unlawful.

(2) Nothing contained in this Act
or in any of the Antitrust Acts shall
render unlawful any contracts or
agreements prescribing minimum or
stipulated prices, or requiring a ven-
dee to enter into contracts or agreements prescribing minimum or
stipulated prices, for the resale of a
commodity which bears, or the label
or container of which bears, the
trade-mark, brand, or name of the
producer or distributor of such commodity and which is in free and open
competition with commodities of the
same general class produced or distributed by others, when contracts or
agreements of that description are
lawful as applied to intrastate transactions under any statute, law, or
public policy now or hereafter in
effect in an State, Territory, or the
District of Columbia in which such
resale is to be made, or to which
the commodity is to be transported
for such resale.

(3) Nothing contained in this Act
or in any of the Antitrust Acts shall
render unlawful the exercise or the
enforcement of any right or right of
action created by any statute, law,
or public policy now or hereafter
in effect in any State, Territory, or
the District of Columbia, which in
substance provides that willfully and
knowingly advertising, offering for
sale, or selling any commodity at less
than the price or prices prescribed
in such contracts or agreements
whether the person so advertising,
offering for sale, or selling is or is
not a party to such a contract or agreement, is unfair competition and is
actionable at the suit of any person
damaged thereby.

(4) Neither the making of contracts or agreements as described in
paragraph (2) of this subsection, nor
the exercise or enforcement of any
right or right of action as described
in paragraph (3) of this subsection
shall constitute an unlawful burden or
restraint upon, or interference with,
commerce.

(5) Nothing contained in paragraph (2) of this subsection shall
make lawful contracts or agreements
providing for the establishment or
maintenance of minimum or stipulated
resale prices on any commodity referred to in paragraph (2) of this
subsection, between manufacturers,
or between producers, or between
wholesalers, or between brokers, or
between persons, firms, or corporations in competition with each other.

Webb-Pomerene Law (1918)

Section 2. That nothing contained in
the Act entitled "An Act to protect
trade and commerce against unlawful
restraints and monopolies," approved
July second, eighteen hundred and

ninety, shall be construed as declaring to be illegal an association entered into for the sole purpose of engaging in export trade, and actually engaged solely in such export trade, or an agreement made or act done in the course of export trade by such association, provided such association, agreement, or act is not in restraint of trade within the United States, and is not in restraint of the export trade of any domestic competitor of such association: *And provided further,* That such association does not, either in the United States or elsewhere, enter into any agreement, understanding, or conspiracy, or do any act which artificially or intentionally enhances or depresses prices within the United States of commodities of the class exported by such association, or which substantially lessens competition within the United States or otherwise restraints trade therein.

Section 3. That nothing contained in section seven of the Act entitled "An Act to supplement existing laws against unlawful restraints and monopolies, and for other purposes," approved October fifteenth, nineteen hundred and four teen, shall be construed to forbid th acquisition or ownership by any cor poration of the whole or any part of th stock or other capital of any corporatio organized solely for the purpose of en gaging in export trade, and actuall engaged solely in such export trade, un less the effect of such acquisition o ownership may be to restrain trade o substantially lessen competition withir the United States.

Section 4. That the prohibitio against "unfair methods of competition and the remedies provided for enforcin said prohibition contained in the Ac entitled "An Act to create a Federa Trade Commission, to define its powei and duties and for other purposes, approved September twenty-sixth, nine teen hundred and fourteen, shall b construed as extending to unfair method of competition used in export trad against competitors engaged in expoi trade, even though the acts constitutin such unfair methods are done withou the territorial jurisdiction of the Unite States.

25

Economic Objectives and Antitrust Policy

Clare E. Griffin

The United States, more than any other Western nation, watche over its economy with a careful eye to try to preserve the kind c environment that will be most conducive to protecting individue economic freedom without sacrificing efficiency. To this end u have antitrust laws and an elaborate set of judicial precedem which have grown up under the laws. The first of these laws was passed in 1890. We tend to accept the regulations flowing from these laws as good, without often reconsidering the premises and assumptions upon which they are based. The following article takes a fresh and unusual approach to such a re-examination of antitrust objectives and, in so doing, provides a good vehicle for a reappraisal of our antitrust philosophy.

More than any other country in the world we place reliance upon the competitive principle as a regulatory and protective force. It is a regulatory force in that it determines what is to be produced and who is to produce it. It provides a spur to efficiency and to progress. It accomplishes these ends, which any interdependent society must accomplish in one way or another, and it does it in a way which infringes to the minimum upon that other cherished ideal of Americans that each should be allowed to manage his own affairs. In short, it is our answer to the central problem of a modern society: how to preserve individual economic freedom in the face of an ever-increasing interdependence.

It is a protective force in that it gives to every individual with money in his pocket an effective veto over the demands of people upon whom collectively he is dependent for his livelihood. The practical ability to say "no" in the economic sphere depends on the existence of reasonable alternatives, which is the essence of competition and the absence of which is the distinguishing feature of monopoly.

Our antimonopoly laws in seeking to preserve this principle are thus dealing with the basic principle that distinguishes our kind of economic system. In recent decades our antitrust administration and law has, perhaps inevitably, become highly refined and complicated. **An Antitrust Policy.** Can we put

Reprinted by the author's permission from a speech delivered to a group of lawyers and students of the subject of antitrust regulation.

aside for the moment some of these refinements and by returning to basic objectives suggest in general and nontechnical terms what in the view of an economist this policy should be? Let us suppose that the people of the United States, represented by its government, wishes to explain this policy to the business community and to those who may want to enter that community.

This imaginary audience is limited to actual and potential businessmen because certain other large groups of the community have by one means or another established immunities for themselves from the requirements of competition. So in our audience certain important groups will be absent. Among these will be the labor unions, the farmers, certain professional groups, and the public utilities. But, even so, we will have a sizable audience consisting of the business concerns of the country who engage in interstate commerce. Might not the address of the day proceed somewhat along the following lines?

We the people of the United States welcome this opportunity to speak to the business enterprisers and the prospective business enterprisers of the country. We recognize that you constitute a very important group, for it is in your hands to direct the efforts of the country to the production of those goods which we all want and upon which our American standard of living rests. This control over the productive resources of the country is so important that in many countries of the world it is felt that it can only properly be entrusted to the government itself. We prefer to place this heavy responsibility upon you who are in a sense volunteering and indeed seeking the opportunity to play this role. We can only afford to do this because we as individuals are going to maintain a careful check upon you and if you do not serve us well you will have to give way to someone else. While we recognize your importance we must have it clearly understood that we are sovereigns. Moreover, we are not going to rely merely upon our individual veto powers, but we are laying down certain rules of the game which are designed to make those veto powers effective. It is to explain those rules in general terms that we have called you together today.

In the first place we want you to compete vigorously and effectively but at the same time fairly. We cannot literally make you compete, for we recognize that competition is partly the result of a competitive attitude which cannot be created by government. We can, however, encourage competition, and we intend to do this by permitting you to gain and retain the rewards of efficiency and progressiveness. We shall recognize that "the successful competitor, having been urged to compete, must not be turned upon when he wins."

On the other hand, we recognize that in a contest there will be losers as well as winners. We will not use the antitrust laws to preserve competitors from the results of a fair contest. To this last observation some of you may be thinking that if competitors are not thus preserved the result may be that only one winner is left and then competition will have disappeared. To this several replies can be made. One of these, for example, might be the corporation income tax. But preserving competition must not be confused with preserving particular competitors.

Finally, if this policy of refusing to protect competitors seems unduly harsh, we would remind you that after all no one asked you to be a business man. If you want security, serenity, and peace of mind we would suggest that there are many other lines of activity which would probably suit you better. It is our view that in this country the conduct of a business enterprise should be a strenuous activity. It involves the assumption of very considerable risks, and if you are to expect the rewards of enterprise you must be prepared to accept the risks. These risks include the possibility that others may be able to perform substantially the same services which you are offering more effectively than you can do. They also involve the possibility that some new form of business organization, such as the chain stores or supermarkets in retailing or new products such as the new light metals, will crowd you out no matter how efficient you may be in performing your old job. Those possibilities are the price of progress, and you must accept them.

In view of this emphasis which we place upon competition you may well ask how we define the term. We pass over some of the definitions of this term employed by the economists as convenient tools of analysis and bearing such terms as "pure competition," "perfect competition," "imperfect competition," and "monopolistic competition." We accept a definition of this term which conforms to common, non-technical usage. By competition we mean rivalry between the members of one economic group for the patronage of members of another economic group. "One economic group" can mean, for example, a group of sellers who are rivals for the patronage of the buyers. In other situations it could mean rivalry of the buyers for the patronage of the sellers. But even this simple statement raises the question of who are to be included in the group of sellers. Must they be various sellers of precisely the same thing? (This is the central requirement of so-called pure competition.) We do not mean that, for if we did competition would be a comparatively rare thing instead of the pervasive force which we desire it to be. One kind of automobile is not exactly like another, but this does not preclude the possibility of very effective competition between the makers of the two. Likewise one metal is certainly not the same as another, but if these metals represent real alternatives, from the point of view of the buyers, then the sellers of those metals can be in effective competition with one another. Of course, this line of reasoning could lead us too far, for in a certain sense everything that is produced and offered to the American people is in competition with everything else. This is true in the sense that the consumer's dollars will be spent for one thing or for another, and in that extreme sense we could say that baby food is in competition with movie admissions. Somewhere between these two extremes a reasonable concept of the "group of sellers" must be found.

This is really a question of defining a market. Do we have in fact one market for Fords and another market for Chevrolets? The manufacturers of these two cars and certainly the dealers know very well that these are not separate markets, but rather that the mass of consumers consider one of the products a very close substitute for the other. The real issue is the question of the closeness and facility of substitution. Is one kind of transparent wrapping material a reasonable substitute for another? If so, the manufacturers of the two should be regarded as in the same group of sellers and the two products as being in competition. In this and other cases the answer is one of marketing fact and can only be determined by an actual examination of the market. The problem is complicated by the fact that for a number of products there are different uses. Thus aluminum may be in very close competition

with copper in the field of electrical transmission. In the field of kitchen utensils, on the other hand, it may be in competition with stainless steel but not with copper. To have effective competition one product does not have to be a close substitute for another at every point or form of use. The important question can be phrased in this way: Does the manufacturer of virgin ingot aluminum, for example, in setting his price and other terms of sale have to take into account the price and terms of sale in the copper and other industries? If as a matter of fact his freedom to enforce any price he wishes *is* effectively limited by the offers of the producers of copper, stainless steel, magnesium, and even of plastics, then we will say that the seller of aluminum is in competition with these others.

Since this question of the range of substitution has been discussed so much of late and is assuming such importance in the practical determination of the presence of competition, it may be well to say a word about the relative effectiveness of competition between precisely identical products and competition between those that are somewhat different. In the classical view, the former was to be preferred. There is, however, a growing recognition by economists, following the lead of the late Professor Schumpeter, that the most effective competition in fact has been that of slightly different products or of producers using different methods. Professor Schumpeter's view implies that the competition of one retail grocery store with another almost identical store in the next block was probably less effective in reducing the costs of retailing and lowering retail prices than was the injection of the chain stores and the supermarkets into the traditional retail pattern. A similar line of reasoning applies to potential competition. A representative of a large American enterprise which has ample financial and managerial resources has told me that at frequent intervals his people have taken a "hard look" at the aluminum industry to see if the margin between costs and prices in that industry would make it attractive for them to enter. The aluminum industry, no doubt, was aware that they were being watched by powerful potential competitors and this might well have had a salutary effect upon their policies. This means that if we wish to preserve the most effective and useful competition, we must take a rather broad view of the group of sellers among whom that competition is presumed to exist.

Our second admonition may be somewhat superfluous since it is implied in the first, but to leave no doubt on the matter we will state specifically that there shall be no agreements, combinations or conspiracies to prevent the normal working of competition. While this remark is not intended to be exclusive we will take a particularly unfavorable view of any agreements as to price or as to division of the market. We recognize that in some lines of trade there will be so few of you that it will be impossible for you to be entirely unware of what your competitors are doing, and we are not going to place the impossible requirement upon you that your own actions should be made without consideration of the actions or possible reactions of others. We will not consider parallelism of action, whether conscious or not, as equivalent to collusion. If, however, we are convinced that such parallelism of action is the result of agreement, tacit or otherwise, we will consider that as a violation of this admonition.

Our third injunction to you is that you must not monopolize or strive to monopolize a line of trade. By this we mean that you are not to conduct your affairs with the object of destroying competitors. We recognize that it is going to be difficult at times for us to distinguish the aggressive striving for improvement, for lower costs and for the offering of lower prices, which are the normal methods of competition, on the one hand, from a desire to destroy a competitor on the other. There are those who believe that the objectives of normal business competition and the objectives of destroying competitors are in fact the same. This we think is not true. The object of competition is to advance the interest of one's own firm; competitors may, it is true, be injured if they cannot maintain the pace, but that is an incident and not the object. Any supposed analogy between business rivalry and war is false on this point, for the object of war is to destroy the enemy almost regardless of injury to yourself.

It is conceivable that a monopoly could be attained or retained by normal and commendable business policies, but we think the cases where this can happen will be rare indeed. For example, it was felt by some at the time when the Ford Motor Company had attained over 50 per cent of the market that there was a very real possibility of it going on to crowd out all competitors merely on the ground of efficiency, resources, and the popularity of its product. Instead of going on to monopoly position it began to slip and its relative decline was very rapid and pronounced, in spite of the fact that there was no apparent decline of efficiency or deterioration of its product. It simply did not (perhaps could not) adapt itself quickly enough to changes in market demand and product improvement. Then there was the great United States Steel Corporation which was highly integrated, backed by large financial resources and which provided some 60 per cent of the steel output. But as new forms of steel were developed and new customers arose they too slipped to a present 30 per cent. Advancing technology, shifting markets and other features of a dynamic economy are potent obstacles to monopoly which is based only on sound business methods and efficiency. Indeed, size itself brings its problems in administration, coordination of activities, adaptation to the needs of different levels of the market and many others—so much so that it is probably a fair generalization that it is more difficult for the largest company to grow by any desired proportion than for one of its smaller rivals to do so. The history of American corporations, particularly the history of the one hundred largest companies of 1900, indicates that in this country even a position of leadership is highly precarious.

In short, monopoly based only on efficiency, progressiveness, and good business methods, while apparently not impossible, is so highly improbable that the danger of it does not deserve to provide an important basis of our antitrust policy. The prohibited monopolizing or attempting to monopolize involves a purpose which can be judged partly by the methods used. We shall not try to spell out here the particular methods which would lead us to the conclusion that there was an attempt to monopolize. In general we can say they are of two sorts, first the acts that have been specifically prohibited in our previous statements such as combinations and agreements and on the other hand those acts which can inelegantly be called business skulduggery, by which we mean acts that violate the accepted ethics and mores of the business community. On the other hand growth of your business on the basis of genuine efficiency will not be prohibited. In this connection, however, bear in mind that efficiency as used here means efficiency in such matters as cost reduction, product improvement and improvements in marketing methods. They do not mean the advantages which a concern may gain by being able to coerce a supplier or buyer. The distinction can be suggested, though not clearly defined, by noting that the former types of efficiencies are cumulative in the sense that the efficiencies of individual companies will add up to an increased efficiency on the whole economy. The other type of efficiency is not cumulative, for it merely represents an advantage that one gains at the expense of another. Another way of describing the distinction is that the former can be called true economic advantages and the latter merely acquisitive advantages.

The subject of bigness is related in the minds of some to the problems of monopoly. The view has been urged upon us that to maintain the necessary conditions for competition, a definite limit, expressed as a percentage portion of the market served, be set for companies. This view has at various times been supported by two contradictory claims: first, that the big businesses are, generally speaking, not exceptionally efficient anyway and nothing would therefore be lost by cutting them down to size. On the other hand, it has been claimed that the big businesses are so highly efficient that they make the entrance of new competitors almost impossible. We consider it unnecessary to decide between these conflicting claims. We reject the suggestion because such a limit on size would constitute a limit upon the possibility of growth. We consider that to say to any business concern that it cannot increase its volume of sales beyond its present volume would have the effect of asking it to act as though it actually had attained a monopoly. We would be suggesting to its managers that they should not improve the quality of their product or reduce their prices or improve their service, for those are the methods that would lead to an increase in size. To ask a business firm to act as though it were a monopoly in order to avoid the legal charge of being one, would surely represent a high order of separation of law and economic reality.

We emphasize this because we believe that the possibility of technological progress both in means of production and in types of goods and in marketing methods is, in an age like this, when science is presenting so many possibilities, the main requirement of an effective society. We believe that this desired progress of the economy would not be encouraged by restricting the possibility of progress and growth of the individual firms in that economy.

The fourth major point on which we would like to clarify our position deals with your pricing policies and practices. Our position on this point is largely a negative one. We say to you that we believe that the freedom to set your asking prices is one of the essential freedoms of a free enterprise system. You may, therefore, ask what prices you wish and offer what prices you wish. This is intended to imply that you may charge different prices to different people if you wish to do so, providing this discrimination in price is not used as part of a scheme to create a monopoly either for yourself or among suppliers or customers. In justification of this latter position we recognize that markets are not "perfect" as the term is used by the economists. On the contrary, competition will often be stronger at some points than at others. These may be different points in the geographic sense or they may be different levels of the market. We may use other devices to try to remove these imperfections of the market, but as long as they exist we recognize that it would be quite natural that you may want to quote lower prices at those points where the competition is more keen than you do at others where it is not so pronounced. In doing this you may either meet, in good faith, the equally low price of a competitor or you may take the initiative in offering the lower price if you anticipate that the competitive conditions in that segment of your market

require it. These competitive conditions which might justify such a discriminatory price may result from the anticipated actions of competitors or they might result from the belief that the prospective buyer is in a position to produce the product himself and that it is necessary to offer a lower price to forestall that loss of business. Or again you may wish to open a new channel of trade which may require discounts consistent with the requirements of that channel. For your protection as sellers we will object if the buyer brings improper pressure upon you to reduce your price. By improper pressures we mean those that would run beyond the degree of competition existing at that point in the market or beyond the economies that you may effect by selling to him rather than to others. But within these general limits you are free to fix your own prices.

This is as far as we are going in our general statement of policy and of what we expect from you. Some of you will surely ask that we be more specific and that we should lay down a definite list of "thou shalt nots." We sympathize with this desire to have the laws so specifically drawn that anyone can certainly know what acts are lawful. It is possible, however, to grant this request only to a very limited extent, and beyond this the policy we have outlined will have to be expressed in rather broad terms. To paraphrase the words of one of our eminent jurists, the antitrust law must have all the generality of a constitutional provision.

There are two major reasons for this. In the first place, it would be practically impossible to specify all of the particular acts which might violate this general policy, and even if they could be listed at any one time, conditions would change and new industries develop which would call for continual revision, not to mention the ingenuity of businessmen and their lawyers in finding ways to violate he spirit of the law without treading upon the letter of it. But the more important reason is that specific acts must in this area be judged by intent or probable effects or both. There seems, therefore, to be no escape from the broad application of the rule of reason. As one writer said: "The price of using the mechanistic *per se* violation doctrine as an escape hatch from the burdens of the 'rule of reason' is too high when one considers the unreality of reducing problems of concentration to a formula."[1]

Economic Tests. From these very broad rules we hope to attain certain results. In a summary way we can say that the desired result is the preservation of competition, but even the competitive ideal is only a means of attaining certain more specific goals.[2] In the first place, we hope to attain a reasonably high level of "efficiency." By this term we mean that business firms and industry shall be operating at a level of costs as low as the existing state of the arts permits. We believe that competition is likely to encourage this result, for it will reward the more efficient and penalize the less efficient and indeed eliminate some of these from the race altogether. But efficiency refers to performance relative to the known methods of production. That is, in the economist's term it refers to the existing "state of the arts."

A second and more important requirement is progress; that is, that the state of the arts should be continually advancing. While efficiency is a static concept referring to a state of affairs at a given point of time, progress is a dynamic concept. The distinction gains importance because the form of competition which would require a reasonably high level of efficiency may not be the form which will be most conducive to progress. For example, one of the features of the economist's picture of perfect competition is that new and better methods of production or types of products would be copied immediately by all others in the field: but if that condition could conceivably be attained it would probably serve to discourage progress. The reason for this is that progress is made by experimentation which always involves a degree of risk. The assumption of this risk by business enterprisers can only be justified on the expectation that more than normal profits will be obtainable at last for a limited period of time. Therefore, some limitations upon perfectly prompt imitation must be welcomed. These limitations may be imposed by our patent system, or by the length of time required to attain the necessary "know-how," or by the delay and natural obstacles that exist against newcomers who would like to enter the field or perhaps by other means. This paradoxical requirement that some brakes, natural or legal, upon progress are necessary to encourage progress must be borne in mind in trying to determine what degree and kind of competition we are seeking in particular cases.

In the third place, we hope from the preservation of competition to secure a socially useful profit pattern. We deliberately use this expression instead of saying that we seek to restrict the amount of profits. We think that a socially useful profit pattern is one which will be characterized by variety in which the more efficient and progressive firms will receive rather substantial profits, the mediocre firms moderate profits, and the inefficient firms no profits at all. In general we believe that profits should be the reward for superiority. They are the

[1] S. C. Oppenheim, *A New Look at Antitrust Enforcement Trends*, Commerce Clearing House, Inc., New York, 1950, p. 77.
[2] These objectives and their relation to antitrust problems are developed in greater detail in Griffin, C. E., *An Economic Approach to Antitrust Problems*, American Enterprise Association, 4 E. 41st St., New York, 1951.

reward for being better, not merely for being good. This differential feature of profits is an essential part of the competitive ideal.

In the fourth place, we believe that competition should yield a situation in which there will be reasonable ease of entrance on the part of newcomers into any field of trade. By "reasonable" in this case we mean that there should be no restraints upon entrance other than those that are imposed by the nature of the industry itself. It is quite evident that entry into the steel industry cannot be as easy as into the retail grocery business. Not only are there obstacles in fact to entering such an industry as the steel industry, but it is socially desirable that these obstacles should exist. For, after all, the starting of a new enterprise in that industry requires the use of millions of dollars of capital and the time and services of thousands of men. These are, so to speak, valuable social assets, and they should not be lightly committed. An advantage indeed of the private enterprise system is that the restraining effect on these natural obstacles is scaled very nicely to the value of the resources that are involved.

Thus we can say that a good industry or a good company is one that shows these desired characteristics: it will be efficient; it will be progressive; the profits yielded will be justifiable on the ground of superior performance; and the ease of entry will be as great as the natural conditions of the industry permit, that is to say, there will be no artificial or arbitrary restraints. Surely some economists would want to add to this list of the tests of a good industry, but I am satisfied that all of them would include these four in their lists.

What significance do these standards have from the point of view of antitrust administration and policy? Without treading too seriously upon the territory which properly belongs to the lawyer can we not say that these are among the objectives which public policy seeks; and second, that, since these are the results which we would hope to attain from effective competition, their presence or absence at least in any marked degree would have some evidentiary value in determining whether the competition itself exists? I can hardly imagine these four tests being met if there were any substantial degree of monopoly.

26

Antitrust in an Era of Radical Change

Max Ways

It would be fatuous to argue that a segment of society as important as the economic segment should not be controlled in some manner by the political agency through which society controls its various institutions in the best interests of greatest number. But it would be equally fatuous to argue that controls imposed in 1890 and 1914, when conditions were immeasurably simpler, are necessarily appropriate to today's economic conditions. Yet a majority of otherwise well-informed people seem to take this position. They have made a fetish of our antitrust laws. This author attempts a fresh look at the environmental situation and proposes a new basis for control over business in the realm of antitrust.

Our sacred cow was born two-headed. Any serious examination of antitrust must start by recognizing that two distinct—indeed, contrary—policies have existed side by side. One policy has protected competition against such practices as conspiracies between firms to fix prices or limit production; this side of antitrust, exemplified by the Addyston Pipe case of 1899 and the very similar electrical conspiracy cases of 1961, has played and should continue to play a helpful part in the ever increasing liveliness and flexibility of the American market. The other antitrust policy has been fearful of change; it has frowned upon the growth of firms, especially by merger; it has sought to preserve the specific structure of markets on the assumption—long since demonstrated to

Reprinted from the March 1966 issue of *Fortune Magazine* by special permission, © 1966 Time, Inc.

be groundless—that the degree of competition is directly proportionate to the number of competitors and inversely proportionate to their average size; it has impaired the legitimate scope of freedom of contract and introduced arbitrary rigidities into the market through which we allocate our resources.

During the last fifteen years the second policy has become more and more dominant in antitrust enforcement. Essentially, this other head of antitrust is anticompetitive and reactionary. Instead of relying upon the market to protect consumers and encourage progress, it substitutes the preferences of public administrators and judges as to how production and distribution should be organized. By trying to shield specific competitors against the effects of competitive innovation, it tends to reverse —or at least to inhibit—that long line of social evolution which has been described as the movement "from status to contract."

Because our economy is so resilient, the measurable practical damage done by this second kind of antitrust policy has not been great—yet. But what of tomorrow?

We can know very little about the business specifics of 1986 or 1996. But some general statements about the next twenty or thirty years can be made with a high degree of confidence. Among them: (1) the pace of change, which broke through a sort of sound barrier around 1950, will continue to accelerate; (2) change will be made up of millions of innovations; many will be based on scientific discoveries and technological inventions; there will also be significant innovations in merchandising, finance, and corporate structure, and those patterns of coordination and decision making that we sum up on the word "management." In short, what we know of the next twenty years is that corporations will need the utmost flexibility because in each year our economy will be more and more involved with innovation. It is this prospect that urgently requires the U.S. to abandon the anticompetitive side of antitrust.

Traumatic Memories

Serious debate of antitrust policy is drowned out by a kind of litany. "What makes the American business system superior to the British and all others?" "Antitrust." "What slakes the public resentment of big business?" "Antitrust." "What preserves us from direct government regulation and maybe even socialism?" "Antitrust."

Beneath this drone of exaggerated and indiscriminate praise, individual businessmen do no more than mutter sullenly— usually when their own oxen are gored.

Corporation lawyers, prosperously immersed in the arcane minutiae of antitrust, fail to raise a public alarm about where antitrust is moving. Such protests as come to the surface are directed against the Attorney General of the day ("Bobby" became an expletive), or upon the chief of the Antitrust Division and the members of the Federal Trade Commission, or upon one jurist or another (Chief Justice Warren has earned the post of head whipping boy).

But this thing, as they used to say in Hollywood, is bigger than all of them. The reactionary side of antitrust has a momentum that is built into court decisions, congressional investigations, and the clichés of public discussion. This trend has picked up speed during the terms of such dissimilar Presidents as Truman, Eisenhower, Kennedy, and Johnson. A White House "friendly to business" cannot reverse the way antitrust has been going. The place to clarify a fundamental national policy is Congress.

In order to lift discussion out of the ruck of legalistic bickering, economistic thumb-sucking, and political personalities, *Fortune* offers the proposition printed above. No doubt, lawyers learned in these matters can improve its wording—if they can spare the time from their clients' antitrust cases. As it stands, however, the purport of the proposition is clear enough: to present the two sides of antitrust as a choice.

Much more is at stake than the level of corporate profits, or the efficiency of the aggregate economy, or its rate of growth. The *quality* of the American future depends on the flexibility of the market framework. If our business system continues to be haunted by hallucinations lingering from American capitalism's traumatic childhood, we will deal clumsily—and perhaps disastrously— with an era of radical change.

Bryan, Brandeis, Bigness and Badness

A glance back at the origins of antitrust may help clarify the choice that now confronts the U.S. In both its good and bad aspects, antitrust was a response to the great change that began in the last third of the nineteenth century. The good side—the confidence in competition and the resolve to foster it—was a brave leap in the dark by a nation that could not be sure of the direction in which modern capitalism would evolve. The bad side—the fear of large business units, new methods, new patterns of trade—was a timid, if understandable, clinging to the circumstantial patterns of an older America. Both elements, side by side, can be clearly seen in the discussion of "the trusts" that rolled through the U.S. between 1880 and 1917.

Many words conspicuous in that discussion—including "trust," "monopoly," and "competition"—had split meanings; antitrust history is an exercise in unscrambling unintentional puns. "Trust," for example, meant originally a quite specific device by which stockholders in competing companies ended competition by pooling their voting stock in the hands of a board of trustees. But "trust" was also widely used to mean *any* large business corporation. "Trusts" in the first meaning—along with price-fixing agreements and other anticompetitive practices—were regarded by many lawyers and businessmen of the day as "conspiracies in restraint of trade," which had been illegal under common law. A practical difficulty was that the courts of the states, which normally enforced such common-law principles, could not readily get their hands on these huge new combines; they leapt across state lines and operated a nationwide business system. Without an act of Congress, federal courts had no solid authority to enforce the common-law prohibition against agreements in restraint of trade. Many who supported the Sherman Act of 1890 saw it as plugging a loophole in the federal-state structure. They reasoned that in the new business world, as in the old, competition would protect the public and stimulate progress. The good side of present antitrust policy is descended from this position.

But their interpretation of antitrust fell a long way short of satisfying that part of the public clamor which used the word "trust" to mean everything that was large, new, and different in business. Theodore Roosevelt understood—perhaps sooner and better than anyone else—the political dilemma involved in the two usages of the word "trust." In 1900, as governor, he told the New York Legislature: "Much that is complained about is not really the abuse so much as the inevitable development of our modern industrial life. We have moved far from the old simple days when each community transacted almost all its work for itself and relied upon outsiders for but a fraction of the necessaries, and for not a very large portion even of the luxuries, of life. Very many of the antitrust laws which have made their appearance on the statute books of recent years have been almost or absolutely ineffective because they have blinked the all-important fact that much of what they thought to do away with was incidental to modern industrial conditions, and could not be eliminated unless we were willing to turn back the wheels of modern progress by also eliminating the forces which had brought about these industrial conditions." As a politician, T.R. was responsive to that element in popular antitrust feeling which was simply resentment of change. But when it came to practical antitrust policy he moved very cautiously because he believed that at bottom the people wanted progress even more than they wanted "the old simple days."

The young Walter Lippmann, writing in 1914 and using the word "trusts" in the broad sense of modern business organizations, brilliantly described popular reaction to the change. The trusts, he said, had come "into the life of the simple American community as a tremendous revolutionary force, upsetting custom, changing men's status, demanding a readjustment for which people were unready. Of course, there was antitrust feeling; of course, there was blind desire to smash them. Men had been ruined and they were too angry to think, too hard pressed to care much about the larger life which the trusts suggested." Lippmann understood that William Jennings Bryan represented resistance to change. "Bryan . . . thought he was fighting the plutocracy; as a matter of fact he was fighting something much deeper than that; he was fighting the larger scale of human life. . . . What he and his people hated from the bottom of their souls were the economic conditions which had upset the old life of the prairies, made new demands upon democracy, introduced specialization and science, had destroyed village loyalties, frustrated private ambitions, and created the impersonal relationships of the modern world."

This "antitrust" state of mind, which Lippmann called "conservative," had little knowledge of or faith in market competition. In the old, simple life only a small proportion of goods and services had ever passed through a competitive market. The village blacksmith was a small businessman who had a local monopoly. The village general store was a retail conglomerate, and in the absence of competition it could indulge in all kinds of administrative inefficiencies— e.g., the new clerk's ignorance that the proprietor kept the nail keg behind the pickle barrel. Louis Brandeis, one of the

most influential voices in developing the reactionary side of antitrust, never really believed that, under the stimulation of increasing competition, corporate management was reducing administrative inefficiencies; instead, he seemed to feel that a thousand nail kegs would be hidden behind a thousand pickle barrels. Brandeis believed that in very big corporations inefficiencies would be multiplied; therefore, if big corporations made profits this fact could be explained only by assuming that size gave them illegitimate "market power" to insulate them from their small competitors.

They Ran Harder

This sort of thinking widened the split that had opened between two meanings of the word "monopoly." Originally, it had meant an exclusive right, granted or protected by the Crown, to do business in a certain commodity in a defined area. (All enduring European cartels were to have this element of government protection.) In the U.S. of 1880–1917, however, monopoly began to take on a very different meaning, which is at the root of many of our present antitrust difficulties. Section 2 of the Sherman Act is directed against "every person who shall monopolize, or attempt to monopolize or combine or conspire with any other person or persons, to monopolize any part of the trade or commerce among the several states . . ." Does "monopolize" refer to a set of practices intended to erect artificial walls against competition? Or does the statute forbid a company to attain in the course of the competitive race a large share of a line of trade? Under the influence of the Bryan-Brandeis type of "conservatism," the word "monopolize" has tended to move more and more toward the latter meaning. *Fortune*'s proposition is intended to move it back toward the first meaning.

The greatest source of confusion, however, lay in the different applications of the word "competition." When in the late nineteenth century the U.S. entered a genuine market economy, businessmen were not immune to the general feeling of insecurity. The late nineteenth century's notorious conspiracies in restraint of trade were efforts to flee the rising uncertainties of intensified competition. These conspiracies all broke down, whether because they had been outlawed by Section 1 of the Sherman Act or because of technological developments.

But the main line of U.S. development in the twentieth century found very different answers to "the problem of competition." The corporation, with the principle of limited liability, compensated for the mounting risks that had become too great for individual proprietors and unlimited partnerships. If accelerating change undermined the security of a company, the company's response was to run faster—not to try to stop the change. If the new technology required huge investment, the corporation's response was to grow by plowing back profits, attracting new capital and by mergers with other companies. If huge technological plants required specialization, the corporation was to develop professional managers to coordinate the specialists. In short, twentieth-century business evolved in exactly the opposite direction from the repressive spirit of the old conspiracies. Instead of limiting production and suppressing innovation in order to raise prices, modern corporations place a tremendous emphasis on increasing sales volume by vigorous merchandising, by the search for new markets, by cutting costs; they spend billions on research and development to create new products and services; they rely on the diversification of product lines, rather than on the suppression of innovation, to defend the company against the increasing vulnerability of *any* product to competition.

The Rise of Consumer Power

The economy of 1900 was dominated by trade in the necessities of life. A family needed food, clothing, fuel, in quantities that could not be produced and distributed at a cost far below the family's income. There was not much consumer choice—or "power"—in that situation. The family could not resist a rise in the price of bread by shifting its purchasing to overcoats, even if the price of overcoats was falling. Demand in all three markets was "inelastic." A monopoly position in any one of them could by raising prices siphon off what little difference there might have been between family income and the cost of subsistence.

The twentieth century's enormous increase in productivity—and therefore in real wages—changed all that. In the U.S. today the basic subsistence requirements of 1900 can be purchased for less than 20 percent of an average family's income. We have raised our standard of "necessary" purchases to include home furnishings, non-utility clothing, etc. In this area of "secondary needs" today's consumer can at least postpone purchase if he finds the current price of one "need" less attractive than another. Above this, now, lies a third level, the vast domain of "discretionary" goods and services. Competition in this area jumps over the old market boundaries; as the economists say, these discretionary markets are subject to a high degree of "cross elasticity of demand." The beer competes with the candy; the trip to Miami competes with the violin lessons for Junior. This increase in demand elasticity—and therefore in the buyer's power to resist monopoly—has far outstripped any increase in "market power" that may have accrued to large corporations.

Back in 1902 an economist, Simon N. Patten, foresaw that the power of the great corporations would be limited by "the consumers' power of substitution." The chemists, among others, vindicated him. Synthetics hover menacingly over just about every raw material except gold, which is protected—at a low level —by some rather odd governmental arrangements. Progress has done most of antitrust's work by sharply reducing the chance that "market power" can arbitrarily raise prices.

By ignoring the whole range of fundamental changes that have come over the U.S. economy and by looking only at the percentage shares of large companies in narrowly defined markets, the Brandeis tradition insists that competition has been decreasing. In order to make it appear that a given company has an inordinately large share of a market, the government's usual tendency is to define "market" as narrowly as possible. If you assume that aluminum wire doesn't compete with copper wire (the Alcoa-Rome Cable case, 1964), that a commercial bank doesn't compete with another commercial bank twenty miles away (Philadelphia Bank, 1963), that a retail shoe market could be arbitrarily defined as any city of 10,000 with its "immediately surrounding areas" where both the merging companies had stores (Brown Shoe, 1962), then of course, you can prove quite a lot of "concentration." By setting up the rules of proof as if the U.S. market today were as tightly compartmentalized as in 1890, you can give some color of truth to the charge that U.S. business has become oligopolistic. Antitrust policy is still riding on a quest to rescue the maiden, Economic Freedom; but the girl has long since been liberated by other hands and now has fourteen daughters livelier than their mother.

The Great Scouring-Pad Case

Don Quixote wasn't exactly crazy; he had just arranged his mental life so that he could see what he wanted to see. Sometimes events in the actual world of business intrude abruptly upon antitrust's La Mancha. The government had no sooner won the Paramount Pictures case, after years of complicated market analysis, than television came on the scene to prove that the movie industry as a whole was not exactly immune from competition. Within a few years television not only changed the structure of the entertainment industries but also caused an upheaval throughout the world of advertising. Television is the biggest and best-known postwar example of the effect of innovation on the U.S. economy. But every year there are tens of thousands of smaller examples of how innovation can transform a relatively stagnant business situation into one marked by agitated competition. Frequently, the increased liveliness is triggered by a merger.

Consider the great scouring-pad case pending, as this was written, before the Federal Trade Commission. For many years two medium-sized companies, S.O.S. and Brillo, doing a nearly equal business, accounted for more than 95 percent of the steel-wool pads sold to housewives for cleaning pots and pans. During this period the competition between Brillo and S.O.S. does not appear to have been intense; there were few important changes in product design or in production or merchandising methods. At the end of 1957, General Foods, which had not previously been in the household cleanser business, bought S.O.S. No challenge came from Washington. During the next two years sales of S.O.S., relative to Brillo's, slumped. General Foods then took several steps to revive its ailing property, steps that did not depend upon General Foods' vast size or market power but simply on its managerial brains. It turned the S.O.S. account over to a different advertising agency; then it followed the agency's recommendations for some changes in the product and the advertising pitch. Because investigators found that housewives associated the red soap in S.O.S. pads with rust, the soap was changed to blue; to call attention to the sizable amount of soap in S.O.S., a TV commercial showed a soap pad being whipped into a sort of meringue in an electric mixer. Brillo fought back with a plastic pad called "Dobie" and a disposable pad called "Paddy." General Foods, after a fumble with something called "Handigrips," countered "Paddy" with "S.O.ettes." General Foods' tactics worked. S.O.S. overtook Brillo and spurted ahead, even making big gains in the New York market, where Brillo's share had run as high as 84 percent.

Clearly, competition was heating up in scouring pads. But the FTC was not pleased. In 1963 it issued a complaint charging that the six-year-old merger of General Foods and S.O.S. violated the Clayton Act because it "tended to create a monopoly." In its complaint the FTC had little to say about what was actually going on in scouring pads. Instead, it stressed the size of General Foods and carried on about such matters as the company's possession of more than 50 percent of the markets in coconut and "edible gelatins (excluding ready-to-mix desserts)." The FTC displayed its solicitude for the status quo ante by asserting that the merger had "upset and realigned adversely, and threatens to upset and realign further, the competitive structure of the household steel wool industry." This fell deed, said the complaint, had been achieved through General

Foods' "economic power, merchandising prowess and extensive advertising and promotion S.O.S.'s share of the steel-wool scouring-pad market had risen from 51 percent at the time of the merger to 57 percent at the time of the complaint. The FTC asserted that monopoly was on the march.

But was it? At the initial hearing before the FTC's examiner, evidence showed that innovation had been breeding in another part of the teeming forest of American business. Scouring pads made with materials *other than steel wool* were attracting a rising share of the housewife's money. General Cable had a copper pad called "Chore Girl"; Kurly Kat Corp. had a plastic pad called "Flip" and two copper pads called "Kurly Kate" and "Kopper Kate"; Du Pont was in there with "Combo," made of nylon; Colgate-Palmolive had test-marketed a nylon pad called "Colgate-Ajax"; General Mills had a plastic pad called "Ocelo"; Minnesota Mining and Manufacturing was marketing "Scotch-Brite" and building a plant to make "Rescue" (both of nylon). Lever Brothers, Procter & Gamble, American Home Products, and a host of small firms were reported considering getting into the cleaning-pad free-for-all. Some monopoly!

The FTC's examiner was not impressed. He defined the market in which S.O.S. was sold as that for "steel wool scouring pads." He cited the indubitable fact that the physical properties of steel-wool pads are different from those of non-steel pads. But do their *uses* differ? The FTC's lawyers said "we must conclude" that non-steel pads are used only for cleaning china and glassware, but the lawyers did not produce evidence to back this up. General Foods denies that it is the case. Store managers, who probably know more about housewives than do FTC lawyers, mingle steel-wool pads and non-steel pads on their shelves, indicating that they think its all one market. Advertising for the non-steel pads directly attacks steel pads as out of date. Prices of several non-steel pads are obviously set up to compete (on a per-time-used basis) with steel pads. In short, against a mountain of evidence that all scouring pads compete with all other scouring pads in an exceedingly lively market, the FTC's lawyers and the examiner, intent on showing monopolistic concentration, decided that steel wool stands impregnably alone in its ability to clean pots and pans. If so sweeping a claim were publicly made on behalf of S.O.S. or Brillo, the FTC would probably crack down on it for deceptive advertising.

On the Point of a Needle

Many government briefs and judicial opinions contain ingenious economic analysis and show an impressive ability to relate old legal precedents to new sets of facts. Yet these admirable exercises are suffused with unreality. Everybody now laughs at the medieval schoolmen who engaged in complicated speculation on how many angels could dance on a needle point. The schoolmen did this as a kind of mental calisthenics; they were not attempting to regulate a seraphic oligopoly. The FTC, the Antitrust Division, and the federal judges, however, aren't kidding.

The trouble is that the sophisticated analytical techniques they employ, though impressive in a purely academic sense are being hopelessly outstripped by the increasing fluidity and complexity of the U.S. economy. The scouring-pad situation is about as simple as modern business can get; the mind reels at the prospect of antitrust lawyers and economists arguing over whether X's lasers really compete with Y's masers.

It is significant that market-structure analysis as used in antitrust cases always distorts the facts in one direction—toward a simpler, more primitive, more stagnant economic picture than the situation that actually exists. In the present state of the science, economic analysis cannot handle more than a small fraction of all the variables and contingencies needed for a sound *legal* judgment on changing market structure in any particular "monopoly" case. And the analysis tends to ignore the element around which competition in fact increasingly centers—managerial brains.

The Creative Gale

The economist who best appreciated the central role of management in the modern economy was Harvard's great Joseph Schumpeter. Writing in the 1930's and 1940's, he foresaw that the future U.S. economy would live in a self-generated "gale of creative destruction." He believed that the excellence of an economy would and should be measured by its innovative capacity rather than its size. As Schumpeter used the term, innovation did not mean the ability of science to discover new truths or of technology to invent new things. His "innovation" is an *economic act* by which a new product or a new service or a new production or merchandising method is introduced to actual use. One of management's most important functions is calculating the relative risks and rewards of possible innovations. At any point in time there are millions of potential innovations, many of them arising from advances in science and technology. These compete with one another for birth. A decision to attempt a certain innovation is based on calculations about how it will fare in competition with other offerings, old and new. Before and after the decision, management assembles and coordinates the work of scientists and technicians from many specialized fields, along with the judgments of merchandisers and of men who deal with the markets for capital. Rivalry between corporations centers on management teams that compete with one another to find new ways of cutting costs, increasing volume, modifying old products and introducing new ones. The general market "allocates resources" by awarding different levels of profits to the winners and losers of this race.

Given Schumpeter's views about the decisive role of management, it is not surprising that he expressly foresaw the importance of mergers for American business. He understood, of course, that some operations require heavy capital investment under a unified management; but his thought on mergers went much further than a justification of bigness. Schumpeter's view of the innovating society puts the accent on flexibility. The merger technique is one that a management can use to develop the abilities it has, or to acquire abilities it needs to take advantage of new opportunities, or to protect itself by product diversification when the "gale of creative destruction" blows hard upon its existing business. In the innovating society, no company can expect to maintain indefinitely a given product line or a given market position or a given technology or a given set of marketing methods or a given set of financing arrangements.

Here is an example of a merger where present antitrust policy would play down the socially valuable motives while imputing "monopolizing" motives:

Company A has a group of scientists and engineers who have developed a narrow line of products in a specialized field of electronics. Starting from scratch six years ago, company A has achieved a profitable volume of $20 million a year. Its product line looks safe over the next three or four years—but beyond that, who knows? Its research and development people, still fecund with ideas, may come up with another series of inventions; but this second series, unlike the first, may not find an avidly waiting market. The second series may require vigorous selling, a skill that company A has not needed to develop. The second series may require financing on a scale unknown to the brief history of company A. It may require a great increase in numbers of employees, bringing problems of union negotiations of which company A is innocent.

Company B is also in electronics. It is older and bigger—say, $250 million a year. Some of its products compete directly with the present products of company A. Company B has a vigorous merchandising arm and a good reputation in the markets for capital. Its present product line looks fairly safe over five or six years. But its R. and D. seems tired, sterile. It decides that acquisition of company A will stimulate its research, while it can supply the broader managerial deficiencies of company A.

Antitrust policy, as now practiced, would tend to ignore all these considerations of managerial balance and efficiency and concentrate upon one fact: A and B are competitors in certain markets; therefore a merger between A and B is a horizontal merger that would "reduce competition"—meaning only that it would reduce the number of competitors in a narrowly defined market. Antitrust policy would say that if company A needs merchandising and financing expertise, let it go into the executive market and hire the men *individually;* if B needs scientists, let it do the same. This answer displays an ignorance of how work is organized in this society. A first-rate R. and D. department is far more valuable than the sum of the individual skills that make it up. So is a first-rate sales department or a treasurer's office. Company A's inventiveness might be aborted long before it could build, man by man, its merchandising and financial skills. And company B's capacity for introducing innovations might be wasted for lack of technological inventiveness.

Merger of A and B can be defended as socially desirable on grounds of efficiency. In a static economy this desideratum might be overbalanced by the danger of monopoly. But on the actual line of this economy's movement the danger that a merged A and B could garner the fruits of monopoly approaches zero.

Forbidden Fruit Is Not Always Sweet

To point out the social value that may inhere in mergers is not to argue that all mergers make good business sense. Of the 2,100 mergers consummated last year quite a few may turn out to be mistakes. There are days when the financial pages of the newspapers are so full of corporate acquisitions—rumored, achieved, or frustrated—that it seems as if the urge to merge is reaching orgiastic levels. Some top executives, apparently afflicted with corporate satyriasis, charge up and down the country, pawing the ground and snorting as they search for another sleek little company with which to mate. Questions inevitably arise as to whether these executives' attention is adequately fixed on the business they already have.

But preventing businessmen from making mistakes is not the proper function of the antitrust laws. If certain executives become so eager to show growth by acquisitions that they bite off more than their management capacity can handle, if they pay more than an acquisition is worth, the market will punish them—as it has already punished some incautious corporate giants. Indeed, if the hand of antitrust were lifted from the merger field, some executives might place merger decisions more on the basis

of sound business judgment and less on the basis of what their antitrust lawyers think they can get away with. The appetite for forbidden fruit is ever careless of the fruit's quality.

Another artificial stimulus to merger arises out of the tax structure. High rates of individual income taxes inhibit holders of common stock from making vigorous demands on corporations for higher dividend payout ratios. Because capital-gains rates are lower than ordinary income rates, stockholder interest tends to concentrate on corporate "growth," which may increase the market value of stock faster than it increases dividends. Some eager corporate managers view acquisition as a shortcut to "growth." If this situation distorts the total market unduly, its remedy lies in reform of the tax laws rather than in tougher antitrust policy to reduce the number of mergers.

There is no reason to suppose that the wrong motives for corporate acquisitions account for more than a minor fraction of the present wave of mergers. Essentially, the merger movement is a rational and constructive response by the business community to the increasing liveliness and fluidity of the economy. This rational effort by business to prepare itself for tomorrow's conditions is colliding head-on with a more and more restrictive antimerger policy that does not adequately appreciate the pressure of change.

Antitrust enforcers are fond of pointing out that of last year's 2,100 mergers less than thirty have been challenged (so far) by the Antitrust Division or the FTC. This comparison is supposed to show critics that the business system couldn't possibly be damaged by antimerger policy. That cat won't jump. Recent Supreme Court decisions go so far in prohibiting specific mergers that *any* potential merger of two substantial, healthy companies is logically subject to challenge under the new precedents. Uncertainty about whether a given company—or its competitors—will be permitted to merge pervades all councils of business strategy.

The "Social and Moral" Argument

The trustbuster has in his arsenal one reserve weapon that transcends economics. When he fails by economic analysis to show that some company, escaping the competitive discipline, has damaged the public, he can always shift his ground to the "social and moral" argument against bigness—an argument that goes all the way back to the William Jennings Bryan era. This argument rests upon one interpretation of "equality" as a social goal. It prefers a society of many small producers because it fears "the concentration of political or social power in the hands of a few men."

In antitrust law the classic expression of this fear of bigness is a passage in Judge Learned Hand's opinion in the Alcoa case. He brushed aside as irrelevant Alcoa's attempt to show that it had not *acted* as if it were a monopoly, that it had not engaged in "predatory practices" or gouged the public. Moving to the "higher" ground, Judge Hand said: "Congress . . . did not condone 'good trusts' and condemn 'bad' ones; it forbade all. Moreover, in doing so it was not necessarily actuated by economic motives alone. It is possible, because of its indirect social or moral effect, to prefer a system of small producers, each dependent for his success upon his own skill and character, to one in which the great mass of those engaged must accept the direction of a few."

This quotation encapsulates fundamental mistakes about the nature of the modern corporation. It assumes that today's business unit is simply a magnification of the village general store where the proprietor "directed" his obedient clerk; this way of looking at modern business inevitably results in a picture of concentrated power.

But the regimentation and loss of freedom that Hand feared is not characteristic of large-scale business. The actual development of the modern corporation disperses power to many individuals within a unified decision-making structure. The head of a modern corporation is hedged about with new limitations upon his power. He is rarely, for instance, in any significant sense the owner of the business. The rise of professional management, distinct from the shareholders but answerable to them, has created a fundamental check-and-balance situation unknown to early capitalism and to the old law of private property. A more recent and equally important trend has been the dispersal of power *within* management. In a complex modern organization a subordinate is not the "agent" of his boss. Managers far below the top level of a large contemporary corporation have power that inheres in their skills, rather than in the delegation of a superior. They are not so much "directed" as given responsibility and opportunity to initiate, to decide, and to coordinate activities that a chief executive officer would be helpless in handling. More and more work that is entirely "directed" from above is performed by machines and computers. Millions of little managers within large modern corporations have more actual scope for individual choice and decision than the "independent" small farmers, artisans, and small tradesmen of the nineteenth century had.

The U.S. public, which may be more in touch with reality than antitrust lawyers, seems to sense that business power is not being concentrated "in the hands of a few men." Once upon a time every banker and bootblack knew the names of Vanderbilt, Rockefeller, Morgan, Harriman, Carnegie. He knew what business each was in and what kind of man each was. These men were giants in the land and their tremendous concentration of economic power carried with it a threat of inordinate political and social influence. But the man in the street today is not likely to know the names of Frederic G. Donner, Michael L. Haider, Fred J. Borch, Albert L. Nickerson, and Donald J. Russell, who are the chief executive officers of companies doing an annual business in excess of $40 billion —a sum that makes the sales of the old Standard Oil Trust look like a hot-dog stand. If your barber can identify the companies headed by the names above, he should stop cutting hair and come write a gossip column for *Fortune*.

What the Proposition Means

Because opportunity is expanding and power is more and more widely distributed in this economy, *Fortune's* proposition for a new antitrust policy would end the effort to crawl back into the past. It would not allow courts to infer an offense against competition from size or market share or to assume, even in horizontal mergers, that a "restraint of trade" had occurred because the number of competitors had decreased and their average size increased.

The proposition would also mean that in vertical mergers—i.e., those that involve a supplier and a customer—the government could no longer void the acquisition on the ground used, for instance, in the case of Consolidated Foods' merger with Gentry Inc., a processor of dehydrated garlic, onions, and capsicum. The Supreme Court dissolved the merger because it was concerned that Consolidated might discriminate in favor of a supplier that bought its garlic, onions, and capsicum

from Gentry. If evidence showed such a danger to be real, a court, instead of dissolving the merger, should issue an injunction forbidding the merged companies from unfair discrimination. In other words, the court's action should be aimed at illegal acts rather than at a corporate structure.

As for conglomerate mergers, public policy ought to welcome them. The trend to conglomerates allows corporate capital or mangerial skill to be applied in new markets that might otherwise languish for lack of these ingredients.

On similar grounds, joint ventures, where two or more companies form a third, should be welcomed. In the Penn-Olin joint-venture case the Supreme Court, intent on increasing the number of competitors, speculated that *each* of the parent companies might have entered the market (chemical salt in the southeastern U.S.) if they had not combined. The two companies might have had sound managerial reasons for preferring joint venture—reasons that the Justices of the Supreme Court are not qualified to assess and should not be made responsible for assessing.

We cannot know that the future requires big corporations, any more than we can know it will be best served by small ones. We can know that the future requires innovation and flexibility and that the market, including the merger market, provides a better framework for them than central government planning would. We have three choices: we can substitute planning for the competitive market; we can keep the market, while distorting its action by government intervention on the false premise that the vigor of competition is determined by the number and size of competitors; or we can recognize that we are moving, year by year, into a more truly competitive and more innovative society in which we will not need and cannot afford the restrictive side of antitrust.

How to Get Rid of Hypocrisy

The real "social and moral" danger to this society is that we will continue to pursue our present line of economic development while keeping alive in antitrust policy a set of ideals, derived from the Bryan-Brandeis form of conservatism, which denigrate the business we have. If these ideals were valid, if we could have independence and freedom *only* with small business units, then we ought to scrap our present system and sacrifice some part of our material prosperity for our social, political, and moral

ideals. When we do not do so, millions of Americans—conspicuously including college students and professors—accuse the society of hypocrisy.

There is indeed a gap between what we do and what we say—through antitrust—that we believe. But this is because the ideals are too firmly anchored in the particular experience of a past society. Every year the business system cries out more loudly for men of independence and character to take on the massive new burdens of decision making in an innovating society. As we enter a period of accelerating change we will have social and moral problems grave enough without carrying on our backs the trauma of 1880–1917.

27

The Antitrust Chief Dissents

Donald F. Turner

This and the preceding article are companion pieces. Mr. Ways made certain proposals for altering the philosophy of antitrust regulations, and in this article Mr. Turner defends the present philosophy and administration of controls. The articles are particularly good in that the opinions expressed are quite largely based on substance rather than emotion, which so often is the case in ideological matters of the kind here involved. The issue, furthermore, is important and promises to increase in importance as technology develops and large organizations become even more common. The realistic difference is not between whether to exercise control over the business economy, but what kind of control to exercise. We would probably make more progress on this matter if the issue could be clearly focused on the issue of how rather than whether to control.

I will not go so far as to say that *Fortune*'s analysis is nonsense, or that the proposal based upon it would be folly. I doubt that any one of us knows or could know enough about the facts to warrant conclusions so strong. However, I have no hesitancy in saying not only that no affirmative case has been made out for the proposition which *Fortune* suggests, but also that the best economic information and thinking available to us indicates that a strong anti-merger policy, at least insofar as horizontal-type mergers are concerned, is almost certainly right.

There is no doubt that some conceived and still conceive of the Sherman Act and Section 7 of the Clayton Act as weapons against bigness per se, as protectors of small business come what may, and as protectors of what were and are thought to be great social values. But so long as such sentiments are not allowed to override judgments based on competitive concepts, it seems to me that the presence of such diverse motives is totally irrelevant to the question whether the law, as economic policy, is silly or wise.

The principal purpose of antimerger law is to forestall the creation of, or an increase in, market power. Its purpose is to preserve competitively structured markets insofar as natural forces will permit. I need only briefly restate the traditional reasons which are mustered in support of such a policy. If we can avoid the creation of undue market power, by and large we expect to achieve better market performance—better in terms of lower prices, higher quality products, and innovations both in product and in technology. We also expect to minimize the misallocation of

Reprinted from the April 1966 issue of *Fortune Magazine* by special permission; © 1966 Time, Inc.

resources that results from monopoly or oligopoly pricing.

Consequently, if there is validity in this traditional economic reasoning, an anti-merger law clearly makes sense, even based almost entirely as in Philadelphia Bank, on structural considerations. For there is obviously a polar distance between our present law on horizontal mergers and a law, as proposed by *Fortune*, that would make mergers lawful "unless they spring from a manifest attempt to restrain trade."

If there is validity in the traditional competitive analysis, a tough antimerger law is not going to do any significant harm to the economy, even though, as I have argued repeatedly elsewhere, it must be based on general rules that are bound to stop some mergers that in fact are innocuous or even somewhat beneficial. For a tough rule on horizontal mergers does not stop the economy from achieving the principal objects with which the antitrust critics are concerned. If we exercise reasonable restraint in formulating rules on other kinds of mergers, a tough rule on horizontal mergers simply shuts off some merger alternatives, not all. It may indeed in some instances prevent the merger which would most readily accommodate efficiency gains; but there seems to be little doubt that in many cases superiority of the substantial horizontal merger in this respect will be at best marginal and there may be no superiority at all.

Moreover, even if the general body of merger prohibitions went well beyond its present scope, the avenue of internal growth remains open and this is the avenue by which many if not most firms have achieved whatever economies there are in large size. There seems to be little reason to believe that any significant economies will long go unrealized because this or that merger has been prohibited. Again, this is not to say that there will never be a case in which growth through merger is more advantageous to the economy than internal growth or expansion. There undoubtedly will be some such cases, but if we are right in being concerned about undue concentration in markets, it is more than a fair guess that the gains from a strong antimerger policy will far outweigh the losses.

The economic purpose of an antimerger policy is precisely the same as the purpose behind the antitrust prohibitions on such anticompetitive agreements as price fixing. The purpose is to prevent, wherever natural economic forces do not compel it, development of the concentrated market structure that produces the same adverse effects on performance as those produced by price fixing and similar agreements.

The Effects of Concentration

I now turn to the question whether our traditional analysis, which looks with disfavor upon concentrated market structures, is no longer valid—or at least no longer sufficiently valid to make a strong antimerger policy worthwhile. The most important assertions in the *Fortune* article seem to be these:

(1) That concentration in the production of a particular product is of little or no significance because of interproduct competition; (2) that traditional analysis "tends to ignore the element around which competition in fact increasingly centers—managerial brains"; and (3) that in creating large-size companies mergers usually produce greater efficiencies, most importantly in research and development.

As for interproduct competition, it no doubt does impose ceilings on the power of the manufacturers of a particular product to raise prices. If the products are close enough substitutes and the costs of production are comparable, the ceiling may be as tight as would be imposed by additional sellers of precisely the same product. But what conclusions can be drawn from this? There is of course the well-recognized fact that antimerger law and antimonopoly law will often involve some rather difficult problems of market definition, and that these problems should be approached in a rational way.

But it seems to me preposterous to suggest that we should cease to be concerned about concentration in the production of a particular product simply because the existence of other products narrows the range of price exploitation that otherwise would obtain. Though, to quote *Fortune,* "beer competes with . . . candy," a monopoly or an oligopoly in the beer industry would still have power to raise price well above competitive levels before any significant number of customers would decide to quench their thirst with Hershey bars. And the fact that aluminum wire competes with copper wire and that many copper and aluminum products compete with steel products simply does not mean that concentration in any one of these industries has no impact on the price of its products or has no impact on other aspects of competitive performance. Therefore, it does not mean that antitrust concern with concentration has lost its *raison d'être.*

Indeed, it would not be entirely facetious for me to suggest that those who praise the virtues of interproduct competition do not really take themselves all that seriously. Even the editors of *Fortune* continue to praise the virtue of making price-fixing agreements unlawful. Yet price-fixing agreements among producers of the same product would be a matter of no consequence if interproduct competition denied producers the power to raise prices.

That significant increase in concentration in the production of particular products will normally lead to less competition is strongly supported by empirical evidence. A study by Professor Joe S. Bain on the relation of profit rates to industry concentration in forty industries defined more or less along traditional product lines shows a significant correlation between higher than average profits and high concentration. Another more recent study shows that among industries with medium entry barriers (again defined along traditional product lines), the industry that is more highly concentrated shows higher profits. A recent thorough study of the banking industry also shows that concentration of banks in a local market goes hand in hand with higher interest rates—a direct correlation between concentration and a higher price for the product sold, in this case, money.

Were it correct, as many assert, that increased concentration does not lead to diminished competition, either because of interproduct competition or for any other reason, it remains for them to explain why it is that even among industries with stationary demand and constant output, those that are highly concentrated set prices significantly higher than costs plus normal profit. To repeat, what evidence we have tends to support the commonplace conclusion that significantly increased concentration means diminished competition and the extraction of monopoly profits from the consumer.

Economies of Scale

Let me now turn to the contention that traditional analysis "tends to ignore the element around which competition in fact increasingly centers—managerial brains." I can only say that the contention if true (and I don't believe it is) seems to me to be largely irrelevant to the appropriateness of antimerger policy unless

management is so scarce a resource that it can only be utilized to full advantage by permitting levels of concentration well beyond what other economies of scale would dictate. I know of no evidence that management is that scarce a resource. But even if we suppose that first-class management is so scarce that we should encourage a greater concentration of business assets than we now have, it seems clear that valid competitive considerations would still dictate directing such further concentration toward conglomerate forms rather than permitting underutilized management to fulfill itself by substantial horizontal mergers.

I should like to turn now to the question of whether economies of scale generally are so significant that an abandonment or substantial curtailment of antimerger policy is in order. Let me summarize some of the evidence. One statistical study, which was carried out some years ago, concerned the relationship between corporate size and profit rate among manufacturing corporations. The primary finding of this study is that average profit rates increased as firm size grew to approximately the $5-million total-asset mark, but that once this level had been reached profit rates were constant or even tended slightly downward. In short, among corporations with assets exceeding $5 million, profit rates are not crucially dependent on firm size. If it were true that better managers tended to concentrate in larger firms, or that economies of scale were continuous, then profits should increase with size throughout the whole of the distribution. The statistics, however, simply do not bear this out.

The Limits of the Argument

In a study whose results appear to be typical, Professor Bain set out to measure statistically the extent of scale economies within twenty of the leading manfacturing industries. By this, I mean he attempted to measure the minimum size of plant which was sufficiently large to realize all of the engineering and technical savings which are associated with mass production. Having done this, he examined whether concentration was greater or less than appeared to be required for optimal efficiency. His conclusion was this:

"Referring to the first four firms in each of our industries, it appears that concentration by the large firms is in every case but one greater than required by single-plant economies, and in more than half of the cases very substantially greater." This finding indicates that an active merger policy intended to limit increases in market concentration is unlikely to result in lower efficiency, that an antimerger policy and efficiency are not in conflict.

Bain's study deals with economies of scale within fixed technologies, and the critics of antitrust merger policy quite properly suggest that we need also to concern ourselves with the relationships between competition and technological innovations. By no means the first to do so, *Fortune* refers admiringly to the writings of Professor J. A Schumpeter, who advanced the view that some combination of large firm size and monopoly is required if firms are to invest substantial funds for innovation. While Schumpeter's writings are strong and lucid, and there is a good deal of implicit appeal to the arguments which he makes, we still need to ask ourselves whether this approach has empirical as well as theoretical justification, and if so just what the limits of the argument are.

We have had several studies designed to test the validity and dimensions of the proposition that both the amount of research and the efficiency of research are correlated with size of firm. I believe it is accurate to say, on the basis of these studies, that once we get a firm large enough to do significant research at all there are no evident economies of scale either in research per size of firm or in research productivity for any given amount spent. It is indeed true that larger firms are much more likely to have research laboratories than small firms. Nevertheless, among firms which do have research organizations, small firms tend to spend *proportionately* as much as their larger counterparts, and in some instances they spend more.

Research and Innovation

Another most interesting study showed that between 1899 and 1937 the industries in which labor productivity increased most sharply were those characterized by declining concentration. Not only was this true, but industries of low concentration showed better performance than those with high concentration. Since we frequently presume that research and innovation are directed toward lowering costs, leading thereby to higher levels of output per man-hour, those studies suggest that increasing concentration has not led to more innovation but rather that the opposite may have been the case, and that "it is the competition of new rivals within an industry, not the competition of new industries, that is associated with rapid technological progress."

The last question which deserves comment is whether large firms and large research laboratories are necessary for *efficient* research activity. The argument here is that even if smaller firms spend proportionately as much as or more than their large rivals on research and development, smaller laboratories are inherently less efficient than their larger counterparts and turn out relatively less in the way of innovations. There is no overwhelming evidence on the point because of the difficulties involved in measuring output of research laboratories. Here again there are undoubtedly situations in which research of any kind requires expensive facilities which firms below some minimum size could not afford. However, two studies suggest that in general there is little reason to suppose any persistent economies in large size. Indeed, they suggest the contrary.

The proposition that the factual premise for an antimerger policy has disappeared rests on little more than sheer assertion; the weight of the evidence we have indicates that there is about as much justification today for an antimerger policy directed against substantial horizontal mergers as there ever has been. In this connection I cannot but point out again that antimerger law, even if stretched well beyond its present bounds, leaves open most alternatives whereby any advantages of large size may be legitimately obtained. All in all, the costs of being too lenient on mergers still appear to be higher than the costs of being too strict.

28

A Debate: The Quality Stabilization Bill

Stanley C. Hollander and James L. Fri

Our antitrust laws make collusion over price a violation which cannot be condoned by any extenuating circumstances. It represents what lawyers call a per se violation, and the courts have been uniformly strict in judging cases of price collusion. As written, this provision of the Sherman Act applies to collusion over prices at the retail level as well as all other levels. However, Congress and certain business groups have never been quite as sure of their position in regard to retail price maintenance as about other forms of price collusion. Congress has passed so-called fair trade legislation which has been substantially undermined by court interpretations, and now it is considering a quality stabilization bill which would authorize manufacturers to set prices on their goods when sold by middlemen. Although this would not involve overt collusion, it would have similar consequences with respect to a manufacturer's products at the retail level.

In the two articles that follow the two sides of the controversy are presented. Like controlling the size of businesses, this is an issue concerning which emotions run high. It also represents a significant issue on which informed people should have reasoned opinions.

The Case *For*, by James L. Fri

From a careful reading of testimony on the quality stabilization bill, a reasonable conclusion is that the conflict is not so much between opponents and proponents as it is between knowledge of the realities of present-day marketing and outmoded theories and concepts.

Anyone examining the provisions, and particularly the limitations, of the proposed act must conclude that the arguments put forward by its opponents are largely based on unfounded premises not inherent or implied in the language or intent of the act itself. They also err in setting up hypothetical situations that would not materialize within the highly competitive environment of today's marketing operations.

The primary purposes here are to identify some of the basic issues and to evaluate the relative significance of the facts and the theories as expressed by opponents of the bill. The following three points will be emphasized:

First, price stabilization of trademarked products at the retail level under the quality stabilization bill is completely compatible with the concept of free and open competition.

Second, an economy requiring unrestricted price competition at the retail level is destructive of the consumer's best interests because it places a premium on misrepresentation, deception, and consumer exploitation. Price of product is meaningless unless related to quality of product; the discount form of merchandising reverses all of the creative and constructive quality-building

Reprinted from *Business Horizons,* Spring 1964, Vol. 7, No. 1, pp. 5–20, by special permission.

forces inherent in the brand-name system of distribution.

Third, opponents of the quality stabilization bill, whether representatives of the Department of Justice, professors of marketing, or newspaper editors, have themselves been deceived or otherwise are a party to the deception of Congress and the consumer when they cite "estimates" and "projections" allegedly showing that enactment of this bill would result in increased prices to consumers, except on those well-known products that have been used as loss leaders to create deceptively an image of low-cost retailing.

The Provisions

The bill deals with the consumer's guide to value—trademarked and branded goods in free and open competition. Its purpose is to promote quality and price stabilization, to define and restrain certain unfair methods of distribution, and to confirm, define, and equalize the rights of producers and resellers in the distribution of competitive trademarked goods.

First and foremost, the bill is purely *permissive.* It is completely voluntary for the manufacturer, the reseller, and the consumer. No one can force the manufacturer to use the quality stabilization law, the reseller to handle the quality-stablized product, or the consumer to buy it.

The bill would give practical statutory implementation to the unanimous decision of the U.S. Supreme Court in the Old Dearborn case. In that decision, the court held that the owner of a brand or trademark, who has spent years and fortunes in research, development, and promotion to build consumer acceptance, has a continuing property right in his brand or trademark. Furthermore, he has a right to protect his good name and reputation from abuse in unethical advertising or reselling of the branded product.

The bill names three circumstances under which the owner of the brand name or trademark may revoke the use of his trademark: (1) if the seller has used the trademark in "bait" merchandising practices; (2) if he has advertised, offered for sale, or sold goods bearing the trademark at prices higher or lower than those established by the owner of the brand name or trademark; or (3) if he has published misrepresentations concerning such trademarked goods with intent to deceive the public.

It is important to note that the bill affects only the use or abuse (in advertising, selling, or misrepresenting) of the trademark, not the sale of the physical product itself. As the U.S. Supreme Court pointed out in the Old Dearborn case, nothing can "prevent the purchaser from removing the mark or brand from the commodity—thus separating the physical property, which he owns, from the good will, which is the property of another—and then selling the commodity at his own price, provided he can do so without utilizing the good will of the latter as an aid to that end."[1]

The bill covers only products in direct competition with other similar products in an open market. Thus, by specific language of the bill itself, the consumer is safeguarded against arbitrary or noncompetitive marketing practices. Before any trademark owner can take advantage of the proposed act, goods usable for the same general purpose must be available to the public from other

[1] *Old Dearborn Distributing Company* v. *Seagram Distiller's Corp.* (1936), 299 U.S. 195.

sources, and such goods must be in free and open competition.

Excluded from the operation of the bill are products sold to or by any governmental agency—federal, state, or local; products sold to charitable, educational, medical, and religious organizations; sales under court order, such as in bankruptcy proceedings; and sales of damaged, deteriorated, defaced, or secondhand goods when plain notice of the condition of the goods is given to the consumer. In addition, the bill exempts sales of prescriptive drugs for medicines.

Quality and Value

Price of a product is meaningful only in relation to its quality. Price and quality go together to make up *value*. Under the normal functioning of a free, competitive enterprise system—free from the pressures of monopoly at either the production or retail level—the consumer looks to the manufacturer because quality control is in his hands.

Those experienced in actual production and marketing know that for most consumer goods the retail price does not, per se, give dependable indication of its real quality. It is only when such price is related to a known quality or grade that the consumer can use price as a guidepost.

These guideposts are meaningful and useful to the consumer only when a manufacturer (or a distributor or retailer) clearly identifies the product by trademark or brand name and when he also establishes or suggests a realistic retail price for each quality or grade. By such identity the seller voluntarily assumes responsibility for satisfactory performance in open competition with other products within the same price range. Thus, to maintain these values, the goods must compete primarily in the laboratories and testing departments before they are offered for sale.

Under such a policy, there is aggressive competition to build up to a quality or value rather than down to a price; consequently, in both national trademarked products and distributor house brands, the consumer gets much more real value for her money. This basic concept motivates and governs all effective brand-name merchandising and promotion down to the retail level.

The discount form of merchandising reverses practically all of the creative and constructive forces inherent in the brand-name system of distribution. By its very nature, it is admittedly predatory in that its motivating force is sapped from the energy and goodwill developed by brand-name manufacturers and retailers by heavy investments, research, and promotion.

From the marketing point of view, the primary purpose of this bill is not only to encourage manufacturers and retailers to compete openly on quality rather than just on price. Its more important purpose is to give them specific protection on their investments in establishing quality and developing more helpful guideposts for the consumers in evaluating quality.

An Outmoded Concept

One basic concept that has hampered realistic consideration of this bill is the contention that free and open competition cannot coexist with price stabilization at the retail level. At the recent hearings, an economist and teacher said with considerable finality that "price maintenance at the retail level and an effective competitive system are incompatible." Efforts to evaluate this bill by such an outmoded concept tend to throttle constructive consideration of it.

Proponents of this theory should go into the marketplace and see the competitive forces in action, including the rugged competition in today's market among such large distributors as chain stores, mail-order houses, and cooperative buying organizations. For years these large distributors have been marketing under their own house brands with price stabilization at the retail level and with complete control of merchandising policies from the manufacturer to the consumer. Under such a policy, competition for consumer patronage is on "value for money" rather than on the lowest price for the same trademarked item.

As far as the marketing processes and competition are concerned, the brand names of these large distributors perform a function identical to the brand names of manufacturers. They represent more than one-third of all trademarked goods sold in the United States. Certainly, this is tangible evidence of effective free and open competition at the retail level as far as the consumer is concerned. Under the provisions of the quality stabilization bill, the same unrestricted forces of competition would be in effect on national brands.

The consumer accepts or rejects all prices, quality stabilized or not, house brand or not. If she does not like the price, she buys a competitive product. Under quality stabilization, the combination of quality plus price must be right for the consumer or the manufacturer will lose his market.

The forces that actually control prices of consumer goods are very well summed up in the following words:

> Competition will always continue to play a major role in American business. This fact should help to allay the fears of retailers who are maintaining that such things as fair trade legislation will raise the cost of living. . . . The danger of reputable product manufacturers raising their prices

to unconscionable heights is remote when one considers that competition between them would effectively prevent such action. The law of supply and demand, never formally enacted or repealed, will tend to be the over-riding element in all price actions.[2]

A False Charge

Apparently relying on the press release distributed by Paul Rand Dixon, Chairman of the Federal Trade Commission, before his testimony before the Senate Commerce Committee, the Scripps-Howard newspapers editorialized: "Dixon called the bill by its right name—a price-fixing device." But when questioned by the Senate Commerce Committee, Dixon had to admit that the quality stabilization bill cannot be used unless the product is in free and open competition:

> Senator Hartke: Under this proposed bill, isn't it true that if there is no item in free and open competition available that the item could not be in this category of having an established price?
> Mr. Dixon: This protection is built in. If a man had absolute monopoly—if he sold all the canned peaches in America, if he was the only source, *he couldn't fix the price under this bill.*[3]

The charge that the bill would permit price fixing is totally groundless, yet it has been the most useful and oft-repeated of the scare slogans used against the bill. As Senator Eugene McCarthy pointed out:

> The reason this [price-fixing] allegation crops up is because the opponents of quality stabilization shut their eyes to a simple but fundamental distinction. To permit one manufacturer of a brand-name competitive product, a mattress, for example, to control the use of his trademark, is far different than to permit all mattress manufacturers to get together and fix prices. The former is permitted under quality stabilization. The latter is *not* permitted under quality stabilization. The former *promotes* competition. The latter *destroys* competition.[4]

Another unfounded contention regarding the economic effects of the quality stabilization bill is that price stabilization at the retail level would prevent consumers from benefiting from lower prices made available by "more efficient retailers" and by "innovators of new merchandising techniques," and would "protect inefficiency." These statements imply that the prices used by stores making use of the discount appeal are a reflection of greater efficiency. They are not. Instead, such discount prices are deliberately used to create an image of low-margin retailing.

The present form of discount selling is no more a new type of retailing than was piracy on the high seas a new form of commerce in the early days of trade. Both are unlawful seizure or appropriation of the property of others. The major difference is that in piracy at sea the government was not hesitant in coming to the aid of the shipper—the owner of the merchandise. Today, some departments of our government not only fail to protect the property rights of the

---

[2] "The Merchant's View," *New York Times*, Oct. 6, 1963.

[3] From transcript of Hearings before a special subcommittee on the Quality Stabilization Bill S-774, Senate Commerce Committee; 88th Cong., 1st and 2nd sess. (Hearings not yet concluded), p. 366.

[4] From a speech before the National Retail Hardware Association on July 16, 1963.

lawful owner of well-established brand names, but they give wide and misleading publicity to the illusion of savings available in stores that use sharply discounted prices deceptively to attract customers.

Mythical Savings

The Department of Justice is the primary source of the allegation that enactment of this bill will result in higher prices to the consumer of 19 per cent to 27 per cent; theorists project this to claim the quality stabilization act will cost the consumer as much as $14 billion a year.

Where did the figures of 19 per cent to 27 per cent come from? The Department of Justice in 1956 had the F.B.I. look for the "savings opportunities" on selected items in eight cities. Almost obscured in the Department's report are the two significant words, "savings opportunities."

Propagandists also completely ignore the significant admission in 1959 by Robert A. Bicks of the Department of Justice regarding its alleged survey: "However, it has not been our contention that savings of 27 per cent were possible on all items within the retail outlets surveyed. *The survey merely disclosed that such savings were available on the specific items surveyed to those prudent consumers interested in best buys.*"[5]

Estimates of huge price increases to consumers are based almost entirely on the unwarranted assumption that consumers are enjoying billions of dollars of net savings under the present form

of merchandising, which offers little price stabilization of national brands at the retail level.

That such estimates of savings are in large part mythical can convincingly be demonstrated by simply examining the Justice Department's procedures in obtaining the results. Anyone acquainted with the discount form of merchandising should know that if this study had included all items sold by these same stores, customers would have contributed an average of $.25 or more of every dollar. The reason is simple: this type of store operates on a margin of 25 to 35 per cent. True, customers would have made savings on some branded items, but they would have lost most of these savings on other purchases in the same store.

Deeply discounted products—those sold well below the store's needed gross margin—are intended to deceptively create an image of low-cost retailing. No mystery should surround the technique of this form of selling. In order to stay in business, this type of store must realize a minimum gross margin on its total sales just the same as any other retailer. Thus, for every dollar he sells below his required percentage markup, he must sell an equal volume above this markup. In brief, the formula for operating under a discounting policy is simply to surround every deeply discounted item (loss leader) with a sufficient number of profit boosters.

It can safely be concluded therefore that savings on individual discounted items cannot be added together and projected on a nationwide basis as net savings to the consumer. Those who make such estimates are either uninformed in the mechanics of discount selling or are attempting deception.

To assert simply that huge savings accrue by purchasing from discount stores is misleading; it must also be pointed out

[5] *National Fair Trade Legislation—1959,* Hearings Before a Special Subcommittee on Fair Trade of the Committee on Interstate and Foreign Commerce; U.S. Senate, 86th Cong., 1st sess. (Washington: U.S. Government Printing Office, 1959), p. 300.

that unless purchases are limited solely to the identifiable loss leaders, customers will pay about the same price in the discount store as in the regular limited-service stores.

Unless the myth of discount selling is exposed, and the average consumer made aware of the truth about the loss-leader technique, she is in grave danger of losing the most valuable and dependable guidepost heretofore available for judging the relative value of goods offered for sale—the retail price suggested by responsible manufacturers and retailers.

After more than eight years' experience under the discount form of merchandising, it may be concluded that, in total, it has not contributed to improved quality of product, to shopping convenience, or to lower retailing costs in relation to services rendered. Because of its predatory nature, it has instead increased the ratio of low-quality products and, more importantly, has caused manufacturers to decrease their investments in long-range programs of research and informational advertising.

Adherence to a reasonable consumer price by retailers—a price that covers the normal costs of distribution—cannot be considered price fixing or inefficiency in any sense. It is simply an honest and intelligent spread of the actual costs of distribution to all items of merchandise, rather than a deceptive spread of these costs, giving unidentifiable items the larger burden.

The Case *Against*, by Stanley C. Hollander

The proposed quality stabilization bill now before Congress would be a strange law. Its subject matter has little or nothing to do with its title, and most of the nominal beneficiaries of the law appear unenthusiastic about it. It probably will

not help the people who are supposed to be its real beneficiaries, and finally, the law will have to be ineffective to avoid harming the consumer.

The proposed law certainly has little or nothing to do with quality stabilization. The word "quality" does not even appear in the text of the legislation beyond the opening clause which reads: ". . . this Act may be cited as the 'Quality Stabilization Act.'" That phrase is the last reference to quality considerations. But the word "price" makes twenty-six appearances in the relatively short text of the bill. This curious imbalance suggests the true nature of the proposal: the law is concerned with price fixing and not with quality control.

Briefly, the law would amend the Federal Trade Commission Act to permit the owner of a trademark or brand—usually a manufacturer—to set the prices at which all subsequent dealers must sell the products that bear his brand or mark. Essentially, it is resale price maintenance under a new label. Without specific legislative authorization, such vertical price control violates the Sherman Act prohibition on price agreements in interstate trade. The much debated Miller-Tydings Enabling Act (1937) and the McGuire Act (1952), which are now conceded to have failed in their purposes, allow the states to authorize resale price maintenance on wholesale and retail sales within their own borders. The pending bill provides direct federal authority for price maintenance and, in another curious provision, requires those states that do not want price maintenance to pass specific canceling legislation.

Fallacies

The Quality Argument. Although the term "quality stabilization" is essentially subterfuge to overcome the distaste that Congress has always shown for this type of price control, some of the law's advocates do go through a tortuous chain of reasoning to justify the quality label. They say that when some retailers reduce the price of a given product, the other retailers are forced to follow suit, which in turn places pressure on the manufacturer to reduce his wholesale price; but without such pressure, products would be produced and sold at a mystical optimum balance of cost and quality considerations. Therefore, the advocates say, the wholesale price reductions can be obtained only through hidden deterioration in the quality of the product. And so, we are told, retail price reductions are a serious disadvantage for the unwary consumer.

At first glance the proposition seems fairly reasonable. But the supposed price-quality balance is highly questionable, because it suggests that each product has an optimum combination of ingredients, workmanship, and wholesale price, and that any movement away from this combination short-changed the consumer. John W. Anderson, President of Quality Brands Association of America (the successor to the American Fair Trade Council) and the author of the quality stabilization bill, has said:

> It, of course, is not well known to the public that a reduction in the quality of a product to accommodate, for example, even a 10-percent reduction in the factory's price to meet the demands of piratical price cutters, usually reduces the value of that product to the consumer by a good deal more than 10-percent. It is the last 10-percent of cost of labor and material put into a product that carries to the consumer a far greater proportion of the product's value than any other 10-percent. At times an arbitrary cheapening of the prime production costs of a product by 10-percent or

less reduces its value to the consumer by 50-percent or more.[1]

This statement completely ignores the impact of volume changes on unit costs and the fact that the average manufacturer of such price-maintained goods as electrical appliances, fountain pens, and haberdashery regularly offers a series of models, grades, and lines, rather than a single price-workmanship-ingredients combination. Would Mr. Anderson argue that only the manufacturer's top line affords the best dollar-for-dollar consumer value, and that all lower-priced models somehow cheat the customer? How can he reconcile his argument with this statement by a close student of the field: "Each feature added to a television set ordinarily commands a price that is significantly above the added cost of the feature to the retailer (and to the distributor and manufacturer as well)"?[2]

Patent medicines and cosmetics are two products for which resale price maintenance has been assiduously cultivated. As everyone knows, material and manufacturing costs are only a fraction of the final price for these products; packaging, administration, research, promotion, and marketing constitute a large part of the expenses. It seems extremely unlikely that price reductions would lead to quality deterioration in this field.

Manufacturers' Involvement. All of this is quite irrelevant, for if manufacturers are as competitive as the resale price maintenance advocates say they are, price disparity at retail (the subject of this law) does not create effective

[1] *Quality and Price Stabilization,* Hearings before the House Interstate and Foreign Commerce Cimmittee, 87th Cong., 2nd sess. (Washington: U.S. Gov't Printing Office, 1962), p. 126.
[2] Alfred Oxenfeldt, "Customer Types and Salesman Tactics in Appliance Selling," *Journal of Retailing* (Winter, 1963–64), p. 14.

pressure for price reductions at the manufacturer level. Any manufacturer knows that reducing his own prices will not end differences in the prices his retailers charge. Let us assume that two retailers, R1 and R2, both handle that popular consumer product, Brand WM1 widgets, which they buy from manufacturer WM1 at $36 per dozen. R1 is a low-margin retailer who takes only a 20 per cent markup on widgets, while high-margin dealer R2 takes 40 per cent. R1's retail price, then, is $3.75, while R2's is $5. Lowering the wholesale price will not help R2. Even if WM1 dropped his price to $28.80 per dozen, R1 would charge $3 per widget while R2 would have to ask $4 to maintain his markup. So even if WM1 wants to help his high-margin outlets, which may or may not be the case, he has no reason to reduce his wholesale price. And yet the whole argument fails if manufacturers do not use wholesale price cuts to respond to competition among their own retail outlets.

Oddly enough, the resale price maintenance advocates always discuss competition among manufacturers with great reverence and describe it as a praiseworthy force. Yet the one inducement for WM1 to lower his own price is competition with other widget manufacturers. Competition among manufacturers, rather than retail competition, would have to stop in order to end downward pressure on prices.

Of course, those manufacturers who are looking for complete shelter from competition might feel that the termination of dealer competition would help end rivalry at their own level. Thus our friend WM1 might well relax if he could be certain that all of his fellow widget manufacturers would enforce the same high resale prices for their widgets that he was setting. Then the consumer would be forced to pay the combined price that WM1 and

high-margin dealer R2 wanted. No alternatives would exist, and all of the safeguards that our competitive system provides would have disappeared. It is not surprising that no reputable consumer organization has endorsed this supposed bit of consumer legislation.

Even though consumers obviously are not seeking the kind of protection this law provides, one might expect manufacturers to be enthusiastic about it. The bill repeatedly refers to the rights it provides for "the owners of brands, names, and trademarks," which in this context means mainly the manufacturers of consumer goods. Although some attorneys regard the principle as very shaky, the law rests on the idea of protecting the trademark owner's goodwill by allowing him to control the prices at which subsequent dealers resell his products.

Some manufacturers, including the producers of some well-known and highly regarded brands, have been ardent and articulate supporters of the legislation. But partly for the reasons we have already noted, the great majority of manufacturers appear unenthusiastic and disinterested in the privileges this law is supposed to bestow. The existing resale price maintenance laws have only been utilized by the manufacturers of less than 10 per cent of all goods sold in retail stores; moreover, some of those manufacturers used price maintenance unwillingly and under coercion. The Antitrust Division has reported a number of instances of retailers exerting collective pressure on their suppliers to force price maintenance, and undoubtedly other such instances have gone unreported. The recent histories of a number of trades contain example after example of manufacturers who have paid lip service to price maintenance but have continued to cultivate low-margin outlets. The records of Congressional hearings and reports on resale price legislation over the years constantly indicate that the support for this type of price control has come from *some* manufacturers' and *many* retailers' associations. Quality stabilization bills made little progress in Congress until the influential National Association of Retail Druggists transferred its support to the pending legislation from the rival price maintenance proposals that would have used somewhat different legal mechanisms to accomplish the same result.

Retailing Change

After examining the fallacies in the ostensible purposes of the quality stabilization bill, we come to the core of the matter. American retailing has been in ferment for a little over a century, and the rate of change in retailing has accelerated in the last thirty or forty years. During the entire period some traditional merchants have always sought laws that would stop change and progress in distribution. From 1850 to 1890 many wholesalers lobbied for state and city licensing ordinances designed to keep manufacturers' salesmen from calling on the retail trade. During the same period, wholesalers and retailers united to fight the department store and the mail-order house. Ridiculous nuisance ordinances were advocated, such as laws requiring a store to have a separate main exit for each department. Then at the turn of the century, the battle turned toward the chain stores. State after state was persuaded to adopt anti-chain store tax bills, some of which still remain on the books. In recent years this traditionalist campaign has been directed at the supermarket, the chain store, the self-serve retailer, and the discount store.

The campaign, particularly intense in the drug trade, has been designed to keep the more efficient retailers from passing operating savings on to their customers. In essence, price maintenance requires each retailer, regardless of whether his costs are high or low, to charge the same price for maintained goods as every other retailer. The consumer cannot save on her purchases of maintained goods by patronizing self-service stores, or forgoing charge account privileges, or being willing to travel to busy, central locations, or even by selecting the more skilled and able retailers. Price fixing curtails her freedom to choose among feasible alternatives. Thus resale price maintenance becomes a tax on the consumer for the benefit of the inefficient or high-cost dealer. Practically every survey ever made, with the exception of those commissioned by drug trade groups, has shown that branded goods sell at higher prices when placed under price maintenance. From its recent and very thorough investigation of the alcoholic beverage trade in New York, the Moreland Commission concluded that price maintenance had placed an enormous trade tax on liquor consumers in that state.

Paradoxically, the legislation may not benefit even the retailers as much as they think it will. In the short run, it will, of course, provide protection against vigorous competitors. In the long run, if the minimum resale prices are enforced, more and more dealers may enter the market to take shelter under the manufacturers' price umbrellas. As a result, each store will obtain a smaller and smaller share of the total market. The consumer is thus forced to pay higher prices, yet each retailer's total profit may easily decline instead of increase. Only where there are restrictions on entry, as in the liquor trade and in some aspects of the drug business, is the retailer assured of enjoying the monopoly tax that the consumer is asked to pay. This decline in profit as dealers multiply is one reason why the druggists fight so vigorously to keep grocers and other outlets out of aspirin and other packaged drug lines. In some cases, fixed prices for the manufacturers' brands have encouraged the large retailers to develop their own private brands, despite the slow and expensive processes of development and promotion. Private brands can also hurt the manufacturer of nationally branded goods, the supposed beneficiary of this bill. However, if private brands appear, the consumer is not as seriously at a disadvantage as she would be in a market consisting solely of price-fixed items. In any event, the net effect of resale price maintenance is to introduce unnecessary and wasteful complications into the economic process.

Almost all of the dynamic economies of Western Europe and North America have moved, or are now moving, against resale price maintenance because of the brake it places upon innovation and progress in distribution. The British government, which in 1957 abolished a particularly vicious system of collective price maintenance administered by trade associations, has now declared its intention of prohibiting the individual resale price fixing that the quality stabilization bill would encourage in this country. The British Board of Trade finds that price maintenance tends to keep prices above the competitive level and is inflationary and "against the public interest." Canada, Sweden, Norway, France, and Denmark have all prohibited resale price fixing, and the Netherlands government is now reported as also opposed. In West Germany federal authorities have the right to review and reduce all preset resale prices.

Objectionable Features

In addition to resale price maintenance in general being undesirable, the bill now before Congress contains several particularly objectionable features. In an attempt to plug the loopholes and correct the weaknesses of previous laws, the authors of the bill may have laid the groundwork for future trouble. In the McKesson case several years ago, the court ruled that a combination manufacturer-wholesaler who tried to set resale prices for other wholesalers was engaging in a horizontal conspiracy in restraint of trade and could not enforce his prices against his own competitors. The proposed law provides that an integrated firm may dictate resale prices for the goods it sells to its competitors. In another provision designed to deal with a different type of difficulty that arose under the earlier laws, the quality stabilization bill stipulates that the price set for an assortment or bundle of goods need not be the same as the total of the prices set for each item in that assortment or package. Put the two provisions together, and a variety of interesting possibilities develops. What might stop a record manufacturer, for example, from setting a very high minimum price for individual records to build up prestige for his label, and then establishing a direct-by-mail record club at very low prices? Where would this leave the independent record dealers?

The current version of the act states: "Each such currently established resale price and resale price range shall be uniform at each level of distribution, except for reasonable marketing costs." The House committee that reported out the bill says this means that the price must be uniform throughout the country, except for transportation and other geographic cost differentials. But the present language was substituted for much more specific references to transportation costs in the committee process, and there is no way to tell now how future courts would interpret this provision.

The list of such objectionable and questionable features goes on at considerable length. Some of these defects in the legislation may be eliminated or improved by amendment or in the conference proceedings between the two houses of Congress. Or, conceivably, some of the defects may be aggravated in the process. There is no point in dwelling on details, except insofar as they illustrate the difficulties of trying to apply retrogressive legislation to a progressive situation. Nor is there much point in dwelling on what perhaps is a matter of aesthetics: it seems inappropriate to adopt so grossly mislabeled a piece of legislation as an amendment to a law designed to prohibit misrepresentation. The fundamental objection to resale price maintenance, and hence to this bill, is that it is designed to interfere with progress in distribution.

29

Robinson-Patman: Dodo or Golden Rule?

Business Week

It should be recognized that our antitrust legal structure was not planned at one time, nor as a consistent whole. Different parts of the structure were passed in response to problems that appeared serious at various phases of the business cycle. During the "big depression" of the 1930's, when demand was slack, large buyers could and did extort exhorbitant discounts from anxious sellers. To protect sellers, who were in a relatively weak bargaining position at the time, Congress passed the Robinson-Patman Act, which, among other things, made it illegal to grant more of a discount than could be justified by the cost savings directly attributable to the order. In more normal times this law has seemed to many to be in basic conflict with other parts of the antitrust laws and to discourage price competition, which usually is counted on to regulate competition. However, the law has proved to have remarkable survival power and it continues to be administered—often in ways that could never have been anticipated by its proponents. The present article is a good example of the kind of criticism that this law engenders.

The following encounter took place recently in the executive offices of one of the nation's leading manufacturers of toilet articles:

A young product manager, dapper and eager, grabbed the doorjamb of the

Reprinted from the November 12, 1966, issue of *Business Week,* by special permission. Copyright © 1966 by McGraw-Hill, Inc.

company lawyer's office and swung himself into the room.

"Pete, I've got a problem," he said. "If I run a $1 promotion on shaving cream in Market Area 22, do I have to do the same thing in 21 and 23?"

"All I can say is it all depends," the lawyer, said cautiously. "Take a look at my memorandum."

"Yeh, yeh, I know," replied the production manager, swinging out of the office again, frustration in his voice. "Memo No. 37,658."

Serious doubts. The cloud of doubt left in the product manager's mind is, in a nutshell, the story of the Robinson-Patman Act—a statute passed by a Depression Congress in June, 1936, and still the most controversial antitrust law on the books. Its enigmas—compounded rather than clarified in 30 years, and not likely to be solved soon—create serious doubts for businessmen, who must consider the law's provisions in making every buying, pricing, and promoting decision.

Responsible law professors, lawyers, and jurists have admitted not just doubt but horror at the law and its administration. Epithets for Robinson-Patman range from "a hodgepodge of confusion and inconsistency" to "the Typhoid Mary of antitrust." The Federal Trade Commission's enforcement methods have been described as "increasingly fitful, fretful, inconsistent, petulant, will-of-the-wispish, and—like the fabled dodo bird, it seems—proceeding in ever-decreasing concentric circles.

The law has its defenders, of course. Representative Wright Patman (D-Tex.), the still-influential, 73-year-old congressman, who sponsored the statute, calls it "The golden rule of business"— one designed to "give little business fellows a square deal." To FTC Chairman Paul Rand Dixon, the law's critics are greedy malcontents, "who want to live by the law of the jungle—and in the jungle it's the biggest gorilla that wins."

Dissenter. Amid the debate, there's a crescendo of voices urging that, after 30 years, the time is ripe to reevaluate the act, to see what changes in drafting or administration would make it work better. The latest call came from FTC's own great dissenter, Commissioner Philip Elman, who insists businessmen should no longer have to make everyday pricing decisions at their peril.

As enacted, the law was aimed at ending discriminatory pricing. Its main target was the large food chain that could elicit discriminatory low prices from suppliers, and, with the resulting advantage, push smaller competitors out of the market. "One certain big concern," Patman has said, "had really caused the passage of this act"—Great Atlantic & Pacific Tea Co., Inc.

Changes. Robinson-Patman outlaws both the granting and soliciting of discriminatory prices or promotional allowances. Included in the act are sections spelling out circumstances under which price differences among different customers are legal, and which may be cited in defense. Most critics concede the need for an antidiscrimination law, and acknowledge that selective price favors can be a tool of monopoly. Their charges center not on need, but on what they consider sloppy draftsmanship and bad administration.

The thrust for change—coupled with continuing invective on both sides—raises practical questions, not mere esoteric arguments in legalese: Is the act doing the job it was intended to do? Have businessmen learned to live with it? Is it widely ignored? Do businessmen really want change, and if so, is there any likelihood they will get it?

I. Snare of Enforcement

Many question whether Robinson-Patman has achieved its intended goal

Although passed mainly to prevent large buyers from gaining decisive advantages over competitors, the statute came out of the drafting process focusing more on the seller than on the buyer. And it imposed such heavy burdens on FTC that it has been largely ineffective against big buyers. Of more than 1,100 cease-and-desist orders issued in Robinson-Patman history, only 30—or less than 3%—have been against buyers.

Even when buyers have been attacked in recent years, the decisions have left themselves open to a curious criticism: that they have been aimed not at giant companies but at small businesses, and that they have prevented lower prices to cooperative buying groups of small concerns formed to compete with larger companies.

Joe's Bar or GM. Indeed, a recent study by the Yale Law Review concluded that FTC enforcement over the years has generally focused on small businesses. A former FTC attorney believes this is at least partially because "it's a lot easier to proceed against Joe's Bar & Grill than against General Motors." Others believe small businesses are caught in the Robinson-Patman trap because they are "unsophisticated" or "unwary" or can't afford the time and money for omnipresent advice from legal counsel.

Perhaps the most glaring example of what some believe to be backward enforcement occurred in the garment industry. As garment makers tell it, they are small businesses selling to giant retail buyers, some of whom alone do three times as much business in a year as all the women's coat and suit makers.

"When a big buyer comes into the shop," says Joseph L. Dubow, executive director of the New York Coat & Suit Assn., "he doesn't stop in the showroom; he goes straight to the stockroom. He may see 700 garments there. He says:

'I can use 500. How about taking an ad in the Times?' "

In Seventh Avenue language, the buyer was saying: "You pay for an ad in the New York Times to tell people my store is carrying your garments, and I'll buy 500 of them."

Pressures. The manufacturer knows that to give a cooperative advertising allowance to one customer and not give a proportionate one to all others is illegal. "But he's under pressure to move the goods, to pay the rent, the mills, the workers," says Dubow, "so he gives in. He knows if he doesn't, somebody else will."

To halt rampant price discrimination in the industry, FTC put some 300 garment makers under cease-and-desist orders. As Chairman Dixon relates it, "a large group" of apparel makers themselves asked for the orders, believing this to be "the only way to stop discrimination."

Has it worked? Dixon says FTC has gotten "excellent compliance," but Dubow, who opposes the orders, maintains that pressures for discriminatory advertising allowances and resulting violations continue to be rife. He urges that FTC attack not suppliers, but buyers, "the seat of economic power."

The other side of this coin, as noted by Elman, is that the apparel makers, forbidden to fix prices in hotel rooms, may be using FTC chambers to achieve the same goals. He is suspicious of "the alacrity with which industry members have accepted the preferred boilerplate orders"—the agency's blanket cease-and-desist edicts.

Anti-antitrust? This is not the first suggestion that Robinson-Patman is an anti-antitrust law. A law school dean once called it a "price-fixing statute hiding in the clothes of anti-monopoly and pro-competition symbols."

Former FTC economist Corwin D.

Edwards argues that the strong pressures of big buyers for lower prices—the haggling and bargaining of the marketplace—is often the main force in lowering "sticky" prices. And the Robinson-Patman Act, he says, has lessened the buyer's pressure and increased the seller's resistance. A lawyer for a large food manufacturer contends that nothing would make his company happier than perfect enforcement of the act.

II. Maze of Compliance

Since the act focuses primarily on sellers, they have been saddled with immense problems of proving themselves free of violations. Companies that can afford it have lawyers holding their salesmen's hands on every pricing decision, shepherding every new promotional plan from cradle to grave.

Whether challenged by FTC or not, companies spend millions analyzing whether they come within various legal defenses. Could a price reduction to one customer and not to another, for example, be justified by:

- Differences in cost?
- The fact that it would cause no injury to competition anywhere along the line of distribution?
- Meeting a rival supplier's price?

The law wasn't designed to prevent buyers from getting lower prices based on more efficient distribution methods, so it contains a so-called cost-justification proviso exempting price differences based on cost savings. General Electric Co. spent $100,000 cost-justifying its quantity discount structure on radio and television tubes. Colgate-Palmolive Co. spent a similar amount justifying a new system of discounts on toilet articles. Both studies, in the form of thick books,

are gathering dust in corporate files just in case FTC raises a challenge.

Creative Accounting. The cost accounting necessary to meet FTC standards differ widely from that needed to keep ordinary business records. Yet there is no FTC-approved method of cost justification, so companies are forced to create their own.

The commission, in general, is highly critical of company cost allocation, making the defense practically useless to businessmen in formal proceedings, although cost studies have been useful in persuading the FTC staff not to bring a case. Frederick M. Rowe, a well-known and often critical legal expert on Robinson-Patman, calls the cost defense "a bonanza for accountants," but "fool's gold" for affluent respondents.

Figuring out whether a price reduction to one customer may hurt another can be a harrowing experience. Consider the case of a chemical company making vinyl acetate, which is used as a raw material in paint emulsions and has half a dozen other applications. One of the company's customers uses the raw material to make an acrylic emulsion; another uses it to make a polyvinyl acetate emulsion—both paint bases.

When one customer presses for a lower price on vinyl acetate, the question arises whether the supplier may give it to him without giving the same break to the other customer. Ultimately, this question boils down to whether acrylic-based paints compete with the polyvinyl acetate type; if they do, the favored customer would have an advantage over his rival. Multiply the soulsearching the chemical company must go through in this case by every product in its line, and you have a measure of the intricacy of Robinson-Patman.

It is similarly a tricky business to define the limits of the provision of the law allowing a supplier to cut his price to a customer if he does it "in good faith to meet an equally low price of a competitor." The acrobatics caused by this "meeting-competition" defense have filled volumes in FTC's files.

Take the hypothetical example of Oil Company A competing with Oil Company B in a local gasoline market, say, Norfolk, Va. If B lowers the wholesale price of gasoline to its service stations in the area, it sets off a chain reaction: B dealers lower retail prices, taking gallonage from A dealers. Stung by the loss, A's dealers complain. Discontented dealers, coupled with declining sales, give Company A a headache, but in the light of Robinson-Patman, what can A do?

Under company policy, A will not pick up the phone to ask competitors what they are charging, for this kind of discussion could lead to accusations of price-fixing. Thus, A faces a dilemma: It must learn what B's price is in order to cut its own price to protect injured dealers and, at the same time, prove it's meeting—but not beating—a lower price "in good faith."

So, A dons its Sherlock Holmes cap, and dispatches salesmen to ask B's dealers for a copy of their invoices. This may take two or three days, and dealers may be reluctant. By the time A has the documentation it needs, the price may have gone back up.

Volatility. These problems are common in the oil industry, and similar ones are faced in other industries where pricing is volatile. A food company lawyer laments that if his concern scrupulously followed the Robinson-Patman Act in a rapidly fluctuating market, "our computer would break down in protest."

The problem became so acute in gasoline marketing that FTC eventually abandoned half a dozen cases that had gone through long and costly hearings to embark on an industrywide approach. Now, 18 months have passed since FTC held comprehensive hearings to resolve

the problem, with testimony filling 1,030 pages—in fine print. Although many businessmen are waiting eagerly for solutions, FTC hasn't said a word about gasoline since.

III. Routes of Escape

While many businessmen complain about Robinson-Patman, others just ignore it. And the law's prolix provisions are easily avoided. A soap manufacturer concedes privately that it gets around the requirement of proportional promotional allowances by fashioning plans the smaller customers won't like and can't use. "Every once in a while I tell [company executives] they've got to throw in one [promotion] everybody will like," says the concern's lawyer. "Otherwise it'll look suspicious."

Painfully slow enforcement of the law expands the compliance gap. "By the time FTC uncoils itself and does something," a rubber-company attorney says, "it's at least four or five years, and that's little solace to the guy who's been done wrong." Four Justices of the Supreme Court roundly criticized FTC last term for conducting proceedings that wend their "leisurely way toward a wearying conclusion."

FTC Discord. And the credibility gap is widened by the open breach within FTC between Elman and the four other commissioners. Adding to the confusion, the Justice Dept., which long has shown an allergy to Robinson-Patman, often disagrees with the commission on its enforcement.

Besides invective, constructive alternatives to Robinson-Patman have been offered. The current Justice Dept. antitrust chief, Donald F. Turner, proposed a new price-discrimination law while he was teaching at Harvard University. More than a decade ago, the Attorney

General's National Committee to Study the Antitrust Laws suggested that Robinson-Patman difficulties might be eliminated by more sensible enforcement, but few agree on what this means and fewer believe FTC has achieved it. Recent attempts at industrywide enforcement, where the case-by-case method had broken down have met with little success so far.

Slim Chances. Despite the constant urgings of respectable jurists that the law be repealed, reassessed, or rewritten, mounting to a hue and cry in the statute's 30th year, there is little hope that it will be. For this there are a number of reasons:

Many businessmen would rather live with the known than take a chance on another congressional enactment. Many who would take that chance are reluctant to advocate revision openly, fearing their support would automatically taint the appeal with "big business" overtones. And, finally, chances are slim that any meaningful revision would be condoned by small-business advocates in Congress, even though "little business fellows" have been mauled by the backlash of FTC enforcement.

C

Social and Ethical Issues

30

What Are the Social and Ethical Responsibilities of Marketing Executives?

James M. Patterson

During most of its history business has not been greatly concerned over its social and ethical responsibilities. It has been criticized to some extent for its limited concern, but businessmen have seemed to assume that society expected business to produce the maximum amount of goods and services at the lowest cost and that society would be tolerant of its social and ethical behavior if it did that well. Basically, this was probably true when goods were in short supply and therefore highly prized. However, today we are entering a new era of relative plenty, and there are signs that society is raising its expectations of businessmen in these areas. They will do well to respond to these rising expectations. The following article discusses the guideposts that businessmen may follow in this somewhat trackless wilderness.

There is no specific, concrete guide to responsible action for marketing executives, beyond a sort of "watered-down" commercial version of the Golden Rule.

Reprinted by special permission from the *Journal of Marketing*, national quarterly publication of the American Marketing Association, Vol. 30, No. 3, July 1966, pp. 12–15.

Let us face the fact that the search for a general set of rules defining the social responsibilities of marketing is misguided in principle and doomed to fail.

Instead of asking, "What are the social responsibilities of marketing?", the question might better be, *"What workable guides are available to help a marketing executive to evaluate alternative courses of action in a specific concrete situation?"*

Responsible Actions

The really difficult problem of defining responsible marketing actions lies in those everyday marketing activities that raise simple questions of *equity, fairness,* and *morality*—not just questions of legality. To quote from Howard Bowen's classic questions about the responsibilities of businessmen,

> Should he conduct selling in ways that intrude on the privacy of people, for example, by door-to-door selling . . . ? Should he use methods involving ballyhoo, chances, prizes, hawking, and other tactics which are at least of doubtful good taste? Should he employ 'high pressure' tactics in persuading people to buy? Should he try to hasten the obsolescence of goods by bringing out an endless succession of new models and new styles? Should he appeal to and attempt to strengthen the motives of materialism, invidious consumption, and 'keeping up with the Joneses'?[1]

The marketing executive faces nagging questions, about the propriety of attempting to *manipulate* customers, and in particular of the ethics of using emotional and symbolic appeals in various forms of persuasive communication. The list of problems might go on and on, but these examples serve to suggest the type of marketing actions in question.

For those who would act responsibly, the answers to such questions are not at all clear-cut, with the "good guys" lined up on one side and the "bad guys" on the other. How, then, is the marketing executive who actually wishes to behave responsibly to find his way through the labyrinth of ethical and moral issues? Instead of trying to give general an-

[1] Howard R. Bowen, *Social Responsibilities of the Businessman* (New York: Harper and Brothers, 1953), p. 215.

swers to questions that have not yet been asked, the objective should be for the harassed marketing executive to frame his problem in such a way that he can solve it for himself.

Abstract general rules offer little or no guidance to a marketing executive to frame his problem in such a way that he can solve it for himself.

Abstract general rules offer little or no guidance to a marketing executive who is concerned about the quality of the tire he is forced to produce if he is to make a profit in the $12 price-line, or about the extent of headquarters intervention into the internal operations of his company's franchised dealers. What he needs is an approach, or way of thinking about these issues, which will help him to determine whether this particular decision with respect to product quality or that particular form of intervention is in some sense "wrong" or "unfair."

This search for the responsible course of action is not a problem unique to business and marketing. It is central to all areas of social thought and action. Consequently, the marketing executive might profitably borrow approaches and insights from other areas.

Three obviously relevant areas immediately come to mind: *ethics, law,* and *political theory*—ethics, because "right" conduct is a central concern; law, because it attempts to administer justice by means of specific case decisions; and political theory, because of its traditional concern with power and its regulation.

Ethics

As a branch of philosophy, ethics has been concerned for centuries with standards for decision-making and right conduct. Consequently, one would expect ethical writings to be an important source of guidance to the marketing executive in determining responsible courses of action.

Unfortunately, though, the connection between ethics and policy is not quite so clear-cut as one would wish. In fact, so long as ethics is looked to for answers, the decision-maker remains in the difficult position of having to apply abstract ethical principles to specific concrete situations which seldom if ever quite fit the general definition.

Take, for example, the moral commandment, "Thou shalt not steal." Is it stealing for a marketing executive to accept a gift from a supplier? The marketing executive is forced to resort to "common sense" to guide his decisions.

However, Wayne A. R. Leys, in an important book on ethics, argues that if policy-makers were to read philosophical ethics for critical or deliberative questions instead of conclusive answers, they would correct many sources of bad judgment.[2] He approaches ethics much as John Dewey did—not so much as a command to act in a certain way, but as a tool for analyzing a specific situation.[3] In other words, right and wrong should be determined by the total situation and not by the rule as such.

Here are some "deliberative questions," representative of those Leys derived from some of the different systems of philosophical ethics.

A. *Utilitarianism:*
  1. What are the probable consequences of alternative proposals?
  2. Which policy will result in the greatest possible happiness for the greatest number?
B. *Moral Idealism:*

1. Is the practice right? Is it just? Honest?
2. Does the policy put first things first?
3. Can you will that the maxim of your action should become the universal law?
4. Are you treating humanity as an end and not merely as a means?
C. *Instrumentalism:*
  1. What will relieve the conflicts and tensions of the situation?
  2. Does the proposed solution anticipate consequences in the larger environment as well as the immediate situation?

In effect, Leys would have us abandon the principles-approach in favor of the case-approach. This may not be bad advice. Perhaps if the marketing executive were to ask similar deliberative questions about a proposed policy, he too would find them of value in defining the responsible course of action. He might ask, for example, "Would it be desirable if *all* firms adopted this practice?"

Law

In his attempts to determine the responsible courses of action, the marketing executive should also consider law as a potential source of guidance.

In an important book, Edmond Cahn notes that judges, under the official guise of deciding technical legal issues, are frequently required to assess moral interests and to resolve problems of right and wrong.[4] Thus, he concludes that the great body of case law should be regarded as a rich repository of moral knowledge that is continually being reworked and refined.

One section of Cahn's book, dealing

[2] Wayne A. R. Leys, *Ethics for Policy Decision* (Englewood Cliffs, New Jersey: Prentice-Hall, Inc., 1952).

[3] John Dewey and Charles Tufts, *Ethics* (New York: Henry Holt and Co., 1932), p. 310.

[4] Edmond Cahn, *The Moral Decision* (Bloomington, Indiana: Indiana University Press, 1955).

with what he calls the "Radius of Loyalty" is especially relevant to the marketing executive in his search for workable guides to responsible action:

> The most valuable moral lesson the law can teach concerning loyalty (responsibility) is the lesson of relations. . . . The duty always remains a function of the relation. . . . By the same token, there can never arise in anyone's moral life an indefinite, unlimited duty of loyalty to any one creature or institution. Loyalty—however light or intense it may be—always has reference to a defined and specific relation. . . .[5]

Those familiar with the distinction between the liability of a common carrier, an ordinary bailee, and a trustee will recognize this "rational" principle in action. Perhaps this "lesson of relations" can also be applied to marketing.

Clearly a customer is related differently to a firm than is an employee, or a supplier, or even an audience-member who watches a sponsored television show. For that matter, even different customers are likely to have different relationships with a firm. If responsibility is in fact a function of a *specific relationship* involving a *specific kind of transaction*, then a more precise definition of the exact character of a customer-relationship might help to clear the air of nebulous admonitions to management to act responsibly.

Another approach for the marketing decision-maker was developed in an earlier book by Cahn.[6] In *The Sense of Injustice* he notes that over the years the frustrations attending the traditional search for abstract justice nearly led to its abandonment.[7] He further notes that were it not for the "sense of injustice" —that sympathetic reaction of outrage, horror, shock, resentment, and anger— society would be left entirely without empirical guidance in its search for a path to justice. He continues:

> Why do we speak of the "sense of injustice" rather than the "sense of justice"? Because "justice" has been so beclouded by natural law writings that it almost inevitably brings to mind some ideal relation or static condition or set of perceptual standards, while we are concerned with what is active, vital, and experiential in the reactions of human beings. Where justice is thought of in the customary manner as an ideal mode or condition, the human response will merely be contemplative, and contemplation bakes no loaves. But the response to a real or imagined instance of injustice is something quite different; it is alive with movement and warmth in the human organism.[8]

It follows that the responsible marketing action is the one that does not arouse the executive's "sense of injustice." Often when a time-worn trade practice is looked at in this light, one can see that it is not "fair," and this means that reform can be instituted. The change in the grading of items for export so that they now conform to domestic standards is a classic example of how an established practice is changed to reduce the "sense of injustice."

Political Theory

The third example comes from the area of political science.

[5] Same reference as footnote 4, at pp. 151–152.

[6] Edmond Cahn, *The Sense of Injustice* (Bloomington, Indiana: Indiana University Press, 1949).

[7] Same reference as footnote 6, at p. 13.

[8] Same reference as footnote 6, at p. 13.

Over the years political theorists have been concerned, among other things, with devising ways to subject potentially arbitrary power to the "Rule of Law," that is, to ensure that discretionary government power will be exercised responsibly.

Granting the differences in degree, this concern is quite similar to the concern of those who seek to ensure that discretionary market power will also be exercised responsibly. And it is demonstrable that *structural* limitations on potentially arbitrary power work better than *substantive* limitations.

Take, for example, the Anglo-American constitutional experience. Minimum reliance was placed on substantive limitations, that is, on generalized prescriptive commands of the "thou shall not" variety, while maximum reliance was put on an intricate set of structural "checks and balances."

Of course, there is a Bill of Rights; but much more important have been such structural limitations as the separation of certain key powers among the various branches of the federal government, the reservation of other powers to the several states, and the creation of a representative government which consciously reflects the variety and diversity of interests affected by governmental power. *In fact, the success of the Anglo-American experience is much more due to emphasis on structural rather than substantive limitations.*

The success of this structural approach argues strongly for its application in the realm of private power. Instead of attempting to specify elaborate codes of conduct, the wiser strategy would be to attempt to develop a set of structural limitations on private power, to ensure that it will be exercised responsibly, that is, in accordance with the legitimate purposes of society.

But this may not be as easy as it sounds. For example, the concept of separation of powers may have no application in the private sphere. And of course, it is not at all clear what structural forms are appropriate for recognizing the legitimate interests of the various constituencies affected by the firm's marketing decisions—or for that matter which constituencies ought even to be recognized.

Still, we are not entirely without structural precedent in the private sector. Several structural limitations have already been developed which give various constituent interests a "say" in the determination of those corporate policies which vitally affect their own interests. Collective bargaining, for example, structurally recognizes the interests of the employee constituency in corporate decisions relating to the terms and conditions of employment. Similarly, General Motors' dealer councils give structural recognition to the franchised dealer's interests in certain GM distribution policies.

But clearly the prime example of a structural limitation in the private sphere is *market competition*. Certainly competition is by far the most important and most pervasive structural limitation on the exercise of private market power.

And yet this is not an altogether effective limitation; and a certain amount of potentially arbitrary discretion remains. In fact, it is this element of freedom from competitive control that raises the whole problem of business responsibility in the first place.

Some Implications

If competition worked perfectly, by definition there would be no discretion in the marketplace, and therefore no need for the businessman to bother thinking about which course of action is the responsible one. However, an element of market power persists in all markets; and even the most vigorous enforcement of antitrust laws would be unlikely to increase the effectiveness of competition to the point where marketing decisions would be controlled in every detail.

Certainly attempts should be made to improve the performance of competition as a structural limitation on potentially arbitrary corporate discretion. In fact, effective competition is much to be preferred over substantive limitations in the form of government-imposed codes of conduct. The marketing executive ought to try to improve the effectiveness of *the structural limitations of competition,* simply to forestall potential impositions of *substantive limitations by government fiat!*

But even beyond improving market competition as a structural device for reflecting the interests of customers in the making of decisions more "responsible," nonmarket structural arrangements are needed to reflect those interests the market fails to register.

For instance, customers' interests in the firm's marketing decisions might be partially recognized by the voluntary appointment of a representative "Customer Review Board," which would consider and react to most proposed marketing decisions. At minimum, this would provide the firm with a useful

"sounding board" for testing proposed courses of action.

It might also be possible to select a representative sample from a firm's customer list, and then to use survey techniques to "tap" these customers' opinions as to contemplated marketing actions. This, too, would serve as a source of guidance in management's search for responsible marketing practice.

In neither case, however, would management be bound to abide by the opinions of the customer group. Still, if there were negative reactions from a representative group of customers, management would find this helpful.

The important point is that structural limitations on potentially arbitrary power have been so eminently successful in the public area that their application in the realm of private power deserves careful consideration.

This proposal for dealing with the problem of social and ethical responsibility in marketing has been a mere "prologue." The most important problems remain.

Clearly, the possibilities of developing new structural arrangements that will effectively recognize customers' legitimate interests in the marketing decisions of the firm have only begun to be explored. And of course, the actual workability of the ethical and political approaches in specific cases remains to be tested.

31

Shopper Is Damned . . .
in Grey Tints

E. B. Weiss

*Marketing is sure to be in the forefront of the developing con-
troversy over the ethical responsibilities of business, because
marketing is the point at which the business operation, with its
urge for profit, makes contact with the masses of consumers and
their desire for value at low price. This friction is productive of
many and serious ethical confrontations. The author of the accompanying article points out to businessmen that the past legalistic
approach will not be adequate to the changing circumstances.
The article is better at highlighting the problem than at indicating
its solution.*

In a Chinese "fortune" cookie, I found
a tiny strip of paper with the legend:
"The buyer needs 1,000 eyes, the seller
not one."

Today's shopper has less need today
for 1,000 eyes as protection against outright fraud. But "fine-type" evasions of
simple business ethics, which are now
the great shopper puzzlement, are common enough to make 1,000 eyes quite
handy. Indeed, "grey-area" marketing
practices are more prevalent than ever
before in the history of modern marketing.

For many years, marketing has believed—or professed to believe—that
"Let the buyer beware" had been more
or less decently interred decades ago.

So today we have Truth-in-Packaging
—Truth-in-Credit—the whole "protect-
the-consumer" movement. The Federal

Reprinted from *Marketing Insights*, Vol. 1,
No. 4, October 24, 1966; Advertising Publications, Inc., Chicago, by special permission.

Trade Commission continues to hand
down cease-and-desist orders—and the
Better Business Bureaus, if compelled to
assess the net result of years of policing,
might be induced to confess that "business" really is not very much "better."

It is true that out-and-out fraud is not
remotely as prevalent in marketing as it
was years ago. But whatever vacuum its
departure created has been amply filled
by "grey-area" marketing practices.

Ironically, decades ago the clear-cut
frauds were rarely perpetrated by the
corporate giants of yesteryear. These
frauds were almost exclusive with industry's petty riff-raff. Today, however,
legally correct, but ethically dubious
marketing practices seem to have become
almost the hallmark of our large consumer goods manufacturers.

Yet, top management in most of our
consumer goods corporate giants is not
merely keenly aware of its modern social
responsibilities—it tends to be acutely

conscious of its social obligations in a sophisticated society.

For example, Lammot du Pont Copeland, president of E. I. DuPont de Nemours & Co., recently said:

> Management, it seems to me, must reach for a balanced solution within the framework of one unassailable precept; business is a means to an end for society and not an end in itself, and therefore business must act in concert with a broad public interest and serve objectives of mankind and society, or it will not survive.

In speech after speech in recent months executives have urged their associates to take a more active role in politics and civic affairs, to join the war against poverty, to improve relations with government, academic circles and students. The social responsibility theme seems suddenly to have gathered a steamroller momentum. A new generation of corporate managers—many of them self-critical of past performances—envisions a wider role for business than has been traditional.

"Legality" Is a Panacea

New attitudes in the business community, which many observers believe are belated, appear to be designed to avoid what could be a collision between the forces created by the vast postwar technological advances, the new economics, the expanding role of government, the new and still growing sophistication of our society and finally, the so-called "campus revolt" which has been underscored by the evident decision of large segments of the student body to avoid business in its future life.

The increasing social awareness of our sophisticated society with respect to business practice (and especially on campus where employment in business

has lost much of its lure) makes it essential that business take ever greater strides to demonstrate its responsible and progressive involvement in the life of the nation, and the world. But in some instances, the new corporate philosophy has yet to percolate down to marketing. In marketing, the too common tendency is to ask: "Is it legal?" If the answer is affirmative—then presumably marketing has demonstrated its responsibility to society.

Recently, the New York Times asked 52 leading executives to express their views on these matters. The sampling found every executive who replied emphatic in stating his belief that business had a social responsibility beyond providing quality goods and services to consumers. But in the area of marketing, management's directives have tended to equate "social responsibility" with "legality." The legal department thus has become the arbiter of "social responsibility" in its relationship to marketing programs.

This was—and is—an essential first step. But it is only a first step. And because the necessary additional steps have been taken in some corporations, the marketing function continues to limit its "social responsibility" to an answer to the question: "Is it legal?"

In the Journal of Marketing, James M. Patterson, in an article significantly entitled, "What Are the Social and Ethical Responsibilities of Marketing Executives?" wrote the following opening sentence: "There is no specific, concrete guide to responsible action for marketing executives, beyond a sort of 'watered-down' commercial version of the Golden Rule."

That is precisely why marketing will now have to keep a wary eye on the proposals for new Truth-in-Marketing legislation. Clearly, marketing is now confronted with the spreading ramifications of the protect-the-consumer movement which, in time, will lead to still more legislation restricting market practices.

Directives Needed

In brief, a sophisticated society is now just beginning to say to the top management of consumer goods corporations: "Elimination of marketing frauds is no longer adequate implementation of social responsibility. Now you must eliminate the 'grey areas' of marketing practice. This is your new social responsibility—and a social responsibility that the more sophisticated segments of our younger generations are seriously concerned with."

Where downright fraud is involved, stringent laws now offer reasonably effective protection for the unwary as well as the wary. But what about those grey areas between fraud and the golden rule—between what is legally permissible and what is morally and ethically wrong? It is for this vast and growing grey marketing area that management must evolve and issue socially responsible directives.

Practices subtly devised to operate within these grey areas seldom break laws (although this will change as laws are passed to shield the public against credit malpractices, against package malpractices, etc.). But they are now as inimical to the public weal as was outright fraud in the days when marketing's robber barons rode high, wide, and handsome.

A Marketing Strait Jacket

History records the incident of a medieval butcher being paraded through the streets for selling wormy meat, his face close to a horse's tail. But today's common practice of hiding a 12% to 14% instalment loan rate behind a semantic camouflage that makes it appear to be 6% invited few reprisals—until recently when "truth in credit" became an issue.

"A New England conscience," a friend from that part of the country once explained to me, "rarely keeps a man from doing what he knows he shouldn't do—it simply prevents him from enjoying it as much." However, easy conscience in marketing is not at all a New England exclusive.

There is a decided tendency in marketing to use the words "legal" and "honest" interchangeably. When the marketing executive says that most marketing programs are "honest," what he really means is that most marketing programs operate within the law. But legality is no longer the major concern in marketing. The moral law is now the great issue in marketing!

If marketing does not exercise a greater degree of statesmanship, then marketing will ultimately put itself into a regulatory strait jacket as rigidly confining as that which restricts banking, the railroads, and our utilities.

Marketing, today, is in process of becoming a quasi-utility! Only enlightened statesmanship can enable marketing to avoid the legislative strangulation that is the typical lot of the quasi-utility.

Significantly, the National Industrial Conference Board—an industry-financed study group not especially noted for a deep concern with the public weal—published a presumably objective analysis of business morality, as differentiated from conformance with the letter of the law. In the board's report, such incriminating comments as the following appear:

> Over 95% of the companies surveyed do not use any special means to detect departures from expected standards of business conduct by employees. . . .

A frequently expressed reason for not making a special effort to uncover unethical behavior is the difficulty of doing so. As a rubber company executive puts it: "We believe, so long as we must depend on humans, that there is no procedure or series of controls which will automatically prevent or uncover unethical practices!"

Three-fifths of the cooperating companies report that they have not issued general written statements of ethical principles to guide employees in the conduct of company business. There may not be a dozen corporations that have laid down a truly modern, socially responsible code of marketing ethics—as differentiated from a legal code.

Execs Set Company Morals

Business management holds some naive notions on this subject. For example, that same NICB report notes: ". . . the moral tone of the corporation, as set by the actions of its top executives, is the most important single determinant of employe ethics. Employes soon know what kind of a company they are working for, and behave accordingly in the public interest."

That, of course, assumes an unimpeachable degree of integrity at the highest management level as well as at the marketing level. That is a pretty big assumption—especially in a competitive society.

It is entirely obvious that the merchants of trash, who still dominate tv programing, act as if the public interest did not exist. Their policy is one of the viewer be damned.

In the grey area of marketing practice, too often the attitude is the shopper be damned.

Politicians may be more interested in the vote-getting appeal of shopper unrest than in the merits of their complaints. But politicians do know that the consumer is restless. This is the crux of the matter. Unfortunately, this incipient revolt by the shopper has been more impressed on the minds of politicians than on the minds of too many marketing executives.

The intelligent consumer does not deny that he is healthier and more comfortable than at any time in history. But the shopper tends also to be aware that technological change, and the growing complexities of living, are making it increasingly difficult to buy wisely. And shoppers are clearly showing signs of resenting the hurdles placed in their shopping path by grey-area marketing practices.

Major segments of the public are now unquestionably more adept at spotting outright frauds. But the race between sophisticated unethical marketing and the sophistication of the shopper still gives marketing the inside track.

And recognition of this blunt fact is directly responsible for the emergence of protect-the-consumer legislation—marketing's handwriting on the wall.

Supporting evidence comes from a citadel of business conservatism—the Harvard Business Review. An article in that publication includes this pungent conclusion: "The philosophy of the day, in considering borderline cases involving public taste, fair dealing, and full and accurate information, too often seems to be: 'This is the deal—can we get away with it?'"

"Can we get away with it?" does not refer to the legal aspects of marketing. Not at all. The reference is to marketing practices whose ethics or morality may be questionable. Well, a more sophisticated society, especially the younger and better educated segments, is now beginning to say: "That is not a modern concept of social responsibility." The voice of the young, intelligent consumer is rising in the land. It cannot be squelched—and this is "his master's voice" for marketing. And if marketing doesn't hearken, Congress and state legislatures most certainly will.

D

Fashion

32

Readings on Fashion

Edward Sapir

One of the pervasive and growing forces in present-day marketing is fashion. We tend to think of fashion in terms of clothing, because it is here that fashion reaches its pinnacle. However, a moment's thought will show that fashion today permeates almost all goods and services which consumers buy, and even invades the field of industrial goods. Consider, for example, the fashion changes in pots and pans—from enamel to cast aluminum, to drawn aluminum, to copper-bottomed, to copper-covered—without any real functional difference. Also, a comparison of machine tools will often show little difference but streamlining. Here, then, is a tremendous force that influences business decisions in countless ways, yet it is only superficially understood by businessmen and scholars. In the following article an eminent sociologist discusses fashion and custom, the background social force within which fashion operates.

Custom

The word *custom* is used to apply to the totality of behavior patterns which are carried by tradition and lodged in the group, as contrasted with the more random personal activities of the individual. It is not properly applicable to those aspects of communal activity which are obviously determined by biological

Reprinted by permission of The Macmillan Company from The *Encyclopaedia of Social Sciences*, Vol. 4, pp. 658–662, and Volume 6, pp. 139–144. Copyright (Vol. 4) 1959, (Vol. 6) 1960, by The Macmillan Company.

considerations. The habit of eating fried chicken is a custom, but the biologically determined habit of eating is not.

Custom is a variable common sense concept which has served as the matrix for the development of the more refined and technical anthropological concept of culture. It is not as purely denotative and objective a term as culture and has a slightly affective quality indicated by the fact that one uses it more easily to refer to geographically remote, to primitive or to bygone societies than to one's own. When applied to the behavior of one's own group the term is usually limited to relatively unimportant and unformalized behavior patterns which lie between individual habits and social institutions. Cigarette smoking is more readily called a custom than is the trial of criminals in court. However, in dealing with contemporary Chinese civilization, with early Babylonian culture or with the life of a primitive Australian tribe the functional equivalent of such a cultural pattern as our court trial is designated as custom. The hesitation to describe as custom any type of behavior in one's own group that is not at once collective and devoid of major importance is perhaps due to the fact that one involuntarily prefers to put the emphasis either on significant individualism, in which case the word habit is used, or on a thoroughly rationalized and formalized collective intention, in which case the term institution seems in place.

Custom is often used interchangeably with convention, tradition and mores, but the connotations are not quite the same. Convention emphasizes the lack of inner necessity in the behavior pattern and often implies some measure of agreement, express or tacit, that a certain mode of behavior be accepted as proper. The more symbolic or indirect the function of a custom, the more readily is it referred to as a convention. It is a custom to write with pen and ink; it is a convention to use a certain kind of paper in formal correspondence. Tradition emphasizes the historic background of custom. No one accuses a community of being wanting in customs and conventions, but if these are not felt as possessed of considerable antiquity a community is said to have few if any traditions. The difference between custom and tradition is more subjective than objective, for there are few customs whose complete explanation in terms of history does not take one back to a remote antiquity. The term mores is best reserved for those customs which con-

note fairly strong feelings of the rightness or wrongness of modes of behavior. The mores of a people are its unformulated ethics as seen in action. Such terms as custom, institution, convention, tradition and mores are, however, hardly capable of a precise scientific definition. All of them are reducible to social habit or, if one prefers the anthropological to the psychological point of view, to cultural pattern. Habit and culture are terms which can be defined with some degree of precision and should always be substituted for custom in strictly scientific discourse, habit or habit system being used when the locus of behavior is thought of as residing in the individual, cultural pattern or culture when its locus is thought of as residing in society.

From a biological standpoint all customs are in origin individual habits which have become diffused in society through the interaction of individual upon individual. These diffused or socialized habits, however, tend to maintain themselves because of the unbroken continuity of the diffusion process from generation to generation. One more often sees custom helping to form individual habit than individual habit being made over into custom. In the main, group psychology takes precedence over individual psychology. In no society, however primitive or remote in time, are the interactions of its members not controlled by a complex network of custom. Even at an early stage of the palaeolithic period human beings must have been ruled by custom to a very considerable extent, as is shown by the rather sharply delimited types of artifacts that were made and the inferences that can be drawn from some of these as to beliefs and attitudes.

The crystallization of individual habit into custom is a process that can be followed out theoretically rather more easily than illustrated in practice. A distinction can be made between customs of long tenure and customs of short tenure generally known as fashions. Fashions are set by a specific individual or group of individuals. When they have had a long enough lease of life to make it seem unimportant to recall the source or original locality of the behavior pattern, they have become customs. The habit of wearing a particular style of hat is a fashion subject to fairly rapid change. In the sphere of language custom is generally referred to as usage. Uncrystallized usages of speech are linguistic fashions, of which slang forms a particular variety. Food habits too form a well recognized set of customs, within which arise human variations that may be called fashions of food and that tend to die out after a brief period. Fashions are not to be considered as additions to custom but rather as experimental variations of the fundamental themes of custom.

In course of time isolated behavior patterns of a customary nature tend to group themselves into larger configurations which have a formal cohesion and which tend to be rationalized as functional units whether they are such historically or not. The whole history of culture has been little more than a ceaseless effort to connect originally independent modes of behavior into larger systems and to justify the secondary culture complexes by an unconscious process of rationalization. An excellent example of such a culture complex, which derives its elements from thousands of disparate customs, is the modern musical system, which is undoubtedly felt by those who make use of it to be a well compacted functional whole with various elements that are functionally interdependent. Historically, however, it is very easy to prove that the system of musical notation, the rules of harmony, the instrumental techniques, the patterns of musical composition and the conventional uses of particular instruments for

specific purposes are independently derivable from customs of very different provenience and of very different age, and that it is only by slow processes of transfer of use and progressive integration of all these socialized modes of behavior that they have come to help each other out in a complex system of unified meanings. Hundreds of parallel instances could be given from such diverse fields of social activity as language, architecture, political organization, industrial technique, religion, warfare and social etiquette.

The impermanence of custom is a truism. Belief in the rapidity of change of custom is exaggerated, however, because it is precisely the comparatively slight divergences from what is socially established that arouse attention. A comparison of American life today with the life of a mediaeval English town would in the larger perspective of cultural anthropology illustrate rather the relative permanence of culture than its tendency to change.

The disharmony which cumulatively results from the use of tools, insights or other manipulative types of behavior which had enriched the cultural stock in trade of society a little earlier results in change of custom. The introduction of the automobile, for instance, was not at first felt as necessarily disturbing custom, but in the long run all those customs appertaining to visiting and other modes of disposing of one's leisure time have come to be seriously modified by the automobile as a power contrivance. Amenities of social intercourse felt to be obstructive to the free utilization of this new source of power tend to be dismissed or abbreviated. Disharmony resulting from the rise of new values also makes for change in custom. For example, the greater freedom of manner of the modern woman as contrasted with the far more conventionally circumscribed conduct of women of generations ago has come about because of the rise of a new attitude toward woman and her relation to man. The influences exerted by foreign peoples, e.g., the introduction of tea and coffee in occidental society and the spread of parliamentary government from country to country, are stressed by anthropologists more than by the majority of historians and sociologists as determinants of change. Most popular examples of the imposition of fashions which proceed from strategic personalities are probably fanciful and due to a desire to dramatize the operation of the more impersonal factors, which are much more important in the aggregate than the specific personal ones. With the gradual spread of a custom that is largely symbolic and characteristic of a selected portion of the population, the fundamental reason for its continuance weakens, so that it either dies out or takes on an entirely new function. This mechanism is particularly noteworthy in the life of language. Locutions which are considered smart or chic because they are the property of privileged circles are soon taken up by the masses and then die because of their banality. A much more powerful and exact knowledge of the nature of individual interaction, particularly as regards the unconscious transfer of feeling, is needed before a really satisfying theory of cultural change can be formulated.

Those customs survive the longest which either correspond to so basic a human need that they cannot well be seriously changed or else are of such a nature that they can easily be functionally reinterpreted. An example of the former type of persistence is the custom of having a mother suckle her child. There are numerous departures from this rule, yet both modern America and the more primitive tribes preserve as a custom a mode of behavior which obviously lies close to the life of man in nature. An example of the latter type of persistence, which may be called adaptive persistence, is language, which tends to remain fairly true to set form but which is constantly undergoing reinterpretation in accordance with the demands of the civilization which it serves. For example, the word robin refers in the United States to a very different bird from the English bird that was originally meant. The word could linger on with a modified meaning because it is a symbol and therefore capable of indefinite reinterpretation.

The word survival should not be used for a custom having a clearly defined function which can be shown to be different from its original place and significance in culture. When used in the latter, looser sense the word survival threatens to lose all useful meaning. There are few customs among us today which are not survivals in this sense. There are, however, certain customs which it is difficult to rationalize on any count and which may be looked upon as analogous to rudimentary organs in biology. The useless buttons in modern clothing are often cited as an example of such survivals. The use of Roman numerals alongside of Arabic numerals may also be considered a survival. On the whole, however, it seems safest not to use the word too freely, for it is difficult to prove that any custom, no matter how apparently lacking in utility or how far removed from its original application, is entirely devoid of at least symbolic meaning.

Custom is stronger and more persistent in primitive than in modern societies. The primitive group is smaller, so that a greater degree of conformity is psychologically necessary. In the more sophisticated community, which numbers a far larger total of individuals, departure from custom on the part of a few selected individuals, who may in turn prove instrumental for a change of culture in the community at large, does not matter so much for the solidarity of the group to begin with, because the chance individual of the group finds himself reinforced by the vast majority of his fellow men and can do without the further support of the deviants. The primitive community has also no written tradition to appeal to as an impersonal arbiter in matters of custom and therefore puts more energy into the conservation of what is transmitted through activity and oral tradition. The presence of documents relieves the individual from the necessity of taking personal responsibility for the perpetuation of custom. Far too great stress is usually laid on the actually conserving, as contrasted with the symbolically conserving, power of the written word. Custom among primitive peoples is apt to derive some measure of sacredness from its association with magical and religious procedures. When a certain type of activity is linked with a ritual which is in turn apt to be associated with a legend that to the native mind explains the activity in question, a radical departure from the traditionally conserved pattern of behavior is felt as blasphemous or perilous to the safety of the group. There is likewise a far lesser division of labor in primitive communities than in our own, which means that the forces making for experimentation in the solution of technical problems are proportionately diminished.

In the modern world custom tends to be much more conservative in the rural districts than in the city, and the reasons are similar to those given for the greater persistence of custom among primitive peoples. The greater scatter of the rural population does not generally mean the more intensive individual cultivation of the forms of custom but rather a compensatory effort to correct the threats of distance by conformity.

Within a complex community, such as is found in modern cities, custom tends to be more persistent on the whole in the less sophisticated groups. Much depends on the symbolism of a custom. There are certain types of custom, particularly such as are symbolic of status, which tend to be better conserved in the more sophisticated or wealthy groups than in the less sophisticated. The modern American custom, for instance, of having a married woman keep her maiden name is not likely soon to take root among the very wealthy, who here join hands with the unsophisticated majority, while the custom is being sparsely diffused among the intellectual middle class.

The varying degrees of conservatism in regard to custom can be illustrated in the behavior of a single individual because of the different types of social participation into which he enters. In England, for instance, the same individual may be in the vanguard of custom as a Londoner but insistent on the preservation of rural custom as a country squire. An American university man may be disdainful of customary opinion in his faculty club but be meekly observant of religious custom on Sunday at church. Loyalty or departure from custom is not a simple function of temperament or personality but part and parcel of the symbolism of multiple participation in society.

Custom is generally referred to as constraining force. The conflict of individual will and social compulsion is familiar, but even the most forceful and self-assertive individual needs to yield to custom at most points in order that he may gain leverage, as it were, for the imposition of his personal will on society, which cannot be conquered without the implicit capture of social consent. The freedom gained by the denial of custom is essentially a subjective freedom of escape rather than effective freedom of conquest. Custom makes for a powerful economy in the learning of the individual; it is a symbolic affirmation of the solidarity of the group. A by-product of these fundamental functions of custom is the more sentimental value which results from an ability to link the present and the past and thus to establish a larger ego in time, which supplements with its authority the larger ego represented by the community as it functions in the present.

The formulation of customs in the sphere of the rights and duties of individuals in their manifold relations leads to law. It is not useful to use the term law, as is often vaguely done in dealing with primitive societies, unless the enforcement of customary activity be made explicit, being vested in particular individuals or bodies of individuals. There are no societies that are wholly free from the binding force of implicit law, but as there are also many primitive societies which recognize some type of legal procedure it seems much better to speak of law only in the latter case. There are, for instance, few American Indian tribes in which customary obligations are recognized as a system of law that is capable of enforcement by the community. Psychologically law prevails, but not institutionally. This is in rather sharp contrast to the legal procedure which has been developed by the majority of African tribes. Here there is not merely the law of custom in an implicit sense but the perfectly explicit recognition of rules of conduct and of punishment for their infringement, with an elaborate method of discovering guilt and with the power of inflicting punishment vested in the king. The example of African law indicates that the essential difference between custom and law does not lie in the difference between oral tradition and the written formulation of custom. Law can emerge from custom long before the development of writing and has demonstrably done so in numerous cases. When custom has the psychological compulsion of law but is not controlled by society through the imposition of explicit penalties it may be called ethics or, more primitively,

mores. It is difficult to distinguish law and ethics in the more simple forms of society. Both emerge from custom but in a somewhat divergent manner. Mundane or human sovereignty becomes progressively distinguished from socially diffused or supernatural or impersonal sovereignty. Custom controlled by the former is law; custom controlled by the latter is ethics.

The agencies instrumental in the formation of custom are for the most part quite impersonal in character and implicit in the mere fact of human interrelationships. There are also more self-conscious agencies for the perpetuation of custom. Among these the most important are law and religion, the latter particularly in the form of an organized church and priesthood. There are also organizations which are sentimentally interested in the conservation of customs which threaten to go out of use. In the modern world one often sees a rather weak nationalistic cause bolstered up by the somewhat artificial fostering of archaic custom. Much of the ritualism of the modern Scottish clans is secondarily rather than lineally conservative.

If complicated forms of conscious manipulation of ideas and techniques which rule the modern world are excluded from the range of the term custom, the force of custom may be said to be gradually lessening. The factors which favor this weakening of custom are: the growing division of labor with its tendency to make society less and less homogeneous; the growing spirit of rationalism, in the light of which much of the justification of custom fades way; the growing tendency to break away from local tradition; and, finally, the greater store set by individuality. The ideal which is latent in the modern mind would seem to be to break up custom into the two poles of individually determined habit on the one hand and of large scale institutional planning for the major enterprises of mankind on the other.

Fashion

The meaning of the term fashion may be clarified by pointing out how it differs in connotation from a number of other terms whose meaning it approaches. A particular fashion differs from a given taste in suggesting some measures of compulsion on the part of the group as contrasted with individual choice from among a number of possibilities. A particular choice may of course be due to a blend of fashion and taste. Thus, if bright and simple colors are in fashion, one may select red as more pleasing to one's taste than yellow, although one's free taste unhampered by fashion might have decided in favor of a more subtle tone. To the discriminating person the demand of fashion constitutes a challenge to taste and suggests problems of reconciliation. But fashion is accepted by average people with little demur and is not so much reconciled with taste as substituted for it. For many people taste hardly arises at all except on the basis of a clash of an accepted fashion with a fashion that is out of date or current in some other group than one's own.

The term fashion may carry with it a tone of approval or disapproval. It is a fairly objective term whose emotional qualities depend on a context. A moralist may decry a certain type of behavior as a mere fashion but the ordinary person will not be displeased if he is accused of being in the fashion. It is different with fads, which are objectively similar to fashions but differ from them in being more personal in their application and in connoting a more or less definite social disapproval. Particular people or coteries have their fads, while fashions are the property of larger or more representative groups. A taste which asserts itself in

spite of fashion and which may therefore be suspected of having something obsessive about it may be referred to as an individual fad. On the other hand, while a fad may be of very short duration, it always differs from a true fashion in having something unexpected, irresponsible or bizarre about it. Any fashion which sins against one's sense of style and one's feeling for the historical continuity of style is likely to be dismissed as a fad. There are changing fashions in tennis rackets, while the game of mah jong, once rather fashionable, takes on in retrospect more and more the character of a fad.

Just as the weakness of fashion leads to fads, so its strength comes from custom. Customs differ from fashions in being relatively permanent types of social behavior. They change, but with a less active and conscious participation of the individual in the change. Custom is the element of permanence which makes changes in fashion possible. Custom marks the highroad of human interrelationships, while fashion may be looked upon as the endless departure from and return to the highroad. The vast majority of fashions are relieved by other fashions, but occasionally a fashion crystallizes into permanent habit, taking on the character of custom.

It is not correct to think of fashion as merely a short-lived innovation in custom, because many innovations in human history arise with the need for them and last as long as they are useful or convenient. If, for instance, there is a shortage of silk and it becomes customary to substitute cotton for silk in the manufacture of certain articles of dress in which silk has been the usual material, such an enforced change of material, however important economically or aesthetically, does not in itself constitute a true change of fashion. On the other hand, if cotton is substituted for silk out of free choice as a symbol perhaps of the simple life or because of a desire to see what novel effect can be produced in accepted types of dress with simpler materials, the change may be called one of fashion. There is nothing to prevent an innovation from eventually taking on the character of a new fashion. If, for example, people persist in using the cotton material even after silk has once more become available, a new fashion has arisen.

Fashion is custom in the guise of departure from custom. Most normal individuals consciously or unconsciously have the itch to break away in some measure for a too literal loyalty to accepted custom. They are not fundamentally in revolt from custom but they wish somehow to legitimize their personal deviation without laying themselves open to the charge of insensitiveness to good taste or good manners. Fashion is the discreet solution of the subtle conflict. The slight changes from the established in dress or other forms of behavior seem for the moment to give the victory to the individual, while the fact that one's fellows revolt in the same direction gives one a feeling of adventurous safety. The personal note which is at the hidden core of fashion becomes super-personalized.

Whether fashion is felt as a sort of socially legitimized caprice or is merely a new and unintelligible form of social tyranny depends on the individual or class. It is probable that those most concerned with the setting and testing of fashions are the individuals who realize most keenly the problem of reconciling individual freedom with social conformity which is implicit in the very fact of fashion. It is perhaps not too much to say that most people are at least partly sensitive to this aspect of fashion and are secretly grateful for it. A large minority of people, however, are insensitive to the psychological complexity of fashion and submit to it to the extent that they do merely because they realize that not to fall in with it would be to declare themselves members of a past generation or dull people who cannot keep up with their neighbors. These latter reasons for being fashionable are secondary; they are sullen surrenders to bastard custom.

The fundamental drives leading to the creation and acceptance of fashion can be isolated. In the more sophisticated societies boredom, created by leisure and too highly specialized forms of activity, leads to restlessness and curiosity. This general desire to escape from the trammels of a too regularized existence is powerfully reenforced by a ceaseless desire to add to the attractiveness of the self and all other objects of love and friendship. It is precisely in functionally powerful societies that the individual's ego is constantly being convicted of helplessness. The individual tends to be unconsciously thrown back on himself and demands more and more novel affirmations of his effective reality. The endless rediscovery of the self in a series of petty truancies from the official socialized self becomes a mild obsession of the normal individual in any society in which the individual has ceased to be a measure of the society itself. There is, however, always the danger of too great a departure from the recognized symbols of the individual, because his identity is likely to be destroyed. That is why insensitive people, anxious to be literally in the fashion, so often overreach themselves and nullify the very purpose of fashion. Good hearted women of middle age generally fail in the art of being ravishing nymphs.

Somewhat different from the affirmation of the libidinal self is the more vulgar desire for prestige or notoriety, satisfied by changes in fashion. In this category belongs fashion as an outward emblem of personal distinction or of membership in some group to which distinction is ascribed. The imitation of fashion by people who belong to circles removed from those which set the fashion has the function of bridging the gap between a social class and the class next above it. The logical result of the acceptance of a fashion by all members of society is the disappearance of the kinds of satisfaction responsible for the change of fashion in the first place. A new fashion becomes psychologically necessary, and thus the cycle of fashion is endlessly repeated.

Fashion is emphatically a historical concept. A specific fashion is utterly unintelligible if lifted out of its place in a sequence of forms. It is exceedingly dangerous to rationalize or in any other way psychologize a particular fashion on the basis of general principles which might be considered applicable to the class of forms of which it seems to be an example. It is utterly vain, for instance, to explain particular forms of dress or types of cosmetics or methods of wearing the hair without a preliminary historical critique. Bare legs among modern women in summer do not psychologically or historically create at all the same fashion as bare legs and bare feet among primitives living in the tropics. The importance of understanding fashion historically should be obvious enough when it is recognized that the very essence of fashion is that it be valued as a variation in an understood sequence, as a departure from the immediately preceding mode.

Changes in fashion depend on the prevailing culture and on the social ideals which inform it. Under the apparently placid surface of culture there are always powerful psychological drifts of which fashion is quick to catch the direction. In a democratic society, for instance, if there is an unacknowledged drift toward class distinctions fashion will discover endless ways of giving it visible form. Criticism can always be met

by the insincere defense that fashion is merely fashion and need not be taken seriously. If in a puritanic society there is a growing impatience with the outward forms of modesty, fashion finds it easy to minister to the demands of sex curiosity, while the old mores can be trusted to defend fashion with an affection of unawareness of what fashion is driving at. A complete study of the history of fashion would undoubtedly throw much light on the ups and downs of sentiment and attitude at various periods of civilization. However, fashion never permanently outruns discretion and only those who are taken in by the superficial rationalization of fashion are surprised by the frequent changes of face in its history. That there was destined to be a lengthening of women's skirts after they had become short enough was obvious from the outset to all except those who do not believe that sex symbolism is a real factor in human behavior.

The chief difficulty of understanding fashion in its apparent vagaries is the lack of exact knowledge of the unconscious symbolisms attaching to forms, colors, textures, postures and other expressive elements in a given culture. The difficulty is appreciably increased by the fact that the same expressive elements tend to have quite different symbolic references in different areas. Gothic type, for instance, is a nationalistic token in Germany, while in Anglo-Saxon culture the practically identical type known as Old English has entirely different connotations. In other words, the same style of lettering may symbolize either an undying hatred of France or a wistful look backward at madrigals and pewter.

An important principle in the history of fashion is that those features of fashion which do not configurate correctly with the unconscious system of meanings characteristic of the given culture are relatively insecure. Extremes of style, which too frankly symbolize the current of feeling of the moment, are likely to find themselves in exposed positions, as it were, where they can be outflanked by meanings which they do not wish to recognize. Thus, it may be conjectured that lipstick is less secure in American culture as an element of fashion than rouge discreetly applied to the cheek. This is assuredly not due to a superior sinfulness of lipstick as such, but to the fact that rosy cheeks resulting from a healthy natural life in the country are one of the characteristic fetishisms of the traditional ideal of feminine beauty, while lipstick has rather the character of certain exotic ardors and goes with flaming oriental stuffs. Rouge is likely to last for many decades or centuries because there is, and is likely to be for a long time to come, a definite strain of nature worship in our culture. If lipstick is to remain it can only be because our culture will have taken on certain violently new meanings which are not at all obvious at the present time. As a symbol it is episodic rather than a part of the underlying rhythm of the history of our fashions.

In custom bound cultures, such as are characteristic of the primitive world, there are slow non-reversible changes of style rather than the often reversible forms of fashion found in modern cultures. The emphasis in such societies is on the group and the sanctity of tradition rather than on individual expression, which tends to be entirely unconscious. In the great cultures of the Orient and in ancient and mediaeval Europe changes in fashion can be noted radiating from certain definite centers of sophisticated culture, but it is not until modern Europe is reached that the familiar merry-go-round of fashion with its rapid alterations of season occurs.

The typically modern acceleration of changes in fashion may be ascribed to the influence of the Renaissance, which awakened a desire for innovation and which powerfully extended for European society the total world of possible choices. During this period Italian culture came to be the arbiter of taste, to be followed by French culture, which may still be looked upon as the most powerful influence in the creation and distribution of fashions. But more important than the Renaissance in the history of fashion is the effect of the industrial revolution and the rise of the common people. The former increased the mechanical ease with which fashions could be diffused; the latter greatly increased the number of those willing and able to be fashionable.

Modern fashion tends to spread to all class of society. As fashion has always tended to be a symbol of membership in a particular social class and as human beings have always felt the urge to edge a little closer to a class considered superior to their own, there must always have been the tendency for fashion to be adopted by circles which had a lower status than the group setting the fashions. But on the whole such adoption of fashion from above tended to be discreet because of the great importance attached to the maintenance of social classes. What has happened in the modern world, regardless of the official forms of government which prevail in the different nations, is that the tone-giving power which lies back of fashion has largely slipped away from the aristocracy of rank to the aristocracy of wealth. This means a psychological if not an economic leveling of classes because of the feeling that wealth is an accidental or accreted quality of an individual as contrasted with blood. In an aristocracy of wealth everyone, even the poorest, is potentially wealthy both in legal theory and in private fancy. In such a society, therefore, all individuals are equally entitled, it is felt, so far as their pockets permit, to the insignia of fashion. This universalizing of fashion necessarily cheapens its value in the specific case and forces an abnormally rapid change of fashion. The only effective protection possessed by the wealthy in the world of fashion is the insistence on expensive materials in which fashion is to express itself. Too great an insistence on this factor, however, is the hall mark of wealthy vulgarity, for fashion is essentially a thing of forms and symbols, not of material values.

Perhaps the most important of the special factors which encourage the spread of fashion today is the increased facility for the production and transportation of goods and for communication either personally or by correspondence from the centers of fashion to the outmost periphery of the civilized world. These increased facilities necessary lead to huge capital investments in the manufacture and distribution of fashionable wear. The extraordinarily high initial profits to be derived from fashion and the relatively rapid tapering off of profits make it inevitable that the natural tendency to change in fashion is helped along by commercial suggestion. The increasingly varied activities of modern life also give greater opportunity for the growth and change of fashion. Today the cut of a dress or the shape of a hat stands ready to symbolize anything from mountain climbing or military efficiency through automobiling to interpretative dancing and veiled harlotry. No individual is merely what his social role indicates that he is to be or may vary only slightly from, but he may act as if he is anything else that individual phantasy may dictate. The greater leisure and spending power of the bourgeoisie, bringing them externally nearer the upper classes of former days, are other obvious stimuli to change in fashion, as are the gradual psychological and economic liberation of women and the greater opportunity given them for experimentation in dress and adornment.

Fashions for women show greater variability than fashions for men in contemporary civilization. Not only do women's fashions change more rapidly and completely but the total gamut of allowed forms is greater for women than for men. In times past and in other cultures, however, men's fashions show a greater exuberance than women's. Much that used to be ascribed to women as female is really due to women as a sociologically and economically defined class. Women as a distinctive theme for fashion may be explained in terms of the social psychology of the present civilization. She is the one who pleases by being what she is and looking as she does rather than by doing what she does. Whether biology or history is primarily responsible for this need not be decided. Woman has been the kept partner in marriage and has to prove her desirability by ceaselessly reaffirming her attractiveness as symbolized by novelty of fashion. Among the wealthier classes and by imitation also among the less wealthy, woman has come to be looked upon as an expensive luxury or whom one spends extravagantly. She is thus a symbol of the social and economic status of her husband. Whether with the increasingly marked change of woman's place in society the factors which emphasize extravagance in women's fashions will entirely fall away it is impossible to say at the present time.

There are powerful vested interest involved in changes of fashions, as has already been mentioned. The effect on the producer of fashions of a variability which he both encourages and dreads is the introduction of the element of risk. It is a popular error to assume that professional designers arbitrarily dictate fashion. They do so only in very superficial sense. Actually the have to obey many masters. Their designs must above all things net the manufacturers a profit, so that behind the more strictly psychological determinants of fashion there lurks a very important element due to the sheer technology of the manufacturing process or the availability of a certain type of material. In addition to this the designer must have a sure feeling for the established in custom and the degree to which he can safely depart from it. He must intuitively divine what people want before they are quite aware of it themselves. His business is not so much to impose fashion as to coax people to accept what they have themselves unconsciously suggested. This causes the profits of fashion production to be out of all proportion to the actual cost of manufacturing fashionable goods. The producer and his designer assistant capitalize the curiosity and vanity of their customers but they must also be protected against the losses of a risky business. Those who are familiar with the history of fashion are emphatic in speaking of the inability of business to combat the fashion trends which have been set going by various psychological factors. A fashion may be aesthetically pleasing in the abstract, but if it runs counter to the trend or does not help to usher in a new trend which is struggling for a hearing it may be a flat failure.

The distribution of fashions is a comparatively simple and automatic process. The vogue of fashion plates and fashion magazines, the many lines of communication which connect fashion producers and fashion dispensers, and modern methods of marketing make it almost inevitable that a successful Parisian fashion should find its way within an incredibly short period of time to Chicago and San Francisco. If it were not for the necessity of exploiting accumulated stocks of goods these fashions would penetrate into the remotest corners of rural America even more rapidly than is the case. The average consumer is chronically distressed to discover how rapidly his accumulated property in wear depreciates by becoming outmoded. He complains bitterly and ridicules the new fashions when they appear. In the end he succumbs, a victim to symbolisms of behavior which he does not fully comprehend. What he will never admit is that he is more the creator than the victim of his difficulties.

Fashion has always had vain critics. It has been arraigned by the clergy and by social satirists because each new style of wear, calling attention as it does to the form of the human body, seems to the critics to be an attack on modesty. Some fashions there are, to be sure, whose very purpose it is to attack modesty, but over and above specific attacks there is felt to be a generalized one. The charge is well founded but useless. Human beings do not wish to be modest; they want to be as expressive—that is, as immodest—as fear allows; fashion helps them solve their paradoxical problem. The charge of economic waste which is often leveled against fashion has had little or no effect on the public mind. Waste seems to be of no concern where values are to be considered, particularly when these values are both egoistic and unconscious. The criticism that fashion imposes an unwanted uniformity is not as sound as it appears to be in the first instance. The individual in society is only rarely significantly expressive in his own right. For the vast majority of human beings the choice lies between unchanging custom and the legitimate caprice of custom, which is fashion.

Fashion concerns itself closely and intimately with the ego. Hence its proper field is dress and adornment. There are other symbols of the ego, however, which are not as close to the body as these but which are almost equally subject to the psychological laws of fashion. Among them are objects of utility, amusements and furniture. People differ in their sensitiveness to changing fashions in these more remote forms of human expressiveness. It is therefore impossible to say categorically just what the possible range of fashion is. However, in regard to both amusements and furniture there may be observed the same tendency to change, periodicity and unquestioning acceptance as in dress and ornament.

Many speak of fashions in thought, art, habits of living and morals. It is superficial to dismiss such locutions as metaphorical and unimportant. The usage shows a true intuition of the meaning of fashion, which while it is primarily applied to dress and the exhibition of the human body is not essentially concerned with the fact of dress or ornament but with its symbolism. There is nothing to prevent a thought, a type of morality or an art form from being the psychological equiv-

alent of a costuming of the ego. Certainly one may allow oneself to be converted to Catholicism or Christian Science in exactly the same spirit in which one invests in pewter or follows the latest Parisian models in dress. Beliefs and attitudes are not fashions in their character of mores but neither are dress and ornament. In contemporary society it is not a fashion that men wear trousers; it is the custom. Fashion merely dictates such variations as whether trousers are to be so or so long, what colors they are to have and whether they are to have cuffs or not. In the same way, while adherence to a religious faith is not in itself a fashion, as soon as the individual feels that he can pass easily, out of personal choice, from one belief to another, not because he is led to his choice by necessity but because of a desire to accrete to himself symbols of status, it becomes legitimate to speak of his change of attitude as a change of fashion. Functional irrelevance as contrasted with symbolic significance for the expressiveness of the ego is implicit in all fashions.

V

The
Marketing
Mix

A

General Marketing Strategy

33

Creative Marketing Strategy

Harry L. Hansen

Often management is a process of reacting to immediate and urgent problems. Any managerial process is in danger of degenerating into a "fire-fighting" operation unless the managers have clearly defined an objective and have planned a strategy for reaching that objective. This article contains suggestions for forming such a plan in the field of marketing.

In order not to avoid but to delimit future arguments, I should define the meanings of the three words in the title of this talk. By creative I mean the combination of two or more usually disparate ideas into a new whole that has greater value than the original two ideas. By marketing I mean the discovery and definition of consumer needs, the translating of these needs into product or service specifications, and the delivery of these products and services to the people. By strategy I mean the employment of all resources

to the attainment of an objective. I do not mean by strategy the more specialized meaning sometimes used in the theory of games which says strategy is a plan of action so complete that it cannot be upset by man or nature. My definition is less elegant and implies that strategy may be unsuccessful. I have no illusion that these three definitions are definitive. Nevertheless they are workable, and they do provide a framework within which I can talk.

Marketing Strategy

Let us think now about the question of marketing strategy and begin with

Reprinted from *Boston Conference on Distribution*, 1959, pp. 54–57, by permission of International Marketing Institute, Soldiers Field, Boston 63, Massachusetts.

the origin of strategic thinking, the art of war. There is no absolute agreement as to the principles of military strategy, although the world has a long record to look at, and military critics and historians have been working on the problem for centuries. For instance, over two millenniums ago the Chinese Sun-Tze set down 13 principles of strategy. Napoleon had 115 maxims for warfare; General N. B. Forrest in our own Civil War had one: "Get there fustest with the mostest." Today the United States is said to have nine principles; Great Britain and Russia, ten. More or less common to these last three lists are principles involving the objective, the offensive, cooperation or unity of command, mass or concentration of force, economy of force, maneuver, surprise, security, and simplicity. Because you may be curious, Great Britain's tenth is "administration" and Russia's, "annihilation."

The fact that the military critics and historians have failed to come to any clear-cut agreement may temper our enthusiasm for finding strategic principles in marketing. But if it is difficult to agree on strategic principles, it is an excellent exercise to attempt to formulate them which I will try to do briefly now. Here are some of my favorites.

The first and most important principle to my mind is *the strategy of the objective*. Managements and companies can be successful of course without having carefully spelled out objectives, but they are sometimes sacrificing greater success by failing to go through this difficult process. Parenthetically I think we should assume that to seek merely to make more profits is so general a goal that it hardly qualifies as an objective. As a useful exercise I suggest that when you return from the Conference you ask your fellow executives individually to write down what the objectives of your company are or should be. Compare them and you may be in for a shock. They are likely to be very diverse, suggesting that in fact you and your colleagues are not united toward any specific goal. Also these objectives are likely to be general, such as to increase sales. No military commander can plan on the basis of an objective such as "win the war." Nor can you as marketers work your best without having a fairly precise and definable objective and scheduling your steps toward it.

The Strategy of the Offensive. Those who have studied warfare know that the secret of successful campaigns is attack, not defense. It is true that history gives us examples of how strategies of retreat or containment have exhausted an enemy, but these are the exceptions to the general rule. And the recent history of distribution in the United States has shown how traditional distribution forms have ultimately had to take the offensive to survive. For instance, the supermarket and the discount house were first fought defensively and unimaginatively and on a limited scale by the chains and the department stores. Ultimately it was necessary to move aggressively and to adopt the very tactics of these new competitors that were once decried. And so I want to suggest to you that the old proverb, the road is better than the inn, is one that may have a useful meaning to marketing strategy. The thing to do is to move out and study your competitor; to find out its strengths and use them where you can and not to retire behind your analysis of its weaknesses. Move your policies and you move your people.

Closely related is another principle of marketing strategy and that is *the acceptance of change*. I have suggested to you earlier that most of us, if not all, have a continuing urge to develop routines, to find a place where we can come to rest, to seek a competitive niche where we can face successfully all comers over a period of time. Perhaps no policy can be more self-deceiving than that which announces the rules under which a company will compete. So comforting, so intelligent, indeed, to define what will be done! But these statements are often based more upon the successes of the past than we would wish to admit. I am somewhat inured as perhaps you are of being frequently told that a revolution is upon us in retailing, in consumer income distribution, and so on. Indeed it would be more appropriate to say a revolution would be here if these changes were not occurring. The meaning of this immutability of change to the marketer is that he must be continually anticipating, exploring, probing, in contrast to reacting to, resisting, and withdrawing.

The Strategy of Total Force. No one denies the fact that military plan involves the mobilizing of a vast array of resources in order to bring them to bear upon a chosen objective. There are many supporting arms and services involved and a multitude of tasks to be integrated. The military commander must blend these together into a united effort. So also must the marketing commander with his arms and services: salesmen, advertising, market research, product planning, pricing, distribution, and the like. Unfortunately in too many companies these marketing arms and services move forward not as a complete integrated team but as a loose confederation of allies more or less having the same objective in mind.

The Strategy of Economy of Force. A commander, military or marketing, is seldom in a position where he has available to him all the resources he needs. Furthermore, it is always necessary for him to have an uncommitted reserve, as the case may be, in funds, equipment, or people. The need for this reserve makes it necessary for him to husband his resources and to make his commitments match the objectives to be taken with some margin, of course, to insure success. There is a selectivity in what he does. In fact I believe selectivity is so important that it might be considered a separate strategy. Now in both the military and marketing fields, experience is heavily relied upon in making the decisions. But experience can be more or less valuable, and it becomes more valuable as we control experience. The argument for market and marketing research can be seen in a new light, to my mind, if we view its objective as that of determining economy of force. Unfortunately the amount of marketing funds spent to obtain sales objectives is greatly out of balance when compared to the amount of funds spent to research the effectiveness of what is done. Research is a tool that can sharpen objectives and problems, and this sharpness is a first step toward developing economy of force.

As one of the key principles of marketing strategy, I would suggest *the strategy of communication.* By communication I mean the exchange of information by any means. Generally speaking, this principle is not recognized in its powerful entirety by marketing organizations. The closest approach to it is essentially a partial one: a market research department is created, sales analysis work may be done as part of the market research activity, or perhaps this work is done as an additional duty by accounting personnel, and a sales vice president periodically makes reconnaissance sorties into the field. But these separate activities, and they are usually such, show no strategical grasp of the communication function. There are facts, ideas, concepts, call them what you will, which need free and easy circulation from the market to the master strategists; and, conversely, there needs to be a free flow in the opposite direction. But any of us sitting here this morning knows that this free communication is often seriously blocked.

The Strategy of Maneuver. There are times in the conduct of military and marketing campaigns when the commander has so committed his forces that there is nothing for him to do but to turn the campaign over to providence. But this is a course of events that is to be avoided at all costs. We must preserve the ability to maneuver, to scrap old plans and improvise new ones, to meet the changing shock of battle and competition. In order to be in this happy position, two things are necessary: effective communication and resourceful and independent tactical commanders. I have already referred to the strategy of communication. Now as for these commanders and the inability to maneuver, it should be clear that a substantial amount of training and decentralization of decision-making is necessary. We are all familiar with the dictum to place the decision-making as close to the action point as necessary. This is the essence of maneuver.

The Strategy of Time. There is a time, or more commonly several times, to strike, and to strike at a particular time requires two things: (1) continual and careful planning of the steps that are necessary to initiate an action; (2) continual alertness to the opportunity. Proper timing is one of the most subtle of the marketer's administrative skills. Let me take one aspect of timing alone. The marketer must not lag behind the needs of the market with his new product introduction—but perhaps he can a little if he chooses to minimize his risks of innovation. He must not move appreciably ahead of what the market will accept—but perhaps if he is not a little ahead, he maximizes his risk. What is his timing strategy? Lack of such a strategy can condemn a marketing organization to a mediocre performance.

I want to suggest to you finally and quickly that if *simplicity* is a principle of grand strategy in warfare, it is also one in successful marketing. Simplicity depends upon thinking through objectives so that there is no confusion as to what they are. But there is more to simplicity than that. Simplicity involves a ready understanding in an organization as to what is intended, and this cannot be obtained without a great deal of interaction between the planners and the doers. The simplest concept can become a most confused one when it is communicated to line people without adequate allowance for mutual discussion.

34

A Model of Non-price
Competitive Strategy

Jon G. Udell

*Classical economic theory postulated price as the predominant,
and almost only, element of competitive strategy. Even a cursory
examination of the business world reveals that nonprice forms of
competition not only are important, but appear to be increasingly
important. Although businessmen have known this and have acted
accordingly, we have had no theory about how nonprice elements
of strategy could and should be employed. The author of the
following article presents the outline of such a theory, arguing that
the "product-market" is the dominant influence in nonprice competitive behavior.*

Business management often chooses to emphasize the non-price facets of competitive strategy. This emphasis does not imply that price is not important; it is, and always will be, as long as we have a quasi-free enterprise economy. However, the non-price facets of competition, given a reasonable level of prices, may often be more important than pricing.

In the past few decades a number of non-price variables have been added to the classical and neoclassical theories of firm behavior. Edward Chamberlin introduced product differentiation and the monopolistically competitive market structure.[1] Joe S. Bain presented the concept of limit pricing and the condition of entry.[2] William Fellner emphasized the roles of uncertainty and firm recognition of interdependence.[3] The works of these and other economists are significant contributions, but they fall short of providing an adequate theory of non-price competitive strategy. With only a few exceptions, these theoretical developments have one thing in common —they relate firm behavior to the market structure of the industry. Certainly the behavior of a firm may be influenced by the size and number of its competitors, the degree of recognition of interdependence, and the amount of collusion among the competitors. Bringing these factors into the theory of firm behavior is necessary, but these factors alone do not ex-

Abridged from *A Model of Non-Price Competitive Strategy* (Madison, Wis.: Bureau of Business Research and Service, University of Wisconsin), Wisconsin Selected Papers, Vol. 1, No. 1 (July, 1963).

[1] E. H. Chamberlin, *The Theory of Monopolistic Competition,* Cambridge, 1958.

[2] J. S. Bain, *Barriers to New Competition,* Cambridge, 1956.

[3] W. Fellner, *Competition Among the Few,* New York, 1960.

plain *how* a firm will compete (or should compete) for the consumer's dollar.

It is the author's hypothesis that the theory of non-price competitive strategy, to be realistic and useful, must take into consideration the nature of a firm's product and the characteristics of the buyers for that product. For example, one would not expect a producer of newsprint (an industrial good) to compete in an identical manner to a producer of perfume (a consumer non-durable). And a comparison of the structures of the newsprint and perfume industries would not explain the differences between their marketing strategies. For this reason it is suggested that the "product-market" be incorporated into the theories and models of firm behavior.

I. Defining the "Product-Market"

It is proposed that the "product-market" is the dominant influence in non-price competitive behavior. The "product-market"—the nature of a product in relation to the characteristics of the buyers and potential buyers for that product—may be delineated according to five interrelated variables.

1. Knowledge of the buyer.
2. Technical nature of the product.
3. Value of typical purchase.
4. Effort of the buyer.
5. Purchaser's buying motive.

Knowledge of the Buyer

Knowledge of the buyer is defined as the level of comprehension and understanding that the purchaser has in regard to the product and particularly its want-satisfying power. This would include the buyer's comprehension of the product's composition, functioning, and applica-

tion. However, as the definition implies, primary emphasis is placed upon the buyer's knowledge of the ability of the product to satisfy his wants and needs (physical and psychological). A comprehension of composition, functioning, and application are necessary only to the extent that they aid the buyer in judging a product's utility to him.

This knowledge is a matter of degree, in that perfect comprehension and understanding are never attainable. For example, even though the purchasing agent of Wisconsin Power and Light Company would not have perfect knowledge of the composition and burning properties of various types of coal, he would have a high level of knowledge relative to the typical homeowner who purchases coal to heat his residence.

Technical Nature of the Product

Technical nature of the product is defined as the complexity of a commodity from the point of view of the consumer or industrial user. From the point of view of a homemaker buying wrapping paper for mailing packages and other household uses, paper would be considered a relatively nontechnical product. She would not be concerned about the intricate complexities of various paper compositions, nor would she need any special technical information in order to use the paper. However, paper would be considered a technical product by the General Electric Company when their production department purchases special paper to use in the insulation of electrical transformers. In short, as it affects competitive strategy, the technical nature of the product is measured according to the point of view of the customer or potential customer to whom the firm wishes to appeal.

Value of Typical Purchase

The value of the typical purchase may be defined as the amount of money involved in the average (modal) sales transaction. The amount of money will, of course, be a product of the price of the commodity times the typical quantity sold per transaction. It is not necessary that any or all of the quantity be delivered at the time of the sales transaction, i.e., formulation of the sales contract. For example, a tool manufacturer might receive an order from the United States Army for $100,000 worth of inexpensive wrenches, the wrenches to be delivered to various places over a considerable period of time. In this instance, the value of the sale would be $100,000.

In cases where the quantities sold vary greatly, a point estimate of the typical sale would not be realistic. In this case the range of typical sales values is the appropriate measure to use.

Effort of Buyer

Effort of the buyer is defined as the amount of time, expense, and consideration which the typical purchaser puts forth to acquire a given product. For example, when Mr. Jones desires a package of cigarettes, he is not willing to put forth a great amount of effort to obtain a specific brand or to buy from a specific vendor. He usually will make his purchase at the most convenient retail outlet. This is true, by definition, of all convenience goods.

On the other hand, when Mr. Jones decides to purchase a new automobile, he is willing to put forth a substantial amount of time, expense and consideration in the effort to obtain an automobile which best meets his needs and desires for the price paid. This is true, to a greater or lesser extent, in the case of

shopping goods and specialty goods, and even more true in the typical industrial goods transaction where the time and effort of a number of corporate executives may be involved.

Purchaser's Buying Motive

Buying motives are those impulses and considerations within the consumer which induce the purchase of a product. All goods are purchased for their estimated utility—that is, the buyer's estimation of their capacity to yield personal satisfaction, or their productivity—their capacity to yield a profit or to operate an institution.

Purchasers' buying motives may be classified to two extremes, those which are *psychologically functional* and those which are *operationally functional*. Psychologically functional buying motives are those which flow indirectly from the anticipated performance of the product and from the mind of the consumer. The satisfaction of these motives yields the purchaser emotional and psychological utility. This utility is only indirectly derived from the product's performance. Furthermore, the psychological satisfaction may be received at the buyer's conscious or sub-conscious level of thought. If a young lady received psychological satisfaction from a bottle of Chanel No. 5 perfume because a beautiful girl embraced by a handsome gentleman was pictured in an advertisement for the perfume, she probably is receiving psychological satisfaction at a sub-conscious level. However, if the satisfaction is primarily derived from her recognition of the social prestige of Chanel No. 5, she is receiving psychological satisfaction at the more conscious level.

In contrast to psychologically functional, the operationally functional product buying motives are those influences in the purchase which flow directly from the anticipated performance of the product, their satisfaction being derived from the product's physical performance. The majority of product buying motives for industrial goods fall within this class. For example, a road construction company purchases a new dump truck because it will serve the firm by hauling construction materials. A consumer's operationally functional buying motive may be illustrated by a Michigan homeowner's purchase of an efficient oil burner to heat his home.[4]

It is important to recognize that the buying motive, or motives, inducing a purchase can seldom be classified as entirely psychological or entirely operational. Even in the purchase of industrial goods, both types of buying motives may be operative. This is illustrated by the sales success that electronics concerns have experienced by introducing fashion and styling into the design of electrical computers.[5]

Given these two major classifications or types of buying motives, the question arises to what constitutes a good or optimum purchase. An optimum purchase is one in which the balance between operationally functional and psychologically functional buying motives provides the buyer with a maximum amount of satisfaction (in terms of utility or profits) for the money expended. This assumes, of course, that the product fulfills the anticipations of the purchaser.

[4] One may more simply characterize buying motives as "operational" and "psychological." However, the author has used the additional word "functional" in order to emphasize that psychological buying motives may be just as functional and reasonable as operational buying motives.

[5] *Wall Street Journal*, "Electronics Concerns Use Styling, Color to Achieve Product Identity, Boost Sales," October 13, 1960, p. 1.

II. The Propositions of the Product Market

With the five attributes of product-market defined, two inversely related hypotheses concerning the non-price competitive behavior of the firm are proposed:

1. The importance of the product facet of competitive behavior varies directly with the value of the typical purchase, the efforts of the buyer, the technical nature of the product, the knowledge of the buyer, and the importance of operational buying motives. In other words, the higher the value of the typical sale, the greater the purchasing efforts of the buyer, the more technical the product (as defined from the consumer's point of view), the greater the knowledge of the buyer, and the more important the operational buying motive—the more important will be the product facet of non-price competition.

2. The importance of the sales efforts facet of competitive activity varies inversely with the value of typical purchase, the efforts of the buyer, the technical nature of the product and the knowledge of the buyer, while varying directly with the importance of psychological buying motives. In short, the importance of sales efforts tends to be associated with low values of typical sale, the lack of purchasing efforts by the buyer, less technical products, a low level of buyer's knowledge, and the predominance of psychological buying motives.

Symbolically, the hypotheses may be expressed by the following equations:

$$(1) \quad PS = a_0 + a_1 V^{n_1} + a_2 E^{n_2} + a_3 T^{n_3} + a_4 K^{n_4} + a_5 O^{n_5}$$

$$(2) \quad SE = b_0 - b_1 V^{m_1} - b_2 E^{m_2} - b_3 T^{m_3} - b_4 K^{m_4} + b_5 P^{m_5}$$

where a_i, $b_j \geq 0$; i, j ≥ 1 and:

PS = Importance of Product and Service

SE = Importance of Sales Efforts

V = Value of Typical Purchase

E = Effort of the Buyer

T = Technical Nature of the Product

K = Knowledge of the Buyer

O = Strength of the Operationally Functional Buying Motives

P = Strength of the Psychologically Functional Buying Motives

The importance of sales efforts and product is determined by the combined effect of the values of all the attributes. However, for purposes of practical analysis, it might be convenient to evaluate the effect of each attribute and then to estimate the combined effect of all the attributes.

It should be pointed out that the role played by each attribute is not necessarily 20 percent of the total importance of the five variables. In practice, the relative importance of each variable would be estimated on the basis of past experience, observable facts, and management intuition.[6] Also, it is possible for the value and importance of a variable to change. For example, in recent years the automobile has declined in importance as a status symbol. A considerable portion of the social prestige which once accompanied the ownership of a large, powerful and expensive automobile has been transferred to other products, such as boats and homes. As a result, the psychologically functional buying motive, although still present, does not play as important a role in automobile purchasing as it once did.

A second major point concerning the

[6] Mathematical measurements and analysis may make it possible to make a more precise evaluation of the product-market and the causal relationships involved. At this introductory stage no such attempt is made.

two propositions is that the importance of one facet of non-price competitive strategy does not preclude the coexisting importance of the other. The value of some of the product-market attributes may favor product, while other attributes favor sales efforts. Also, the predominance of one type of buying motive does not preclude the importance of the other type of buying motive. The buying motives prompting the purchase of the automobile illustrate this point. Performance, reliability, economy, safety and other operationally functional buying motives may be the most important in the purchase of an automobile. However, this does not prevent the desire for design, pleasing colors, prestige, and other psychological factors from strongly entering into the purchasing decision. In short, the sum of the attributes for each product-market is different. At the one extreme the product-market will favor only sales efforts, and at the other extreme the product will be of sole importance. Between these hypothetical extremes an infinite number of gradations (combinations) exist.

In light of the above comments, it is obvious that the two propositions are not, from a theoretical point of view, as rigorous as one might desire. The exact importance of each attribute cannot be judged "a priori," and the resulting importance of the two facets of non-price competition cannot be precisely determined. However, the propositions do provide a theoretical approach for explaining and predicting the optimum non-price behavior of the firm. Having obtained measurements (perhaps estimates) of the value and importance of each of the product-market attributes, and having evaluated their combined influence, the firm's management can estimate the optimum balance of product and sales efforts to use in its marketing strategy.

B

Marketing
Information

35

Better Management of
Market Information

Kenneth P. Uhl

This article deals with the subject of marketing information. The author makes a good case for the necessity of marketing information as a complement to the marketing concept. The current interest in the subject suggests that it is the kind of activity that is likely to be undertaken by the more progressive firms; if they find it profitable, their success will induce the early followers to emulate them. Gradually the laggards will adopt the practice of systematically analyzing marketing information, and then marketing information will have become a standard part of business practice.

Many executives have been dismayed to discover that corporate excellence in production and finance alone has not led to success. Excellence in marketing is also needed. As a result, the marketing function has been elevated to the vice-presidential level, and many firms have begun to orient their activities to their customers' needs. It has been hoped that this increased emphasis on marketing, popularly called the marketing concept, would promote the needed marketing excellence—but all too frequently it has

not. Instead, marketing problems have continued to grow larger and become more difficult.

Attempts at solutions have been many, and successes have been few. A common response has been to restructure marketing organizations. Older and simpler line-and-staff structures have been strengthened with more staff specialization and changes in titles and authority bases. Multiproduct firms have created merchandising offices and have experimented with brand managers or product managers. Multimarket firms have experimented with varying degrees of geographical decentralization and have installed various

Abridged from *Business Horizons,* Spring 1966, Vol. 9, No. 1, pp. 75–82, by special permission.

territorial marketing managers who have been charged with profit responsibility. But success has been spotty, at best, and improvement is still needed. This author's contention is that the handling of marketing information must be better managed—and the focus is on how to do it.

To begin, extensive rethinking is required about both the use and the management of marketing information in the firm. In terms of use, management must insist on planning, organizing, directing, and controlling the marketing function through information as a replacement for "management" by intuition. This means that necessary information must be both available and used.

In terms of management, the old separate segments of intradepartmental information programs are largely unmanageable as composite programs. Instead, new facilities and new organizational structures must be envisioned and installed. The need for such correction has been overwhelmingly obvious to executives who have gained control over production, finance, and other areas through the development and use of information programs.

Similar, if not greater, gain can be accomplished in marketing. Enough has been learned by some firms to indicate that marketing fat can be converted to muscle through the development and use of adequate marketing information programs. The need for marketing information improvements is obvious; the emphasis here will be on plans and programs to bring about such improvements.

Marketing Information Entity

The basic structural weakness in virtually every ill-informed firm has been the absence of one entity for processing marketing information. Such firms have been typified by the presence of uncoordinated bits and pieces of the information function scattered here and there. Marketing information as an activity has seemed to be everywhere; it has belonged to no one and has received little development and use by these firms. As a result, they do not consider marketing information an activity that is manageable or even worthy of management. The marketing concept has not been developed sufficiently to make management see the need for composite marketing information systems.

A fundamental requisite for better managed marketing is that the scattered information activities be both perceived and managed as an entity. That is, these activity components must be (1) identified throughout the organization, (2) thought of as being parts of a whole, and (3) managed as an information unit.

These components, furthermore, must be managed through a single, separate, and centralized office. One director must be responsible for the entire marketing information program in all of its scattered locations. Through such an arrangement all marketing information activities can be managed as a system—a system which by its very nature must circulate and function internally and wherever the firm wishes to market its offerings.

There is no single precise description of the activities, responsibilities, and authorities of marketing information offices, nor is there one organizational arrangement that is patently superior to all others. Some broad guidelines, however, can be applied to a multitude of specific situations.

Establishing an Information Office

The office of marketing information must assume broad and pervasive responsibilities. Specifically, it must be responsible as consultant, coordinator, and controller for each of the basic marketing information components—searching/ securing, analyzing, transmitting, storing, and using. Some difficulties do result, because of the traditional treatment of the marketing information function.

The last component, the *using* function, is the most demanding and the least aided by recent technological advances in information handling. Basically, to manage the using function, the director's office must know who needs what information, when, and why. Knowing "why" is essential if the office is to serve as both manager and consultant. The office must make known to users the firm's information resources, including their costs;[1] it must be able to evaluate information requirements and requests and to moderate and temper those which appear unreasonable. To do this the office must have the capacity to discern which offices should have what information. It must also be able to consult with using units relative to what information they should be using and how they should use it. In other words, to information users, the office should be synonymous with both marketing information and its effective use. The director serves as a consultant to the organization, though, like the company attorney, he has the obligation to be authoritarian when more than advice is needed. Finally, the using component dominates and dictates to the information system. The system exists solely to facilitate better management— better management through more and better information availability and use.

[1] Some of the problems of cost and benefit estimating are discussed in R. S. Alexander, "Let's Have a Marketing Research Done," *Journal of Business*, Seton Hall University (December, 1963); David W. Ewing (ed.), *Effective Marketing Action* (New York: Harper and Bros., 1958), pp. 219–23; and Wroe Alderson and Paul Green, *Planning and Problem Solving in Marketing* (Homewood, Ill.: Richard D. Irwin, Inc., 1964).

The components of *searching/securing, transmitting, analyzing*, and *storing* must be completely under the guidance of the marketing information office. These four components, while different in form, are similar in how they should be managed. The overall task of the office is to see that each component is present in correct capacity, properly allocated in the organization, and performed with necessary efficiency—all relative to the needs of the using units. In other words, the office must see that there is not too little or too much searching/securing, transmitting, analyzing, and/or storing capacity relative to the using needs of the organization, and that capacity is properly allocated and efficient. Continuing audits of the information components relative to users' information requirements provide the information office with the guidance it needs for the management of the marketing information function.

This is not to suggest that all four of these activities should be performed by the information office. Clearly, it would be a most unusual organization and situation in which these four components could be centralized within an information office or any other single office. Their management must be centralized, but the actual operations are likely to be located in many different departments. Each activity should be located where it can be performed most efficiently, relative to the needs of the using units.

Some of the activities must be largely centralized in the information office, while others can be performed far more efficiently in a number of locations. For example, at a minimum, the information office must serve as a central information index and know rather precisely what information is available and where. In this case, information may be stored in various locations throughout the firm. However, random access memory storage units, computers, and electronic transmission facilities have opened up new possibilities for massive centralization of information storage.[2]

About the same statements can be made about information analysis. Simple analysis encourages performance in securing and using units. However, more complex, more difficult, or more burdensome numerical problems suggest the advantages of centralized analysis and use of specialists and computer facilities. Also, more complex nonnumerical analysis calls for use of specialists. A case in point is the type of analysis and synthesis performed by brand managers in developing advertising proposals. And a not-to-be-forgotten objective of the information manager is to get each necessary information component performed efficiently. This goal requires, among other things, seeing that each is performed by the correct unit.

The searching/securing and transmitting components must be carefully controlled because of their diverse and widespread nature. Gerald Albaum, an information research expert at the University of Arizona, has clarified the diverse nature of information by classifying it into two categories: planned and unsolicited.[3] The planned type can be assigned to various offices based on source contacts and searching/securing capacity. Where these do not permit use of noninformation offices, these supply components can be assigned to the marketing information office. For example, a sales group may have both the capacity and the source contacts to actively search/secure and transmit information on competitive pricing patterns. In contrast, the same sales group would not have the capacity to search/secure customer segment profiles or to gauge product images. These tasks, therefore, would normally accrue to a special marketing information group.

Unsolicited (that is, incidental) information, in contrast to planned information, cannot be anticipated relative to specific kind, source, timing, or availability. For example, a competitive firm may be planning to lower the price on its entire product line by 20 per cent. Receipt of this information prior to initiation of the action certainly would be useful, but is not normally available. Much marketing information cannot be anticipated.

Searching/securing and transmitting incidental information calls for (1) information sensitivity by all members of the organization, (2) transmission channels direct enough that small scattered facets have a chance for meaning and survival by reaching a central assembly point while they are still alive, and (3) in general, an organizational environment that encourages incidental information sensitivity, receptiveness, and transmission. The eyes, ears, and other senses of the organization obviously cannot be centralized. But to create the necessary environment and facilities requires centralized management of the information function.

It has been shown that a single, separate marketing information office must exist to make one person responsible for all marketing information within the company. And because both the information-using units and the supplying components are scattered, the emphasis of information management must be on coordination and consultation, but with the element of control vested in the office. The office must oversee the entire area of marketing information. The director must be concerned with company-

---

[2] While numerous articles and books are available, a single publication containing views of both academicians and businessmen is: George P. Shultz and Thomas L. Whisler (ed.), *Management Organization and the Computer* (New York: The Free Press of Glencoe, Illinois, 1960).

[3] Gerald Albaum, "The Hidden Crisis in Information Transmission," *Pittsburgh Business Review* (July, 1963), p. 1.

wide management of all of the marketing information components. Parts of these components may be largely centralized and therefore under the immediate control of the information director. Others, because of their locations, must be managed somewhat less directly through numerous overlays. In this latter and more difficult control situation, the success of the information office will be largely dependent on its ability to gain recognition as the marketing information specialist.

Conclusions

The fundamental requisite for better managed marketing is that the marketing information function be both perceived and managed as an entity. In terms of the information components, there must be a single, separate, and centralized management of the marketing information program. That is, the entire program—all of its components, all of its facets, all of its scattered locations—must be the responsibility of one director. His responsibilities must be broad and pervasive, for this control situation is not an ordinary one. The information director must be responsible as consultant, coordinator, and controller of each of the information components. Some of these components may be largely centralized and consequently under the direct control of the director. Others must be managed somewhat less directly through numerous overlays. In this latter and more difficult control situation, the office must gain recognition as the ultimate source of information know-how.

Three locations can be considered for the information office. Firms with strong, well-received, well-respected company-wide marketing research offices may be able to broaden them into marketing information offices. Another suitable location is the merchandising office. This office will have the best chance for success where it has had considerable exposure and experience in management of information activities. Finally, in some firms the information office simply cannot be located in the marketing structure because the prevailing information climate is just too suppressive. In such situations creation of company-wide information offices, including the marketing information office, seems to be the best way to cope with a very difficult, but all too common problem. And even firms with favorable information climates may be better able to develop and use information systems that are managed from company-wide information offices.

In the past few years much has been written about the impact that computers and other improved information handling facilities will have on organizational structures and on management. Some have viewed the advances and concluded that they will result in massive centralization with almost no middle management, while others have said that the advances will encourage the use of more decentralized forms of organization.[4]

A relevant focal point that has been implicit in this study is that the new technology—particularly information analysis, storage, and transmission—will be an immense aid to information management and, in turn, to information use. Random access memory storage units and computers and accompanying accessories and know-how will both permit and encourage (if not dictate) increased recognition of information

[4] For example see Edward McCreary, "Countertrend to Decentralization: Top Management Tightens Controls," *Dun's Review and Modern Industry* (July, 1959), pp. 32–34; and Harold F. Smiddy, "Managerial Decision-Making," *Advanced Management* (November, 1958), p. 10.

systems, per se, as well as increased centralization of information functions. But clearly, total centralization of the system would be most unusual because of the nature of its basic components. Finally, neither massive organizational centralization nor decentralization is likely to be dictated by (1) increased use of the new technology, (2) management of the information system as an entity, or (3) increased centralization of the information system. Instead, improved information systems will facilitate many organizational forms—forms that will take their shapes based on market needs and problems, not on information restraints.

Top management's success in remedying its marketing malady through a central information office depends largely on the extent to which it is able to:

1. Locate and develop the marketing information office outside the influence of the old line marketing group
2. Locate within the office as much of the marketing planning and control activity as is necessary to ensure effective use of the office
3. Restrict information duplication and back-up activities in the marketing division once they are assigned to the information office (that is, allow marketing management no alternative information aid)
4. Establish a company-wide information office and structure to contain the marketing information office.

36

Distribution Costs and Marketing Decisions

James Don Edwards

Cost-accounting methods have been much less extensively and less successfully applied to the marketing process than to production. There is no denying the greater difficulty of applying cost accounting to marketing. And in past years, when additional sales came with relative ease, management was acting properly in putting its major emphasis on those functions which promised to increase sales volume, even though their cost might not be precisely known. Today, however, and most probably in the future, a company, in order to be competitive, must spend its marketing dollars as efficiently as competitors do or it will lose position and profit in the buyers' market, which threatens to become increasingly intense. The next reading suggests the broad outline of the accounting methods that can be used as tools in a more careful control of marketing programs.

It has been estimated that distribution costs account for about fifty-one percent of the cost of the consumer dollar while production costs comprise the other forty-nine percent. This does not mean that every firm incurs its total costs in this ratio. Each individual firm is only a single link in the chain which extends from the producer to the consumer. The manufacturing firm may incur a much greater proportion of production costs, but there remains the task, with the concomitant costs, of distribution.[1] This task must be carried out by someone.

In spite of the relative importance of distribution costs, accounting for distribution has not been developed to as great an extent as production cost accounting. Yet it is recognized that this field is one in which economy through cost control is badly needed, for it is the basis for programming of market action.[2] Few manufacturers know exactly how much it costs to sell a particular product to a particular type of customer in a specific location. And the number of producers who know how much it *should* cost to make a similarly particularized sale is even smaller. Nevertheless, such information is essential to good control of company costs, and the greatest possible cost saving to an individual firm may be made in this area in which most firms lack adequate knowledge.[3]

The explanation of this situation is probably twofold. Historically, the need for detailed distribution cost accounting is a comparatively recent one. It arises from the increasing importance of distribution occasioned by concentration of production with expansion of markets and from the greater need for efficient distribution due to increased competition in distributive activity. This will be especially important in the future because the second type of factor, accounting for the slower rate of development of distribution cost accounting, is a function of the inherent nature of distribution as contrasted with production.

Production of similar products by different firms involves very similar methods in many cases. In contrast, distribution of such products may be performed efficiently in a number of different manners. Distribution methods also are generally much more flexible than are production methods. A large outlay for productive facilities of a specific type usually ties the firm to a certain narrow range of production alternatives for a considerable period. Distribution methods are normally readjusted by shifting from one combination to another as a continuing process. Another point of difference lies in the relative importance of psychological factors. Production is much more subject to mechanical control than is the reaction of a customer to a salesman's efforts. All these factors point to the lack of standardization of distribution activities. Without some degree of standardization, performance can only be measured by highly subjective evaluations.[4]

Still another difficulty is that of securing basic information. There are no timekeepers or inspectors on hand when a salesman contacts a prospective customer. This is still further complicated by the fact that the marketing mix includes not only personal selling, but

From *Business Topics,* Michigan State University, Vol. 8, No. 2, Spring, 1960, pp. 15–20, by special permission.

[1] J. Brooks Heckert, "Back to Distribution Costs," *The Journal of Accountancy* June, 1945, p. 456.
[2] Editorial, "A Study in Distribution Costs," *The Journal of Accountancy,* January 1946, p. 6.
[3] Paul W. Atwood, "The Manufacturer Looks at His Costs of Distribution," *The Accounting Review,* March 1934, p. 28.

[4] James W. Culliton, "The Management Challenge of Marketing Costs," *The Harvard Business Review,* January, 1948, p. 81.

advertising and sales-promotion as well. These, in turn, are complicated by the fact that they tend to have residual benefits. For instance, a shoe advertisement run by a retail store not only generates sales immediately, but still may be influencing shoe sales months later when viewers or listeners decide they need shoes. Even when the basic cost information is available, the job of interpretation is extremely difficult. Distribution costs, to a much greater degree than production costs, contain many joint and indirect items which must be assigned to specific results. Indirect costs are troublesome in production accounting; they are even more so in distribution.[5] But the need for adequate distribution cost accounting is so great that these difficulties must be overcome, as many of the problems of production cost accounting have been.

Distribution Costs

Distribution costs have been defined as all costs necessary to get the order from the customer, deliver the goods, account for them and collect the account.[6] This is a reasonably broad definition but not the broadest possible, because in essence marketing begins with the determination of increasing wants and the delineation of market opportunities. It is certainly easy to argue that product design is a marketing function and its costs marketing costs. In one sense, all justifiable costs are distribution costs. Theoretically, the objective of the firm is to maximize profits. This can only be done through sales at a price greater

than cost. If, then, the distribution of its product at an advantageous price is the primary objective of the firm, all activity should be directed toward that objective and all costs incurred may be viewed as contributing to the distributive process. On the other hand, it could be argued at least equally well that all justifiable costs are production costs. This argument would contain the implicit shift of meaning of production from production of goods to production of utility as measured by revenue.

Types of Utility

The economist usually recognizes four types of utility; form, place, time and possession. Production, as commonly defined, involves only the creation of form utility. Distribution, in the usual sense, refers to the providing of time, place, and possession utility. At any rate, such functions as sales promotion, shipping, and collecting are as productive of revenue as is the fabricating process, since all are essential to profitable operations. But accounting classification or division is based in general on responsibility. In most manufacturing concerns, the management organization is divided into the three broad functions of production, distribution and finance. It is always difficult to say which function is the major one. Since all three are essential in some degree, any attempt to rank them resolves into a priority question like that of the chicken and the egg. This situation is becoming more complex today because of the increasing tendency to specialize administrative functions.

In addition to contributing toward marketing efficiency, the use of distribution cost accounting makes it legally feasible to charge different prices to different types of customers, thus passing on to customers the advantages of buying in those quantities or by those

[5] J. Brooks Heckert, *The Analysis and Control of Distribution Costs*, Ronald Press, New York, 1940, pp. 15–17.

[6] William B. Castenholz, "Selling and Administrative Expense Analysis as a Basis for Sales Control and Cost Reduction," *The Accounting Review*, June 1931, pp. 125–29.

methods which result in saving to the seller. Without adequate distribution cost accounting records, the seller may run afoul of the Robinson-Patman Act if he engages in differential pricing when selling to different customer types.

Stages of Cost Handling

The cost accountant must handle company costs through three major stages. He records costs as they are incurred, traces costs in terms of internal activity, and assigns costs to periodic revenue.[7] It is in the second and third stages of this sequence that the treatment of production and distribution costs differs. The tracing of costs within the firm must be done on the basis of some type of cost-unit. For production costs, the unit is usually a specific quantity of the product, as a single automobile or a ton of steel. For distribution costs the unit is not so easily chosen.[8] Only a few business costs are incurred on a clearcut unit of product basis. Some material, labor, packaging and delivery costs can be related directly to the units of product to which they apply. Other costs are incurred by the enterprise as a whole as a necessity of being in business. These "bread-upon-the-water" costs are not clearly identified with units of product sold. The problem of separating costs jointly incurred for the sale of several types of product and of separating results which jointly stem from one such cost thus arises. This is the crux of the distribution cost challenge.[9]

Sorting Distribution Costs

One method of sorting distribution costs is based on the function for which the costs are incurred. The entire marketing effort is divided into such component functions as direct selling, advertising, warehousing, transportation, credit and finance, etc. Each of these functions is then broken down into still further divisions until many costs can be segregated directly at incurrence. Costs which cannot be apportioned directly must then be spread on the basis which is assumed to reflect most clearly the benefit derived from them by the various functions.[10] Classification of costs by functions does not, in itself, provide a measure of efficiency nor exert control over costs. However, it is a useful first step in that direction. The comparison of actual costs incurred to perform a function with the costs which should have been required does provide such a measure. Comparison is facilitated when costs are classified by function rather than simply by the nature of the expense, such as rent, wages, etc.[11] But the functional method is a broad one. Its utility depends upon the complexity of the process of distribution required. If many products are involved and the marketing effort is great, the functional method of analysis may not be sufficiently specific to provide adequate control.

A Further Breakdown

To provide the more specific information needed for effective cost control, distribution costs can be broken down

---

[7] W. A. Paton and A. C. Littleton, *Introduction to Corporate Accounting Standards,* American Accounting Association, Chicago, 1940, p. 119.

[8] C. Rufus Rorem, "Differential Costs," *The Accounting Review,* December 1928, p. 341.

[9] James W. Culliton, *op. cit.,* pp. 79–82.

[10] Paul G. Brown, "Analysis and Control of Distribution Costs," *The Journal of Accountancy,* September 1948, p. 237.

[11] Donald R. Longman, *Distribution Cost Analysis,* Harper and Brothers Company, New York, 1941, p. 46.

	Usual Method	Using Standard Distribution Cost
Sales	$100,000.00	$100,000.00
Deduct—Cost of Goods Sold	60,000.00	60,000.00
Gross Profit	$ 40,000.00	$ 40,000.00
Deduct—Selling and Administrative Expense (Actual)	35,000.00	
Standard Distribution Costs		25,000.00
Net Profit	$ 5,000.00	$ 15,000.00

into still finer classifications. The combination of direct and indirect allocation again is used to divide functionalized costs according to any of a number of unit bases. Some of these bases are the commodity sold, the type of customer, the channel of distribution, and the territorial or organizational divisions. This type of classification provides a much closer measure of efficiency and technique of control. For example, the actual cost of a specific channel of distribution in selling a given quantity of Product A to small customers in Territory 2 is much more significant for purposes of control than is the total cost of distribution. The methods of indirect allocation used to spread the functionalized costs to these unit-bases are highly important. They will vary according to the particular cost under consideration and the unit-base to which applied. But the utility of the resulting information is a function of their validity in managerial decision making and pricing. The problem is not a simple one, and, as with indirect production costs, it is probably most satisfactorily solved when attacked on an individual-firm basis.

Defense of Standards

When this sort of analysis is correlated with the study of sales potentials and actual sales results, it can reveal misdirected sales effort and costs which are not justified by results. This information is the foundation of distribution cost control, but in and of itself it is not enough. The proper direction of sales effort does not insure the optimum result. Even profitability is not conclusive evidence of efficiency.[12] The efficient firm may be unprofitable while the inefficient may prosper for a time.

Not only what has happened but also what should have happened must be known for the proper measurement of performance. The decision as to what should have happened can be expressed in budget form or through the use of distribution cost standards. The fact that criteria of satisfactory performance are needed is undeniable. The chief arguments against standard distribution costs hinge on the difficulty of their determination and their questionable validity once determined. These arguments probably can never be resolved in general, but must be decided on the basis of particular cases. Need for a basis of comparison is a strong argument in support of standard distribution costs. Another interesting brief can be made for distribution cost standards based on the use which can be made of them to resolve the cost or expense question connected with distribution expendi-

12 J. Brooks Heckert, *op. cit.*, p. 208.

tures.[13] To determine the gross profit on sales, the cost of goods sold is deducted from total sales. This cost of goods sold figure is supposedly a true cost since it includes not only direct costs but also allocated indirect costs.

Overcoming Conflict in Treatment

In the case of deductions from gross profit to arrive at net profit, it may be held that there is no relation between the amounts deducted and the actual sales. The selling, financial and administrative costs used represent all expenditures of this type made during the period even though it is apparent that some such costs could have had no relation to sales booked during the period. The accountant is likely to rationalize to the effect that actual expenditures alone are reliable as a measure of such costs. At the same time, he will argue forcefully that the cost of sales figure is a true one though it is probably entirely divorced from the actual production expenditures of the period. The use of distribution cost standards to overcome this conflict in treatment can be illustrated by a simplified profit and loss statement. A standard rate of 25¢ per dollar of sales is assumed. Obviously, some disposition must be made of the $10,000 difference between actual and standard distribution costs. If this difference represents avoidable error, it should be written off as a business loss. If, when added to the standard cost figure, it presents a more accurate picture of normal distribution expense it should be so treated. But if it represents expenditures made in the ordinary course of operations to stimulate distibution in succeeding periods, it

should remain on the books as a deferred item.

The Ultimate Goal

It must be admitted that where distribution costs regularly recur in similar amounts, no great distortion in results is created by handling them as period costs. However, a similar statement could be made with regard to production costs, which would obviate the need for inventory accounting. The period cost concept would not be widely accepted for the reason that the methods of handling indirect production costs are well established on a unit of product basis while a widely accepted technique for deferring distribution costs has not been devised. Most accountants would agree that if it is possible to determine the period actually benefited by selling effort it is logical to treat distribution costs as prepaid expenses, but the accountant usually feels that the relation to future periods is not sufficiently definite and clear.[14] It should be the task of cost accountants to develop means whereby such relationships can be determined at least as definitely as those connected with production costs. This task can be restated as the elimination of the distinction in treatment between product costs and expenses or period costs. The truly significant relationship is the one existing between justifiable expenditures which produce revenue and the revenue produced. Costs of revenue, rather than costs of goods and cost of being in business, attain the position of prime importance when the artificial barrier of the accounting period is removed. It is the third step in the cost accountant's activity, the matching of costs to revenue, which is the ultimate

[13] William B. Castenholz, *The Control of Distribution Costs and Sales,* Harper and Brothers Company, New York, 1930, pp. 151–61.

[14] Howard C. Greer, "The Technique of Distribution Cost Accounting," *The Accounting Review,* June 1931, p. 136.

goal. The first two steps, the recording of costs and tracing of cost conversions within the firm, are only instrumental to it.

37

The Most Dangerous Game in Marketing

Jaala Weingarten

The rate of failure among new products put on the market is usually estimated to be in the neighborhood of four out of five. One commonly accepted way of improving the odds for a company launching a new product is to test-market it thoroughly—often in more than one market, to be sure that the results are reliable. This testing procedure is costly, but many companies have been willing to absorb the costs in order to improve their prospects of success. However, a new problem has arisen recently. Competing companies have taken advantage of the time lag introduced by test-marketing to launch their own versions of the new product without the precaution of testing. They have been successful often enough to have cast some doubt on the advisability of employing the test-market procedure. The following article gives an interesting account of this new phenomenon.

A short time ago, Lever Brothers Co. came up with what it thought was a marketing coup. After spending a great deal of time and money on research and development, the company developed a new table syrup called "Mrs. Butterworth" that featured the addition of butter. Smacking its lips over an anticipated major breakthrough, Lever Brothers put the product on the test market. Result: "Mrs. Butterworth" caught the eye of a major rival, and by the time Lever

Brothers was ready to go national, so was the competitor.

Lever Brothers' unfortunate experience is by no means rare in the hazardous world of test marketing. Many another company can relate a similar tale of woe. For lurking in the path of the test marketer are all the booby traps that ingenious rivals can rig up. "It is," says one insider, "the most dangerous game in marketing."

But why should a company's attempt to prove out a product be so fraught with peril? The major reason, of course, is that great driving force of the U.S. economy itself: competition. For when a new product is test marketed, all its secrets are bared long before it can hope to make a national impact. "Tipping the mitt," says Robert S. Wheeler, vice president and marketing director for Corn Products Co., "can be one of the greatest calamities to befall a marketer."

Marketing men recall, for instance, the case of Procter & Gamble's "Head & Shoulders" shampoo. While P&G was working up a preliminary lather in the test market, a smaller drug company, noting the product's quick acceptance, flooded the market with its own shampoo, hastily concocted but identical in concept, thus giving its larger competitor an unwelcome scrubbing.

In another instance, a giant food company came out last year with a fruit-filled toast waffle. Hailed by the manufacturer as a new taste sensation, the product was test marketed in selected areas around the country at a cost of a half-million dollars. The waffle caught on at once with consumers; housewives, apparently, could hardly wait to pop it into their toasters. Its future looked most appetizing.

There was just one thing wrong: the waffle looked good to the competition too. So good, in fact, that another large food concern, enviously watching its sales in the test stores, bought up a supply, put them under a microscope— and soon went into national production with an exact replica. "It did not cost them a nickel to test it," says a third marketer who watched the drama from the sidelines, "and they beat the original product to the national market by six months. Moreover, their duplicate caught on immediately. And now the first manufacturer, after investing all the work and money, is dragging along with a second-place brand."

Equally diabolical is the competitive maneuver to create a state of euphoria in the test marketer by gobbling up quantities of his product off the shelves.

This tactic, of course, is meant to give the tester false confidence. Frequently it also robs him of the chance to run his product through the laboratory again to get rid of flaws the test-market period is supposed to spotlight. This stratagem is often responsible for a product's failure once it goes national after a "successful" run in the test market. By then, of course, it is too late.

Another favorite technique of competitors is price-cutting. Robert Wheeler, a frequent critic of test marketing, cites the case of Procter & Gamble's Crisco Oil. When it went on the market, a smaller company fought back by reducing the price of its own similar product. P&G, in turn, retaliated by cutting the price of Crisco while it was still on the test market—presumably in the belief that the tiny rival could not possibly sustain the low price. To its discomfort, however, the other product continued to sell at reduced price. "Whatever timetable P&G had for profit," says Wheeler, "was out the window."

Flourishing and Proliferating

But despite the heavy costs, occasionally astronomical losses and other perils, test marketing is not only flourishing but proliferating. In 1966 alone, outlays for this purpose ran to more than $1 billion. The irony of it all is pointed up by Edwin M. Berdy, director of market research for Bristol-Myers' Hillside division. "Like it or not," Dr. Berdy argues, "test marketing, imperfect and fallible as it is, still remains the only gauge we have to determine a new product's future."

Agrees President Harrison F. Dunning of Scott Paper Co.: "We are for it because it is the only way you can find out if you are, in fact, filling a real consumer need."

And competition, while ever present, is by no means the only culprit. Many a new-product disaster stems from a company's childlike faith in certain marketing myths—such as the belief in a "typical" consumer. As one battle-weary veteran puts it: "The fact is, there is no such thing anymore as a typical test market."

For one thing, the U.S. market has grown both more complex and more segmented. Then, too, the steady parade of new products and the changing ethnic population mix make it increasingly difficult to gauge potential success accurately by using scattered markets that usually represent no more than 2% to 3% of the nation.

Too, many marketers criticize the excessive use of favorite test cities (such as Rochester, New York, Hartford, Connecticut and Columbus, Ohio). "As time goes on," says President Charles T. Pope of American Chicle Co., "it is increasingly difficult to find test markets that are not simultaneously serving as test sites for many other brands—sometimes even for kindred products. This raises a question as to how realistic the marketing environment is."

Test marketing sometimes goes awry even when a site is specially chosen to test a particular product. A case in point was the recent testing of a new lubricant for outboard motors by Dow Chemical Co. The lubricant was tested in Florida and Michigan. Florida was particularly chosen because the company thought that a warm-weather state, in which the product would have to stand up under continuous use, would prove the most demanding test. And the lubricant was a marketing success.

But the story was quite different in Michigan. Although the lubricant sold well and worked well during the summer, the following spring the company discovered that in the colder northern climate it had congealed, allowing the outboard motors, idle all winter, to rust. The rusting problem, of course, never came to light in Florida where the motors were in year-round use.

More often, though, test marketing fails because of excessive zeal. All too often, the product manager or marketing manager himself causes a snafu. The process goes something like this: To get the backing he needs for a pet project, the product manager goes to top management with his estimate of the test-market results. These he hopefully extrapolates on a national scale—"with nice big black figures in the lower righthand corner," notes one executive —to convince management that the undertaking is worth a further investment.

Once he gets the go-ahead, says the critic, the man responsible for the project naturally has more than an objective interest in its success. And to get the kind of results he needs to justify management's continued confidence, his philosophy now is that the test market "must succeed at any cost."

It is not difficult to "rig" a test market—through aggressive sales to retailers, hypoed advertising or excessive use of coupons. But the picture changes considerably when the product, after ringing up its test "success," goes national. Then it must stand on its own feet. "Many a manager," the critic maintains, "has sabotaged his own product by too eager tactics."

"To get accurate projections," says Bristol-Myers' Edwin Berdy, "you have to knock off 10% for overzealousness on the part of the product people, sales personnel and store management."

Another form of self-sabotage is insufficient product and market research. Too often, say the critics, shortcomings hidden behind an aggressive test-market introduction come to light only on the national market. For example, one well-known produce manufacturer tried out a meat in the test market, where it sold very well. Nationally, however, it flopped. The failure remained a mystery until a researcher visiting a delicatessen discovered that under the fluorescent glare in the display case, the meat turned blue. During the test marketing, under ideal display conditions, this failure had not come to light.

Far too many products, says market researcher Jack A. Gold, hold up well in test marketing because they are displayed under optimum conditions but "die" under more normal conditions. "Research on the life of the product, its storage future and its durability on the shelf should rank equally with other aspects of market research," he says.

Perhaps one of the most assiduous protesters in the field is Kimberly-Clark Corp. "We don't go on the market," says Gilbert Dementis, director of marketing research, "until we have tested the product's concept, studied the competitive situation, developed prototypes and pretested advertising."

"Don't forget," adds Jack Gold, "the test market was also meant to be a marketing laboratory. It is unfortunate that too many marketing people don't do their homework properly."

"Who Needs It?"

In view of all the criticism, it is not unusual to find a growing number of companies who say of test marketing: "Who needs it?" One of the most vociferous is Irving Scharf, the director of marketing for Seagram-Distillers Co., whose 100 Pipers Scotch was introduced nationally without a market test. "We don't believe in it," Scharf says. "If you do your homework well, why should you need a test market? Besides, considering all the pecularities of each market, we had very little to learn from any one."

Indeed, some successful products have

been introduced without test marketing. Among the more recent: Standard Brand's Planters Dry Roasted Peanuts, Colgate-Palmolive's Soaky Fun Bath and Quaker Oats' Aunt Jemima Easy-Pour Pancake Mix. Many companies forgo the test market solely because they feel that product security is paramount. Several years ago, in announcing the introduction of Wondra instantized flour, for example, General Mills President Edwin W. Rawlings admitted that the product was going national because it was the only way the company could get a jump on the competition. "At Best Foods," adds Robert Wheeler, "we are seriously considering going national without test marketing on several projects now on the drawing board."

However, most companies still believe in test marketing. For all its faults, they feel, it represents the only available barometer of a product's worth. One need only consider the fate that has befallen some untested products to understand this viewpoint (for example, a detergent manufactured by a very large and well-known chemical company that was found by consumers to have a kerosene odor and not enough suds).

According to Bristol-Myers' Edwin Berdy, a veteran in the field ("I have no test-market anecdotes to tell—just scars to prove I was there"), probably the best thing that could happen to test marketing would be a frank exchange of experiences and information among its practitioners. "Let's not give up on test marketing," says Berdy, "but, rather, let's identify the areas of softness and correct them as best we can."

As for the future, the advocates of test marketing hardly expect to come up with any startling innovations. But a number of approaches have been designed to more effectively safeguard product security or at least keep competition at bay.

One such ploy is controlled-store

testing. "The likelihood of keeping a marketing innovation confidential, at least from major competitors," says Charles A. Sobel, vice president of market research firm Audits and Surveys Co., "is much greater when its introduction is limited to twenty or thirty scattered stores than if it is tested on a large scale in major cities." Spot coverage is also usually less expensive, and testing a limited sample of stores rather than blanketing whole areas enables the testers to better control such marketing variables as climate and season.

Another approach, originated by Jack Gold, is to take testing directly into the consumer's home. Until this plan, initiated at the Mennen Co. several years ago by Gold, the new product does not appear in stores but is exposed to consumers, along with competitive products, in their homes. At the end of the trial period, consumers are questioned about their satisfaction with the product. They are not even aware that they are trying a new product.

In the final analysis, the experts agree on one thing: there are no moral victories in the marketing field. No matter how well a product fares on any one market, it still must make the grade on a national scale to achieve a conclusive victory. As one marketer tersely puts it: "The name of the game is still profits."

C

Product Planning and Strategy

Leverage in the Product Life Cycle

Donald K. Clifford, Jr.

The product life cycle is one of the most promising concepts to guide managers in making marketing decisions. Unfortunately, many introductory marketing textbooks give this concept only passing mention. This article discusses succinctly the concept and the various stages of the cycle as well as what this means to the marketing manager. Also brought out is the fact that life cycles can be managed. The major portion of the article deals with life cycle management.

Not long ago, a leading packaged goods maker was promoting a brand of toilet soap. Growth had been fair but not spectacular. Finally, product and market tests suggested that an increase in spot television advertising, backed by a change in copy, could help the product to reach the "escape velocity" it needed to become a sales leader. But management, feeling that the funds would be better spent in launching a new product, vetoed the proposal.

The new product was, to be sure, a moderate success. But the promising

Reprinted by special permission from *Dun's Review*, May 1964. Copyright, 1968, Dun & Bradstreet Publications Corp.

soap brand went into a gradual sales decline from which it never recovered. Management had pulled the props out from under the product at a critical point in its growth period.

Again, a product manager at a firm making light industrial equipment felt that his principal product was not getting the sales support it deserved. Unconvinced by the salesmen's claims that the product was "hard to sell," he developed new presentations and sales kits and persuaded sales management to run special campaigns. At year-end, however, volume had shown no improvement. With the power of hindsight, management recognized that this product had long since passed its zenith and that no amount of additional sales support could have profitably extended its growth. Yet the expensive promotion drive had cut into the marketing budgets of several promising new products. In short, management had failed to consider each product's position in its life cycle.

As these two cases suggest, the concept of the product life cycle—familiar as it is to most business executives—is frequently forgotten in marketing planning. Yet there is conclusive evidence that if properly used it can transform a company's profit-and-loss statement. The concept is based on the fact that a product's sales volume follows a typical pattern that can be charted as a four-phase cycle (*see chart, page 249*). After its birth, the product passes through a low-volume introduction phase. During the following growth phase, volume and profit both rise. Volume stabilizes during the period of maturity, although unit profits start to fall off. Eventually, in the obsolescence stage of the product, sales volume declines.

The length of the life cycle, the duration of each phase and the shape of the curve vary widely for different products. But in every case, obsolescence eventually occurs either because the need disappears (as when frozen orange juice hit sales of orange juice squeezers), because a better or cheaper product may be developed to fill the same need (oil-based paint is losing its position in the home to water-based paint, and plastics are replacing wood, metal and paper products ranging from dry-cleaning bags to aircraft parts) or because a competitive product suddenly gains a decisive advantage through superior marketing strategy (as happened to competing products when Arthur Godfrey promoted Lipton Tea and again when the American Dental Association publicly endorsed Procter & Gamble's decay-prevention claims for Crest toothpaste).

The profit cycle of a product is quite different from its sales cycle. During introduction, a product may not earn any profit because of high initial advertising and promotion costs. In the growth period, before competition catches up, unit profits typically attain their peak. Then they start declining, although total profits may continue to climb for a time on rising sales volume. (In the chemical industry, for example, rapid increases in volume often more than offset the effect of price reductions early in the growth phase.)

During late growth and early maturity, increasing competition cuts deeply into profit margins and ultimately into total profits. For instance, as a result of drastic price-cutting, general-purpose semiconductors, once highly profitable, now return so little unit profit that major companies such as the Columbia Broadcasting System and Clevite Corp. have left the business entirely. Finally, in the obsolescence phase, declining volume eventually pushes costs up to a level that eliminates profits entirely.

What does this mean for the marketing manager? At the very least, he should always bear in mind that the factors behind a product's profitability change with each phase of its life cycle, and plot his sales strategy accordingly. Typically, product development and design are crucial in the introduction phase. For industrial products, where customers are slow to change from a proven product, technical superiority or demonstrable cost savings are often needed to open the door. For consumer products, heavy marketing spending may be critical in building volume.

During the growth period, reliability is vital to the success of most industrial products and technically complex consumer products. A well-grounded reputation for quality can win a manufacturer the leading position in the market, as it did for Zenith Radio Corp. in black-and-white television sets. For consumer packaged goods and other nontechnical products, on the other hand, effective distribution and advertising are crucial.

The key requirement during maturity, though harder to define, can be described as "overall marketing effectiveness." Marketing skill may pay off in a variety of ways; for example, by cutting price so as to reach new consumers, by promoting new uses for the product, or

by upgrading distribution. During obsolescence, cost control is the key factor in generating profits. The product of the low-cost producer and distributor often enjoys a profitable "old age" long after its rivals have disappeared from the scene.

But although they are valid within their limits, these generalizations about the product life cycle do not really go far enough. For they fail to take into account a key fact: life cycles can be managed.

Life-cycle management, which adds a

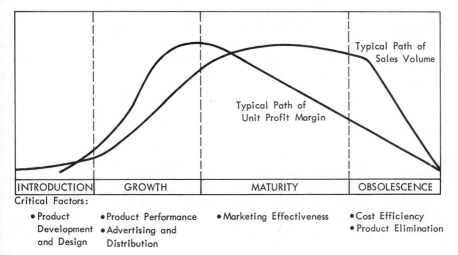

Critical Factors:

- Product Development and Design
- Product Performance
- Advertising and Distribution
- Marketing Effectiveness
- Cost Efficiency
- Product Elimination

Profile of a Product. The wise marketer is aware of the critical factors underlying the course of his product's sales volume and profits. More importantly, he knows how to manipulate those factors to swell earnings. The chart above shows the typical shape of a product's sales volume and profit. The table shows a life-cycle "audit" of a product in early maturity.

Product XYZ, March 1965		Change in Past Year	Average Annual Change Over Past Five Years
Annual sales volume	$28.6 million	+2.5%	+11.8%
Gross margin	31.0%	−5.0%	−17.0%
Profit contribution	9.0%	−5.0%	−12.0%
Return on invested capital	14.0%	−4.0%	−12.0%
Price	$.85/lb.	−$.04	−$.11/lb.
Market share	16.0%	−	+ 8.0%

vital new dimension to the traditional life-cycle concept, has two basic aspects: (1) Controlling individual product life cycles to generate new profits. (2) Controlling the mix of product life cycles in the product line by carefully planned new-product introduction, product-line pruning and allocation of money and manpower among existing products according to their profit potential.

A product's introduction phase can often be shortened by increasing marketing expenditures or securing national distrbution more quickly. In the next phase, growth can be speeded and sales and profits ultimately pushed to higher levels by exploiting additional markets, by pricing the product to encourage wider usage, and by more productive advertising or sales efforts; in short, by more effectively planned and implemented marketing strategy.

Cheating Old Age

But it is in maturity that the shape and duration of a product's life cycle can be changed most radically. Is the product really approaching obsolescence? Or does it merely seem to be because consumers' needs are not being truly filled or because a competitor has done a superior marketing job? The question is crucial, since often the real challenge of "maturity" is not to adapt to it but to change it by revitalizing the product— through repackaging, for example, or by product modifications, repricing, appealing to new users or adding new distribution channels. And often a successfully revitalized product offers a higher return on management time and funds invested than does a new product.

Take, for example, the case of E. I. du Pont, which as a major force in packaging materials has been strongest in cellophane, a product so well-known it has become almost a synonym for

transparent packaging. After World War II, flexible packaging, and cellophane in particular, entered a period of rapid growth. By the 1950's, however, new products began to meet certain packaging needs better. Polyethylene film, for example, was not so easily ruptured in cold weather, and in time it also became lower in price. As a result, cellophane began losing its share of the flexible-packaging market, and it was clear that sales would soon begin falling unless strong corrective action was taken.

Faced with this threat, du Pont launched a series of product modifications. These included special coating to reduce winter breakage and increase protection, new types of cellophane for different products and lighter grades of cellophane more competitive in price with the newer packaging materials. All in all, the customers' choice of cellophane types mushroomed from a handful to well over 100.

The results have been impressive. In the face of widespread prediction of rapid decline, cellophane as a whole has maintained its sales volume—of which the traditional grades now represent a relatively small fraction.

Further testimony to du Pont's effectiveness in lifecycle management is its control of the life-cycle mix of its flexible packaging products. Recognizing the maturity of cellophane, du Pont has developed a strong position in polyethylene and in other new packaging materials. So while maintaining its position by reshaping the life cycle of cellophane, the company has also provided for growth by adding new products to strengthen its product mix.

Another success in life-cycle manipulation was scored in the cake-mix market, where P&G introduced a large number of new cake types. This built sales in three ways. First, by broadening its line, P&G appealed to a wider market. Second, by increasing the variety of cakes, it persuaded women to make them more often. Third, by vastly increasing the number of cake mixes to be stocked in supermarkets, P&G achieved a billboard of cake mixes on shelves that inevitably drew the shopper's eye. In brief, Procter & Gamble increased the demand for cake mix and then filled that demand through the strength of its distribution.

Not all products, of course, can be revitalized in maturity. Maturity is forced upon some products by a basic change in consumer habits or a radically superior new competitor. In such cases it is important to recognize the fact promptly, and to cut back on the time and money invested in the product. In obsolescence, finally, marketing effectiveness is a matter of knowing when to cut short the life of a product that is demanding more than the small share of management attention it deserves.

Not long ago, a small candy company drastically changed its life-cycle mix by eliminating no fewer than 796 of the 800 items in its product line. By putting its muscle behind a single strong growth brand, and maintaining just three other products to offset swings in production, the company shifted its life-cycle balance from early obsolescence to growth. From a marginal producer, it has become one of the most profitable small companies in the confectionery business.

This type of successful product and product-line strategy is clearly the result of imagination, courage and sound judgment. It took imagination and initiative for P&G to expand its cake-mix line rather than modify its prices or advertising approach. It took marketing courage as well as judgment for the small candy company to cut its line by 99.5% rather than seek new brokers or start a fresh promotion program.

These companies, and others like them, were able to manipulate the life cycle of their products by making dis-

ciplined, periodic reviews of their progress. Such reviews should include not only a formal audit of each product's progress and outlook that pinpoints its position in its life cycle, but a profile of the life-cycle mix of the product line as a whole.

Tracing a Life Story

Although the steps involved in the first part of a life-cycle analysis often vary, the following are typical:

- Developing historical "trend" information for a period of three to five years, using such data as unit and dollar sales, profit margins, total profit contribution, return on invested capital, market share and price.
- Tracing trends in the number and nature of competitors, the number and market-share rankings of competing products and their quality and performance, shifts in distribution channels and the relative advantages of competitive products in each channel.
- Analyzing developments in short-term competitive strategy, such as competitors' announcements of new products or plans for expanding capacity.
- Developing (or updating) historical information on the life cycles of similar or related products, to help suggest the shape and duration of the life cycle for the product under study.
- Projecting sales for the product over the next three to five years and estimating an incremental profit ratio for the product during each of these years. The incremental profit ratio is the ratio of total direct costs to pretax profits. Expressed as a ratio—for example, 4.8 to 1 or 6.3 to 1—it measures the number of dollars required to generate each additional

dollar of profit. The ratio typically improves (that is, falls) as the product enters its growth period, then begins to rise as the product approaches maturity, and climbs even more sharply as it reaches obsolescence.

- Estimating the number of profitable years remaining in the product's life cycle and—based on all the information at hand—assigning the product to one of seven positions on its life-cycle curve: introduction, early or late growth, early or late maturity, early or late obsolescence.

Once the life-cycle positions of all the company's major products have been determined, a life-cycle profile of the company's entire product line can be drawn up. It works this way: Management first determines what percentages of sales and profits fall within each of the seven stages of this product life cycle, thus creating a "life-cycle profile" in terms of both sales and profits; it then calculates the change in the life-cycle and profit profiles over the past five years, and projects these profiles over the next five years; and finally it develops a *target* life-cycle profile for the company as a whole.

The target profile shows the desirable share of company sales that should fall within each phase of the product life cycle. It is determined on the basis of obsolescence trends in the industry, the pace of new-product introduction in the industry, the average length of product life cycles in the company's line, and management's objectives for growth and profitability. As a rule, the target profile for companies whose life cycles tend to be short, and for companies aiming for ambitious growth, will call for a high proportion of sales in the introductory and growth phases.

By comparing the company's target profile and its present life-cycle profile,

management is now in a position to assign priorities to such functions as new-product development, acquisitions and product-line pruning. And once corporate effort has been broadly allocated in this way among products at various stages of their life cycles, marketing plans should be developed for individual product lines. Since each product's life-cycle position and outlook has been calculated, marketing executives, from the product managers up to the marketing vice president, have a far sounder basis for setting up individual product plans.

Time for an Audit

To illustrate the use of life-cycle analysis, consider a well-diversified company in the packaging business—a field where new materials and new forms of packaging are being introduced every year and where mature and obsolescent products still account for the bulk of sales volume. As a basis for planning individual product and product-line strategies, this company carried out a life-cycle audit, developing sales and profit information for each of its products.

For product XYZ, a packaging film (*see table, page 249*), sales growth slackened last year. Gross margins, profit contribution and return on investment, which had all been declining since 1959, fell more sharply last year. Prices were largely to blame, but increased costs were also significant. Market share, meanwhile, had doubled in the previous five years, but showed no gain in 1964.

Two new competitors and four new competitive products had appeared, eliminating a former quality advantage of product XYZ. Sales analysis indicated that the top fifty accounts did 82% of product XYZ's volume in 1964, as against 68% five years earlier. In the same period, the total number of customers somewhat decreased. Finally, the incremental profit ratio appeared about to deteriorate from 11–1 to 12–1 in the coming year, rising to 15–1 by 1969.

On the basis of this analysis, marketing executives determined that product XYZ was in early maturity, with at least ten more years of profitable life in prospect. They decided, however, that a further increase in maturity could be offset, and additional growth achieved, if the film's tensile and tear strength could be improved by 25% at no increase in cost—an objective that appeared technically feasible. This then became a major element of their marketing strategy.

In similar fashion, the company developed life-cycle and profit profiles of its entire line. Only 6% of its current sales were represented by products in the introduction and growth stages, a far cry from the target profile of 25% called for (based on the expected length of life cycles in the business and growth and profit objectives). Management therefore decided to step up its acquisition program and new-product development sharply and to eliminate two obsolescent products. These steps cut the share of total volume represented by obsolescent products from 15% to 11%—close to the target profile of 10%.

The depth of life-cycle analysis, and the factors it must consider, vary almost as widely as do company needs, objectives and product lines. There is, then, no reliable formula for weighting the various factors that determine the life-cycle position of a product. But a management that makes good use of life-cycle analysis knows that it is this very flexibility that makes life-cycle analysis such an effective and widely applicable route to profits.

The Death and Burial of "Sick" Products

R. S. Alexander

Great attention has been paid to the subject of new product development and introduction over the past two decades. This is not surprising in view of the fact that the profit potential for a company is much greater in selling differentiated products than in selling homogeneous products. However, product elimination is a necessary counterpart to product addition, and business as yet has paid scant attention to this subject. The article following deals in a theoretical way with this subject that is certain to become a matter of rising concern and importance to businessmen. As yet we do not know much about product elimination on an empirical basis, although since this article appeared, there has been evidence of interest in learning more about the process.

Euthanasia applied to human beings is criminal; but aging products enjoy or suffer no such legal protection. This is a sad fact of business life.

The word "product" is used here not in its broad economic sense of anything produced—such as wheat, coal, a car, or a chair—but in its narrower meaning of an article made to distinct specifications and intended for sale under a separate brand or catalogue number. In the broader sense of the word, certain products may last as long as industrial civilization endures; in the narrow sense, most of them are playthings of change.

Much has been written about managing the development and marketing of new products, but business literature is largely devoid of material on product deletion.

This is not surprising. New products have glamor. Their management is fraught with great risks. Their successful introduction promises growth in sales and profits that may be fantastic.

But putting products to death—or letting them die—is a drab business, and often engenders much of the sadness of a final parting with old and tried friends. "The portable 6-sided, pretzel polisher was the first product The Company ever made. Our line will no longer be our line without it."

But while deletion is an uninspiring and depressing process, in a changing market it is almost as vital as the addition of new products. The old product that is a "football" of competition or has lost much of its market appeal is likely

Reprinted from the *Journal of Marketing*, national quarterly publication of the American Marketing Association, Vol. 28, No. 2, April 1964, pp. 1–7.

to generate more than its share of small unprofitable orders; to make necessary short, costly production runs; to demand an exorbitant amount of executive attention; and to tie up capital that could be used more profitably in other ventures.

Just as a crust of barnacles on the hold of a ship retards the vessel's movement, so do a number of worn-out items in a company's product mix affect the company's progress.

Most of the costs that result from the lack of an effective deletion system are hidden and become apparent only after careful analysis. As a result, management often overlooks them. The need for examining the product line to discover outworn members, and for analysis to arrive at intelligent decisions to discard or to keep them, very rarely assumes the urgency of a crisis. Too often, management thinks of this as something that should be done but that can wait until tomorrow.

This is why a definite procedure for deletion of products should be set up, and why the authority and responsibility for the various activities involved should be clearly and definitely assigned. This is especially important because this work usually requires the cooperation of several functional groups within the business firm, including at least marketing, production, finance, and sometimes personnel.

Definite responsibility should be assigned for at least the following activities involved in the process: (1) selecting products which are candidates for elimination; (2) gathering information about them and analyzing the information; (3) making decisions about elimination; and (4) if necessary, removing the doomed products from the line.

Selection of Products for Possible Elimination

As a first step, we are not seeking the factors on which the final decision to delete or to retain turns, but merely those which indicate that the product's continuation in the product mix should be considered carefully with elimination as a possibility. Although removal from the product line may seem to be the prime aim, the result is not inevitably deletion from the line; instead, careful analysis may lead to changes in the product itself or in the methods of making or marketing it.

Sales Trend. If the trend of a product's sales is downward over a time period that is significant in relation to the normal life of others like it, its continuation in the mix deserves careful examination. There may be many reasons for such a decline that in no way point toward deletion; but when decline continues over a period of time the situation needs to be studied.

Price Trend. A downward trend in the price of a new product may be expected if the firm introducing it pursues a skimming-price policy, or if all firms making it realize substantial cost savings as a result of volume production and increased processing know-how. But when the price of an established product whose competitive pattern has been relatively stabilized shows a downward trend over a significant period of time, the future of that product should receive attention.

Profit Trend. A declining profit either in dollars or as a per cent of sales or investment should raise questions about a product's continued place in the product line. Such a trend usually is the result of a price-factory cost squeeze, although it may be the outcome of a loss in market appeal or a change in the method of customer purchase which forces higher marketing expenditures.

Substitute Products. When a substitute article appears on the market, especially if it represents an improvement over an old product, management must face the question of whether to retain or discard the old product. This is true regardless of who introduces the substitute. The problem is especially difficult when the new product serves the same general purpose as the old one but is not an exact substitute for it.

Product Effectiveness. Certain products may lose some of their effectiveness for the purposes they serve. For example, disease germs may develop strains that are resistant to a certain antibiotic. When this happens, the question of whether to keep or delete the drug involves issues not only of the interests of the firm but of the public welfare.

Executive Time. A possible tipoff as to the location of "illness" in a product mix lies in a study of the amount of executive time and attention devoted to each of the items in the product line. Sick products, like sick people, demand a lot of care; but one must be careful to distinguish the "growing pains" of a new product from the more serious disorders of one that has matured and is now declining.

The six indicators mentioned do not of themselves provide evidence justifying deletion. But they can help management to single out from a line of products those upon which it can profitably spend time and money in analyzing them, with elimination from the line as a *possibility*.

Analysis and Decision Making About "Sick" Products

Although the work of analyzing a sick or decrepit product is usually done by people other than the management executives who decide what to do about it, the two processes are interdependent.

Unless the right factors are chosen for analysis and unless the work is properly done, the decision is not likely to be an intelligent one. Accordingly, these two factors will be discussed together.

What information does a decision-maker need about a product, and what sort of analysis of it should he have in order to render a sound verdict as to its future? The deletion decision should not turn on the sole issue of profitability. Profit is the most important objective of a business; but individual firms often seek to achieve both long-run and short-run objectives other than profit.

So, in any individual case the critical factors and the weights assigned them in making a decision must be chosen in the light of the situation of the firm and the management objectives.

Profits

Profit management in a firm with a multi-product line (the usual situation in our economy) is not the simple operation generally contemplated in economic theory. Such a firm usually has in its product mix (1) items in various stages of introduction and development, some of which may be fantastically profitable and others deep "in the red"; (2) items which are mature but not "superannuated," whose profit rate is likely to be satisfactory; and (3) declining items which may yield a net profit somewhat less than adequate or may show heavy losses.

The task is to manage the whole line or mix so that it will show a satisfactory profit for the company. In this process, two questions are vital; What is a profit? How much profit is satisfactory?

Operating-statement accounting makes it possible to determine with reasonable accuracy the total amount of net profit a company earns on an overall basis. But when the management of a multi-product firm seeks to determine how much of this total is generated by its activities in making and marketing each product in its mix, the process is almost incredibly complex; and the results are almost certain to be conditioned on a tissue of assumptions which are so debatable that no management can feel entirely comfortable in basing decisions on them.

This is because such a large portion of the costs of the average multi-product firm are or behave like overhead or joint expense. Almost inevitably several of the items in the product mix are made of common materials, with the same equipment, and by manpower which is interchangeable. Most of the company's marketing efforts and expenses are devoted to selling and distributing the mix or a line within the mix, rather than individual items.

In general, the more varied the product mix of a firm, the greater is the portion of its total expense that must be classified as joint or overhead. In such a company, many types of cost which ordinarily can be considered direct tend to behave like overhead or joint expenses. This is particularly true of marketing costs such as advertising that does not feature specific items; personal selling order handling; and delivery.

This means that a large part of company's costs must be assigned to products on some arbitrary basis and that however logical this basis may be it is subject to considerable reasonable doubt in specific cases. It also means that if one product is removed from the mix many of these costs remain to be reassigned to the items that stay in the line. As a result, any attempt to "prune" the product mix entirely on the basis of the profit contribution, or lack of it, of specific items is almost certain to be disappointing and in some cases disastrous.

But if a multi-product firm could allocate costs to individual items in the mix on some basis recognized as sound and thus compute product-profit accurately, what standard of profit should be set up, the failure to meet which would justify deletion?

Probably most managements either formally or unconsciously set overall company profit targets. Such targets may be expressed in terms of dollars, although to be most useful in product management they usually must be translated into percentages on investment, or money used. As an example, a company may have as its profit target 15% on investment before taxes.

Certainly *every* product in the mix should not be required to achieve the target, which really amounts to an average. To do so would be to deny the inevitable variations in profit potential among products.

Probably a practical minimum standard can be worked out, below which a product should be eliminated unless other considerations demand its retention. Such a standard can be derived from a balancing out of the profit rates among products in the mix, so as to arrive at the overall company target as an average. The minimum standard then represents a figure that would tip the balance enough to endanger the overall target.

What role, then, should considerations of product profit play in managerial decisions as to deletion or retention?

1. Management probably will be wise to recognize an overall company target profit in dollars or rate on investment, and to set in relation to it a minimum below which the profit on an individual product should not fall without marking that item for deletion (unless other special considerations demand its retention).

2. Management should cast a "bilious eye" on all arguments that a questionable product be kept in the mix because it helps to defray overhead and joint costs. Down that road, at the end of a series of decisions to retain such products, lies a mix entirely or largely composed of items each busily "sopping up" overhead, but few or none contributing anything to net profit.

3. This does not mean that management should ignore the effect of a product deletion on overhead or joint costs. Decision-makers must be keenly aware of the fact that the total of such costs borne by a sick product must, after it is deleted, be reallocated to other products, and with the result that they may become of doubtful profitability. A detailed examination of the joint or overhead costs charged against an ailing product may indicate that some of them can be eliminated in whole or in part if it is eliminated. Such costs are notoriously "sticky" and difficult to get rid of; but every pretext should be used to try to find ways to reduce them.

4. If a deletion decision involves a product or a group of products responsible for a significant portion of a firm's total sales volume, decision-makers can assess the effects of overhead and joint costs on the problem, by compiling an estimated company operating statement after the deletion and comparing it with the current one. Such a forecasted statement should include expected net income from the use of the capital and facilities released by deletion if an opportunity for their use is ready to hand. Surviving joint and overhead expenses can even be reallocated to the remaining products, in order to arrive at an estimate of the effect that deletion might have, not only on the total company net income but on the profitability of each of the remaining products as well. Obviously such a cost analysis is likely to be expensive, and

so is not justified unless the sales volume stakes are high.

Financial Considerations

Deletion is likely not only to affect the profit performance of a firm but to modify its financial structure as well.

To make and sell a product, a company must invest some of its capital. In considering its deletion, the decision-makers must estimate what will happen to the capital funds presently used in making and marketing it.

When a product is dropped from the mix, most or all of the circulating capital invested in it—such as inventories of materials, goods in process, and finished goods and accounts receivable—should drain back into the cash account; and if carried out in an orderly fashion, deletion will not disturb this part of the capital structure except to increase the ratio of cash to other assets.

This will be true, unless the deletion decision is deferred until product deterioration has gone so far that the decision assumes the aspect of a crisis and its execution that of a catastrophe.

The funds invested in the equipment and other facilities needed to make and market the "sick" product are a different matter. If the equipment is versatile and standard, it may be diverted to other uses. If the firm has no need of it and if the equipment has been properly depreciated, management may find a market for it at a price approaching or even exceeding its book value.

In either case, the capital structure of the company is not disturbed except by a shift from equipment to cash in the case of sale. In such a case management would be wise, before making a deletion decision, to determine how much cash this action promises to release as well as the chances for its reinvestment.

If the equipment is suited for only one purpose, it is highly unlikely that management can either find another use for it or sell it on favorable terms. If it is old and almost completely depreciated, it can probably he scrapped and its remaining value "written off" without serious impairment of the firm's capital structure.

But if it is only partly depreciated, the decision-makers must weigh the relative desirability of two possible courses of action: (1) to delete immediately, hoping that the ensuing improvement in the firm's operating results will more than offset the impairment in capital structure that deletion will cause; or (2) to seek to recapture as much as possible of its value, by continuing to make and market the product as long as its price is enough to cover out-of-pocket costs and leave something over to apply to depreciation.

This choice depends largely on two things: the relation between the amount of fixed and circulating capital that is involved; and the opportunities available to use the funds, executive abilities, manpower, and transferable facilities released by deletion for making profits in other ventures.

This matter of opportunity costs is a factor in every deletion decision. The dropping of a product is almost certain to release some capital, facilities, manpower skills, and executive abilities. If opportunities can be found in which these assets can be invested without undue risk and with promise of attractive profits, it may be good management to absorb considerable immediate loss in deleting a sick product.

If no such opportunities can be found, it is probably wise to retain the product so long as the cash inflow from its sales covers out-of-pocket costs and contributes something to depreciation and other overhead expenses. In such a case, however, it is the part of good management to seek actively for new ventures which promise satisfactory profits, and to be ready to delete promptly when such an opportunity is found.

Employee Relations

The effect which product elimination may have on the employees of a firm is often an important factor in decisions either to drop or to retain products.

This is not likely to be a deciding factor if new product projects are under development to which the people employed in making and marketing the doubtful product can be transferred, unless such transfer would deprive them of the earning power of special skills. But when deletion of a product means discharging or transferring unionized employees, the decision-makers must give careful thought to the effect their action is likely to have on company-union relations.

Even in the absence of union pressure, management usually feels a strong sense of responsibility for the people in its employ. Just how far management can go in conserving specific jobs at the expense of deferring or foregoing necessary deletions before it endangers the livelihood of all the employees of the firm is a nice question of balance.

Marketing Factors

Many multi-product firms retain in their marketing mixes one or more items which, on the basis of profits and the company financial structure, should be deleted. To continue to make and market a losing product is no managerial crime. It is reprehensible only when management does not know the product is a losing one or, knowing the facts, does not have sound reasons for retaining it. Such reasons are very likely to lie in the marketing area.

Deletions of products are often deferred or neglected because of management's desire to carry a "full line," whatever that means. This desire may be grounded on sound reasons of consumer patronage or on a dubious yearning for the "prestige" that a full line is supposed to engender. But there is no magic about a full line or the prestige that is supposed to flow from it. Both should be evaluated on the basis of their effects on the firm's sales volume, profits, and capacity to survive and grow.

Products are often associated in the marketing process. The sale of one is helped by the presence of another in the product mix.

When elimination of a product forces a customer who buys all or a large part of his requirements of a group of profitable items from the firm to turn to another supplier for his needs of the dropped product, he might shift some or or all of his other patronage as well. Accordingly, it is sometimes wise for management to retain in its mix a no-profit item, in order to hold sales volume of highly profitable products. But this should not be done blindly without analysis.

Rarely can management tell ahead of time exactly how much other business will be lost by deleting a product, or in what proportions the losses will fall among the remaining items. But in many cases the amount of sales volume can be computed that will be *hazarded* by such action; what other products will be subject to that hazard; and what portion of their volume will be involved. When this marketing interdependence exists in a deletion problem, the decision-makers should seek to discover the customers who buy the sick product; what other items in the mix they buy; in what quantities; and how much profit they contribute.

The firm using direct marketing channels can do this with precision and at relatively little cost. The firm marketing through indirect channels will find it more difficult, and the information will be less exact; but it still may be worthwhile. If the stakes are high enough, marketing research may be conducted to discover the extent to which the customer purchases of profitable items actually are associated with that of the sick product. Although the results may not be precise, they may supply an order-of-magnitude idea of the interlocking patronage situation.

Product interrelationships in marketing constitute a significant factor in making deletion decisions, but should never be accepted as the deciding factor without careful study to disclose at least the extent of the hazards they involve.

Other Possibilities

The fact that a product's market is declining or that its profit performance is substandard does not mean that deletion is the *only* remedy.

Profits can be made in a shrinking market. There are things other than elimination of a product that can be done about deteriorating profit performance. They tend to fall into four categories.

(1) **Costs.** A careful study may uncover ways of reducing factory costs. This may result from improved processes that either eliminate manpower or equipment time or else increase yield; or from the elimination of forms or features that once were necessary or worth-while but are no longer needed. The natural first recourse of allocating joint and overhead costs on a basis that is "kinder" to the doubtful product is not to be viewed with enthusiasm. After reallocation, these costs still remain in the business; and the general profit picture has not been improved in the least.

(2) **Marketing.** Before deleting a product, management will be wise to examine the methods of marketing it, to see if they can be changed to improve its profit picture.

Can advertising and sales effort be reduced without serious loss of volume? A holding operation requires much less effort and money than a promotional one.

Are services being given that the product no longer needs?

Can savings be made in order handling and delivery, even at some loss of customer satisfaction? For example, customers may be buying the product in small orders that are expensive to handle.

On the other hand, by spending more marketing effort, can volume be increased so as to bring about a reduction in factory cost greater than the added marketing expense? In this attempt, an unexpected "assist" may come from competitors who delete the product and leave more of the field to the firm.

By remodeling the product, "dressing it up," and using a new marketing approach, can it be brought back to a state of health and profit? Here the decision-makers must be careful not to use funds and facilities that could be more profitably invested in developing and marketing new products.

(3) **Price.** It is natural to assume that the price of a failing product cannot be raised. At least in part, its plight is probably due to the fact that it is "kicked around" by competition, and thus that competition will not allow any increases.

But competitors may be tired of the game, too. One company that tried increasing prices found that wholesalers and retailers did not resent a larger cost-of-goods-sold base on which to apply their customary gross profit rates, and that consumers continued to buy and competitors soon followed suit.

Although a price rise will not usually add to the sum total of user happiness, it may not subtract materially from total purchases. The decison-makers should not ignore the possibility of using a price reduction to gain enough physical volume to bring about a more-than-offsetting decline in unit costs, although at this stage the success of such a gambit is not likely.

(4) **Cross Production.** In the materials field, when small production runs make costs prohibitive, arrangements may sometimes be made for Firm A to make the *entire* supply of Product X for itself and Competitor B. Then B reciprocates with another similar product. Such "trades," for instance, are to be found in the chemical business.

Summation for Decision

In solving deletion problems, the decision-makers must draw together into a single pattern the results of the analysis of all the factors bearing on the matter. Although this is probably most often done on an intangible, subjective basis, some firms have experimented with the formula method.

For example, a manufacturer of electric motors included in its formula the following factors:

Profitability.
Position on growth curve.
Product leadership.
Market position.
Marketing dependence of other products.

Each factor was assigned a weight in terms of possible "counts" against the product. For instance, if the doubtful item promised no profits for the next three years, it had a count of 50 points against it, while more promising prospects were assigned lesser counts. A critical total for all factors was set in advance which would automatically doom a product. Such a system can include other factors—such as recapturability of invested capital, alternate available uses of facilities, effects on

labor force, or other variables peculiar to the individual case.

The use of a formula lends an aura of precison to the act of decision-making and assures a degree of uniformity in it. But obviously the weights assigned to different factors cannot be the same in all cases. For example, if the deletion of a doubtful product endangers a large volume of sales of other highly profitable items, that alone should probably decide the matter.

The same thing is true if deletion will force so heavy a writeoff of invested funds as to impair the firm's capital structure. Certainly this will be true if all or most of the investment can be recaptured by the depreciation route if the product stays in the mix.

This kind of decision requires that the factors be weighted differently in each case. But when managers are given a formula, they may tend to quit thinking and do too much "weighing."

The Deletion of a Product

Once the decision to eliminate a product is made, plans must be drawn for its death and burial with the least disturbance of customer relations and of the other operations of the firm.

Such plans must deal with a variety of detailed problems. Probably the most important fall into four categories: timing; parts and replacements; stocks; and holdover demand.

Timing. It is desirable that deletion be timed so as to dovetail with the financial, manpower, and facilities needs for new products. As manpower and facilities are released from the dying product and as the capital devoted to it flows back into the cash account, it is ideal if these can be immediately used in a new venture. Although this can never be completely achieved, it may be approximated.

The death of a product should be timed so as to cause the least disturbance to customers. They should be informed about the elimination of the product far enough in advance so they can make arrangements for replacement, if any are available, but not so far in advance that they will switch to new suppliers before the deleting firm's inventories of the product are sold. Deletion at the beginning of a selling season or in the middle of it probably will create maximum customer inconvenience, whereas at the end of the season it will be the least disturbing.

Parts and Replacements. If the product to be killed off is a durable one, probably the deleting firm will find it necessary to maintain stocks of repair parts for about the expected life of the units most recently sold. The firm that leaves a trail of uncared-for "orphan" products cannot expect to engender much good will from dealers or users. Provision for the care and maintenance of the orphan is a necessary cost of deletion.

This problem is much more widespread than is commonly understood. The woman who buys a set of china or silverware and finds that she cannot replace broken or lost pieces does not entertain an affectionate regard for the maker. The same sort of thing is true if she installs draperies and later, when one of them is damaged, finds that the pattern is no longer available.

Stocks. The deletion plan should provide for clearing out the stocks of the dying product and materials used in its production, so as to recover the maximum amount of the working capital invested in it. This is very largely a matter of timing—the tapering off of purchase, production, and selling activities. However, this objective may conflict with those of minimizing inconvenience

to customers and servicing the orphan units in use after deletion.

Holdover Demand. However much the demand for a product may decline, it probably will retain some following of devoted users. They are bound to be disturbed by its deletion and are likely to be vocal about it; and usually there is little that management can do to mitigate this situation.

Sometimes a firm can avoid all these difficulties by finding another firm to purchase the product. This should usually be tried before any other deletion steps are taken. A product with a volume too small for a big firm to handle profitably may be a money-maker for a smaller one with less overhead and more flexibility.

Neglect or Action?

The process of product deletion is important. The more dynamic the business, the more important it is.

But it is something that most company executives prefer not to do; and therefore it will not get done unless management establishes definite, clearcut policies to guide it, sets up carefully articulated procedures for doing it, and makes a positive and unmistakable assignment of authority and responsibility for it.

Exactly what these policies should be, what form these procedures should take, and to whom the job should be assigned are matters that must vary with the structure and operating methods of the firm and with its position in the industry and the market.

In any case, though, the need for managerial attention, planning, and supervision of the deletion function cannot be overemphasized. Many business firms are paying dearly for their neglect of this problem, but unfortunately do not realize how much this is costing them.

40

Firms Trying to Profit from Inventions Often Face Many Obstacles

Lee Berton

In theory, a patent gives the holder seventeen years of uncontested use of the patent grant. This sounds as if the holder has monopolistic control over a market for an extended period. However, as the accompanying article demonstrates, the protection is much less than the typical person is likely to assume and its effective life is apt to be much shorter than seventeen years. Because the purpose of patent protection is to give the holder enough protection to induce inventors to invent and make their inventions commercial, the protection should be long enough to accomplish this result but not long enough to return the inventor an exhorbitant profit. Our patent system achieves the result in only a very rough fashion. Although some of the practices described in the article are of dubious legality and more questionable ethics, they do at least help to pass on to consumers the benefits of invention faster in many cases.

As every inventor knows, two umbrellas shield him against the expropriation of his ideas by others. As every patent attorney knows, the inventor can get soaked under either of them.

The first is simply security—keeping mum about valuable ideas that haven't yet been patented, an umbrella the wise inventor raises himself. The U.S. Patent Office helps by keeping confidential all its applications for patents. When it does grant one, the second umbrella unfurls; the patent is made public, but its issuance gives the holder a 17-year monopoly on the rights to his invention.

Reprinted from *The Wall Street Journal*, June 26, 1968, by special permission.

All this might seem to give adequate protection, but often it does not. Talks with patent attorneys, inventors and others reveal myriad ways in which security is breached and patent protection ripped to shreds, by fair means and foul, in the ceaseless conflict that goes on over the rights to valuable ideas.

It is a struggle the public seldom sees; some battles are fought in court but most are not. Also, just about anything goes. Intelligence is gathered at scientific conferences. Merger talks are started with no intent of merger. Paper barricades are set up in the Patent Office. Attorneys shop for the "right" court in which to press patent suits. Back-scratching deals are made quietly.

And both sides use industrial spies—men like U. O. Cumming, an ordinary-looking New Yorker who has posed as everything from a reporter to an accident victim in digging out information for his clients, among them the nation's largest corporations and patent law firms.

It's a bizarre war with no de-escalation in sight. "With today's fierce competition, some companies are forced to use devious methods to obtain the patent plans or trade secrets of others or they'd be put out of business," says Reynold Bennett, an attorney and director of the patents committee of the National Association of Manufacturers.

"Designing Around" a Patent

A patent strategy can be devious without being considered unethical, of course. For example, a firm eager to market a product patented by a rival can often "design around" the rival's patent and get one of its own. This is perfectly legal and is even encouraged; indeed, that's why patents are made public—to encourage their widest possible use and to stimulate further improvements in the technology they cover.

In keeping with this viewpoint, the Patent Office takes a very liberal view of what is novel and useful enough to warrant patent. A few changes here and there, and one company can get a patent on a product similar to that of another firm. In 1960, inventor Albert Mintz got a patent on a safety door chain with key lock and got it manufactured by a Long Island, N.Y., firm. But a Brooklyn company designed around the Mintz patent by making some changes in the lock. Now R. Russell Dock, patent counsel to Mr. Mintz, hopes to help his client design around the Brooklyn firm with still another modification.

The advantage of "designing around"

is that the company doing so successfully can avoid taking out a license from, and paying royalties to, its competitor. The latter, however, can make such circumvention a lot tougher by filing for a long string of patents covering different aspects of the same invention. This not only gives him more protection against "designing around" but may also be used as a smokescreen to fool other companies; Patent Office procedures make it difficult to track down numerous patents on a product, and even if the patents are known, it's difficult to tell which ones are being used—particularly if a manufacturing process is involved.

A Loose-Lipped Researcher

Consider Zefran, an acrylic fiber made by Dow-Badische Co., a 50%-owned subsidiary of Dow Chemical Co. Dow-Badische has dozens of patents dealing with the manufacture of Zefran, but will not say which of them are actually being used. The company also won't say why it maintains so many patents, but a rival firm says Dow-Badische obviously is striving for the widest possible patent protection of its basic manufacturing method while trying to "obfuscate" it at the same time.

There are, of course, plenty of ways to find out things your rivals would prefer kept under wraps. A loose-lipped researcher at a trade show or scientfic conference can give his opposite numbers at other firms some good leads; he may also drop a few tips in the course of job shopping or in scientific papers written for technical journals.

"Scientists are wonderful and talented people, but they seem to have an absolute mania, stimulated by sales and business people, for immediate telling the world about any idea that occurs to them," sighs John R. Shipman, a patent attorney for International Business Machines Corp.

There are shadier ways of getting the information, too. One corporate attorney tells of a chemical firm that failed to protect valuable, patentable secrets because it didn't discover until too late that someone had planted a spy camera in one of its Xerox machines to snap pictures of documents being duplicated. Asked if the chemical firm was his own company, the attorney declined comment.

Intelligence about ideas that are patentable but that aren't yet covered can be used to deprive a competitor of many years of royalty income—and sometimes even the patent he might otherwise have obtained. Say, for example, that ABC Corp. finds out that a rival has developed or is developing a new widget. ABC speeds up its own widget development (perhaps borrowing a couple of ideas filched from its competitor) and applies for its own patent.

If its rival has an application in, too, the Patent Office has to decide which party deserves the patent. The date of filing is of no consequence; under present law, the party that can demonstrate it was the first actually to invent the product or process gets the rights to it. So ABC, even though it filed later, might be able to undercut its rival if it could prove, through documented laboratory experiments, records of factory prototype work and the like, that it was first with the invention.

Even if it can't do so, and its rival finally wins, ABC may have saved a tidy sum. A major "interference"—the Patent Office's term for a situation in which different parties make duplicate claims for the same invention—can take many years to resolve—and until a patent actually is issued, the invention in question can be used by anyone without payment of royalties.

Du Pont Co., for example filed a patent application in 1952 on a method for treating plastic film with ozone so it would accept ink printing. By 1955, the Patent Office had no less than 11 other applications for a similar patent. After a seemingly endless round of examinations by the Patent Office and a court challenge by two of the 11 other parties, Du Pont got its patent—in 1966. Its competitors had been able to use the process for 14 years without paying Du Pont a penny.

Of course, it could have been an accident that 11 others filed. Leon Wolinski, the researcher who developed the process for Du Pont, says the need for it was well-recognized in the entire plastics and chemicals industry. But he still finds the patent applications by 11 other inventors "an amazing coincidence."

In seeking information about a rival's innovative ideas, a number of firms adopt the phony merger ploy. Norman Jaspan, a management consultant who specializes in industrial security, says: "Many a proposed merger you've read about was never intended to be but was proposed as a means of filching a company's secrets."

The filcher, taking a sudden interest in another firm, naturally wants to inspect its assets—including its patent applications and patent holdings themselves. Though patents are public, it is far easier to learn the patent holdings of a company in merger talks than it is to track them down in the Patent Office. Once the supposed suitor has the information he wants, he breaks off talks—and may attack the other company's patents and steal its ideas.

Turning Cagey

Once burned, twice shy, seems to be the reaction of many victims. "We used to let everyone who was interested in buying us look at our patent applications, but we had an ugly experience with a competitor and we're playing it cagey now," says the patent counsel for a small Eastern firm.

Of course, playing it too cagey can mean loss of a juicy purchase offer from an earnest buyer. One way to be careful without discouraging honest suitors is to insist that the checking of patents and patent applications be done by an independent attorney and not by the would-be acquirer's staff; the outside counsel can tell the suitor all he really needs to know without exposing the other firm to undue risk.

A good many companies are adopting this defense. Thomas Wilson, who heads the 40-man patent department at W. R. Grace & Co., says the phony merger ploy "is becoming a touchy issue" and reports that a number of acquisition prospects approached recently by W. R. Grace have asked for outside counsel. Grace has made a dozen acquisitions in the past four years.

Some firms scorn deception altogether and make an all-out, frontal assault on a rival's patents, seeking to invalidate them or force the holder to grant special favors to the attacker. If the attacker is a big firm and the defender a small one, or an individual with limited resources, the battle is often a one-sided affair with a predictable outcome.

"Not every company has $100,000 or $200,000 to fight a patent case, and that's often what it takes to see it through if a big firm with huge financial resources is attacking an important patent," says Peter L. Tailer, a New York patent attorney who represents many independent inventors and smaller companies.

Searching for "Prior Art"

The big firm may harass the small one with claims of prior invention, seek-ing to get the small firm to cave in under the prospect of a lengthly, expensive court battle. Or it may make a thorough search for "prior art" that could invalidate the patent on the invention it covets.

"Prior art" means previous inventions similar or identical to the one in question. The Patent Office searches for such inventions before it grants patents, but it does not pretend that its inspection is a truly exhaustive one; with 3.3 million patents on file and more than 89,000 applications flowing in annually, the Office simply cannot make a complete search. So a determined attacker may well uncover the existence of a previous invention, one so similar to the invention he wants to market that the patent on the latter may be seriously questioned.

The attacker may also seek out indications that the invention had been made public or had actually been used more than a year before patent application had been made for it. Under present law, proof of such use of public knowledge (disclosure in, say, a technical journal) more than a year before filing also can scrap a patent.

A patent holder who feels himself threatened has a few cards to play, too. If he thinks his patent is shaky, he may find a "patsy." The "patsy" is a firm that agrees to take a license on the invention in question in return for a special favor of some kind from the patent holder. The reasoning is that if other firms see the patsy taking a license with no questions asked, they will be less apt to challenge the patent themselves.

One attorney tells of a big consumer products firm that keeps in reserve a smaller company which has agreed to take any licenses that are meeting "resistance" from the big firm's rivals. "The small company rolls over and plays dead, agreeing to pay the standard license fee to the big firm. Then it gets compensated by getting business from one of the big company's divisions," explains the attorney.

He requests anonymity. "For heaven's sakes," he says, "I'd be run out of the business if anyone knew I'd spilled the beans."

A more common defensive measure is to threaten the attacker's customers with legal action for patent infringement, in hopes they can be persuaded to stop buying the product in question and force the attacker to back off. (Patent infringement actions can be brought against customers of an infringer as well as an infringer himself; since the customers often lack the financial and other resources of the infringer, they may be more susceptible to pressure.)

If the attacker is undeterred, if the patent is a key one and if the defender feels he has a good case, the whole matter may land in court. The defender may file an infringement suit or, less often, the attacker may beat him to the punch by starting a legal action to challenge the validity of the patent.

Either way, the odds seem to favor the attacker. According to a recent study by a Congressional subcommittee, 79% of the cases that reached U.S. circuit courts of appeal in infringement or validity actions in 1966 resulted in findings that the inventions involved weren't worthy of patent protection. (Patent cases are tried in U.S. district courts, but appeal to the circuit court is made in most cases.)

Patent attorneys believe that Federal district and appeals courts are now reflecting the influence of two 1966 Supreme Court decisions. In these, the high court indicated that it believed patents should be issued more scrupulously and cover only really new and important advances.

Faced with unfavorable odds in court, patent holders try to select those jurisdictions with the best record in upholding patents and avoid those with the

worst. This "forum shopping" centers on the circuit courts of appeal, where the final decision in most patent cases is made.

A patent holder can pick the appeals court he wants by pressing his suit against customers of the infringer who do business in that jurisdiction. He can avoid the "wrong" court the same way.

Steering Clear of the Third Circuit

One Pennsylvania electrical parts maker, for example, has filed 25 infringement suits in the past eight years but has been able to avoid the U.S. Third Circuit Appeals Court, whose jurisdiction includes district courts in Pennsylvania, Delaware and New Jersey. According to the firm the Third Circuit Appeals Court had the poorest record for upholding patents of all 10 of the appeals courts in the 1959–63 period, the latest for which it has figures. The Third Circuit Appeals Court upheld only 2%, says the company.

Blatant forum shopping has its dangers. If it is clear that the plaintiff is simply trying to duck one court or wring a favorable verdict out of another, a judge who feels his jurisdiction is the proper one in which to try the case may throw out the patent. "Mainly, it depends on whether the judge takes offense," says one attorney.

Actually, neither attackers nor defenders go into court at all if they can help it; patent litigation is too expensive and time-consuming. An attorney at Kenyon & Kenyon, a big Wall Street law firm specializing in patent litigation, estimates that 80% of the patent squabbles it handles are settled out of court.

If the attacker is mainly bluffing, but meets a resolute defense, he may give up the fight and meekly take a license from his erstwhile foe. If he has some solid evidence that might invalidate the patent, and it is the defender who is bluffing, the latter is the one who surrenders. There also are a number of special deals that can be—and often are —arranged.

Not What It Seems

Just recently, for example, a Midwest maker of construction equipment halted its attack on another firm's patent for certain parts (the attacker had been making and selling them without permission) and took out a license from the patent holder. This looks like capitulation, but it isn't.

Under the license, the Midwestern firm agreed to pay the patent holder 5% of its sales of the parts, a standard royalty—but it also is required to pay no more than $1,000 in a given year. In reality, the lincensee is paying only $1 in royalties for every $750 in annual sales, a negligible amount.

According to the patent attorney for the attacker, the other firm "accused us of infringing their patent, but we showed them prior art that knocked that patent." The patent holder then begged the attacker to take out a license anyway, at the "ridiculously low" terms later agreed on and to keep mum about the prior art.

This course enables the patent holder to go on collecting a straight 5% royalty from other license holders, on a patent that would probably be declared invalid if challenged. And the Midwestern firm, at a price of only $1,000 a year, has been spared the far heavier cost of legal action.

Such back-scratching sometimes draws the fire of Federal antitrusters—when they can find out about it, that is. In May, Union Camp Corp. and Bemis Co. were fined $75,000 and $50,000 respectively on charges that they had conspired to use an invalid patent in such a way as to keep competitors from making a certain type of paper bag with a mesh-covered window. The president and patent attorney of Union Camp were also fined $5,000 apiece. The companies and individuals involved pleaded no contest.

Patents as Trading Material

Sometimes companies find it possible to settle their differences through a cross-licensing deal. Under such an arrangement, a company accused of infringement may offer the accuser use of one of its own patents if it can keep on using the accuser's. In some cases, neither firm pays royalties, and both enjoy the use of each other's technology.

Obviously, the firm with a big storehouse of patents is going to be able to use this and similar defensive techniques most effectively. A number of firms have big patent portfolios, using them not only as a source of income (sale of the patents or royalties from licensing), but as trading material, too.

Among patent attorneys, Ford Motor Co. has a reputation as a hoarder of patents with considerable skill in their defensive deployment; the firm has more than 1,500 active patents, many having little or nothing to do with its manufacturing businesses. Ford won't comment on the defensive use of them, preferring to discuss its formal program to offer licenses as a source of income.

The settlement of many a patent squabble, in court and out, often rests on the evidence unearthed by private detectives and others retained as industrial spies. U. O. Cumming, the New Yorker with a knack for impersonation, is one of the busiest; he has been involved in thousands of cases since 1927, and he claims that there are few industrial plants he hasn't been able to infiltrate.

Mr. Cumming works both sides of the street. One week, a patent holder suspecting infringement may ask him to find out which of the attacker's customers is buying the product in question; the next a different attacker may retain him to help prove that a certain patent is invalid. Just recently, posing as a trade magazine reporter, he wormed a damaging admission out of a patent holder who was suing Mr. Cumming's client for infringement.

"The holder had filed for his patent in 1958," related Mr. Cumming, "but inadvertently slipped by telling me he had commercially used the item patented in 1956 (well outside the one-year limit on use or public disclosure prior to a patent application). My testimony to that effect is currently being used in court by my client to get the patent thrown out."

On another occasion, he was hired by a patent holder to get evidence of infringement. As Mr. Cumming tells it, he simply called the president of the alleged infringer and told him that he had been involved in an auto accident outside the plant—just outside a section of it where Mr. Cumming believed a certain machine was in operation, a machine thought to be infringing the patent in question.

Saying he needed substantiation from witnesses who might have seen the fictional accident, Mr. Cumming got a list of the names of employees working in that section. One of them eventually gave testimony on the operation of the machine, and Mr. Cumming's client won his infringement suit.

41

Market Segmentation as a Competitive Strategy

Nelson N. Foote

Market segmentation is the process of so designing or featuring a product or service that it will make a particularly strong appeal to some identifiable subpart of a total market. In a sense, manufacturers have always segmented their markets, because different products appealed to different types of consumers. However, historically the process has been largely accidental. Today it is becoming more common for companies to design products for specific market segments or to adapt products in such a way that they will appeal more strongly to a segment which happened to like it in the first place. The article which follows gives an interesting and insightful glimpse of the process of market segmentation as seen by an executive of a company which has practiced segmentation somewhat systematically.

Let us assume we have made the discovery that consumers of ice cream differ significantly in their preferences for chocolate, strawberry and vanilla. And let us assume that these flavor preferences are not distributed randomly among all kinds of people, but are differentially associated with some other characteristic of customers for ice cream, such as hair color, and that these associations are substantial in degree and practical to ascertain. For example, let us say that brunettes tend strongly to like chocolate, redheads to favor strawberry, and blondes, vanilla. Finally, let us imagine that this pattern is just that simple and orderly—product differences nicely match customer differences.

Then what?

What is the businessman who wants to sell ice cream in this market to do about our findings? Is he to conclude that he should offer all three flavors, the same as the rest of the industry, lest he forego any important source of sales? Or should he try to serve only blondes and brunettes, since there are not enough redheads to make serving them profitable? Or should he seek to establish a reputation as the producer of the finest Dutch chocolate ice cream, so that he captures nearly all that segment of the market? Or should he go after the great mass of vanilla fans, through upgrading this lowly flavor with a French accent? Or should he take account of his newness or smallness in the industry and challenge the incumbent giants of the trade by introducing pistachio or frozen custard? Or should he offer the normal product line of his industry but allow some major chain of retail outlets to apply its store brand to his product? Should he go after the door-to-door trade

A paper presented at Consumer Market Segmentation Conference, American Marketing Association, February 24, 1967. Reprinted by special permission.

with a very short line—like Neapolitan only—or open his own chain of soda fountains with 28 flavors? Or should he be creative and try to think up some utterly new way to exploit his knowledge of differing customer preferences, since all these strategies—and more besides—are already in use today in the ice cream business?

Plainly, even if one knew far more than is known already about patterns of correlation between product and customer differences in any particular market, it takes a lot of thinking and doing before this knowledge can be turned into a calculated competitive strategy. Meanwhile we find examples of marketing managers who have very successfully employed a strategy of market segmentation, quite without the resources of detailed information that as professional marketers we like to think are indispensable to decision-making in matters of such complexity and risk.

It seems important throughout discussion of market segmentation to recognize that the main source of interest in the concept is its potential value as a competitive strategy. There may be quite a number of people in this audience whose interest is in promoting the sale or purchase of data regarding the stratigraphics of consumer choice. But unless these data can be put to practical use in improving or defending the market position or profits of their user, only the data seller will benefit, and he not for long. So my self-chosen assignment here is to bear down on the task of thinking out the use of such data in actual marketing management. Although I make my living as a marketing researcher, I think that we need more thinking on this matter as much as we need more research.

Immediately, however, the question arises of who is going to discuss competitive strategy in public—especially in the presence of competitors of his own firm—save in empty generalities. A salesman of research data, or representatives of advertising agencies or media, might set forth some hypothetical tactics of market segmentation as a means of soliciting business. But other than personal vanity or the desire to solicit another job, what would induce someone connected with a manufacturer or a retailer to disclose his thinking about competitive strategy? The incentives of professional exchange of technique, or the teaching of younger members of the fraternity, are not sufficient justification. Many kinds of professional know-how are properly kept proprietary by the firm which paid for their development. If market segmentation is to be analyzed publicly and candidly from the standpoint of an actual competitor in a market, it has to be justified by some benefit that it will bring to this competitor. If it were not my conviction that in fact it is to the benefit of every competing firm that market segmentation be discussed publicly in terms of its implications for competitive strategy, you would not be listening to these words at this moment.

Moreover, we can go one step further and declare that market segmentation as a competitive strategy is also in the interests of customers. If it were not—if it did not offer customers a firmer base for choice among competing offerings and a wider array of genuine choices—it would not work as a competitive strategy. Like any deal, market segmentation is good business only when both parties to the transaction benefit. Market segmentation is thus in effect a logical extension of the basic principles of marketing.

The process of market segmentation, however, when approached as a task of formulating and executing a marketing strategy, involves matching not merely customer characteristics and product characteristics, but a tripartite matching of customers and offerings *and* the array of competitors in the market, as seen from the standpoint of any one competitor within this constellation. If we think of offerings by competitors as expressions of their differing *capabilities,* it will not only be easy to remember the three C's —*customers, competitors* and *capabilities* —but the full task of developing a strategy is more clearly pushed into view.

Let me illustrate concretely by referring to one of our most respected competitors in the Chicago area, the Zenith Radio Corporation. Zenith won a preeminent position in the television receiver market some ten years ago by becoming established in the minds of consumers as the leading exemplar of product reliability. Its policy of manufacturing products of good workmanship goes back many years, but during the middle Fifties many consumers became quite concerned to identify the set that would, they hoped, give them the least trouble from breakdown. That was when Zenith's market share soared, until it surpassed the erstwhile industry leader's. Servicemen and the radio-TV specialty stores with which they are associated lent vigorous aid. Zenith's management and its advertising agency pressed the opportunity that had widened for them. But Zenith had not adopted product reliability as a self-consciously opportunistic, short-term tactic. As fas as is known, Zenith's strategy was not derived through marketing research, although marketing research by competitors soon verified its efficacy. After some delay, other competitors raised their quality control standards, but none has been able, coming in later on a me-too basis, to emulate Zenith's success. One could quibble about some details of Zenith's reputation—whether hand-wiring is in fact more or less reliable than printed circuits, whether reliability has not been confused to some extent with repairability, whether Zenith sets any longer enjoy the lowest breakdown rate—but from the marketing standpoint, Zenith remains king among that segment of the set market which emphasizes reliability above other virtues when buying sets. The quality standards of the whole industry were forced up by Zenith's success, an outcome of obvious benefit to the consumer, but of at least equal benefit to all the other competitors in the industry, whose personnel devote their whole lives to their industry and much prefer feeling proud of their occupation to feeling ashamed of it.

The meaning of the Zenith example would be very incomplete, however, if we paid attention only to the success story and failed to note that there are many other virtues in television sets which consumers prize besides reliability. If there were not, it would be hard to explain why the Zenith brand share at its zenith rose barely above a fifth of the market. To be sure, Zenith may have preferred its profitability to the greater volume it may have deliberately foregone by upholding a price premium. On the other hand, maybe not; a price premium is just about the loudest advertisement for quality there is.

Meanwhile Zenith's major rival did not simply decide it had to emulate Zenith, but staunchly pursued its strategy of industry statesmanship through the introduction of color, achieving handsome victory and reward from matching its offering with the rising wants of all those customers who were reaching for color in magazines, movies, photography and other visual media. Alongside these two industry leaders were certain other manufacturers, one of whom has done well by stressing portability and personalization, another by treating the television set as a major piece of furniture, and so on. What is important here is that several competitors held their own or improved their position, even during the period of greatest success by Zenith and RCA,

not by seeking to manufacture some hypothetically optimum television set, but by addressing themselves to some substantial segment of the market which *they saw themselves as peculiarly fitted to serve.* The firms which got shaken out during the past dozen years—among which some were big for a time—or which severely lost position can best be described as undistinguishable in their capabilities and offerings, hence undistinguished by consumers.

Now what has been added to the understanding of market segmentation by the example of television receivers? What has been added that is indispensable is the element of competitive capability—a virtue that one particular competitor pre-eminently possesses— which matches a substantial or rising consumer want. In colloquial terms, what have I got that the other guy hasn't, and which the customer wants badly enough to walk a mile for it?

A few years back, we looked at some commonplace demographic characteristics of television customers arrayed by the brands they tended to favor. When we looked at these demographic characteristics simultaneously, certain results were far more revealing in combination than singly. Only a limited example— because here we are indeed verging on the disclosure of competitive intelligence: we found that one highly meaningful segment of the market— meaningful in terms of sensitivity of discrimination among brands—consisted of households below the median in years of schooling but above the median in income. For convenient reference we called them merely the new-rich, obviously an inexact term. One particular brand seemed to be designed and advertised and priced—properly overpriced, as it were—specifically for this segment, and in fact it enjoyed at that time an inordinate share of their setbuying. Now that company has not noticeably changed its offerings during recent years—they still seem pointed toward the new-rich segment—but its brand share has dwindled substantially. It appears that people with more money than schooling nonetheless are able to learn from experience and do upgrade their taste, given a little time.

The moral of this example is that market segmentation has to be viewed as a continuous process, and marketing strategy has to keep in step with the changing structure of the market. While this implication is probably obvious, perhaps less obvious is the corollary that, just as consumers learn, it is necessary for competitors to exercise differing capabilities from those which may have won them success in the past. And here we come to a matter which lies beyond not only research but also ordinary logic and in the realm of managerial will. Who is to tell a manufacturer that he is capable of doing something he has not done before, and of doing it better than any of his other competitors? By definition, the ordinary kinds of evidence are lacking, because there is not past experience to be projected forward.

In the course of interpersonal relations among individuals, a teacher or a parent may tell a child that he possesses talents he did not previously recognize; the child may then adopt this observation as a conviction about himself which empowers him to demonstrate that it is true. All of us are familiar enough with instances of this outcome not to need to debate whether they occur. The faith of a coach in an athlete, of a critic in a writer, of an employer in an employee, of a wife in a husband, is often the ingredient which brings out a latent capability. Because so little is understood about the process, we cannot make it happen on demand. We are fortunate to recognize it when it does happen, even more so when we spy the opportunity beforehand and do not waste it, for ourselves or for others. Even further beyond present understanding is the possibility of specifying here a reliable formula whereby the management of a company can truly discern those latent talents in its own organization which can be mobilized more effectively by itself than by any of its competitors to satisfy some important emerging customer want.

I do know this, however: recognition of such a talent feeds on itself; it is a cumulative process—a benevolent spiral. I am positive that when the management of Zenith found itself being recognized by consumers for its virtues of good workmanship, it was immensely stimulated to push further in that direction. Thus one of the most valuable functions of marketing research in implementing a strategy of market segmentation is to listen to what is being said about a company by its customers in terms of recognizing its special talents. Developing something that is already there—watering a plant that is already growing, to mix a metaphor—is surely much easier and more likely to succeed than trying to create new capabilities out of whole cloth—or, for that matter, borrowing the garments of others, in the sense of imitating or acquiring another company and offering that as an expression of one's own capability.

Part of the growing sophistication of consumers is their increasing interest in the character of the organization they are dealing with. At General Electric we are acutely conscious that certain of our competitors, whose products are no better and sometimes not as good as ours by any measure or product quality, nonetheless enjoy the preference of certain customers. This problem repeatedly confronts the manufacturer who finds himself in competition with retailers who handle only store brands. The whole fascinating issue of what is going to emerge as private branding widens its sway is too vast to open up here. Yet it deserves mention here as constituting market segmentation on an utterly different axis from market segmentation on the axis of product features and brand images.

Segmentation varies in degree as well as in kind. The famous case of the ordinary salt which "rains when it pours" illustrates a valued product feature which has maintained for a particular brand a large and stable market share for many years, while conferring on consumers a valued satisfaction for which they are quite willing to pay a price premium and a rewarding degree of brand loyalty. Many such product features are easily imitated, however, and the reputation for distinctiveness originally achieved may dissolve in the minds of consumers despite advertising. The impermanence of minor product features as a source of competitive distinctiveness and effective market segmentation is a conspicuous failing of the current picture in package goods competition. Like rock-and-roll music, there is too little difference between the new ones and the old ones to make much difference. The proliferation of trival product differences which appeal to trivial differences among consumers and represent trivial differences among the capabilities of their makers is in effect a mockery of the theory of market segmentation. This proliferation of trivial differences provokes denunciation by producers, retailers and consumers alike as market fragmentation rather than segmentation, and makes an industry vulnerable to the outsider who commences to segment on a different axis. The effective response to the trivialization of market segmentation, however, is not to abandon it as a strategy. To do that would be to abdicate all initiative to competitors. The way out of the expensive waste of trivial segmentation is to engage in serious segmentation, which means segmenta-

tion on a larger scale or even on another axis.

Serious, large-scale innovation seems often to come from outside an industry rather than inside. Examples like General Motors in locomotives, Volkswagen in autos, IBM in typewriters, Corning in housewares, Lestoil in detergents, come to mind. Rivalry within a going constellation of competitors seems often to lead to implicit imitation, even when everyone involved is convinced that he is trying to be different from everyone else. How this result occurs is not hard to discern. Close rivals tend very easily to magnify the importance of small differences, whether initiated by themselves or others. If created by another, a close competitor often feels he must come up with a rival innovation but only of corresponding scale.

One detects nothing very distinctive about Silvertone television sets, to mention another respected Chicago competitor. Viewed as manufactured products, they are close to the industry's average line. But where Zenith stresses the reliability built into the product, Sears stresses the services offered by the stores in which Silvertone sets are bought—the promptness of repair service, the easy credit, the ample parking, the special sales well advertised in local newspapers or direct mail. That is, Sears segments the market on another axis from Zenith. But thus far Silvertone has encroached far less upon Zenith's clientele than upon the portions of the market occupied by companies whose offerings are less distinctive.

We shall come back to this intriguing question of how far the competition of store brands with manufacturer brands may go before some equilibrium is reached. Some companies as yet have a less urgent private-brand problem anyway, like the auto and gasoline firms and the sellers of services—insurance, banking, air travel, lodging, dry cleaning—which distribute through their own exclusive retail outlets. So for some moments longer let us stay within the sphere of competition among manufactured products and nationally-advertised brands.

Assuming this sphere, we can now state our main hypothesis in further detail: Market segmentation works best as a competitive strategy—contributes most to the success of competitors and the satisfaction of customers—when product and brand and maker are closely identified in the minds of all concerned.

If we were to assume that one by one more competitors in a market choose particular segments as the customers especially to attract, on the basis of correct appraisal of their own special capabilities to satisfy these segments, then the competitors who do not make such deliberate choices will find themselves increasingly confined to the miscellaneous and dwindling residue. As alluded to in our first example, such a development is to some extent a description of what has already happened in some markets, so we may be prophesying simply an intensification of current tendencies rather than anything new under the sun. In other words, self-conscious segmentation may become not only a means of success but the price of survival in a market.

Beyond the ordinary criteria of survival or success as measured in profitability and market share, however, are some other benefits of segmentation to an industry and the various competitors in it. We have mentioned the feeling of pride in their occupation and the quality of its products which most people desire in their life work. Some other benefits of belonging to an industry which steadily adds to the values it offers its customers also deserve explicit recognition. They include the fact that being bested by a competitor whom one respects is easier to accept that being bested by a com-

petitor whom one does not respect. There is a good deal of satisfaction to the producer as well as the consumer in seeing an industry progress over time through advanced applications of science and technology. In an industry plagued with cut-throat price competition instead of value competition, imitation is almost inevitable, because no one can afford the research and development required for innovation. In the vicious downward spiral which obtains in such an industry, jobs are insecure because companies are insecure, and morale and morality seem to decline together. Enough examples spring to mind. An industry trapped in such a spiral, worst of all, has rarely been able to reverse it without outside help, as from major suppliers. DuPont, for example, has struggled quite nobly to raise the plastics molding industry from its swamp. Customers themselves, especially in recent years, have sometimes under these conditions willingly paid substantial premiums for quality and reliability, and this has brought a turnabout, but not before the damage became painful to all concerned.

Both competitors and customers share the benefits of stabilized markets wherein strong degrees of mutual loyalty exist between particular companies and particular segments of customers. Distribution and advertising costs are significantly lower under conditions in which repeat sales make up a high proportion of total sales. The model line of any competitor can be shorter, yet his volume nowadays may be higher, than when he tries to carry everything everyone else in the industry offers. All phases of marketing are much more intelligently, effectively and efficiently conducted when companies and customers, having chosen each other with care and sophistication, can rely on each other's growing discrimination, and sypathetically anticipate the orderly, developmental unfolding and matching of their future wants and capabilities. Some marketing researchers even envision a paradise in which companies will spend as much money in listening as in talking, and will make more money doing so.

Let us commence to summarize while rejecting a few additional elements into this consideration of market segmentation as a competitive strategy. Our first proposition was that any approach to market segmentation which dealt only with matching customer characteristics with product features was seriously incomplete. The very incentive for exploring market segmentation is to gain advantage—to seek some basis for customer preference—against the array of other competitors and their offerings in a particular market. If one plays only with customer characteristics and product features, he may arrive at the notion of some optimum product for an average customer—in effect, a recipe for reducing his product to commodity status, hence the very opposite of market segmentation, which implies product differentiation. But if he goes to the opposite extreme, and tries to equal or surpass the total array of differing products offered by all competitors to all segments of his market, he courts the usual fate of me-too-ism, while suffering impossibly mounting marketing costs. Hence he must seek to identify those offerings which most appeal to some desirable segment of the total market and simultaneously express those capabilities in which he is strongest. The problem of choice here is analogous with that of the boy who must seek distinction from a brother who excels him athletically and another who excels him academically: what talent can he develop which, though different, will seem equivalent in the eyes of those whose approval they seek? To be all things to all people, to excel in every virtue, is impossible; to be average in all means indistinguishability. Achieving only trivial

distinctiveness is a barely-veiled form of imitation, although it can immensely add to promotional expense in an industry. Hence the evolution of a criterion for selecting which customer segments and matching product distinctions to pursue must come from, and be disciplined by, correct identification of the real strengths and weaknesses of the company itself, as compared with other competitors in its market.

Companies, like individuals, sometimes involuntarily suffer crises of identity, as when merged with other companies. A company embarking upon market segmentation as a competitive strategy is deliberately precipitating a crisis of identity. In place of identity, however, which seems to apply only to the maker of a product rather than to a triple set of interrelations, I believe the concept of theme is more applicable and explanatory of the common element which has to be discovered or invented to match customer characteristic with product feature with company capability. The so-called total marketing approach in its sophisticated form seems finally to come forth with such recognizable themes. The theme of *ease of use* of essentially highly-technical equipment has served Kodak for generations, and recurs in numerous notable expressions —from the Brownie to the Instamatic, from the ubiquitous yellow box to the universally recognizable name itself. It illustrates how versatile in its manifestations a theme can be.

But just as product innovation can be trivialized through pointless small variations which make no real contribution to anyone, the concept of theme can be trivialized also—and in fact is, whenever some advertising agency tries to adorn an advertiser with a superficial image that has no real structural relationship to customer segments, competitive constellation or company capabilities.

The concept of theme is useful in

teaching marketing and market segmentation to managers whose experience has been in more exact fields. It helps to avoid the mental blocks that arise when segmentation is grasped as a series of pigeonholes in which various kinds of customers are filed for separate treatment, whereas the manager is eager for all the sales he can get from any source whatever, and finds it hard enough to devise one marketing strategy without having to devise many. To return to our main example, the television receiver market, the theme of reliability can be applied by one manufacturer to all the models in his line, and throughout all the functions of marketing in his total marketing program. But the same manufacturer could hardly pursue simultaneously with equal thoroughness and equal success such contrasting themes as modern and traditional cabinetry, portability, technical innovation and retail convenience, although he may keep pace with the industry average in these respects. Market segmentation does not deal with water-tight compartments, but with emphases sufficiently simple and distinctive to win notice and preference among customers to whom they are important, without alienating customers by being deficient in the other virtues which they more or less take for granted.

In terms of demographic and other statistical dimensions by which customers and products may be differentiated, the possibilities for market segmentation are troublesomely infinite. But when the problem of choosing a theme to emphasize is disciplined by attempting to match customers, competitors and capabilities, these troubles are usually reduced to very few choices that are actually open to a particular firm—though hopefully at least one. The real difficulties of choice are not statistical but spiritual—the anguish of facing up to the fact that if a company is going to move in one direction, it must forego moving in all the others. Such a decision comes especially hard in diversified companies, yet some diversified companies have achieved real synergy through this discipline.

Once this clarifying commitment has been made, its effect on everyone in the organization is to release spontaneous ingenuity in its implementation. A good theme stimulates numberless applications and suggestions, furnishes a guide in numberless subordinate decisions, and eases numberless chores of communication, both inside and outside.

Not only does a positive theme help to mobilize an organization in pursuit of its marketing objectives, and heighten their satisfaction, but it wins respect from competitors, even while strengthening and securing its position against them. Spirit is harder to imitate than matter; hardware is easy to copy, but the spirit of a whole organization is not. The competitor who wishes to emulate the success of a competitor's dominant theme must, instead of echoing it, come up with an equivalent theme that uniquely fits himself to his situation— that matches his own three C's.

We did promise to come back before closing to that matter of competition between the retail sphere and the manufacturing sphere, as an example of market segmentation along radically different axes. It was partly a matter of convenience to set this question aside, and partly a matter of conviction. One observes that retailers, regardless of size, seem to want to sell what their customers want to buy. If these customers show no very pronounced preferences among the offerings of various manufacturers, it is probably because there is no very pronounced basis for preference among the competing products. And when this is so, the manufacturers of these more or less indistinguishable commodities are most vulnerable to the substitution of store brands for manufacturer brands.

Retailers can compete with retailers in the sale of commodities, by offering store values instead of product values; manufacturers cannot. But when a real basis for product preference exists, the preferred brands either show up on the retailer's shelves, or the retailer is forced to forego substantial business to his competitors who will stock the preferred products. A&P is not about to discontinue Campbell's soup or Heinz ketchup or Jello or other items of this character.

Competition is far from dead among retailers. And as long as competition among retailers exists, manufacturer brands which offer distinctive values to customers will find the way to those customers, if not through one channel, then through another. In a competitive society, the customer will not be denied his choice between less satisfaction and more.

Hence the problem of the manufacturer in confronting the rise of private branding is only in part a task of confronting changes in his environment. The other half of the task is to confront himself and his need for continuous learning and development of his own distinctive capabilities. It is the birthright of the manufacturer to determine the character of his product.

Nowadays we have the phenomenon of the publisher who dreams up an idea for a book and then hires someone to write it. Such offerings by publishers, however, are so poorly received by critics and readers that they have become known as non-books. In the same sense, we might speak of products which no longer portray the identity of their makers as non-products. But the consuming public will always remain more responsive to the author than to the publisher—to the manufacturer than to the middleman—if only the maker will put himself into his product. That is the one point I wanted to be sure got included in today's discussion of market segmentation.

42

Spotlight on Psychographic Market Segmentation

Grey Matter

The concept of market segmentation is a reasonably recent development in the field of marketing. Where it has been employed it has usually been a segmentation of the market on the basis of demographic (population) statistics. In fact, the market for many products is segmented psychologically as well. People whose population characteristics may be alike may be different from each other psychologically, or vice versa. These psychological characteristics often have marketing significance. It is to this kind of market segmentation that the present article is addressed.

Pages of business literature, whirlwinds of words from convention rostrums, extol the value of market segmentation as *preferred* strategy in today's marketing planning. And for many businesses this is *sound advice*. Unfortunately, as so often happens, the tendency of people is to be swept along by currents, thus *overlooking* rich opportunities.

To most marketers "market segmentation" means cutting markets into *slices* —demographically, geographically, according to economic status, race, national origin, education, sex and other established criteria. But the idea of relating marketing strategy to *psychological* differences among consumers has been slow to germinate. We call it "Psychographic Market Segmentation." The strategy of isolating a market by selecting people who react *en masse* to a particular *emotional appeal* or who share common *behavioral patterns* has been overshadowed by the concentration on *easily* discernible market divisions such as youth, sex, financial status, education, location and others.

Break Traditional Boundaries

Psychographic segmentation breaks across the boundaries of these traditional market sectors and discovers a homogeneity of linkage among people who have been considered as belonging to *diverse* markets. For example, the assistant principal of a school and a truckman may be earning identical salaries and perhaps living not very far apart. They may also be in the same age group and of the same ethnic origin. But *emotionally* and *psychologically*

Reprinted from *Grey Matter,* November, 1965, Vol. 36, No. 11, a Bulletin on Thoughts and Ideas on Advertising and Marketing, issued by Grey Advertising, Inc.

they may be at opposite poles. Psychographic segmentation places them into the marketing segments in which they belong *psychologically*. Conversely, a family in the middle forties in age and middle-income status may have the same outlook and youthful *attitude* as a young newly-formed family unit. Psychologically, they belong in the youth market segment for many products.

The *profit potential* in psychographic segmentation of markets is greater than is generally realized and those advertisers who see these opportunities clearly, and exploit them skillfully, are scoring and will score triumphs, while those who continue to dissipate competitive energy only on established notions of market segmentation may find themselves on a "me too" merry-go-round.

Fables and Foibles

Every departure from herd thinking seems to create a mystique which acts as a *barrier* to the less venturesome. This is true of psychographic segmentation, too. For instance, the prevailing notion in marketing circles is that an appeal to a limited group is of necessity limited in its impact. Holders of this view fail to realize that there are no rigid boundaries circumscribing people's attitudes. On the contrary, these are fluid, and an idea tossed into what seems to be a tiny pool more often than not ripples out in widening circles until what appeared to be a small market becomes a huge market.

Let's take the case of Maclean's tooth paste. These marketers reasoned that since 70% of the population is concerned with tooth decay, it would be sound strategy to aim at that part of the remaining market (30%) composed of people who are psychologically or emotionally more concerned with "whiteness," the cosmetic effect of brushing their teeth, than with cavities. The success of this maneuver in gaining a share of the tooth paste market beyond their expectations is well known to the marketing world.

A Shift on a Giant Scale

The foible still lingers that it's tactically unsound for a company to aim products and promotion at *specific* markets while its overall strategy is to court the *mass market*. The weakness of this stance is best illustrated by the automobile industry.

Let's go back five years or so. A significant *under-the-surface* trend in mass consumer marketing almost went unnoticed by automobile manufacturers. For many years planners in this giant industry focused on *bigness, flashiness and standard designs* until "the peas-in-a-pod" appearance of automobiles became a subject of universal comment. Meanwhile the small foreign car began making inroads and seemed to be the answer to *mass marketing* of automobiles. But, in reality, the consumer mass market was breaking into psychological segments. Differing groups of people were demanding greater *differences* in automobiles than the industry had heretofore realized.

In 1962 the marketing world sensed a *new trend* in the action of Chevrolet. (Actually the trend was not new. It had been going on unnoticed by most advertisers.) But the automobile industry made it new in *magnitude,* if not in conception. It made the shift on a giant scale . . . a shift away from look-alike products to a strategy of fitting products and advertising to "psychographically" segmented markets as a means of obtaining a larger share of the *total* mass market. This marketing philosophy was explained by Semon E. Knudsen, Chev-

rolet's manager, in these words: "Four distinct lines of products, appealing to four different segments of the buying public, give a choice of product to fit most needs, either *emotional* or practical." (The emphasis is ours.)

This was recognition of market segmentation based on *psychological* as well as practical needs of people. The success of this philosophy for Chevrolet is history. Its significance is in the *thrust* it gave to psychographic market segmentation in the automotive industry which will be felt throughout the marketing world.

The impact of Chevrolet's action is especially evident in the advertising of all the competitors in the so-called "mass brands" of the industry: Chevrolet, Ford, Plymouth and Rambler. Take Plymouth. Under the umbrella "There's something for everyone in Plymouth '66," each brand aims at a specific psychological target while not neglecting its economy status:

> The new "elegant" VIP is a "limousine in looks, power and ride. But it's a Plymouth in price."
>
> The "Bold Fury . . . a great big beauty."
>
> Barracuda is a new version of the "fast-back . . . if you go in for bucket seats."
>
> The Valiant "really lets you live within your budget."

At this point we'd like to make it clear that we are *not* passing judgment on the *advertisements per se.* We're merely commenting on the *psychographic market segmentation* they represent.

Interestingly, Russell Baker, famed columnist of the New York Times, undoubtedly with a twinkle in his eye, comments on the psychographic segmentation of automobile marketing in this manner: "It is becoming harder and harder to buy a new car without psychiatric help. As the ads for the new models show all too clearly, what Detroit is now selling is not so much a car as a personality."

Enter the Dissenters

But there are those who pooh-pooh the whole *idea* of market segmentation. Professor William H. Reynolds, of the University of Southern California, writing in the September-October 1965 Harvard Business Review, says that psychological market segmentation is nothing more than variety marketing with a different name. He brushes aside the evidence of *success* of this approach with the statement: "Granting the existence of subcultures, there is an amazing uniformity to the American culture from border to border."

We're not so naive as to ignore the influence of the *norm* on the buying behavior of the individual. Nor do we overlook mass motivation as a generator of sales of mass products. Our point is that to overlook *Psychographic Market Segmentation as a marketing strategy for many mass products means missing rich profit opportunities*. A *myopic attitude* about the homogeneity of the American consumer can lead to losses, for the desire of the individual for change and for self-expression has become ingrained in the American character.

Even in suburbia (the alleged symbol of uniformity of living) there is a restless urge to be *different* while conforming to the community pattern. There are social, intellectual and economic islands in apparently homogeneous suburban towns. The urge to *differ* is often much more powerful than the desire to conform.

The noted sociologist, David Riesman, of the University of Chicago, put his finger on the problem when he said: "Differentiation is as strong as homogenization in the market, and the very effort to get *everybody* will alienate *many* bodies."

Summing It All Up

For companies with limited budgets it may be a matter of *survival* to discover and concentrate on a segment of the market which presents the richest potentials. But for large volume advertisers, too, it is often sound strategy to aim at *groups* instead of shooting the works at the mass.

In the dynamic expansion which our economy is undergoing, the mass consumer will become more *complex*, more puzzling and less mass. The tremendous increase in population will result in larger heterogeneous groups of consumers who will have to be taken into account in marketing strategy. However, there will be *less need* for trying to find the *mass* consumer. For specific segments of the market can be large enough in themselves to be cultivated profitably by mass marketers. Fact is that even today astute advertisers are finding it profitable to pick segments of the market and to develop them deeply and intensively.

Aiming advertising at the mass consumer may be the only effective strategy for many products, but it often results in a *sameness* of products and advertising which *dilutes* advertising effectiveness. Certainly research will have to apply itself more and more to *finding* and *identifying* psychographic segments of the market, each large enough to return a handsome profit to the marketer.

43

Factors Motivating Consumer Choice of Private Brands

Robert S. Hancock

During the past decade there has been a great increase in the use of private or distributor brands by retailers. Much of this growth, which may well continue in the future, can be directly associated with the increasing importance of mass merchandising through large-scale retailers. This increase in the use of private brands is significant for all types of marketing institutions. The accompanying article looks at the factors which seem to foster the use and acceptance of private brands by retailers and consumers respectively. One interesting assertion made by the author is that consumers tend to associate the fulfillment of their needs with a retailer, and not with a manufacturer. If this is true, many manufacturers should take another look at their present branding policies.

For the purposes of our discussion this afternoon, it is preferred to use the term "private brands(s)" as indicated in your program. In so doing, private brands are regarded as synonymous with "distributor brands," "controlled brands," "wholesaler-retailer brands" and other similar terms. Each of these terms seem to have identical meanings as they all denote the ownership of a brand by a wholesaler or retailer and the marketing institution having ownership control assumes, if not the total merchandising task, a major portion of it.

Reprinted by special permission from *Marketing Concepts in Changing Times*, edited by Richard M. Hill, Proceedings of the 42nd National Conference of the American Marketing Association, December 1959.

Growth Patterns of Private Brands

The growth of private brands is a counterpart of large-scale retailing. When or where private brands originated is not known, but a number of our present-day corporate chains commenced buying by specification before the turn of the century. A rather strong and definite pattern of private brand growth was apparent in the 1920's and this continued until World War II. Setbacks in the development of private brands occurred during World War II and the immediate post-war years, when materials were scarce and production rates could not be maintained for private brands. There has, however, been a very strong resurgence of private brands during the past decade and this growth has every indication of continuing. It is this recent resurgence that has generated the concern of leaders in the retailing *industry*. Hence, for manufacturers and distributors affected by private brands, it is both timely and desirable to inquire into the marketing strategy that has been successful in motivating consumers toward private brands.

Before inquiring into this marketing strategy let us clarify the fact that private brand growth is a counterpart to large-scale retailing. Most of our retailing developments center on the vast size to which some retail organizations have grown. We all know that relatively few of the nation's retailers account for the bulk of the annual retail volume. Furthermore, only about 3.5 per cent of the retailers reach an annual sales volume in excess of one-half million dollars. Few of these, though, have the sales volume and executive talent to enter the private brand field. There has, however, been the startling growth during the last few decades of a few hundred retail firms whose sales volumes now fall into the "multimillion dollar class" and six corporate chains whose sales volumes now fall into the "more than a billion dollar" category. During this same period, the corporate chain, voluntary chain, and retailer-cooperative have made their mark. Mass merchandising developments as spearheaded by these organizations have created many of the conditions which have tended to make private brands a logical course of action. These same retail firms have the financial strength and know-how to undertake the expensive demand-creating operations necessary to build private brand acceptance on a grand scale.

Associated with these developments has been horizontal integration, i.e., the expansion into many retail outlets. This has contributed the assurance of a high and sustained sales volume which is as essential to the success of a private brand as it is to a manufacturer's brand. Vertical integration is another condition contributing to the development of private brands. Retailers with sizable sales volumes have found it advantageous to assume some manufacturing and wholesaling functions or to specify clearly their own requirements for their brands.

These developments, then, have contributed to the fundamental conditions which were necessary before a retailer could embark on a widespread private brand program, or before he could successfully exploit the advantages of private brands.

Factors Which Favor the Use and Acceptance of Private Brands

Without exception, this study found that a successful private brand hinges on the existence of either customer need, or the fact that customer goodwill and confidence in the retailer is so strong that consumer acceptance of the private brand is assured. Of course retailers are in a much better position than manufacturers when it comes to recognizing customer need and in building his confidence in the store and merchandise lines. There is no doubt that a number of our largest retailers have done just that. In other words, it is contended that consumers strongly associate the fulfillment of their needs with a retailer, and not (as commonly held by some) with the manufacturer who most often is at a distant place from the consumer-retailer community.

Recognizing the above basic considerations, large-scale retailers have found that in order to maximize their efforts to meet consumer need, satisfaction and service, it is necessary to have a marked degree of control over the products they sell. In doing this, private brands are recognized as an integral part of a well-rounded and effective merchandising policy, for without them either gaps, or marked deficiencies in their merchandising policies, or both, would occur. The firms involved in our study recognized three important merchandising gaps, and a like number of marked merchandising deficiencies, all of which could be wholly or partially overcome with their own brands. The merchandising gaps are:

1. *Price and quality gap*—A product of equal or higher quality at a lower price is needed to satisfy consumer demand.
2. *Ensemble and family of products gap* —A complete ensemble, or a family of products cannot be obtained economically by buying manufacturers' brands, and to have coordination of quality, style (or design) and price in order to create a uniform appeal, private brands are necessary.
3. *Prestige gap*—No appeal to the prestige market can be made with a manufacturer's brand.

The marked deficiencies in merchandising effectiveness are:

1. A product or merchandise line is unstable because the line is sold by discount retailers, the price is unstable and subject to price cutting; or the line may be fair traded and this depresses the merchandising possibilities for the firm.
2. A manufacturer's brand either is not available or is weak in public acceptance; or if available, it has spotty distribution.
3. The cost of distribution of the manufacturer's line is too high or the distribution policies of the manufacturer do not coincide with those of the retailer, and hence greater distribution efficiency in the form of lower costs may be had by developing the private brand.

Some of the above factors are obviously stronger than others in motivating consumers. Certainly consumers are very likely to be more influenced by the product values they can feel and observe, rather than the "hidden values." It is quite clear that the three "gaps" and the closing of them by retailers are strong factors in motivating consumers. On the other hand, the latter group of factors are really merchandising policy matters and as such are not usually discernible by consumers. One thing seems certain—it is the entire complex of factors, rather than any single one, that has made possible the adoption of private brands by large-scale retailers. In turn, these same factors have had an important role in the widespread acceptance of these brands by consumers.

Private Brand Pricing

Because price and other factors of appeal account for much of the success of the acceptance of private brands, these factors are worthy of additional elaboration. The pricing of a private brand at a price lower than a manufacturer's brand of comparable quality is a typical example of the strategy employed. When customers are able to compare the merchandiser's brand and price with a manufacturer's brand and price, there is the obvious tendency for the price-conscious customer to select the lower-priced product. But, great care must be taken so as not to price the item too low. For example, one general merchandising company reported having purchased a large quantity of men's sweaters which retailed at $12.95 in competing stores. This firm replaced the label with its own and featured the sweaters as a $12.95 value for only $4.98. They failed to sell these sweaters in great quantity until such time as they moved the price up to $7.98 and then featured them as a $12.95 value. Such experiences as this indicate to retailers that the price of a private brand cannot be set so low as to cheapen it in the consumer's mind.

For the most part, we found that it is typical for private-brand merchandise to sell for less, particularly when a comparable manufacturer's brand is also displayed. Frequently, the private brand is shown to its best advantage when the retailer is able to display it prominently along with manufacturers' brands. This, in fact, is a very common practice and is used for such diverse products as appliances, grocery products, cold cream, and aspirin.

If, however, price is set at the same level as the manufacturer's brand, additional accessories or quality features are promoted heavily so that, relatively, the private brand is lower priced. An example of this technique was found in one department store which featured private brand shirts at the same or higher prices than manufacturers' brands. In this instance the higher-count broadcloth, stronger buttons and better workmanship were features which attracted the customer from the manufacturers' brands to the store brand. Prestige lines which have experienced considerable growth and acceptance usually have no comparable manufacturer's brand to compete against. Therefore, their reputation and value are usually supported by a prestige price. This is the exception to the more common policy of relatively low price. Many department stores have such lines.

Appeal is not on price alone, however, but also on value. Value is a function of both price and quality. If the customer accepts the stated policy of many private branders, e.g., "We have private brands only if we can offer the customer the same quality at a lower price or a higher quality at the same price," the greater value appeal is stronger than price or quality alone.

While price remains one of the strongest appeals, pricing has other advantages for the merchandiser. Price lining, for example, is easier to accomplish when products are tailored to specifications which are in accord with customer needs. To the customer, general price lining is an inducement to shop at the store which has definite price lines— price lines at levels which are acceptable to him.

Some retailers have found that vacuums existed at both the high and low ends of their price lines, with manufacturers' brands occupying a strong position in between. By filling these gaps with their own brands, a broader product and price appeal can be made. Such a broadening of the line exploits more completely the needs of the consumer. Women's shoes, house furnishings, and coffee are examples of products for which stores may have multiple private brands. Department stores frequently have separate brands for the Basement Store.

Pricing is closely allied to some other aspects of successful merchandising, namely fair trade and the need to control price. Fair trade which helped to foster the development of private brands, also fostered price competition as the historical margins on many lines became unrealistic and eventually broke down. This brought with it an expansion of discount selling and other aggressive competitive practices.

Without control over price the retailer may find himself selling at prices which do not afford a margin high enough to cover operating expenses. This was found to be one of the problems faced by department stores in the sale of major appliances. To compete with discount houses, department stores may be forced to sell appliances at a very small markup. A private brand retailer confronted with this problem may have a much wider margin on his own brand. He can stabilize his price at a lower level and still have sufficient margin to undertake aggressive merchandising profitably. When retailers merchandise on a price basis, control over price is essential to their success. Without control over price, they may be faced with an intolerable margin squeeze.

Creating Product and Store Distinctiveness

Finally, one very important hidden advantage results from the closing of the gaps just outlined. This advantage is *product* and *store* distinctiveness. Distinctiveness is a product of private brands not usually recognized by the casual observer. Large scale retailers clearly recognize that any retailer is at a competitive disadvantage unless he can create an image of distinctiveness for his products and his establishment. The merchandising of manufacturers' brands by large-scale retailers in all likelihood stimulates the demand for the brand in other stores as well. "Why should we advertise manufacturers' brands heavily and increase sales of those brands in other stores, when we can promote our private brands and our store's exclusively?" and "We feature our own brands so as to offer products that are distinctive—products that are different—from manufacturers' or competitors' brands," are the typical views of large-scale merchandisers. These retailers have clearly recognized the value of distinctiveness and this is one of the reasons they have developed private brands. But, more importantly this has given them a "captive" customer.

While distinctiveness may at first seem incongruous to private brands, this is an important success factor in retailing. To create distinctiveness, private branders fill the gaps at the high and low ends of the price lines, or develop brands in direct competition with moderately-priced manufacturers' brands. In this way stores refrain from becoming so similar to their competitors that they have little or nothing different to offer their customers. What then, is the force that attracts trade? Most of the really successful merchandisers have created a distinctiveness which has built their large volume of trade. Private brands enable merchants to create distinctiveness of product and store which is not possible through location, interior design and layout, promotion, or the use of commonly-handled manufacturers' brands.

The distinctive private brand can be a promotional aid which will help to attract customers away from competitors. This may be a price difference or quality difference, or it may be store loyalty built upon a succession of purchases of private-brand merchandise. The mixing of both manufacturers' brands and private brands has given some retailers a maximum appeal. Even those units with 90 or 95 per cent of their volume in private brands recognize the advantage of the mix, if for no other purpose than objective comparison by the consumer.

The Outlook for Private Brands

All signs point to the conclusion that private brands are in the ascendancy. Among these signs are the continuing growth of large-scale retailing and the steadily growing use of private brands. The same is true of department store groups and more centrally-owned chains. Voluntary chains, retailer-cooperatives and consumer cooperatives are today even more deeply engaged in private brand development.

The ever-present consumer interest in

price favors the expansion of private brand business and the extension of private brands into comparatively new areas. Among these are house furnishings and even such products as clocks and watches, jewelery, silverware, and photographic equipment. Private brand developments in these lines are in the infancy stages.

Our study amply demonstrates that private brands can be sold on a high-price prestige basis as well as in competition with manufacturers' lower-priced brands. Retailers, therefore, have an opportunity in many lines to use several private brands at different price levels.

Leading private brand users have developed a high degree of customer loyalty and trust in their brands, and this good will in turn can carry them to new heights in the use of private brands. Product distinctiveness of this type is an asset as unique as it is valuable, and retailers are certain to capitalize on it.

As long as private brand users exercise care in the selection of their lines, supervise closely the quality of their products, and price their brands intelligently, consumer interest in private brands will perhaps remain high.

The exact growth pattern is difficult to predict. Where private brands are deeply entrenched, the rate of growth may be comparatively slow, but even this is uncertain because of the interrelationships between private and manufacturable for private brands are filled out. However, such a plateau, if there is to be one, is certainly not in sight, as the way toward further expansion seems wide open.

There is no prospect that private brands will in any sense drive out manufacturers' brands, however. Both types of lines are certain to increase in dollar volume with our expanding economy. Department stores, chain stores, and even the mail order houses will not be able, and in fact may have no desire, to cut off manufacturers' brands. Some consumers for various reasons will always prefer manufacturers' brands in certain fields. Good merchandisers will meet their customers' needs, whatever they may be, and many customers will continue to call for manufacturers' brands. In fact, if manufacturers become increasingly disturbed about the growth of private brands they will attempt to strengthen the competitive position of their own brands.

It is clear, therefore, that the competitive struggle between manufacturers' and private brands will continue. Private brands have some strong advantages, but manufacturers will also be keen and quick to exploit their own brand positions.

44

The Battle of the Brands

Leon Morse

In marketing literature a distinction is always made between national brands and private brands. This terminology is unfortunate because the terms are not dichotomous. Frequently, and increasingly, private brands are national in their market coverage. In fact, the battle between manufacturer's and distributor's brands is growing in intensity and the indications are that distributor brands are slowly increasing their market share where they have historically been strong and are invading new product categories. The following article puts the battle issues into clear focus by citing specific examples.

"We are located in one of the most fiercely competitive markets in the nation," the supermarket executive cried. "The loss leaders in this area are hot enough to scald you. It is not uncommon to take a loss of 20 to 25 cents on every pound of coffee during a weekend special. I think that when the price differential in favor of the private brand reaches the levels I have mentioned, the battle gets too unequal. We cannot even compete by giving away our entire profit on the national-brand label."

No mere special pleader, the man who uttered these words at a recent grocery manufacturers convention is a very significant figure. He is President George W. Jenkins of Florida's 74-unit Publix Super Markets, Inc., and perhaps better than anyone else he put into perfect focus the

Reprinted by special permission from *Dun's Review*, May 1964. Copyright, 1968, Dun & Bradstreet Publications Corp.

battle currently ranging between the retail (private-label) brand and the national (manufacturer's) brand. Too, Jenkins ably summed up the way the private-label brands have carried the war into the camp of the national brands in the nation's department stores, supermarkets, drugstores and other outlets.

There can be little doubt that the retail brands are indeed on the offensive. "In the last ten years the volume of business done by our 12,000 member stores in private labels has doubled," admits William Burston, manager of merchandising of the National Retail Merchants Association. "The smaller stores do 4% of their volume in private labels. But their greatest impact has been in the larger stores: many of them run as high as 8%—and some 10%—in private brands. And this pie is not a whole one. Many of the department store products are completely unbranded."

The shelves of the supermarkets bear

the same marks of invasion. As far back as 1958, a study by the A. C. Nielsen Co. found that supermarkets did 25.6% of their business in brands other than national (included in this figure, of course, were some regional brands too). The record of success of the Great Atlantic & Pacific Tea Co., with 25% of its total volume in private labels is well known. And private labels have also been proliferating along the aisles of such other major supermarket chains as Safeway Stores, Acme Markets, Food Fair Stores and the Kroger Co.

As alarming as this trend is, one other movement has brought even more concern to national-brand manufacturers: the phenomenal increase in private-label business among the nation's wholesale cooperatives, the companies that deal with grocery outlets. Two examples make the point: in five years, New York's Staff Supermarket Associates has built a $16-million business by servicing member stores with private labels: Chicago's Topco Associates, a buying organization for 29 small and medium-sized supermarket chains throughout the country, has a private-label volume of $200 million in foods, houseware, soft goods and health and beauty aids.

The movement toward private brands in all types of consumer goods is continuing to grow. Although drugs and cosmetics are so universally distributed that it is difficult to estimate private-label volume, clear trends are shaping up here too. Thus Marrud Inc., the nation's largest operator of leased drug and cosmetic departments in discount houses, does 7% of its business in private labels, and expects to do 10% by 1964. So confident is Marrud of the future of retail labels, in fact, it is planning to broaden its operations on a grand scale. From being merely a discount-department operator, Marrud has bought a plant and now intends to make drugs and

cosmetics for itself and for other retailers.

To established manufacturers, of course, such practices smack of what at least one of them has referred to as "piracy." Such charges bother Marrud's balding President Jacob Margolis not at all. "I'll be blunt about it," says Margolis, "it's an accepted practice. As soon as a product proves itself and it's permissible, we take it to one of our suppliers and ask him to duplicate it."

Marrud is not alone. What is worse, from the viewpoint of the manufacturers, is that some of the nation's largest retailers share the views of Jacob Margolis. Moreover, they command sufficient technological muscle among their suppliers to even beat name brands to the punch when the stakes (and the potential volume) warrant it. Just one example: Sears' color television, which the company had ready for market long before many national-brand makers were willing to even attempt the gamble on color.

Why the Rebirth?

All this, of course, only serves to bring up one nagging question: What is behind the present resurgence of private brands? Historically, of course, they are nothing new on the retailing scene, having made their appearance during the 1920s. Then, though, they made hardly a dent in the sales of national brands until the 1930s and the Depression, when price became paramount for the consumer. But even in those dismal days they were of little threat to the "names." One of the few to really hit the dominance of the national brands was A&P's still-active Ann Page label. And a few drugstores, called "pineboards," were hastily set up to discount name brands and sell their own private labels.

But these two diverse examples really

constituted the bulk of the private-brand drive; with the exception of Ann Page and a few other products, consumers did not take readily to them. Then they died almost entirely when every spare inch in the nation's plants swung over to defense production during World War II.

Why, then, the return to life? The answer lies in the thin margins that have best both retailers and manufacturers in recent years. From the retailing point of view, of course, much of today's thin-margined selling came from the discount house. It was this new form of merchandising that wrecked the fair-trade laws by cutting prices on national brands. Bait merchandising became the order of the day; self-service took over virtually everywhere; profit margins went down and volume went up.

Such giant retailing combines as Sears, Roebuck, and J. C. Penney (Montgomery Ward had other troubles), armed with their own brands, were more than equal to the challenge. But the sluggish traditional department stores and the variety stores, not quick enough to react to new currents, took the full brunt of this onslaught.

Once the stores did wake up, however, they quickly followed Sears' and Penney's lead in developing the store brand (an old, but effective, weapon that is best described as an "exclusive" private brand). Here, directed by their buying groups, they were able to purchase in sufficient quantity to gain considerable price leverage from manufacturers. In effect, then, the retailer, moving with greater emphasis into the private-brand business, added an impetus all their own. Three of the most adept at this game: Federal Department Stores, R. H. Macy Co. and Allied Stores.

Yet why were they so overwhelmingly successful? Indeed, why have all the private brands succeeded to such a marked degree when the bulk of them

went down to such miserable failure even during the 1930s?

In part, it is the consumer himself who has changed. His loss of brand loyalty has been chronicled time and again. So has his lack of respect for a "name." "Today's consumer is more sophisticated," explains Professor Malcolm P. McNair of Harvard's Graduate School of Business Administration. "This consumer figures all the angles, looks for the advantageous price, has declining allegiance to brands and institutions, does not necessarily accept any one retailer as his purchasing agent."

Competition, and the thin profit margins that accompany it, has accelerated the movement. "I've seen it happen frequently," observes bespectacled Murray Hillman, senior vice president in charge of planning for top advertising agency McCann-Erickson. "A manufacturer will have a dominant position in the market but then slowly begin to add to the price of his product without creating additional consumer benefits. A few such small increases add up, and when the product gets high enough it becomes vulnerable. Then the private label moves in and undercuts him. There is a difference in price that the market can tolerate—in many cases as much as 20%—but it must be justified by product improvement."

Added to these factors is still another consideration. Nobody has studied the failure-and-success cycle of the private brands more closely than the men who make them today, and they have put their finger on the quality that, along with lesser consumer sophistication, spelled their doom during that earlier marketing period. Simply put, that quality was the retail brands' lack of quality. With the exception of a few reputable brands like Ann Page, the private label on all too many of the products was simply a mask for their lack of quality.

By and large, this mistake has not been repeated in the 1960s. "We've got a better iron than General Electric," claims Frederick L. Devereux, own brands marketing manager of Allied Stores. "We know. We tested them both at the United States Testing Laboratory."

While General Electric undoubtedly would contest that point, there is no doubt that the private-brand makers have learned their lesson on quality. Says George Doherty, vice president of Topco Associates: "We've got to have a strong quality base to our sales effort. We say, and we can prove, that well over 90% of the products we buy from manufacturers are modified to our specifications to get better quality. We tell them what we need to satisfy our customers. We're not content to sit back and just order."

Cooperative wholesalers and buying organizations are even going so far as to make something of a fetish of testing. Topco Associates has 25 people in its testing laboratory. Hundreds of products are tested at the Boston laboratories of Dr. Herbert Shuster for Staff Supermarket Associates. And quality insignias are to be found on a wide variety of private-label products.

There is also, of course, the stature of the companies that now manufacture private brands. "Gone are the days when the private-label supplier was a small manufacturer in a loft," says Benjamin Abrams, president of Emerson Radio & Phonograph Corp. "Retailers these days can count on getting the brands from major manufacturers. Private label is a growing business. We've got to face the reality and come to terms with it."

There is little doubt that the private-label manufacturers have moved out of the loft. When J. C. Penney went into hard goods, for example, its vice president of distribution, William L. Marshall, took particular note of the men soliciting his company's business. "What

impressed me," he noted, "was the caliber of the men who made the presentations to us. They were all part of the top management group. It was plain that management was driving for our business. They were leading their aces and giving us the full treatment."

And though there remain notable holdouts, some of the most respected names in manufacturing are now in private brands. These include the Hotpoint division of General Electric, the Hoover Co., SCM Corp., Goodyear Tire & Rubber, the Kelvinator division of American Motors, Westinghouse Electric, Magnavox, Union Carbide, Bell & Howell, Eastman Kodak, Genesco, Norwich Pharmacal and Rexall Drug and Chemical.

Indeed, the retail brand business has grown so large that the past decade has witnessed the emergence of major manufacturers whose sole function it is to produce for this market. One of these companies, the Franklin Manufacturing Co. division of Studebaker Corp., is shooting for a volume of $75 million in 1964; another, Colonial Corp. of America, is aiming at $100 million.

Part of the reason for the increase of "name" manufacturers is that they have learned how to vary the product mix. "We make certain that our products sold through our distributors are distinct from those with the retail label," says Charles J. Gibson Jr., president of the Gibson Refrigerator division of the Hupp Corp. "Take the 'air sweep' feature of our air conditioners: it isn't available to retailers."

The Holdouts

There are, as noted, a few holdouts who stoutly refuse to produce private-label goods. In this group are Maytag Co. and Frigidaire division of General Motors. Claire Ely, vice president in charge of sales and marketing for Maytag, sums up the case for the hold-outs. "We do not believe," says Ely unequivocally, "in offering competitors the same merchandise under a different name. We believe dual manufacture is distasteful to our dealers, and we will not manufacture for this market."

Many executives put their objections in far, far stronger language. Not long ago, President Edgar M. Bronfman of Joseph E. Seagram & Sons issued a raging indictment of the private brand-ers. "Roaming the seas of free enterprise," he cried, "they use the precious charts which our national brands have plotted. Muscling in under their price flag, they maraud the markets which you and we and all the others have developed with untold billions of dollars in product improvement and research. They free-load from our hard-won franchise—and drain from our costly advertising."

The Brand Names Foundation is the offical spokesman for this point of view. Its budget in 1963 was increased to $750,000, and it has stepped up its numerous promotions, including Brand Names Week. In various speeches, Albert Messer, its president, echoes Bronfman. "Who will do the preselling?" asks Messer. "Who will create the traffic and product development? Who will develop such money-saving devices as palletizing and traypacking if the private label continues to proliferate?"

The retailers have their own answer. "They call us parasites," snorts George Doherty of Topco Associates. "Yet what does a manufacturer do when his com-petition comes out with a new product? He does the same thing as us: he hurries out and has it copied. That's the way American business works—unless you can protect your product legally."

Nevertheless, some of these charges do have merit. Retailers do use coopera-tive advertising funds furnished them by manufacturers to advertise their own

retail brands. And while manufacturers pay retailers the national rate for co-operative advertising, the retailers pay the local rate. The difference in the two rates is frequently used by the retailers to advertise their own label.

And retailers have contributed little to product innovation. Yet it must be pointed out that this gradually is chang-ing. Sears, for example, has already placed the first thermoelectric refrigera-tor on the market. Franklin Manufactur-ing calls its Avanti refrigerator the first with any significant design changes. J. C. Penney claims to have pioneered the first washers with baked-enamel finishes and the first mothproof blankets.

When they face each other across store aisles, of course, both private and national brands have their own weapons. The manufacturer's brand has at its command the high-powered national media of television and magazines that presumably presell the consumer. But the retailer's brand has control of the store and that all-important shelf placing and the use of local advertising—as well as standing in the community, no mean factor in closing many sales.

In truth, the private brand has been adding to its array of weapons. Private-label packaging, for example, has shown dramatic improvement in recent years. Marrud's hair-spray container recently competed against top aerosols at the annual packaging show of the Chemical Specialty Manufacturers Association. Allcolor Co.'s "open-end" slot makes it possible to select any number of tissues from its package—an improvement asserts the company, over similar national brand packages.

Marrud has also added more sophisti-cated marketing techniques to its pack-aging; for example, before new store labels are introduced, they are tested with shoppers. Too, the company offers coupons (discount slip inside a product) and "cross ruffs" (two related products, such as a toothbrush and toothpaste, packaged together and priced particularly low to encourage sales). A favorite ploy of United Whelan Corp. is to create a comparison display of name brands against its own private brands, showing the already great price discount; then to offer an additional 10% discount for purchasing two or more of its store brands.

A Few Problems

Yet marketing the private label in retail stoes is not without its difficulties. One of the most critical points, not unnaturally, is the sales clerk. Not only is he more familiar with manufacturers' labels, he is proselytized by the manufacturers' representatives who repeatedly stress the advantages of their products. Moreover, the manufacturer's brand generally has been presold through advertising; as a result, it usually is an easier sale for the clerk, as he well knows.

"Several people in my department do nothing but visit stores trying to stimulate our sales clerks to sell *our* brands," says Fred Devereux of Allied Stores. R. H. Macy makes its house brands even more enticing for the clerk: prizes go to those who are particularly successful merchandisers of Macy's brands. The Frederick Atkins buying office publishes a newsletter to highlight the achievements of those of its stores with the largest increase in store-brand sales.

Can there, though, be such a thing as a winner in the battle of the brands? On the face of it, there cannot. Certainly, both have grown so large that neither need fear disappearing from the marketing scene entirely. But it seems quite clear that the battle between them is growing in intensity. Indeed, both sides have taken to the Government in their zeal for victory.

Thus a major attack on retail branding is being mounted in the United States Congress through the recently introduced Quality Stabilization Bill. This bill, in effect, would reinstitute fair trade by providing that if names and trademarks are used on a product, the seller must abide by the price the manufacturer puts on it; if the retailer wishes to discount the product, he must replace the manufacturer's label. If such a bill should be passed, of course, the discounter could not cut prices on name brands and the traditional retailer's need for retail brands might lessen.

The manufacturers, on the other hand, have been handed a jolt by several decisions made by the Federal Trade Commission. In the first case, the FTC held that the Borden Co. discriminated illegally by selling brand evaporated milk at a higher price than the same milk marketed under other labels. The Borden defense was that advertising added value to the product.

In the second case, the FTC required that Procter & Gamble Co. dispose of the Clorox Co., which it had acquired. The FTC maintained that P&G would only bring greater efficiencies in marketing and advertising to Clorox. Where products are similar, it declared, such efficiencies do not result in benefits to the consumer who pays for them in higher prices.

The FTC, in these cases, evidently took the position that once a product reaches a certain level of acceptance, advertising does not become a benefit to the consumer, but an expense. Both cases take strong positions against advertising. With the power of advertising minimized, however, manufacturers would be gravely handicapped; so both companies are appealing these cases.

Thus the cold war between manufacturer and retailer seems destined to continue without a winner. It appears that the private brand is here to stay, and the manufacturer's brand will just have to make a place for it on the shelf—and learn how to compete with it.

45

A Theory of Packaging in the Marketing Mix

William R. Mason

In today's highly competitive economy, packaging is playing an increasingly important role in the marketing of more and more products. The current annual expenditure in the United States for this activity is about $20 billion.

In making its packaging decisions, management must decide upon the role its package is to play. This is not a simple decision, for a package performs many interrelated functions, some of which may be conflicting. Management's basic decision, therefore, becomes one of choosing the functions deemed most important and determining how completely the package is to perform each. The author of this article outlines a basic theory to guide management in choosing among the many possible mixes of packaging attributes. The basis of this theory is the assertion that the major purpose of a package is to influence or control the location of product storage within the marketing channel.

It is axiomatic that the job of packaging is to sell. But after that banality has been voiced, what guides to management judgment—what theories, if you will—influence the choice of a package?

This article is not a check list of features that should be built into a package, but a rough guide to basic judgments management must bring to bear in its choice of packaging before

Reprinted from *Business Horizons*, Summer 1958, Vol. 1, No. 3, pp. 91–95, by special permission.

the particulars of type face, combination of colors, package count, or printing method are up for decision.

The critical judgments that must be made on the packaging choice concern the "mix" of packaging attributes best able to perform, in different degrees, the particular functions of the package that are believed to be important to sales. The basic judgment in choice of packaging is, "What jobs should the package do, and how completely should it do each?" The answers to the lesser decisions can fall into place once the "mix" of desirable packaging attributes has been determined, once the assignment of basic functions desired of the package has been made. Frequently, too much effort and time are devoted to making lesser decisions, usually on questions of graphic art rather than this basic judgment.

The packager may accept as a guide, when making basic decisions on product "mix," that:

> The major purpose of any package is to influence or control the location of product storage within the marketing channel.

"Storage," as I am using the term, means the holding of goods for future use at any level along the marketing channel, *including the level of the ultimate consumer.* Even at the ultimate consumer level, the product may be stored in several places—sugar, for example, may be stored on a shelf or on the table. The packager is interested in getting the bulk of his product's storage as near as possible to the point of ultimate use.

The functions of the product's package are:

Protecting the product.
Adapting to production line speeds.
Promoting the product.
Increasing product density.[1]
Facilitating the use of the product.
Having re-use value for the consumer.

The performance of a package in the first two of these basic functions is relatively easy to measure through physical testing procedures. And, because it is comparatively easy to evaluate the degrees to which these functions are fulfilled by any package under consideration, such measurement is very common. Today, it must be a rare package that reaches its market without being

[1] That is, increasing the ratio of product volume to package volume.

rated objectively on its degrees of protection and production line adapability. However, these ratings seem to be applied too often without consideration of the package's ability to fulfill its other possible functions.

There are four other major jobs that the package can do at least partially; these should be assigned priority by company management, but often they seem to be neglected.

All packages have the opportunity to perform, at least partially, each of these functions. But it is an unusual package that performs each to the same degree. That the package gives a superior performance of one function does not necessarily mean that it will give a superior performance of another. Because he needs to choose a package, the packager, whether he recognizes it or not, must assign priorities to the value of each of these functions to further his product's sale and use.

To illustrate, it is usually easy to create a package that has uniquely promotable features quite aside from graphic arts; that is, a package that could eminently perform the promotional function. But something else has to give. Using such a package may require sacrificing a good job in one of the other areas, for example in adaptability to production lines speeds or in failure to increase package density. In like fashion, it is frequently possible to build a feature facilitating product use into a package—but not always without sacrificing some measure of product protection.

After all, when a package is criticized as a poor sales- or use-builder, it can be criticized fairly only when its performance of *each* of the basic functions is evaluated. A product may seem "overpackaged" simply because the packager's assignment of priorities differs from the critics.

Interrelationships

Let's examine in a little more detail the way each function impinges on the others:

Protecting the Product. Beyond the requirements imposed by various governmental, carrier, and trade practice rulings, there usually are a substantial number of alternatives open to management with regard to product protection —even during the period when the product is in its distribution channel. To illustrate, even though a carrier ruling may require the product's 24-count carton to have a minimum corrugated fiberboard strength of, say, a 100-pound test, a company's management may choose board that meets more severe tests in order to permit higher stacking or use of mechanized materials-handling equipment by certain important handlers at various levels in the product's distribution channel. Accordingly, in such a situation, an opportunity to tailor the product's package to its product-protection job alone is relinquished because of a desire to better the package's performance of its density-increasing and promotional jobs.

But perhaps a more important range of product-protection considerations occurs at the time of product use— especially when the product is partially used. How much protection should the bread wrapper give a partially used loaf of bread? Will incorporating the use-facilitating features of a pouring spout or a tear tape opening require yielding too much product protection?

Adapting to Production-Line Speeds. Sometimes the operating speeds of packaging equipment do not match the speeds of other equipment in the production line. Until recently, for instance, the normal operating speeds of wrapping machinery that would handle polyethylene film did not match the normal production line speeds for many new products. Two or more wrapping machines were often required in a production line, and the results were poor space utilization, greater capital investment, and sometimes greater labor costs. As an alternative to these wastes, the packager "made do" with other types of film that could be handled by high-speed wrapping equipment but lacked some of polyethylene's protective attributes. New types of wrapping machines have largely corrected this situation. But the point is that the freedom of the packagers to better their packages' protective attributes was limited.

The question of a package's adaptability to production line speeds, however, usually crops up before the package is actually used. The packager's advertising agency or his sales department suggests a new package with striking promise of being able to fulfill the promotional or use-facilitating function better than current packaging; but, upon analysis, the suggested new package is found to require either slowdowns in production line speeds or investment in new packaging equipment. The company's management is then obliged to judge whether or not the suggested package's better performance of the promotional or use-facilitating functions justifies the slower line speed or the different packaging equipment.

Promoting the Product. Features may be built into a package which are promotable to consumers, to customers, and to intermediaries in its product's distribution channel. But sometimes a feature desirable for promotion to one of the three is not desirable for one of the others. Features that minimize a retailer's loss or pilferage are, presumably, important to him; but they are not necessarily of any interest to consumers. Features that minimize a consumer's embarrassment at purchase can increase a retailer's stacking or display difficulties and make inventory control more trying.

Even granting a package feature that is promotable regardless of level in its product's distribution or use, incorporation of the feature into the package frequently requires sacrificing some good package performance of one of the other basic package functions. For example, a gift-wrapped set-up box complete with nosegay of artificial flowers is a highly promotable candy package, as is a rigid plastic, reusable package for razors that is large enough to hold a fishing lure. But both packages sacrifice density for better promotion.

Increasing Product Density. This seems to be the area where the packager's sales department on the one hand, and his purchasing and production departments on the other, are most often in disagreement about the choice of packaging. Except on those occasions when the sales department recommends yielding a package's higher density in order to improve its promotional value, the sales department is usually advocating increased package density. It improves relations with carriers; it permits better utilization of space throughout the distribution channel, thus encouraging fuller inventory stocks in the pipeline; and it permits more units to be displayed per assigned running foot of shelf-service display space. But it frequently slows production line speeds and increases per-unit packaging cost.

Usually this issue turns on package shape. The cylinder, for instance, is an efficient package shape for liquids; a given measure of liquid can be packaged cylindrically with less material than is necessary for any rectangular container holding the same amount of liquid. But the normal 12-count (3 x 4 put-up) layer of a 24-count carton will occupy significantly less shelf space if it holds rectangular packages rather than

the same number of cylindrical packages with the same amount of liquid.

But bettering a package's performance of its density-increasing function can inhibit good performance in other areas too. The density of many candy packages, for instance, could be improved significantly, but not without loss of their value as items specifically tailored for re-use as sewing baskets or cookie tins. Increasing density could also lessen the package's value as a promotional vehicle or as a promotable item in itself. Package designers seem better able to build points of brand differentiation into a 12-ounce beer bottle than into the higher density 12-ounce beer can.

Facilitating the Use of the Product. Excluding changes in the graphic art of packages, most package changes in recent years have been in facilitating the product's use. All the changes to tear tapes, pouring spouts, squeeze bottles, aerosol cans, and so forth would have to be included here. And, as is obvious ot anyone exposed to the mass advertising media, bettering the package's fulfillment of this function has proved to be a means of bettering the package's performance in promotion.

In many cases, however, where the use-facilitating function of a package has been improved, a case can be built that some degree of product protection has been sacrificed. And, bettering the package's use-facilitating job sometimes means relinquishing some package value as a re-use container for the consumer. The flow of a viscous liquid perhaps can be directed a little more accurately or easily from the mouth of a narrow-necked glass jar than from a tin can, but packaging the liquid in the glass jar means sacrificing the protection against impact provided by the tin can. The tear tape makes a corrugated carton easier to open but, for many purposes, lessens its value as a re-usable container. Some shaker openings make cleanser or spice packages easy to use but, once used, leave the product exposed.

Having Re-use Value for the Consumer. Perhaps the competition of the various functions of the package for recognition by company managements is most apparent in this area. In recent years, according much recognition to this function of the package seems not to have been in vogue. Typically, designing a package to do its other jobs well has meant slighting its re-use value—the previous illustrations of candy and razors notwithstanding. A package's re-use value generally has suffered with successive changes unless its re-usability has been very promotable.

The Principle, the Corollary, and Recent Trends

How does management know whether it is better to sacrifice a measure of product protection for a more promotable package or to build a use-facilitating attribute into the package instead of a density-increasing attribute?

Assuming that two "mixes" are in conflict or partial conflict, management may find the answer by deciding which will be more likely to push product storage as far from the packager as possible. This is, of course, another way of saying that the basic purpose of a product's package should be as much as possible to maximize product inventory near the point of use or possible use. If neither "mix" holds promise of increasing product inventory at the point of use, does either hold promise of increasing storage at the next level back from the point of use? If neither "mix" aids in getting the product stored on the dining-room table, does either help in getting more of the product inventoried on the kitchen shelves? If neither helps there, which encourages the greater amount of well-placed open display at

retail? If it is a tie between the two package "mixes" at this level, which of the two has promise of encouraging the greater retailer inventory—regardless whether in open display or not?

It follows, then, that the most successful package changes are those whose impact is greatest at a level in the product's marketing one step forward from the level currently storing the channel's largest share of the product.

Most recent packaging changes can be understood a little better if viewed against the backdrop of these generalizations. Interestingly, they explain current trends in package design that, on the surface, seem to be running in opposite directions. For instance, recently some company managements have been increasing package size or package count. Other managements have unit-packaged, lessened package size, or reduced package count. But both apparently contradictory approaches have the same purpose—*to maximize product inventory as close to a point of use as possible.* Let's examine a few recent package changes in light of these generalizations (I am referring to those changes that typically affect more than just the package's graphic art):

Changes Involving Package Size or Count. Proprietary medicine, soap powder, or detergent, beverages, and toilet tissue are among those widely distributed consumer products whose recent package changes have included addition of "king" or "giant economy" size packages to their lines. Table salt, facial tissue, crackers, and cereal on the other hand are among the items distributed in large part through the same marketing channel, which have added smaller-size packages or "unitized" packages to their lines. In each case, promotion turning on "convenience" to the user frequently has accompanied the introduction of the new package size. Where the move has been to increase the package size, packagers are trying to encourage the consumer to maintain inventories of their particular brands far in excess of the consumer's normal needs for the product during any reasonable time span between shopping trips. In effect, the packagers are trying to move a greater share of their channel's total storage function closer to the point of use—from retailer to consumer in this particular illustration. Where the move has been to lessen package size, it is apparent that the packagers are trying to move storage location further forward: to get facial tissues into purses as well as on the vanity; to get brand-identified salt on the dining-room, breakfast, TV, or barbecue table as well as on the pantry shelf; to get half a dozen varieties of cereal in the home rather than in the store in anticipation of a family's vacillating demands. Again, the packagers are trying to move a greater share of the channel's total storage closer to the point of use.

Changes Involving Package Shape. Ice cream and milk, in both powdered and liquid forms, are examples of items that have been undergoing changes from cylindrical to space-saving rectangular packages. In part, at least, the change has been precipitated by increased recognition of the marketing channel's limited capacity to store items under refrigeration and of its eagerness to husband its shelf space. In effect, the change permits a greater share of the inventory to be moved forward.

Changes Involving Packaging Materials. This is the area where packagers' desires to push storage forward probably have been most apparent. And, incidentally, it is in this area that the lie is put to the belief that a package's prime job is protection of the product. If product protection were the prevailing consideration, few if any of certain kinds of change in packaging materials would ever have taken place. For example:

a. *Changes from opaque to transparent materials* usually have been represented as irrefutable evidence of the packager's good faith in allowing his customers to see his product. Understandably, the suppliers of transparent packaging materials have done what they could to further this impression. But conversion from opaque to transparent packaging typically has meant something else as well; *It has been a means of obtaining favorable open display shelf space at retail,* where the product could be seen by the consumers. In effect, it has meant moving part of the storage function forward in the channel from concealed storage or low-traffic locations to prominent, high-traffic locations. Small wonder that such a premium has come to be placed on transparency—even for products not especially attractive to the eye.

b. *Changes from rigid to flexible materials* have almost always meant relinquishing some measure of product protection—and the recent changes from rigid to semi-rigid or flexible packaging are legion. The changes, while requiring some loss of product-protection value, typically have given the product an especially promotable package, one with conspicuous promise of moving product storage closer to a point of use.

Changes Involving Addition of "Ease-of-Opening" or "Ease-of-Use" Attributes. I believe that, where they have been successful, package changes incorporating this kind of feature have tended to move product storage increasingly closer —however slightly—to the point of use. Typically, the movement of storage effected by such "ease-of-opening" package changes has not been at the consumer level in the product's marketing channel; it has been at the retail level. Perhaps it could be argued that the

extremely successful rigid flip-top cigarette package has helped move the
smoker's storage of his cigarettes a little
closer to the point of their use, but the
main value of the package with regard
to its movement of product storage has
been at the retail level. The package,
again, was a means of obtaining a good,
high-traffic position in open display for
the particular brands of cigarette that
pioneered this packaging change. It
was something distinctively new that
could be promoted to the marketing
channel itself—quite aside from its
being amenable to use in effective
promotion to smokers—for brands not
having so extensive or complete retail
inventories as those enjoyed by more
popular brands.

In summary, the choice of a product's
package, no less than the choice of the
total selling effort brought to bear on
the product, has to represent a reconciliation of a variety of functions, each of
which has potential merit in furthering
the sale of the product but all of which
are, in part at least, mutually exclusive.

The most successful reconciliation will
be the one that, to return to our original
axiom, produces the most sales. It will
emphasize that function which pushes
the bulk of product storage one step
farther along the marketing channel and
one step closer to the ultimate consumer.

D

Marketing
Communications

46

Specialize
Your Salesmen!

George N. Kahn and Abraham Shuchman

For many firms, particularly those selling industrial products or those selling consumer goods directly to retailers, the personal selling activity plays a central role in marketing. Unfortunately, the salesman is widely criticized today for his poor performance in the field. The authors of this article suggest that the apparent low productivity of salesmen is because of top management's failure to recognize that salesmen are generally called upon to perform two distinct jobs, each of which calls for specialized aptitudes. One solution to this problem is for companies to organize their sales force on the basis of the task to be performed, rather than on the traditional bases of products, customers, and territories.

The 1960's promise to be a period of more intense competition than current managements have yet experienced. The signals are now clearly discernible:

- A rising flood of new products and imports.
- A growing saturation of markets for older products.
- An increasing invasion of markets by

Abridged from *Harvard Business Review*, January–February 1961, Vol. 39, No. 1, pp. 90ff by special permission.

firms formerly regarded as noncompetitive.
- The spread of automation with its enormous output potential.

These trends emphasize a compelling need for marketing programs that will assure new account development for existing products and maximum efforts for new products, despite massive onslaughts by competitors for whom new customers and new markets are also an urgent necessity. If recent experience is a reliable indicator, managers seeking a hard-hitting program for market development will focus on advertising and other impersonal methods of sales promotion.

For many firms, however, and particularly for firms selling industrial products or selling consumer goods through distributors, the central role has been and will continue to be played by personal selling. Unfortunately, personal selling, aside from the provision of increased staff support, continues to be organized almost exactly as it was a generation ago in the days of the drummer. Territories, products, and sometimes (but not often) customers are the main divisions in current sales organization. Virtually no attempt has been made to organize personal selling on the basis of the task to be performed.

Why has specialization in personal selling stopped with territories, products, and customers? Why has little effort been made to increase the productivity of personal selling by applying one of the basic principles of mass production—specialization by task? The failure arises from a number of misconceptions or badly digested knowledge on the part of top management about the work that field salesmen are asked to perform, and about the requirements for accomplishing this work. Management seems not to have perceived that:

- Salesmen are called on to do not one but two very different jobs.
- The performance of each of these jobs involves different problems and techniques.
- The personnel requirements for satisfactory performance of each of these jobs are very different.
- The difficulties of reorganizing for specialization in the two jobs may be more than compensated for in improved sales performance.

In sum, top management has been

overlooking an opportunity to raise field performance to levels never before achievable, and consequently an opportunity to develop a promotional weapon that could achieve new account development on an unprecedented scale.

Salesman's Two Jobs

First of all, while many executives may sense, or be vaguely aware of, the underlying principle, they do not comprehend the extent or the real nature of it: that in almost every company, and for almost every product, the work of a field salesman breaks down into two distinct jobs—(a) *sales development* and (b) *sales maintenance*.

On the one hand, the field salesman must service and cultivate existing customers. He must preserve and, if possible, expand the volume of business these customers do with his firm by maintaining and building on the favorable attitudes which already exist. He is engaged in a holding operation. The objective of sales maintenance is the *creation of sales* from people who already are customers, and whose habits and patterns of thought are already conducive to such sales.

On the other hand, the field salesman is expected to obtain new customers for his firm as well. He must convince companies that are not now using his firm's products to adopt them. To do this, he must eliminate and alter either the unfavorable or the indifferent attitudes and habits that are a part of the potential customer he is facing. He is engaged in a conversion operation. The objective of sales development is not so much the creation of sales as the *creation of customers* out of people who do not at the moment view his company favorably, and who are undoubtedly resistant to change.

Since these two jobs put such different

requirements on a man, charging a field salesman with both creating sales and creating customers can only result in his undertaking the task he prefers to the detriment of the task he dislikes. The usual result is that among field salesmen, sales maintenance activity drives out sales development activity.

Why? Simply because the latter task is more difficult for the salesman to endure. None of us likes to enter and work in an unfriendly atmosphere in which rebuffs and even lack of common courtesy often prevail, in which we are given no recognition or status, and in which the probabilities of achieving one's objectives, despite the expenditure of considerable effort, are small. But this is exactly the situation faced by a salesman when he is engaged in sales development! As the social scientist would put it, he is a *change agent* in such a situation, and frequently faces a very hostile environment.

On the contrary, most of us prefer to go where we are known and where we know who is who, where we are treated with respect and accepted as an equal, and where the probabilities of achieving our goals without undue exertion are high. This is the situation faced by a salesman when he is engaged in sales *maintenance,* and, being only human, he will prefer to concentrate on the task of sales maintenance and avoid the task of sales development.

Creating Customers

However, failure to create new customers is due only in part to the reluctance of salesmen to devote themselves to this onerous task. Even when salesmen make a real effort, most of them cannot perform the task satisfactorily. The reason is simply that most field men possess neither the temperament nor the skills which the job requires.

As noted earlier, developing new accounts requires the reshaping of the prospective buyers' attitudes, habits, and patterns of thought. Essentially, this is a highly creative task requiring considerable time, talent, resourcefulness, and ingenuity. The talents needed by a development salesman can best be outlined by discussing the succession of stages through which the salesman must work to create a customer:

1. To start with, the development salesman must identify those firms in his territory which are worthwhile for him to attempt to convert, and identify the influential executive in each. He must secure access to these executives for himself, and in many cases for his firm's technical specialists, under conditions which will assure him attention. This signifies that the development salesman must be an analyst as well as a talented tactician who understands that he must approach an executive in terms of the executive's company rather than in terms of the salesman's product.

2. The development salesman must establish with these executives a relationship in which he is perceived as a source of possible help in solving company problems. To achieve this, the development salesman must be capable of understanding his prospects to the degree that he can communicate both his appreciation of their problems and an image of himself as a source of help in solving such problems.

3. He must motivate prospects to change by helping them become aware of a need for change. He must be able to develop an appetite in the prospect when he is not hungry, by fostering a constructive discontent with things as they are. Since prospects, generally, are satisfied with their present behavior, he must disturb prospects' satisfaction with the status quo.

To accomplish this, he must have the talent and ability to create a situation in which each prospect *can learn for himself*, rather than be told or shown that he has problems and needs which can be better solved and satisfied.

4. He must transform a readiness to change into an actual change in behavior. This transformation, the keystone of the entire development process, requires that the salesman be able to arouse in prospects the intention to change as well as the conviction that the suggested change is appropriate. It means, as well, that the development salesman must encourage and support prospects while they deliberate the change and try to put it into practice.

5. However, securing an initial order or even a short sequence of orders does not signal, as too many marketers seem to believe, the end of the development process. Making a sale is not equivalent to creating a customer. The prospect may still very quickly become—with little provocation—a tenant of the inactive customer file. Consequently, the development salesman's job remains unfinished. He must still convert his prospect's action into habit. The salesman's final goal, therefore, is to stabilize the change he has created.

To do this, the development salesman must have sufficient awareness to reinforce his prospect's conviction that the innovation is wise by providing as much reassurance as possible. He must be capable of generating for his prospect both the experiences and the information which emphasize the advantages of the innovation.

Maintaining Sales

Once the purchase of the salesman's product has become habitual, the strategic objective of the development process has been achieved. The work of sales development is finished and that of sales maintenance begins. When the prospect has been converted to a customer, then the motives and objectives of the seller shift. Keeping the customer and making him a better customer are now a salesman's goals. His aim is to preserve and build on the foundation of confidence and acceptance established in the development process.

What the maintenance salesman seeks, therefore, is not change but *constancy*. His selling strategy is defensive rather than offensive. His selling tactics must be designed, not to break through established positions, but to make his own position entrenched and secure, impregnable to the assaults of competitors. In maintaining and strengthening customer loyalty and preference, the maintenance salesman starts from a well-prepared and propitious vantage point. He not only possesses much vital information but is supported and aided, in addition, by many forces in his customer's psychological and organizational environment:

1. He knows directly or has been thoroughly briefed about the customer's operations, organization, and personnel.

2. Even if he has not done the development work himself, he has ready access to key executives and is perceived as a source of help.

3. He derives advantage from his customer's conservatism and inertia, from his customer's characteristic fear of and resistance to change, and from his customer's feelings of comfort and security, engendered by the knowledge that the salesman's product and firm perform well.

4. He is aided by his customer's reluctance to seek a new supplier as long as the present one is doing an acceptable job. This is due, at least in part, to the knowledge that such a search and accommodation to a new product is costly in time, money, effort, and psychological strain and tension.

Thus, the conditions and circumstances under which the maintenance salesman works are far different and far more favorable than those under which the development salesman works. The principal task of the maintenance salesman is to keep his customers content with and happy in their relationship with his firm. It is to preserve and deepen his customer's satisfaction with the status quo. This satisfaction lasts for a time, after the intensive development work that produced it. But it is like a fire. It is lit; it burns; it is warm. It needs fuel. It does not last forever unless it is fed, regularly and carefully. The fire can be made to burn even more brightly through the use of two additives—friendliness and personal attention. Maintenance salesmen must have the happy ability to inject humor and warmth into the customer's business life.

Customer Service

The basic fuel for the fire of customer loyalty, however, is service. It is making the customer's work less difficult by being helpful and useful in improving his job performance. It is aiding him to solve his problems and assisting him to move toward the promotion of greater profits that is his goal. It is, in other words, doing such an effective job *for* the buyer that he himself wants to and actually helps the salesman to do an effective job *with* him.

For the *industrial* maintenance salesman this means that he must know the applications of his product better than do the customer's own technicians. He must know not only every conceivable use—and limitation—of his product, but the engineering behind it and the possibilities of complementary and competing products. He must understand his customer's processes and operations so well that he knows precisely where his product can and cannot be used as well as

how it must be used in order to yield maximum benefit.

The maintenance salesman working among *distributors* and *dealers* has similar needs. This means that he must be intimately acquainted not only with the general practices and problems of the trades to which he is selling, but also with the specific practices and problems of each customer. Moreover, he must be able to spot weaknesses and wastes in these practices, come up with practical suggestions for eliminating them, and help provide the skills needed to accomplish this elimination.

But comprehensive knowledge of products, processes, and trades is only one requirement for success in maintaining selling. In addition, the maintenance salesman must be the communicator of cogent and important market information and a crossbreeder of ideas. For industrial products he must be able to keep abreast of technological developments that can affect both his own and his customer's markets. He must be able to evaluate the impact on his customer's markets of these developments as well as of trends in competing industries.

Similarly, the salesman working in intermediate markets must be able to supply information about what is being sold by whom, how it is being sold, and who is doing the buying. Beyond this, he must be able to serve as an exchange medium for merchandising and promotional ideas. He must be alert to novel ideas and approaches used effectively by creative and pioneering jobbers or dealers and must take these to other distributors or dealers.

The Big Difference

Maintenance and development salesmen both need such talents as facilitate the acquisition, analysis, use, and communication of information. However, while they both must be able to apply these talents and skills to the products, markets, and operations of the customer company, the development salesman must be able to apply them under much more difficult conditions to an audience with very different attitudes.

The ability to obtain and communicate information about customer products, markets, and operations is, in most instances, sufficient for success in maintenance selling. It is by no means a sufficient condition for success in development work. On the contrary, the *sine qua non* of success in new account development is the ability to obtain, understand, and use information about the prospect himself; about his needs, fears, aspirations, and perceptions; about his prejudices, loyalties, ambitions, and enthusiasms.

The really critical abilities are the faculties to acquire, understand, and use not "technical" information or objective facts, as is the case for maintenance selling, but psychological information or subjective facts; and, equally important, to communicate and bring about effective communication between others. The crucial talents and skills of the development salesman are qualities that a maintenance salesman requires only to a very limited extent and perhaps not at all— such traits as empathy, a sharp "third ear," introspective skill, and superior intelligence.

There are other talents and skills which a development salesman must have and a maintenance salesman need not have. The former must be a creative strategist, a tactician capable of designing and implementing original, effective sales approaches and sales presentations —"custom-tailored" for each prospect and for each person influencing the purchase. He must be able to mobilize and exploit skills, knowledge, and ideas of technical and missionary specialists. As a result, the development salesman is required to be alert and active, with an inventive imagination, and a sensitivity to or feel for the appropriate deed and the appropriate time. He requires resourcefulness, ingenuity, much tact and skill in interrogation, and the administrative skills needed to plan, organize, coordinate, direct, and control the work of others.

Born, Not Trained

Thus, there are real and very substantial differences between the talents and skills which determine success in development selling and those which determine success in maintenance selling. But this fact in itself, although interesting, is certainly no revelation to some marketing managers. *What is really significant* (and has not been apparent to managers, however) *is that most of the qualities needed for successful development selling cannot be acquired.*

No amount of training can provide these qualities if a man does not possess them. A man has them or he does not. If he has them, training can develop and strengthen them; it can improve their use. But if he does not have them, training will not give them to him. Clearly, an adult who is not emphatic, introspective, or sensitive to subtleties of expression cannot be taught to be so.

We have no means for increasing an adult's intelligence, imagination, resourcefulness, or ingenuity. Training can provide information, skills, and technical competence; but training, in the usual sense in which this word is used, cannot enable a person to develop new and different personality and character traits. This is what would be required in order to make most salesmen real development salesmen.

Conclusion

The application of specialization by task to personal selling can provide an opportunity to raise field performance to levels never before achievable, and consequently an opportunity to develop a promotional weapon that could achieve new account development on an unprecedented scale. Such specialization must focus around the fact that the work of a field salesman is really two distinct jobs: sales development and sales maintenance.

The objective of sales maintenance is the creation of sales from people who already are customers, and whose habits and patterns of thought are already conducive to such sales. The objective of sales development is not merely the creation of sales, but the creation of customers out of people who do not at the moment view the company or its products favorably, and who are undoubtedly resistant to change.

In effect, these two jobs require men of different calibre and sentiments. Maintenance and development salesmen both need talents which facilitate the acquisition, analysis, use, and communication of technical information. However, the development salesman must, in addition, have the ability to obtain, understand, and use information about his prospects' needs, fears, aspirations, perceptions, prejudices, loyalties, ambitions, and enthusiasms. One might call this key quality *social perceptiveness,* and what is really significant is that it cannot be acquired or taught.

As a result of the scarcity of such talented men in personal selling, the best method for ensuring thorough new account development with the best use of all selling talent available is to have salesmen specialize in the maintenance or development jobs, and not try to do both.

This specialization will undoubtedly create problems that will require careful management attention. But the rewards of specialization will more than offset the difficulties of transition periods between salesmen, rivalries between the two sales forces, and the development of performance standards.

47

The Salesman's Role Revisited

James A. Belasco

The function of a salesman varies greatly depending upon whether he is working in a seller's or a buyer's market. In a seller's market the salesman can identify closely with his employer because sales are relatively easy to make and his role is primarily that of presenting the goods forcefully. In a buyer's market the buyer has many options open to him. Consequently, to get him to buy his product, the salesman must be very attentive to his needs and desires. The changes that have occurred in the selling situation have not been widely recognized; as a result, one hears much criticism of present-day salesmanship. This article points out some of the sociological and psychological problems inherent in the salesman's role.

Salesmen Wanted
Must be aggressive, self-starter, able to work with people. High earnings for the right man.

This advertisement, or variations thereof, appears in newspapers throughout the United States. Yet a great many of the applicants chosen will not be able to fill the job adequately.

Most marketeers know that the costs of this inefficient hiring process are high. It may cost as much as $8,200 direct out-of-pocket to place a trained salesman in the field.[1] Many selection problems may be traced to a *unidimensional* view of both the salesman's job and the person who fills it. Most current selection procedures focus on such intellectual dimensions of both job and worker as abilities, education, and experiences required.

Yet evidence indicates that jobs pose other demands as well. For instance, Jasinski's study of assembly-line workers,[2] Whyte's study of engine-room operators[3] and waitresses,[4] Rosen and Rosen's study

of union stewards,[5] Trice's study of night watchmen,[6] and Tannenbaum's study of factory workers[7] all reflect the importance of the emotional and interactional dimensions of jobs.

However, the factors that determine job success are not necessarily the intellectual dimensions which most selection devices are designed to measure. Rather, job success may depend upon the match between the incumbent's personality and the temperamental demands of the job.

The Salesman's Job Re-examined

In an effort to gain insights into the multidimensional nature of the salesman's job, the author spent considerable time in two different companies interviewing and observing salesmen and sales managers. This resulted in some new avenues of thought which might be useful in selection procedures.

Intellectual Demands

The intellectual demands of a job may be subdivided into three separate di-

Reprinted from the *Journal of Marketing*, national quarterly publication of the American Marketing Association, Vol. 30, No. 2, April 1966, pp. 6–8.
    [1] *Wall Street Journal*, November 18, 1964, p. 1.
    [2] Frank J. Jasinski, "Technological Delineation of Reciprocal Relationships: A Study of Interaction Patterns in Industry," *Human Organizations*, Vol. 30 (Summer, 1956), pp. 24–28, at p. 25.
    [3] William F. Whyte, *Men at Work* (New York: Irwin-Dorsey, 1961), p. 53.
    [4] William F. Whyte, *Human Relations in the Restaurant Industry* (New York: McGraw-Hill Book Company, 1948).

    [5] Hjalman Rosen and Hudson Rosen, "Personality Variables and Role in a Union Business Agent Group," *Journal of Applied Psychology*, Vol. 41 (April, 1957), pp. 131–136, at p. 131.
    [6] Harrison M. Trice, "Night Watchman: A Study of an Isolated Occupation," *ILR Research*, Vol. 10 (November, 1964), pp. 3–8, at p. 8.
    [7] Arnold S. Tannenbaum, "Personality Change as the Result of an Experimental Change of Environment," *Journal of Abnormal and Social Psychology*, Vol. 55 (November, 1957), pp. 404–406.

mensions of intelligence, job knowledge, and problem-solving ability.

Intelligence may be further divided into verbal ability, numerical ability, spatial ability, and mechanical ability. Some evidence indicates that salesmen must be in the top 30th percentile of the general population in verbal ability.[8] Specific sales occupations may involve a combination of verbal ability with one or two other dimensions of intelligence. However, beyond this minimum amount no linear relationship exists, between the intellectual ability of the applicant and his probability of job success. Other considerations appear to come to the fore, including the emotional demands of the position.[9]

Emotional Demands

It is necessary to understand the emotional demands that a salesman's position makes upon him. First, he has an extremely broad role with many divergent role partners. He may occupy at any one time the role of persuader, serviceman, information-gatherer, problem-definer, advocate, information-reporter, expediter, coordinator, traveler, scheduler, display-arranger, and customer ego-builder.

In addition, the salesman may occupy several roles at once. In the course of one sales call he may gather marketing information, persuade the customer, arrange a product display, and expedite a special order. He deals with a wide variety of role partners, ranging from

[8] John B. Miner, *Intelligence in the United States* (New York: Spring Publishing Company, 1957); John B. Miner and John E. Culver, "Some Aspects of the Executive Personality," *Journal of Applied Psychology*, Vol. 39 (October, 1955), pp. 348–353 at p. 352.

[9] John B. Miner, *The Management of Ineffective Performance* (New York: McGraw-Hill Book Company, 1963), p. 23.

production workers to secretaries to engineers to vice-presidents.

After all, the salesman serves as the link between at least four different groups. He is linked with his own sales-management group; with the balance of the organization upon whom he must depend for fulfillment of his orders; with the customers whom he services; and with other salesmen, both within his company and elsewhere.

Each group imposes certain behavioral expectations on him. Oftentimes the expectations of one group will be in conflict with those of the other. The placing and expediting of a special order for a new customer is an excellent example of the potential conflicts. The customer places the order and expects that the salesman's company will deliver the order on schedule. Sensing the opportunity to add a new account, the salesman exerts pressure to get the order delivered on time. This pressure may take the form of calls to the production manager and possibly even a visit to the plant; and the production group is likely to resent this.

The salesman's role is unusual in that it exists so far apart socially, psychologically, and physically from the dependency support of the usual "man-boss" relationship. With the possible exception of the president, the salesman's role is perhaps the most independent role in the organization.

Furthermore, in the performance of his many roles, the salesman faces three specific role conflicts. First, there is the *conflict of identification*, which arises out of the multi-group membership of the salesman. As the salesman works with the customer, it is reasonable to expect that he will identify with the customer rather than his company. However, when he returns to his company, the salesman must drop the identification with the customer and identify again with the company. This constantly shifting focus of identification poses a role conflict. The sales convention is one method of increasing the salesman's identification with the company.

The identification conflict, in turn, gives rise to the *advocacy conflict*. When the salesman has identified with the customer, it is logical to expect that he will seek to aid the customer by advocating the customer's position to the other groups with which he is linked. While this function may be very important and may be actually encouraged by the salesman's superiors, it places the advocator in a very difficult position.

The salesman also faces the *conflict inherent in his dual role as an advocate* for both the customer and his company, and his pecuniary interest as an entrepreneur. As an entrepreneur paid on the basis of sales volume, he has a decided interest in selling as much as possible in the shortest possible time. However, he may uncover facts overlooked or unknown to the customer which indicate that difficulties in the customer's organization will limit his product's usefulness. If the salesman informs the customer of these observations and that in all probability the product will not fully meet the customer's needs, obviously the salesman runs the risk of losing the sale and the income that goes with it.

In short, as a result of the large number of roles which the salesman occupies and his linkage with several different groups, he is faced with *potential conflict*. This conflict may be translated into *actual role conflict* when the salesman's role partners do not agree about how they expect him to act in given situations; and the salesman's behavior is highly visible to the role partners with the divergent expectations. This relationship between role consensus, observability, and actual role conflict is illustrated in the accompanying diagram.

Amount of Actual Role Conflict

		Observability	
		High	*Low*
Role	High	medium	low
Consensus	Low	high	medium

The different people with whom the salesman interacts have differing expectations of him. Therefore, role consensus is low. At first glance, because of the wide geographic differences separating many of the salesman's role partners, it would seem that individuals holding conflicting expectations would be unable to observe the salesman's behavior which did not conform to their expectations. However, many training-and-control activities enable the company to observe more of the salesman's behavior. For instance, the frequent accompaniment of the sales manager on calls with the salesman increases the visibility of the salesman's actual field behavior to the company. This high visibility coupled with low role consensus leads to a considerable amount of role conflict for the salesman.

On balance, then, the salesman's job poses two emotional demands on him: first, the ability to manage a high level of role conflict; and second, the ability to tolerate and manage social ambiguity with few organizational or group supports.

Interactional Demands

Closely related to the emotional demands of a job are its interactional demands.[10] First the job demands a person with a wide range of behaviors and flexibility in adapting his behaviors.

[10] See Elliot D. Chapple and Leonard R. Sayles, *The Measure of Management* (New York: The Macmillan Company, 1961), pp. 114–141.

The salesman must be able to talk at considerable length some times and be a quiet listener at other times. He must be able to move easily from one situation where he is dominant to another where he is dominated. In short, his role requires him to adapt to a large number of differing personalities with a wide range of possible behaviors.

Second, the intensity of social contact fluctuates widely. The salesman may encounter an entire hour of intense negotiations with a customer which will then be followed by a two-hour period of almost no social contact during which time he travels to another appointment and waits for the next customer. He must be able to be highly active at times and highly inactive at others.

As a result, he is constantly shifting from an inner-directed focus, dwelling largely on himself, to the other-person customer-directed orientation during sales calls. This may result in a considerable amount of inner stress.

In fact, a fourth interactional demand is the ability to withstand stress. First, there is the stress of meeting new personalities or situations. Second, there is the stress engendered by competition; and the salesman must manage this high-level stress without permitting it to limit his flexibility or range of behaviors.

In addition, his role requires him to show a high degree of persistence. This is necessary in situations when he refuses to be discouraged by the customer, as well as in the situation where he may try for months to make a sale, only to lose it at the last moment. In other words, the salesman must be able to sustain his level of activity and flexibility in spite of discouragements.

Implications

What is the significance of the above analysis as to selection and placement of salesmen?

The answer is that many of the current procedures and concepts are not far-reaching enough. Both man-analysis and job-analysis need to be broadened in scope to include the emotional and interactional dimension of both. Selection instruments must be devised which gather information about the applicant in terms of his personality requirements. Then, a "fit" must be found between the total demands of the job and the personality requirements of the individual.

In addition, decreased control might be indicated. A small increase in selectivity can lead to a large decrease in control costs.[11] Perhaps salesmen could be freed of some aspects of the nonproductive control activities, such as call summaries, planning sheets, and trip reports.

In summary, a new way of looking at salesman selection is proposed. This implies the need for research on job descriptions and requirements which emphasize the temperamental dimensions of jobs, plus selection devices which gather information about the applicant in terms of these temperamental dimensions. The point is that we need to know far more about the emotional and interactional demands which specific jobs pose for salesmen.

[11] Amitai Etzioni, *Modern Organization* (Englewood Cliffs, New Jersey: Prentice-Hall, Inc., 1964), p. 64.

48

Advertising's Place in the Economy of Abundance

Fairfax M. Cone

Business critics usually reserve their sharpest barbs for an attack on advertising. This is probably because the institution of advertising calls attention to itself and is the focal point of all the profit-making objectives which preceded it. Most of the attacks on advertising can only be understood properly if they are seen as criticisms of the market-place economy. Of course any perceptive person would have to concede that there are faults and excesses in advertising, but there are also faults in labor relations and accounting practices. These call for correction rather than abandonment. But the loudest critics would eliminate persuasive advertising. In the following article the author, one of the best-known advertising spokesmen, discusses some of the critics and criticisms of advertising.

I. The Present

Certainly the most puzzling aspect of the abundant life in America, which is the guiding light of most ambitious people everywhere, is the criticism that is heaped upon it by unenthusiastic observers. For one thing, it is fairly certain that these would have been the severest critics of the economy of scarcity and severity that characterized the American society until the first decades of this century. For another, these are the people most concerned with poverty, illiteracy and all manner of political and economic frustration in the undeveloped countries.

The trouble seems to be that our rich,

Reprinted from *Printer's Ink*, June 14, 1963 (copyright 1963 by Printer's Ink Publishing Corp.).

free-choice economy doesn't work exactly the way these observers want it to. Since their solicitude for the individual can scarcely admit that there may be some national unwisdom in the full exercise of his choice, it is argued that the foolish choices are not, as a matter of fact, the individual's at all, but instead the result of manipulation by hidden and godless persuaders and corruptors of the public taste. The principal means by which this corruption is accomplished is held in these critical circles to be advertising, and the attacks upon it are widespread.

I have no doubt at all that dishonest men make dishonest advertising. It is much harder to have this published than it was once, and it is difficult to have it broadcast nationally; still advertisers do try and sometimes they succeed briefly, in fleecing some part of the public. But the charges against advertising that have only been leveled and never proved apply not to specific arts or advertiser aims that may be against the public interest, but to the basic freedom of our people to exercise their own judgment and their own choice.

Thus does the case against advertising move into the area of social alarm and sociological distress. The case has been put with varying degrees of heat and reason by a number of well-known observers and critics of contemporary life in the English-speaking countries where the much-vaunted standards of living are highest; and they see these as false standards, maintained by advertisers for the satisfaction of their own cupidity.

This seems a large charge.

The clearly demonstrable fact is that the advertisers are all the businesses in America which are engaged, either directly or indirectly, in satisfying the needs and a great many desires of 190 million people who are assured from birth, as their American heritage, anything legal for which they can produce the money to pay.

The principal objection to this seems to be that a number of English and American historians, economists and ecclesiastics simply don't like it. They adhere to the Puritan traditions of another time; they fear public self-destruction, through over-indulgence; and they believe this is made imminent by the requirements of business and industry to exploit an unthinking public entirely in their own interests.

Reference is made frequently to the opinions of the English historian, Arnold J. Toynbee, who states with no exceptions at all that "Advertising is an instrument of moral, as well as intellectual, mis-education. Insofar as it succeeds in influencing people's minds, it conditions them not to think for themselves and not to choose for themselves.

"It is intentionally hypnotic in its effect. It makes people suggestible and docile. *In fact it prepares them for a totalitarian regime!*"

The italics and the exclamation mark are my own. But let us allow Dr. Toynbee to go on:

"The destiny of our American civilization," he has written, "turns on the issue of our struggle with all that Madison Avenue stands for more than it turns on the issue of our struggle with Communism."

Madison Avenue's first aim, he says, is "to captivate us without allowing us to become aware of what is being done to us." If this proves impossible, Madison Avenue resorts to "sheer bullying, and it will carry this, if necessary, to the third degree," Dr. Toynbee charges.

"Producing and disposing of the maximum quantity of consumer goods was not the purpose of the American Revolution. What is more, it is not the true end of man . . . If one generation does not eventually revolt against the present attempt to impose this objective upon us, it can be foreseen that our children or our children's children will revolt against it," he adds.

Reference is made frequently, also, to the opinions expressed about advertising by the American historian, Arthur Schlesinger Jr., the distinguished Harvard professor of history who is an assistant to President Kennedy, and to John Kenneth Galbraith, the Harvard economics professor who was President Kennedy's first ambassador to India, who holds that advertising is essentially an economic waste with some dire implications for our future. These are the same implications and maledictions expressed by Arnold Toynbee, and I wouldn't repeat them were it not for one thing: Professor Schlesinger and Professor Galbraith add some economic questions to the dismissal of advertising by their British colleague on the grounds of immorality and irreligion, and these have been widely disseminated.

Here, again, I wish these men had stuck to the known facts about advertising and not undertaken to give it responsibility for a whole system of economy in which it is only a part.

II. The Past

In his essay "The Big Decision—Private Indulgence or National Power?" (1960), Arthur Schlesinger Jr. asserted that: "We have committed ourselves—rather, we have permitted our leaders to commit us—to the fatuous thesis that private spending is always more 'intelligent' and more 'useful' than public spending. We are in trouble [this was an election year and Mr. Schlesinger was of the opposition] not because of ineluctable circumstance, but because of voluntary choice. We can change this situation any time we want to. It is not obligatory, for example, to spend three times as much money on advertising as on higher education."

It is possible that without the private spending that Mr. Schlesinger is unable to accept as more desirable than public spending—and that, axiomatically, is dependent to a considerable extent upon advertising—education, which is financed largely by profits from business and by taxes on business, would get drastically less.

It is J. Kenneth Galbraith's opinion, as this is stated in "The Affluent Society" (1958), and constantly and frequently referred to, both pro and con, that ours is a nation of unprecedented wealth whose economic theory and viewpoint, forged in what was virtually another world of poverty and the need for efficient production, now are obsolete.

"No one would wish to argue," he says, "that the ideas which interpreted this world of grim scarcity would serve equally well for the contemporary United States. Poverty was the all-pervasive fact of that world. Obviously, it is not ours. One would not expect that the preoccupation of a poverty-ridden world would be relevant in one where the ordinary individual has access to amenities—foods, entertainment, personal transportation and plumbing—in which not even the rich rejoiced a century ago."

But then, Professor Galbraith adds, "So great has been the change that many of the desires of the individual are no longer even evident to him. They become so only as they are synthesized, elaborated and nurtured by advertising and salesmanship, and these, in turn, have become our most important and talented professions."

When he states that: "Wants can be synthesized by advertising, catalyzed by salesmanship, and shaped by the discreet manipulation of the persuaders" he is putting on exhibit a belief in the effect of carnival magic upon bumpkin credulity that shows nothing but contempt for the intelligence, the will, and the wisdom of the great mass of American citizens.

He pictures these citizens with something less than love and sympathy as they enjoy their foolish affluence:

"The family which takes its mauve and cerise air-conditioned, power-steered and power-braked automobile out for a tour passes through cities that are badly paved, made hideous by litter, blighted buildings, billboards and posts for wires that should long ago have been put underground. They pass on into the countryside that has been rendered largely invisible by commercial art . . . They picnic on exquisitely packaged food from a portable ice box by a polluted stream and go on to spend the night at a park which is a menace to public health and morals. Just before dozing off on an air mattress, beneath a nylon tent, amid the stench of decaying refuse, they may reflect vaguely on the unevenness of their blessings. Is this, indeed, the American genius?"

If this isn't a picture of futility, I wouldn't know one. But even admitting the valid criticism within the general exaggeration of this picture (I am particularly allergic to city litter and blight and the dotting of any countryside with billboards), I am unable to accept this as a picture of anything but Mr. Galbraith's disrespect for the average American and his taste.

There are some very strong dissenters from the Toynbee-Schlesinger-Galbraith party line.

Men as far apart politically and economically as Leon Keyserling, chairman of the council of economic advisors to President Truman, and Dr. Raymond J. Saulnier, chairman of President Eisenhower's council of economic advisors, refute it with equal vigor. They reject the proposition that money spent for private wants must divert money from public needs. Instead they believe that each dollar spent on private wants effectively *produces* money for public needs through nothing more than our existing system of taxation.

Says Leon Keyserling: "It's a fantastic misanalysis to picture consumer goods and public needs as opposing forces.

"We hear on one side from one brand of reactionaries that we can't have the national defense we need because this would hurt our private economy. We hear from those whom I regard as equal reactionaries on the other side, although they have a new patter, that we can't afford to make progress in our private economic lives under our American system . . . because we need public services."

Dr. Saulnier concurs. "Sometimes I get the impression that they [Toynbee, Galbraith, etc.] are talking about a new set of blue laws," he has said.

According to George Reisman, at the City College of New York, "The proof that Galbraith offers of the unimportance of production is the fact that had they not been advertised, there would have been no demand for a great many products now being produced. Without advertising and salesmanship to 'contrive' a sense of want for them," he declares, "the marginal utility of such products would have been zero.

"The absurdity of this standard is immediately evident," Reisman continues. "If a man is suffering from pneumonia, need he never be told of his need for penicillin? If a man desires to travel, need he never be told of the existence of automobiles, airplanes, railroads and steamships and from whom they or their services are available? If a man desires artificial light, need he never be told of the existence of electricity and electric lights and where to obtain them? Or if he is hungry, need he never be told of the hundreds of different kinds of food and where to come by them? Or must men be born with a knowledge of all these things and where to acquire them, before they can be considered to satisfy non-'contrived' wants?"

I suppose it is implicit in their writings and their speeches that the proponents of public vs. private spending have no personal wish to dictate anything. They are simply on the side of things intellectually and morally good as they see these, and against what they consider to be an evil and growing materialism. Nevertheless, they question the ability of many people to withstand the attractive forces of this materialism that advertising embodies and they would like to expunge it.

George J. Stigler, Walgreen Professor of American Institutions at the University of Chicago, believes that if we accept the proposition that people are essentially foolish in disposing of their income and easy prey to any kind of advertising, we are likely soon to believe that these same people are stupid in other ways.

"It is a very short step," he says, "to say that not only are they incompetent in disposing of their money, but that they obviously are incompetent of disposing of their votes intelligently."

Professor Stigler's remarks are excerpted from an article by Henry Hazlitt in Newsweek and they are from the text of a discussion of the Galbraith book at a meeting of the Mont Pélerin Society, an international group of economists, in Germany.

The summary rejection in the society's report on John Kenneth Galbraith's proposition is made by Friedrich A. Hayek, who is also a distinguished economics professor at the University of Chicago. "The first part of [his] argument is, of course, perfectly true: We would not desire any of the amenities of civilization —or even the most primitive culture— if we did not live in a society in which others provide them. The innate wants are probably confined to food, shelter and sex. All the rest we learn to desire because we see others enjoying various things.

"To say that a desire is not important because it is not innate is to say that the whole cultural achievement of man is not important . . . How complete a *non sequitur* Professor Galbraith's conclusion represents is seen most clearly if we apply the argument to any product of the arts, be it music, painting or literature.

"For over a hundred years we have been exhorted to embrace socialism because it would give us more goods. Since it has so lamentably failed to achieve this where it has been tried, we are now urged to adopt it because more goods after all are not important."

When Dr. Toynbee and Professor Galbraith talk about moral and intellectual miseducation to make people suggestible and docile, and about wants that are synthesized by advertising and shaped by the manipulation of the persuaders, they fail to explain either how this miseducation is directed, what wants are synthesized, or how the manipulation is accomplished. So let us get down to brass tacks.

The largest of the various classifications of advertising is local advertising in newspapers, which represents 24.3 per cent of all advertising (1962 figures). This is divided about 70–30 between retailers' advertising and classified advertising. The latter are individual efforts by single persons for the most part, and while there may be larceny in the minds of some of these people, there is no professional attention of any kind, good or evil, involved in the want ads' construction. Retail-store advertising has as its sole purpose moving some of the goods that fill the store aisles and counters into the homes where the newspapers go. Everything that is represented may be seen in the stores and *is* seen in the stores, and the advertising that urges its purchase is invariably written in terms of prices and specifications for goods whose desirability has already been established.

One of the facts that is consistently overlooked (and one that shows the naivete of many of the emerging critics) is the overriding demand by the retailer that a market exists for everything he stocks. By the same token, it is vital that a market exists for everything a manufacturer makes. The development of markets is quite different from the existence of markets: The potential that was developed in the case of frozen orange juice was possible only because the potential was there in annoyance (squeezing) and in variations in quality and price of the fresh fruit.

The market for all frozen fruits, vegetables and juices was characterized by these same considerations of quality, price and the lengthening of the seasons, and it can hardly be maintained seriously that it was miseducation that resulted in their establishment as standard menu items in millions of American homes. Advertising can scarcely be accused of synthesizing a desire for the convenience and variety of canned and powdered soups.

Ever since Good Housekeeping magazine introduced its famous (and hard to get) Seal of Approval, products that were denied this were equally unwelcome in most other magazines. Thus, since magazine advertising was a vital element in success, unapproved products were virtually dead as a factor in the national stream of distribution.

Local radio (3.6 per cent of the total) and local television (2.4 per cent) seem to be the least likely of all to synthesize wants or to employ hidden persuasion or any other manipulation in projecting these wants into sales and acquisitions. There is no degree whatever of subtlety. The promise is entirely to satisfy desires as they exist.

Manufacturers' advertising, and the advertising of insurance and transportation companies, publishers, motion picture producers, and hotels and resorts, which is called *national* advertising, are itemized in the total U.S. advertising bill as follows: in television 11.8 per cent; in magazines 7.9 per cent; in newspapers 6.7 per cent; in radio 2.2 per cent; in outdoor 0.9 per cent.

The total of all this advertising is almost exactly the same as the total for retail advertising in newspapers.

In the matter of subversion and manipulation, charges against this national advertising are circumstantial and ephemeral. The generalities of the professors and the ministers that are echoed throughout numerous high schools, where "The Waste Makers" has been given the stature of a historical document, are for the most part restate-ments of Vance Packard's own generalizations.

Probably the most remarkable and most frightening of the suggestions in the first Packard book was that advertising people had got deep into hypnotism, subliminal persuasion and motivational research, to ensnare the American public and render it incapable of withstanding the advertisers' appeals.

Unfortunately, words like subliminal and sub-threshold and hypnotic are frightening words, particularly when they are used in connection with persuasion and manipulation, and the grouping of motivation research in the same fearsome category has made this another subject of very real concern and suspicion.

The truth about motivation research is probably stated better by Pierre Martineau, the perceptive and skillful director of the research and marketing department of the Chicago Tribune, than by anyone else in the field:

"There is every reason why motivation and communication should be systematically studied. If it is possible to probe such areas, certainly the selling strategy and the copy appeals will be infinitely more effective when they are directed toward potentially powerful motive forces instead of completely irrelevant motives; when the basic themes are not violating any underlying governing attitudes; when the overtones are consistent with the predominant social and psychological currents in our style of life; when the product personality becomes clear-cut and meaningful."

Surely this is somewhat short of diabolical.

It is sometimes amazing how difficult it is for even the shrewdest minds in advertising and selling to decide on procedure. But even when this is not the case, careful business people insist on the verification of their experience and their convictions by up-to-date research.

It would be foolish to maintain that the world was waiting for either the miniature marshmallow or the paper towel that resembled a sponge. But I think it is wrong to complain that the desire for such improvements is synthesized by advertising.

I must confess that I can summon up no feeling of guilt whatever for having planned, written, or otherwise shared the responsibility for more than $1.5-billion worth of advertising for a number of products that cannot by any stretch of the imagination be called essential.

Pat Steele, in pleading guilty to a life very much like my own, wrote in an advertisement for Young & Rubicam something that sounds little different from Professor Hayek.

"The complex thing we call civilization," he said, "is made up of luxuries. An eminent philosopher of our time has written that great art is superior to lesser art in the degree that it is 'life-enhancing.' Perhaps something of the same kind can be claimed for the products that are sold through advertising.

"They enhance life to whatever degree they can.

"Indeed that is the purpose of our unique and restless economy. It is fundamentally devoted to the production and distribution of things people don't need. Among them are toothpaste, electricity, outboard motors, artificial satellites and education.

"Without advertising that economy cannot exist."

The fact that the Toynbees, the Galbraiths, et al., lash out as they do at advertising without differentiating between good advertising and bad, between retail-price advertising and national product advertising, between personal want ads and impersonal radio and television solicitation, and between service advertising (with recipes, health infor-

mation and such) and advertising for such pure luxuries as furs, diamonds, pearls, perfumes, or even motorized can openers, pencil sharpeners, pepper grinders and tooth brushes, establishes a disdain for the facts of advertising that is shocking in professional men.

Note Dr. Toynbee's words: "The moral that I draw is that a way of life based on personal consumption, stimulated by advertising, needs changing— and there 'are dozens of possible alternatives to it. For instance, we could still have full employment in the economically advanced countries if we gave up advertising and restricted our personal consumption to, say, the limits that present-day American monks and nuns voluntarily set for themselves, and if we then diverted our production to supply the elementary needs of the poverty-stricken three-quarters of the human race, working for this obviously worthwhile purpose would bring us much greater satisfaction than working, under the stimulus of advertising, in order to consume goods that we do not need and do not genuinely want."

It is impossible for me to draw any other conclusion than that Dr. Toynbee would shut off advertising not because advertising itself is bad but because its use in the stimulation of ideas with which he disagrees might thus be dramatically curtailed.

I note fewer and fewer references to Harvard's David Riesman and Yale University's David Potter by these present-day commentators on American life as we know it. Riesman's "The Lonely Crowd" and Potter's "People of Plenty" were generally cited by the apprehensive members of the community ten years ago because they had commented thoughtfully on what they both considered a disturbing trend away from originality and individuality that was growing in the American psyche. Neither one had any question but what advertising contributed to this, nor do I; for the standards of living that advertising promotes are just that, and as these have been attained they have tended to standardize concepts, too.

But I think this is temporary.

There are some things most people want that represent a good deal more than just the hankering for material goods that the detractors of our society and our economy find so distressing, and which they blame advertising for stimulating. This hankering, which is an irrepressible desire and a challenge, is the natural consequence of the American deal that promises any man anything he can earn.

This is what the reformers evidently hope to change.

But I think they will not succeed.

III. The Future

I think there will be too many people who are dedicated to the national promise, who are convinced that there is nothing immoral in opulence, who think there is no better preparation for philosophic contemplation than ridding one's life of interfering thoughts and wants and conflicts, many of which are necessarily material.

For my own small part I am happy to suggest to a new generation of women that they can have any color hair their hearts desire with an expert, inexpensive hair treatment. I am happy to suggest to these same women, and their sons and daughters and their husbands, that the application of a tanning lotion before sunning will prevent sunburn. I am pleased to tell the whole family, too, about a deodorant soap that "stops perspiration before it starts" by removing the bacteria that are the cause of the odor. I firmly believe that while 15 cents' worth of chalk, soda, salt and soap will make the equivalent of a dollar's worth of toothpaste, it has only been the consistent advertising of the toothpastes through the last 20 years that has made American young people pay attention to their teeth; the boy-meet-girl formula of much of this advertising may leave something for the professionals to desire, but it has been more effective than all the strictures of all the dentists who ever lived. Whereas the dentists offered only advice, the advertisements suggested tangible and appealing rewards.

The list of unnecessities could go on and on. Who needs canned luncheon meats or TV dinners, self-polishing waxes, ballpoint pens, greeting cards, transistor radios, remote-control television, electric shavers?

In the decade ahead more than 13-million people will be added to the labor force. By 1975 the total availability of workers will reach 93-million. If they don't make things for one another, things far over and beyond necessities of a Spartan life, the ranks of the unemployed will surely be greater than the number of workers.

This is a picture the bleakness of which could only be compared with the Middle Ages.

49

Is Advertising Wasteful?

Jules Backman

The following article is a condensation of a rather comprehensive survey of competition in advertising made by the author under a grant from the Association of National Advertisers in 1967. I considers the main criticisms leveled against advertising and attempts to answer them as effectively as possible with fact presently available. On this emotionally charged issue it would be impossible to satisfy everyone that any study was objective, but this one represents a good attempt at objectivity.

With some exceptions, economists generally have criticized advertising as economically wasteful. All the criticisms are not so extreme as one widely used economics text which states:

"Overall, it is difficult for anyone to gain more than temporarily from large advertising outlays in an economy in which counteradvertising is general. The overall effect of advertising, on which we spent $14 billion [actually $15 billion—JB] in 1965, is to devote these productive resources (men, ink, billboards, and so forth) to producing advertising rather than to producing other goods and services."[1]

Most critics do not go this far in condemning advertising. However, the do emphasize that advertising may be wasteful in several ways: by adding unnecessarily to costs, by an inefficient use of resources, by promoting excessive competition, and by causing consumer to buy items they do not need. Thi article brings together the scattered criticisms of advertising and answers to them and thus presents an overview of the debate in this area. The nature of these criticisms and the significance of waste in a competitive economy are firs reviewed. Attention is then given to the vital informational role played by adver tising, particularly in an expanding economy. Advertising is only one alter native in the marketing mix, and hence its contribution must be considered among alternatives rather than in abso lute terms.

Reprinted from the *Journal of Marketing*, national quarterly publication of the American Marketing Association, Vol. 32, No. 1, January 1968, pp. 2–8.

[1] George Leland Bach, *Economics*, Fifth Edition (Englewood Cliffs, New Jersey: Prentice-Hall, Inc., 1966), p. 437. See also Kenneth Boulding, "Economic Analysis," Volume 1, *Microeconomics*, Fourth Edition, Vol. 1 (New York: Harper and Row, 1966), p. 513.

Variations on a Theme

The criticism that advertising involve economic waste takes several forms.

Competition in Advertising

The attack usually is centered on competition in advertising which some critics state flatly is wasteful.[2] Others have been concerned about the relative cost of advertising as a percentage of sales. Sometimes an arbitrary percentage, such as 5%, is selected as the dividing line between "high" and more "reasonable" levels of expenditure.[3]

Such cutoff points are meaningless, since the proper relative expenditures for advertising are a function of the product's characteristics. It is not an accident that relative advertising costs are highest for low-priced items which are available from many retail outlets and subject to frequent repeat purchases (for example, cosmetics, soaps, soft drinks, gum and candies, drugs, cigarettes, beer, etc.).

Particularly criticized are emotional appeals, persuasion, and "tug of war" advertising where it is claimed the main effect is to shift sales among firms rather than to increase total volume of the industry. For example, Richard Caves states: "At the point where advertising departs from its function of informing and seeks to persuade or deceive us, it tends to become a waste of resources."[4]

In a competitive economy competitors must seek to persuade customers to buy their wares. We do not live in a world where a company stocks its warehouse and waits until customers beat a path to its doors to buy its products. If this is all that a business firm did, we would have economic waste in terms of products produced but not bought as well as in the failure to produce many items for which a market can be created. In the latter case, the waste would take the form of idle labor and unused resources.

Inefficient Use of Resources

Economists have criticized advertising most vigorously as involving an inefficient use of resources. This criticism has been directed particularly against advertising where the main effect allegedly is a "shuffling of existing total demand" among the companies in an industry. Under these conditions, it is stated, advertising merely adds to total costs and in time results in higher prices. There undoubtedly is a shifting of demand among firms due to many factors including advertising. But this is what we should expect in a competitive economy. Moreover, there are many products for which total demand is increased (for example, television sets, radio sets, cars, toilet articles) for multiple use in the same home. In the sharply expanding economy of the past quarter of a century there are relatively few industries in which total demand has remained unchanged.

It must also be kept in mind that the resources devoted to competitive advertising usually are considered to be wasteful "in a full-employment economy" because they may be utilized more efficiently in other ways. Thus, the extent of "waste" involved also appears to depend upon whether the economy is operating below capacity. This point is considered in a later section.

[2] Nicholas H. Kaldor, "The Economic Aspects of Advertising," *The Review of Economic Studies,* Vol. 18 (1950–51) p. 6.

[3] Joe S. Bain, *Industrial Organization* (New York: John Wiley & Sons, 1959), pp. 390–91. See also *Report of a Commission of Enquiry Into Advertising* (London England: The Labour Party, 1966), p. 42. The Reith Report defined "substantially advertised products" at 5% or more.

[4] Richard Caves, *American Industry: Structure, Conduct, Performance* (Englewood Cliffs, New Jersey: Prentice-Hall, Inc., 1964), p. 102.

Adds to Costs

Sometimes, it is stated that if advertising succeeds in expanding total demand for a product, the result is a shift of demand from other products, the producers of which will be forced to advertise to attempt to recover their position. The net result of such "counter-advertising" is to add to costs and to prices.

But all increases in demand do not necessarily represent a diversion from other products. Thus, an expanded demand for new products is accompanied by an increase in income and in purchasing power flowing from their production. Moreover, during a period of expanding economic activity, as is noted later, the successful advertising may affect the rate of increase for different products rather than result in an absolute diversion of volume.

Creates Undesirable Wants

Another variation is the claim that advertising is wasteful because it ". . . creates useless or undesirable wants at the expense of things for which there is greater social need. When advertising makes consumers want and buy automobiles with tail fins, tobacco, and movie-star swimming pools, there is less money (fewer resources) available to improve public hospitals, build better schools, or combat juvenile delinquency."[5] It is claimed that many these types of products are useless and anti-social. Criticism of advertising is nothing new. In the late 1920s Stuart Chase claimed: "Advertising creates no new dollars. In fact, by removing workers from productive employment, it tends to depress

output, and thus lessen the number of real dollars."[6]

These are value judgments reached by the critics on the basis of subjective "standards" which they set up. "What is one man's meat is another man's poison," as the old saying goes. The real question is who is to decide what is good for the consumer and what should he purchase?

In a free economy, there is a wide diversity of opinion as to what combinations of goods and services should be made available and be consumed. Obviously, tastes vary widely and most persons do not want to be told what is best for them. In any cross section of the population of the country there will be a wide disagreement as to what constitutes the ideal components of a desirable level of living. Each one of us must decide what purchases will yield the greatest satisfactions. We may be misled on occasion by popular fads, advertising, or even advice of our friends. But these decisions in the final analysis are made by the buyers and not by the advertisers, as the latter have found out so often to their regret.

Competition and "Waste"

The critics of advertising are really attacking the competitive process. Competition involves considerable duplication and "waste." The illustrations range from the several gasoline stations at an important intersection to the multiplication of research facilities, the excess industrial capacity which develops during periods of expansion, and the accumulations of excessive inventories.

There is widespread recognition that inefficiencies may develop in advertis-

---

[5] "Advertising and Charlie Brown," *Business Review*, Federal Reserve Bank of Philadelphia (June, 1962), p. 10.

[6] Stuart Chase, *The Tragedy of Waste* (New York: The Macmillan Company, 1928), p. 112.

ing as in other phases of business.[7] Mistakes are made in determining how much should be spent for advertising —but these mistakes can result in spending too little as well as too much.

We cannot judge the efficiency of our competitive society—including the various instrumentalities, such as advertising —by looking at the negative aspects alone. It is true that competition involves waste. But it also yields a flood of new products, improved quality, better service, and pressures on prices. In the United States, it has facilitated enormous economic growth with the accompanying high standards of living. The advantages of competition have been so overwhelmingly greater than the wastes inherent in it that we have established as one of our prime national goals, through the antitrust laws, the continuance of a viable competitive economy.

Informational Role of Advertising

Advertising plays a major informational role in our economy because (1) products are available in such wide varieties, (2) new products are offered in such great numbers, and (3) existing products must be called to the attention of new consumers who are added to the market as a result of expansion in incomes, the population explosion, and changes in tastes.

The most heavily advertised products are widely used items that are consumed by major segments of the population. This does not mean that everyone buys

every product or buys them to the extent that he can. Some of these products are substitutes for other products. For example, it will be readily recognized that cereals provide only one of many alternatives among breakfast foods. In some instances, heavily advertised products compete with each other like, for example, soft drinks and beer. In other instances, additional consumers can use the products so that the size of the total market can be increased (for example, toilet preparations).

Potential markets also expand as incomes rise and as consumers are able to purchase products they previously could not afford. As the population increases, large numbers of new potential customers are added each year. Continuous large-scale advertising provides reminders to old customers and provides information to obtain some part of the patronage of new customers. The potential market is so huge that large scale advertising is an economical way to obtain good results.

In addition, the identity of buyers changes under some circumstances and new potential buyers must be given information concerning the available alternatives. It has also been pointed out that some of these products are ". . . subject to fads and style changes" and that ". . . consumers become restive with existing brands and are prepared to try new varieties." Illustrations include cereals, soaps, clothing, and motion pictures.[8]

The consumer has a wide variety of brands from which to choose. Product improvements usually breed competitive product improvements; the advertising of these improvements may result in an increase in total advertising for the class of products.

[7] Committee on Advertising, *Principles of Advertising* (New York: Pitman Publishing Corp., 1963), p. 34; and Neil H. Borden, "The Role of Advertising in the Various Stages of Corporate and Economic Growth," Peter D. Bennett, editor, *Marketing and Economic Development* (Chicago, Illinois: American Marketing Association, 1965), p. 493.

[8] Lester G. Telser, "How Much Does It Pay Whom To Advertise?", *American Economic Review, Papers and Proceedings* (December, 1960), pp. 203–4.

When any company in an industry embarks on an intensified advertising campaign, its competitors must step up their advertising or other sales efforts to avoid the possible loss of market position. This is a key characteristic of competition.

On the other hand, if any company decides to economize on its advertising budget, its exposure is reduced and its share of market may decline if its competitors fail to follow the same policy. Thus, for some grocery products it has been reported that ". . . competition within a sector may have established a certain pattern with regard to the extent of advertising, and any company dropping below this level faces possible substantial loss of market share."[9]

These results flow particularly if the industry is oligopolistic, that is, has relatively few producers who are sensitive to and responsive to actions of competitors. However, as the dramatic changes in market shares during the past decade so amply demonstrate, this does not mean that the companies in such oligopolistic industries will retain relatively constant shares of the market.[10]

The informational role of advertising has been succinctly summarized by Professor George J. Stigler:

> . . . Under competition, the main tasks of a seller are to inform potential buyers of his existence, his line of goods, and his prices. Since both sellers and buyers change over time (due to birth, death, migration), since people forget information once acquired, and since new products appear, the existence of sellers must be continually advertised. . .

[9] National Commission on Food Marketing, *Grocery Manufacturing*, Technical Study No. 6 (Washington, D.C.: June, 1966), p. 14.

[10] Jules Backman, *Advertising and Competition* (New York: New York University Press, 1967), Chapters 3 and 4.

This informational function of advertising must be emphasized because of a popular and erroneous belief that advertising consists chiefly of nonrational (emotional and repetitive) appeals.[11]

Elsewhere, Professor Stigler has pointed out that ". . . information is a valuable resource," that advertising is "the obvious method of identifying buyers and sellers" which "reduces drastically the cost of search," and that "It is clearly an immensely poweful instrument for the elimination of ignorance. . . ."[12]

Often this information is required to create interest in and demand for a product. Thus, it has been reported:

> . . . to a significant degree General Foods and the U.S. food market created each other. Before a new product appears, customers are rarely conscious of wanting it. There was no spontaneous demand for ready-to-eat cereals; frozen foods required a sustained marketing effort stretching over many years; instant coffee had been around for decades, supplying a market that did not amount to a tenth of its present level. General Foods' corporate skill consists largely in knowing enough about American tastes to foresee what products will be accepted.[13]

Similarly, J. K. Galbraith, who has

[11] George J. Stigler, *The Theory of Price*, Third Edition (New York: The Macmillan Company, 1966), p. 200.

[12] George J. Stigler, "The Economics of Information," *The Journal of Political Economy* (June, 1961), pp. 213, 216, 220. See also S. A. Ozga, "Imperfect Markets Through Lack of Knowledge," *Quarterly Journal of Economics* (February, 1960), pp. 29, 33–34, and Wroe Alderson, *Dynamic Market Behavior* (Homewood, Illinois: Richard D. Irwin, Inc., 1965), pp. 128–31.

[13] "General Foods Is Five Billion Particulars," *Fortune* (March, 1964), p. 117.

been very critical of advertising, has recognized that:

> A new consumer product must be introduced with a suitable advertising campaign to arouse an interest in it. The path for an expansion of output must be paved by a suitable expansion in the advertising budget. Outlays for the manufacturing of a product are not more important in the strategy of modern business enterprise than outlays for the manufacturing of demand for the product.[14]

We live in an economy that has little resemblance to the ideal of perfect competition postulated by economists. However, one of the postulates of this ideal economy is perfect knowledge. Advertising contributes to such knowledge. Thus, in such an idealized economy, even though advertising may be wasteful it would still have a role to play. But in the world of reality, with all its imperfections, advertising is much more important. Advertising is an integral and vital part of our growing economy and contributes to the launching of the new products so essential to economic growth.

How Much Is Informational?

In 1966, total expenditures for media advertising aggregated $13.3 billion.[15] It is impossible to determine exactly how much of this amount was strictly informational. However, the following facts are of interest.

- Classified advertising was $1.3 billion.
- Other local newspaper advertising, largely retail, was $2.6 billion.

- Business paper advertising was $712 million.
- Local radio and TV advertising was $1.1 billion.
- Spot radio and spot TV advertising was $1.2 billion.
- National advertising on network TV, network radio, magazines and newspapers was $3.7 billion.
- Direct mail was $2.5 billion.

Classified advertising and local advertising are overwhelmingly informational in nature. Certainly some part of national advertising also performs this function. These figures suggest that substantially less than half of total advertising is of the type that the critics are attacking as wasteful;[16] the exact amount cannot be pinpointed. Moreover, it must be kept in mind that a significant part of national advertising is for the promotion of new products for which the informational role is vital.

From another point of view, even if there is waste, the social cost is considerably less than suggested by these data. Thus, in 1966 about $10 billion was spent on advertising in newspapers, magazines, radio, and television; another $746 million was spent on farm and business publications. Without these expenditures, these sources of news and entertainment would have had to obtain substantial sums from other sources. It has been estimated that ". . . advertising paid for over 60% of the cost of periodicals, for over 70% of the cost of newspapers, and for 100% of the cost of commercial radio and TV broadcasting."[17]

[14] J. K. Galbraith, *The Affluent Society* (Boston, Massachusetts: Houghton Mifflin Company, 1958), p. 156.
[15] This total excludes a miscellaneous category of $3.3 billion.

[16] For the United Kingdom, the "disputed proportion" of advertising expenditures has been estimated at about 30% of the total. Walter Taplin, *Advertising, A New Approach* (Boston, Massachusetts: Little, Brown & Co., 1963), p. 126.
[17] Fritz Machlup, *The Production and Distribution of Knowledge in the United States* (Princeton, New Jersey: Princeton University Press, 1962), p. 265.

Thus, advertising results in a form of subsidization for all media of communication. Without it, these media would have to charge higher subscription rates or be subsidized by the government or some combination of both.

Advertising and Expanding Markets

Economic growth has become a major objective of national economic policy in recent years. Rising productivity, increasing population, improving education, rates of saving, and decisions concerning new investments are the ingredients of economic growth. In addition, there must be a favorable political climate including tax policies and monetary policies designed to release the forces conducive to growth.

Advertising contributes to economic growth and in turn levels of living by complementing the efforts to create new and improved products through expenditures for research and development. One observer has described the process as follows:

> . . . advertising, by acquainting the consumer with the values of new products, widens the market for these products, pushes forward their acceptance by the consumer, and encourages the investment and entrepreneurship necessary for innovation. Advertising, in short, holds out the promise of a greater and speedier return than would occur without such methods, thus stimulating investment, growth, and diversity.[18]

Among the most intensive advertisers have been toilet preparations (14.7% of

[18] David M. Blank, "Some Comments on the Role of Advertising in the American Economy—A Plea for Revaluation," L. George Smith, editor, *Reflections on Progress in Marketing* (Chicago, Illinois: American Marketing Association, 1964), p. 151.

sales), cleaning and polishing preparations (12.6%), and drugs, (9.4%). The markets for these products have been expanding at a faster rate than all consumer spending.

Advertising appears to have contributed to an expansion in the demand for these products and to the growth of our economy with the accompanying expansion in job opportunities and in economic well-being. There may have been some waste in this process—although all of such expenditures cannot be characterized as wasteful—but it appears to have been offset in full or in part by these other benefits.

The charge of large-scale waste in advertising appears to reflect in part a yearning for an economy with standardized, homogeneous products which are primarily functional in nature. An illustration would be a refrigerator that is designed solely to be technically efficient for the storage of food. However, customers are also interested in the decor of their kitchens, in convenience and speed in the manufacture of ice cubes, in shelves that rotate, and in special storage for butter. These are additions to functional usefulness which "an affluent society" can afford but which a subsistence economy cannot.

Advertising in a High-Level Economy

The concept of waste must be related to the level achieved by an economy. Professor John W. Lowe has observed that "Perhaps a good deal of the 'wastefulness' assigned to advertising springs from the fact that a large part of the world's population cannot consider satisfying *psychological wants* when most of their efforts must be devoted to *needs*."[19] (Italics added.)

[19] John W. Lowe, "An Economist Defends Advertising," *Journal of Marketing,* Vol. 27 (July, 1963), p. 18.

In a subsistence economy, scarcity is so significant that advertising might be wasteful, particularly where it diverts resources from meeting the basic necessities of life. Such an economy usually is a "full employment economy" in the sense that everyone is working. But the total yield of a full employment subsistence economy is very low, as is evident throughout Asia, Africa, and South America.

Professor Galbraith has noted that, "The opportunity for product differentiation . . . is almost uniquely the result of opulence . . . the tendency for commercial rivalries . . . to be channeled into advertising and salesmanship would disappear in a poor community."[20]

In the high level American economy, there usually are surpluses rather than scarcity. The use of resources for advertising to differentiate products, therefore, is not necessarily a diversion from other uses. Rather, it frequently represents the use of resources that might otherwise be idle both in the short run and the long run and thus may obviate the waste that such idleness represents.

The Marketing Mix

The concept of waste cannot ignore the question—waste as compared with what alternative? Advertising cannot be considered in a vacuum. It must be considered as one of the marketing alternatives available. Generally it is not a question of advertising or nothing, but rather of advertising or some other type of sales effort.

It is a mistake to evaluate the relative cost of advertising apart from other marketing costs. It is only one tool in the marketing arsenal which also includes

[20] John K. Galbraith, *American Capitalism: The Concept of Countervailing Power* (Boston, Massachusetts: Houghton Mifflin Company, 1952), pp. 106–07.

direct selling, packaging, servicing, product planning, pricing, etc. Expenditures for advertising often are substituted for other types of selling effort. This substitution has been readily apparent in the history of the discount house. These houses have featured well-advertised brands which were presold and, hence, virtually eliminated the need for floor stocks and reduced the need for space and many salesmen.

Advertising is undertaken where it is the most effective and most economical way to appeal to customers. It is a relatively low cost method of communicating with all potential customers and this explains its widespread adoption by many companies. To the extent that less efficient marketing methods must be substituted for advertising, we would really have economic waste.

Summary and Conclusions

There is wide agreement that the informational role of advertising makes a significant contribution to the effective operation of our economy. There is also agreement that inefficiency in the use of advertising is wasteful, as are other types of inefficiencies that are part and parcel of a market-determined economy. The gray area is so-called competitive advertising, largely national, which is the main target of those who insist advertising is wasteful. Although precise data are not available, the estimates cited earlier indicate that the charge of competitive waste applies to substantially less than half of all advertising expenditures.

Competition unavoidably involves considerable duplication and waste. If the accent is placed on the negative, a distorted picture is obtained. On balance, the advantages of competition have been much greater than the wastes.

Advertising has contributed to an expanding market for new and better products. Many of these new products would not have been brought to market unless firms were free to develop mass markets through large-scale advertising. There may be some waste in this process, but it has been more than offset by other benefits.

When burgeoning advertising expenditures are accompanied by expanding industry sales, there will tend to be a decline in total unit costs instead of increase, and prices may remain unchanged or decline. In such situations, it seems clear that advertising, while adding to total costs, will result in lower total *unit* costs, the more significant figure. This gain will be offset to some extent if the increase in volume represents a diversion from other companies or industries with an accompanying rise in unit costs. Of course, such change is inherent in a dynamic competitive economy.

Advertising expenditures have risen as the economy has expanded. At such times, the absolute increase in sales resulting from higher advertising expenditures need not be accompanied by a loss in sales in other industries. This is par-

ticularly true if a new product has been developed and its sales are expanding. In that event, new jobs probably will be created and help to support a higher level of economic activity generally.

The claim that resources devoted to advertising would be utilized more efficiently for other purposes ignores the fact that generally we have a surplus economy. All of the resources used for advertising are not diverted from other alternatives. Rather, it is probable that much of the resources involved would be idle or would be used less efficiently. Even more important would be the failure to provide the jobs which expanding markets create.

Finally, advertising does not take place in a vacuum. It is one of several marketing alternatives. The abandonment of advertising could not represent a net saving to a company or to the economy. Instead, such a development would require a shift to alternative marketing techniques, some of which would be less efficient than advertising since companies do not deliberately adopt the least effective marketing approach. On balance, advertising is an invaluable competitive tool.

50

Advertising—A Critic's View

Colston E. Warne

This article is a statement of the views of a long-time critic of the practice of advertising. It is a vigorous presentation of the typical views of many critics of promotion in marketing. Because the views are held by many intellectuals, whose number certainly is not diminishing, it is incumbent upon marketing students to give the specific objections serious thought. If advertising is ever to gain complete intellectual respectability, the points at issue will have to be dealt with individually rather than in blanket fashion. The reader is urged to do this as the points are presented by the author.

In the face of repeated attacks from educators, Congressional committees and journalists, the advertising fraternity has veered between a posture of a misunderstood and aggrieved innocent and that of a repentant sinner. In response, some of its leaders have launched fervent appeals for basic reform. Others have mounted intensive campaigns to refute critics and to demonstrate the essential purity of the guild. From the earliest days of organized advertising associations, extreme candor has featured discussions in the advertising press. Such utterances as "Our house is not clean," "We need a rededication to truth," "Let's kick out the scoundrels who are besmirching our profession," will be heartily applauded at advertising conventions. And, equally applauded, will be able spokesmen like Messrs. Harding and Britt who attempt to exorcise advertising's challengers by applying an aura of righteousness and essentiality to the industry.

At the present time, we are witnessing a re-rededication to truth in advertising and to the "unsoiled sale." This is accompanied by public relations campaigns to correct the unfavorable image of the industry. Yet exposé books continue, Congressional hearings bring out dubious practices in ever-widening fields of sales persuasion and, as the consumer continues his nightly television fare of pseudo-scientific comparisons with Brand X, a crisis of confidence besets the whole industry. Significantly, after recent exposés, it has become far less possible for the leading agencies to

Reprinted from *Boston Conference on Distribution*, 1961, pp. 61–65, by permission of International Marketing Institute, Soldiers Field, Boston 63, Massachusetts.

proclaim that the trouble stems from a small and notorious fringe of marginal operators.

Payola of one kind or another seems to have become the accepted *modus operandi* in a good deal of merchandising effort. And advertising, itself, has taken on aspects of a form of payola in its cooperative advertising and advertising allowance programs. It is certainly no secret within the industry that these bribes to retailers for shelf space and special in-the-store attention in the form of advertising allowances are on the increase. In the old days, it used to be spiffs and PM's—push money paid directly by the brand advertiser to the retail clerk for each sale of a given brand. This principle of spiffs and PM's has now spread throughout distribution in the form of the advertising allowance. Or to put it another way, in the name of advertising, the presumed objectivity of the sales clerk with respect to competing brands within a given store has been corrupted. Thus the final sale, the last opportunity for products to stand, one against another in open competition, has been subjected to a truly subliminal manipulation.

In fairness, one should state at the outset of this discussion that we are not concerned here with the intentions of advertisers. The careful critics of advertising have to be concerned, first and foremost, not with what the advertisers believe they are doing, but with what the actual effects of these activities are on the market place. To be sure, a single generalization can scarcely encompass the total effect of the various aspects of this $12 to $13 billion industry which includes within itself the employment of partisan persuasion to diverse ends.

What must concern the observer today, however, are some of the broad scale or "mountain-range" effects. Many of these effects of advertising which disturb serious commentators have to be viewed in the context of the burden that historical and technological development has placed on this industry.

None of us must overlook the fact that the rapidly evolving industrial revolution which transferred our population from the farm to metropolitan areas in a short thirty years created a social vacuum in product knowledge. Man does not live by bread alone, but certainly man does live and must live with the goods he uses to sustain his existence. Furthermore, daily and countless exchanges of goods and services and the manner in which we deal with each other when we make these transactions contribute a compelling impact on the nonmaterial aspect of our lives. The ethics of a culture, as Toynbee has recently suggested, can be, and are often, expressed most poignantly at the point of exchange of goods and labor in the accent placed on prevalent values in the market place.

During the past fifty years, while modern technology has been not only drawing modern man away from the farm but flooding his life with new and complicated products, the social problem of acquiring the knowledge needed to adjust to the selection and use of these products fell, without either planning or forethought, on the shoulders of an infant advertising industry just growing out of its space-peddling stage. Through no fault of its own, advertising was unaware of the implications in the task that more or less by accident was handed over to it. Nor was the advertising industry alone in its lack of awareness. After all, it was not until the 1920's that social commentators began to sense the threat of mis-allocation of resources that was implicit in turning over the

function of providing product information to the partisan efforts of competing brand advertisers. Indeed, only in the 1920's did what we call the consumer movement, or consumer consciousness, first begin to develop vigorously. Even today, neither our sociologists nor our economists have paid much attention to the broader significance of advertising. Thus in the days of 1929 excesses, when *Liberty Magazine* carried in one issue as many as 19 different testimonials from Mabel Norman, the general reaction was a naïve one—how could anybody believe that Mabel Norman honestly meant her praise for 19 different brands of goods—and our sensibilities were offended at the vulgarity of the display. No one foresaw then that the appeal to irrationality in the choice of goods was far more serious than the vulgar aspects of testimonial advertising.

We have gone far since that day. Practitioners of advertising have eaten the fruit of a new tree of knowledge. Many today openly proclaim their objective to be appeals to the irrational or the irrelevant. I doubt, however, if even those who have paid out the highest fees to motivational researchers have actually intended thereby to destroy the theoretical basis of a free enterprise system. These very same advertisers who hold that sales appeals must be irrational point with the next breath to those sales as "votes for advertised goods"—as public acclaim of their efforts. They cannot have it both ways. If sales must be achieved through irrational means, then those sales are the empty votes of a disenfranchised electorate and merely represent consumer manipulation to producer-dictated ends. In the absence of rationality in purchase, consumer sovereignty becomes a meaningless concept. And here the critics of advertising must point out that any weakening or destroying of the effective exercise of consumer sovereignty is a serious attack on this vital balance wheel in our economy.

We stand today as the giant consumer among nations. And the advertising industry with an unwitting recklessness has immodestly boasted of its role as the chief creator of our immense capacity to devour goods and services. Unlike most of advertising's defenders, however, I would not so unfairly lay all the blame for the mounting waste of our natural resources on Madison Avenue's fashionably draped Brooks Bros. shoulders. I would say, however, that insofar and by as much as advertising does succeed in destroying rational choice of goods by appealing to irrational motives, it is contributing to the time when we may find ourselves a have-not nation with respect to important resources and is also substituting tinsel for substance in our living standards. Thus, I feel compelled to say that perhaps the first and most serious question that the critics of advertising are now raising about the manner in which this industry currently functions is its conscious or unconscious assault against the exercise of a meaningful consumer sovereignty.

The claim has been made that a waste of resources in the form of unstable goods, built-in obsolescence, meaningless product differentiation, a wasteful distributive system, speeded-up replacements, not to mention the costs directly linked to advertising appeals, are necessary extravangances to keep the economy afloat. If this be true, if it is indeed necessary that we must maintain a vast business-sponsored WPA, a gigantic make-work movement in order to keep our economic system functioning, then the time has come for us to face this most lamentable fact and to call it by its real name—a make-work program. I, for one, do not believe that American ingenuity has been so strained that only through this kind of mounting outlay of men and resources can we manage to keep ourselves functioning economically. But if we *do* have to shore ourselves up with a make-work program, then I would also have to say that there are other areas of activity (low cost housing, for example) where it seems to me the task would be more productive and less wasteful. I would further comment that we seem historically to apply the advertising make-work stimulus in inflationary times and taper it off in recessions.

Aside from this promotion of waste through attempts to destroy consumer sovereignty, perhaps the second most disturbing feature of advertising as it functions today lies in the area of monopoly power it has placed in the hands of the most substantial spenders (or shall I say investors in advertising). The national advertising outlay is not evenly divided among contenders for custom. It bulks with a very heavy weight at the top. I have frequently read in the advertising press the statement that it is difficult if not impossible today to launch a new brand of food or drug without the outlay of as much as $10 million. If this is true, and the statement appears generally valid, then what we face is a fantastic tax upon freedom of market entry. And in addition to this restriction of access to the market that advertising exercises, there is also that other monopoly aspect of its functioning—namely, through irrational sales appeal, advertising attempts to grant any given brand advertiser an aura of incomparable quality for his product. Thus it is not one toothpaste or another, but love vs. fear; and not one cigarette or another, but tars and nicotine vs. taste. Here is where the much-sought-after brand loyalty enters the picture. It is one of the great claims of the advertising practitioner that he can conjure up one degree or another of brand loyalty by the magic of images. Obviously, to the extent that partisan advertising alone creates brand loyalty, it creates a non-competitive market situation. It is little wonder that in recent years we have seen a flight from price competition into promotional rivalry and that along with that flight has come fewer ounces in the package, a lowering of product quality control, an increase in promotional costs, and a rapidly stepped-up wave of mergers in the consumer goods field. Not only the small company but the middle-sized company stands a decreasing chance to survive in a period when market survival depends upon the magnitude of promotional outlays rather than upon efficient production reflected in lower prices. By providing in our society few significant sources of product information beyond those in the hands of partisan persuaders, we have not only made it ever more difficult for the consumer to be able to exercise rational choice, but we have also constricted opportunities for entrepreneurship.

There is, however, an avenue by which we may be able to rid ourselves of what appears to be a growing hardening of the arteries in this section of our economic system. I refer to grade labeling and the development of product standards. There is probably no idea more abhorrent to most of organized advertising. In areas where we have had objective grades established for goods, advertising has not ceased to function. It has tended to be a different kind of advertising with more emphasis on price than glamour, but it has certainly functioned as a market factor in the distribution of such goods as eggs, turkeys, milk and ice cream, to name a few of the very few product areas where some objective standards of quality have been established and enforced. To be sure, established objective grades for quality tend to open up the market to the smaller firms. That Grade A on the frozen turkey gives the small processor a place in the supermarket counter right next to the big brander and often an opportunity to win the sale through a lower price. The small contender, once he has an entry to the market, can sometimes make his own mark with his prices.

In those areas of production where advertising plays a dominant role—food, drugs, cosmetics, tobacco and liquor—there is little in the literature of economics to lend credence to the belief that the largest concerns are the most efficient. And in meat packing, for example, it appears that bigness is an acutely crippling weight on efficient functioning. Even in autos, judging from the hearings before the Senate Committee on Monopoly, the biggest producers do not report the lowest costs. I do not want to get into that murky area of optimum plant size here, but I do think that the advertising industry counts too heavily on our lack of sophistication when it offers as one of its justifications for its existence the statement that advertising is responsible for mass production. Mass demand cannot be said to have been the egg to the production chicken. The overfed and too-long nurtured immodesty of advertising is most evident in this industry argument. Mass production did not flow from a copywriter's pen. It is, rather, a total cultural achievement. Its technology has come from our common heritage in the development of science. Its fortunate development here on our shores centrally stemmed from (1) a wealth of natural resources; (2) one of the widest free trade areas in the world in the early part of the century; and (3) the development of the economics of scale in competitive production. The centralizing impact of advertising has today carried production concentration far beyond the point dictated by the requirements of this mass production and has had a blighting effect upon traditional competition.

In recent years, moreover, fictitious prices have become illicit marketing sirens not only of fringe companies but of major concerns. Through the advertising of exorbitant pre-ticketing levels and subsequent price cuts, the consumer has been asked to believe that an article is made to sell at a higher sum in order to induce him to buy it at a fraction of that price. This sort of advertising practice represents the unfortunate transfer of the ethics of a going-out-of-business sale to the center of the market place.

Still another practice which has recently heaped condemnation upon advertising has been deceptive packaging—a practice which has also amply demonstrated that the package is itself a most effective advertising medium. Senator Hart's revelations of last summer vividly demonstrate that consumers are today deeply disturbed over the attempt of companies to avoid rational price comparison by jiggling the size and weight of branded goods, with a bold assist from specialists in package design. The overweening aim has been not to serve the consumer but to develop display values which will insure "sales vitality."

Yet still another indictment should be added. There is such a thing as saturation in advertising. Granted that this informational agency, properly employed as an accurate and descriptive educational mechanism, has a real and substantial place in our culture, this does not delegate it to subject human consciousness to the shrieking of an oriental bazaar. Even Grand Canyon would be spoiled if a thousand hawkers were permitted to proclaim the superlative virtues of each outlook spot. Too much is too much, particularly when embellished at times by miracles not yet discovered even by scientists. Herein lies the need for a consumer manifesto which would include as a minimum the acceptance of these basic elements:

1. The new communication media—radio and television—were not created for advertising. The airwaves are owned by the consuming public and the costs of radio and television, whether indirectly assessed through advertising or directly through the cost of electricity and television acquisition and maintenance, are consumer costs. Advertisers are there incidentally as nonpaying guests in the home and are not to be obnoxious, long-winded, stupid or inane. Program content is rightfully not the creature of the advertiser dedicated by his dictates to cater to the lowest common denominator of mass taste.

2. The countryside belongs to the consumer, not to the advertiser. There is no inherent right to create incessant affronts to the human eye every hundred yards along a highway—a procession of billboard slums.

3. Newspapers and periodicals have their central responsibility to their readers, not to their advertisers. This responsibility is compromised whenever dubious standards of advertising acceptance prevail or where choice is warped by planted stories designed to sell, not to inform.

4. Legislative and self-regulatory efforts to impose truth in advertising and to ban false and misleading advertising, though possessed of great merit, have thus far proven notoriously ineffective. They need to be improved. No prohibitions on false advertising, however drastic, can suffice to compel advertising to play its essential role in our culture. Truth in advertising is not a residue left after the elimination of falsehood. Advertising has ever been prone to discover new techniques of subtle deception wherever prohibitions have been imposed. What is today needed is the application of a supplementary approach.

5. Specifically, I propose a policy of *caveat venditor*—let the seller beware —a policy to be enforced by our social and legal institutions. Succinctly, I start on the premise that an advertisement should be a warranty to the purchaser of

the price and quality of an article. Thus the burden of proof as to an advertising claim will lay squarely upon the seller of a branded good. A claim should be accurate and complete as to all essential details and should constitute a full disclosure of both the merits and demerits of the good in its intended use. Advertising should not be poised on the slippery edge of irrelevance, misrepresentation or deception. The obsolescent and socially destructive idea of *caveat emptor* should be appropriately buried as a relic of the days of simple markets and well-understood commodities.

This suggestion that the seller be held legally bound by his statements (including the clear implications that these may give to the ordinary consumer) is by no means a revolutionary one. It has been already incorporated into a number of court opinions and is beginning to find a place in economic and judicial attitudes. It should now be fully integrated into the legal structure. Full disclosure in one form or another has already emerged in declarations of ingredients in foods and drugs. Hazardous substances have to have full warnings on their labels. Moreover, the drift of court opinion has been toward the acceptance of the principle that the manufacturer in placing a product upon the market assumes a responsibility to the consumer which goes beyond the mandate of *caveat emptor*.

In conclusion, let me state that I know of no consumers who are not willing, even eager to be told with accuracy and candor about new or truly improved products, or for that matter to have their memories jogged about the merits of existing products. The consumer has no quarrel with advertising as such. His basic quarrel is simply that this medium has been misused. As a whole, it has not been designed to inform but has been powered for a lesser objective—the promotion of brands. And being so powered,

it has less often led to consumer enlightenment than to consumer bewilderment.

It is all very well for advertising partisans to plead that only one out of five Americans is disgusted with its actual performance and that, in the main, the nation is well content with the toothy blondes who greet them with beckoning hands filled with the fruits of our culture. Correct it may be that the majority of the consumer "electorate" basks contentedly in the advertising sun. Yet I would suggest to you that the revolt against advertising has come from opinion leaders and that the rise of the American educational levels may well extend the area of alienation.

Mr. Harry Harding of Young and Rubicam in a recent speech (*Purpose: Growth,* presented at the 1961 AAAA Annual Meeting, April 22, 1961, White Sulphur Springs, West Virginia) reiterates the basic fallacy in the thought of the advertiser in affirming that the consumer will not act without persuasion or force. I doubt this. Must life be made meaningful solely by the efforts of specialists in stimulation who, in quest of self-profit, seek to coax or cajole? Has not the most important force—that of self-initiation—been omitted? Do you, for example, need the advertiser to shape the profile of your values? I seriously doubt it.

It should be accented that it is not the critic of advertising who wishes to establish a standardized consumer after his own image. A discerning critic wishes more deliberative choice, more autonomous human beings who operate in an environment which, with truthful information sources, fosters freedom of choice and free competition of ideas in the market place, not the pre-conditioned "standard package" of acceptable goods of the advertiser. It is advertising that is concentrating its techniques upon the manipulation of human personality into profitable molds. To be sure, it is no hidden persuader. It is instead a private agency of human conditioning of not inconsiderable power, designed generally to create an image of sterile optimism, an obsession with material things, with change, with motion, and with superficial appearance. Its failure to date has not been so much in craftsmanship as in its failure to recognize that accurate advertising is a phase of educational experience and should maintain the standards of education—it should be fact-faithful, presenting the imperfections as well as the advantages; it should have perspective; it should be tentative and as unbiased as possible. Artificial product differentiations and romantic fantasies may for a time capture unthinking consumer loyalty. If, however, our culture is to have vital meaning and survival power, these techniques must prove no substitute for unadulterated truth.

51

Economic and Social Responsibility of Advertising Men

Earl W. Kintner

The author of this article spent about twenty years with the Federal Trade Commission and finally served as its chairman. Members of that agency probably see more of the seamy side of advertising than anyone in the country. In view of his experience it is interesting to read his views on the responsibilities of advertisers.

Fourteen billion dollars of advertising annually is a powerful economic force. This force has played a mighty role in building and sustaining our American system of free competitive enterprise, which has produced the highest standard of living ever achieved by free people in the history of the world.

As our ability to produce goods has increased through mechanization and higher productive efficiency, distribution and consumption have become important

Reprinted from *Printer's Ink*, December 24, 1965. Copyright 1965 by Decker Communications, Inc.

problems. All these gains of mass production and advanced technology would go for naught without a means of reaching a market of potential consumers. Customers must be sought and taught, often persuaded, to move up in the living scale. Personal selling is one way. But we are now manufacturing mountains of goods which are of better quality and are produced more economically than ever before. Personal selling must be augmented by mass selling in order to bring these goods to the consumer.

Advertising should and indeed does acquaint the public with new products and new methods—products and methods which in most cases are safer, easier and cheaper. We can readily see the force of advertising as it applies to our system of free enterprise. It provides the opportunity for new companies and new products to flourish and grow; at the same time, advertising helps the manufacturer with an established name to maintain his position. The result of this process is to increase the overall freedom of individual consumers to choose among different products.

Mass selling means advertising, which multiplies the personal salesman by millions. Advertising is to distribution and consumption what improved machines are to production. Advertising is the accelerator which puts speed and power into sales. Sales mean more income for more people. In turn, these people desire more goods and services, not only for the basic needs of food, clothing and shelter, but for the enjoyment of leisure hours, for the opportunities of participating in communal and cultural activities. Without this accelerator, advertising, we could not have the kind of life we enjoy in America today.

A summary definition of the social responsibilities of advertising would, at a minimum, embrace these three elements:

1. To function as an efficient instrument of free and fair competition by focusing public attention on the demonstrable merits of competing products and services.
2. To foster innovation by affording new entrants to the market place an efficient means for winning public acceptance.
3. To furnish to consumers the information necessary for intelligent choices.

These responsibilities are affirmatively stated. Viewed negatively, we may state the summary in this way:

1. To avoid perverting free competition by using advertising as an unfair method of competition. Disparagement of worthy competitors or the diversion of sales through deception are obvious examples of foul competition.
2. To avoid the use of deception or the exercise of market power to stifle innovation. Advertising can be used as a tool of monopoly, just as it can be used as an instrument of free competition.
3. To avoid flooding consumers with false and misleading statements which pervert the right of free choice. The economic damage to consumers produced by such practices is vicious; the weakening of public confidence in a free-enterprise economy resulting from such practices is a far greater vice.

Obligation to Tell the Truth

The functions of advertising must be tuned to an overriding obligation. That obligation, in essence, is to speak the truth. Speaking the truth involves something more than the mere avoidance of the half truth, and that is the inclusion of the fact that is essential to the formation of an accurate judgment of the qualities of the article or services described. The difficulty comes in the reconciliation of purpose with obligation. There is a constant tension in any form of activity that seeks to win attention from competition, but if we say that attention cannot be won honorably, then we admit that advertising is an improper social activity. It is the firm opinion of the author that there is no need to make such an admission.

Advertising bears a basic responsibility to trusting consumers—consumers who themselves are the beneficiaries of the rising sophistication in American life. As the levels of public education and public taste rise, so must the minimum standards of advertisers rise. The proverbial advertising man who addresses his pleas solely to twelve-year-olds is becoming obsolete, as indeed he should. This individual does a disservice to himself, his product, his industry and, most important, to the increasingly aware consumer.

Advertising has never been able to sell an inferior product for a prolonged period of time. Too often we give the consumer too little credit for his ability to see fraud, deception and trickery. But the American consumer soon gets wise to chicanery, and fraudulent purveyors of shoddy and shady merchandise have to close up shop and move elsewhere, or else find new tricks and gimmicks. As a matter of fact, even worthy products have had to give up the ghost because for some reason or other the public would not accept them. The consumer has always exercised and is exercising today a censorship over advertising, because falsely advertised products find it harder and harder to make advertising pay off. It seems absolutely certain that the manufacturer of good products, prompted by advertising in good taste, will dominate the advertising scene long after the opportunist has withdrawn his shadily advertised product from the market or has given up business completely.

Showcase of Free-Enterprise System

A further aspect of the overall role of advertising lies in the inescapable fact that advertising is the showcase of our free-enterprise system to all the world. This showcase reveals itself both in the United States and overseas. Our mass media are capable of reaching into the most remote corners of the world; indeed the day has come when an American television commercial may be viewed simultaneously in Europe. Surely, in this perspective every businessman must realize the importance of truthful advertising conducted in good taste. Here in the United States, on display to visiting diplomats, students and tourists, is the giant showcase of American wares and a full-scale presentation of how they are sold. Let us take a concrete example— that of foreign diplomats stationed in our nation's capital. As soon as they arrive, they get the treatment: "Dear Friend" letters by direct-mail sellers, double-spread ads of sensationally reduced prices, breathless bargains barking out of their TV and radio sets, and the yellow pages of the telephone book offering an infinity of "free" inspections and "guaranteed" service. To these persons, some of them highly influential, Washington offers an illustration of our free-enterprise system, not as we preach it but as we practice it. And any instance of business chicanery carries a far greater impact on them than on us. We recognize skullduggery as the handiwork of an individual or, at most, of a corporation; they regard it as a revelation of national degeneracy. Nor is such superficial judgment peculiar to foreigners in America. Just ask an American tourist his opinion of the national character of the country where he paid for a pearl and got a white marble.

We may view advertising and its impact as a small skirmish in what has been described as the "battle for men's minds." In such a context it is certain that the picture of American free enterprise is badly dirtied by offensive and deceptive advertising. Just as certainly, we can and must realize that our picture is strongly bolstered by truthful advertising that is presented in good taste.

Finally, in analyzing the role of advertising in our economy, we must conclude with a note of caution. All intelligent businessmen realize that advertising has many critics. Much has been said about the sins of advertisers, their agencies, and the media. On the other hand, many good and constructive things have been done by responsible groups in the advertising industry. . . . Of course, the good work being done by some does not justify the shortcomings of others which may not yet have been corrected. But the value of legitimate advertising to our economy is too important to permit the abuses of some to bring the entire industry into general disrepute. Certainly there are some jackals on the fringes of advertising, as in any other industry. Law enforcement agencies such as the Federal Trade Commission were created to root out the weeds, but there is danger in harming the carefully cultivated plants by the misapplication of weed killer. Care must be exercised in combating the evils found in some advertising, lest in the process all advertising be harmed. This would be a catastrophe, not only to advertising, but to our entire economic system.

Importance of Reputation

At this moment millions of purchasers are making millions of buying decisions. It is fair to surmise that in the great bulk of these transactions the purchaser is buying a reputation. In some instances it will be the reputation of the manufacturer; in others, that of the retailer; in still others, that of an advertising medium. But in each instance reputation is an important factor. Therefore, the preservation of a reputation for propriety and decency is a matter of intense self-interest. Temptations in the market place can be severe, but no businessman with a shred of dignity can for one moment imagine that any material gain is worth the destruction of his own pride, his own code of ethics, and his own sense of vocation. Thus, advertisers must insure that every message bearing their imprint

is a truthful message. Every medium must insure that no false voices speak through it. And the creators of advertising must assume a special professional responsibility.

Professional responsibility extends far beyond the mere avoidance of legal penalties and observance of legal boundaries. Professionalism means a willingness to respectfully disagree with one's client; a willingness to recommend an unobjectionable program; and, yes, to resign from the service of the client if he persists in violating the ethical precepts of his adviser. If advertising men and women develop this sense of professionalism, and if advertisers absorb the lesson that good will and public reputation slowly and painfully acquired can easily be dissipated by an ill-advised and offensive short-term campaign, public respect for advertising will be assured.

Professional Responsibility Required

The acceptance of professional responsibility requires courage. It also requires a sense of one's own worth and dignity, and a sense of the importance of one's work. The man who works only for money can have no true dignity. The man who is prepared to sacrifice everything for financial gain can have no pride in his work. If advertising is to become something more than the rat race described in popular novels, then each individual in the industry must demonstrate that he can exercise professional responsibility.

During the few years which have elapsed since the rigging and payola scandals and the resulting highwater mark in public cynicism, a host of advertising men and women have come to appreciate the necessity for individual responsibility. It is true that these individuals are tested in the privacy of offices; responsible actions induced by these restraints receive no publicity. On the other hand, harmful actions by individuals who recognize no restraints inevitably command public attention. Nevertheless, careful and impartial observers of advertising can detect a perceptible increase in the ranks of those who stand for honest advertising.

Many excellent publications serving the advertising industry, such as Advertising Age, Broadcasting, Sponsor, and Sales Management, have strongly supported self-regulatory programs in the industry. This has been done both through education on the problems of advertising and encouragement of voluntary solutions by the industry. Advertising Age, for instance, carried a series entitled "Advertising We Can Do Without," which featured advertisements forwarded by readers which seemed to cross the lines of truth and good taste. In the series the magazine reproduced the actual ad, thus exposing the advertiser and his defects.

Of all the trade publications, however, one deserves special mention. Printers' Ink, founded in 1888, has traditionally played a leading role in the movement for truth in advertising. In its earlier days, this publication led the successful fight for the adoption of a model advertising statute by the states. Printers' Ink also strongly supported the development and growth of Better Business Bureaus. In recent years it has launched other programs for truth and taste in advertising. It published a candid series of articles designed to alert advertising to the scope of the problem, to spell out the dangers of laxity, to pinpoint responsibility for action, and to show what action could be taken. These articles prove that Printers' Ink which may be thought of as the editorial conscience of the advertising industry, is very much alive to its self-appointed, historical role.

Entire Industry on Trial

To conclude this section on self-regulation in advertising, the author must remark that the entire advertising industry is on trial. It has been on trial since late in 1959; it will continue to be on trial for a long time into the future. In large measure the outcome of this trial rests with the advertising industry. If it succumbs to ineffectual handwringing or cynicism or intransigence in the face of the public interest, a bitter outcome is certain. The only way to avert that outcome is to demonstrate responsibility. In whatever way we wish to define the function of the advertising industry, that function must include as an indispensable element the duty to tell the truth in a tasteful manner.

Advertising men and women must find within themselves a belief in their capacities to meet responsibilities. It was John Stuart Mill who said that "one person with a belief is equal to a force of ninety-nine who have only interest." As we have seen, many in advertising have demonstrated that they have beliefs. But the work cannot stop. The demonstrations must continue and increase in scope and effectiveness. Only in this way can persons in advertising show—as they must—that they are determined to be responsible citizens in a free society.

The public and moral responsibility of advertisers and those who serve the industry must in turn be shared by the advertising media—newspapers, magazines, periodicals, radio, and television.

The question whether the Federal Trade Commission should hold media legally responsible for deceptive advertising has been a subject of much public comment. This possible extension of legal responsibility is a matter involving serious policy considerations. It is the firm hope of the author that the Commission will never find it necessary to name an advertising medium as respondent in a deceptive advertising case. If federal and state authorities engage in the sort of vigorous enforcement which is necessary, and if the whole of the advertising industry, in cooperation with all advertising media, does the proper job of intensive self-regulation, it would seem that this serious legal step need not be taken.

The mere fact that the recent crisis in public confidence had its origin in television does not mean that other media can or should relax. First of all, practical consideration of self-interest dictate against such an answer. Visual deception in a television commercial may have an immediate impact upon public confidence in all television commercials, but the cynicism thus aroused may also result in a skeptical attitude toward printed assertions of advertisers. No medium can afford complacency toward problems of other media.

Just as nature abhors a vacuum, so does a civilized society abhor a vacuum in the imposition of needed restraints. It is important to realize that the failure of one source of necessary restraints will result only temporarily in the absence of restraint; the pressure of public opinion will soon force the needed contribution from another source.

Pressures for increased governmental control of advertising have been building in recent years. It is possible that these pressures will result in controls more extensive than really ought to be necessary to insure that advertising's responsibilities will be met. The best defense against such pressures is a demonstration that individuals and groups within the advertising industry can meet their responsibilities on a voluntary basis. The record in this regard is encouraging, but the hard work must continue.

Alternative Is Government Control

I believe in self-regulation. A free man can and will accept responsibility as well as privilege; free men recognize that freedom means responsibility. Some advertising men have adopted a cynical attitude toward self-regulation. One of these pessimists said, "Talk of self-policing leaves me very cold." Another told a prominent magazine that only the Federal Trade Commission had the power to clean up advertising and that to suggest any other means was to invite futility. This attitude is as dangerous as it is false. Certainly, vigorous enforcement of prohibitions against false advertising by the Federal Trade Commission is a must, but individual integrity is also a must. If industry fails to accept its responsibility for truthful advertising, then we can secure truth only by massive government control. This alternative is appalling, because, at bottom, those businessmen who pass their moral responsibilities on to the government are advocating a police state. It is difficult to believe that effective trade regulations can be brought about only by a Gestapo. Individual integrity is the mortar cementing the foundations of our system of government. If the mortar cracks and crumbles in spots, it can be repaired. But the house will not stand without mortar.

In short, the goal of ethical advertising can be reached. The Federal Trade Commission and state law-enforcement officials can provide the sanctions that are an indispensable part of any civilized activity. The men of advertising can, in cooperation with the media, guide their efforts by firm ethical standards, thus providing the largest contribution. Consumers and consumer-protection groups, by public education and by vociferous protest against tasteless advertising, can achieve ever-higher levels of good taste. If all of these social entities perform conscientiously and efficiently, then we can provide one more illustration that the complex balance of forces that is the American system can respond to challenge without surrendering individual freedom.

52

How Advertising Shapes Decision

Dr. Ernest R. Dichter

Advertising plays a vital role of shaping consumers' decisions to buy goods and services of all kinds. By so doing, it performs an important economic service to both producers and consumers. The author, a well-known consulting psychologist, discusses some of the important psychological and material factors that affect the buying behavior of consumers; he then looks at the impact of advertising on people in regard to these basic factors.

People get involved in discussions about Advertising at the drop of a hat. At cocktail parties, business luncheons, almost any gathering where words are bandied about, Advertising is a topic. Unfortunately, such discussions all too frequently center around obnoxious commercials, the high cost of advertising, the moral issues. Few people outside the advertising profession, however, give really serious thought to the impact of Advertising on people. In the following I shall develop some of the important points I feel should be considered in this respect.

Reprinted from REPROS, edition No. 16 by courtesy of the Bureau of Education and Research, Advertising Federation of America, and by special permission of Ernest Dichter, President, Institute for Motivational Research, Inc.

1. Advertising Structures the World

Advertising structures our physical environment and our world of objects. We cannot understand or digest the world in its chaotic stage. We need classification and order. This need for organization exists already in the child. The child needs fairy tales to classify people into good and bad groups.

But objects, too, need grouping. Ever since earliest childhood, we have been surrounded and have lived with hundreds, eventually thousands, of objects. We play with dolls, electric trains, enjoy our first shoes, and love to ride in a car. When we start watching television, we are beginning to be influenced by Advertising—long before we know how to read. It is our first knowledge and information about the world and the country we live in. It is our first orientation. We see a picture on television of the cereal we eat. We are informed that other children are apparently eating the same cereal. This orientation-function is carried through in later years in many details, for the world of objects is confusing in its variety and its multiplicity. As a form of communication, Advertising organizes these contacts with objects.

2. Advertising Helps in Growing Up

American people are moving ahead continuously, at least in an economic sense. This means that a whole new generation literally moves into a higher income bracket every few years and, as a result, into a higher class. In many of our motivational research studies we learn that a series of problems confront this new middle class. They must learn how to behave as members of their new class. This means they must learn how to buy.

In its various forms, Advertising represents a course in education. For example, a family considers buying new furniture. Before purchasing, they read all manner of advertising material. The end result of this procedure is training—learning to recognize important values in the field of furniture. They also learn to understand what constitutes good and bad furniture, for Advertising provides them an education in taste. Among other things, they learn how to check on claims, what criteria to use to decide for themselves whether a bed, a table, a chair, is or is not well constructed.

Our growing up process goes on and on. The average person is not aware of the help he really needs to readjust to the continuous problems of living.

Our relationship to the objects we surround ourselves with is an extremely important part of these problems.

3. Advertising Teaches Critical Judgment

Possibly one of the most unexpected results of Advertising is that it teaches people to rely upon their own judgment. This is brought about by a multitude of conflicting claims. To enlarge upon this somewhat, sometimes six different cigarettes may be advertised on television within the short span of one or two hours. Each claims to be milder, to have less nicotine, to include a better filter than the others. Contrary to what is normally expected, it isn't so much the specific commercial which has or does not have an impact. Instead, it is the comparison which the viewer and consumer makes of various claims that produces the final impact. The modern consumer discards very rapidly all statements which seem to wash each other out and hunts for specific facts which permit him to discover for himself what the true difference is between the different cigarettes. In a sense, he doesn't believe any of the advertising claims, but he learns what he should look for in them.

4. The Soul of Products

Ever since primitive days, mankind has had more than a rational relationship to products and materials. Entire cultural and historical periods are characterized by materials. We distinguish between the stone age, the bronze age, the iron age. Very possibly we could carry this forward to the plastic age, the electronic age. And each one of the materials to come out of its particular age possesses a life of its own—leather, wool, silk, wood, copper—all involve a different set of emotions. Silk is elegant, aristocratic, refined. Wool is comforting and warming.

Advertising facilitates the contact

between people and products—helps also to discover the soul of many materials and objects. When a copywriter attempts to describe the beauty of a dress or an elegant pair of shoes, it is necessary to probe deeply for the real emotional nucleus of the product. In a sense, he is the novelist, the dramatist, the poet of *objects*. Were it not for Advertising in our world, this emotional communication with *things* would be very poorly covered. Certain novelists and dramatists in the legitimate fields have, of course, long recognized the importance of building an appropriate psychological background for their stories and plays. They have talked about the meaning of a set of china, a house, the way a woman dresses, the pleasure of a cigar. On a mass scale, however, only in Advertising do *objects—things* in general—take the center of the stage.

Our world has bcome much more complex and kaleidoscopic. We have to establish contact with a much larger number of objects, materials and products than ever before.

Advertising builds a bridge which permits us to understand, familiarize ourselves with these new materials and products. We learn to accept the magic of an electric dishwasher as we used to believe in the magic of a sword, of a potion.

Objects have played a larger role in our lives than we like to admit. Ever since Eve's apple, we have used tangible things to express our emotions and our desires.

5. Advertising Creates Images

The word "image" (or the personality of a product) has become a by-word in modern advertising. The true meaning here is simply that we do not buy the technological aspects of a product alone, instead we buy the promise of continued quality and the reputation of a manufacturer and consumer experience. A brand, or a make, of a particular commodity, is both a written and signed guarantee by the manufacturer. At the same time, when surrounded with the effects of a continued advertising effort, it is total exposure of all these things a company and its products stand for and permits me, the consumer, to choose the type of product with the kind of image I think best matches my own.

In a sense, we have re-established the direct contact a consumer formerly enjoyed with the maker of an object, the Master Builder. Thus the brand of a product is the signature of the man who carved the table and of the man who designed the table which the manufacturer presents to his buying public.

6. Better Products Are Taken for Granted Because of Advertising

Insofar as innumerable products are concerned, many of our motivational research studies disclose that quality standards are taken for granted by the vast majority of people. A good part of the credit for this should go to Advertising.

Advertising is democratic. It exposes and places all messages out into the open. The average consumer realizes that if he pays practically the same amount of money for the different makes of refrigerators, he gets about the same values. He also knows that most refrigerators are quite good today. The same thing is true about cars, shoes, food items, etc.

Not too long ago I saw an advertising mention in South Africa on toilet tissue. It was guaranteed to be processed from clean, new fiber only.

This kind of reassurance is happily no longer necessary in this country. The consumer is convinced that toilet tissue is never made from dirty or used fibers or rags. To advertise today that milk is fresh or that only clean equipment and materials were used in a canned product is very like a restaurant advertising that dishes are being washed after every meal.

"Of course," says the customer. "They would land in jail if they didn't." One of the interesting effects of this reliance on basic good quality created through modern Advertising, has been the necessity to sell more by emotional means— by the creation of an image, as discussed before—and by attempting to create a direct desire for a new product or a new device. It is important to understand motivations and we must appeal to prospective buyers by emotional means as well as by rational arguments. At the same time, actual product improvement and new product development is the outgrowth of the wide advertising of many products.

7. Creation of Constructive Discontent

Advertising is accused of making people want things they do not really need. This raises a very complex argument. What *do* we really need? If we were to buy only those things that are absolutely necessary, we'd all soon be once again living in caves. We may or we may not wear anything. If we do, we could all wear overalls of one type or one color. On the other hand, for literally thousands of years our lives have been enriched by a myriad of products that were "not necessary." Adornments, protective devices, elaborate food and fine furniture have even graced the daily lives of some of the most primitive tribesmen. The heights were even reached during the early days of Egypt, Greece, and Rome.

The answer, then, to the accusation

that advertising makes people wan, things they do not need is: "Yes, indeed!"

Far from being immoral, I believe thi continuous push towards what I ca*l* *constructive discontent* represents a ver*y* important aspect of human progress If people are permitted to be conten and satisfied with their present statu and their present possessions, then th*e* need to motivate them toward new an*c* better lives, toward progress, would b*e* distinctively lessened.

Our life is a continuous fight betwee*n* wanting, on the one hand, to go back t*o* the womb, or discover a South Pacifi*c* island where we can have utter relaxa tion plus 100 per cent security and, o*n* the other hand, the desire to becom*e* independent and more mature as a*n* individual. While some excesses as *a* creation of frivolous obsolescence migh*t* be deplored, technological developmen*t* is so rapid and the desire of people fo*r* new things is so great that Advertisin*g* has become a vital form of communica tion and a vital tool for keeping up th*e* pace of continuous progress.

Advertising is a necessary part o*f* modern life. It is essential in a free enter prise system, keeping up the competitive spirit of our economic system as well a*s* the constructive discontent and competi tiveness of our individual lives.

Advertising is even needed in a planned economy, such as Russia. Moder*n* manufacturing needs communicatio*n* with the public. Advertising plays thi*s* role.

Upon closer examination, even th*e* issue of material goods versus spiritua*l* values is rather meaningless. Is th*e* acquisition of a book *spiritual* or *material*? Does the purchase of a new dress *uplift* *your spirit* and help you to enjoy lif*e* more, or is it *object materialism?*

In the final analysis, it is up to th*e* individual whether he or she buy*s* something new or replaces a product fo*r* empty reasons (such as keeping up with the Joneses) or to satisfy a basic, human desire for new experiences and a richer life.

Advertising coordinates the hundreds of thousands of products which are available to us as three-dimensional, intangible expressions of our real world. Each act of buying, in miniature form, is an act of creation, an expansion of ourselves. The impact of advertising is to make this object world accessible, understandable, organized and desirable.

A product can be an expression of the pursuit for happiness if the goals of the country as a whole are clearly defined as not simply the accumulation of material wealth but the enrichment of life, self-realization and inner freedom. The most essential quality of a modern, democratic society, in itself, can become the subject of social persuasion: Advertising.

E

Price Determination and Administration

53

Price Formulation

Gerald Albaum

Economists and businessmen have both shown an interest in the subject of pricing, but their interests have been quite different. The economists have discussed the theory of pricing with very little concern over how the function is carried on in practice. The businessmen, by contrast, have practiced pricing but have shown remarkably little interest in the theory of the process. In this article the author attempts to bridge the gap between theory and practice

I. Introduction

Setting the price of a product or service is an inevitable part of marketing management, particularly that aspect known as product planning and development. Some of the other steps may, in certain cases, be by-passed but a product cannot go to market without its price tag. Furthermore, remembering that some type and level of profit is the ultimate goal of business, the price must be right or a company will make less profit than it might have. This is as true if the price is too high as if the price is too low. Too low a price quite obviously gives away profit. The same is true of

Condensed from Gerald Albaum, *Price Formulation*. Tucson, Arizona: Division of Economic and Business Research, University of Arizona, November 1965.

too high a price although in this case it works out through a reduction of sale and is less obvious. In fact, many businessmen seem to have a curious blind spot on this point which inclines them to assume that setting a high price is erring on the safe side. A few moments reflection on this point should convince one of its error, and further thought directed toward its economic consequences suggests that an economy-wide policy of setting "safe" high prices will have the effect of restricting the gross national product. . . .

II. Theoretical Guides Are Needed

One can recognize the vital importance of proper pricing and still be in doubt as to how to determine price in a particular case. Due to the importance of the pricing problem as well as the role price plays in our free enterprise market economy, there definitely is need for a *realistic* and *useful* theory to guide businessmen in determining what price to charge for the product(s) offered for sale.[1] Historically, businessmen have relied on economists to provide theoretical guidelines. However, the economists have not been of great help. Their theories leave much to be desired, except perhaps as "normative" theories to guide businessmen operating under the stated assumptions which delineate the operating world.[2] Their *method of analysis* and the analytical tools they use appear to be more useful than the actual results achieved by them. Thus, "the main contributions to practical pricing of . . . theoretical analysis are to point out the kinds of demand and cost relations that have to be guessed, and to show how these functional relations should be used to indicate the most profitable price."[3]

[1] For a discussion of the role of price in a market economy see W. Allen Wallis, "The Price System," *Modern Marketing Thought.* J. H. Westing and Gerald Albaum (eds.), (New York: The Macmillan Company, 1964), pp. 263–266; Federal Reserve Bank of Chicago, "The Role of Prices in a Market Economy," *Business Conditions,* November 1961, pp. 3–5; and Federal Reserve Bank of Philadephia, *The Price System,* Series for Economic Education, January 1962.

[2] In all fairness to economists, it should be pointed out that the driving force behind the development of their theories was not specifically to help businessmen set a price. Rather, the purpose was to explain the forces—and the relationships among these forces—that affect price, and to show the role price plays in the operations of the firm. However, regardless of intent, the fact remains that businessmen have relied upon economists for guidelines to help them in determining a price.

[3] Joel Dean, *Managerial Economics,* © 1951, p. 406. Reprinted by permission of Prentice-Hall, Inc., Englewood Cliffs, New Jersey.

Importance of Pricing

While pricing is an integral aspect of marketing it is sometimes held to be less important than most businessmen believe it to be. There is some evidence to support this viewpoint.[4] In a study of 200 producers of industrial and consumer goods, Udell found that only 50 percent of the respondent firms indicated that pricing was one of the five most important policy areas in their marketing success. The most important activities in the success of the firms contacted relate to the product and to sales effort. Udell attributes the relatively low ranking of pricing to three factors:[5]

1. In today's competitive economy, *supply*—or production capacity—*generally exceeds demand;* and, therefore, nearly all sellers are forced to be either completely competitive or almost collusive in their pricing. Because there may be little or no freedom for a company to deviate from the market price, heavy reliance must be placed on product differentiation and sales effort.

2. *The relatively well-to-do consumers of today are interested in more than just price.* They are interested in product quality, distinctiveness, style, and many other factors which lead to both physical and psychological satisfaction. . . . It is only logical that consumer-oriented managements would choose to emphasize products and sales efforts in an attempt to satisfy consumer desires.

3. *It is through successful product differentiation that a manufacturer may obtain some pricing freedom.*

[4] Jon G. Udell, "How Important Is Pricing in Competitive Strategy?". Reprinted from the *Journal of Marketing,* national quarterly publication of the American Marketing Association, Vol. 28, No. 1 (January 1964), pp. 44–48.

[5] *Ibid.,* p. 45.

Products known to be identical must be priced identically in the market place. A departure from identical prices would result in all patronage going to the seller or sellers with the lowest price.

Although price may not be as important as many people believe, the businessman nonetheless must set a price. Thus, it is a decision area of marketing, and as such, deserves the diligent attention of business executives. . . .

III. Questions About Economists' Theory

With non-essential modifications and refinements economists' theory has been held by many to be an explanation of what the typical businessman tries to achieve as a pricing objective. Many economists also hold that it is a useful tool which businessmen use or should use in determining the level of the price to be set. Other economists believe that the theory explains the way a business firm is pushed or pulled against its will.

Our primary concern with the economist's theory of pricing can be expressed in the form of the simple question: Is the technique a useful one to the businessman? It would be pleasant to think so because the scheme is so precise and neat. Anyone charged with pricing responsibility would find it comfortable to have so exact a scheme to follow—even though the data on which it is based might be hard to obtain. Careful analysis, however, raises some basic issues about the soundness of the concepts and theory.

The Demand Curve

First is the concept of the demand curve. It is a simple matter to draw the demand curve with an assumed slope from zero to capacity volume. It is quite another matter to establish the level, shape and slope of the curve *in fact*. A firm has no experience with sales volume at either very high or very low prices and cannot afford to experiment with prices at these extremes. At best, a firm knows the demand only at the price presently being charged for its product, and perhaps also at a few other discrete points. Moreover, the knowledge about demand is quite inexact, even within a narrow range of the present price. Without precise knowledge about the demand curve it is impossible to plot the location of the marginal revenue curve, since the marginal revenue curve is derived from the demand curve. The relationship between demand and pricing is discussed in more detail in Section V.

The Average Cost Curve

A second issue concerns the shape of the average unit cost (AUC) curve. Economists have almost invariably assumed it to be a U-shaped curve. This assumption, however, has been based on reason rather than on empirical evidence.[6] Some years ago a survey among top business executives seemed to show quite clearly that businessmen act as if the curve either declined all the way to plant capacity or declined until just before capacity was reached and then increased gradually until capacity was reached. (Of course, once capacity is reached the average costs increase infinitely).[7] In this study approximately

[6] The reasoning is that in the short run, average unit cost is derived from short run production functions with increasing and diminishing returns to scale.

[7] Wilford J. Eiteman and Glenn E. Guthrie, "The Shape of the Average Cost Curve," *American Economic Review*, Vol. XLII, No. 5 (Decemeber 1952), pp. 832–838. The

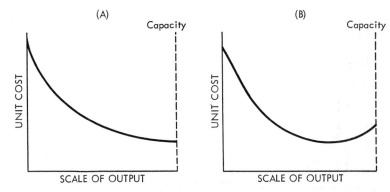

Figure 1. Shape of the average cost curve. (Source: See Footnote 7.)

61 percent of the respondents believed their average cost curve looked like that shown in Figure 1A, and 34 percent felt their cost curves were similar to the one presented in Figure 1B.

If this assertion about the shape of the average cost curve is true, its implications are devastating to the theory, for if the demand curve and the average unit cost curve slope to the right at the same rate, the marginal revenue and marginal cost curves derived from these curves will not intersect and therefore *cannot be used as price determinants.* Similarly if the average cost curve declines more rapidly than the demand curve and their related marginal curves should happen to intersect, such intersection would have *no valid pricing significance* since, at that point, costs would be declining faster than revenue.

Even if the assertion by Eiteman and Guthrie about the shape of the average cost curve is not true *in fact*, the value of the theory to the business executive who has to determine a price is questionable. Managerial decision regarding price and volume of product to produce are made on the basis of what executives

validity of this study was seriously questioned by some economists (see *American Economic Review*, Vol. XLIII, No. 4, Part I, September 1953, pp. 621–630), but on issues not of concern in this paper.

think is true and not on the basis of what is true.[8]

There is further evidence that tends to destroy the validity of the U-shaped average cost curve. Johnston, using his own study of many industries in the United Kingdom and analyzing the results of the main empirical studies of cost functions that had been made during the period 1936–1960 concludes that:

1. The various short-run studies more often than not indicate constant marginal cost and declining average cost as the pattern that best seems to describe the data that have been analyzed.

2. The L-shaped pattern of the long-run average cost emerges so frequently from the various long-run analyses.[9]

[8] Wilford J. Eiteman, *Price Determination in Oligopolistic and Monopolistic Situations*. Ann Arbor, Michigan: Bureau of Business Research, School of Business Administration, The University of Michigan, 1960 (Michigan Business Reports, No. 33), p. 5. This idea was perhaps first implied by Chamberlain in his famous case of the slope of the demand curve—that is, businessmen in making decisions assume the demand curve has a certain slope while, in fact, the slope is entirely different.

[9] From *Statistical Cost Analysis* by J. Johnston, p. 168: Copyright © 1960 by McGraw-Hill. Used by permission of McGraw-Hill Book Company. See Chapter 5

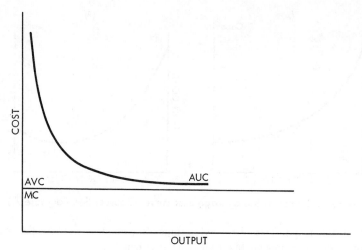

Figure 2. Empirical average cost curve.

Figure 2 depicts the shape of the average cost curve that emerges from these empirical cost studies. (AUC is as defined previously, AVC is average variable cost, and MC is marginal cost).

Marginal Concepts

A third problem cöncerns the concepts of marginal cost and marginal revenue. Businessmen simply do not think in these terms. As far as marginal costs are concerned, businessmen have similar concepts, such as out-of-pocket or direct costs. However, there is nothing similar to marginal revenue. Generally, businessmen are more used to thinking in terms of *total* costs and revenue, and in some cases *incremental* costs and revenues.[10] It cannot be stated definitely which of the concepts—total or incre-

mental—a pricing executive should use. As will be shown later, in the case of costs both concepts can be used. The determining factor is the objective the firm wishes its pricing to achieve and the strategy employed in this endeavor.

Profit Goal

A fourth, and even more fundamental, question is whether the typical firm does or should try to make the largest possible profit *today*. To do so may invite competitors into the field and could result in lower profits over the long term. In economists' terms this is known as short run vs. long run maximization of profit. The theory is based on the assumption that one should maximize short run profits and purports only to tell one how to do this. It is of small significance to anyone worried about market position or potential competition rather than today's profit.

---

for a discusion of the main studies during the period 1936–1960.

[10] Incremental costs and revenue are somewhat similar to marginal costs and revenue. The difference between the two is that marginal cost and revenue are concerned with infinitesimally small changes in costs and revenues, resulting from volume changes, while incremental cost and revenue

---

are finite changes resulting from decisions of many types not necessarily operating through changes in volume [W. Warren Haynes, *Pricing Decisions in Small Business*, (Lexington, Ky.: University of Kentucky Press, 1962), pp. 14–15].

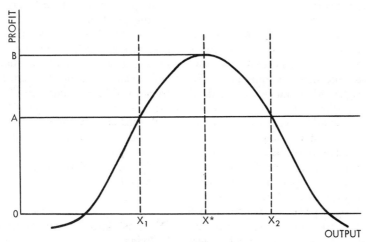

Figure 3. Profit curve.

A more realistic and useful approach is to view business managers as desiring to earn only satisfactory profits in the short run. Once the minimum acceptable level of profit is determined, whether it be stated in terms of money or some target return, then the firm has a range of output alternatives from which it can choose the most profitable one (assuming no other considerations are involved, such as liquidity, the desire for business stability and peace or various humanitarian factors).[11] Figure 3 shows the traditional profit curve for a firm. Although it is drawn continuous it should be recognized that the alternatives actually evaluated by a firm are finite and small in number. If OA represents the minimum acceptable level of profit, then any output within the range OX_1 and OX_2 would be acceptable to the firm. Since there are only a small number of alterna-

tives evaluated the selection of OX^* with the maximizing profit OB would be solely up to chance. A businessman would never really know if he had, in fact, achieved OB level of profit.[12]

Traditional theory and much of the discussion it has generated seem to imply that only one goal is involved, regardless of what it may be. Such an implication was refuted in a study of 20 large corporations.[13] In this study, it was found that while one goal is dominant in most companies, there were also collateral goals. Thus, price-making by any one firm was not always ruled by a single policy or goal.

[11] For a discussion of pricing objectives see E. Jerome McCarthy, *Basic Marketing: A Managerial Approach* (Homewood, Illinois: Richard D. Irwin, Inc., Rev. Ed., 1964), pp. 806–821; and Robert F. Lanzillotti, "Pricing Objectives in Large Companies," *American Economic Review*, Vol. XLVIII, No. 5 (December 1958), pp. 921–940.

[12] This approach using satisfactory profits as the basis of price decisions is quite similar to that known as Revenue Maximization developed by William Baumol, *Business Behavior and Growth* (New York, The Macmillan Company, 1959). A simplified discussion of this is found in C. E. Ferguson and Juanita M. Kreps, *Principles of Economics* (New York: Holt, Rinehart and Winston, 1962), pp. 534–539. Very simply, Baumol's hypothesis is that the chief goal of large, oligopolistic firms is maximizing total revenue, subject to earning a certain minimum level of profit.

[13] Lanzillotti, *op. cit.*

The Right Price

A final, and perhaps the most serious, criticism of the economist's theory is that it assumes each firm has the same objective and there is one price that is the right price under any and all conditions—the price that maximizes profits. Put another way, it assumes that price can be statistically and mathematically determined based on a given set of considerations or factors. Anyone who has had experience with pricing will recognize that this is not true to life. The right price for Reynolds' ball point pens was the wrong price for Eversharp. Reynolds apparently was willing to make a quick profit and leave the field whereas for Eversharp the price should have been designed to gain and hold a substantial share of a new market. In retrospect it would appear that a short run maximizing of profits was the wrong objective for Eversharp since the company merely helped open up a market which others then took over. Thus it should not be assumed that each firm had the same objective.[14]

Conclusion

The point seems to be that successful pricing involves an important element of strategy over and above the considerations of cost and demand. To put it in terms of an analogy that is currently popular, pricing involves the theory of games. In a game of poker, for example, the cards one holds are known (even more fully than costs and demand) but the right way to play the hand depends as much on the moves and counter-moves of opponents as upon the cards. This strategy, which involves anticipating and reacting to opponents, is as important in pricing as in poker. Any pricing theory which leaves out this element of

[14] See *Ibid.*, pp. 924–927.

strategy cannot realistically explain pricing practice.

One should not conclude from this discussion that cost and demand are either irrelevant or unimportant. Rather, cost and demand define the limits or extremes within which an executive should exercise strategy. The good executive will want the most precise data available on both costs and demand, but the measure of his success lies in how wisely he develops and executes his strategy. . . .

IV. Cost and Its Relationship to Price

In tribute to the economist's theory it should be pointed out that it gives full and equal recognition to both supply and demand factors. It is an unfortunate fact that typically businessmen elevate supply (or cost) considerations to a position of dominance. This over-emphasis on cost probably results from the fact that demand data are hard to obtain and such as can be secured are of uncertain accuracy. By contrast, the accountant stands ready to supply cost data on short notice and in almost any form required. These cost figures also have a comforting appearance of precision. The pricing executive who uses unit cost figures should constantly remind himself that for pricing purposes the apparent precision of unit cost data may be specious. For example, most manufacturing operations today involve elements of *joint cost*. Suppose that scrap metal is produced in large quantities as a necessary part of one operation and that this scrap could be used as an important raw material for another product. The accountant might charge this material for costing purposes as scrap, as new metal, or at some intermediate figure. For pricing purposes the proper cost would depend on such things as the amount of by-product scrap, its alternative intra-company uses, whether competitors had the same possibility of using by-product scrap, etc. These considerations change with time and the danger is that the accountants set up their cost allocating methods under one set of conditions and they persist after conditions have changed. Unless the pricing executive is sensitive to these changes he runs a real risk of using misleading cost data.

The same kind of point can be made with respect to overhead or fixed costs. The accountant will, and should in the normal course of costing, allocate overhead costs on some pro-rata basis to all processes and products. For pricing purposes, however, overhead costs must be viewed in the light of plant utilization. If facilities are being fully used no product should be sold that covers less than full cost—direct and overhead. If facilities are not utilized fully, a product may be sold that covers less than full costs, provided no better use can be found for the facilities.

It might also be observed that frequently when a company is breaking into a new market its full cost figure would indicate the need for a high price because of the likely small volume while getting established. If this high price were charged it would insure a small volume and probably damn the venture. Under such circumstances the only relevant full cost figure would be one based on an assumed satisfactory volume after successful market entry.

Another point to be kept in mind about full costs is that they can be calculated only on the basis of some assumed volume. Overhead costs can only be converted to a unit basis by dividing totals by some volume figure. To be conservative, as he is by nature, an accountant tends to assume a small, "safe" volume and thereby arrives at a high full cost figure and if this cost figure is used to set the price it tends to bear out the

accountant's original conservative assumption. The following comment by Huegy on this point is pertinent:

> . . . price decision cannot be the simple product of cost accounting and arithmetic—cost accounting facts are history; prices are in the future. At some time, of course, estimates of future costs must be placed alongside proposed prices. But costs are affected by volume, and volume is affected by price, so perhaps management has to assume some desired price and volume relationship and let costs become the result rather than the cause.[15]

Business executives in general have a decided tendency to think of full costs as a level below which they will not price. Economists acting as business consultants tend rather casually to suggest *direct costs* or *incremental costs* as a minimum standard for pricing. Probably both positions are extreme. In defense of the businessman it can be said that no profit (i.e., net profit) can be made unless full costs are first covered. He also must concern himself with the competitive effects of direct cost pricing. What starts out as direct cost pricing for a marginal segment of business may, through competitive chain reaction, come to lower prices on a major part of his business. In other words, the businessman has to worry about starting a price war. In the economists' defense it can be shown that under conditions of excess plant capacity (where the markets can be segmented or hermetically sealed) it is possible to increase total profit by selling at less than full cost. In fact, one can show at the extreme that where the product is in existence

---

[15] H. W. Huegy, "Price Decisions and Marketing Policies," *The Environment of Marketing Behavior*, Robert J. Holloway and Robert S. Hancock (eds.), (New York: John Wiley & Sons, Inc., 1964), p. 293.

and threatened with obsolescence there is *no* cost floor for pricing purposes. Here the retailers' expression applies, "You have to sell it or smell it!" The truth, in this controversy, as usual, lies somewhere in the middle. The alert pricing executive will not lightly depart from full cost as a price floor but he will always seriously contemplate the possibility of backing down toward direct or incremental cost as the floor and in unusual cases will recognize that anything that has been spent is "sunk cost" and has no relevance at all to pricing.

The foregoing statement leads to a final observation on cost and pricing which, as a point of view, is more important than anything that has been said. In our economic system the *value* of a product rather than its *cost* is the basis for pricing. Cost serves only as a benchmark to the seller, indicating to him whether the price the buyers will pay is profitable enough to warrant engaging in the business. This point needs emphasis because historically prices have been justified or condemned by measuring them against cost. Moralists from ancient times to the present have talked about "just" or "fair" prices by which they have meant prices that exceed full cost by not more than a socially acceptable rate of profit. It is true that over a period of time competition will tend to equate price and cost. (Economists call this the normal price.) This tendency, however, does not and should not operate in the short run in a free enterprise market economy. In such an economy price is the regulator that directs the flow of the economy's resources into the fields where consumers most desire them. This will only happen in a free market economy where price is allowed to regulate if prices in those areas are permitted to provide attractive profits during an interim period to compensate for risk and initiative. This point needs special emphasis in connection with product development since it is precisely in this area that price and cost should be the least closely related.

V. Demand or Value and Its Relationship to Pricing

A pricing executive then, in addition to considering costs of various kinds, should try to establish the value of the product as accurately as possible. In a sense this amounts to attempting to establish the demand schedule for the product, which in the geometric approach involves determining the level, slope and shape of the demand curve. There is little to be gained, however, in defining the curve at its upper or lower extreme since it is unlikely that profitable operations are possible at either extreme.

Value should be measured in terms of *product utility*, translated into monetary terms. Thus, pricing is a continuous process of adjusting product price to the fluctuating utility of the last prospective buyer so as to make him a customer. When estimating the demand curve one should stratify the market. This involves determining the number of prospects who will buy at several levels of price. The pricing executive then should select the strata he is interested in. The resulting price gives the last prospect an amount of utility or value equal to the price charged while all others will have a "surplus" in that they would be willing to pay a higher price.

Methods of Estimating Values

Determining the value of a product to prospective buyers is by all odds the most difficult and least developed phase of pricing.[16] The obvious, but superficial, way of doing it is to use a *questionnaire* method and ask likely buyers how much they would be willing to pay for a product. Prospects in the ultimate consumer market cannot give useful responses to questions of this kind when they are suddenly confronted with an artificial buying situation unless, of course, there is some "customary price" that they expect to pay for the general category of products involved. Ultimate consumers generally buy to satisfy emotional needs which mature only after time and exposure to the products. There is further difficulty of translating an emotional want into dollar terms. Some experimental attempts to do this have been made in terms of *barter*. A consumer is confronted with a variety of known products in the approximate price range and is then asked in turn whether he would choose the product under consideration in preference to others. Or, as a reward for cooperating in a research study by answering a series of questions about an unrelated subject, the consumer is offered a gift that he can select from several items. This approach gives the consumer a price frame of reference, but does not overcome the fact that the product has not had time to acquire emotional significance.

In the industrial goods field users are more often of help in suggesting a price. Since the product has a measurable value to the industrial user he can, with sufficient motivation and effort, give a close approximation to the value of the product to him. It is important, however, to be on guard against the inherent bias of the industrial user in favor of a low price, and it is difficult to know how much to allow for this bias.

A technique being used with greater frequency in recent years is *experimental* (or test market) pricing. In essence this involves the selection of two or more comparable markets in which different prices are charged during a test period.[17] It is then assumed that variations in sales are attributable to the differences in price. This method of measuring value has much to recommend it since it comes close to creating a true market situation. Its limitations are that it is expensive, time-consuming and involves the highly uncertain assumption that all of the many other factors among the test markets were and remained constant. In addition, where a product is new and perhaps not even covered by a patent, security is probably quite important and it may be unwise to expose the product to even a limited market. Nevertheless, the test market method deserves consideration where time and expense permit the planning of a very careful experiment.

In general, perhaps the most feasible method of measuring a product's value is to compare it with the closest substitutes available. The prices of these substitutes provide a point of departure. The pricing executive still faces the sensitive but critical task of measuring the product's distinctive features in terms of dollars. Quite clearly, this approach is best for product improvements. In terms of frequency of occurrence the procedure covers a substantial majority of cases, but it affords little guidance for those rare product innovation oppor-

[16] See Wroe Alderson and Paul E. Green, *Planning and Problem Solving in Marketing* (Homewood, Illinois: Richard D. Irwin, Inc., 1964), pp. 247–252.

[17] This method can also be used under simulated market conditions. In general, when the experimental method is used under such conditions a variant of the questionnaire method is also used. See Jack Abrams, "A New Method for Testing Pricing Decisions," *Journal of Marketing*, Vol. 28, No. 3 (July 1964), pp. 6–9; and Edgar A. Pessemier, "A New Way to Determine Buying Decisions," *Journal of Marketing*, Vol. 24, No. 2 (October 1959), pp. 41–46.

tunities. For such cases the pricing executive has little to guide him but *experience* and *intuition*.

Finally, for a product that has been available in the market for a long time, *statistical analysis* of past price-volume relationships may provide a way of estimating a demand schedule. By using regression analysis, a manager can analyze the relationship of past sales to price changes over time or cross-sectionally analyze sales and prices where regional differences in price exist at any point in time.[18] Such analyses can be useful in forecasting the effect of future price changes, particularly if the market for the product has not been significantly affected by varying extraneous influences. One serious limitation to the value of this approach is that price changes may have been too infrequent and too narrow to yield a range of volume response to price broad enough for planning purposes in the case of time series, and in the case of cross-sectional data regional price changes may lack enough variability to establish a meaningful demand schedule.[19] This method has been most successfully used for agricultural products.

VI. A Conceptual Framework

At this point one might say that the boundaries of the pricing problem have been staked out. The executive knows his various cost resistance points at one extreme and something about the product's value (or what the traffic will bear) at the other extreme. His job is to pick the right price in the gap between the

cost "floor" and the demand or value "ceiling." Unfortunately, there is no one right price since there are other factors which influence the price decision. This section discusses some of the more important influencing factors other than cost and value and integrates all of the factors into a simple conceptual framework.

Competition

Reaction of competitors is often the crucial consideration imposing practical limitations on pricing alternatives. Certainly, the sales volume attainable for one firm's products depends upon the prices of competitive products as well as upon its own price. By competitive products is meant substitute products, regardless of whether they are considered to be in the same "industry." The executive responsible for pricing must decide whether to price above, at the same level of, or below competition.

In addition to present competitors, potential competitors must be considered. Of relevance is the height and importance of the barriers to entry and competition— i.e., how easy and cheap it is to get into the business and compete effectively. Obviously, the more significant the barriers the more pricing freedom for an executive, and the higher up in the gap toward the value ceiling his price can be. Examples of barriers an executive can use to shelter himself from competition, in addition to the "natural" barrier caused by the amount of investment it takes to get into the business, are having a product distinctiveness, a brand prominence and a well-established channel of distribution which gives greater dealer strength. Each of these makes it that much harder for present and potential competitors to influence effectively the pricing decision.

---

[18] Statistical analysis can also be used to analyze experimental data. A good example is found in Milton H. Spencer and Louis Siegelman, *Managerial Economics: Decision Making and Forward Planning* (Homewood, Illinois: Richard D. Irwin, Inc., Rev. Ed., 1964), pp. 136–141.

[19] Alderson and Green, *op. cit.*, p. 248.

The Marketing Mix

If a firm is to achieve maximum success, there must be consistency among all its policies. Since price is but one element of the marketing mix, pricing decisions must be made in light of the intended policies for the other elements if a well-integrated and balanced marketing program is to be achieved. Thus, wherein the gap between cost and value a price should be is influenced by the overall marketing program. For example, a company's channel of distribution may be affected by its price decision:

. . . middlemen are parties directly affected by pricing decisions. The price that might maximize profits for the firm might cause huge losses in money and morale among the dealers and distributors. Computing the long-run costs under such circumstances frequently involves "guesstimating" in a type of political theory of games situation.[20]

The Law and Public Policy

In making a price decision, the executive cannot be unaware of certain public policy considerations. For one thing, price may have somewhat of an effect on the public relations of the firm. Too high a price at certain times may create consumer ill will to the extent that the long run growth of a firm is hampered.

Perhaps more important than public relations, however, is the influence of government antitrust regulation. For many companies, such regulation more

or less limits the gap between cost and value. Notable among business firms whose pricing is directly influenced by antitrust legislation are those involved in the electrical price-fixing conspiracy of a few years ago. The pricing alternatives available to the firms in the electrical equipment industry are severely limited.[21]

Dominant firms in an industry also have their pricing freedom restricted by federal government regulation. The major concern is the effect of pricing policies on market share. Any change in price by a large firm having the effect of increasing its market share may bring antitrust prosecution on the grounds of there being a tendency to monopolize the market. Whether such action will be taken by the government depends upon whether the greater market share exceeds some maximum tolerable level set by the regulatory agencies. A case in point is General Motors whose share of the automobile market generally fluctuates in the range of 50–55 percent. Any appreciable increase in their market share, say to 60 percent or more, will certainly be scrutinized by the federal government.

Other Influencing Factors

Competition, the marketing mix and public policy are not the only factors affecting where in the gap between cost and value the price might fall. They are perhaps the most important, but on occasion others exert a strong influence as is suggested by Oxenfeldt and Baxter:

There may be a wide space between the cost floor and the demand ceiling. In that case, bargaining skill rather

[20] Charles M. Hewitt, "Pricing—An Area of Increasing Importance." From *Marketing Management and Administrative Action* by Steuart Henderson Britt and Harper W. Boyd, Jr. (eds.), Copyright © 1963 by McGraw-Hill Book Company, p. 325.

[21] See J. Howard Westing and Jon G. Udell, "Pricing and the Antitrust Laws," *Michigan Business Review*, Vol. XIV, No. 5 (November 1962), pp. 6–11.

than economic factors may fix the position of a price, or the firm may gain by charging a low price, perhaps because this will mean many future sales. An omnibus formula can scarcely respond to situations of this type. Nor can it weigh the eagerness of particular customers or the merits of a particular product. Such factors strengthen the case for using individual decisions to modify the formula's figure for profit.[22]

Summing It Up

Figure 4 best summarizes what has been said. The value of a product to the last prospective customer fixes the ceiling while cost sets the floor. However, there are two cost floors—one set by direct or incremental costs and one set by full costs. In any price decision, the appropriate cost floor depends upon the objective involved. Between the cost floor and the appropriate value ceiling is a gap. Wherein this gap to set the price depends upon such factors as the nature and type of competition, the overall marketing program to be used and public policy considerations.

Although Figure 4 and the accompanying discussion present value as being greater than total cost this need not be the case. In fact, since the approach presented involves stratifying the market, there are certainly strata for which the value of the product is less than total cost and even strata for which value is less than direct or incremental cost. Where value lies relative to cost in any individual situation depends upon the market strata selected. However, unless a firm is in a distressed situation such as having an obsolete product it

[22] Alfred R. Oxenfeldt and William T. Baxter, "Approaches to Pricing: Economist vs. Accountant," *Business Horizons*, Vol. 4, No. 4 (Winter 1961), p. 89.

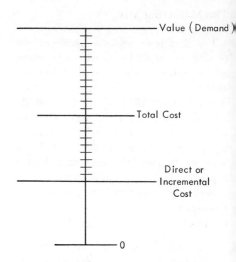

Figure 4. The anatomy of a price.

will not choose strata whose value is less than direct or incremental cost, while it may select strata that value the product at a level less than total cost—at least in the short run.

The conceptual framework presented here certainly is not the sole answer for the firm's pricing problems. It is, however, a useful guide for the executive having responsibility for pricing. Moreover, it should help to understand better the various objectives and strategies a firm might have in its pricing. This is important since the right price depends upon the objective the company has and the strategy it proposes to employ in reaching that objective. . . .

VII. Conclusion

This paper attempts to present a conceptual framework that will aid business executives in pricing their products. As a starting point the contribution made by economists is evaluated. Necessarily, such an evaluation has had to be somewhat superficial and arbitrary in that only the traditional theories of perfect and imperfect competition have been touched upon. Quite obviously, economists have advanced much farther than these simple theories. The justification for concentrating on these two theoretical formulations is that they are perhaps the most readily understood and are used as the basis of economic theory taught by universities. Thus, the young college graduate enters the business world equipped with such knowledge.

The questions raised concerning the economists' theory serve as the building blocks for formulating the conceptual framework. At no point are there any rigid rules or mechanical formulas presented. The conceptual framework presented tries to incorporate *all* the major factors having an influence on price, something that is not done by the economists' theory. The nature of these factors as well as the fact that they are important is suggested in the answer to the question of when does a price decision have to be made. In answering this question it is important to keep in mind that the decision does not necessarily have to involve a change in price

—it may also mean that no action is to be taken. Considering this, it is perhaps more accurate to restate the question in terms of when a review and evaluation of price has to be undertaken.

Quite obviously, this problem arises initially when a new product is to be introduced. In addition, the problem arises frequently in connection with one or more of the following situations:

1. Changing costs
2. Product changes
3. Changes in the actions of competitors
4. When government forces it either directly or indirectly
5. Changes in the nature of demand
6. Changes in general business conditions

There is no simple solution to a business manager's pricing problems and this paper is no exception. At best it contributes a point of view to guide a manager in this endeavor. However, it does raise certain relevant questions the pricing executive must answer for himself. Determining a price for a specific product is still an individual job. . . .

54

A Planned Approach to New Product Pricing

Stephen J. Welsh

The pricing of new products is a challenge to marketing management. Because of the great number and magnitude of uncertainties associated with new products, the pricing process is inevitably complex and difficult. The accompanying article describes one approach to the problem. This approach employs certain features of some of the accepted and widely used methods of pricing. The author states that his approach involves a logical order and rational sequence of actions to be taken by the pricing executive, but that this should not be considered a substitute for sound executive judgment.

Recently there has been much discussion about pricing and the various methods of pricing: cost-plus pricing, demand pricing, differential pricing, and even intuitive pricing. In this discussion of a planned approach to new product pricing, a portion of each of these various techniques is employed.

New products, for our present purposes, are those which represent a major innovation and which are new to the industry. This excludes products which are new only in the sense that a specific company has not manufactured them before. By this definition, the market for a new product is undefined at the outset; not all the potential applications are known; the market experience of directly competing products is not available; channels of distribution have yet to be chosen; appropriate markups are undetermined; and there will be an almost complete lack of cost experience. Moreover, potential customers are full of questions about a new product: Will it really work? For how long and with what reliability? How soon might major improvements be made? How might improvements affect the value of the purchase? Will prices come down substantially, and how soon?

Uncertainties like these can materially influence the price a customer might be willing to pay, and the amount of time, effort, and expense involved in selling them. Thus, there are many difficulties that are peculiar to new product pricing. On the other hand, there is an advantage: putting a price on a new product is a task that *cannot* be ducked.

Reprinted from *Pricing: The Critical Decision,* American Management Association Management Report No. 66, pp. 45–57, by special permission.

Too often, with established products, we manage to avoid a systematic review of our pricing problems and opportunities, rationalizing that, after all, we do have the product priced and that since the price has served us for some time, let's carry it on a little longer. A new product, obviously, does not permit us this luxury. It is price-less, and before we can go to the market, we must put a price on it—for better or worse, wisely and deliberately, or by cut and try.

Preliminary Considerations

The pricing job should start very early, ideally when the product is in the concept stage. If someone hands us a prototype and says, "Here, put a price on it," it's already too late, for much of our money has already been spent. The price determines the return on investment, and the estimated return should determine our decision to invest in development. So price planning, logically, should be done at the very beginning.

The reasons for bringing out a new product should be clearly in mind before we attempt to price it. It is easy to jump to the conclusion that our objective is to maximize profit. Although this is an important element in any pricing situation, a company may have other objectives. They may include the following:

1. To load a manufacturing facility more fully or eliminate or reduce a seasonal load problem. The manufacturer of TV antennas may decide to introduce a novel item of tubular lawn furniture.
2. To broaden the line and thereby employ more fully a selling or distribu-

tion facility or asset. This is common practice in the food field: a truck that delivers bread and cake might as well deliver a line of cookies.

3. To use the new product as an entree into new industries for other, broader lines. A manufacturer of conveyors may develop a better rock-crusher primarily as a way of getting into the construction market.

4. To complete a line in order to remove a competitive disadvantage represented by present gaps.

5. To provide a vehicle for the sale of complementary products.

In some of these situations, a price structure designed to maximize profit could work against the accomplishment of the company's real objectives. Hence, price structure or policy must be clearly related to over-all marketing objectives and strategies.

Steps in New Product Pricing

Assuming that this relationship has been defined, we are ready to approach our new-product pricing decision. Let us assume that our primary objective is the achievement of maximum profit for a single product or line. This goal is suggested not necessarily because it is the most frequently encountered but because it involves us in the full range of complexities that are present in most new-product pricing problems.

The approach involves seven steps; these steps are designed to develop, in logical sequence, the answers to three key questions:

1. How much will how many customers be willing to pay for how much of the product—in other words, how would our sales volume vary as a function of our price?

2. What is the least we can profitably charge—that is, what does our cost picture look like at various levels of output?

3. What risks are involved? More specifically, what threats should we anticipate from our competitors, and what might they be able to do to us and when?

Perhaps one day our operations researchers and computer people will develop formulas which will take all of these factors precisely into account and come up with a single "best answer." But for the present, all we can hope to do is to secure as much information as we can which will guide us in formulating sound human judgments.

Step 1: Approximate the Impact of Price on the Volume We Might Expect to Achieve. We know that there is a relationship between the price we set on our product and the volume we might hope to achieve with it. The economist tells us that a typical price-volume relationship theoretically looks like the diagram in Exhibit 1. At a high price, only a small volume is likely. As price declines, volume can be expected to increase—probably to a point of market saturation, beyond which there will be no additional volume. Although this is a highly theoretical representation of the relationship, it can be a useful starting point for our thinking, since, by definition, our new product, at least for a time, permits us to enjoy the monopolistic position the economist had in mind.

Getting practical mileage out of this concept depends on the fact that any new product, however novel it may be, does have alternative or indirectly competitive products. This fact introduces a few variations into the original demand curve, at or near price levels of these alternative products, as is shown in Exhibit 2. These alternatives are key elements in our thinking, because what

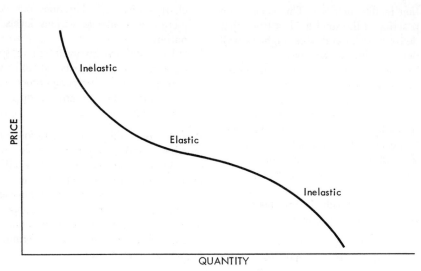

Exhibit 1. Single-stage demand curve.

a customer will pay us for a new product necessarily reflects the price-performance package which we offer him as compared with that of competing products.

For our new product and for each competing product, there are two primary factors determining relative attractiveness to potential customers: performance and price. We can develop reasonably accurate information on our performance, competitor performance, and competitor price, and this will enable us to reason in at least approximate terms about the remaining unknown—namely, the price of our new product. We go about this by taking the following substeps:

1. What is our product? Our product must be defined—not in terms of its construction, chemical formulation, or any similar physical description but rather in terms of what it will do—that is, its performance characteristics: how durable is it? how beautiful? how convenient? how efficient?

2. What are the applications for our new product? Obviously, the advantages or disadvantages of our product in comparison with alternative products depend upon the use to which it will be put. A new fabric, for example, which will pass water vapor but shed water droplets is one thing in rainwear applications, another in battery separators, something else in bandages or surgical dressings, and still another when used as a filtering medium. The performance requirements differ in major ways, and the products with which our new product will be competing for use will vary from one of these application areas to the next.

3. What are the alternatives? We don't have to consider each one, but it is important to spot the principal ones from which we can expect competition in each of our use areas.

4. In each of these applications, what are the customer's performance requirements, and what is their relative importance? In other words, what are the major product characteristics which appear likely to govern the selection of product to be used.

5. What are the prices of the alternatives, and how well do they fulfill the

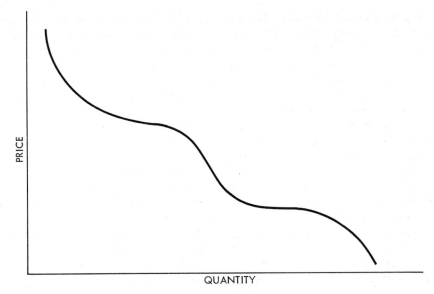

Exhibit 2. Two-stage demand curve.

product requirements of customers? With some few exceptions, reliable price information on these products is easy to come by. On product performance, extensive field research with users is often necessary to give us the answers we need.

6. How does our product perform in comparison with these alternative products? Here, comparative engineering tests and the whole range of product testing techniques can come into play.

7. On the basis of this information, what would seem to be the "threshold" price for our product? Let's define threshold price as that price which appears likely to secure for our product real consideration on the part of the consumer. It involves the premium a customer would be willing to pay for the performance characteristics of our product compared to those of the alternative products.

Exhibit 3 is a threshold price chart for a real industrial product which we have studied and which we can call

"supersynthetic resin." The chart summarizes a good deal of the information developed in the preceding steps. For each of two applications, it shows present price levels of two alternative materials and a judgment on maximum threshold price for supersynthetic resin in the markets represented by these two uses. In one application, supersynthetic is clearly inferior to both alternatives, and the magnitude of the inferiority finds expression in the distance between the two lines representing the alternatives and the line representing supersynthetic.

By this time in our analysis, the chances are that we have conducted many comparative engineering tests and have done appropriate product testing in the field. We may have used a mass of detailed data from salesmen. Perhaps we have even done some test marketing at several prices. In essence, we have been applying to our product, in advance, the kinds of appraisals involved in value analysis, to borrow a notion from the purchasing field.

Step 2: Appraise Marketing Requirements and Broadly Define Marketing Plan. We now should have some idea of the size of the market which might exist for us at several price levels. We have no idea, however, of the timing required to penetrate this market. This element of timing is most important—first, because we must later consider the impact of competition upon our pricing strategy, and, second, because the rate at which we develop sales volume could materially influence our costs.

To some extent, the rate at which we can penetrate a market depends on the characteristics of the product and its market. For example, if our product requires a long period of testing by customers, our rate of developing significant commercial volume would be relatively slow. Similarly, seasonal variations of our proposed market might have a bearing on the matter.

Let's assume that our new product is a novel business machine, an improved collator based on a new principle and having substantially superior operating characteristics. First of all, we must recognize that, besides the engineering of the product itself, there are a number of other features to be decided. These include such matters as service contracts, guarantees, and whether the collator should be sold or leased.

Next, obviously, we must decide which segment of the market (the various application segments of the total market as well as the geographic segments) to approach first and what sequence these segments should follow. We must determine those who have the principal influence in purchases of equipment of this kind—systems people, purchasing people, engineering personnel, management personnel—and the message we should use to reach them.

With this kind of information in hand, we are prepared to start thinking about appropriate channels of distribution and to appraise the kinds of activity required to establish this distribution. Simultaneously, we will be making our judgments on the role and relative importance of advertising, promotional

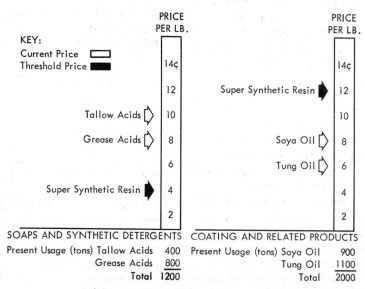

Exhibit 3. Threshold price comparison.

activities, publicity, field sales, participation in trade shows and conventions, and other means to be used in introducing the product into the market.

Outlining the marketing plan will give us some insight into the selling costs and expenses, which will become important to us later as a significant cost factor, and it will also provide a basis for judgment regarding the rate at which we might expect to penetrate the market under this plan.

Step 3: Plot Growth Curves at Several Selected Price Levels. When we have pulled together our tentative marketing plan, including its timing, we are then ready to prepare a chart like the one in Exhibit 4. Since we have now introduced the time element, this chart shows several growth curves, one for each price level, summarizing our judgments concerning the rate at which we might be able to develop sales volume at these different prices. These growth curves assume (1) execution of the tentatively established marketing plan; and (2) continuation of present competitive conditions. More specifically, they assume that in the future, as at present, we will

have no directly competing products, and that there will be no changes in competing products, their performance specifications, or their prices.

Step 4: Approximate Cost Data. There is some evidence that the importance of cost has been overdone in many pricing situations. Many companies still use price formulas based almost entirely on cost considerations. Although cost certainly is an important factor in new product pricing, a better balanced viewpoint recognizes that cost is principally significant in determining whether the new product is economically feasible and whether it should be introduced at all. It is important in developing a price floor, in other words. However, since cost obviously has an important bearing on pricing, we are now ready to draw some judgments on unit costs.

Development of approximations of unit manufacturing cost is a relatively simple job, if we have estimates of sales volume and rate and if no undue precision is required at the time. The manufacturing costs of direct labor, materials and supplies, purchased components, equipment required, and over-

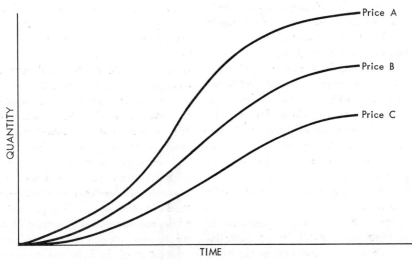

Exhibit 4. Projected product sales patterns.

head can be developed in approximate terms on the basis of the predicted volume levels. The basis for estimating the elements of sales and administrative expense is provided in the action program in those areas which have already been broadly defined.

Exhibit 5 shows the kind of chart that can be prepared from the foregoing information. It represents our unit costs plotted against time. Although the basic data would necessarily be developed in terms of volume, we have already developed approximations of volume against time, and consequently this form of presentation can be readily prepared. Emphasizing the time factor is important, since we must now appraise competitive capabilities, and time is an essential factor.

Step 5: Appraise Capabilities of Competitors, Including Timing. In the previous step, we were proceeding on the assumption that there would be no change in the competitive environment, but we know that this is not true. Sooner or later competitors will be attracted to our market, and there is always the possibility that additional alternative products or materials may be developed or that changes may be made in the offerings or price of currently available alternative materials.

But in trying to evaluate these threat or risk factors, how can we tell what course future events will take? While we cannot tell with certainty, there are some things we can do to forecast the impact of future competition. As in the military world, to try to appraise our rival's intentions is a philosophical pursuit of dubious value. But we can appraise his capabilities—usually with fair accuracy.

There are two key questions in appraising the capabilities of potential competitors: (1) what will he do to us

and how long will it take him to do it? and (2) how effectively and at what cost does it appear likely he can do it? In this step, we are looking primarily for an answer to the first of these questions—the timing on which we might anticipate competition. In the step to follow, we will turn our attention to the relative advantages or disadvantages that competitors may have in our market and the costs at which they might be able to operate.

In trying to estimate the timing with which competitive forces may come into play, a useful place to start is with the "requirements" for successful operation in the business. If our competitor is to operate successfully in the market, he must meet the same requirements as we do. Consequently, we must now take each major functional area (research and development, manufacturing, and sales) and form some judgments about the amount of time he might need to spend in each in order to enter and operate in our market.

In the research and development area, we can readily evaluate the patent situation, which may provide some clue regarding the probable timing or conditions of direct competition. Further, through a realistic appraisal of the magnitude of the technological innovation which we have made and perhaps with some insight into the direction our competitor's research is taking, we can arrive at a reasonably good estimate of the amount of time he should require to duplicate our accomplishment. Another pertinent point in this research-and-development appraisal is the amount of opportunity for additional product research and development which remains to us. In other words, is it possible that, while our competitor is getting to where we are now, we can proceed with further exploration of the field and consequently

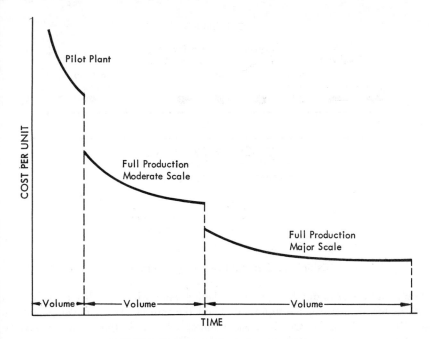

Exhibit 5. Our projected cost patterns.

stay a jump or more ahead of him? Similarly, we can appraise his capabilities to meet the manufacturing and sales requirements of the operation. An interesting question in the sales area is the extent to which we might have been able, by virtue of being first, to sew up key distribution agencies or facilities.

As the result of such analysis, it is possible to prepare a chart like the one in Exhibit 6. Such an analysis of competitive capabilities needs to be made as objectively as possible. We should be careful not to overestimate the amount of time it would take our competitors to match us. On the other hand, it is important not to sell short the accomplishment made by our own technical or manufacturing people.

Step 6: Estimate Competitors' Costs. The purpose of this step is to obtain some estimates of the unit costs our competitors might incur, for comparison with our own. While it may seem difficult enough to try to forecast our own unit costs over a period of time without taking on the almost impossible problem of computing our competitors' costs, we are not seeking great precision in these estimates. Our principal need is to evaluate the major differences between their costs and our costs in meeting the requirements for successful operation in this busines. If, for example, it appears likely that a competitor can copy or otherwise match our performance without duplicating the extensive research and development we have put into it, this is certainly an important plus for him. If his manufacturing equipment will permit him to manufacture much more economically than we can and perhaps with a lesser additional investment, this also becomes a significant consideration. Or if either of us has major advantages in distribution or marketing organization or marketing contacts which would be extremely time

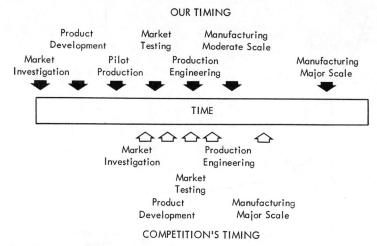

Exhibit 6. Competitive timing program.

consuming and costly to duplicate, these, too, are factors which can be appraised in broad but useful terms. On the basis of judgments (or speculation, if you will) of this kind, it is possible to prepare a chart something like the one in Exhibit 7.

Step 7: Decide on the Price. By this time, we have surrounded ourselves with a good deal of information, even if it is only approximate, that should be helpful to us in answering the three key questions with which we started, and we are prepared for Step 7, which is to make some price decisions. Here, as always, we have some choices to make:

1. We can decide between a skimming strategy or a penetration strategy .
2. We can decide to get as much profit as we can as soon as we can or, if our estimate of the competitive situation gives us enough time, we can attempt to maximize our profit with a somewhat lower price schedule.
3. We can establish a price that will discourage competitors and yet not discourage ourselves.

Some of the bases for our decision have been assumed. For example, in Step 2 we tentatively established a mar-

keting plan which predicted both costs and the rate of market development we might achieve. At this point it would be desirable to review the plan and its indicated results and, if necessary, devise several alternative plans leading to different costs and rates of penetration, so that profitability of the various plans may be compared.

This kind of analysis should be continued during the introductory stage of the product's life. As additional information accumulates, it can be plotted in the same way as a means of reviewing the correctness of your pricing strategy on a continuing basis.

Pricing Guideposts

The following suggestions may help summarize the points we have been discussing:

1. Begin your pricing analyses early in the product-development process. Ideally, price thinking should begin before any money is invested, and preferably as soon as the product idea is conceived as possible.
2. Consider cost, certainly, but as a limit

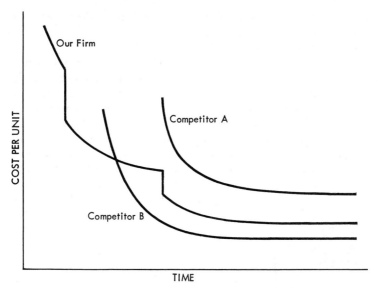

COST PER UNIT

Our Firm

Competitor A

Competitor B

TIME

Exhibit 7. Our projected costs vs. those of competitors.

or floor on price. In itself, cost is not a sound basis for determining price.

3. Do not try to be precise at this point. Only those differences that are substantial should be considered. To be successful, this approach should be applied in a series of successive approximations. In this way, obvious disqualifiers come to the fore quickly, before a great deal of time and effort has been expended.

4. Take a broad view of pricing. Since there is no facet of the business which is not reflected in the pricing process, representatives of all functions must participate in the program.

5. Get, and maintain on a continuing basis, detailed information about competitive products, prices, markets, and strategies. The sales organization is a good source of information of this kind, and it is all too often overlooked in a company's over-all planning for new product development and introduction. The intelligence function of many companies is very weak.

6. Don't try to avoid using your judgment. The pricing procedure de-scribed requires judgment, but it has the advantage of requiring a number of small judgments, thereby reducing the number of broad jumps involved in the process.

7. Get your product-line policies and plans in order. Most pricing binds grow out of unsound or poorly policed product-line policies or faulty business objectives. A lack of such policies and objectives is behind most situations in which there is a failure to set a price which will yield an adequate profit before competitors get under way.

The approach suggested in this paper is difficult, complex, and time consuming. But the problem is a crucial one, and we should be willing to devote to it an effort which is commensurate with the magnitude of the individual project. Another approach is to guess. We all like to guess with a few dollars, but guessing wrong with hundreds of thousands of millions of dollars is another matter. The cost of not performing this task in a rational, comprehensive manner is very high indeed and probably explains in part the magnitude of the statistics we have all seen about the proportion of failures in new product ventures.

The complexity of the problem and the scope and difficulty of handling all of the manifold considerations makes a persuasive argument for limiting new product development to projects of substantial significance. The effort required to evaluate a product or establish a sound pricing policy for a $20 million product line does not substantially exceed the scope of work required for a $50,000 line.

The seven steps outlined above are not a method but an approach involving a logical order and rational sequence for considering a wide range of highly important factors. They cannot substitute for executive judgment but can furnish those making the judgments with the kinds of materials they need for soundly based decisions on new product pricing.

55

An Operational Approach to Product Pricing

Bill R. Darden

Pricing has always been a highly subjective and an inexact technique. Businessmen have relied upon the marketplace to bring about any corrections that might be necessary. Undoubtedly there has been an overreliance upon the adjustments that would be achieved through the market mechanism. The market may force a lowering of a price that has been set at an unduly high level, but it will not raise a price that has been set too low—at least, not in the short run. The following paper is aimed at improving the pricing process by suggesting an operational approach to the subject that provides a formal vehicle to quantify the pricing hypotheses of businessmen.

The best brains in the business and academic worlds labor to provide the product pricer with a repertoire of sophisticated techniques and approaches, and he continues pricing products in his

Reprinted from the *Journal of Marketing*, national quarterly publication of the American Marketing Association, Vol. 32, No. 2, April 1968, pp. 29–33.

usual manner. While the economist expounds use of concepts of demand and marginal analysis, the pricer uses experience, intuition, and cost-plus. While the statistician calls for probability and payoff tables, the pricer uses experience, intuition, and cost plus. While the professional expounds the use of price elasticity and cross-elasticity concepts, the pricer again uses experience, intuition and cost-plus.

Obstacles to Optimal Product Pricing

Why does the pricer persist in this "irrational" behavior? This question seems to evoke answers from academicians and professionals that are as "irrational" as the pricer's behavior. Actually, the answers are simpler than presupposed and are all in the form of obstacles to "optimal" pricing. Some of these obstacles are:

1. The pricer does not have the time, nor the interest, to read and digest the latest literature on pricing, even if it were directly applicable in practice, which it is not.
2. In many cases the objectives of the pricer may be quite different from the objectives assumed in the literature for arriving at optimal guides to action.
3. The typical pricer usually has many product lines, and in each product line he may have many products. Thus, the time that he may allot to pricing each product may be very small.
4. Also, while the pricer recognizes that many products are substitutes or complementary to each other, he has no way to quantify or measure these effects properly.
5. The product pricer also has problems in determining competitor reactions to price strategies. The direction and degree of *price* reactions is a prime trouble area.
6. Again, the pricer does not have the methods, time, or money to measure demand curves or other consumer response curves properly. From experience, intuition, and judgment he must make hypotheses about future

decision relationships. Future positive feedback increases the belief in these hypotheses, while negative feedback decreases the belief in these hypotheses. With negative feedback, the pricer begins to investigate his "key" hypotheses, sequentially, and these may be revised.

The above "obstacles" do not begin to show the difficulties of the "complete" pricer. The "complete" pricer must deal with all the myriad combinations of price, advertising, sales promotion, personal selling, place, and product. Heuristically, he must hypothesize about the degree to which competitors will react to his price change and in what form this reaction will occur. The product pricer must "guess"—on the basis of his present hypotheses—what blend of marketing decisions will go best with a given price, and he must in turn determine what effect the given price will have on the sales of other products in the product line (both in the short run and in the long run). To continue with the latter thought, the product pricer must coordinate pricing policy with channel decisions, product decisions, and promotion decisions. *This coordination must take place through time*, not only at a point in time (as economic analysis often assumes).

It is not surprising, then, that the product pricer cannot predict the quantity demanded for a given price during a given period. However, it is probable that the product pricer does use an implicit, informal method of determining a sales volume range for a given price. Thus, it is believed that most product pricers *do* consider more than cost and turnover in pricing. It is hypothesized in this paper that many pricers use experience and intuition to arrive operationally at hypotheses which serve as a basis for price making. The purpose of this paper, then, is to for-

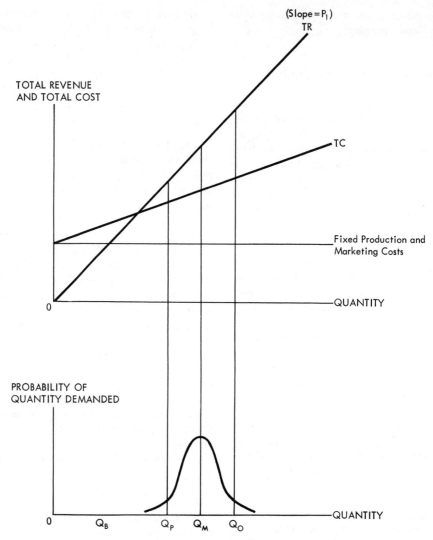

Figure 1. At a given price (P₁), the use of three volume estimates to fit a beta probability distribution.

malize, heuristically, an operational approach to pricing, given the beliefs of the pricer.

Profit Variance and Price Limits

The central concept of the proposed pricing approach is exemplified in Figure 1. Assuming some given price, P_1,

the breakeven chart in Figure 1 can be easily produced. The typical marketing executive will determine the most likely quantity demanded at P_1—in this case, Q_M. Now the marketing student determines the most likely profit at Q_M, as well as the breakeven quantity, Q_B. This approach is likely to be repeated for several prices, yielding respective profit and breakeven quantities for each price. Actually, the marketer is using repetitive breakeven analysis to feel out demand.

In addition, the marketer may determine optimal advertising and sales promotion for each price, which in turn also affects the profit and breakeven quantities received for each price. It is also recognized that the final most likely price is that which reflects judgments about competitive reactions.

Now the price investigator can estimate for a given price a pessimistic quantity demanded and an optimistic quantity demanded. These estimates are Q_P and Q_O, respectively, for price P_1 in Figure 1. Thus the pricing specialist has three sales volume estimates at a given price, P_1: a most likely estimate (Q_M), a pessimistic estimate (Q_P), and an optimistic estimate (Q_O).

Rationale and Uses of Quantity Estimates

In the Program Evaluation and Review Technique, commonly called PERT, the planner is faced with the problem of estimating times required for accomplishing particular activities. In order to draw upon the judgment and experience of the superintendent or foreman in charge of completing the activity, and at the same time eliminate bias, the planner asks for three time estimates. These time estimates include an optimistic estimate, a pessimistic estimate, and a most likely estimate. In the cases of optimistic and pessimistic estimations, the planner counsels the estimator to choose times that have a chance of 1 in 100 of occurring. The rationale behind this counsel is that such estimates can be used to approximately fit a beta probability density function to the time occurrence of the given activity.

The same rationale lies behind the estimations of Q_P, Q_M, and Q_O at P_1 in Figure 1. The marketer is unsure what future volume will be generated by the projected marketing mix (including, of course, the price, P_1). For example, the degrees to which competitors may react, the change in marketing environment, and changes in company implementation effectiveness are all subject to varying degrees of change. However, using the three quantity estimates and assuming a beta probability distribution, the price-maker can determine a sales volume which stands a 50–50 chance of occurring. This volume will be called "largest expected volume" and is denoted by Q_E. Borrowing from PERT network analysis, the following formula yields an approximation of Q_E, using the three quantity estimates:

$$1. \quad Q_E = \frac{Q_P + 4Q_M + Q_O}{6}$$

An important characteristic of this approach is the flexibiilty of the beta distribution. It allows the volume estimator to make the extreme volume estimates asymetrical around the most likely volume, if he so chooses. Thus, the probability distribution fitted to the volume estimates may be positively skewed, negatively skewed, or symetrically distributed.

Variance of Sales Volume

In addition to yielding the "largest expected volume" for a given price, this "operational approach" produces a good estimate of the volume variance. Using again the volume estimates at P_1, the marketer can compute this approximate variance with Equation 2 shown below:

$$2. \quad \sigma^2 = \frac{(Q_O - Q_P)^2}{36}$$

Price Range and the "Operational Approach"

The major strength of the "operational approach" lies in its ability to draw on the experience and judgment of marketing specialists in the firm. The knowledge in regard to competitor reactions, market changes, consumer behavior, and company implementation effectiveness should to a great degree be reflected in the estimates of volume at a given price. Using a repetitive approach, the same analysis can be made for several prices.

Specifically, the pricer wishes to determine some upper and lower limits for prices that must be investigated. Figure 2 shows a special type of demand curve (or curves). This demand curve actually represents three demand curves: the first (D_O) indicates optimistic quantity estimates at various prices; the second (D_M) shows most likely sales volume at all prices; and the third (D_P) shows pessimistic estimates. These three curves generate three total revenue curves in Figure 2: the optimistic revenue curve, the most likely revenue curve, and the pessimistic revenue curve.

The marketer begins at a high price level, decreasing the price until at a given price (in this case P_1) the pessimistic quantity estimate generates only enough revenue to just break even (BEP_1). At a higher price P_{1+}, the volume Q_{P1-} will not cover costs and a lower price P_{1-} the volume Q_{P1+} will generate profits. The price (P_1) which accompanies Q_{P1} becomes the upper price limit, ensuring the firm that it will do better than break even over 99% of the time at this price.

In order to establish a lower price limit, in Figure 2, the marketer lowers the price past P_1 until a price is reached which allows the pessimistic revenue curve to break even again (BEP_2). At P_2, such a situation occurs and this price,

again, will generate profits 99% of the time.

The marketer has now "bracketed" the feasible prices available to him. This price range may be so small that the respective quantity estimates of the two extreme prices may overlap; however, this seems unlikely in most cases.

The price range determined above provides a very conservative price zone for analysis. Actually, there are other criteria which provide a wider range of prices for investigation. For example, the product pricer could determine the upper and lower price limits on the basis of the largest expected quantity estimates. The probability of breaking even using this criterion (at either price limit) drops from .99 to .50. Another criterion, the most likely quantity estimate, provides a compromise, most likely guide, and, depending upon the individual industry and market, may prove the most feasible criterion for most firms.

After the upper price limit $(P_1 = P_U)$ and the lower price limit $(P_2 = P_L)$ have been determined, the firm may wish to find the largest expected quantities and the quantity variances at each price limit. From this information, the largest expected profit can be determined at both P_U and P_L as shown below.

$$Q_{E1} = \frac{Q_{P1} + 4\, Q_{M1} + Q_{O1}}{6}$$

Expected Profit $= PR_E = Q_{E1}\,(P_U) -$ TFC $- (V)Q_{E1}$
Where V = Average Variable Cost
TFC = Total Fixed Cost

Now the same information can be determined at the lower end of the price bracket.

Implications for Pricing Strategy

The "operational approach" provides the product pricer with a formal vehicle

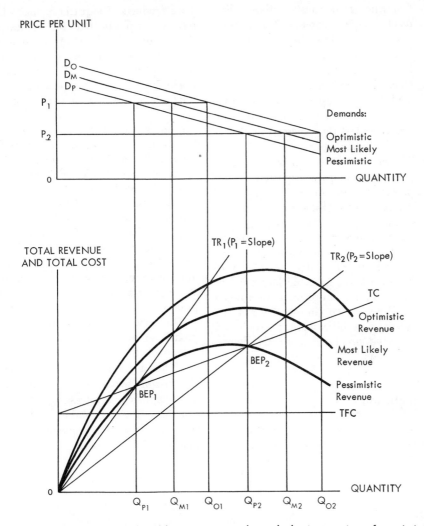

Figure 2. Determination of feasible price range through the interaction of pessimistic, most likely, and optimistic demands with cost curves.

to summarize and integrate his various hypotheses into a clear picture of economical alternatives. Some considerations for the pricer are:

1. The quantity estimates for the upper price limit and the lower price limit may overlap. For example, the upper limit may have an optimistic quantity estimate of 500,000 units, while the lower price limit may have a pessi-

mistic quantity estimate of 499,000.

2. While Figure 2 assumes that costs remain constant in determining the upper and lower price limits, this assumption is not necessary. Thus, the pricer can change marketing blends to optimize some given objective at each price without changing the usefulness of the operational approach.

3. The use of three quantity estimates for a given price *does not* require

that pricing specialists within a firm reach complete agreement as to forecasted sales. Thus, the difficult problem of "consensus" in pricing is largely overcome.

4. Once the product pricer has "bracketed in" the upper and lower price limits, he can use a sequential approach to test the expected profitability of intermediate prices.

5. The product pricer can not only compute and compare expected largest profits, but he can also compute and compare quantity and profit variances at various prices. There is no guarantee that quantity variances will be similar at different prices; therefore, a product pricer may be willing to accept a lower expected largest profit at some price in exchange for a much smaller variance (in other words, the pricer may be willing to trade off expected profit for a greater degree of certainty).

Conclusion

In general, the product pricer must use experience, intuition, and cost to price products. The pricer cannot wholly rely on sophisticated techniques and theory for optimal pricing of products. If it can be accepted that product pricers must rely on "operational" techniques for pricing then it would appear that one of the principal tasks of the marketing academician is the exploration of these approaches. Thus, major contributions can be made to marketing by providing marketing management with operational approaches which allow the executive to efficiently use his hypotheses about the decision situation. Bayesian decision theory is one move in this direction; however, the complexity of its methodology, as well as the problem of determining subjective probabilities for the various alternative outcomes of a given price strategy, prohibit its use by most product pricers.

This paper presents an operational approach to pricing that takes into consideration the above complexities and provides a formal vehicle to quantify the pricing hypotheses of businessmen. The approach involves no change in thinking. However, the methodology does allow use of a sequential approach and probability theory.

56

When Is Price
Reduction Profitable?

Clare E. Griffin

Many business firms, particularly those in oligopolistic industries facing a decline in consumer demand for their products, have been criticized for failing to reduce prices. The critics assert that lowering prices would lead to increased demand and greater profits for the companies in question, because the demand for their products is elastic with respect to price. Although lower prices would undoubtedly generate increased revenue, whether profits are increased depends upon the cost structure, particularly the relationship between fixed and variable costs.

The accompanying article analyzes the feasibility of a price reduction for a firm operating under the conditions mentioned above. The author contends that when costs are taken into account, a very high price elasticity of demand would have to exist in most manufacturing industries to warrant reducing prices, at least in the short run.

How often have we heard, at Congressional hearings or other public meetings, criticism of businessmen for failing to reduce prices, especially in the face of declining demand. This criticism is directed in particular at large firms operating under conditions of oligopoly (i.e., where a few large concerns share most of the market). A specific target for this criticism has been the automobile industry. For example:

Walter Reuther proposed, about two years ago, that the automobile manufacturers should reduce prices by $100. This, he argued, would be good for the

country and would actually be profitable to the companies.[1]

John Blair, at one time chief economist to the Kefauver Committee on Antitrust and Monopoly, has taken the position that if automobile producers fully recognized the elasticity of demand, they would be more likely to reduce prices in their own interest. Blair quoted with approval Sir Denis Robertson as saying that in his experience businessmen almost invariably regard the demand for their industry's product as extremely inelastic.[2]

[1] *Hearings before the Senate Subcommittee on Antitrust and Monopoly*, 85th Congress, Second Session (Washington, Government Printing Office, 1958), p. 2225.

[2] *American Economic Review*, papers and

Abridged from *Harvard Business Review*, September–October 1960, Vol. 38, No. 5, pp. 125 ff., by special permission.

How much truth is there in such assertions? That is what I would like to examine in this article. Specifically, I shall discuss, from the point of view of business policy, the feasibility of price reduction as a means of stimulating sales in the short run. Even more specifically, I want to question the feasibility of price reduction for maintaining profits or reducing losses in an oligopolistic industry in the face of a real or threatened general decline in consumer purchases of the product in question.

Exaggerated Elasticity

It is difficult to know whether businessmen do, in fact, underestimate the degree to which sales volume will increase as a result of reduced prices. But it is true, in any event, that business critics do exaggerate the effects that price elasticity of demand has or should have on price reduction. The chief reason for this is a relative neglect of the cost side of the problem.

In an industry where there are few producers of products that consumers regard as closely comparable, a price reduction by one important producer will almost necessarily be met by the others. Whether, under these circumstances, a price reduction would maintain or increase profits depends on two questions:

1. What will be the effect of the price reduction on demand and thus on revenues? (This is the problem of demand elasticity.)
2. What effect will this change in volume have on costs? (This is the problem of cost elasticity.)

Naturally, both questions must be considered by a manufacturer in determin-

proceedings of December 1958 meeting of the American Economics Association, May 1959, p. 444.

ing whether a price reduction will be in his own interest.

I would argue that in most manufacturing industries the elasticity of demand would have to be very high indeed to lead producers into price reductions. Further, in most cases where manufacturers refrain from reducing a price when they know the reduction will be matched by competitors, this decision does not imply a general tendency to underestimate the elasticity of demand.

Of course, when I refer to price elasticity, I mean the relation of demand to price in a moderate range around existing prices—say a 10% price change up or down from the existing market price. Similarly, when I discuss the ratio of fixed to variable costs subsequently, I refer to production within a restricted range around the usual percentage of theoretical capacity. No practical purpose is served by departing unrealistically from reasonable price changes and from usual capacity percentages.

Increasing Revenue

Let us consider in some detail the automobile industry which, in many ways, is fairly representative of American heavy industry. It will be illuminating if we work out the implications of the studies of demand mentioned by John Blair, which indicate a price elasticity for new automobiles ranging from 1.2 to 1.5. These studies seem to imply that this would justify a price reduction. What the 1.5 figure means, for example, is that the increased demand will be one and one-half times as great as the decreased price, or that a 1.0% decrease in price would produce a 1.5% increase in demand. (Strictly speaking, the coefficient is a minus quantity, for the quantity bought varies inversely with price. However, it seems easier to neglect minus signs, and this fairly common practice will be followed here.)

This particular estimate for automobiles represents the limit that has been mentioned by independent researchers; the usual estimate is substantially less than this. Various studies have been made, and they are summarized in the report of hearings before the Kefauver Committee. During these sessions various experts offered estimates of the coefficient of price elasticity of demand for automobiles which ranged from a low of 0.6 to a high of 1.5.[3]

Let us accept for the moment the largest of these figures as an indication of the reaction of demand to a price change and ask whether it would be profitable for an automobile manufacturer to reduce the list price of a line of cars by, say, $100. Assuming that the average price of the line is $2,500, let us place the anticipated sales volume at this price at 1,000,000 cars. We will also assume that a price reduction by one producer will be met by others, so that we are not considering a relative price advantage but the effect of a general price change. How will volume and revenue be affected? Consider this:

A price reduction from $2,500 to $2,400 is 4%. With a demand elasticity of 1.5 this would indicate a resulting increase in sales of 6% (i.e., 1.5 x 4%). So volume would be increased from 1,000,-000 to 1,060,000 cars, and sales and revenue would be affected as follows:

At price of $2,500,
1,000,000 cars × $2,500 =
$2,500,000,000
At price of $2,400,
1,060,000 cars × $2,400 =
$2,544,000,000

Thus, we would have increased rev-

enue by $44,000,000. This is where much popular reasoning, as well as that of some economists, ends. The conclusion is hastily drawn that if the manufacturer really recognized the degree of elasticity, of if he were not overly cautious or just plain stupid, he would seize this opportunity to increase revenue.

The Key Is Costs

Of course, revenue alone is not the objective; rather the maintenance of profit is the ultimate goal, and to estimate this we must consider costs as well. This is the point often overlooked by those who criticize business, especially the mass-production industries. Overestimating the role of increased volume in reducing unit costs, they forget that the true effect on total costs of producing the additional 60,000 cars will depend on the ratio of fixed costs to variable costs.

What is a reasonable estimate of the ratio between fixed and variable costs in heavy industries? Here are some good approximations:

In the automobile industry, my own interviews indicate that the ratio would be on the order of 15% to 20% for fixed costs and 80% to 85% for variable.

For the United States Steel Corporation (when operating at 80% of capacity), the ratio has been estimated at 18.5% for fixed, 81.5% for variable.[4]

In the production of pig aluminum, the ratio has been placed at 15% for fixed and 85% for variable.[5]

In order to consider what happens to

[3] *Hearings before the Senate Subcommittee on Antitrust and Monopoly,* 85th Congress, Second Session pursuant to S. Res. 57 and S. Res. 231, p. 3215.

[4] Study by Theodore O. Yntema included in *Hearings before the Temporary National Economic Committee,* Part 26, p. 14058.

[5] Nathanael H. Engle, *Aluminum, An Industrial Marketing Appraisal* (Homewood, Illinois, Richard D. Irwin, Inc., 1944), p. 208.

cost in our illustrative case, let us accept, for purposes of our anaylsis, a fixed-variable cost ratio of 20 to 80, thus taking again the upper limit of the estimated range which would be most favorable to the price reduction proposal.

We assumed as our starting point a price of $2,500 and a volume of 1,000,-000, thus yielding a revenue of $2,500,-000,000. Now if we assume that unit costs are $2,300, there is a total cost of $2,300,000,000 and a profit of $200,000,-000. If the 20 to 80 ratio of fixed to variable costs exists, this total cost then breaks down to fixed costs of $460,-000,000 (20% of $2,300,000,000) and variable costs of $1,840,000,000 (80% of $2,300,000,000), or $1,840 per car.

If we reduce the price to $2,400, revenue will, as indicated before, become $2,544,000,000, but the number of cars produced and sold is increased from 1,000,000 to 1,060,000. Costs will become:

Fixed cost	$ 460,000,000
Variable ($1,840 × 1,060,000)	1,950,400,000
	$2,410,400,000

Profits can be determined thus:

Revenue	$2,544,000,000
Costs	2,410,400,000
Profit	$ 133,600,000

Thus, while the price reduction produced an increase in revenue of $44,-000,000 (from $2,500,000,000 to $2,544,000,000), it reduced profits by $66,400,-000 (from $200,000,000 to $133,600,-000). Expressed in unit terms, the price reduction led to reduced revenue per car of $100, and to reduced cost per car of only $26.42. Cost at the larger volume, therefore, would be $2,273.58 instead of $2,300 at the old volume. Obviously, *the additional cars are not free goods,* and anyone who makes recommendations as to price policy on

the basis of revenue only—or on the assumption that the reduction in revenue per car will "naturally" be offset by the larger volume—is being decidedly unrealistic.

Theoretical Profits

It is true that there might be some theoretical demand elasticity that would justify a price reduction even when considering the cost factor. It is true, also, that the higher the percentage of costs remaining fixed, the lower would have to be the coefficient of elasticity. However, assuming the 20% fixed and 80% variable cost ratio, the elasticity of demand under the conditions assumed above would have to be 4.46, in order to justify a price reduction.[6] This is about three times the elasticity found in any of the studies of the automobile industry.

In concrete terms, an elasticity of

[6] The following equation can be used to determine the elasticity of demand required for a given price reduction (leaving profits unimpaired) when the ratio of fixed and variable costs within the range of volume contemplated is known:

X = per cent increase of volume required
Y = price reduction in dollars
P = profit per car at the old price
C = cost per car at the old price
V = per cent of variable cost at present level of production

$$\text{Therefore } X = \frac{Y}{P - Y + (1 - V)C}$$

and the coefficient of elasticity will be

$$\frac{X(P + C)}{Y}$$

In the above example, then:
Y = $100
C = $2,300
P = $200
V = .80

$$\text{Then } X = \frac{100}{200 - 100 + .20 \times 2,300} = 17.86\%$$

and the coefficient of elasticity will be

$$\frac{17.86(200 + 2,300)}{100} = 4.465$$

demand of 4.46 would mean that the effect of adopting a price of $2,400 instead of a price of $2,500 would be to increase the purchase of new cars by 17.84%, that is, from the assumed 1,000,-000 cars to 1,178,400 cars (4.46 × 4% reduction = 17.84%).

In determining whether (on a common-sense basis) this result might possibly follow, we must bear in mind that this is not a question of cross elasticity, which expresses the effect of a price change by one competitor which is *not* met by the others. What would happen if one manufacturer of a large proportion of the cars in a certain price class were to set this lower price and his competitors, conveniently for him, chose to remain at the higher price? This is indeed another question, but not a very realistic one, for the other manufacturers almost surely would meet the lower price.

At any rate, when Reuther and economists refer to elasticity of demand, they mean general elasticity for the product of an industry—not cross elasticity which arises from a competitive differential in prices. Thus, the conclusion is inescapably that if businessmen deny that a price reduction of 4% by all the producers would probably increase demand by 17.84% they are neither stupid nor ignorant of the workings of demand elasticity.

From a consideration of elasticity and fixed and variable costs, some other observations can be offered:

1. *The elasticity required to maintain profits varies inversely with the margin of profit at the point of departure.* If, in the above illustration, we had assumed the same original price of $2,500, a cost of $2,000 (instead of $2,330), a profit per car of $500, and the same ratio of fixed to variable costs, the elasticity required to maintain profits would have been 3.125 instead of 4.46.

2. *If in two situations the unit profit in dollars is the same, but in one instance it is a smaller percentage of cost or price, required elasticity in that case will be greater.* This generalization is suggested by the fact that if we assumed the original price to be $2,800, cost $2,300, and profit $500 (as in the immediately preceding example), the required elasticity would have been 3.256.

3. *The greater the price reduction, the greater must be the coefficient of elasticity.* Leaving all other factors the same as in the original example, let us contemplate a price reduction of $200 instead of $100. For profits to remain unimpaired in this case an elasticity of 5.42 would be required.

The fact that a higher elasticity is required to justify the larger price decrease follows, of course, from the fact that—with the relation of fixed and variable cost assumed here—the effect of a volume increase is greater increase in total costs than in total revenue. This divergence becomes greater as the price reduction is increased, and therefore a still larger elasticity would be required to offset this effect.

The conclusion is that the effect of a general price reduction on demand— what we have called price elasticity— is not great enough in the automobile industry to induce a price reduction when account is taken of the effect that increased demand has on costs.

There are, of course, many factors affecting people's demand for new cars. One of these (which, unfortunately for policy makers, is not subject to direct influence by the companies) is the level of consumer income. This effect of income on demand can be called "income elasticity," and for this too the coefficients have been estimated. All five of the studies cited at the Kefauver Committee hearings also estimated income elasticity, and in every case it was more pronounced than price elasticity.

The estimates ranged from a low of 2.1 to a high of 4.2.[7]

This coincides with the common-sense observation that people will buy more new cars when their incomes are going up and, I would add, when their confidence in the future is high; in the opposite conditions, a price reduction will not do the trick. This is especially true in the automobile industry because most prospective customers have a car; therefore their refusal to buy a new one this year does not deprive them of transportation. In a sense, a new car for such persons is a luxury, and durable luxuries are not purchased even at reduced prices when the public is uneasy about the future. For this reason, it is difficult to buck the effect of a recession with a price reduction.

Price Dynamics

The concept of elasticity is commonly and properly used in economics in a static sense: i.e., it is concerned with the effect of price on effective demand at a given time with all other factors remaining inactive. Consistent with this concept, it is better to think of alternatives at a certain point in time rather than while changing from one time to another. When we phrase the problem in this way and give due attention to the costs incurred in producing the additional units, I think we must conclude that it is vain to expect voluntary price reductions in most oligopolistic industries purely in the hope of increased demand resulting from the price change itself. There are, of course, other reasons that may prompt a price reduction, but that is another story.

[7] *Hearings before the Senate Subcommittee on Antitrust and Monopoly*, 85th Congress, Second Session pursuant to S. Res. 57 and S. Res. 231, p. 3215.

Expanding the Market

But prices and price elasticity can also be viewed in a dynamic sense, and businessmen frequently do view them in that way. Thus, a price reduction, especially a radical one, may under some circumstances have a profound effect in expanding the market over a period of time. The expansion may be one not only of degree but of kind. For example, if a new product is put on the market at a high price (fully justified by unit costs), it may tap but one level of potential demand. There may be other, much larger potential demand levels in lower price ranges. A bold and imaginative policy of reaching to those lower levels could bring rich returns. Consider the chemical industry as an illustration:

A new synthetic fiber, for example, may be so costly and high priced that it is used only for surgical and other very limited purposes. By dropping the price in anticipation of reduced costs, the hosiery and fine apparel markets may be reached; still further down the price scale, the rug, carpet, and industrial markets may be tapped.

This familiar story is basic to the epic of Henry Ford and other pioneers in the automobile industry who sharply dropped the prices of automobiles in the second decade of this century. The decline in the price of automobiles from 1909 to 1916 was radical indeed: the national average of wholesale prices dropped in this period from $1,250 to $604. And the revenue of the industry (wholesale value of U.S. production), rose from $160 million to $921 million.[8]

This is a story that has fired the im-

[8] Ralph Epstein, *The Automobile Industry* (Chicago, A. W. Shaw Company, 1928), p. 314.

agination of generations of businessmen, greatly to our national advantage. It is also the favorite example of critics who urge present-day businessmen to act along the same lines. It is good that the example should be remembered, but like any prescription it cannot be applied indiscriminately. The situation that existed in the early days of the automobile industry was a very special one that ordinarily comes but once, if at all, to an industry.

Mass Production Myths

Now what about the ratio of fixed and variable costs for U.S. manufacturing industries generally? We have become so impressed with the advantages of mass production that we assume additional products can be manufactured with very little incremental cost. The real advantages of mass production do not properly lead to this conclusion; they concern the effectiveness with which labor can be employed, supplies obtained, and the production process arranged. They do not imply that once plants and equipment are set up, additional output units will roll off the machines at very little extra cost. This misconception leads to much fallacious reasoning on the part of the public.

In manufacturing industries generally —even where there is a large investment in plant and equipment—the variable costs greatly exceed the fixed costs. In the automobile industry, the estimate has already been made of 15% to 20% for fixed costs and 80% to 85% for variable costs. That some ratio of this kind should be expected is suggested by the published figures of the automobile companies which indicate the distribution of the revenue dollar. Specifically:

It is indicated that 50% or more of

every dollar taken in by the larger companies is spent on materials and supplies purchased from outside sources. The figures also suggest that another large item, around 25%, is the payroll, most of which, of course, is for hourly rated workers and will be influenced by the number of workers employed and the hours for which they are employed. Thus, both of these items vary almost directly with volume. On the other hand, salaries, depreciation, maintenance, and interest payments are in the short run relatively fixed. But the total of these items is proportionately small. These comments suggest why, contrary to wide popular opinion, the fixed costs in this industry play a minor role.

I stated earlier that these figures seem to be fairly representative of American manufacturing industries. True, in some industries the ratios will be affected by the degree of integration. For example, we would expect a petroleum company that limits itself to refining to have high variable costs represented by its purchases of crude oil. On the other hand, the consolidated statements of some of the larger integrated companies, covering costs and expenses of production and distribution, indicate a pattern not radically different from that shown by the industries mentioned.

Again, outside of the industrial field, public utilities do, of course, show a higher percentage of fixed costs, as do the railroads. But in most heavy industries the fixed-variable cost ratio will approximate that of the automobile industry. All these comments on fixed and variable costs have assumed a moderate range of volume. If the proposed price reduction has a *very* extensive effect on volume, new facilities will be required. Probably this would mean new plants; and, if optimum plant size has been attained, this would not lead to lower unit costs. Indeed, during a period of inflation, the addition of new facilities would raise costs. Also, unit cost might advance because of increased pressure on suppliers, the necessity of attracting to the area a large number of new workers, and more overtime work. Three points of caution, however, should be noted:

1. Just because increased volume in manufacturing industries is not usually a sufficient reason for voluntary, industry-wide price reduction, advantages of large volume production should not be questioned. The major economics of scale, which explain the effectiveness of large firms in some industries, rest on a multitude of factors such as greater specialization of functions, the nature of the market, distribution methods made possible by large-scale operations, and the like. But a moderate increase in volume such as might result from a feasible price reduction will neither make possible nor enhance these normal advantages of scale.

2. The low price elasticity which may preclude a price reduction under conditions of oligopoly does not imply that a price advance is feasible. One reason for this is that a price reduction will almost certainly be met by competitors, while a price advance may or may not be followed. Herein lies an essential difference between monopoly and oligopoly. The monopolist is free to move his price up or down at will. The oligopolist may move his price *down*, but he may increase it only if such a move gains the approval of his competitors who may have different ideas about the economically feasible price.

3. Although the above argument throws doubt on certain reasons for price reduction as a means of combating declining sales, it by no means implies that there are not any reasons. Most of them involve some of the various, subtle competitive pressures which exist in

modern industry and which some think are more potent and socially useful than the simple price competition of "like with like" envisioned in the model of perfect competition.

Conclusion

On the basis of this discussion, let me end by suggesting a few generalizations:

When a price reduction can and probably will be matched by competitors, its effect on total volume (i.e., demand for the whole industry) must be considered.

The increase in the number of units sold, together with the reduced unit price, determines revenue. If the elasticity of demand is smaller than 1.0, revenue will decline; if it is larger than 1.0, then the revenue increases. (This, of course, is the meaning of "unit elasticity.") If the revenue declines with larger volume, the argument against the move is obvious and conclusive.

If there are close substitutes whose prices are not reduced, the elasticity is likely to be greater than 1.0; hence, the revenue will increase with a price reduction. Revenue is less likely to increase if the product is unique (or nearly so) in meeting the desires of the market or if the price of substitutes is also reduced.

If revenue is increased by a price reduction, there must, of course, be an increased volume produced for sale. The cost of producing these additional units must be subtracted from the increased revenue to determine the effect on profits. To maintain profits, the unit costs of the added product must decline by more than the price reduction. The possibility of this occurring is increased by a high ratio of fixed to variable costs. In most manufacturing industries, fixed costs are a smaller proportion of total costs than the public commonly assume them to be. In this fact lies the chief source of error in reasoning about the feasibility of price reduction.

Mainly, this discussion has viewed the short-term effect (one or two years) of a moderate price reduction (up to about 10%). A radical price reduction extending over a period of years presents another problem. On the demand side, in such cases, there may be large, untapped sources of demand at lower price levels; on the supply side, radically new methods of production may be made possible by larger volume. Such conditions explain the occasional success of increasing profit by reducing price, especially in the early days of an industry. This potentiality should not be disregarded in such industries, but the special circumstances accompanying its success must be observed.

F

Channels of Distribution

57

Are Channels of Distribution What the Textbooks Say?

Phillip McVey

In the study of marketing we tend to assume that policies and practices all originate with the manufacturer and that he has the power to do what he chooses. It is true that for the past thirty or forty years the manufacturer has been the dominant institution in the economy and that to put some order into a very complex process certain simplifying assumptions must be made. However, the following article adds a touch of realism to marketing by pointing out that the neat pattern assumed to exist in connection with channels of distribution is, at best, a tendency.

Perhaps Wroe Alderson said as much as is safe to say when he described a marketing channel as a group of firms which "constitute a loose coalition engaged in exploiting joint opportunity in the market."[1]

Reprinted from the *Journal of Marketing*, national quarterly publication of the American Marketing Association, Vol. 24, No. 3, January 1960, pp. 61–65.

[1] Wroe Alderson, "The Development of Marketing Channels," in Richard M. Clewett (editor), *Marketing Channels for Manufactured Products* (Homewood, Illinois; Richard D. Irwin, Inc., 1954), p. 30.

Theory and Actuality

Certainly too much is said about channel relationships in many published textbooks for businessmen and students, if one is to look for proof in current marketing practice. The picture usually given is one of long lists of various types of middlemen and facilitating agencies, which differ minutely but precisely in functions performed. Alignments of particular types are presented as "right" or "customary" for a given commodity or type of producer. Furthermore, it is often implied that it is the producer who selects all the links in the channel and establishes the working arrangements with them, down to and including the outlet which sells his goods to the final user.

Several popular college textbooks in marketing illustrate this manufacturer-oriented approach to channel planning.[2] One reason for fairly standard treatment of channel-building is that the growth of marketing knowledge has proceeded from a description of the activities of existing business firms, leaning heavily on data provided by the U.S. Censuses of Wholesale and Retail Trade. The framework appears orderly and well planned. But little recognition is given to the probability that some channel sequences "just grew" like Topsy, without direction or intent of known parents.

The Census method of counting, whereby each separate establishment is assigned to a single traditional category on the basis of a *major-portion-of-dollar-volume* rule, tends to produce more orderliness in the picture than probably exists. It tends to obscure a great deal of "promiscuous distribution" and channel-jumping. The Census rule, like the Procrustean bed of Greek mythology, effectively reduces the number of categories into which firms are sorted, and avoids hybrid, nondescript classifications.

Yet hybridity is too common among marketing firms to be ignored. For example, almost any wholesaler will do some business at retail; similarly, it is not uncommon for a broker to find himself holding title to a given lot of goods,

thus becoming temporarily a merchant middleman. A realistic classification may require the use of relative terms to identify types of operation, according to a range of variables—for example, the *degree* to which a firm caters to a given customer group, or the *frequency* with which a function is performed.

Further study of marketing textbooks may lead a reader to conclude that: (a) middlemen of many types are available to any manufacturer in any market to which he wishes to sell, and within each type there is an ample selection of individual firms; (b) the manufacturer habitually controls the selection and operation of individual firms in his channel; and (c) middlemen respond willingly as *selling agents* for the manufacturer rather than as *purchasing agents* for a coveted group of customers to whom the middlemen sell.

Yet none of these conclusions is entirely valid.

In a product line such as fashion apparel, a garment maker may have an extremely limited choice of types of middlemen: the selling agent, the broker, the direct-buying retailer, or the chain store buying office. The general absence of service wholesalers from this line of trade is not correctible by manufacturers' *fiat*.

In a particular market area, the choice may be even more limited. Of individual firms of a given type, there may be no choice at all. These limitations arise, of course, because of the free choices made by the middlemen as to locations, customer groups, and product assortments they elect to sell.

[2] Examples are found in T. N. Beckman, H. H. Maynard, and W. R. Davidson, *Principles of Marketing,* sixth edition (New York, The Ronald Press Company, 1957), pp. 44–45. C. F. Phillips and D. J. Duncan, *Marketing Principles and Methods,* third edition (Homewood, Illinois; Richard D. Irwin, Inc., 1956), p. 562. M. P. McNair, M. P. Brown, D. S. R. Leighton, and W. B. England, *Problems in Marketing,* second edition (New York, McGraw-Hill Book Company, Inc., 1957), p. 66.

Is the "Channel" an Academic Concept?

Integrated action up and down a channel is a rare luxury in marketing. Why? It may be that the "channel of distribution" is a concept that is principally academic in usage and unfamiliar to many firms selling to and through these channels.

Instead of a channel, a businessman is likely to concern himself merely with suppliers and customers. His dealings are not with all of the links in the channel but only with those immediately adjacent to him, from which he buys and to which he sells. He may little know nor care what becomes of his products after they leave the hands of some merchant middleman who has paid him for them and released him to return to problems involving his special functions. A manufacturer may not even consider himself as standing at the head of a channel, but only as occupying a link in a channel that begins with his suppliers.

Policies

Choice of a channel is not open to any firm unless it has considerable freedom of action in matters of marketing policy. Other areas of policy seem to be treated with more respect. For example, it is well recognized that a *price* policy is an authoritarian privilege open only to those sellers who possess power to withhold goods from the market in considerable quantities, or who have the choice of alternative markets and the means to solicit them. Usually a differentiated product is necessary. Therefore, a wheat farmer can seldom have anything resembling a price policy.

Likewise, a *design* policy is meaningful only when variations in product characteristics have been understood and accepted by customers to be of significance. Manufacturers of semifinished or component parts, or of textile "gray goods" cannot enjoy this luxury in most cases.

Similarly, the selection of a multi-stage channel is not the prerogative of a manufacturer unless his franchise is coveted by the middlemen he seeks, as being more valuable to them than their franchise would be to him.

Names such as Sears Roebuck & Company, Macy's, or Kroger mean a great deal more to the customers of these retailers than do the brand names of most of the items sold in their stores. These firms control the channels for many products, even to the point of bringing into existence some manufacturing firms needed to fill gaps in their assortments. In the same manner some national wholesalers, holding the reins of a huge distributive system, are more powerful than either their suppliers or their customers. In such extreme cases the power position is obvious. The big company, regardless of its position in the channel, tries to make its plans and policies effective by taking the initiative for co-ordinated action.

Uncertainty Among Smaller Firms

As to the many thousands of middle-size and small companies that truly characterize American marketing, the power position is speculative, vacillating, and ephemeral. Strength in certain market areas, the temporary success of a product, ability to perform a certain needed type of financing or promotional effort—these and similar factors enable companies to assume power.

On the other hand, financial reverses, an unfortunate sales campaign, or even the lack of accurate market news—these factors can shift power elsewhere, possibly to another link in the channel or to another firm in the same link. In any case, the opportunity of any firm is contingent upon the willingness of others to use it as a link in the channel.

Comparison with Advertising Media

Selection of middlemen has been likened to the selection of advertising media. In both instances the task is to find a vehicle which has an existing coverage (or circulation) which coincides with the market desired. A region blanketed with a neat mosaic of distributors' territories will appear on a map much like the same region covered by television stations.

However, there is an important difference. Seldom does an advertising medium restrict its availability. The advertiser's product need not be sold first to the medium on the grounds of self-interest. Only occasionally will a middleman accept any product he is offered. The requirement that he invest his own money and effort forces him to be selective in terms of probable outcome or profit. No seller can afford to neglect the task of selling *to* the middlemen he seeks, as well as *through* them. Nearly every comprehensive campaign of consumer advertising allots substantial effort to dealer promotion and distributor promotion. Indeed, much consumer advertising is undertaken primarily for the stimulating effect it will have upon middlemen.

Middlemen's Reactions

Middlemen's reactions to new-product offerings probably deserve more attention from manufacturers than usual. Wholesalers and retailers, as well as agent middlemen, enjoy an excellent position from which to make keen judgments of a product's probable successes within local markets. Free from the manufacturer's proclivity to "fall in love with the product," but not primarily concerned with its ultimate usage characteristics, middlemen who are alert merchandisers can look at the product with an eye to salability alone.

Yet it is common practice for manufacturers to force acceptance with a heavy barrage of consumer advertising, introductory high-markup offers, free merchandise, combination deals, co-operative advertising schemes, and the like. These may have the effect of "mesmerizing" middlemen, and of clouding the issue of the product's own rate of initial acceptance.

Lack of effective vertical communication in most channels is a serious deterrent. Possibly no other proof of the weakness of manufacturers' control over channels is so convincing as their inability to obtain facts from their own ultimate and intermediate markets. Information that could be used in product development, pricing, packaging, or promotion-planning is buried in nonstandard records of middlemen, and sometimes purposely secreted from suppliers.

Channels research is one of the most frustrating areas of marketing investigation, since it requires access to data collected by firms which are independent, remotely situated, and suspicious. Unless given incentive to do so, middlemen will not maintain separate sales records by brands sold. Extracting the needed figures by preferred units of measure is often a hopeless task. To get such data, one producer of pipe tools adopted a device commonly used with electric appliances: a "warranty registration" questionnaire attached to the tools. Ostensibly designed to validate users' damage claims, its true purpose was to discover where, when, how, and by whom the tools had been sold.

Communication downward from the manufacturer is also faulty, placing in doubt the claim that all links in the channel are bound together by common objectives. For example, it is seldom practical to disclose a forthcoming promotional plan in all its details and to ask the middlemen whether the plan will be timely, acceptable, and supportable by their efforts. To do so would jeopardize the advantage of surprise, usually a significant competitive stratagem. Yet the value of synchronized, co-ordinated action on any new plan by all firms in the channel is obvious.

Middlemen's Views

Channel Building

To the extent that any middleman can do so, he should think of himself primarily as a purchasing agent for his customers, and only secondarily as a selling agent for his suppliers. The planning of his product line will proceed from an analysis of a finite customer group in which he is interested . . . to the selection of goods capable of satisfying those needs . . . and then to the choice of available suppliers who can provide those goods. Of course, he may actually begin his assortment with one or more basic products, chosen by him as a way of defining the area of customer needs in which he elects to deal.

From that point on, however, his chief stock in trade becomes not the franchises of important suppliers, but rather his customer group. He is interested in selling any product which these customers desire to buy from him. The attractiveness of any new offering by a supplier is not to be judged by the size of the markup or commission, nor the unusual nature of the product, nor details of its manufacture, nor the promises of manufacturer's advertising support.

The key question is: Does it fit the line? That is, does it complement the other products that he sells, in terms of salability to precisely the same group of buyers? His list of customers is probably less subject to intentional revision

than are many other aspects of his business. Is it not at this point, then, that channel building starts?

Some unusual product combinations may result from this approach. A manufacturers' agent selling baby garments in the Southwest took on a line of printed business forms, which the small retailers on whom he called were seeking. An Omaha wholesaler successfully added grocery products to his liquor business. A Cleveland distributor of welding equipment rejected a portable farm welder offered by his principal supplier, since he had no contact with farmers, but was interested in carrying a line of warehouse tractors and lift trucks.

Approach to New Products

In some cases a middleman may deem it worth-while to shift from his current customer group to a new list of prospects, in order to find a market for a particularly promising new product. In the main, however, he will not do so. His approach to new prospects is based on their close similarity to those now on his customer list. To all these persons he attempts to become known as a helpful specialist in a well-defined set of recurring needs. The scope of his line, and the interrelation of products in it, must be known to the bulk of his customers. Scrambled merchandising, or stocking of unrelated items, will tend to split his market into many small groups.

Assortment Sales

Furthermore, the middleman attempts to weld all of his offerings into a family of items which he can sell in combination, as a packaged assortment, to individual customers. His selling efforts are directed primarily at obtaining orders for the assortment, rather than for individual items. Naturally the greatest *numbers* of his transactions will seldom be made in this way; but often his greatest volume and more profitable sales to "blue-chip" accounts will be assortment sales.

Catering to assortment sales has considerable significance to channel operation, because of the kind of sales service which a middleman can offer a single product supplier is affected thereby. Since he is relatively disinterested in pushing individual items, the middleman is criticized for failure to stress a given brand, or for the poor quality of his salesmen's product knowledge, his disuse of suppliers' advertising materials, his neglect of certain customers (who may be good prospects for individual items but not for the assortment), and even for his unrefined systems of record keeping, in which brand designations may be lost.

The Middleman as an Independent Market

The middleman is not a hired link in a chain forged by a manufacturer, but rather an independent market, the focus of a large group of customers for whom he buys. Subsequent to some market analysis of his own, he selects products and suppliers, thereby setting at least one link in the channel.

After some experimentation, he settles upon a method of operation, performing those functions he deems inescapable in the light of his own objectives, forming policies for himself wherever he has freedom to do so. Perhaps these methods and policies conform closely to those of a Census category of middleman, but perhaps they do not.

It is true that his choices are in many instances tentative proposals. He is subject to much influence from competitors, from aggressive suppliers, from inadequate finances and faulty information, as well as from habit. Nonetheless, many of his choices are independent.

As he grows and builds a following, he may find that his prestige in his market is greater than that of the suppliers whose goods he sells. In some instances his local strength is so great that a manufacturer is virtually unable to tap that market, except through him. In such a case the manufacturer can have no channel policy with respect to that market.

58

Do Your Distribution
Channels Need Reshaping?

A. L. McDonald, Jr.

*A channel of distribution presents an unusual—perhaps unique—
organizational problem to the businessman. Legally the members
of the channel are independent, but they must be so well integrated into the total marketing organization of a company that
their actions will not frustrate the company's objectives and strategies. The problems created by the channel of distribution were not
great in the past, when the manufacturer gave up his interest in
his product once it left his hands. Today an efficient manufacturer
with an advertised brand dare not lose interest in his product until
after it has been satisfactorily used by the consumer. This projected interest in his product adds a new dimension to marketing
in that the channel of distribution must be managed to assure that
it is operating as the manufacturer expects. This problem is discussed in the following article.*

It was late Friday afternoon in the
office of Lester Wadsworth, an elderly
Kansas City farm equipment dealer.
Larry Richardson, the new regional manager of Benson Tractor Company, had
just broken the news that his company
was adding a distributor in the Kansas
City area. According to his figures,
Wadsworth's sales would not suffer. But
Wadsworth, who had enjoyed an exclusive franchise for many years, was not
taking the decision with good grace.

"Twenty-seven years I've been selling
Benson tractors," he was saying. "It's the
better part of your lifetime, Larry. Bart
Benson and I have come a long way
together. We've done a lot of business,

Abridged from *Business Horizons*, a publication of Indiana University, Summer 1964,
Vol. 7, No. 2, by special permission.

and we've shot a lot of duck up at Bart's
place in Michigan. I know Bart pretty
well, Larry. He doesn't have any use
for a salesman who isn't out to break
every record that's in the book. But
Bart's a pretty sound, conservative guy.
Sure, he's for growth. But somehow the
Benson Tractor Company has stuck with
Les Wadsworth for twenty-seven years,
while the bright young fellows with the
big ideas about expanding distribution
have come and gone. It's worth thinking
over."

Richardson took a week to think it
over and then phoned Wadsworth to tell
him that the decision stood. Within a
month the new distributorship was a reality, and within a year Benson tractor
sales in the Kansas City region rose 40
per cent. Wadsworth's sales had not suf-

fered by the loss, but he was still bitter.

Few sales executives are eager to walk into a disagreeable situation like this. Even on the top management level, taking action on a distribution problem is apt to be hard, uncomfortable work. For that reason, many companies avoid it until their distribution channels have turned into profit drains.

The Hands-Off Attitude

It would be hard to find a businessman today who is unaware of the vast changes taking place in distribution patterns or who would deny the key importance of distribution to his company's marketing success. In practice, however, operating executives are strongly tempted to stand pat, often despite recognized soft spots in the distribution structure. Understandably, the executive whose experience and knowledge are limited to traditional channels is apt to be especially reluctant to take the personal risk involved in disrupting long-standing distributor relationships. For the greater the potential benefits of a change, the greater the penalties of a mistake are likely to be.

An equally basic reason for this hands-off attitude is that the very idea of actively *managing* distribution channels is foreign to the great majority of companies. This is understandable enough. Distribution channels are, after all, outside the company and beyond management's direct control. Distribution policies cannot be administered like other management policies; working with and through independent middlemen is a job of negotiation rather than supervision. Management cannot get its way by issuing directives. It must rely on persuasion.

In addition, organizational factors tend to perpetuate the *status quo*. In most companies no one is responsible, in any real sense, for distribution development.

In theory, the top marketing or sales executive bears this responsibility, but in practice it is often fragmented and neglected. Sales managers straining to meet the current quota are unlikely to make distribution changes that might hurt the current quarter's sales. Marketing executives have more exciting and seemingly more profitable projects to think about— new product development, advertising budgets, and sales promotion campaigns. Not having time or staff to spare, they are seldom inclined to invest the necessary effort in improving distribution. And what marketing department considers itself adequately staffed?

Quite naturally, then, management comes to regard its distribution structure as a framework within which the company is obliged to work. "That's the way it is in the trade. We've got to go along," an outsider may be told if he questions some aspect of distribution policy. Yet trade conditions, after all, are nothing more than the sum of the activities of a multitude of individual enterprises, whose only common purpose is profit. There is nothing immutable about "the way it is in the trade." In fact, experience suggests that a company that makes a disciplined, carefully planned effort to manage its distribution channels can often come very close to writing its own ticket in the marketplace.

Seizing the Initiative

. . . Ordinarily, of course, a company with long-established distribution channels and commitments has no freedom to strike out with a fresh strategy. For such a company, successful major distribution change frequently is a complex, time-consuming, and delicate process. But management's determination to shape distribution channels to the company's needs, rather than passively acquiesce to the distribution *status quo*, is the secret of more than one outstanding marketing success story.

Recent studies of major consumer and industrial marketing problems by Mc-Kinsey & Company confirm that the quickening tempo of market change is creating an ever increasing range of un-exploited distribution opportunities. To exploit these opportunities, a company must first recognize them. But it is un-likely to do so without an intensive re-examination of its present distribution strategy in relation to the dynamics of its market. Such an analysis may uncover profit opportunities that can be realized by a minor modification in the existing dealer structure—or it may dictate a completely revised marketing program, calling for a fresh approach in sales pro-motion, advertising, and selling effort.

Because no two companies have iden-tical distribution practices and problems, the pattern of improvement opportunities uncovered by an evaluation of channels is always unique. Geographical area, class of customer, prevailing trade prac-tices, and company warehouse locations are only a few of the considerations that may affect the right distribution mix. Moreover, since it is so intimately linked to other aspects of the over-all market-ing program, distribution strategy often influences or even determines advertis-ing, promotion, pricing policies, product warranties, or sales strategy. In this area of marketing, perhaps more than in any other, easy answers are dangerous.

For all the difficulty of generalizing about distribution problems, though, we can distinguish five broad types of op-portunities that may be disclosed by a basic evaluation of channels and meth-ods. These are (1) filling in distribution "holes"; (2) revitalizing the distribution network; (3) developing a multichannel system; (4) switching strategy; and (5) creating a new channel.

Filling the Holes

It is a practical fact that no distribu-tion network stays intact for long. In the normal course of market change, dis-tributors add new lines, drop others, and sometimes change their businesses entirely to take advantage of new opportunities. Thus, gaps in coverage develop. Among companies operating in fairly stable mar-kets, whose distributor relationships have settled into comfortable routine, these gaps are especially likely to go unde-tected.

Most manufacturers, of course, keep "current" distribution maps on file, show-ing complete coverage of all their im-portant markets. For three years one such company, a maker of automobile accessories and supplies with a loyal and long-established dealer network of auto-motive accessories stores, had been suf-fering a steady loss of market position in this growth business. Its regional man-ager in upstate New York decided that an informal audit of competitive activi-ties in his area might throw some light on the problem. Accordingly, he had his salesmen survey every retail outlet in his region. The survey showed that the rapid growth of service stations selling competitors' lines had cut deeper into his dealers' market share than he had ever thought possible.

The regional manager took his evi-dence to headquarters and convinced top management of the need for a nationwide distribution survey. Its findings were conclusive: the company's market share had shriveled because it had seriously underestimated the rapid growth in several key areas of service stations selling competitive lines.

Why had no one discovered this situation earlier? The reason was plausible enough: Most of the company's local sales managers valued the good relations they had with their existing dealers too much to be interested in making changes so they tended to play down the growing importance of service stations. In market coverage, consequently, the distribution network so neatly plotted on the map at corporate headquarters was full of holes.

The lesson this particular manufacturer learned the hard way is one that applies to almost any company selling through independent distributors: over a three- to five-year period, the distribution network is almost certain to develop serious flaws unless management has a program for keeping it in good repair.

This, of course, is primarily a job for sales management. If salesmen are really interested in building and sustaining distributor relationships, serious gaps will not go undetected for long. But merely writing the responsibility into salesmen's job descriptions is not enough. To most salesmen, the pressures of meeting the current quota and earning bigger commissions or bonuses are far more urgent than the tedious job of keeping tabs on distributors. Unless it is made a meaningful part of their job performance, it is almost sure to be neglected.

The problem is insidious, but once uncovered it is not difficult to correct. Moreover, it usually offers management an opportunity to add fresh strength to the distribution network rather than merely plugging the gaps. Simply by attacking this problem, many manufacturers have significantly stepped up the effectiveness of other marketing activities, particularly advertising, by gaining a broader base of market exposure.

Revitalizing the Network

Effective management of a distribution network, however, means much more than simply keeping the holes plugged. It demands an awareness of the eco-nomics of each distributor, based on his discount structure and selling costs. It also requires constant alertness to the relative performance of individual distributors.

Often a manufacturer is confronted by the problem of getting more effort out of his good distributors and replacing those who will not do an adequate job. To do this successfully, management must be able to grade the performance and potential of its distributors and target the support program at the growth candidates. It is just as important to face up to the task of replacing the losers, even when their volume is substantial.

Improving the performance of existing distributors is a task that can be approached in many ways. However, all tie in directly to the other aspects of a total corporate marketing program, frequently depending on other parts of the program for their success. For example, financial aid, in the form of inventory, equipment, or accounts receivable financing, will sometimes provide the means for the smaller distributor to expand his volume. Sometimes a new cooperative advertising plan will tip the scales to gain better distribution support. And in certain cases, specialized sales support to assist in dealing with big customers will greatly strengthen a distributor's performance.

Developing a Multichannel System

The natural instability of distribution networks is, of course, more than matched by changes in the marketing environment. The so-called distribution revolution of recent years and shifts in consumer buying habits have immensely complicated the distribution patterns of many manufacturers. To take a simple example, screwdrivers used to be sold through hardware wholesalers to retail hardware stores and a few other retailers. Today they can be bought in discount houses, department stores, variety stores, automotive accessories stores, and even in some drug marts and supermarkets. Examples like these are so familiar that many manufacturers regard them as history, forgetting that similar changes—less spectacular but no less pervasive—may be taking place in their own businesses today.

Manufacturers who have traditionally relied on general-line distributors are often especially slow reading the message of market change. The decision to supplement a network of general distributors with other channels—for example, brokers and direct sales in the food business—will admittedly complicate the life of marketing management. But, as the examples of General Foods and Campbell Soup show, this decision can be profitable. Both companies have begun to use independent food brokers to supplement the activities of their large company-operated sales forces on certain product lines.

Often the task of designing a multichannel distribution system is thrust upon a manufacturer bringing out a new product that cannot be profitably marketed through traditional channels. Adding a new distribution channel for the new product frequently affects relationships with the old distributors and may even call for a redesign of the whole marketing program.

Again, a company may find itself with a multichannel distribution system on its hands overnight in the wake of an acquisition. When the acquired company makes a product closely related in some way to that of the acquirer, management needs to look twice before concluding that its own distribution setup can be relied on to handle the new line. If the patterns of retail coverage for the two

lines differ significantly, or if the move would divert selling effort from the company's established product, ways may have to be found to meld the two networks into a workable multichannel system. Here again, the necessity of understanding the distributor's profit economics can hardly be overemphasized.

Switching Distribution Strategy

Usually management realizes the need for a basic shift in distribution strategy only when it faces an acute marketing problem—shrinking market share, declining profitability, or unexplained failure to reach realistic growth targets. Such a shift can take many forms: replacing brokers with direct salesmen, eliminating distributors and selling direct to key retailers, and replacing direct salesmen with distributors in markets that cannot economically support direct sales coverage, among others. In any case, a shift in strategy is most often stimulated by changes in retail patterns.

A well-known manufacturer of household products had brought out an improved version of its main product line in the early 1950's. It won a strong position in hardware stores, then the established channel for products of its type. For a time, the company's sales curve rose steadily. Then a new change occurred: food stores taking on houseware items began to cut deep into his hardware store sales. Like its competitors, this company saw what was happening. Unlike them, however, it feared that adding food brokers to its distribution network would alienate its hardware distributors. Management's reluctance to change cost the company dearly. Within ten years, 75 per cent of all sales for its type of product had moved into food stores where its retail coverage depended on spotty, missionary selling by hardware distributors. Moreover, hardware retailers made no effective efforts to give the company's line special support. As a result, its market share had dwindled alarmingly.

The solution to this manufacturer's problem was simple enough, at least in principle: sell to the food chains through food brokers. Once the details had been worked out, management did not have to wait long for the effect on sales. Today this company is selling more through both food stores and hardware outlets. It has more than regained its earlier market share, but the company will never regain the profits it lost by delaying the decision to reshape its distribution policy until it became a matter of survival.

A classic example of a planned shift in distribution channels is furnished by a well-known maker of pharmaceuticals that brought out an important new dietary product a few years ago. It introduced the product through its traditional drug channels. Then, after the product's image had been established in the consumer's mind and the market buildup was well under way, it shifted the bigger share of the distribution to food stores in time to meet competitive imitations and exploit popular demand. Largely because of this carefully timed shift, the product's success was tremendous. And the company has since succeeded in maintaining the two channels —drug wholesalers and food brokers— side by side with surprisingly little friction.

Creating a New Channel

Unlike the opportunities discussed so far, the creation of a new distribution channel is apt to be the result rather than the cause of a major new marketing strategy. It reflects management's decision to meet a market demand, present

or potential, that cannot be economically satisfied through existing channels.

The task of creating a new channel from scratch is a formidable one. Moreover, because sound distributor relationships take time to build, the profit payoff may be slow in coming. The first step, of course, before a new channel is even designed, is to analyze the entire sequence of selling operations to determine the most economic division of sales functions between manufacturer and middleman. This, of course, means analyzing the economics of the proposed distributors' operations, for a new channel cannot be effectively set up and developed into a marketing force unless profit incentives are provided at every stage of the selling operation.

Some years ago, a large food manufacturer saw the opportunity to build a new business in the institutional field by marketing a key product to institutions —hotels, restaurants, cafeteria chains, and the like. The food brokers who handled its sales to supermarkets and grocery chains, however, were not equipped to sell to institutions. In fact, no ready-made distribution channel existed to suit the company's needs, so it set about creating one.

Through want ads and other recruiting methods, the company screened nearly a thousand candidates and found some two hundred individuals with suitable backgrounds and adequate capital to invest in an exclusive franchise. The new system was a network of wagon delivery distributorships, each designed to service from scores to hundreds of local eating places. The company provided liberal assistance in financing trucks and setting up the franchisees' books. It held training seminars for the new distributors. Its salesmen spent much time helping them get under way.

Three years later, sales of the product to institutions had almost tripled. At this point, the sales growth leveled off.

Investigation showed that a number of wagon distributors, having achieved their personal income goals, had lost interest in further growth. Others had taken on different lines and were devoting less effort to this manufacturer's product. Still others were losing ground because they had not kept pace with the increased sophistication of the food service managers in the institutions they served. In short, the supervision exercised by the sales force at the start had faded to the point of ineffectiveness.

Obviously, the remedy was to recognize that the salesman's key functions had now become the training, motivation, and guidance of the distributors. To this end, the company began reorienting its sales force, setting new selection standards, and adjusting sales objectives to meet the new requirements. Within a year, its institutional sales were again climbing at an acceptable rate.

Grasping the Opportunity

Before a company can begin to estimate what it might gain by a thorough overhaul of distribution channels, it must assemble and evaluate information going beyond distribution and extending into areas so basic that the answers may have long been taken for granted. Because objectivity and sound critical judgment are necessary to explore these questions, responsibility for the project should be assigned to someone who combines the best marketing judgment with the least personal stake in the distribution *status quo*. Facts—not the opinions of headquarters executives—are the only basis for a sound evaluation, and facts should not be obscured by defensive explanations.

Any examination of distribution channels should provide a firm, factual basis for a recommended improvement program. As in most marketing situations, however, there are usually alternative routes to improvement, and management should insist on a reasonable choice among them.

Before choosing among the alternatives, however, management should carefully price them out according to (1) cost of implementing the recommended change; (2) cost of providing sales and marketing support to the new distribution network, as against that of the old; and (3) sales and profit results that can realistically be expected. It should also check the feasibility of these alternatives by talking about them with present and prospective distributors.

Once having made the decision, management should not look for immediate results to justify it. It may be months before the corporate sales curve shows a positive response. Almost invariably, a thorough evaluation of distribution channels requires a substantial investment of top management confidence. Soundly conceived and executed, this investment can pay off handsomely in long-term marketing effectiveness.

59

New Strategies to Move Goods

Business Week

Until recently physical distribution has received little managerial attention. It was recognized as a necessary activity, but seemed to be one with little glamour and a low payoff. Suddenly this has all changed. Physical distribution has become the avant-garde activity in the field of marketing. Part of its current attraction lies in the fact that management has only recently recognized the magnitude of physical distribution costs. The availability of new techniques in warehousing, data processing, operations research, and transportation are probably even more important as explanations of the new interest in what is fashionably called logistics. The next article is an interesting account of many of the things that are happening in this field.

In most modern factories today, everything is beautifully organized. Components flow together in a purposeful and orderly manner with little waste motion or material.

Then the finished product reaches the shipping dock. And chaos begins.

In many cases, the product moves by inappropriate means of transportation, often in undesired quantities. It may well be protected by the wrong kind of package. It is almost sure to be picked up and put down needlessly. It is stored in warehouses that may be badly located for today's shifting markets or nòt needed at all. And it is likely to be controlled by the wrong kind of paperwork.

Cost Battle. Moving and storing goods on their way from mine and mill

through various subassemblies and assemblies to their final markets costs anywhere from $50-billion to $75-billion a year—$100-billion if paperwork costs are included.

This is now the third highest cost in doing business, trailing only the payout for materials and labor. Factory automation has proceeded so far that now there's little that can obviously be done to reduce the cost of these two. But with profit margins always under pressure, a new attack has to be launched somewhere.

That's why distribution is the next—some say possibly the last—place where truly significant savings can be achieved.

A New Concept. Smart, far-sighted companies are already going after those savings by attacking antiquated methods and high costs of distribution. These companies are applying the order and system that prevail inside the factory to the shipment of finished goods. As the movement spreads, a new era of sophisticated distribution techniques is dawning.

This new revolution is made possible by new tools and techniques in transportation, materials handling, packaging, order processing and inventory control. It grows out of such things as jet cargo planes, larger and more versatile freight cars, container ships, broad interstate highways, and—perhaps most of all—high-speed computers with an insatiable capacity.

But the revolution is far more than the sum of all these. It is an intellectual rather than mechanical revolution.

And a New Job. Management for the first time is learning how to use all these gadgets as part of one huge, interrelated system. A new kind of executive position at the policymaking level is appearing alongside sales, production, and finance.

The fact that this new responsibility must be carved out of other executives' empires is the cause of much friction in the changeover. Nevertheless, for most companies, it is becoming inevitable.

Increasingly, one man is being handed the responsibility for getting the proper amount of the right kind of a product to a place where demand for it exists, at the time it exists, and at minimum cost. That is the true import of the revolution in what some people call physical distribution and others call business logistics.

The specific responsibilities usually combined in the new department are: traffic and transportation (that is, deciding among trucks, rail, water, or air, and the rates and routes most suitable); warehousing; materials handling; protective packaging; order processing; production planning; inventory control; customer service; market forecasting; and plant and warehouse site selection.

Many into One. Formerly, everything that occurred in most of these areas was so helplessly detailed and complex that the human brain simply couldn't comprehend it all as one single system. Each area was set apart and left to a specialist often in lower middle management who was looked upon by top management with some respect, but whose chances of promotion to higher levels were not the best.

Order processing was part of sales, warehousing was part of production, transportation was autonomous, and so on. Costs were kept separately and often allocated to the wrong place. Each fragment was interested in keeping its own cost down, little realizing or caring that higher costs in its activity could result in lower total costs.

Though the human brain still can't take in all the detail and paperwork involved in treating physical distribution as one system, computers can. That is one of the extraordinary things happening today. The need for doing an incredibly complex job becomes unmistakably apparent just at the moment management has developed the tools that enable it to perform the job.

New Basis for Decisions. Now companies can feed the intricate detail of purchase orders, shipping instructions, freight charges, damage claims, insurance, invoices, inventory costs, stock levels, customer complaints, and everything else into a machine so that, at last, total distribution costs can be understood.

With this new information, management has for the first time an intelligent basis for deciding where to make trade-offs:

- Whether to reduce warehouses and go to air freight.
- Whether to hire more clerical people, speed up order processing, and then

take advantage of slower, cheaper transportation.

- Whether to hold back and combine shipments to take advantage of lower truckload and carload rates at the risk of decreasing customer service.
- Whether to switch products from one factory to another to fill otherwise empty company-owned trucks.

The list of possible variations is endless. So new, in fact, so big and mysterious is the whole idea that one of its major prophets, George C. Smith, distribution manager of Du Pont's Fabrics & Finishes Dept., likes to describe it as the "witchery of physical distribution."

Explosive Impact. Witchery or science, its effects will be explosive. Once a company puts into operation a sophisticated physical distribution program, its costs can plummet so abruptly and its customer service improve so rapidly that it gains a significant edge over its competition. Since no one else can allow a competitor to keep such an advantage, the physical distribution concept is bound to spread like a prairie fire.

Already, some Wall Street analysts are taking it into account, and are including in their study of any company an investigation into its distribution philosophy and methods.

As the concept spreads, companies that for decades have sat secure in geographical areas other producers couldn't economically reach will find their territories invaded by competitors from halfway around the world. By the same token, they can push their own markets into their competitors' backyard.

New Ballgame. Certainly, different kinds of transportation companies will have to tailor their services to fit into the total distribution concept. For them, it will be practically a new experience. The ancient advantages held by railroads, truckers, water carriers, and airlines can often be upset by new equipment and tighter, more customer-oriented service.

By and large, there will be less need in distribution for the independent middleman, if all he does is provide intermediate halts in the flow of goods to market. But for those who can speed products on their way while cutting distribution costs, the future is assured.

The need for salesmen will be greater than ever—but they will have to know more about their own products and their customers' needs. In short, they will have to sell. The function of order taking will be fulfilled by computers talking to each other.

Most important, the distribution revolution will free capital for more profitable uses than inventory carrying. For the long run, the implications of this are enormous. Thanks to a greater control of inventories at every step in the distribution line and a faster reaction time when inventories do get out of line, both companies individually and the economy as a whole will run a smoother course.

The Road Is Difficult but the Payoff Big

Everyone caught up in the excitement of the physical distribution revolution agrees on one thing: Its purpose is to increase profits. But agreement ends there. The distribution roads leading to this objective can be many and diverse, often taking off in opposite directions.

Today, with money expensive and hard to get, most retailers and wholesalers don't want to carry any larger inventories than they have to. A manufacturer finding a way to make fast, dependable deliveries can thus gain a big competitive edge. Many manufacturers are gaining that edge—and boosting sales and profits or winning new markets—by a total overhaul of their distribution systems.

Paradoxical. For a company like Norge Div. of Borg-Warner Corp., in the highly competitive consumer products field, a key consideration was to improve dealer service. U.S. retailers can choose among many kitchen appliance makers, so the manufacturer that provides the retailer with the greatest profit margins will have his appliances displayed and pushed.

Norge found that the somewhat paradoxical way to greater profits was to increase its own warehousing costs—because this led to more-than-offsetting increases in sales, as well as to lower dealer inventories.

In general, what Norge did is representative of the thinking of many consumer products companies with relatively high-cost products.

In a completely different field Hammond Valve Corp., a small company in the Chicago area that makes bronze valves, took a similar road. Hammond, which used to distribute its line through jobbers, discovered five years ago that it could boost profits by improving its service to its ultimate consumers. So it opened six regional warehouses. Now it takes two days to service a customer's order, instead of six weeks.

The results parallel Norge's. "Our sales have more than doubled in the last five years," says Morris R. Beschloss, Hammond's youthful president. Greatly increased volume and lower unit production costs, he says, have far outweighed the added costs of operating warehouses.

Paperwork and Warehouses. This doesn't mean that for manufacturers the blueprint for the distribution revolution is more warehouses.

For some, on the contrary, it means fewer warehouses. It can mean going to air freight as innumerable manufacturers, such as Raytheon Co. and American Optical Co., have done. Or it can mean using a truck or boxcar as a rolling warehouse if the transportation company can be relied upon for dependable deliveries.

The Gillette Co., maker of the world's largest-selling brand of double edge razor blades and safety razors, was faced by a staggering assortment of changes in its business: diversification into a broad range of toiletry products, a shift of its main distribution channels from drug and tobacco chains to grocery chains, introduction of stainless steel blades by competitors.

Gillette took to air freight to rush its own new blades to market, but this added to costs, cut profit margins. Finally, by way of a management study group and a computer model of the distribution system, Gillette found its answer: a total revamping of paperwork. By cutting down the number of days it took to process an order, the company could return to low-cost surface freight for routine shipments, yet keep up delivery schedules. In a sense, the transportation pipeline took on a part of the function of a warehouse.

It All Depends. Johnson & Johnson, maker of bandages and surgical supplies, also came up with faster order-handling procedures, rather than speedier shipment, as the solution to its problems. "We used to ship to every part of the country every day of the week," says John F. Varley, director of sales and distribution services. Now J&J holds back shipments to take advantage of full truckload rates, as against costlier LTL (less-than-truckload-lot) charges.

Even so, it finds service just as fast. By shipping a whole truckload at a time, J&J avoids repeated intermediate handlings that might cause soiling, delay, or loss. "Everything was rushed before," says Varley. "Now everything is on a scheduled basis, and when we have a true emergency we can handle it efficiently.

But it all depends; in the complicated world of physical distribution, one man's meat is another's poison. Singer Co., the sewing machine maker, took off in exactly the opposite direction from J&J.

Singer, which used to ship its machines once a month, has lately upped this to four times a month. "We pay higher LTL rates, but this is more than offset by lower inventories in stores," says George L. Cwik, assistant manager in the transportation services department. Since most of Singer's 1,600 sewing centers are in high-rent districts, low inventories are a gain even if they mean high freight rates.

Counting up the Payoff. If the solutions to the distribution problems are often opposite to each other, there's no doubt where they all aim—to greater profitability through such sales increases as Hammond Valve's doubling in five years, or such savings as the 30% cut in five years in distribution costs that Singer has set as its goal.

Xerox Corp., which switched to a comprehensive distribution organization in May, 1963, tots up some massive gains. Xerox needs to maintain a huge amount of supplies for its office copying machines. Formerly, it worked out of 40 sales branches, each with its own inventories of paper, chemicals and machine parts.

Then a small group of officers, making a study of this setup, found it extremely wasteful; the group discovered that 80% of the items in the inventories were slow movers, and that many could be stored at one location and air-freighted as needed. In the end, the group determined that 92% of the company's customers could be served adequately from just seven distribution centers in the U.S. and Canada.

As a result, supplies in the distribution pipeline were cut in half. "In May, 1963, we were processing 1,000 orders a day," says Andrew Price, manager of corporate distribution; "now we're processing 4,000 and we're still shipping 92% of today's orders today."

One inside estimate of what the new distribution organization has meant to Xerox—even though the payroll in the department has grown from nothing to more than 3,000—is that it has added $9-million to net profits in three years.

Fertilizer. It's not only in high-cost, high-value manufactured goods that innovations in physical distribution build a big payoff. Very often it is in the field of low-cost bulk commodities that more efficient distribution gives a real competitive edge.

Take fertilizer as a good example. "The price of a ton of phosphate rock at the mine is about $7, while the costs of warehousing, shipping, and handling frequently total an additional $11," says Anthony E. Cascino, vice-president for the Agricultural Products Marketing Group at International Minerals & Chemicals Corp. "If we're not aggressive, innovative, imaginative, and resourceful, and one of our competitors is, and discovers a way to cut his distribution costs by $3—we're dead."

IMC uses long-term deals to cut costs and invade new markets. It mines phosphate rock in Florida, potash in Canada. Through a long-term lease of 4,000 hopper cars and a long-term ship charter, it can now sell phosphate in Canada and potash on the U.S. East Coast, two markets it never served before.

Another long-term deal—with the Rice Growers' Assn. of California, a farmers' cooperative—lets it ship Florida phosphate to California as a return cargo in a ship whose primary job is carrying California rice to Puerto Rico. And it can sell the phosphate in California at $2 a ton less than when Idaho phosphate producers had that market tied up.

But, says Cascino, citing the $14-million to $16-million commitment in hopper cars and ship charters: "You've got to have a lot of courage mixed in with your innovation."

On the Retail End, the Computer Is King

Sweeping changes and innovations in physical distribution are by no means confined to industrial and manufacturing companies. Most marketing companies in the retail field have an even greater need to streamline their distribution setups.

But if manufacturing companies must each chart a laborious road through the distribution tangle, the miraculous computer offers to those in the retail field a ready-made key to the future. The computer bids fair to turn retail distribution inside out.

Inventory by Computer. Using computers as tools, Walgreen Co., led by its director of physical distribution, Robert G. Smith, with the wholehearted backing of top management has instituted one of the most advanced warehouse inventory control systems anywhere.

Walgreen, the nation's largest retail drug chain, has nearly 500 supermarket-type drug stores in 36 states and Puerto Rico, each containing something like 20,000 items; it has a chain of discount stores and junior department stores in the South; and it services about 1,900 franchised "agency" stores.

Just one of the things its electronic data processing system does is to analyze once a week the stock status of each item in all of Walgreen's stores and warehouses. If the inventory of an item reaches what the computer has previously determined is a reorder level, out comes a requisition card. All these cards then go back into the equipment. Then, the computer can search out other items from the same source that might be ordered at the same time for volume discounts or lower freight rates, even though their levels aren't yet critical.

The computers give Walgreen so much information about every single product going through its stores that vendors are often embarrassed to find Walgreen knows more about a product's acceptance than they do.

Crosstalk. Computers are not only mines of information; they can tell each other what they know. One of the most exciting prospects in distribution comes from the possibility of two companies' computers talking to each other.

California Packing Corp. is currently teaming up with a pair of large grocery chains in two "direct ordering tests." The idea, says F. H. Bergtholdt, Calpak director of distribution, is to try out "computer-managed inventories and direct wire communications between customer and manufacturer."

"The customer's computer determines what, how much, and when to buy," explains Bergtholdt, "and the order is transmitted from the customer's data processing center to Calpak's data processing center."

All the Way. Several other food processors, too, are trying out computer-to-computer systems. If the tests succeed, the next step may well be to tie in a third computer, the transportation company's.

As stocks in a supermarket chain's warehouse neared a predetermined reorder level, the chain's computer would not only alert the producer, it would also alert the railroad or trucker to have equipment ready at the loading dock.

Then, the computers would follow the boxcar or trailer across the country, making nightly reports on its whereabouts. If and when such a system reaches perfection, big grocery chains could even do without warehouses, shipping directly to stores. Only shelf space and a back room in each store would be needed. Already, some venturesome chains are experimenting in this direction, though still on a primitive basis.

If there's one thing clear from the experience of companies in the distribution revolution, it's this: Building the complex elements of physical distribution into a "total system" is an intricate job.

Computers may offer retail marketers an indispensable tool, but they provide no ready-made construction chart. Just dumping responsibility for distribution on one man or department isn't enough, either.

When a corporation president decides his company needs an integrated distribution system, how does he go about the job?

Companies have undertaken it in a number of different ways. At Xerox, a thorough study of the company's distribution was made by a small group of officers. At Singer Co., President Donald P. Kircher called key executives from all over the world to New York in October, 1963, for a redistribution seminar to set cost-reduction goals. International Minerals & Chemicals put its corporate imagination to work. Norge and others turned to management consultants for guidance.

How a Company Blazes the New Trail

When a company decides to overhaul its distribution system, though, the first thing most executives do is to set up a mathematical model of the company. Hard and expensive as this is, it's easier and cheaper than getting locked into an unworkable system.

To be complete, believes Wendell M. Stewart of the management consulting firm of A. T. Kearney & Co., such a model must show more than shipping and storage charges, packaging and order processing costs.

"It must go all the way into the marketplace," he says, "and find what products are hot sellers, what the demands are and where they originate. It must also go back into the factories and find which are the most efficient production lines for each product."

When the model is completed—and this can take a year or more—the next step is to set management objectives. It is possible, for example, to give every customer one-day service on every item —but the cost may be prohibitive. Within limits that can be programmed into the model, the best service at the lowest cost can be determined by varying such factors as number, size, and location of factories and warehouses, and speeds and rates of different kinds of transportation.

It's also important for companies to remember that transportation rates are not fixed. They can often be lowered by negotiation or threats. Building existing rates into a model, therefore, can destroy the value of the whole exercise.

A model that's correctly formulated can bring to light warehouses serving wrong territories or territories with wrong boundaries, and can suggest that some products are being made in the wrong plants. It can keep a company from adopting a distribution system its customers can't use; if a customer can't store a whole barge load of a product, there's no point in building a distribution system around barges.

Not in a Day. Once the model is built and the computer begins to turn out the trade-offs and compromises that will most nearly achieve a company's long-term objectives, the company can start moving.

According to Robert S. Reebie, former New York Central vice-president and now an independent consultant, it's best to make the move to a comprehensive physical distribution program in a series of short steps. Trying to get there all at once, he feels, is sure to ruffle too many feathers, upset too much existing capital investment, and multiply the chances for mistakes, endangering the success of the whole thing.

Repeat Engagement. When the long-range objective is finally attained and the distribution system is churning out better service to customers at lower cost, many a company finds it's time to start over again. For there's one law of the new distribution revolution that can't be repealed: Physical distribution needs constant attention and renewal.

Fundamental changes are coming so fast in every phase of distribution that no system, however good, can be permanent; a competitor may be already working on a better one. Besides, no wide-awake company's business stands still, and growth can upset even the best-designed program.

Inundated. Rapid growth is sending a flock of major companies to Arthur D. Little, Inc., for a total distribution blueprint, according to David Boodman, a senior staff member at the management consultant company. "In just the last half year," he says, "we have been inundated."

Boodman feels many of these companies have grown so fast that such things as inventory control got out of hand; one company had grown four times over in eight years. Inventory control is Boodman's forte—and fixing optimum inventory levels and maintaining them is one of the most difficult yet essential parts of the distribution revolution.

Changes in products or outlets, diversification, and acquisitions can also upset a previously smooth flow—as Gillette found—or provide a spur to seek new patterns. Anti-freeze, to cite another example, formerly sold primarily at filling stations, now goes mostly through supermarket checkouts, changing the manufacturers' distribution patterns.

Sometimes a change can bring a distribution bonus. When Singer acquired Friden, Inc., the San Leandro (Calif.) maker of calculating machines, it discovered that a private truck fleet would pay off. Now Singer trucks carry sewing machines to California and calculating machines back to the East. With its own trucks, protective packaging requirements are less.

Transportation Strips Down for the Race

The spur that is driving industrial and marketing companies to the new concept of distribution comes not only from internal change. It comes also from the technological upheaval that is transforming the means of distribution. Nowhere are the effects of the revolution in physical distribution more evident than in transportation—and the rapidity of change in this area is speeding up the entire process.

The changes affect truck, rail, ship, and air alike—and they all point to faster, more efficient, less expensive delivery of goods.

Bigger and cheaper. For truckers, the substantial completion of the interstate highway program within five years will mean sharp reductions in maintenance cost as trucks get free of tangled traffic. Reduced costs could mean lower rates.

Bigger and heavier trailers will be allowed—again permitting reduced costs and rates. The so-called double-bottom rig, in which a tractor hauls a semi-trailer and full trailer, is being legalized in more and more states. Even a triple-bottom rig is now under test.

With superhighways crisscrossing the map, with bigger, faster trucks manned by teams of drivers who alternate driving and sleeping, the average rig will be able to double the distance it travels in a night. This means manufacturers can double their marketing area—or cut inventories and storage space in existing areas.

Look, No Wheels. The larger, so-called "damage free" freight car which is posing a challenge to distribution specialists and making over entire industries is only one example of railroad modernization.

In coming years the rails will develop containerization to higher degrees of efficiency. Dramatic as the story of piggybacking and its 20% annual growth has been, leaving the wheels off trailers and carrying only the big boxes will make things still cheaper and faster. Each flatcar will hold more than two containers, and a lower center of gravity will permit more speed. For shippers, again, this means wider distribution, or reduced inventories.

So-called unit trains—semi-permanently coupled trains that shuttle back and forth between one shipper and one consignee—will have an even broader impact as their use spreads among shippers of bulk commodities, particularly coal and grain. By avoiding intermediate freight yards, these trains improve dependability and cut costs.

As their use grows, intermediate storage facilities, notably for grains, may no longer be needed, or may be needed in different spots. And as rates on heavy, bulk materials come down, it may prove desirable to move plants away from raw material sources, closer to markets.

On the Water. Even more dramatic changes will flow from continuing improvements on inland waterways. Central Oklahoma, for example, is to have a 9-ft. deep canal. Old locks on existing canals will be enlarged. Dallas and Fort Worth will be connected to the Gulf of Mexico.

Bulk materials will flow along these waterways at ultra low costs. Industries needing coal, ores, oil, and chemicals at cheap prices, or the low-cost electricity made possible by water-borne coal, will flock to canal and river banks. New communities built for their workers will create new distribution patterns.

On the ocean, container ships are about to become significant in international commerce. Ocean containerization is still hesitant and riddled with problems, but in coming years it will be fast, frequent, and efficient. Shipping, packaging, and insurance costs will plummet. Many domestic producers will find overseas markets opening up—but overseas producers will also find more U.S. markets feasible.

World Shrinkers. Perhaps most sweeping will be the changes in air cargo. The short-and medium-range jets that are already crowding the skies have a limited passenger appeal late at night. Any flight that takes off after 10 p.m. is apt to arrive at an unsalable hour. So, many of these planes are being made convertible for night cargo duty.

This huge increase in air freight capacity will drive down air freight rates —and as some rates descend close to those of surface carriers, the industry will grow at rocket speed.

Most short-range planes will feature cargo pallets interchangeable with those of long-range cargo jets. A pallet loaded in, say, Terre Haute can be flown to Chicago, put intact on a big jet for

Frankfurt, Germany, arrive there next morning.

Within six or seven years airlines will be flying truly huge cargo planes similar to the Boeing 747 and the Air Force's C-5A, capable of lifting up to 110 tons per plane, up from about 45 tons today.

Says the economist Eliot Janeway: "I behooves every corporation in America now making commitments for new plant and warehouse capacity around the world to keep a sharp eye on the job the C-5A will be doing by the time today's commitments go on stream."

The Total Cost Approach to Distribution

Raymond LeKashman and John F. Stolle

Marketing has not been noted for making its decisions and planning its programs on the basis of careful cost analysis. In the past it usually appeared to marketing executives that the market opportunities were so limitless that a dollar could be spent much more productively in a somewhat planless attack on this burgeoning market than in methodical analysis of individual and alternative costs. Today marketing executives are being forced to be more cost-oriented because the markets do not appear so limitless and the costs are larger. The accompanying article is a discussion of this newer approach to marketing planning.

The more management focuses the company's efforts on cutting distribution costs, the less successful it is likely to be in reducing the real costs of distribution. This apparent paradox is no abstract or armchair play on phrases. It explains why so many companies have diligently pruned distribution costs—in the warehouse and in inventory, in order processing and in transportation—only to find that these hard-earned savings are somehow not translated into improved profit

Condensed from *Business Horizons*, a publication of Indiana University, Winter 1965, Vol. 8, No. 4, pp. 33–46, by special permission.

margins. They have been watered down or actually washed out by increases in other costs scattered throughout the company.

It is these "other costs," motley and miscellaneous as they first seem, that turn out on closer analysis to be the real cost of distribution. They never appear as distribution costs on any financial or operating report, but show up unidentified and unexplained at different times and in assorted places—in purchasing, in production, in paper-work processing—anywhere and everywhere in the business. When these gremlin-like costs are traced to their roots, however, one finds that they are, in fact, all intimately interrelated, linked together by one common bond. They all result from the way the company distributes its products.

It is this aggregation of distribution-related costs—rather than what mangements usually mean when they complain about the cost of distribution—that represents the important and increasing drain of distribution on earnings. These are the costs—rather than those usually defined and dealt with as distribution costs—that have eluded even the most earnest cost-cutting drives. Because of its size and its elusiveness, this cost complex remains for many companies a promising profit-improvement potential. [The appendix to the article provides additional information on costs—Eds.]

The Total Cost Approach

When to Use It

For earnings-minded managements, the dimensions of this profit potential, and a practical technique for tapping it, have now been tested and proved. A handful of companies have faced up to the across-the-board impact of distribution on costs and profits. They have accomplished this by applying an approach—we call it the "Total Cost Approach"—that is designed to convert these intangible and intricate cost interrelationships into tangible dollar-and-cents improvements in profit margins.

A major food manufacturer, after applying effectively an assortment of rigid cost-cutting techniques, has found that this new approach is enabling the company to add 1.7 per cent to its margin on sales.

A major merchandiser, already enjoying the benefits of advanced distribution techniques, found that this same new approach could cut from its corporate costs an additional $7.5 million—3 per cent of the sales value of its products—while at the same time significantly improving service to customers.

At Du Pont, a company well known for its general management excellence, this same new approach underlies the announcement that programs recently instituted are expected to cut $30 million from its total cost, a 10 per cent reduction of the costs attributed to distribution.

These success stories shed some light on how distribution drains profits—and on what can be done about it:

The real impact of distribution on profits is much greater than most managements think. In companies in which distribution-connected costs have been studied, they turned out to be significantly greater than management estimated—as much as from a third to a half of the selling price of the product.

This untapped profit-improvement potential exists because these costs lie in a managerial no-man's land, where they can increase because they are outside the scope of responsibility or control of any operating executive. These distribution-related costs are not strictly the responsibility of the man in charge of distribution, because they are costs of purchasing, manufacturing, or some other function of the business. But they cannot be dealt with effectively by the executive in charge of these other functions because they are actually caused by distribution decisions, for which only the man in charge of distribution has any responsibility. They are the result of complex interrelationships involving all of the functions of the business. Distribution lies at the crossroad of these complex interactions, and that is what is so different about distribution. In no other function of the business can decisions made at the operating level look so right and be so wrong.

These costs will not respond to the usual cost-cutting approaches. Management has achieved near miracles in cutting costs in one function of the business after another, including costs within the distribution function, notably in warehousing, transportation, and order-filling. But conventional cost-cutting approaches are limited to costs that fall within any one operation of the business; for cutting these costs, management can hold some executive responsible. Distribution-related costs are organizational orphans, beyond the reach of even the most diligent, skillful cost-minded executives.

These costs will respond only to a high level across-the-board re-examination of how distribution affects the total costs and total profits of the business, and of what management action is necessary to tap this profit opportunity.

Thus the problem and the opportunity are deposited squarely on the desk of the chief executive. The purusit of these added profits has to get its start, its support, and its sanctions at the top management level. With this high-level effort, even companies that have tightened and tidied their distribution operations can greatly increase earnings by a frontal attack on the basic framework of their distribution decisions and practices.

This broad, basic approach has a continuing payoff, for once the most profitable pattern of distribution has been defined for the present operations of the business, management has in its hands a yardstick for measuring the impact on total profits of any proposed management move. This makes it possible to define the impact on total profits of a new plant or a new product, or a cluster of new customers, and so makes it possible to determine what changes in distribution—if any—will ensure peak profits from these new ventures.

What is this total cost approach? What is new about it? Why have we not heard more about it?

The Approach Simply Stated

This approach sounds simple. First, analyze the distribution impact on each cost of the business, and select for more detailed study those activities the cost of which is significantly affected by distribution policies and practices. *Second,* develop the data necessary to measure the profit impact that alternative distribution decisions would have on each of these activities. *Finally,* determine which distribution decision will maximize profits.

Obviously, if it were as simple as it sounds, more companies would long ago have beaten a path to this better mousetrap. Three sets of facts explain why this has not been so:

1. The impact of distribution on costs is more difficult to unravel than is the effect of other business decisions. All functions of a business are somewhat interrelated, but distribution is more complexly intertwined with each. And it is these interrelationships—rather than the costs of the distribution functions per se—that are the cause of high distribution costs and the key to understanding and reducing these costs.

2. Because corporate accounting has historically been oriented to finance and production, rather than to marketing or distribution, the operating reports that guide managerial action do not tot up in any one place the full impact of distribution on costs. The real cost of distribution never stares management in the face.

3. Even where managements have become aware of these costs and their impacts on profits, there was until recently very little that anyone could do about the pervasive effects of distribution. Even a relatively simple problem in distribution system design can involve hundreds of bits of information that interact in thousands of ways. So there was no way of dealing with the distribution cost complex until techniques were developed to manipulate this mass of material as a single integrated entity.

This last is, in fact, the major reason why these distribution-related costs have continued to rise and to depress profit margins throughout our economy. And for that same reason the total cost concept remained until recently a topic for textbook discussion, theoretically provocative but of little practical use. But techniques have been developed to deal with information in these quantities and with interrelationships of such complexity. They have converted this sound but previously unworkable concept into a practical management approach.

Conclusions

Experience not only confirms the practicality and profitability of the total cost approach, but it also defines some clear-cut guidelines for managements who propose to put this approach to work. Experience in applying this approach suggests, too, that a number of additional considerations need to be clarified.

The fact that this substantial profit opportunity exists in a company is no implicit criticism of its operating management. No traffic manager or transportation specialist can be expected to deal with a problem the roots of which extend far beyond his sphere into manufacturing and marketing. Nor can the best warehouse manager be expected to come up with solutions to problems the causes and conditions of which extend from purchasing and supplier relationships at one extreme, to customer service considerations at the other. Even those companies that have centralized distribution responsibility in the hands of a single high-level executive rarely can provide this executive with the wide range of supporting capabilities and indepth experience necessary to deal with this profit potential.

Nor does the fact that the necessary action requires top management support mean that the chief executive has to become an expert in the complexities of the mathematical tools involved, any more than he has to become knowledgeable in computer technology or the relative merits of the hardware and software. No one intends to suggest that management has to do or know anything specific or technical about distribution. What is required is management's insistence that something be done, by someone with the appropriate capabilities and experience.

In this sense, the challenge of the total cost approach has another interesting management meaning. The relentless and increasing impact of distribution on profits is one of a growing category of management problems that are not going to be solved satisfactorily within the framework of traditional organizational and decision-making approaches. The most effective solution to any company's distribution problem requires looking at the company as a whole and dealing with the profitability of the entity. More and more, management is being faced with problems requiring this kind of across-the-board attention.

At the same time new concepts, new techniques, and new technology are becoming available that are peculiarly able to cope with this very kind of problem. The more we learn about the computer and about such techniques as simulation, the more apparent it is that they are used to fullest advantage when they are used to deal with problems like these for which no other problem-solving technique is truly appropriate.

There is every reason to believe that with the increasing complexity of modern businesses and the mounting competitive pressures in their environment, the ability of companies to forge ahead and to grow profitably may have a direct relationship to the ability of management to put these new tools and their vast new capabilities to work. In the days ahead, competition between companies may in large measure reflect the skill with which competing managements take advantage of these new management tools.

Appendix

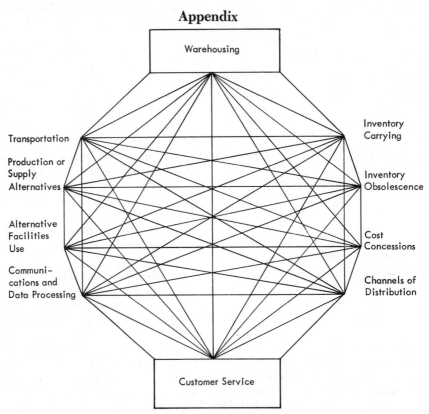

THE REAL COST OF DISTRIBUTION

The real cost of distribution includes much more than what most companies consider when they attempt to deal with distribution costs. In a sense, any major distribution decision can affect every cost in the business and each cost is related to all the others. Our experience indicates that the following ten cost elements and interrelationships are the ones that are most likely to prove critical in evaluating the impact of alternative distribution approaches on total costs and total profits.

Warehousing. To provide service through the company's chosen channels of distribution, some warehousing is required, involving from one in-plant warehouse to a multiple-unit network dispersed across the country. Service usually becomes better as the number of warehouses, is increased, at least up to a point. However, as the number of warehouses increases, their average size decreases; this will begin to reduce the efficiency of service to customers. Also, costs increase. Thus, any change in the three variables—number, type, or location of warehouses—will affect both service and costs.

Inventory Carrying. The ownership of inventory gives rise to costs for money, insurance, occupancy, pilferage losses and custodial services, and sometimes inventory taxes. Depending on the business involved, this group of costs may range from 10 per cent to 30 per cent of average annual inventory value. Customer service will be improved by keeping inventory at many storage points in the field near to customers, but this will increase total inventory and the cost for carrying that inventory. Thus, inventory carrying cost is closely linked to warehousing cost and customer service.

Inventory Obsolescence. If (at a given level of sales) total inventory is increased to provide better customer service, then inventory turnover is decreased. Also, the greater the "pipeline fill" in the distribution system, the slower the inventory turnover. This automatically exposes the owner to greater risks of obsolescence and inventory write-down. This is a particularly important cost for companies having frequent model changeovers, style changes or product perishability.

Production or Supply Alternatives. Production costs vary among plants and vary with the volume produced at each individual plant. Plants have different fixed costs and different unit variable costs as volume is increased. The decision of which plant should serve which customers must give weight not only to transportation and warehousing costs, but also to production and supply costs; these will vary significantly with the volume allocated to each plant.

Cost Concessions. A special aspect of production or supply alternatives arises from the fact that distribution decisions can affect costs otherwise incurred by suppliers or customers. For example, when a retailer creates his own warehouses, this may free suppliers from packing and shipping small quantities or from maintaining small local warehouses in the field. A retailer who establishes his own warehouse network may be able to recoup some of these costs by negotiation with the supplier.

Channels of Distribution. The choice of distribution channels profoundly affects the nature and costs of a company's sales organization, its selling price and gross margin structure, its commitment to physical distribution facilities. These in turn will affect production and supply costs.

Transportation. Changing the number or location of warehouses changes transportation costs, sometimes in unanticipated and complex ways. For example, an increase in the number of warehouses may initially reduce total transportation costs; but past some determinable point, the cost trend may reverse because of the decreasing ratio of carload to less-than-carload tonnage.

Communications and Data Processing. These costs vary with the complexity of the distribution system and with the level of service provided, including costs for order processing, inventory control, payables, receivables and shipping documents. These costs rise as more distribution points are added to the system. Additionally, as the cycle time or response time of the communications and data processing system is shortened, costs of this service are increased.

Alternative Facilities Use. Changes in inventory requirements or in other aspects of the distribution operation will change space requirements and utilization in a plant-warehouse facility or a retail store. Space used for distribution may be convertible to selling space which yields incremental sales and profits. In the case of retail business, this is actually a variation of the customer service factor since it increases the availability of goods with which to fill customer requirements.

Customer Service. Stock-outs, excess delivery time, or excess variability of delivery time all result in lost sales. Any change in the distribution system will influence these elements of customer service, and therefore must either gain or lose sales for the company. These effects, while difficult to measure, must be considered part of the real cost of distribution.

G

Financing and Credit

61

The Great Credit Pump

Carl Reiser

The subject of trade credit has been largely ignored in marketing literature, which is unfortunate because this aspect of credit is quite significant in the total economy, and manufacturers are finding that the cost of granting credit to middlemen is increasing. This article presents an overview of trade credit. As the author points out, the problem facing many manufacturers is how to use credit as a sales tool without paying too high a price for sales. Different techniques are available to accomplish this objective, including the captive finance company.

One of the most significant and least discussed statistics in the U.S. economy is the total of outstanding trade credit, the short-term credit that business extends to business. Estimates put it at nearly $10 billion more than the entire federal budget for 1963, some $20 billion more than the total value of all U.S. corporate bonds outstanding at the end of 1961, and about two and a half times the gross national product of Canada. It is in the neighborhood of $100 billion. But even more dramatic than its sheer size is its growth rate. In the decade between 1951 and 1961, while the U.S. gross national product, measured in current dollars, grew 58 percent and nationwide sales grew 37 percent, trade

Condensed from the February 1963 issue of *Fortune Magazine* by special permission; © 1963 Time, Inc.

credit expanded by just about 100 percent.

A no less striking fact is that U.S. manufacturers are the main source of this credit. They account for about half of the total. The remainder comes from wholesalers, service industries, and the entire complex of other nonfarm businesses put together. But the figure does not adequately state the entire investment in credit by U.S. producers of goods. For, in addition to short-term trade credit, they also extend to their customers untold billions of dollars in long-term credit through a number of different devices, such as the "captive" finance company. All together, the amount of credit supplied by manufacturers is far greater than that provided by the banking system, which at last count had some $42 billion in commercial and industrial loans outstanding. Since the banks are the base of the whole credit system, the manufacturers can be viewed as a great pump, vastly increasing the volume and velocity of the credit on which U.S. business operates.

The question arises: How did U.S. industrial corporations, whose main function is to produce goods, get into this formidable side business of financing trade? This raises other intriguing questions. Who, for example, pays for this credit? Or to put the question in the form that is of surpassing interest to business, who *should* pay for it? And in view of the extraordinary growth of trade credit, there is a still more important question from the over-all economic standpoint: Is it dangerous?

A Competitive Weapon

In answering these questions it is necessary first to examine the characteristics of trade credit and the reasons for its phenomenal growth. (This article will discuss long-term credit later.) Trade credit is strictly short-term credit extended by a seller of goods or services to a commercial customer—e.g., by a manufacturer to another manufacturer or to a wholesaler or retailer, or by a wholesaler to a retailer. It is entered on the current-assets side of the seller's books as a receivable. (It sometimes appears technically as a "note," a term commonly used in the jewelry trade among others.) The great bulk of trade receivables arises from sales of goods on open-account credit, where the buyer is expected to pay according to accepted trade terms. A typical statement of such terms is "two-ten-net-thirty"; translated, this means that the buyer has thirty days to pay, but if he pays in ten days, he gets a cash discount of 2 percent. There are other kinds of receivables, of course. Goods are often sold, for instance, on dating plans, whereby the customer accepts seasonal merchandise ahead of time and gets an extended time in which to pay. And there is consignment selling, in which the seller does not expect payment for goods until the customer actually sells them.

In part, the tremendous proliferation of these devices in recent years can be explained by the current vogue for doing things on the cuff, whether it is buying a home, eating out, or taking a jaunt by air. So much attention has been fixed on the phenomenal growth of consumer borrowing that hardly anyone noticed that trade credit was growing even faster, and today has roughly twice the volume of consumer credit. This suggests that there are some powerful economic factors, independent of mere fashion, at work. What has happened is that trade credit has become an increasingly essential weapon in the sales arsenal.

Customers demand a longer time to pay for their purchases and the sellers have had to go along with this in order to get the business. In fact, they vie with one another in offering easier and easier terms, because in a number of businesses such competition has become at least as meaningful as price and quality competition, sometimes more meaningful. In hardly any business or trade have the traditional, decades-old credit terms been officially changed. But in instance after instance the seller quietly grants the buyer a longer time to pay, or the buyer quietly avails himself of more time. "We don't grant the credit," says the executive of a steel supply company ruefully. "The customers take it."

The Undercapitalized Middleman

The conditions that enable the customers to "take it" were created by the emergence of the "short-order economy," described earlier in this series (*Fortune,* August, 1962). The burdens and costs of distributing goods are constantly being shoved back onto the producer. Wholesalers and retailers want to hold as little inventory as possible, and many of them would prefer not to pay for goods until they have actually sold them. They get their way because, in this economy of abundance, a producer frequently can hope to gain an edge only by catering more generously than his competitor to the needs of potential buyers. . . . Selling is more and more a matter of providing services that enable the customer to do *his* business more profitably.

By and large, both the middleman and the retailer in U.S. distribution are undercapitalized. They lack the assets and the credit ratings on which to borrow money cheaply. (Trade debt actually accounts for roughly *half* the borrowings of wholesalers and retailers.) Manufacturing corporations—especially the larger ones that are responsible for the bulk of U.S. industrial output—have huge assets and excellent credit ratings. They borrow at prime rates, and with a relatively plentiful cash flow, have ready access to cheap money. Consequently, the pressure is on them to take more and more of the job of financing the flow of goods through the distribution pipeline.

The whole subject of trade credit has been largely ignored until very recently by economists, and the over-all effects of this massive movement of money are little understood. However, one thing seems quite certain: The broad economic effect of trade credit tends to be strongly countercyclical. Consumer credit, on the other hand, generally rides with the cycle; when consumers feel an economic pinch they tend to stop buying on credit and start paying their debts. Bankers also become cautious in recession, and they tend to pull back in periods when money is tight. But trade credit tends to

expand under both circumstances, as the customers clamor for more and easier credit and the suppliers, pushed by intensified competition, give in to the pressure.

This is not just a supposition. It has been documented in an exhaustive study on trade credit made by Dr. Martin H. Seiden, director of the Bureau of Economic Analysis, a New York consulting firm. Dr. Seiden notes that in the recession of 1954, when total sales volume fell $15.2 billion and bank credit fell $300 million, trade credit helped to offset the contraction by increasing $4.1 billion. On the other hand, when the monetary authorities sought to tighten credit in the 1955 boom, trade credit increased by $10.7 billion, while bank credit was expanding by only $6.3 billion.

The Lenient Sales Departments

But it is one thing to say that trade credit has proved a nice cushion against the relatively mild recessions of the past decade and quite another thing to predict that it can keep on growing at its present rate without posing an ominous threat to the economy. The question is: How sound is this credit structure?

A fair answer must take into account that in any company there is a conflict of interests, between the sales department, which above all wants to make a sale, and the finance or credit department, which takes a more orthodox view toward granting credit—how much and to whom. Inevitably, companies end up by taking a more lenient view toward a credit risk than would, say, a banker. In most trade credit there is no down payment, no lien on the goods, no collateral. The National Bureau of Economic Research reported last year [1962] that the dollar volume of trade-credit losses currently exceeds more than a billion a year. This probably exceeds the dollar losses in all other forms of credit combined.

Most companies, however, report that they are not concerned by their loss rates and it is unlikely that the overhanging threat of that $100 billion in trade credit would become a real menace unless the economy took a sharp turn downward. In that case, of course, it could have a spreading effect as devastating as the collapse of credit had in the 1929 depression.

The disturbing element in the situation is that in the recent past credit has been growing faster than sales. This trend shows no signs of abating, but there is no reason to assume that it will continue indefinitely Conditions might change. For example, expansion of informal trade credit has undoubtedly been encouraged by the fact that the nation's total money supply in relation to the G.N.P. has gone back to the level of the Twenties, now that the excess liquidity generated during World War II has been worked off. As economic activity "grew up" to money supply, access to credit through existing financial institutions became more difficult and encouraged the resort to substitute devices. But the rein on the money supply can get looser as fears of inflation fade and the balance of payments is brought under control. Also, the competitive conditions resulting from today's buyer's market could well change. If manufacturers begin to find that their capacity is stretched, they might be less willing to give such generous payment terms.

In some areas of business, creditors have already begun to sense the need for caution. In retailing, the great discount revolution . . . has produced a number of new operators who are skating on very thin ice. Typically, many discounters use trade credit to finance growth; they buy goods on credit, turn the goods over, put the money into new goods and stores, and count on a further fast turnover to pay off their suppliers. Turnover is the key to discount operation, and it gives the discounters a considerable power over suppliers, who are so eager to get the discounters' volume business that they are willing to extend credit well beyond the limits of prudence indicated by a retailer's assets and working capital. According to Dun & Bradstreet, which regularly surveys some 200 discounters, the median figure for discount stores showed current assets at one and a half times debt in 1961. (Department stores, by contrast, had current assets of roughly three and a half times debt.) There has been a disturbing number of bankruptcies among discounters, and some suppliers are trying to tighten up credit terms.

Another trouble spot is the highly competitive construction industry, notably in home building. There is, at last, a trend toward concentration in what has always been a fragmented industry dominated by many small operators. "Many of the tract builders have become economic giants who buy in big gobs and have bargaining power," says one supplier to the building trades. "They can get quantity prices and move large volumes at low margins." But smaller subcontractors in particular are being squeezed because they make cutthroat bids to land contracts. The credit problem posed by these undercapitalized businesses, working on ever slimmer margins, is worsened by the manner in which builders and contractors are paid —in stages leading up to a completion payment that gives them their profit. A hard-pressed contractor will obviously make his suppliers wait for their money until *he* gets paid. Almost every supplier to the building trades reports that his receivables are disturbingly extended, and getting worse.

How to Cut Prices Quietly

The average age of receivables for all U.S. manufacturers rose from about thirty-five days in 1956 to nearly forty-five in 1962, according to the National Association of Credit Management. The pressure to extend trade credit, however, is by no means uniform throughout the economy. For manufacturers of mass-produced, high-consumption, high-turn-over items such as food and toiletries, credit is not a big factor in selling. Velocity is the important thing, and the producers have concentrated on stream-lining their distribution systems, speeding up shipment, reducing inventory, and moving the goods through to the consumer. The retailer orders, sells, pays for the goods on the usual terms, and orders more goods. Receivables held by Colgate-Palmolive, for example, simply tend to rise in proportion to sales.

But the story is quite different in a whole cross section of other U.S. businesses, from electronics to machinery, from textiles to chemicals. A big aluminum company reports that, in 1962, 29 percent of its trade accounts were over-due as against only 15 percent in 1955. The average age of receivables held by a major electrical manufacturer, to take another example, has jumped from forty days to more than fifty in the past five years.

The cost of carrying this liberalized credit obviously concerns these manufacturers. In general, they consider it an inevitable cost of getting more business. In a sense, the terms and conditions of sale are part of the price of the goods. Many businessmen are frank to admit that the easy extension of credit is equivalent to juggling prices. "The basic problem," says the chief financial officer of an electronics company, "is that most of the industry has excess capacity. So what can it do to sell more goods? It can use credit so that it amounts to a price concession."

There is a tactical advantage in so using credit. An outright price cut immediately alerts the competition, but credit can be extended quietly here and there without anyone's noticing, at least for a while. Some companies are worried about where this eventually leads to. "What does this giveaway generate?" asks an executive of a major steel company. "It doesn't generate more business because eventually everybody else will do it." And he adds, "Too much credit is about the worst thing that can happen."

"You Can't Do This to Joe Doakes"

Many corporations accept the role of financier reluctantly. The extension of credit is, after all, an investment of money—frequently of considerable sums that could otherwise be used elsewhere in the business, perhaps in new production facilities. This investment is increasing just when industry is trying its best to cut down other distribution costs, notably the cost of holding inventory. The distinction between inventory and receivables is becoming fuzzy. It makes little difference to a manufacturer whether he holds his products in his own warehouse until his distributor has orders for them, or pushes them along to the distributors, who won't pay him until he has sold the goods. Either way, the manufacturer gets hit with the cost.

The problem many manufacturers are facing is how to use credit as the vital sales tool that it is without paying too high a price for their sales. It is a highly complex problem, one that can no longer be solved simply at the level of the credit manager and his gimlet eye for credit risks.

An obvious way to solve it would be

to charge the customer for the use of the money, with the double purpose of getting some return on the investment and at the same time forcing the laggard customers to pay up sooner. Some firms do charge interest on open-account credit when the customer extends his payment beyond the usual trade terms. Many companies have thought about doing that, but have shied away because, in the words of one corporate executive, "It would cost more to administer than it would be worth. Anyway, you're not going to make it stick. The customer says, 'Your lousy equipment isn't working,' or 'You didn't ship this piece,' or so forth. 'You can't do this to Joe Doakes,' says the sales department. 'He's a big customer.'" One of the country's major steel-supply companies once tried charging a fee on overdue accounts, but shortly abandoned the idea. The competition didn't go along, and besides, the company found that when a customer had to pay interest, he simply let his bill run, so that it was harder than ever to collect the overdue amount.

In some industries, however, it *is* often possible to put credit on a self-sustaining basis. A good example is in commercial electronics, particularly the manufacture and sale of tubes, semiconductors, and other components. This is a relative new business, and by and large, the distributors of these products are undercapitalized. Furthermore, it is a highly competitive business, due to the pressure from imports and the declining market for tubes. The result has been an enormous demand for easy credit, and the standard trade terms in the business (thirty days net) have become meaningless. Distributors now get as much as 120 or 180 days to pay—or longer. Manufacturers have recognized the problem for what it is, and in effect try to regularize the whole situation by extending formal inventory loans over longer periods. Under one such plan, for example, the

manufacturer extends one- to three-year credit, at 6 percent per annum, to the distributors who will carry its line of components. The manufacturer recognizes this as virtually an advance of equity money to its customers. "They started out short of equity," says the financial vice president. "Now they're short of business."

Westinghouse uses a variant of this technique, not only for electronic components, but for a number of other products. "When the terms go from thirty to ninety days," points out an executive, "the manufacturer doesn't get any interest. It means a ballooning of working capital. The demand is for credit at no cost—to the customer. With capital equipment, normal trade practice is net thirty days. But this gets abused, and we keep hearing, 'I want two years to pay.' So what we want to say is, 'Our standard terms are thirty days, but we have a financing plan of up to five years.' We try to *sell* the customer on financing, since that gives him longer to pay."

How to Make a Profit on Credit

As the man at Westinghouse points out, "Financing of consumer goods has been going on for years. But in the last few years a lot of these techniques have been applied to industrial goods." The device Westinghouse ultimately adopted in 1954 in order to formalize its medium- and long-term credit arrangements was a captive finance company, the Westinghouse Credit Corp., which offers a wide range of leasing and financing arrangements to its customers. A number of other leading industrial corporations have done the same thing.

The captive finance company gives a corporation many advantages, one of the most important being that it clears a mess of receivables off the parent company's books. It also segregates the corporation's credit-financing problem, and puts it under the management of financial experts who presumably are free of pressure from sales departments. It gives industrial companies a direct and easy contact with the money markets. And it makes it feasible for a corporation to amortize its credit costs, and even to make a profit on credit.

The device has some limitations, however. It is highly useful in such fields as transportation equipment, appliances, and capital goods—where purchases are commonly financed over relatively long periods. It is not so useful in such areas as food, though captives have been set up even there.

The captive does *not* spare the manufacturer the need to make an investment in credit; it is simply a different kind of investment, one that often brings a direct return. Not every corporation finds it a satisfactory way to commit its money. Recently Motorola got rid of its captive credit company, in which it had a $40-million investment. The captive was set up to finance the installment sale and leasing of Motorola's two-way radio systems. But the company found that it could use the investment more profitably elsewhere. E. P. Vanderwicken, vice president and treasurer, says: "We're going to be in new businesses we don't know about yet. The alternator is doing away with the generator in cars, and semiconductors are making the vacuum tube obsolete. Over the next ten years there will be many new businesses to go into, almost all better to be in than the finance business."

Everyone Wants a Piece

One factor that is making the finance business less attractive in some cases is the development of strong competition. Once U.S. manufacturers were lonely pioneers in merchandising credit; no one else wanted to touch it. International Harvester developed the farm-equipment market through credit. General Motors helped build the mass market for cars by setting up General Motors Acceptance Corp. (in 1919), to finance the purchase of cars both by dealers and consumers. Fruehauf created a market for trailers when the banks and other institutional lenders were leery of the infant trucking industry. The captive credit companies still perform useful functions that other finance institutions won't or can't perform. They provide a steady source of credit for customers when bank money dries up in tight-money periods or in recession. In the case of agricultural-equipment makers, the captives supply copious drafts of credit in rural areas where the banks are too small to do the needed job. Also, banks, independent finance companies, and others do not like financing dealer and distributor inventories, which is less profitable than the financing of consumer paper.

But generally speaking, everyone is now eager to get into the fields pioneered by the manufacturers. Many banks, independent finance companies, and old-line factoring concerns have diversified their financing activities, and are now competing with one another—and with the captives—for industrial or consumer time-installment business. Big finance companies have entered the leasing business, where they compete with Westinghouse Credit Corp. The banks, once so conservative, have become perhaps the most aggressive of all. As their source of funds has shifted more and more from demand to time deposits, raising the cost of their money, they have sought more profitable business. In the past five years their share of the new car-financing business has risen from about 40 percent to nearly 50 percent.

This new competition is having an interesting and significant impact on the nature and use of captive companies, and on their function in the marketing scheme of the parent companies. The auto industry offers a very dramatic illustration of what can happen.

Ford's "Last Resort"

For years, as one auto executive recently remarked, the auto industry "had it made" insofar as the smooth distribution of its product went. Broadly speaking, the sale of cars to the dealer was on a sight-draft basis. The factory made the cars; the dealer paid for them when he took delivery. The carmakers themselves were in the enviable position of carrying virtually no finished inventory at all. Indeed, in earlier years the dealer had to pay for the cars as they came off the production line, though this was modified after the mid-1930's when the carmakers began to give free transit time while the car was en route to the dealer.

. . . G.M.A.C. long gave General Motors dealers an advantage over the dealers of the other carmakers, who did not have their own captive companies. G.M.A.C. today [1963] finances, at wholesale, some 74 percent of the cars handled by its dealers, and about 22 percent of the cars sold by them on time payments to consumers. Its dollar share of total U.S. new-car installment paper is about 17 percent, nearly equal to that of all independent finance companies combined (they have about 20 percent). This situation galls the independents, who would like to have Congress pass an antitrust law severing G.M.A.C. from G.M.

A few years ago Ford, which had chafed under G.M.'s competitive advantage, decided to do something about it. (Ford had started a captive in 1928 but soon sold it to C.I.T. Corp., which han-dled most of the Ford business there-after.) Several developments in the car business seemed to make some move imperative, not the least being the enormous proliferation of new car models and types, which threatened to balloon dealers' inventories. (Many large dealerships require an average inventory of around $200,000; some require $500,000 or more.) This began to give G.M.'s one-half of 1 percent margin on wholesale paper a very real significance. First Ford tried to get the independent finance companies to bring their rates down to meet G.M.A.C.'s. But, says Theodore O. Yntema, the chairman of Ford's finance committee, the company had no luck. "The largest independent finance company [C.I.T.] told us bluntly it would not meet G.M.A.C. rates" So, in a move that Yntema has described as a "last resort," Ford three and a half years ago re-entered the finance business by setting up Ford Motor Credit Corp.

Ford's bid has been costly and it offers a nice illustration of what is required when credit is used as a sales tool. The company had to build a nationwide credit organization of some 100-odd branch offices, and the start-up costs have been high. Ford has plunked $25 million in capital stock into the subsidiary, plus $75 million in paid-in surplus. As of 1961, on receivables of $160 million, Ford realized a minuscule net income—$64,159—and it will be some time before it reaches a desired yield of, say, 10 per cent on its investment.

But the rewards have been great, too. F.M.C.C. has already achieved a very signal victory. It has been responsible for driving down finance-company rates on auto financing to a level comparable to G.M.A.C.'s, which is what Ford had in mind in the first place. What Ford didn't particularly have in mind but has resulted is a benefit also to Chrysler and other dealers.

A $250-Million Bump

Meanwhile the carmakers, like other manufacturers, came under pressure from their customers (the dealers), who insisted on passing back some of the burden of carrying inventory. A little more than a year ago, with the introduction of the 1962 models, G.M. dramatically reversed the industry's hoary no-inventory policy. It initiated a free-wholesaling plan that in effect puts the autos into the dealer's showroom on consignment up to fifteen days. The other carmarkers, of course, were compelled to introduce similar plans.

The effect was arresting. The move automatically transferred dealers' debts on G.M.A.C.'s books, where they yielded interest, to the parent company's books, where they didn't. This increased G.M.'s receivables by a whacking $250 million, pushing its total receivables of all kinds to slightly under a billion dollars. Ford's receivables were bumped more than $200 million.

Detroit's experience shows how, even in a mighty industry enjoying one of its most prosperous periods, the manufacturer has to keep the massive and costly pump of trade credit at work.

VI

Special
Areas

A

Industrial Marketing

62

Systems Selling: Industrial Marketing's New Tool

Thomas J. Murray

An emerging marketing technique in the field of industrial market-ing is systems selling. According to the companies that have placed their marketing emphasis on systems selling, systems are described as combinations of products and services designed to perform a complete function for the customer. Because, as the author of this article points out, the key to any system sale is identifying the problem to be solved for a customer, this tool is really nothing more than an application of the marketing concept to industrial marketing. This article suggests that systems selling has a bright future. However, not enough time has elapsed to make a final judgment.

When C. Ray Harmon was brought in as assistant to the president of Los Angeles' Electronic Specialty Co. in 1955, he found the firm floundering along with a few components on its production lines, a meager $1.6 million in sales and only $72,000 in profits. The company had just gone public after an erratic eleven-year existence, and its growth prospects in the electronics mar-ket were not particularly bright. Harmon, however, came armed with a reputation

Reprinted from *Dun's Review,* October, 1964. Copyright 1968, Dun & Bradstreet Publications Corp.

as a "hatchet man" whose specialty was chopping off operating inefficiencies. More important, he brought with him a plan to change the entire profile of the concern.

In just nine years, Harmon's idea has transformed a sluggish outfit into a thriving operation. Sales are expected to top $85 million this year, and earnings will probably exceed $1.6 million. And what was Harmon's plan? It was to develop full lines of compatible products and services that could be tied together and marketed in packages called "sys-tems." His method: spin off all unrelated items and build a full "systems" capability for the firm through acquisitions.

Electronic Specialty's experience, while unusually successful, is by no means an isolated case. The systems approach to industrial marketing has sent a quiet revolution rippling through the ranks of American business. Scores of companies have placed their marketing emphasis on selling systems, or, as they are often described, combinations of products and services designed to perform a complete function for the customer. The upshot is a dimming of the traditional role of many suppliers as mere vendors of off-the-shelf items and a concomitant growth in their ambitions to act as project contractors who move in and solve problems.

Big firms such as Allis-Chalmers, Honeywell and General Precision, as well as medium-sized and small concerns, such as Dorr-Oliver, Taylor Instrument, Ajax Magnethermic, Hobart Manufacturing and Rohr Corp. to name but a few, are trying to become all things to their customers. From their wide range of goods and services, these companies are now providing start-to-finish systems designed, engineered and packaged to perform integrated functions ranging from manufacturing to material handling and from data processing to distribution.

Among the more complex systems are General Precision's fully automatic pressure pumping and inventory measuring system for huge petroleum tank farms and Ajax Magnethermic's fully integrated continuous-casting system for the processing of nonferrous metals from raw materials to finished product. Somewhat simpler systems include the total power propulsion package engineered for and installed in commercial jet transports by Rohr Corp. and the full refrigeration, heating, ventilating and air-conditioning package designed and sold by Hussmann Refrigeration to supermarkets.

For most of these firms, the big push toward systems selling in the industrial market is of very recent vintage and in many cases involves some of the same corporate integration achieved at Electronic Specialty. Thus, with companies such as Allis-Chalmers, which began its drive about four years ago through the acquisition of a joint interest in a systems company, or with General Precision, which combined two hardware companies in 1962 to enhance its systems capability, or with Ajax, which bought two concerns with compatible product lines in 1958, the shift to this has involved a step-by-step development of their capabilities. Says William Terry, general manager of Allis-Chalmers' electrical apparatus and systems division: "Every expansion of our plants is geared in some way to further development of this systems concept."

Why is everybody getting on the systems-selling bandwagon? For the most part, it is due to an emerging awareness among marketing men that industrial buyers are searching for greater value for every purchasing dollar. Says Conrad Jones, vice president at the wellknown management consulting firm Booz, Allen & Hamilton: "In the future, you'll find more customers thinking in terms of doing more business with fewer suppliers. You can't satisfy a customer with just a product. We think selling a total package of satisfaction is the way of the future."

More specifically, the reasons for the upsurge of interest in this marketing strategy range over the full spectrum of recent industrial developments:

- Intensifying competition has caused suppliers to search out new ways to market their goods, hence the accent on selling whole packages of products and services with its promise of more sales, fuller use of capacity and greater turnover.

■ An increasing awareness on the part of industrial firms that the machinery and techniques required for a modern plant are so complex, they can rarely understand all their own needs, much less buy and install the equipment on their own.

■ The need for greater reliability of technical machinery and processes is forcing industrial buyers to lean heavily on the quality of equipment purchased, hence the demand for greater supplier responsibility.

■ The realization of small industrial firms, caught in a competitive squeeze, that they can no longer afford to think in terms of individual components.

Spurred on by these developments, vendors have been promoting, advertising and selling this systems concept with ever-widening emphasis. And yet, for all the hoopla surrounding the trend, there is really nothing new about it at all. Its origins can probably be found in the approach of the Bell System more than fifty years ago when American Telephone & Telegraph President Theodore Vail looked upon the telephone not as a product to be sold but as a total communications system with a variety of integrated services. Similarly, heavy-equipment manufacturers such as General Electric and Allis-Chalmers decades ago were putting together combinations of their equipment and services to perform complete cycles on production lines.

What is new, however, is the increasing integration of automation with manufacturing and processing functions and all the allied operations of a contemporary industrial facility. Suppliers view the possibilities of applying some form of automation to their products as virtually endless. "In ten years," says George W. Downs, director of systems sales at General Telephone's Automatic Electric Co., "it will be fantastic. Soon all processes will be automated."

Moreover, applications of the systems approach in the military market have provided a powerful impetus to its growth in the industrial field. The skills, advanced technology and marketing ability acquired in servicing defense contracts have begun to give many companies new outlets to the commercial market. "In one case about two years ago," points out Electronic Specialty President William H. Burgess, "we discovered that a system we had been building for a defense contract was applicable to the industrial area."

But for all the emphasis on the term *systems,* there is considerable objection in some quarters to the glibness with which it is used. To Harold A. Wolff of Booz, Allen & Hamilton, the packages being sold by most suppliers are not, despite their claims, systems. "They're just selling related products," insists Wolff. "There's nothing new about that. It's just fundamental marketing know-how."

And certainly there is no unanimity among suppliers themselves on a precise definition of the term they have begun to use so freely. In fact, at a seminar organized by the American Management Association, representatives of several leading manufacturers found themselves at odds about what systems selling is. Finally, after much wrangling, says Lester M. Gottlieb, manager of marketing plans for IBM's data-processing division, a consensus was reached. The definition: "It is marketing based on the consideration of a customer or prospect's needs together with a proposal of a solution for his problem," relates Gottlieb. "This is opposed to coming in with a product and creating a need for it. Or to put it simply, it's really just problem-solving." Nevertheless, until a more precise term is coined, the prevailing trend among suppliers is to describe the concept they are using as systems selling.

Whither Objectivity?

There is, of course, some question about whether a company selling its own equipment in the design and installation of a system can be truly objective in its solution to a customer problem. "The nub of this thing is objectivity," asserts President Allan Harvey of Dasol Corp., New York management consultant firm. "There is a fundamental conflict of interest here and a question of whether a firm has developed the best solution to a client's problem."

By way of answering this charge, most firms assert that they are staking far too much of their reputation on such sales to chance such a risk. To George F. Lambeth, Dorr-Oliver marketing manager, for example, project responsibility means that the firm can insure the quality and performance of its product and thus enhance its prestige. Moreover, management likes the fuller corporate identity that goes with the sale of a system rather than a mere product, and regards its installations as a showcase to spur further sales.

The advantages accruing from this marketing tool do not stop there. Right off the top is the obvious boost it gives to sales. "Ours have grown by one-third," claims Ralph L. Shapcott, president of General Precision's industrial controls division. Adds Donald T. Gregg, manager of Taylor Instrument Co.'s contract and construction division: "Over several years now it has added an appreciable portion to our volume, perhaps as much as 10%." And reports Nathaniel T. Holzer, vice president of marketing at Los Angeles' Redcor Corp.: "You might say that our climb from just $300,000 in sales just two years ago to over $4.5

million this year is largely a result of this approach."

Equally heart-warming to its practitioners is the broader line of products the systems approach can spawn. A vendor's capabilities can be stretched to produce new items for integration in more elaborate systems or in further improvements to an original installation. Also, the competitive edge it gives a firm is so compelling, it is almost sufficient reason in itself for switching to a systems approach. Since sale of a total system involves a long-term marriage between vendor and buyer, the supplier is virtually assured of being the one continuing source of parts and service. Says one marketing executive, with an almost diabolical grin: "It's positively Machiavellian, isn't it?"

For all firms marketing such packaged programs, the one enduring benefit is an overall improvement in customer relations. The intimate relationship that develops between both parties, together with the solution that a supplier brings (hopefully) to his client's problems, molds a special tie that is unlike anything in more conventional vendor-customer relationships.

Organizing a company for the systems approach to marketing involves, in many cases, a thoroughgoing overhaul of its operations—from management outlook to sales procedures in the field. At Electronic Specialty, the basic decision started at the very top and was predicated on the belief that an acquisition program was the essential route to building up the required product lines. The firm has since picked up some twenty firms with compatible products, including a complete marketing organization for its selling, and has developed a full engineering capability to handle its design and application programs.

One major problem that can trouble the multidivisional company getting into the systems business is coordinating the various activities of each division. This problem has been solved at Electronic Specialty by the creation of a position called system project manager, an outgrowth of military and aerospace marketing practices. Notes IBM's Lester Gottlieb: "This is a fairly prevalent solution among systems companies. Making him [the system project manager] responsible for the whole project is one of the most efficient ways to coordinate the activities of each group and to optimize the total corporate point of view."

The actual selling process also calls for a radically different approach. For one thing, sales personnel must completely revamp their thinking away from the traditional product orientation. Says Taylor Instrument's Donald Gregg: "You're working on higher echelons, perhaps even with corporate officials. You rarely discuss the comparative merits of your hardware. You focus on your competence, your reputation and your ability to perform."

For most companies this has meant the establishment of special training programs for sales personnel. At Allis-Chalmers, says William Terry, sales people are brought into headquarters four times a year for special seminars that continuously build up their technical competence and familiarity with new developments.

But not every company agrees with the training approach. At Dorr-Oliver, for example, an official says the company does not contemplate any special training for its salesmen. "For those still oriented in their thinking toward equipment rather than a process," he explains, "we have to convince them to change their approach themselves. It won't happen overnight, of course, but they just have to learn to educate themselves."

Still another development is the increasing use of team selling. Involving

as it does in most cases a very high price tag and a relatively complex package of equipment, a systems sale calls for presentation by at least a systems engineer in addition to the regular sales personnel. At Ajax Magnethermic, says marketing manager Marvin E. Hackstedde, the field sales people, all of whom are graduate engineers, are backed up by specialized inside salesmen who follow through on an assigned product area all the way from the initial approach to the prospect to the final installation of a complete continuous-casting system.

But, as more than one observer has pointed out, the systems approach is still so relatively new in its expanded use that there is really no genuinely adequate training ground for systems engineers. "There is an extreme lack of qualification in this field and it is dangerous," warns John W. Field, director of the management information services department for The Diebold Group, a leading management consultant specializing in automation problems. "Words can be sold, but not performance. An intimate knowledge of many disciplines is required for this kind of work, but the demand for trained people hasn't been gratified with adequately trained personnel. What we need are analytical generalists."

In at least one case, that of General Precision's industrial controls division, a likely spawning ground for this new breed of technician is in the customer's own engineering department. According to one General Precision spokesman, the division has found that the man in an equipment user's engineering department who has already been responsible for putting together machinery to solve problems and is familiar with all the functions of the firm's technical operations is, in effect, a systems engineer. "Getting him on our side, however, is the problem," said the official.

Identify the Problem!

While this problem is certainly a knotty one for suppliers, an even more critical one is the very heart of any system sale: identifying the problem to be solved for a customer. In many cases, prospects are not even aware of the exact trouble they are having and throw the full responsibility on the supplier. Depending on the relative complexity of the problem, sales engineers steeped in the lore of production and technology may be able to pinpoint the trouble at an initial session. Or, as in most of today's highly complex situations, the customer will have to provide the supplier with all the knowledge about his process for a full study and evaluation. "When you go into a customer's plant, you have to know every step of his process," says Allis-Chalmers' Terry. "You can't apply computers and controls until you have an intimate knowledge of the whole process."

To most suppliers, this initial step is the most crucial moment in a potential sale. Embroiled as they are in bidding for many contracts, they feel that an early foothold in determining a customer's requirements is absolutely imperative; otherwise, as some vendors complain, they may spend thousands doing the groundwork only to find the prospect using someone else's specifications and purchasing the equipment from a competitor. "We have met situations," claims a Dorr-Oliver official, "where our preliminary engineering for a proposal was taken by the prospect and used to purchase equipment elsewhere."

To minimize the chance of such occurrences, systems sellers must carefully size up each prospect. At Allis-Chalmers, for example, where proposal costs run from $10,000 to as much as $50,000, marketing people calculate their risks very carefully. Says Terry: "We have to decide if we have a reasonable chance of getting the contract. This is very selective selling." Agrees IBM's Gottlieb: "To stay profitable, there is one overriding guideline: propose only when there is a reasonable chance of getting the order."

If proposals have proven costly to some firms, so too has the development of the systems themselves. Notes Taylor Instrument's Gregg: "This is high-risk stuff. Many of these things have never been done before, and it's awfully difficult to cost them out. We've been too prone to base prices on customer intent; yet this has been too obscure in many cases." Adds David P. Wilkinson, Electronic Associates vice president of planning: "If you can sell some stock solution over and over again via a system, then it's possible to make a profit out of this systems business. Otherwise, a systems company really has a tough time of it."

No less pressing a problem is the need to educate the customer in the limits and potentials of his system. Lack of comprehension has frequently led to misuse of an installation and consequent complaints to the supplier about the quality and performance of his equipment. "Many clients simply don't understand what their system is, what it does and what it can do," laments Redcor's Nat Holzer. "We have launched a customer education program and are beefing it up with a continuing documentation program. As far as we are concerned, it's becoming more and more the responsibility of the manufacturer to teach the customer completely about his system."

One further ramification of this education process, says George M. Muschamp, vice president for engineering at Honeywell's industrial products group, is fully informing the customer that if he is to take on a complete system he may have to accept some reorganization that goes deep into company operations.

Obviously, then, systems selling is not in any way a simple undertaking. For, as one marketing executive points out with almost painful memory: "It usually takes about three years of hard, hard work to convert fully to the systems approach to selling. Moreover, it calls for an unlimited amount of patience, conviction and perseverance."

Left unsaid in that statement are many obstacles. Among them: the enormous task of pulling together products and services that relate; the costly job of gearing production to meet neatly dovetailed schedules; the tough problem of finding or training adequate engineering and sales forces; the backbreaking effort of coordinating autonomous divisional activities; and the continuing task of keeping customers satisfied with a full line of services.

Despite these obstacles, the trend to systems selling is gathering strength and spreading. In fact, some marketing authorities, such as Roger Ball of Chicago's Roger Ball & Associates and Booz, Allen's Conrad Jones, predict that it will eventually move into the consumer market. Ball envisions companies selling housewives complete storage and maintenance systems for their households. Jones points to the upcoming S. C. Johnson & Son (Johnson Wax) nationwide car-wash chain, with its complete wash and wax capability, as a variation on the systems-selling theme.

But it is to the industrial market that most companies look for the most advanced strides. Just getting off the ground as it is in most cases, the systems approach has already endowed its practitioners with a rewarding glimpse of what can be done for a host of industries, from chemicals to transportation. More important, as Automatic Electric's George Downs puts it: "This is really the infancy of something new in industry. Its future will be fabulous."

A Customer Is a Company's Best Friend

Edward McCreary Jr. and Walter Guzzardi Jr.

Trade relations is the new euphuism for reciprocity—the practice under which special advantages are granted by the buyer in consideration of the special advantages granted by the seller. It is a practice that is almost universally practiced and at the same time almost universally deplored. The objection to it, of course, is that it substitutes nonmeasurable for measurable considerations. Under reciprocity both parties, and the public, may all be losers. The article which follows gives an interesting account of the practice and indicates its somewhat dubious legal status.

When a businessman's eye alights upon a good customer, some remarkable emotions stir in his breast. Important among them is what one executive describes as "an instinct as old as time": the desire to please. One way to please, of course, is to buy the products the customer himself may have for sale. Friendship thus finds a convincingly material expression, and ties are more firmly cemented. Such reciprocal arrangements ("just good business logic," as one businessman calls them) are often above reproach. Occasionally, they have a dubious moral tone, and may be the subject of cynical comment from competitors who may be left out in the cold. And once in a while the practice of reciprocity comes under direct legal attack. But undeniably, reciprocity can serve the common interests of the participants—who may prefer to avoid publicity in their dealings, but are evidently willing to risk it: about 60 percent of the companies on FORTUNE's 500 list now employ managers whom they euphemistically call "trade-relations men," and who adroitly, and more or less openly, conduct reciprocal affairs.

In some industries—notably those that have long been dominated by big companies—reciprocity belongs to a traditional way of life. Oil and steel companies long ago accepted it as an important influence on their business conduct. The kinship between a bank and its depositors is close, and well understood—so well, indeed, that one knowledgeable observer expressed considerable surprise when a New York bank recently failed to award the contract for its new building to a large depositor who was also a contractor. (The depositor promptly took his banking business elsewhere.) In the invest-

Reprinted from the June 1965 issue of *Fortune Magazine* by special permission; © 1965 Time, Inc.

ment community reciprocity is common practice: underwriting firms share good issues—and poor ones—with one another, and mutual funds parcel out their brokerage business to the houses that evince most interest in selling the funds' shares. Such relationships are part of long-standing custom.

Especially interesting is the way that reciprocal relationships are multiplying all through U.S. business these days, and being pursued with new techniques and formal organization. There are a number of reasons for the increase. Estopped from vertical growth, big companies have branched out horizontally into other industries, becoming more and more diversified until they have found themselves with a long list of suppliers in one hand and a long list of products for sale in the other. That conglomerates should move to make the most of the possibilities they perceive in such a situation seems only natural and practical. And the spur of competition from the corporations it meets as it enters new markets also urges on a company to use the reciprocal weapon, which one young manager describes as "another arrow in our quiver."

Alongside of and partly in response to those pressures, new managerial practices are emerging that also contribute to the escalation of reciprocity. Computers are supplying the information about who is buying from whom, and who is selling to whom, and what products are being exchanged in what volume—a complicated and changing body of knowledge that has to be spaded up before reciprocity, in its modern form, can be thoroughly and intelligently applied. The return to centralization of policy-making authority is helping to assure that deals will not be made, or strangled, by salesmen or purchasing agents in the boondocks, where views of company interests are liable to be parochial. And that authority is being personified in a new kind of manager—a man who joined the managerial cast of characters to fill a genuine need, and who by his performance has enlarged reciprocity's scope. Such "trade-relations men" are sprouting just about everywhere in U.S. industry. Properly interpreting that development as a vote of confidence, the trade-relations men now unabashedly put their names and titles on their doors, and speak freely about their functions. In a curious move, some have even gone so far as to organize a trade association—although they attend association meetings with a characteristically wary enthusiasm.

It is inevitable that the Federal Trade Commission and the Justice Department should be watching the expansion of trade relations with considerable and rather special interest. The government's position and attitude on the subject is being determined by the outcome of a couple of important cases, one of which is a Supreme Court case. For the moment, it seems that the government is resolved to bear down whenever a diversified company makes an acquisition that enables it to use its reciprocal powers in such a way that smaller firms could be squeezed out of the market.

Some other reciprocal practices, however, for the present seem safe from government action. Where two big chemical companies of roughly the same size and strength, for example, buy from and sell to each other intermediate products, the practice is likely to go unchallenged. And where a small supplier buys from his big customer—for instance, when a small company that is selling most of its product to Sears, Roebuck makes a point of going to Allstate for its insurance—no immediate legal action by the government is foreseen. But these are only hazardous generalities. Much of trade relations belongs to a gray legal area. Each deal, even those that are accompanied only by the gentlest and most subtle kind of suasion, must stand on its own merits.

A New Way to Take Richmond

Comfortably en route to Richmond, Virginia, Paul L. Davies, chairman and chief executive of the big conglomerate, FMC Corp., was both satisfied and expectant. His company's machinery division had just received a $35-million contract from the Defense Department for armored aluminum personnel carriers. Davies was on his way to place with Reynolds Metals, at the time troubled by excess capacity, an order for tons of aluminum plate.

But Davies was going not only as a potential buyer. FMC's chemical division is a large producer of soda ash and caustic, which are used in the making of alumina. Davies was therefore looking forward to a mutually beneficial agreement, in which he would place a large order for aluminum and would book in return an order for the sale of substantial amounts of soda ash and caustic.

On his arrival Davies received a rude shock. Richard Reynolds told him that the company had already made provision for its soda-ash requirements. After dwelling on the size and importance of the order he had to place, Davies returned to New York. He indicated that he would be awaiting some further response from Reynolds before he settled on how he would parcel out his aluminum order among the major producers.

As he guessed he would, Davies soon got the word he wanted. Reynolds made some changes in its soda-ash arrangements. FMC could sell Reynolds quite a bit of it, after all.

All this took place in 1959. Present-day practitioners of the art of trade relations profess to be shocked by

Davies' tactics, which they say they regard as too direct. The objective of the professional trade-relations man, of course, remains what Davies' was: to use the company's buying power to open new markets. It is true that Davies succeeded in doing that. It is also true that the deal he made was very large. Still, trade-relations men would insist, such pragmatic tests are not the only ones to be applied. There are more subtle and less hasty ways to get things done. There is a more delicate vocabulary to employ. There are the attitudes of people in both organizations to think about, and considerations of future business to weigh. In short, there is a whole new art to be practiced.

Hold on to the Boss's Ear

The t.r. man, who is a creature of the organization and not, like Davies, its prime mover, has many elements to put on the scale. Initially, he has his own position in the hierarchy to worry over. Where he ranks in the company varies widely from one corporation to another. Generally, he strives—like just about everyone else—to be close to the top, and to have the ear of the boss. In some companies the special functions he performs have brought him to that eminence. But even there he is unlikely to have more rank than sales or purchasing vice presidents who have their own views about what the company should be doing, and their own feelings about their provincial authority. And those men—who are at least the peers of the t.r. man—know the path to the big office, too. Caution is obviously called for.

Yet the t.r. man's caution is shot through with a kind of ingenuity, too. The prototype t.r.—and every one alive differs in some way from the prototype —tends to move behind the corporate scenes, not on the center of the stage. He may be self-effacing. He avoids harsh words or final actions: "This is a man who can always come back," says one witness of the t.r. man in motion. He may maintain a façade of humility. Yet under the surface he has the classic confidence of the Christian who holds four aces.

Because he represents so elemental a fact in business life the t.r. in action can be an impressively effective figure. But his job is liable to begin prosaically enough. The t.r.'s first concern is to make certain that "friendly" companies—by which he means companies that his organization buys from—include his firm as a possible supplier on their purchasing lists. With many multilayered and multidivisional companies turning out a profusion of products, that is not always easy to ascertain. The t.r. needs a steady flow of recent information on the subject. And he needs personal friends— very likely the t.r. men of other organizations—whom he can call with a friendly word of reminder. "Friendly" is very much a part of his lexicon.

There is also a converse function. The t.r. keeps his educated eye traveling down the lists of his company's purchases. His intent, of course, is to see that they are made from the right people whenever possible.

With that kind of basic information in hand, the t.r. is ready to get things rolling. The earlier he can make his arrangements, the more influential he can be. As an example, Kaiser Aluminum & Chemical buys tires in considerable number from General Tire & Rubber. Kaiser now has a plant in Louisiana just coming on stream that will be selling a component used in plastic foams. General Tire uses that component in one of its divisions. Quick to recognize General Tire as a prospective customer that would also be receptive to overtures, Kaiser's t.r. made an approach to his opposite number, John Ragsdale of General Tire, who notes: "Maybe we can do business with each other. We're talking about it." Meanwhile Ragsdale is already doing his part to build the friendship. In Palo Alto, California, a General Tire subsidiary is a major contractor for construction of a giant linear accelerator that will require thousands of tons of concrete. Says Ragsdale: "Kaiser Cement would like to supply the cement for the job. I'll help them make the proper contact."

Take a similar instance. General Tire buys a lot of construction material from Johns-Manville. General Tire also makes a film that, somewhat modified, might be sold to Johns-Manville for its production of pressure-sensitive tapes. General Tire's salesmen weren't making much headway in getting a share of Johns-Manville business—until Ragsdale gave his sales force a boost by making one of those phone calls. He says now: "Our product is in test. And we're getting every opportunity to move into that market."

Often t.r. men, because of the number and special positions of their friends, are the first to find out about a new sales opportunity. Alcoa buys a good deal of fuel oil and lubricants from a big oil company. In a general discussion with his oil-company counterpart, Jack Hamilton, t.r. for Alcoa, was telling the oil-company man about some of the new uses of aluminum for construction. "Then," recalls Hamilton, "he told me about a new office building they were putting up. He gave me the right man to call so that our people could put together a proposal. I don't know how on God's green earth I'd make that contact except this way. We got the business—we earned it. And next time we met the same man told me subcontracts were about to be let for a refinery they were building. He gave me the name of the

general contractor and the production engineer."

Like many others, the t.r. for H. K. Porter, C. P. Stewart Jr., makes it a major part of his job to look out for construction of new plants by suppliers. He gets the names of contractors and engineers on the project. He passes that information on to his salespeople. While they are making their best sales effort, the t.r. emphasizes to the prospective buyer that his company has a special position.

Insight from a Bumped Head

While t.r. men can help their salesmen, they sometimes bump heads with their purchasing agents, who may not have the insight into some situations that t.r.'s have. For example, one of Anaconda's big customers was having trouble making sales to Anaconda's wire-and-cable plant at Hastings-on-Hudson. The plant's purchasing agent, no doubt for reasons that seemed good from his point of view, just wasn't heeding that customer's salesmen. So Anaconda's t.r., E. F. Murphy Jr., who is a headquarters vice president of the company, called the plant's manager. Murphy said to him: "I suggest you see them. They may mean nothing to you, but they mean a lot to Anaconda Aluminum, and to some other divisions."

The t.r. men can also put their influence to work on the purchasing agents of other companies. When Stauffer Chemical, from which Anaconda buys a wide range of chemicals, announced that it was building a plant in Wyoming, Anaconda was surprised to learn that the specifications called for the use of a competitor's mining-machine cable. Murphy called to the attention of Sam Emison, marketing vice president for Stauffer, the fact that Anaconda, which Murphy said "makes the best mining-machine cable in the country," wouldn't even have a chance to bid on Stauffer's business. The communication of Emison to his company's engineers is not recorded. But the next day the specifications were changed so that they called for the competitor's cable "and/or approved equal." Says Murphy: "That's all I asked for." Anaconda won the bid, and sold Stauffer the cable.

The t.r. man, of course, cannot always come back with everything he hopes for. He is liable to be frustrated, for one thing, by other t.r. men, who may represent companies with stronger positions. In that case, the t.r. who came looking for a substantial deal may go home pleased if he succeeds in carving out even a small part of what he wanted—but more than he had at first. "Suppose I find out that another company has the inside track on a piece of business," muses Stewart of H. K. Porter. "Right away I ask 'Is it still open? Do we get a chance?' I know that if we go in on an equal basis, we're probably going to lose. So maybe we can get consideration for some part of the business." One way to do that is explained by George Polzer of Witco Chemical: "When another company has the business tied up on a t.r. basis, I may say 'Look, this is the only product we make that you can buy from us, so why not buy it? You can still buy something else from that other company.'"

The t.r. men can sometimes land a new account for their company by a special kind of triangulation. When Witco Chemical tried to sell some of its products to a steel company, it could not make any reciprocal appeal, since Witco buys very little steel. However, Witco buys a lot of fabricated drums used for shipping chemicals, and the drum manufacturer is a big steel consumer. Says Witco's t.r.: "Since our drum supplier buys from Republic Steel, he asks Republic to give us some consideration." Because of possible legal complications,

however, other trade-relations men are wary of such tertiary deals.

$8 Million in One Hand

As with other managerial practices, some companies set up their trade-relations departments when they saw the practice working for others. St. Regis Paper, in the 1950's, was the dominant company in the manufacture of multiwall paper bags. Not until Crown Zellerbach, Owens-Illinois Glass, and others moved in with their purchasing power did St. Regis step up its own efforts to use its reciprocal potential. When a large metal company was building an $8-million plant on the West Coast, it let out all the contracts, and then found that it couldn't sell the contractors wire and fabricated metal for its own building. The chairman of the board said at the time: "By God, the next time I have $8 million in one hand, I'm going to make sure I have something in the other." Shortly after that the company appointed its first t.r.

The new attention commanded by reciprocity does not mean that it is the dominant element in every business arrangement. Reciprocity, after all, is only one part of the complicated formula that governs large sales; it must be considered, but so must many other criteria. One t.r. man veered away from an attractive offer because, he recalls, "I didn't like the way it was presented. He made it black and white, with none of the normal functions of sales and purchasing. If it had been handled differently, we would have opened some doors, and let the thing develop naturally. But a cold-turkey deal—no, sir."

All t.r. men also point out that they prefix their pitch with an essential phrase: "All things being equal, we want to be considered." The conditions that must be equal are price, quality, and service—and the greatest of these is price, because it is potentially the area where any special consideration is obviously and demonstrably illegal. "We never talk price," the t.r. men say in a chorus. Generally, and doubtless with considerable truth, t.r. men say that they have served their most important purpose after they have won an equitable hearing for their company.

Without flatly denying the t.r.'s point that "all things" must be equal, one sophisticated businessman adds some illuminating qualifications to the premise. "The buyer often makes the low man—he can determine who is going to come in with the low bid, just by making special demands. We used to use one contractor all the time, because he was consistently the low bidder. Now I've told my people to make sure that someone else is the low bidder every once in a while. I don't want to kill off the competition." In a realistic footnote, he continues: "Horse trading will go on to the end of the world. When you're small they call it chiseling. When you're big they call it negotiating."

The Closed Circle

Trade relations, while helping big companies, can hurt little ones. A big company, after all, constitutes in itself an important market for a great many products. Between giants, the awkward danger that one company or the other will come to depend too much on reciprocity is lessened. General Tire's trade-relations man, for example, says frankly that his work moves most smoothly when he deals with companies as large and as diversified as his own.

Thus trade relations between the giant conglomerates tend to close a business circle. Left out are the firms with narrow product lines; as patterns of trade and trading partners emerge between particular groups of companies, entry by newcomers becomes more difficult. Such crystallization, however, is constantly being broken up by technological advances: new products and processes lure companies away from stable relationships. Competition from foreign companies also works against a hardening of trade patterns. Were it not for such factors, the U.S. economy might end up completely dominated by conglomerates happily trading with each other in a new kind of cartel system.

The Highest Judge of All

Militantly aligned against any such eventuality is the power of the government. The Federal Trade Commission and the Justice Department are not directly attacking all aspects of the practice of reciprocity. Instead, they are moving against the process of diversification by merger. When a powerful company acquires a smaller one, the smaller, which now has a parent bristling with reciprocal strength, may come to dominate its industry. This, federal regulators say, is exactly what they are determined to prevent. Section 7 of the Clayton Act is the main legal basis for the government's actions.

In September, 1957, General Dynamics acquired Liquid Carbonic Corp., the leading U.S. producer of carbon dioxide. General Dynamics' chief customer at the time was the government, but the company had as its suppliers hundreds of subcontractors that might be converted into customers once it had acquired Liquid Carbonic. After it had done so, the trade-relations program began to unfold. General Dynamics compiled a "vendor book" that listed 40,000 suppliers which had sold General Dynamics more than $10,000 worth of goods or services the previous year. Vendors were approached. General Dynamic's divisions were even asked how much soda pop they bought; soft-drink makers use large amounts of carbon dioxide. Liquid Carbonic's management expressed the hope that members of General Dynamics' board of directors would marshal "their vast contacts in business" to help reciprocity along.

The vigorous effort in trade relations, however, soon stirred some equally vigorous opposition. The larger divisions of General Dynamics rebelled against the need for acting in the interests of Liquid Carbonic. General Dynamics' director of procurement warned his top management that he was "concerned about the concerted effort on the part of Liquid Carbonic to secure business from our suppliers by consideration of reciprocity . . . Our relationship with the Air Force and suppliers could be disturbed by the disclosure of such practices." The purchasing agent for a supplier of Convair, a General Dynamics division, described the pressure being put on him as "degrading coercion."

When the Justice Department moved in, it claimed that General Dynamics, by its use of reciprocity, was unfairly reducing competition in the field. The government asked for divestiture of Liquid Carbonic, and for an injunction to prevent General Dynamics from engaging in any similar action in the future. In response, the company argued that its exertions in the name of reciprocity were not a substitute for selling but aimed at creating an atmosphere in which Liquid's salesmen could attempt to sell." The company cited the further argument that its trade-relations effort was not, in the end, very successful. General Dynamics contends that the alleged increase of $1 million in sales attributed to trade relations is greatly exaggerated, but that, even if true, the increase would amount to only 1/300th of the market for industrial gases at the time. Liquid Carbonic, General Dy-

namics says, had 27.3 percent of the carbon dioxide market when it was acquired, and after three years of trade relations had lifted its share only to 28.4 percent and, in the course of the three years, Liquid Carbonic took a great deal of the time and attention of General Dynamics' top management.

The Power Is Enough

In its case against Consolidated Foods, the government is taking a similar tack—attacking trade-relations practice through antitrust. The FTC is objecting to the acquisition by Consolidated Foods —a company that processes food and operates chains of grocery stores—of Gentry, Inc., a producer of dehydrated garlic and onion. The government charges that Consolidated Foods was able to influence its suppliers to buy from Gentry, and so reduced competition. Consolidated Foods has responded by cheerfully admitting that it tried to use its reciprocal power to help Gentry along. The only thing is that this leverage didn't work, the company says. Over eight years Gentry's share of a rapidly expanding garlic market was reduced by 12 percent. The company says competition obviously was not impeded.

To that the government has a ready response. For one thing, it suggests that for some years the quality of Gentry's product did not improve to meet the competition, and that Gentry would have lost even more heavily without the aid of reciprocal arrangements. More important, the government insists that after Gentry was acquired, Consolidated Foods had the tacit power to reduce free competition. Whether effectively used or not, possession of that power, says the government, is enough to make the merger illegal.

The Supreme Court has now upheld the FTC. "Reciprocity in trading as a result of an acquisition," said the Court, "violates section 7 of the Clayton Act if a probability of lessening of competition is shown." On that basis, if it so chooses, the government may be able to pry apart many mergers already accomplished, as well as to impede new ones.

An Association Born of Irony

In view of the possible legal involvements, a great many t.r. men and their company lawyers have always been deep believers in anonymity. It seems ironic, therefore, that many t.r. men belong to a trade association, and that the association came into being on legal advice. At an American Management Association seminar some years ago, an FTC lawyer informally suggested that private meetings of t.r. men could take on a suspicious cast. He recommended that the men of reciprocity form an association, hold meetings with lawyers in attendance, and take minutes of the sessions.

Enough t.r. men agreed so that the association now has 141 members from 135 large companies. But others have steered clear of formal membership. So the association has a large platoon of nonmembers, including the trade-relations men from U.S. Steel, Shell Oil, and G.E. Such nonmembers may show up at a gathering to meet friends and give advice, but they aren't there officially. The resulting situation often leads to ludicrous exchanges like this one, overheard at the meeting last year:

"Hi, Harry. Are you here officially this year?"

"No. I'm here strictly on my own."

"Who's footing the hotel bill?"

"Oh, the company is."

B

Risk Management

64

Market Risk—
An Analytical Framework

Mark R. Greene

A subject that has been relatively neglected in the marketing literature is market risk. In his attempt to convince the reader of the virtues of using a risk framework in decision making, the author of this article looks at some of the more common marketing problems to illustrate the various risk types and handling methods. His conclusion that future managers will view decisions as the result of formal analysis of their twin components, expected return and risk, is gaining wider acceptance.

It is well recognized that managers in general prefer to ignore or minimize the possible effects of wrong decisions. While this situation is understandable, it may lead to financial disaster. It is the contention here that marketing managers should pay much more attention to the analysis of market risk than is usually the case. Some of the avenues for a fruitful exploration and analysis of market risk are pointed out in this article.

There is little scientific documentation of the precise extent to which marketing managers ignore or minimize the risks they assume. It is not popular to publicize failures. There is surprisingly little published about the real causes of even such celebrated marketing failures as the Edsel or the Studebaker. There is even less known about the marketing planning and risk analysis which preceded these failures. Donald Tull recently demonstrated that a systematic upward bias tends to exist in the forecasts made on sales and profits for new products.[1] In a survey of 16 manufacturing firms which introduced 63 new products over the period 1955–63, Tull found that the upward forecasting error was relatively high for both profits and sales, but the

abridged from the *Journal of Marketing,* national quarterly publication of the American Marketing Association, Vol. 32, No. 2, April 1968, pp. 49–56.

[1] Donald S. Tull, "The Relationship of Actual and Predicted Sales and Profits in New Product Introductions," *Journal of Business,* Vol. 40 (July, 1967), pp. 233–250.

average error for profit forecasts was about double the average of error for sales forecasts.

The Theoretical Role of Risk in Marketing

One way to describe the marketing function is to interpret it as that process in which the marketing manager continually seeks ways to convert market uncertainties into risks which can be objectively measured and thus handled efficiently either by insurance, transfer to specialists, or by consolidation. Those residual uncertainties which cannot be measured must be borne by the entrepreneur. The competitive process in free private enterprise can be viewed as one in which competitors in the market continually seek to reduce risks. The methods used might include such diverse tactics as price fixing, exchange of marketing information, merger with a competitor, industrial spying, reciprocity, insurance, or patent protection. Marketing science may be said to constitute that body of knowledge which deals with ways of handling marketing risks.

Some definitions and classifications of risk are needed at this point.

Risk Categories

Risk may be defined as the uncertainty surrounding the occurrence of an event which may cause a loss. Different aspects of risk can be classified under three general headings as follows:

I. Financial effects of risk.
   A. Pure
   B. Speculative
II. Ways in which risk may be measured or evaluated.
   A. Objective

   B. Subjective
      1. The risk taker
      2. The risk averter
III. Ways of dealing with risk.
   A. Combination
   B. Avoidance
   C. Transfer
   D. Loss prevention
   E. Knowledge
   F. Assumption

I. Pure risk is the uncertainty surrounding the occurrence of events which can produce *only a loss*, if they should occur. Examples of such events are fire, windstorm, theft, successful negligence suits, and accidental injury or death of a key man. Most pure risks are insurable. Speculative risk concerns those uncertain events which may produce *either* a loss or a profit, if they should occur.[2] Most market risks are speculative. As has been shown, marketing managers generally tend to overlook or minimize the possibility of loss, whether they are dealing with pure or speculative risk.

II. Risk may be further analyzed in accordance with the susceptibility of risk to a process of measurement or evaluation. In some situations the events producing losses occur in a repetitive fashion and lend themselves to analysis by way of probability distribution. In such cases the mean loss and variance can be determined and the whole problem handled by statistical analysis. In these cases risk can be viewed as a concept in variance, that is, the possible deviation of actual from probable or average result. The coefficient of variation, the ratio of the standard deviation to the mean, offers one way of assessing the range of error acceptable to marketing management. If the number of events is large enough this relative error range tends to de-

[2] A. H. Mowbray and R. H. Blanchard, *Insurance* (Fifth edition; New York: McGraw-Hill, 1961), p. 6.

crease. Under the "law of large numbers" the marketing manager may determine in advance the degree of error he is willing to accept and the "confidence level" with which he is satisfied in making his decision. Given these parameters he may then estimate the number of events required for each level of confidence and each range of error. The process is directly analogous to the statistical inference problem in sampling procedures. The type of risk which lends itself to combination in this manner has been called *objective risk.*

Objective risk is high when the number of events to be faced which might cause loss are too varied or too few to permit the averaging process to operate to eliminate "large" variations of actual from predicted results. Objective risk is low when the opposite conditions exist. Objective risk may include both pure or speculative risks. Thus, fire, windstorm, expected sales results for an old product in a new market, and cost of compensating a large number of salesmen are examples of events which lend themselves to reduction by combination.

As an illustration, the marketing manager may measure the degree of acceptable objective risk by a confidence interval estimate of a given error range in a forecast of sales for an old product in a new territory. Suppose that the break-even level of sales is 900 units. The acceptable objective risk is "there shall not be more than a 55% chance that sales will fall below 10% of the expected levels, or in any case below 900 units." The marketing manager may have had sufficient past experience with new products such as this in other territories to estimate the mean and standard deviation of the distribution of sales, or he may make such estimates from a consumer survey or from results in a test market. Suppose he estimates the mean to be 1,000 units, the standard deviation

to be 100 units, and the distribution to be normal. In such a case his objective risk criterion would not be met because he can be only about 84% sure that his sales will not fall below 900. In repeated events there is about a 16% chance that sales will fall below 900, since under the assumption of a normal distribution of sales, "68% of the time" actual sales may be expected to fall within one standard deviation of the mean.

Where the events producing possible losses do not occur repetitively, analysis of the measurement problem is more difficult. The importance of the risk tends to be related to subjective factors and has logically been termed *subjective risk.*

Subjective risk is concerned with the assessment of those uncertain events which cause loss, but for which no ready statistical measurement is known to the risk perceiver. Subjective risk refers to the mental attitude toward risk when an uncertain event is perceived by the decision maker. There are two broad classes into which decision makers may fall—the *risk averter* and the *risk taker*. The risk averter tends to perceive a high degree of risk in any decision he makes, while the risk taker tends to perceive a low degree of risk. Obviously there are many intermediate degrees of willingness to take risk. The risk taker is more inclined to "take chances" while the risk averter is more likely to take the "safe" way out. The risk averter is more likely to be conscious of the risks he faces than is true of risk takers. The risk averter may or may not be aware of all of the facts surrounding an event which would tell him what the probability of occurrence is or what the financial loss might be if the event did occur. He is often dealing with a single event, instead of a large group of repetitive events. Research findings and other information about the market may not necessarily change a risk averter into a risk taker, but this may increase the willingness of the risk averter to take more risk than he would without such information.

It has been fairly well established in the psychological laboratory that risk taking conduct tends to be fairly consistent as a personality pattern.[3] It was hypothesized by Friedman and Savage,[4] and supported by Mosteller and Nogee,[5] that mental attitudes toward risk can be measured through "utility analysis" whereby a number scale can be developed for any individual to establish the subjective value this individual places on money. Theoretically, in those cases involving uncertain outcomes of marketing decisions, the marketing manager could obtain numerical measurements of the degree of severity of losses to him personally. Also, fairly consistent reactions over time to situations involving risk might be achieved. Subjective risk as discussed here may be differentiated from Frank Knight's concept of uncertainty in that subjective risk, at least in theory, can be measured, whereas Knight defines uncertainty as essentially risk which cannot be measured.[6]

III. Various ways have been developed to handle risks once they have been properly identified and classified. First, uncertain events may be grouped together and prepared for through the process of averaging out expected losses. This has been called the method of combination or consolidation. Examples of combination include commercial insurance, self-insurance, mergers, and diversification. Second, management can avoid those activities which produce the chance of loss in the first place. This method may mean, for example, that entrance into a new territory will be avoided for the time being. Third, management can transfer the risk to others. Thus the risk of inventory price declines might be passed back to a wholesaler or manufacturer through ordering "hand-to-mouth." Fourth, loss prevention activities can be undertaken to reduce the likelihood of the loss producing event or to reduce its severity should it occur. Sprinkler systems in a building, sales training activities, and advertising are all examples of activities of this type. Fifth, marketing research, business information systems, and educational activities may all be viewed as ways to increase the degree of knowledge the decision maker possesses about the uncertain events he faces. With greater knowledge comes greater control over the uncertain event and generally less subjective risk or worry. Attitudes of management toward the potential loss should be measured, if possible. Finally, risk may be deliberately assumed by the decision maker. Generally all decisions involve some degree of residual risk which cannot be handled effectively in other ways and are thus simply assumed.

The logical order of priority of the various way of dealing with market risk is diagrammed in Figure 1. Notice that the first step is to recognize the exposure to possible loss, a step which is often ignored or handled cursorily. Observe also that "calculated risk assumption" of residual losses implies that a decision has been made to accept the residual risk, even though "severe." Such a procedure as outlined in Figure 1 is almost certain to produce a far more refined analysis and sophisticated assessment of market risk than would be possible otherwise.

[3] N. Kogan and M. A. Wallach, *Risk Taking—A Study in Cognition and Personality* (New York: Holt, Rinehart, and Winston, Inc., 1964), Chapter 3.

[4] M. Friedman and L. J. Savage, "The Utility Analysis of Choices Involving Risk," *Journal of Political Economy,* Vol. LVI (1948), pp. 279–304.

[5] F. Mosteller and P. Nogee, "An Experimental Study of the Auction Value of an Uncertain Income," *Journal of Political Economy,* Vol. 59 (1951), pp. 371–404.

[6] Frank Knight, *Risk, Uncertainty, and Profit* (New York: Harper & Row, Publishers, 1965), p. 6.

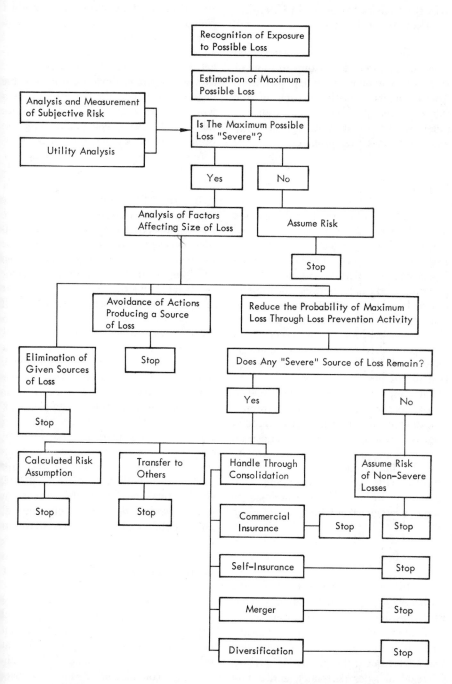

Figure 1. Logic flow chart—marketing decisions involving risk.

Kinds of Risks Inherent in Certain Marketing Problems

As illustrations of risk types and handling methods, let us turn to some of the more common marketing problems. The elements of risk in each of the following activities will demonstrate the potential value of this approach in analyzing marketing problems.

Sales Forecasting

Estimated future sales, on whatever level it may be conducted, may be viewed as a management reaction to risk or uncertainty. Presumably sales forecasting is undertaken to facilitate the planning of physical output, and thus to establish other resource needs such as capital, personnel, and plant capacity. Errors in prediction of major needs can be expensive. It is the goal of management to reduce the degree of error so that profits may be maximized.

Sales forecasting may be described in a risk context as an activity to reduce the degree of subjective risk through increased knowledge of an uncertain environment. If many products are involved, the problem may be one of objective risk, with the marketing manager using the law of large numbers to predict average losses with great accuracy.

Market Segmentation

Identification of those parts of the market which have particular characteristics has long been recognized as an invaluable aid to marketing management. It is through market segmentation that advertising, sales promotion, pricing, selection of sales personnel, and a host of marketing decisions can be made more intelligently. There may be a vast difference, for example, in a pricing and

advertising media decision for a product aimed at a "blue collar" market and a pricing decision for the identical product aimed at an "upper-middle class" market. Market segmentation may be viewed as a management device to increase the degree of understanding of the consumer which in turn helps management reduce the risk of error which might otherwise be made in developing the correct marketing mix for a given sales campaign. Thus market segmentation reduces subjective risk.

In large firms market segmentation may also be viewed as a device to reduce objective risk. Market segments may be viewed as units in a population of consumers from which sales and resulting profits occur according to some predictable distribution, with a mean and variance which can be estimated. If this be true, market segmentation becomes a device to reduce risk through consolidation, permitting management to make confidence interval statements about the likelihood of aggregate success. An important rationale for conglomerate mergers (for example, Textron, General Tire) has been the desire for segmenting markets and reducing the risk of operation by offsetting the losses of one operation against the profits of another, achieving greater stabilization of aggregate profits—in other words, risk reduction through consolidation and through diversification.

Compensation and Training Systems

As a device to reduce risk, some marketing managers tend to favor much greater use of a straight commission system of compensating salesmen than other marketing managers do. The straight commission system is used extensively, particularly in smaller companies. In this way sales effort can be achieved without extensive financial risk since, if no results are obtained in terms of new sales, no commission or other payment is due. Furthermore, many firms make little or no investment in training costs. They can depend on the investments made by others in a prospective salesman's training and experience or perhaps upon the existence of a number of friends and relatives to supply the salesmen with leads.

Use of a straight commission may be viewed as a risk transfer device, and use of a salesman already trained at someone else's expense may be viewed as risk avoidance. Training costs incurred by the firm can be viewed as handling risk through loss prevention activity. In all cases subjective risk is reduced. The firm may view the turnover cost of salesmen hired on straight commission as an average loss, and thus deal with it as a case of reducing objective risk.

Marketing Research

Most marketing research is undertaken to narrow the range of uncertainty within which executive decisions must be made. Marketing research does not eliminate all risk, but in an uncertain environment it does significantly reduce the risk by reducing ignorance.

Similarly, use of a mathematical model may help the marketing manager isolate those variables which have the greatest effect in the outcome of a given decision or to estimate the size of required markets in order to achieve certain other objectives. One of the major advantages of mathematical models is that they permit the decision maker to undertake simulations of real life before financial commitments are made, thus learning vicariously about the uncertain environment of the market. These models become a tool for the reduction of subjective risk by increasing the degree of knowledge.

In those problems lending themselves to sampling procedures, the decision maker may handle objective risk by establishing in advance the level of confidence with which he will be satisfied in accepting or rejecting the hypotheses by which he has framed his questions, as illustrated above in the forecasting example.

Credit Management

Investigation of the credit worthiness of customers before credit is extended, coupled with a policy of limiting the amount of credit, may be viewed as an exercise in risk reduction. Factoring of accounts receivable, purchase of credit insurance, or participating in bank financing plans under which the credit risk is assumed by the bank are other examples of risk reduction through transfer to others. An example of the transfer method of handling risk is also seen in the policy of requiring salesmen to bear part or all of any bad debt losses incurred as a result of their failure to make collections on time or to continue to ship goods to customers when accounts are past due. Marketing managers may decide that a policy of customer diversification is also desirable as a method of reducing the importance of any one account. This is an application of the consolidation principle to reduce risk.

Refusing to sell to certain classes of customers entirely is an example of risk avoidance. Finally, accepting certain credit risks in order to obtain sales that would probably not otherwise be made (for example, credit sales to foreign customers) illustrates risk assumption.

Conclusion

It has been demonstrated that market risk has been a relatively neglected subject in the literature of marketing. By interpreting the various activities of marketing as different examples of risk taking and by examining problems in a risk framework, the marketing manager may make better decisions. One major advantage of using a risk framework in making decisions is that it forces the decision maker to consider those outcomes which might cause disastrous losses to the firm. The normal tendency is to give too much weight to possible *gains*, and insufficient weight to possible losses. However, there is the possibility that due to differences in risk attitudes between top management and middle management, undue weight may be given to decisions involving minimal risk at the expense of potentially profitable decisions carrying only slightly more risk. By a systematic examination of those features of a problem which involve risk, actions can be taken to assess the degree of risk attached to each expected profit level. Action can also be taken to minimize the possible losses which might otherwise occur, through such devices as transfer, avoidance, loss prevention, combination, and insurance.

The marketing manager of the future will tend more and more to view decisions as being the result of formal analysis of their twin components, the expected return component and the risk component.

C

Marketing of Services

65

What Is Meant
by Services?

John M. Rathmell

In an economy both goods and services are marketed. Yet services, although claiming a significant and increasing share of the consumer's dollar, do not receive much attention from marketing writers. The author of this article argues that more marketing attention should be devoted to the services sector of the economy. The reader may question whether the marketing characteristics of services presented in this article are, in fact, as different from those of goods as the author believes, particularly in light of the marketing concept.

Certain concepts and phrases still exist in conventional marketing thought without their meaning being challenged, even though conditions surrounding their origin have changed. The classification of consumer goods into convenience, shopping, and specialty categories is one example;[1] channels of distribution is another.[2]

The ubiquitous phrase "goods and services" is a special example. Most marketers have some idea of the meaning of the term "goods"; these are tangible economic products that are capable of being seen and touched and may or may not be tasted, heard, or smelled.

But "services" seem to be everything else; and an understanding of them is not clear. For example, convenience foods have "built-in-services." Are they services in contrast with foods? A business publication refers to a giant retailer's

Reprinted from the *Journal of Marketing*, national quarterly publication of the American Marketing Association, Vol. 30, No. 4, October, 1966, pp. 32–36.

[1] Richard H. Holton, "The Distinctions Between Convenience Goods, Shopping Goods, and Specialty Goods," *Journal of Marketing*, Vol. 23 (July, 1958), pp. 53–56, and "What Is Really Meant by 'Specialty Goods'?" *Journal of Marketing*, Vol. 24 (July, 1959), pp. 64–66; David J. Luck, "On the Nature of Specialty Goods," *Jour-*

nal of Marketing, Vol. 24 (July, 1959), pp. 61–64.

[2] Phillip McVey, "Are Channels of Distribution What the Textbooks Say?" *Journal of Marketing*, Vol. 24 (January, 1960), pp. 61–65.

new services: leased beauty salons and restaurants, telephone ordering, and in-home selling. Are these institutional rearrangements really services?

And what about service businesses that do not require heavy investment in plant and equipment? Railroads? Light and power utilities?

Marketing's "Goods" Orientation

The marketing discipline has a strong "goods" orientation. In academic courses in marketing, tangible goods are considered, but rarely services to any extent. Yet services represent an area of economic activity that accounts for 30 to 40% of consumer dollar expenditures!

Similarly, many retailers and manufacturers tend to think only in terms of tangible goods; relatively few have broadened their conception of a product to include services. There are exceptions, of course: Sears, Roebuck & Company's entry into the insurance industry, mutual funds, and interior-decorating; the automobile manufacturer's interest in repairing, financing, and leasing.

Table 1. Personal Consumption Expenditures by Type of Product[a]

	1959 %	1964 %
Food and tobacco:		
Goods	100.0	100.0
Services	0.0	0.0
Clothing, accessories, and jewelry:		
Goods	89.1	89.8
Services	10.9	10.2
Personal care:		
Goods	55.3	56.8
Services	44.7	43.2
Housing:		
Goods	0.0	0.0
Services	100.0	100.0

	1959 %	1964 %
Household operation:		
Goods	59.1	57.9
Services	40.9	42.1
Medical care and death expenses:		
Goods	23.3	21.4
Services	76.7	78.6
Personal business:		
Goods	0.0	0.0
Services	100.0	100.0
Transportation:		
Goods	75.5	77.2
Services	24.5	22.8
Recreation:		
Goods	66.4	68.5
Services	33.6	31.5
Private education and research:		
Goods	0.0	0.0
Services	100.0	100.0
Religious and welfare activities:		
Goods	0.0	0.0
Services	100.0	100.0
Foreign travel and remittances net:		
Goods	50.3	39.5
Services	49.7	60.5
Total personal consumption expenditures:		
Goods	61.4	59.2
Services	38.6	40.8

[a] Derived from Survey of Current Business, Vol. 45 (November, 1965), pp. 20–23.

Goods and Services Distinguished

A useful distinction can be made between (1) rented-goods services; (2) owned-goods services; and (3) non-goods services. Also we might think of marketed services as market transactions by an enterprise or entrepreneur where

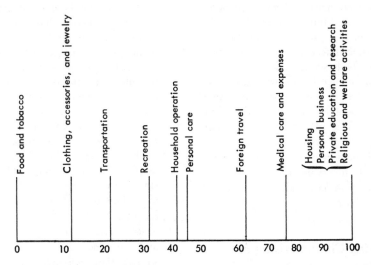

Figure 1. Per cent of major classes of personal consumption expenditures allocated to services—1964. [Source: Survey of Current Business, Vol. 45 (November, 1965), pp. 20–23.]

the object is other than the transfer of ownership of a tangible commodity.[3]

One implicit distinction is to consider a good to be a noun and a service a verb —a good is a thing and a service is an act. The former is an object, an article, a device, or a material . . . whereas the latter is a deed, a performance, or an effort. When a good is purchased, the buyer acquires an asset; when a service is purchased, the buyer incurs an expense.

Another test to distinguish a good from a service is the nature of the product's utility. Does the utility for the consumer lie in the physical characteristics of the product, or in the nature of the action or performance?

Applying this test, there are very few pure products and pure services. The satisfaction, or utility, deriving from a work of art, such as a painting or sculpture, lies solely in the good itself. The benefit, or utility, arising from legal

[3] Robert C. Judd, "The Case for Redefining Services," *Journal of Marketing*, Vol. 28 (January, 1964), pp. 58–59, at p. 59.

counsel proceeds exclusively from the service rendered. In the former, no act is performed; in the latter, no good is involved.

Apart from these extremes, most goods, whether consumer or industrial, require supporting services in order to be useful; most services require supporting goods in order to be useful.

Goods-Services Continuum

Economic products lie along a goods-service continuum, with pure goods at one extreme and pure services at the other, but with most of them falling between these two extremes.

This mixed characteristic is suggested by both Table 1 and Figure 1, even though quite broad categories are considered. Some are primarily goods with service support, whereas others are primarily services with goods support. Most goods are a complex of goods and facilitating services; most services are a complex of services and facilitating goods.

This mixed nature of most economic products is well illustrated by the leasing transaction. If a product is purchased, it is a good; but if it is rented or leased, the rentee or lessee acquires a service.

Yet for the service to have any meaning whatever, a goods component must also be present. Service would contribute time and place utility; the good would be the physical commodity made available and the service would be the act of making it available for a prescribed period of time as an alternative to outright purchase.

Marketing Characteristics of Services

The basic question is—*what are the marketing characteristics of services?* Here are 13 answers:

1. Unlike a good, where monetary values are stated in terms of a price, services are more likely to be expressed as *rates, fees, admissions, charges, tuition, contributions, interest, and the like.*

2. In many types of service transactions, *the buyer is a client rather than a customer of the seller;* the client, when buying a service, figuratively or literally places himself "in the hands" of the seller of the service. Consider, for example, the relationship between the student and the college, the patient and the hospital or physician, the passenger and the carrier. The buyer is not free to use the service as he wishes, as would be the case in the purchase of a good; he must abide by certain prescripts laid down by the seller in order for the service to make any contribution.[4]

[4] For an interesting discussion of relations between clients and client-serving organiza-

3. The various marketing systems in the services category have taken on *highly differentiated characteristics.* Although contrasts do exist in those marketing systems that have evolved for different types of physical goods, they are primarily differences of degree. In the case of services, the marketing of recreation bears little resemblance to the marketing of medical service. As additional examples, there is no apparent relationship between the marketing system for shoe-repair service and for hospital service.

4. Since services are acts or processes and are produced as they are consumed, they *cannot be inventoried,* and there can be no merchant middleman since only "direct" sales are possible. In a number of instances, agent intermediaries are utilized in the marketing of services: insurance and travel agents, for example.

5. The question may be raised as to *the economic nature* of certain products in the services category, for example, payments to charitable and religious bodies and non-profit educational institutions. Are the church on the corner, the college on the hill, and the United Fund Agency downtown economic entities on the supply side? Certainly they compete for the consumer's dollar.

6. There appears to be a *more formal or professional approach to the marketing of many services* (not all, by any means)—for example, financial, medical, legal, and educational services.

7. Because services cannot be mass-

tions see Charles E. Bidwell and Rebecca S. Vreeland, "Authority and Control in Client-serving Organizations," *The Sociological Quarterly,* Vol. 4 (Summer, 1963), pp. 231–242.

Table 2. Magnitude of Some Industrial Services[a]

Type of Service	Gross and Personal Expenditures	Industrial Expenditures
Engineering and other professional services		$ 2,966,000,000
Business services (not elsewhere classified)		$ 8,492,000,000
Corporate sales: telephone, telegraph, etc.	$10,929,000,000	
Less personal consumption expenditures: telephone, telegraph, etc.	−4,720,000,000	$ 6,209,000,000
Corporate sales: electric and gas utilities	$20,197,000,000	
Less personal consumption expenditures: electricity and gas	−8,422,000,000	$11,775,000,000
Corporate sales: railroads	$10,382,000,000	
Less personal consumption expenditures: railway (including commutation)	−454,000,000	$ 9,928,000,000

[a] *Survey of Current Business, Vol. 44 (July, 1964), pp. 16 and 28. Net figures represent corporate sales not only to business but also to government, institutions, agriculture, etc.*

produced, *standards cannot be precise.* Although service procedures may be standardized, their actual implementation will vary from buyer to buyer. Perhaps there will be a standardization of services through the increasing use of service technology at the expense of personalized service, especially in medicine and education; and this would mean that services will follow goods from custom to mass production and standardization.[5]

8. *"Price-making" practices vary greatly* within the services category. Utility and transportation rates are rigidly controlled by public agencies; interest rates display characteristics of price leadership; and some service charges are established on the basis of what the traffic will bear.

9. Economic concepts of supply and demand and costs are difficult to apply to a service because of its *intangible nature.* Moreover, values of some services are difficult to fix. What is the value of the service of a lawyer or a physician in a losing cause as compared with a successful one?

10. *Most fringe benefits* take the form of services: pensions, insurance, unemployment benefits, eye and dental care, psychiatric service; seldom are benefits in the form of goods (such as turkeys at Christmas).[6] If bene-

[5] William J. Regan, "The Service Revolution," *Journal of Marketing,* Vol. 27 (July, 1963), pp. 57–62, at pp. 61–62.

[6] "Why Union Eyes Are on Fringes," *Business Week* (September 12, 1964), p. 60.

fits are created by the employer, in a marketing sense he is selling a product (in lieu of higher wages) to a market segment, his own employees. If the service is created by an outside specialist, such as a life insurance company, the employer is an agent (in a marketing sense) between the seller-creator of the service and the buyer-consumer.

11. There appears to be *limited concentration in the service sector of the economy.* There are few service chains; carriers and utilities are regulated.

12. Until recently, *service firms failed to differentiate between the production and marketing of services.* Performance was equivalent to marketing the service.

13. In the case of services, *symbolism derives from performance* rather than from possession.

Industrial Services

The significance of industrial services in the economy is indicated in the data in Table 2.

Services of Government

The greatest marketer of services in the United States is government. The public sector is becoming a major supplier of that which was once the domain of private enterprises or private institutions. Consider Medicare, urban renewal and slum clearance, public parks and recreational areas, public higher education, and publicly-owned utilities.

Moreover, private sellers of many services are much more controlled by public agencies than are private sellers of goods. It is not much of an exaggeration to say that the mixed economy is divided on a goods-service axis. It is conceivable that most consumer services (excluding personal-care services) eventually will be purchased from public bodies, whereas consumer goods will continue to be purchased from private enterprise.

The Service Challenge for Marketing

Table 1 shows, services are a major component in the economy. McKittrick sees them not only diverting income flow away from manufacturing but also pressuring wages upward because of their relatively greater price increases.[7] Others have cited the lower efficiency in the personal-services sector because of the lower quality of labor in services production, as compared with goods production, and because of the limited opportunities for mechanization.[8]

The distribution of goods is within the province of marketing. But is there the same consensus regarding amusements, health services, and hotels? Should they be treated vertically, within their respective industries and professions—or horizontally, under the marketing umbrella?

In this connection: How are public services marketed? Are there public marketing institutions and procedures? When is the transaction completed? What is the price? What are the terms of sale? The recent promotion campaign to sell the voluntary provision in Medicare to 20 million eligible citizens repre-

[7] J. B. McKittrick, "The Nature of the Involvement of Marketing Management in the Profit Failure," in Charles H. Hindersman, Editor, *Marketing Precision and Executive Action* (Chicago: American Marketing Association, 1962), pp. 75–88, at pp. 81–82.

[8] "Why Service Workers are Less Productive," *Business Week* (November 14, 1964), p. 156.

sents one of the first major attempts to market a government service.

In Conclusion

The increasing percentage of consumer expenditures allocated to intangibles deserves special attention. This is especially true of the marketing of services by public agencies.

But what are services? Certainly any comprehensive approach to the study of services marketing must begin at the conceptual level.

VII

International Marketing

66

A Product Life Cycle for International Trade?

Louis T. Wells, Jr.

In domestic marketing, many managers often find the product-life-cycle concept to be a useful guide in making certain policy decisions. The author of this article proposes a related approach for the executive engaged in international marketing.

The product-life-cycle model is used as the base for a so-called trade cycle, during which the United States begins as an exporter of a product and may finally end up as an importer of the product. In all, four stages emerge as being relevant to the trade cycle. The author claims that the cycle model provides a useful managerial tool in analyzing the future directions of international trade in a product so that the manager may plan early enough for appropriate policies. Because this approach is new, time must pass before assessments can be made concerning the validity of this claim.

The lowering of barriers to international trade has resulted in many opportunities for American companies to profit from exports. Clearly, the businessman needs ways of analyzing the potential exportability of his products and, equally important, tools for predicting which products are likely to be threatened by import competition.

Until recently, the manager was dependent on the explanations of trade offered by the classical and neo-classical economists. Their reasoning generally led to the conclusion that each country will concentrate on exporting those products which make the most use of the country's abundant production factors.

Reprinted from the *Journal of Marketing*, national quarterly publication of the American Marketing Association, Vol. 32, No. 3, July, 1968, pp. 1–6.

The economic theory is elegant—it can be stated mathematically or geometrically and it can be manipulated to yield, under certain assumptions, answers to questions such as what is the value of free trade to a country, or what are the costs and benefits of certain restrictions. So long as the problems posed are of a very broad nature, the theory provides a useful way of analyzing them. However, when the theory is applied to the detailed problems facing the businessman it becomes of limited value.

The Trade Cycle Model

A new approach to international trade which appears most promising in aiding the business executive is closely related to the product life cycle concept in marketing. The model claims that many products go through a trade cycle,[1] during which the United States is initially an exporter, then loses its export markets and may finally become an importer of the product. Empirical studies of trade in synthetic materials,[2] electronic products,[3] office machinery,[4] consumer durables,[5] and motion pictures[6] have demonstrated that these products follow a cycle of international trade similar to the one which the model describes.

According to the trade cycle concept, many products follow a pattern which could be divided into four stages:

- Phase I: *U.S. export strength*
- Phase II: *Foreign production starts*
- Phase III: *Foreign production competitive in export markets*
- Phase IV: *Import competition begins*

A brief look at the reasoning underlying each of these stages will give some clues which will help the businessman to identify the stage in which particular products may be. The concept can then be an aid in predicting the product trade

performance to come and in understanding what actions the manager can take to modify the pattern for certain products and to profit from different stages of the cycle.

Phase I: U.S. Export Strength

What kinds of new products are likely to be introduced first in the. United States? It can be assumed that American entrepreneurs have no particular monopoly on scientific know-how or on very basic technical ability. What they do have, however, is a great deal of knowledge about a very special market—one which is unique in having a large body of very high-income consumers. Products which satisfy the special demands of these customers are especially likely to be introduced in the United States. Moreover, due to a monopoly position of the United States as a supplier of the new products which satisfy these unique demands, they offer the best opportunities for exports.

Empirical studies have failed to show a very simple relationship between demand and invention. However, there can be little doubt that certain products are simply more likely to be developed in America. Automatic transmissions for automobiles promised to be pretty expensive additions to cars. If an inventor considers the chances of his brain child's being purchased by consumers, a U.S. inventor would be more likely to pursue an automatic transmission than a European. The European inventor would more probably concern himself with ideas suitable to European demands. He might respond to high fuel taxes and taxes on engine displacement by developing engines which produce more horsepower per cubic inch. He might develop better handling suspensions in response to the road conditions. An inventor usually comes up with products

[1] For a more complete theoretical support of a similar model, see Raymond Vernon, "International Investment and International Trade in the Product Cycle," *Quarterly Journal of Economics*, Vol. LXXX (May, 1966), pp. 190–207.

[2] Gary C. Hufbauer, *Synthetic Materials and the Theory of International Trade* (Cambridge: Harvard University Press, 1966).

[3] Seev Hirsch, *Location of Industry and International Competitiveness* (Oxford: Clarendon Press, 1967).

[4] U.S. Senate, Interstate and Foreign Commerce Committee, *Hearings on Foreign Commerce*, 1960, pp. 130–139.

[5] Louis T. Wells, Jr., *Product Innovation and Directions of International Trade*, unpublished doctoral thesis (Harvard Business School, 1966).

[6] Gordon K. Douglass, *Product Variation and Trade in Motion Pictures*, unpublished doctoral thesis (Department of Economics, Massachusetts Institute of Technology, 1963).

suitable to his own market. It is even more likely that the final product development leading to commercial production will be achieved by an entrepreneur responding to his own national demand.

Even if an American is most likely to be the first to produce a high-income product, why does he not set up his first plant abroad where labor is cheaper? Certainly for many products the cost of materials and of capital is not sufficiently higher in Europe to offset the advantages offered by cheaper labor. Moreover, the burden of tariffs and freight are light enough now for many items. And the uncertainties of manufacture abroad are diminishing as more American companies gain experience. There are, though, very rational reasons why the American entrepreneur might prefer to start manufacture at home.

At the early stages of a product's life, design is often in a constant state of flux. There is a real advantage which accrues to a manufacturer who is close to the market for his products so that he can rapidly translate demands for design changes into more suitable products. Moreover, these changes often require the availability of close communication with specialized suppliers. Hence, the instability of product design for new products argues for a location in the United States—near to the market and close to a wide range of specialized suppliers.[7] The entrepreneur is less likely to be concerned with small cost differences for very new products. The existence of a monopoly or the significant product differentiation at the early stage of the product life cycle reduces the importance of costs to the manufacturer. The multitude of designs and the lack of standard performance specifications make it very difficult for the consumer to compare prices. Also, in

[7] Same reference as footnote 3.

the early stage of the product life cycle the consumer is frequently not very concerned with price. Success comes to the manufacturer who can quickly adjust both his product design and marketing strategy to consumers' needs which are just beginning to be well identified.

At this point, the American manufacturers have a virtual monopoly for the new product in the world market. Foreigners who want the good must order it from the United States. In fact, wealthy consumers abroad, foreigners with particular needs for the product, and Americans living abroad seem to hear about it very quickly. Unsolicited orders begin to appear from overseas. U.S. exports start to grow—initially from the trickle created by these early orders —to a steady stream as active export programs are established in the American firms.

Phase II: Foreign Production Starts

Incomes and product familiarity abroad increase, causing overseas markets eventually to become large enough that the product which once appealed primarily to the U.S. consumer has a broad appeal in the wealthier foreign countries. Not only does a potential foreign producer now have a market close-at-hand, but some of his costs will be lower than those of the U.S. producer. Imports from America have to bear duty and overseas freight charges —costs which local products will not carry. Moreover, the potential foreign producer may have to invest less in product development—the U.S. manufacturer has done part of this for him. Some measure of the size of his potential market has been demonstrated by the successful sales of imports. Favorable profit projections based on a demonstrated market and an ability to underprice imports will eventually induce an entrepreneur in a wealthy foreign market—usually first in Western Europe —to take the plunge and start serious manufacture. Of course, this manufacturer will, in some cases, be an American subsidiary which starts production abroad, realizing that if it does not, some other company will.

However, the calculations that yield favorable costs projections for competition with imports from the United States in the foreign producer's home market do not necessarily lead to the conclusion that the foreign producer will be a successful competitor in third markets. For many modern manufactured goods he is likely to be at a serious disadvantage due to the small size of his plant in a market where he also must bear the burdens for freight and tariffs. Scale-economies are so important for many products that the U.S. manufacturer, with his large plants supplying the American market, can still produce more cheaply than the early foreign producers who must manufacture on a significantly smaller scale.

During the second stage American exports still supply most of the world's markets. However, as foreign producers begin to manufacture, U.S. exports to certain markets will decline. The pattern will probably be a slowdown in the rate of growth of U.S. exports. The slowdown in the rate of growth of exports of home dishwashers in the last few years as European manufacturers have begun production provides an example of a product in this phase of the cycle.

Phase III: Foreign Production Competitive in Export Markets

As the early foreign manufacturers become larger and more experienced their costs should fall. They will begin to reap the advantages of scale economies

previously available only to U.S. manufacturers. But, in addition, they will often have lower labor bills. Hence, their costs may be such that foreign products become competitive with American goods in third markets where goods from both countries have to carry similar freight and duty charges.

During this stage, U.S. producers will be protected from imports in their domestic market where they are not faced with duty and overseas transportation costs. However, foreign goods will gradually take over the markets abroad which were previously held by American exports. The rate of growth of U.S. exports will continue to decline. The success of European ranges and refrigerators in Latin America points out that these products are in this phase.

Phase IV: Import Competition Begins

As the foreign manufacturer reaches mass production based on his home and export markets, his lower labor rates and perhaps newer plant may enable him to produce at lower costs than an American manufacturer. His cost savings may be sufficient that he can pay ocean freight and American duty and still compete with the American in his own market. This stage will be reached earlier if the foreign producer begins to think in terms of marginal costs for export pricing. If he believes that he can sell above full costs in his home market and "dump" abroad to use up his excess capacity, he may very quickly undercut the U.S. producers pricing on full costs.

During this final stage, U.S. exports will be reduced to a trickle, supplying very special customers abroad, while import competition may become severe. The bicycle is a product which has been in this phase for some time.

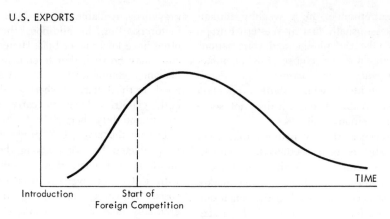

Figure 1. Export cycle.

The Cycle

Thus the cycle is complete—from the United States as a strong exporter to the stage where imports may capture a significant share of the American market. Figure 1 shows schematically the U.S. export performance for an hypothetical product.

The early foreign producers—usually Western Europeans—will face a cycle similar to that of the U.S. manufacturer. As still lower-income markets become large enough, producers in these countries will eventually become competitive —displacing the dominance of the early foreign manufacturers. The manufacture of products moves from country to country in what one author has called a "pecking order."[8]

So far, there are only relatively few examples of the less-developed countries' becoming exporters of manufactured goods. The classic example is standardized textiles. Another interesting example is the export of certain standardized computer components from Argentina. However, the current growth rate of over 12% per year for exports of manufacturers from less-developed countries may indicate that they will soon become

[8] Same reference as footnote 2.

an important factor for the American businessman.

How Different Products Behave

Obviously, the export patterns are not identical for all products. Three variables were critical to the argument supporting the trade cycle concept: the uniqueness of the appeal of the product to the U.S. market, the reduction in unit costs as the scale of production increases, and the costs of tariffs and freight. Differences in these variables will be very important in determining how a particular product behaves as an export or import —and thus what the profit opportunities or threats will be.

High-Income Products

The advantage of the United States in export markets in certain products was said to be dependent on the uniqueness of the appeal of the product to the American consumer. The cycle would be more "stretched out" if this demand is particularly unique. For such products, the U.S. manufacturer will probably remain an exporter for a longer period of

Table 1.   Ratio of Value of 1962–1963 Exports to Value of 1952–1953 Exports

Necessity		Discretionary		Luxury	
Refrigerators	0.47	Automobiles	0.99	Movie Cameras	4.14
Ranges	0.87	Electric Clocks	1.04	Freezers	0.74
Radios	1.42	Still Cameras	4.66	Air Conditioners	3.59
Irons	1.56	Washers	1.35	Slide Projectors	4.66
Televisions	1.04	Vacuum Cleaners	1.78	Dishwashers	8.50
		Mixers	1.25	Outboard Motors	4.18
		Record Players	1.81	Recreational Boats	4.40
Average	1.07		1.84		4.32

$F = 7.0$ (Significant at 0.95 level)

Note: Adjustments for freezer exports to Canada and 1963 still camera exports raise significance to 0.99 level. Same reference as footnote 5.

Source: Classification of products from James Gately, Stephen Gudeman, and George Moseley, "Take-Off Phenomenon," unpublished paper submitted to Consumer Behavior Research Seminar (Harvard Business School, May 27, 1965). Export data from U.S. Department of Commerce, Bureau of the Census, FT 410 Reports.

time and can postpone his fears of import competition.

It is possible to categorize some products for which the U.S. demand is "unique":

Luxury Function. Certainly products which perform functions people are willing to do without until they are comparatively wealthy have a particularly large demand in the United States. Movie cameras and room air-conditioners come immediately to mind. In fact, a classification of consumer durables into luxury, discretionary, and necessity shows a remarkable correlation with the U.S. export performance of the products. Exports increased 330% over a ten-year period for the luxury products, compared to an almost 84% increase for the discretionary items and only a 7% increase for the necessity products. (See Table 1.)

Expensive to Buy. Products that cost significantly more than other products which perform similar functions appeal primarily to a high-income bracket. Electric knife sharpeners are an example of this type of product. A study by Time

Marketing Service[9] showed that 21.5% of households with incomes of over $10,000 (where the heads were white collar, college educated) owned electric knife sharpeners. In contrast, only 11.6% with incomes under $10,000 owned them.

Expensive to Own. Similarly, products that are expensive to maintain or to operate compared to alternative products which perform similar functions are uniquely suited to a high-income market. The American automobile provides an example. The disadvantage of its high fuel consumption more than offsets the advantages of more space and higher horsepower for most low-income foreign consumers.

Labor Saving. Products which save labor by substituting a relatively large amount of capital are particularly appealing to the American market. The high cost of labor, a function of high American incomes, makes it very attractive to

[9] Time Marketing Services, *Selective Mass Markets for Products and Services,* Time Marketing Information, Report No. 1305.

buy items such as heavy road building equipment and computers which substitute capital for labor.

Of course, the businessman can influence the appeal of his products through his product policy. For example, he can build larger or smaller cars, automatic record players or simple ones.

Scale Economies

The trade cycle is also influenced by the amount of savings in cost, which can be achieved by increasing the scale of production. If a small plant is equally as efficient as a large one for a given product, a foreign producer will start to manufacture while his market is still relatively small. U.S. exports will not be as successful, and import competition will probably soon begin.

The effect of scale economies is well illustrated by the cases where a product goes through several stages of manufacture. In refrigerator production, for example, low costs can be reached in assembly operations at a much lower volume than in the manufacture of compressors. This difference shows up in the performance of U.S. exports for one period where exports of completed refrigerators fell drastically, but exports of compressors for inclusion in refrigerators assembled abroad held their own.

Tariffs and Freight

If tariffs or other trade barriers overseas are high for a particular product, foreign production is encouraged. Hence U.S. exports will receive early competition from foreign production. Developing countries have frequently raised tariffs to encourage local production while their markets are still small. However, if the American tariff is high, it follows that the United States manu-

facturers need worry less about import competition.

High freight costs, usually for products which are heavy or bulky compared to their value, tend to discourage trade. Not only will foreign production occur earlier, but foreign competition is unlikely to become a serious threat in the U.S. market. In the extreme cases of very high transportation costs, trade never occurs, or occurs almost entirely along borders where a foreign source is closer than a domestic one. For example, trade in gravel has never been significant because of transportation costs.

Exceptions to the Cycle

Not all products can be expected to follow the cyclical pattern described. The model says little about products which do not have a particularly strong demand in the United States. In addition, for some products the location of manufacture is tied to some particular natural resource—agricultural, to certain types of land; mining and initial processing, to areas containing the mineral. The manfacturing process for some products such as the traditional handicraft goods have only slightly increasing returns to scale. Moreover, some products appear to remain sufficiently differentiated so that price discrepancies play only a slight role. For example, American cigarettes have continued to command a price-premium in Europe.

There are also manufactured goods for which even the U.S. market is not large enough to allow significant scale economies. Such products tend to be produced in various locations close to market clusters, and no one area achieves a large cost advantage. Trade tends to be more on the basis of product differentiation or specialization. However, as demand in the United States grows, a standard version may be produced in quantity, bringing the cost down so that the product moves into the cycle under discussion.

High-performance sports cars and sail boats may be examples of this type product. Until recently, much of the production for such sports cars was located in various areas of Europe and was based on small production quantities. Recently both of these products have seen some large-scale manufacture in the U.S. and significant cost-reductions. General Motors led the way with mass manufacture of the Corvette. More American manufacturers will probably enter the high-performance sports car market and compete with the virtually hand-produced, expensive European sports cars.

The Trade Cycle and Business Planning

Obviously no simple model can explain the behavior of all products in international trade. However, the trade cycle model does appear to be useful for understanding trade patterns in a wide range of manufactured goods. Although no such model should be used by the businessman without a careful examination of individual products, it does provide some very useful hints as to which products might be exportable and which might suffer import competition. The concept can give some clues as to the success of various product policies.

Market Segmentation

The model provides some insights into the role which market segmentation can play in increasing exports and protecting against imports. Design modifications can be made for certain products which can change the appeal of the product to different kinds of customers and thus modify the trade cycle. In fact, the manufacturer often makes such changes for reasons unrelated to international trade but rather as a response to changes in the nature of his home market. As the American consumer becomes wealthier and more sophisticated, and as domestic competition becomes more severe, the manufacturer often makes his products more automatic, more powerful, more luxurious. The marketer may be trying to differentiate his product from those of his competitor, or he may simply be responding to the demands of a wealthier consumer. These changes may make the product more suited to the growing incomes of the American customer, but they will also affect its exportability. The item may become too expensive for the majority of foreign consumers, hastening competition from foreign-produced goods.

This gradual product sophistication may, however, provide some protection against imports in the United States. No doubt, the size and automatic features of the American automobile have had a special appeal to the high-income American market and have consequently held back the flow of imports. The product design has, however, had another effect: simpler, cheaper foreign cars have been able to capture a part of the U.S. market more concerned with economy of operation and lack of style obsolescence than with luxury, fashion, and automatic features—second cars, student cars, etc.

The American automobile industry did not respond to imports by trying to produce a real economy car in competition with the Volkswagen and Renault, but rather produced a middle-range product (the compacts) which competed with Volvo and Peugeot, for example. The move was probably a wise one. No doubt, the producers of the economy cars abroad had reached

cost savings from scale economies equivalent to anything the U.S. producers
could hope to obtain. Moreover, they
had lower labor costs. By choosing to
attack the middle range, the American
manufacturers chose a market where
they could have a scale advantage for
a time, until the higher-income segment
of the European market was so large
that middle-range cars would be more
important. Perhaps the U.S. manufacturers simultaneously created a more
exportable product for the future.

For products where design sophistication consists of adding special features
to a basic model, export versions can be
produced simply by eliminating some of
the extras. Thus, some producers can
extend the exportability of their products while simultaneously satisfying the
more sophisticated needs of their home
market.

The existence of segmented markets
leads to Americans' exporting and importing the same product: exporting
large automobiles to high-income consumers abroad while importing small,
economy cars; exporting large refrigerators while importing small ones for
campers and summer homes. The relative competitiveness of the United States
in 1965–66 in the higher-quality versions of a product stands out well in
the case of home freezers. Prices were
contrasted for comparable home freezers of different sizes in Germany and in
the United States. For each model the
lowest-priced unit was chosen for comparison. The larger models were cheaper
in the United States and the smaller
models in Germany. American manufacturers did not yet need to worry about
imports of large freezers, but they were

already beginning to experience competition from smaller models.[10]

Product Roll-over and Foreign Investment

Of course, the point is finally reached
for many products where design changes
can no longer make the American product competitive abroad or safe from
imports. The U.S. firms may follow two
strategies for survival: a continual product roll-over, shifting resources to new
products more suited to the unique demands of the American market; and
manufacturing abroad to take advantage
of lower production costs and to save
tariffs and transportation charges. The
strategies are not mutually exclusive, but
both require advanced planning and
constant surveillance of the future of
individual products and assessments of
the company's capabilities.

Conclusion

Companies can no longer afford
failure to analyze opportunities for profit
offered by exports and the possible
threats to their own market posed by
imports. The trend of international
events indicates an increased importance
of trade to businessmen. In response to
this changing environment, the manager must have a continuing program to
analyze the future directions of international trade in his products so that
he may plan early enough for appropriate
policies. The product cycle model provides a useful tool in this analysis.

[10] Sears, Roebuck and Co. catalog (Fall
and Winter, 1965) and Neckermann Kata-
log, No. 169 (September 1, 1965–March 1,
1966).

67

Marketing Orientation in International Business

Michael Y. Yoshino

Many business firms are turning to international markets as a source of sales and profits, for reasons of survival, growth, or perpetuation. Many of the ways in which a company can enter an overseas market involve a capital investment. A study conducted by the author of this article reveals that marketing is a neglected area in many international investment decisions. This article attempts to identify some of the reasons for this neglect and to discuss possible consequences. In domestic marketing, companies are well aware of the consequences of ignoring such characteristics as competitive environment, distribution requirements, marketing costs, and marketing experience. These are some of the characteristics that have been largely ignored in international market decisions.

The urge to "go international" has captured the imagination of many U.S. business firms. An accelerating commitment to international business in recent years is dramatically illustrated by the following evidence:

Overseas sale of U.S. companies amounted to 28 billion dollars in 1963, a 50 percent increase over 1959.

U.S. manufacturing investment rose to 15 billion dollars in 1963, a four-fold increase over 1950.

1,897 U.S. firms undertook over 4,644 new foreign activities during the four-year period between 1960 and 1964.[1]

Excellent profit opportunities overseas have lured progressive firms from the advanced nations into international business. As a result, competition in the world market is rapidly taking on a multinational character.

This is reflected in a recent study made by McKinsey and Company, Inc. of one hundred corporations which account for over 40 percent of private corporate U.S. investment abroad. The study reports that the overall pre-tax rate of return of these corporations from overseas operations slipped from 22 percent in 1955 to 14 percent in 1962.[2] The comparable domestic rate in 1962

From *Business Topics*, Summer, 1965, pp. 58–64. Reprinted by permission of the publisher, the Bureau of Business and Economic Research, Graduate School of Business Administration, Michigan State University.

[1] "New Foreign Business Activity of U.S. Firms" (Chicago: Booz, Allen & Hamilton, Inc., 1964), p. 1.

[2] "International Enterprise: A New Dimension of American Business" (New York: McKinsey & Company, Inc., 1962), p. 14.

was 13 percent. The striking difference in profitability once existing between domestic and international markets has all but disappeared.

Marketing Consideration Neglected

In spite of these significant developments, a recent study reveals that marketing remains a neglected area in many international investment decisions. Many operating difficulties recurrently observed throughout this study are traceable to this very fact. In the process of the study, the author conducted intensive interviews with executives of 20 leading American firms at corporate headquarters in the United States, as well as American and indigenous executives abroad. This article attempts to identify probable reasons for this neglect, and discuss possible consequences.

A number of firms studied have made a substantial commitment overseas without carefully evaluating relevant characteristics of foreign markets. One such approach is illustrated in the following example:

A U.S. manufacturer of electronics products was approached by a foreign firm about setting up a joint venture in a promising Asian market. The president saw a demand for the company's products in that market, and was impressed by its growth potentials. He had his staff make cost comparisons with his operations in this country, allowing for the difference in the scale of operations and wage level. He then concluded that the potential profit appeared to be quite attractive, particularly according to the U.S. standard. Once his interest was aroused, he felt time pressure to beat his competitors in

entering the market. He was compelled by the self-generated pressure to establish a beachhead in the market as soon as possible, then devise a strategy to develop it.

Largely ignored in his decision was a host of relevant marketing characteristics such as competitive environment, market maturity, distribution requirements, marketing costs, logistics problems, product policy, promotional facilities, and his prospective partner's attitude toward, and experience in marketing. At the time of this study, the venture, though three years old, was still plagued with problems arising from the inadequate planning surrounding the decision.

Consideration of these and other relevant marketing characteristics should have been an integral part of the entry decision, since these very factors are not only critical in evaluating the attractiveness of a market, but in determining the most suitable entry method, types of production facilities needed, product policy, and the extent of commitments necessary to develop the market.

Evaluation Factors

Evaluation of a foreign market is extremely difficult, challenging the most skilled researcher. In addition, there are two basic factors which prevent marketing-conscious U.S. executives from making objective assessments of a foreign market.

The majority of international investments are traditionally made in economies characterized by severe shortage. For example:

Some time ago, an American automobile manufacturer was evaluating entry into a foreign market. The market was experiencing a tremendous shortage of automobiles of all kinds. Of four hundred thousand motor vehicles operating in the country, 75 percent of the passenger cars and 70 percent of the trucks were at least ten years old. Nearly one-half were 20 years old. According to the official government estimate, the country would need approximately sixty thousand new vehicles every year. Because of the foreign exchange shortage and lack of a domestic automobile industry, annual replacement was only a fraction of the demand.

Under these conditions, where market size is no longer an unknown factor, little need was felt for market forecasting or planning. Moreover, some past international investment decisions have been for a defensive reason to hold the existing local market, which can be no longer reached through exporting.

In spite of much talk about the opportunities of foreign markets, many U.S. executives are not completely free from prejudice about foreign markets. Surprisingly, many still regard international business as a mere appendage to domestic business. International business is segregated from its domestic counterpart and managed by a group of specialists, while the top management concentrates on the domestic operations.

Furthermore, in making investments overseas, there is a danger that top management's attentions are preoccupied with problems such as selecting a partner, negotiating a contract, seeking government clearances, and constructing a plant. The most important consideration of all—market characteristics—is pushed aside.

There is often an implicit assumption that since the company is familiar with marketing problems, its experience is readily transferable to another market. Some feel that since foreign markets are small or relatively unsophisticated, they

can be penetrated with relative ease. Past successes in sellers' markets overseas tend to reinforce this illusion.

Top management's overenthusiasm toward certain foreign projects can also be a problem. While seldom recognized as such, many unwarranted commitments to foreign markets have been made simply because the president "fell in love" with a country on his inspection trip, or an influential member of top management acquired a strong emotional commitment to a given area of the world. Excessive zeal can and has inhibited objective market analysis.

Consequences

The following procedures, with their unsatisfactory results, exemplify neglect of marketing considerations.

Ill-Conceived Entry Strategy. Basically, there are three routes—export, licensing, and direct investments—to enter a foreign market. Obviously there is no one best route under any conditions. Effectiveness of entry depends largely upon the local investment climate and the capacity and the commitment of a particular firm. Thus an understanding of the advantages and limitations of each method is vitally important. These methods must be viewed as alternatives rather than a sequence of developments to be followed. If any firm confines itself, by default, to any one of the three approaches, it is severely limiting its opportunities in a foreign market. There is, however, a perceptibly inflexible attitude among the firms studied toward devising an appropriate entry strategy to meet the particular requirements of the market under consideration. Frequently an entry method is determined prior to market investigation.

While many factors must be considered in developing an appropriate entry strategy, failure to carefully evaluate the market will most likely result in ill-conceived entry strategy. For example:

A large U.S. pharmaceutical firm licensed a new technique to a manufacturer in an Asian market. The licensee promoted the product aggressively and quickly built a substantial volume of business. The U.S. company soon became aware that it was only realizing a fraction of the return, while the licensee was reaping tremendous profit. The situation was particularly regrettable to the American company, since a more direct involvement such as equity participation was entirely possible at the time the collaboration was first proposed. Had the company evaluated the market more carefully, it would have chosen a direct investment route, and could have established itself firmly in this growing market.

When a firm is not aware of the true potential of the market, or lacks a set of carefully thought-out objectives, it tends to neglect proper measures to safeguard its future operations.

In some promising foreign markets, such as Japan, the local investment climate is restrictive as to the scope of activities of any one venture. A single venture, therefore, is unlikely to serve as an effective means for future expansion. Hence it behooves U.S. firms to define with great care the scope and nature of a particular venture to avoid careless overcommitment of future products and technologies. Under these circumstances, a number of narrowly-defined activities would be necessary for diversified U.S. manufacturers to penetrate deeply into a market. Unless this fact is clearly recognized in the beginning and proper steps taken, future

operations in that market would be severely limited.

Ignoring or misjudging the marketing elements critical to the success of the operation. When marketing considerations are neglected in the initial decisions, important marketing decisions are likely to be ignored, or made on a piecemeal basis by nonmarketing executives from the home office, or local executives who lack a proper understanding of marketing.

In the initial phase, the foreign project is usually dominated by production-oriented personnel, because the major problem is frequently viewed as getting the plant into operating condition. These men are understandably preoccupied with production problems and possess little skill or interest in coming to grips with complex marketing issues. Under these circumstances, marketing problems are: ignored, relegated to local partners who have no choice but to follow traditional practices, referred to the corporate headquarters, or based on marketing practices of the U.S. parent organization or its successful foreign subsidiary operating in another market under a different set of circumstances. Any of these alternatives are likely to lead to an unsatisfactory consequence.

One such problem is illustrated in the following example:

A well-known U.S. manufacturer of nondurable consumer goods entered the Japanese market in partnership with a local firm. The decision was primarily based upon the general attractiveness of the situation, data furnished by the Japanese firm, and a one-week, on-the-spot investigation by the assistant to the president of the U.S. company. Unfortunately, performance fell far below original expectations. The U.S. company has unsuccessfully tried a crash program to salvage the operation, including replacement of its top management.

Further examination of this case revealed that the investment decision was made on a superficial analysis of the market, with no attention given to relevant marketing characteristics. It was assumed that Japan, being a compact market of 90 million consumers with relatively homogeneous economic and social characteristics and the highest per capita income and growth rate in Asia, could easily be penetrated. This illusion was further strengthened by top management's impression of a lack of sophistication in marketing on the part of local competitors. Management also overestimated the built-in prestige of U.S. brands in competition with local or European products. These assumptions led to management's failure to commit the necessary resources to the marketing effort. Particularly damaging was the failure to recognize that the critical element in this industry is to cultivate the entrenched and complex channel of distribution.

Another common area of misjudgment is the selection of equipment for a foreign venture. Not familiar with the true nature of competition in a foreign market, U.S. companies find it extremely tempting to equip a new venture with obsolete machines. This action has backfired in some cases. Some firms that had succumbed to this temptation are finding it impossible to compete with local competitors who are equipped with the most modern production facilities.

Limiting the flexibility of future operations. For example:

A U.S. firm which manufactured light industrial machinery began local production in a Southeast Asian market as a result of satisfactory experience with occasional exports. The company was successful in expanding the demand for its products through imaginative promotional programs. Two years later, however, the market was flooded by cheap, local copies of the American product. The American firm has subsequently lost the major share of the market it had created.

What happened here? In shifting to local production, the company management did not bother to evaluate product mix in terms of the market, but decided, by default, that it would manufacture the same product lines it had been exporting. These happened to be the simplest models manufactured for the domestic market. The decision was in part motivated by the U.S. firm's desire to supply the new venture with obsolete equipment sitting idle in one of its American plants. The product decision was made not by the requirements of the market, but the manufacturing capacity of the new venture. It was not until a substantial commitment had been made that the subsidiary learned that their relatively unsophisticated product was within the reach of technology locally available. The only way to overcome the problem was to upgrade the quality of the product. While this was within the technological capability of the firm, it would have required a substantial investment in retooling and the purchase of additional equipment. The local government did not look favorably upon allocating its scarce foreign exchange for this purpose. The company was forced to reduce prices to meet local competitors. At the time of this study, the operation was barely breaking even. This problem could have been avoided had more precise attention been devoted to market characteristics prior to the initial investment decision.

In shifting from export to local production, the assumption is frequently made by the U.S. firm that it should manufacture the *same* product lines exported in the past. This assumption ignores not only local marketing conditions, but also vital differences in the two methods of operation.

Failure to consider local marketing conditions in product decisions severely limits future operating flexibility. The subsidiary is likely to manufacture products, for which strong local competition already exists, which do not reflect the advanced technical skill available at the parent company.

Overlooking Opportunities for Innovations.

It makes little sense for U.S. companies operating overseas to copy local marketing practices, for it is in this area that U.S. firms have a strong competitive advantage over their more tradition-bound, local competitors. However, the manner, as well as the timing, is crucial in introducing marketing innovations. Exclusion of marketing considerations in the initial investment decision overlooks excellent opportunities for introducing new marketing concepts and techniques to foreign operations with a minimum of resistance from the local collaborator.

Most local businessmen interviewed in this study were aware of the advanced marketing concepts and techniques in the United States, and have repeatedly expressed their desire to assimilate them. However, unless this desire is satisfied during the initial period of operation, usually characterized by mutual goodwill, the local collaborators will tend to settle for their traditional practices. Once this happens, they may demonstrate an amazing degree of resistance to any change, as illustrated by the following example:

A well-known U.S. consumer goods manufacturer established a joint venture operation in Japan, but neglected to take the initiative in setting marketing policies for the new venture despite the prodding of the Japanese partner. Lacking conscious formulation, the marketing policy drifted and was eventually improvised by the Japanese partner. When the U.S. parent company became dissatisfied with its performance and attempted to introduce changes in the marketing program, it encountered great resistance. During the early stages, the same suggestions by the U.S. firm would have been more than welcome.

Lack of Clarification.

In setting up a foreign venture, U.S. firms usually make a painstaking effort to retain operating control over production methods, product quality, or financial management. Surprisingly, however, few attempts are made to clarify marketing tasks or responsibilities. This failure has proved to be a major source of conflict in subsequent operations. For example:

A large American manufacturer of consumer goods established a joint venture in an Asian market. The American firm was highly pleased with the performance of its local partner in choosing the plant site, setting up the production facilities, and recruiting the personnel. When production began, however, major differences emerged over marketing policies, particularly in the area of promotions and distribution. Both parties were appalled over the magnitude of the differences and wondered why these had not been detected in the initial exploratory stage.

There are two elements, inherent in the very nature of marketing, which complicate an effective working relationship between American and foreign firms. The first lies in the nature of marketing problems and in the environment in which they take place. While marketing problems can be real and pressing, they are somewhat intangible and elusive. They are difficult to antici-pate, particularly in an unfamiliar oper-ating environment. Moreover, the symptoms of marketing ills are often too subtle to be detected at an early stage. When they are recognized, they are likely to have developed major propor-tions.

Second, there are some important differences in the basic understanding of and attitude toward marketing between American and foreign execu-tives. Potential local partners, partic-ularly in developing countries, are likely to have indifferent or even hostile attitudes toward marketing. To the majority, manufacturing and market-ing, or more accurately, selling, are two distinct activities to be performed by different agencies under different institutional settings. Manufacturers' functions end with the creation of form utility in the narrowest sense of the term. Some even view selling activities with disdain. Even though some "sales" oriented local manufacturers may be highly aggressive and skillful in com-mercial activities, they view their selling functions not in terms of satisfying consumer wants, but as manipulators of markets. They tend to look for an immediate payoff and are reluctant to make long-term investments to develop a market for their products.

Unless these differences are explicitly recognized in the initial phase of the operations, marketing may prove to be a major source of conflict between the partners.

There is no question that American firms have a wealth of accumulated marketing expertise that can be applied abroad. Alert American firms can gain a competitive advantage over tradition-bound local competitors by carefully blending their domestic marketing know-how with more enduring aspects of the local marketing system.

VIII

Management Science in Marketing

68

The Role of Models in Marketing

William Lazer

The concept of the model has become an increasingly powerful interpretive tool in business analysis and decision making. There are many marketing problems to which models have relevance. This article discusses approaches to constructing marketing models, kinds of marketing models, and major uses for models in marketing. The author points out that marketing models are being used more widely than is generally believed, although many applications are not formally called models.

Behavioral sciences and quantitative methods are both in the forefront in the current development and extension of marketing knowledge. It is no mere coincidence that both make frequent reference to two concepts: *models* and *systems*. Certainly models and systems have become powerful interpretive tools.[1]

Models and systems have relevance to such significant marketing problems as: (1) developing marketing concepts and enriching the marketing language by introducing terms that reflect an operational viewpoint and orientation; (2) providing new methods and perspectives for problem-solving; (3) conducting marketing research and designing experiments; (4) developing marketing theories; (5) measuring the effectiveness of marketing programs.

Although they may not be recognized as such, marketing models are fairly widely applied by both practitioners and academicians. The use of analogies, constructs, verbal descriptions of systems, "idealizations," and graphic representations are quite widespread in marketing. For example, pricing models, physical distribution models, models of marketing institutions, and advertising models are useful marketing tools.

Definition of Marketing Models

A model is simply the perception or diagramming of a complex or a system. In marketing, it involves translating perceived marketing relationships into constructs, symbols, and perhaps mathematical terms. For example, an internally consistent set of statements concerning wholesaling, advertising, merchandising, or pricing comprises a model. It relates

Reprinted from the *Journal of Marketing*, national quarterly publication of the American Marketing Association, Vol. 26, No. 2, April 1962, pp. 9–14.

[1] Paul Meadows, "Models, Systems and Science," *American Sociological Review*. Vol. 22 (February, 1957) pp. 3–9, at p. 3.

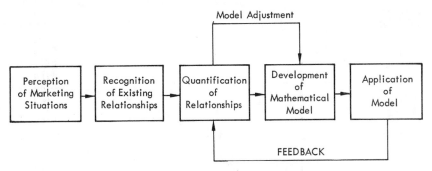

Figure 1. Model building by abstraction.

in a logical manner certain constructs or axioms that are envisaged.

Models are really the bases for marketing theories, since they are the axioms or assumptions on which marketing theories are founded. They furnish the underlying realities for theory construction. Where the perceived relationships are expressed in mathematical terms, we have a mathematical model. In this sense, any consistent set of mathematical statements about some aspect of marketing can be regarded as a model.

All marketing models are based on suppositions or assumptions. These assumptions do not correspond exactly with the real marketing world. Usually they are employed to simplify an existing marketing situation. Therefore, models cannot depict marketing activities exactly. Moreover, no matter how precise mathematical models may be, they do not correct themselves for false assumptions.

Model Building

There are two approaches to the construction of marketing models: *abstraction* and *realization*.[2]

[2] See C. H. Coombs, H. Raiffa, and R. M. Thrall, "Some Views On Mathematical Models and Measurement Theory," in R. M. Thrall, C. H. Coombs, and R. L. Davis, editors, *Decision Processes* (New York: John Wiley and Sons, Inc., 1954), pp. 20–21.

In abstraction, a real world situation is perceived and it is mapped into a model. If it is mapped into a mathematical system, a mathematical model results. This is illustrated by Figure 1.

In abstraction, the model builder must perceive of a marketing situation in a way that permits him to recognize the relationships between a number of variables. For example, he may perceive of relationships between transportation costs, customer satisfaction, and the location of distribution centers; the number of sales calls and resulting sales and profits; the allocation of advertising expenditures and the achievement of favorable consumer response.

Based on this, the model builder will become aware of logical conceptual relationships which he is able to state fairly succinctly and clearly. These relationships may then be quantified through the use of available records and data, experiments, or simulations. The basis for the establishment of a mathematical model is obtained.

Once the mathematical model is determined, it may be applied in "the real world." Feedback will result which will provide the basis for a further alteration of the quantification of the conceptual relationships perceived. It will lead to a refinement and improvement in the mathematical model.

As an example of model building by abstraction, consider the construction of

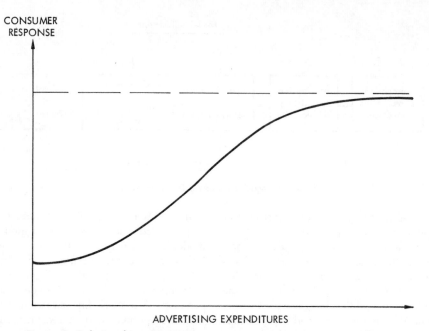

CONSUMER
RESPONSE

ADVERTISING EXPENDITURES

Figure 2. Relationship of consumer response to advertising expenditures.

a model representing consumer response to company advertising expenditures.[3] Through observation, analysis of relevant data, and experience, the model builder may recognize that with little or no advertising expenditures consumer purchases of a product are very small. Then it may appear that, as expenditures increase over a certain range, purchase responses increase quite sharply. While response increases even further with additional advertising expenditures, it is noted that eventually it tapers off and tends toward some limit.

The resulting model may be depicted graphically as in Figure 2. Through research these relationships may be quantified and expressed in terms of mathematical formulas. A model is thus developed which represents the relationships existing between advertising expenditures and consumer response. Such a model has been constructed, and with further mathematical refinements was used to determine the optimum allocation of advertising expenditures.[4] The model also proved to be useful in developing advertising-response curves, analyzing the impact of time lags in advertising effect, evaluating the interaction of competing promotional effort and estimating the impact of varying promotional resources.

Model Building by Realization

In realization, the process of model building is reversed. The model builder starts with a consideration of a logically consistent conceptual system. Then some aspect of the real world can be viewed as the model of the system. It is a process of going from the logical system to

[3] A. P. Zentler and Dorothy Ryde, "An Optimal Geographical Distribution of Publicity Expenditure In A Private Organization," *Management Science*, Vol. 2 (July, 1956), pp. 337–352.

[4] Same reference as footnote 3.

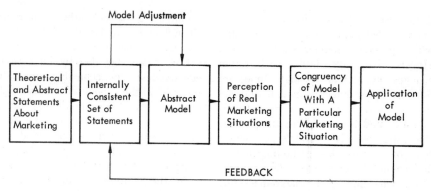

Figure 3. Model building by realization.

the real world.[5] This is portrayed in Figure 3.

Model building by realization may be illustrated by considering the mathematical model known as Markov process. This process is a model that is useful in the study of complex business systems. It studies the present state of a marketing system and what has happened through some transition time. For example, it can be of help in studying the users and nonusers of a product (the present state of the system), and what has happened as advertising is applied over a period (the state transitions). It is a theoretical, logically consistent, and abstract model.

Starting with this model, the model builder may perceive that such marketing situations as the use of advertising to switch brand loyalties of consumers, or to change consumers from the state of nonusers to users, deal with the current state of a system and the transition of the system through time. Therefore, he may use the Markov process to study the effects of advertising impact. As experience from application of the model is developed, feedback will result and the model can be adjusted. In using this procedure, the model builder has gone from a logical mathematical system to the world of marketing.

Herniter and Magee and also Maffei

[5] Same reference as footnote 2, p. 21.

have discussed the application of Markov process models.[6] Their research indicates that such models are extremely useful in determining the choice of promotional policy for maximizing profits in the long run; in specifying the kinds of experimentation required to measure the impact of promotional effort; and in calculating cost and revenue changes resulting from the use of alternative marketing strategies over time.

Kinds of Marketing Models

It is difficult to classify marketing models, since there are many dimensions and distinguishing characteristics that may be used as criteria for classification.

Mathematicians, for instance, might classify marketing models according to the type of equations used. They could distinguish among algebraic, difference-equation, differential-equation, and mixed-difference and differential equation models.[7] Physical models can be

[6] Jerome Herniter and John F. Magee, "Customer Behavior As A Markov Process," *Operations Research*, Vol. 9 (January–February, 1961), pp. 105–122; Richard B. Maffei, "Brand Preferences and Simple Markov Processes," *Operations Research*, Vol. 8 (March–April, 1960), pp. 210–218.

[7] This breakdown is taken from an unpublished paper prepared by Dr. Paul Craig, at

distinguished from abstract models. Loose verbal models may be contrasted with precise mathematical models. Models that take into consideration changes in factors through time are referred to as dynamic models and are distinguished from static models. Deterministic models are differentiated from stochastic models (models in which some of the variables are random factors and cannot be completely determined). Micro-marketing and macro-marketing models exist, as do linear and non-linear models. Perhaps one of the most meaningful distinctions from a marketing point of view is that of goal models and systems models.

Systems Models and Goals Models

A distinction has been made in the behavioral-science literature between *systems models* and *goal models*.[8]

In marketing, a goal model or end-means model starts with a marketing task to be achieved. For instance, it focuses on the marketing objectives and the uses of company resources to achieve them as efficiently as possible. It is the achievement of marketing goals, and not necessarily corporate goals, that becomes important.

The goal model does not lend itself readily to a representation of a multifunctional unit. The marketing department is not viewed as being comprised of a number of different departments with possible

---

the Institute of Basic Mathematics for application to business, sponsored by the Ford Foundation at Harvard University during 1959–1960. The actual classification of models was suggested by Dr. Samuel Goldberg.

[8] Amitai Etzioni, "Two Approaches to Organizational Analysis: A Critique and A Suggestion," *Administrative Science Quarterly*, Vol. 5 (September, 1960), pp. 257–278, at p. 258.

conflicting goals, but rather as one over-all unit with a major goal. The implication here is that if we increase the marketing means, we thereby increase our effectiveness in achieving marketing goals. In this model, moreover, the effectiveness of the marketing department is measured by the devotion to the achievement of marketing goals. Although the goal model is useful, it is Utopian and unrealistic.

In the systems model, the starting point is not a goal. The starting point is the model of a total functioning system, for example, the marketing department. It is the model of a marketing unit capable of achieving goals. The systems model recognizes that there can be many conflicting objectives within an organization and that concessions must be made. In this model, the multifunctional units involved in achieving marketing goals are recognized. This model also considers that some means must be allocated to non-goal directed effort, such as the resources necessary to maintain the marketing organization. Given certain marketing conditions and resources, the main consideration is—how can they be programmed to achieve the optimum for the total business system?

The systems model is the superior model for marketing management. It is the model that the operations researcher uses when he perceives of a business as an over-all system of action when he plans the optimal use of resources. The systems approach to the study of marketing is appearing in the literature and should result in a better understanding of the existing interrelationships among marketing elements, a clearer grasp of marketing behavior, and a more effective allocation of marketing resources.[9]

[9] See Wroe Alderson, *Marketing Decision and Executive Action* (Homewood, Illinois: Richard D. Irwin, Inc., 1957); William Lazer and Eugene J. Kelley, "Interdisciplinary Contributions to Marketing Manage-

Models and Marketing Theory

The terms "models" and "theories" are often used interchangeably. An interesting and useful distinction for marketing can be drawn from an idea expressed by Coombs, Raiffa, and Thrall: "A model is not itself a theory; it is only an available or possible or potential theory until a segment of the real world has been mapped into it. Then the model becomes a theory about the real world."[10] As a theory, a marketing model can be accepted or rejected on the basis of how well it actually works. The actual model itself, however, is "right or wrong" (internally consistent) on logical grounds only.

One can distinguish between models and theories by considering marketing research techniques. A stipulated technique for marketing measurement may be called a model. For example, the forecasting technique known as exponential smoothing, or forecasting by exponentially weighted moving averages, has proved to be a useful forecasting model.[11] As a model, it need only be internally consistent. It is a potential marketing theory.

When data are actually measured by the exponential smoothing technique and are mapped into the model, then the model becomes a theory about the marketing data. The resulting theory may be a good one or a poor one.

The relationship among marketing models, theories, and hypotheses now follows directly. Within a theoretical framework, we are able to test certain hypotheses. The assumptions of a marketing model itself, however, need not be subjected to tests, whereas hypotheses should be tested. It should be noted that assumptions in one model may be hypotheses in another.

Use of Models in Marketing

Five major uses for models in marketing can be suggested.

1. *Marketing models provide a frame of reference for solving marketing problems.* They suggest fruitful lines of inquiry and existing information gaps. Marketing models do this by playing a descriptive role. The descriptive model does not go beyond presenting a representation or picture of some aspect of marketing activity. However, it serves an extremely important function in the extension of marketing thought. The use of flow diagrams in depicting existing relationships or in developing a logical computer program is an example of the use of descriptive models.

2. *Marketing models may play an explicative role, and as such they are suggestive and flexible.* Such models are more than simple metaphors; they attempt to explain relationships and reactions. The marketing scientist not only is interested in describing marketing phenomena and examining them, but he desires to explain existing relationships and frames of references. For example, "switching models" often attempt to explain the relationships between advertising and brand loyalty.[12]

ment" (Bureau of Business and Economic Research, Michigan State University 1959); William Lazer, "Transportation Management: A Systems Approach," *Distribution Age,* Vol. 59 (September, 1960), pp. 33–35; John F. Magee, "Operations Research in Making Marketing Decisions," *Journal of Marketing,* Vol. 25 (October, 1960), pp. 18–24.

[10] Same reference as footnote 2, pp. 25–26.

[11] Peter R. Winters, "Forecasting Sales by Exponentially Weighted Moving Averages," *Management Science,* Vol. 6 (April, 1960), pp. 324–342.

[12] Same reference as in footnote 9.

3. *Marketing models are useful aids in making predictions.* For instance, in answer to the question why models should be used, Bross explains that the real answer to this question is that the procedure has been followed in the development of the most successful predicting systems so far produced, the predicting systems used in science.[13] Marketing practitioners and scientists wish to predict and consequently employ various types of forecasting models and inventory models. These models become more than just an explanation and a representation of an existing situation. They become means of presenting future reality.

4. *Marketing models can be useful in theory construction.* Formulators of marketing models may hypothesize about various aspects of marketing as they might exist. Thereby, we have "reality" as it is hypothesized. Simulation, for example, which really involves experimentation on models, can lead to valuable insights into marketing theory. In the same vein, an ideal may be developed as a model. Although the ideal may not be achieved, it provides a useful vehicle for extending knowledge.

5. *Marketing models may stimulate the generation of hypotheses which can then be verified and tested.* Thereby, it furthers the application of the scientific method in marketing research and the extension of marketing knowledge.

Benefits of Mathematical Models

Why should marketing scientists and practitioners utilize mathematical models rather than other kinds of models?[14] Per-

haps the most important reasons are four:

1. *The translation of a model from a verbal to a mathematical form makes for greater clarification of existing relationships and interactions.* It is a rigorous and demanding task; and conceptual clarity and operational definitions are often achieved. The models developed may also become more generally applicable.

2. *Mathematical models promote greater ease of communication.* Within business administration and related subject-matter areas, there is the difficulty of cross-communication because of the terminology used by specialized disciplines. Through the use of mathematical models, all of the disciplines may be reduced to a common mathematical language which may reveal interrelationships and pertinence of research findings not previously known.

3. *Mathematical models tend to be more objective, while verbal constructs lean heavily on intuition and rationalizations.* Scientific marketing can be advanced through the application of objective mathematical analysis.

4. *Analyses that are not feasible through verbal models may be advanced through mathematical models.* Mathematics provides powerful tools for marketing academicians and practitioners. Mathematics models lend themselves to analysis and manipulation. In the manipulation of verbal models, the interrelationships and logic are easily lost.

Concluding Observations

The usefulness of a marketing model is a function of the level of generalization the model achieves, and the degree of reality it portrays. Symbolization is used in model building to achieve greater internal consistency and more correspondence with reality. The greater

[13] Irwin D. J. Bross, *Design for Decisions* (New York: The Macmillan Company, 1953), p. 169.

[14] Paul Craig, same reference as footnote 7.

the level of symbolization, and the fewer the restrictions, the more adequate and more generally applicable is the model.

For example, it is true that linear-programing models are more abstract, more general, and more valuable than are mere descriptive models representing a factory and warehousing complex. However, it may well be that the linear-programing model is by no means more widely used.

All marketing models are based on simplifications and abstractions. Only by making assumptions is a model molded to fit reality. Sometimes the reality beyond the boundaries of the model, however, is much greater than the reality within the boundaries. The model then becomes severely limited by the assumptions on which it is based.

To be effective, marketing models should be plausible, solvable, and based on realistic assumptions. The current level of model building in marketing is not yet a sophisticated one. It cannot compare favorably with the level of model building in the physical or biological sciences. As the discipline of marketing matures, however, it will use an increasing number of models and will develop more complex models that have broader application.

The Use of Mathematical Models in Marketing

Philip Kotler

The previous article discussed the role of marketing models in general. This article is concerned solely with mathematical models. The author explains and illustrates those quantitative models that hold the greatest promise for decision making in marketing. Such problems as new product development, media selection, and size of sales force represent areas of application of mathematical models. The user is warned that expertise in model building is only half the task; the other half is to find the necessary data. Thus, sophistication in model building must be matched by improvement in the techniques of providing marketing information.

The modern marketing man has to be multilingual, for he obtains his material from many disciplines.

He must be able to converse with *economists* about marginal analysis, elasticity, and diminishing returns; with *psychologists* about projective techniques, latent needs, and nonrational behavior; with *sociologists* about acculturation, social norms, and subcultures; and with *statisticians* about standard error, least squares, and correlation.

Now another language—that of higher mathematics—is needed in marketing. Many marketing men are uncomfortable about this. They do not look askance at mathematical concepts, but they are a bit anxious because of a "language barrier." Fortunately, however, the language barrier is not insurmountable. Linear programing, waiting-line theory, and the like are simply unfamiliar names for some significant ideas.

The purpose of this article is to reduce some of the "mysticism" of the new mathematics by defining its vocabulary and illustrating its central ideas in the context of marketing.

Decision Making

Quantitative analysis is not alien to the field of marketing. For many decades marketing research departments have conducted consumer surveys, prepared sales forecasts, and analyzed sales reports. A few practitioners have even used higher mathematics for complex problem-solving in marketing. But until recently the mathematical "sophistication" underlying the typical research project could be found between the covers of a textbook in elementary statistics. And much of the research has amounted to routine information gathering.

Today the emphasis is changing. The focus of research is on *decision making*, and not fact gathering for its own sake. The belief is spreading that models can be built which identify and relate the key factors in a problem situation, and

Reprinted from the *Journal of Marketing*, national quarterly publication of the American Marketing Association, Vol. 27, No. 4, October 1963, pp. 31–41.

which offer explicit directions for decision making.

Today's marketing executive is asked to distinguish carefully between alternative strategies in making a major decision. Each strategy will lead to one of several outcomes, depending in part upon events beyond the firm's control; and the possible outcomes for each strategy must somehow be weighed, to achieve an estimated value for that strategy. The values of the various strategies must be compared, and the executive must then attempt to select the strategy promising the highest value or payoff.[1]

The Tools of Mathematics

The mathematician carries in his attaché case four basic tools, plus a *potpourri* of special models. His basic tools are *matrix algebra, calculus, probability theory,* and *simulation.*

Matrix Algebra

One tool is *matrix algebra,* by which large arrays of numbers in the form of *vectors* and *matrices* can be manipulated by rules similar to those found in ordinary algebra.

As a miniature example, suppose (6,000, 3,200, 5,000) is a *vector* (for our purposes, a single array of' numbers) whose component numbers represent sales targets in three geographical markets— (say) East, West, and South respectively. Past records show that on the average it takes ½ hour of sales effort

---

[1] Two excellent articles illustrating this approach are Robert D. Buzzell and Charles C. Slater, "Decision Theory and Marketing Management," *Journal of Marketing,* Vol. 27 (July, 1962), pp. 7–16; and Paul E. Green, "Bayesian Decision Theory in Pricing Strategy," *Journal of Marketing,* Vol. 28 (January, 1963), pp. 5–14.

and $1 of advertising expenditure to produce a sale in the first market; ¼ hour of sales effort and $2 of advertising expenditure to produce a sale in the second market; and 1/5 hour of sales effort and $3 of advertising expenditure to produce a sale in the third market. This information can be summarized in a *matrix* (for our purposes a rectangular array of numbers):

	Sales Effort (in Hours)	Advertising Expenditure (in Dollars)
East	1/2	$1
West	1/4	$2
South	1/5	$3

To find the total hours of sales effort and dollars of advertising expenditure required to achieve the geographical sales targets, we multiply the vector by the matrix:

$$(6{,}000, 3{,}200, 5{,}000) \begin{pmatrix} \frac{1}{2} & 1 \\ \frac{1}{4} & 2 \\ \frac{1}{5} & 3 \end{pmatrix}$$

For example, we can call the vector A and the matrix B, and we then proceed to find their product, that is, A • B.

There are definite rules for the multiplication of a vector by a matrix (and for that matter, for the multiplication of two vectors or two matrices, etc.). In the example above, the product A•B is $(6{,}000 \times \frac{1}{2} + 3{,}200 \times \frac{1}{4} + 5{,}000 \times \frac{1}{5}, 6{,}000 \times 1 + 3{,}200 \times 2 + 5{,}000 \times 3)$ or, collecting terms, $(4{,}800, \$27{,}400)$. This new vector is the solution; and it means that the company must have enough salesmen to make 4,800 hours of calls, and also an advertising budget of at least $27,400.

Matrix algebra is essentially a symbolic shorthand for the manipulation of large arrays of data. It affords the advantage of economy in quantitative expression.

Calculus

The second tool which the mathematician brings to marketing is *calculus*. Using *differential calculus,* the mathematician can, among other things, determine what combination of inputs will maximize some output.

A marketing mix is a combination of inputs, such as price and advertising. Suppose that it were possible experimentally to vary the price input and the advertising input while controlling other factors. The effect of these variations on sales could then be recorded, and the profit implied by each level of sales estimated.

The task is to find an equation which best describes how profit varies with variations in price and advertising. A form for such an equation as well as a method of estimating the coefficients (usually "least squares" regression) must be decided upon. Suppose the following equation is found to give a good fit to the data:

$$I = 320 - 2P^2 - 3P + 4PA - 7A^2 + 60A$$

On the left side of the equation is profit (represented by I). Profit is treated here as the *dependent variable,* because its value is conceived to depend upon the values taken on by variables listed on the right side of the equation. These *independent variables* are price (P) and advertising (A). The particular numbers in the equation are constants and coefficients, which are estimated by an appropriate statistical method.

If such an equation can be found, what unique mix of price and advertising would maximize profit? The nonmathematician can use trial and error to arrive at the profit-maximizing mix, but this will be frustrating and time consuming.

The mathematician can determine this mix in a very short time by using calculus. Although this is not the place to explain the procedure, his calculations will show that the optimum price is $4.95, and the optimum advertising budget is $5.7 (in some appropriate unit).

The chief contribution of differential calculus to marketing is to enable a direct determination of optimal action where differential functions are involved. In fact, *marginal analysis* which is applied by economists to all kinds of decision situations—such as determination of the best price, or the number of salesmen—actually is a gross application of differential calculus.

Integral calculus, representing the other branch of calculus, is not used to find the maximum and minimum values of a function, but rather the *area* under a function, among other things. An area can have a meaningful marketing interpretation.

Suppose that on a particular billing date that a department store ranks all of its charge accounts by dollar size. These charge accounts range from $0 to $198. The frequency distribution of all the accounts by dollar size is shown in Figure 1. The shaded area under the curve between $50 and $150 represents the percentage of all accounts falling in this range. How can this area be measured? It does not have the simplicity of a rectangle, triangle, or circle. This area, or other areas under the curve, can be readily measured through integral calculus, provided that the frequency distribution can be represented by a mathematical equation with certain properties.

Probability Theory

The third important tool of the mathematician for use in marketing is *probability theory.*

How should the marketing man

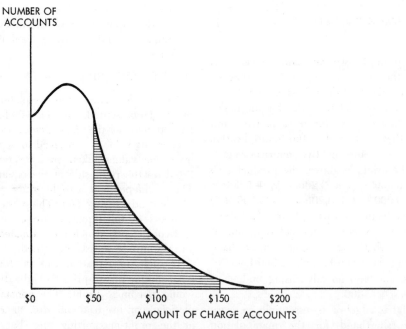

NUMBER OF
ACCOUNTS

$0 $50 $100 $150 $200

AMOUNT OF CHARGE ACCOUNTS

Figure 1. Frequency distribution of charge accounts.

handle the uncertainty that surrounds legislation, consumer intentions, and competitors' acts? He can try to list all the possible consequences of a business move, along with their probabilities. The probabilities can be based on the frequency distribution of past outcomes for similar business moves, or on personal judgment. The assigned probability number must satisfy only two requirements:

1. The probability that a particular consequence will occur is given numerically by some number between 0 and 1 inclusive.
2. The sum of the probabilities of all possible consequences is 1.

Probability numbers can serve as "weights" for appraising various money (or utility) outcomes. Suppose a manufacturer has developed a new product and must hire and train a special sales force to sell it. The number of salesmen to hire will depend upon his estimate of market potential, among other things.

Suppose that he is uncertain whether there is a potential of 2,000, 3,000 or 4,000 units, and he is trying to decide whether to hire 60 or 70 salesmen. Too few salesmen will mean that some potential sales are never realized, and too many salesmen will mean that excess selling costs are incurred. It would help to estimate the profits under different assumptions as to market potential and sales-force size. The estimates will depend upon an appropriate set of assumptions concerning product price, production costs, the effect of the number of salesmen on sales, and selling costs. A hypothetical set of profit estimates is shown in Table 1.

If market potential is 2,000 units, the manufacturer will lose $20,000 with 60 salesmen and $40,000 with 70 salesmen. If market potential is 3,000 units, the manufacturer will earn $50,000 with 60 salesmen, and $40,000 with 70 salesmen. Finally, if market potential is 4,000 units, he will earn still larger profits. In this last case, the profit is higher with 70 salesmen because 60 salesmen are inadequate to tap the full potential.

Should the manufacturer hire 60 or 70 salesmen? By hiring 70, he has the opportunity to gain more but also to lose more. His decision will depend upon the personal probabilities he assigns to the three estimates of market potential. Suppose he quantifies his beliefs as follows: there is a .2 probability that the market potential is 2,000 units, a .3 probability that it is 3,000 units, and a .5 probability that it is 4,000 units. If this were a game of chance which the manufacturer could play repeatedly facing the same payoffs and the same probabilities, and if he had adequate funds, it would be easy to define a good decision rule: choose the act which has the highest *expected monetary value* (EMV). EMV is a weighted average of the alternative profit consequences of an act, the weights being the probabilities assigned to the alternatives. For the example we have:

$$\text{EMV } (60) = -\$20{,}000 \times .2 + \$50{,}000 \times .3 + \$60{,}000 \times .5 = \$41{,}000.$$

Table 1. Estimated Profits for Different Combinations of Market Potential and Sales-Force Size

		Market Potential		
		2,000 Units	3,000 Units	4,000 Units
Decision?	60	−$20,000	$50,000	$60,000
	70	−$40,000	$40,000	$70,000

EMV (70) = −$40,000 × .2 + $40,-000 × .3 + $70,000 × .5 = $39,000.

The results present an interesting paradox. The manufacturer is optimistic about the market potential, and yet EMV is higher with 60 salesmen. His optimism is not quite strong enough.

The use of EMV as a decision criterion in a once-only decision is generally acceptable, if the best consequence is not too great nor the worst consequence too bad. Were the money stakes unusually high for the decision maker, it would be necessary to employ a utility index instead of a money index. This utility index can be constructed from preferences expressed by the decision maker between given sums of money and certain gambles. Instead of the maximization of EMV, the decision criterion would be the maximization of expected utility.[2]

Simulation

The great majority of marketing problems probably will remain intractable to ordinary mathematical solution. For example, the correct price to charge depends upon such elements as the future sales outlook, the possible reactions of competitors, the time lags of these reactions, the intended level of advertising support, ad infinitum. A complex phenomenon is characterized by feedbacks, distributed lags, uncommon probability distributions, and other features which render exact mathematical solutions difficult or impossible. But mathematicians are undaunted: "When all else fails, *simulate!*"

A simulation is essentially a hypothetical testing, as opposed to a field testing, of the consequences of alterna-

tive business decisions. The first step is the construction of a model which spells out how the key variables interact in the situation. The second step is the testing of alternative decisions on the model. Simulations can range from simple paper-and-pencil exercises to full scale computer analyses. The purpose is to speculate on the consequences of changing a price, or dropping small distributors, or introducing a new pattern of trade deals, before risking the irrevocable judgment of the marketplace.

The model used in the simulation may be *exact* or *probabilistic*. In an exact model, the effect of one variable upon another is known with certainty. In a probabilistic model, one of several effects might take place, and we presume to know only their respective probabilities.

Retail inventory control can be used to illustrate a probabilistic model. The problem is to adopt purchasing rules which will balance inventory losses against sales losses. Suppose a supermarket wishes to reconsider its present purchasing policy with respect to one product—for example, eggnog. The daily demand for eggnog fluctuates, and each day of the week has its own demand distribution. Suppose that on a sample of past Tuesdays the number of quarts demanded has varied between 0 and 4, according to the probabilities shown in Table 2.

Table 2. **Probability Distribution of Demand for Eggnog on Tuesdays**

Number of Quarts Demanded	Probability	Monte Carlo Numbers
0	.07	00–06
1	.20	07–26
2	.22	27–48
3	.33	49–81
4	.18	82–99
	1.00	

[2] Robert Schlaifer, *Probability and Statistics for Business Decisions* (New York: McGraw-Hill Book Company, Inc., 1959), Chapter 2.

The third column of Table 2 consists of an allocation of 100 2-digit numbers (between 00 and 99) to all possible events in proportion to their probabilities. Thus, on 7% of the Tuesdays no eggnog will be demanded; so we assign 7 different 2-digit numbers (00 to 06 inclusive) to this event. Likewise, we assign 20 different 2-digit numbers (07-26 inclusive) to the event of 1 quart being demanded, etc.

We now go to a table of *random* digits. The digits are listed in this table in no apparent pattern. The fact is that each of the digits had the same chance of appearing on each trial. While there is no pattern, we know that all the digits will be approximately *equally* represented in a large sample of such digits.

We draw 2 digits at a time. If the first 2-digit number is 43, this can be looked up in the Monte Carlo column in Table 2 and would be interpreted as 2 quarts. In other words, on this Tuesday the demand at the supermarket is 2 quarts. By repeatedly drawing 2-digit random numbers, we can generate a characteristic picture of demand for a succession of Tuesdays.

We can use a different demand distribution, based on store records, for each day of the week. Then we can make assumptions about supply, such as a delivery period every other day and a decision rule to purchase (say) 3 quarts each time. With this information, we can manually or mechanically generate daily demand-and-supply quantities to learn the likely magnitude and frequency of excess inventories and shortages. We compare the average losses incurred under different purchasing rules and choose the loss-minimizing rule.

The probabilistic feature provides realism and has given rise to the name of *Monte Carlo* simulation. In the more complex simulations, a computer is used to produce the random numbers, interpret the events, make the necessary computations, and summarize the results. Computer simulation has been conducted on such marketing problems as media selection; department-store ordering and pricing; site location for retail outlets; and customer facility planning in retail outlets.

The Major Models

The tools of matrix algebra, calculus, probability theory, and simulation are fundamental in setting up and solving many of the models which have been developed to aid marketing executives in decision making. Some of these models are designed for *normative decision making*, and others for the *analysis of a process*. Most of them originated out of operations research activities.

The following models appear particularly "ripe" for marketing application:

1. Allocation models
2. Competitive strategy models
3. Brand-switching models
4. Waiting-line models
5. Critical-path scheduling models

Some of the examples below may seem too simple, if not contrived. However, the examples are illustrative only. Model building is not just a "fun" exercise for those who like to solve puzzles, but can be a serious attack on decision making in business.

Actually the final model for a real decision problem can be quite elaborate and represent a "hooking together" of several elementary models and techniques.

1. Allocation Models

The economic aspect of business decision making is the "allocation of scarce resources to competing ends." In marketing, the scarce resources may be salesmen who are too few to make all the desirable contacts, or advertising dollars which are too limited to produce adequate exposure, or many other possibilities. Nevertheless, a decision must be made on how to allocate or *program* these limited resources to territories, classes of customers, and product lines.

Take, for example, the development of a media plan. The number of available media vehicles is very great. But when any particular product is considered, there are a number of constraints which severely delimit the range of media choice.

First, the advertising budget is finite. Second, the message must be directed at specific market segments (such as mothers in the case of a baby lotion); and certain media vehicles are more effective than others in reaching these segments. Third, the geographical distribution of the market segments imposes restrictions on the choice of media. Finally, the media vehicles or the advertiser, or both, may impose restrictions.

Nevertheless a large number of different media plans would satisfy all the constraints. Of these, which plan will be the most effective? An *effectiveness*

criterion needs to be developed against which every feasible plan can be rated. In media selection, the criterion is the number of expected effective exposures, or some variant of this. *Programing* is one of the mathematical models that can be used for the discovery of an exposure-maximizing media plan.

As an example, a media plan is to be prepared consisting of the purchase of X_1 advertising units of medium 1 and X_2 advertising units of medium 2. Table 3 indicates the relevant characteristics of the two media.

The following constraints are made explicit in a discussion between the media planner and the advertiser:

1. The total advertising budget is $39,600.
2. At least 1,800,000 exposures are to be achieved in region 1, and 7,280,000 in region 2.
3. No more than 2,400,000 exposures are to take place among single women.
4. At least 2,000,000 exposures are to take place among college educated women.

The problem is to find the number of issues of the two media which would maximize the total number of effective

Table 3.   Selected Characteristics of Two Media

	Medium 1	Medium 2
Cost of an advertising unit	$ 2,700	$ 900
Maximum number of units	12	40
Minimum number of units	0	9
Total number of effective exposures per unit	720,000	360,000
Number of effective exposures in region 1 per unit	60,000	100,000
Number of effective exposures in region 2 per unit	660,000	260,000
Number of exposures to single women per unit	100,000	80,000
Number of exposures to college educated women per unit	400,000	40,000

exposures subject to the various constraints. A mathematical statement of the problem is given in Table 4.

Each constraint has been expressed as a mathematical inequality. For example, the budget constraint reads: The number of advertisements purchased in medium 1 (X_1) times their unit cost ($2,700), plus the number purchased in medium 2 (X_2) times their unit cost ($900), must be less than or equal to the budget of $39,600.

The second constraint reads: The number of advertisements placed in medium 1 must not exceed 12. The other inequalities are similarly interpreted.

The constraints have the effect of eliminating most combinations of X_1 and X_2 but there are still a large number of remaining combinations which would satisfy all the inequalities. But only one of these (usually) will also maximize the total number of effective exposures. Mathematical programing is the technique for finding the best solution.

In this simple case, the inequalities could be drawn on graph paper; and this would help to delimit the set of media plans (points) which would satisfy all of the constraints. Then there is a procedure for locating the best plan, the details of which are beyond the scope of this article.

The best plan calls for 8 advertisements in medium 1, and 20 advertisements in medium 2. This plan will cost exactly $39,600 and yield 12,960,000 exposures.

There are several types of mathematical programing. *Linear programing* implies that the criterion and the constraints in the problem can be represented by straight-line segments. The essence of a straight line is that the slope is constant, which means that the ratio of a change in one variable to a change in the other is constant. For example, a linear cost function means that the cost of an additional unit is constant; and a linear exposure function means that the effect of an additional advertising exposure is constant. In other words, diminishing or increasing returns are ruled out in strictly linear models.

Since the assumption of constant marginal returns and costs is patently false in many situations, what explains the popularity of *linear programing models?* The answer is largely that the linear assumption is the easiest to work with and solve. As an additional consideration, many important functions are linear over much of their range.

A number of techniques are available for solving a linear programing problem, once it has been expressed mathematically. *Graphical solutions* are possible when the number of variables is not more than three. Alternatively, the *simplex algorithm* is an all-purpose method. The word "simplex" has nothing to do with "simple"; the *simplex* is a

Table 4. Mathematical Statement of Media Problem

Maximize		$720,000X_1 + 360,000X_2$			
subject to	(1)	$2,700X_1 + 900X_2$	$\leq$	39,600	budget constraint
	(2)	X_1	$\leq$	12 ⎤	
	(3)	X_2	$\leq$	40 ⎟	individual medium usage
	(4)	X_1	$\geq$	0 ⎬	constraints
	(5)	X_2	$\geq$	9 ⎦	
	(6)	$60,000X_1 + 100,000X_2$	$\geq$	1,800,000 ⎤	regional constraints
	(7)	$660,000X_1 + 260,000X_2$	$\geq$	7,280,000 ⎦	
	(8)	$100,000X_1 + 80,000X_2$	$\leq$	2,400,000 ⎤	customer characteristics
	(9)	$400,000X_1 + 40,000X_2$	$\geq$	2,000,000 ⎦	constraints

well-defined mathematical concept which has a geometric interpretation. An *algorithm* is a systematic method for testing various solutions; it guarantees that each successive solution will represent an improvement until the best solution is reached.

The term *non-linear programing* is reserved for a problem formulation where either some constraint(s) or the effectiveness criterion, or both, are not linear. One example is *quadratic programing*, which uses a second-degree curve for some of the constraints or effectiveness criterion, or both.

Integer programing is a variant so named because the optimal solution is constrained to consist of whole numbers. For example, suppose X_1 represents how many salesmen should be hired. If the answer is *not* constrained to be an integer, it could be a mixed decimal such as 9.4. What does it mean to hire 9.4 salesmen? Should the answer be "rounded" to 9 salesmen or 10 salesmen? The solution is not obvious, and the decision may involve a difference of many thousands of dollars. Integer programing is a way of avoiding the ambiguities of fractional answers.

Dynamic programing, the most complicated of the programing variants, is applied to problems where a series of consecutive *interdependent* decisions have to be made. Purchasing decisions, for example, must be made throughout the year; and today's decision must be made in terms of what it implies for the deci-

sion choices in the next period, which in turn will affect the decision choices in the following period, and so on.

In summary, a programing model is applied to problems where there seem to be many different ways to allocate resources. Constraints (usually in the form of mathematical inequalities) are introduced to reduce the number of admissible solutions. Then a search is made for that solution among the feasible set which is optimal in terms of some effectiveness criterion. The programing model holds great promise for aiding in the solution of such important marketing problems as media selection; allocation of sales force; determination of the best product line in terms of a firm's resource base; site location, and selection of channels of distribution.

There are some specialized versions of the programing model which are useful in a marketing context. One of these is the *transportation model,* which defines the existence of several *origins* (such as warehouses) and *destinations* (such as retail stores) and the unit cost of shipping from every origin to every destination. Furthermore, the amount of goods available for shipment from each warehouse and the amount of goods ordered by each retail store are specified. Under the given constraints, the problem is to find which warehouses should ship their supplies to which stores, in order to minimize total transportation costs.

A sample problem is shown in Table 5—try to find the least-cost shipping al-

Table 5. Unit Shipping Costs from Various Warehouses to Various Stores

Warehouse	Store			Warehouse Availabilities ↓
	1	2	3	
A	$5	$3	$6	300
B	$2	$9	$4	200
C	$3	$7	$8	600
D	$6	$1	$4	500
Store requirements ⟶	200	1,000	400	1,600

location by trial and error. Mathematical analysis would show that there is a shipment allocation which would cost only $5,800. It is possible to convert this problem into a standard linear programing problem and then solve it by the simplex method. Alternatively, special techniques have been developed to solve the problem directly, using the format in Table 5.

The transportation model has been used for a number of years in some large companies to develop shipping schedules. It has a useful variant, called the *assignment model,* with promising applications to other problems than transportation. In the assignment model, the number of origins *equal* the number of destinations; and each origin is to be associated with *only one* destination.

As an example, suppose 4 salesmen are to be *assigned* to 4 territories. The salesmen have differing skills, and the territories are in different stages of development. The sales manager makes an estimate of the expected annual sales that would result from each man being assigned to each territory. This information is summarized in Table 6.

There are 24 (4 × 3 × 2 × 1) different possible assignments. Because this is a small-scale example it is not difficult to arrive at the total sales maximizing assignment by trial and error—A3; B1; C4; D2; total sales, $325,000.

In more complex examples, the number of possible solutions increases factorially, and a mathematical analysis is

necessary. Incidentally, the model could be used for assignment of salesmen to other than territories, to different company products, or to different types of customers, for example.

Another problem is known as the *"traveling-salesman" problem.* Although not involving allocation, it has certain similarities to an assignment problem. A salesman must make calls in *n* cities. This means that there are *n* factorial possible routes. One of these routes would minimize the total travel *cost;* and another route (possibly the same) would minimize the total travel *time.* The problem is to find the "best" route in terms of whichever is the stated objective. To date, general solutions are lacking, but certain important theorems have been discovered, such as the fact that the best route never involves any crossing of paths; and mathematical solutions are available where special simplifying assumptions are made. A simulation approach also can be used to search for a reasonable solution.

2. Competitive Strategy Models

Profit outcomes are not only a function of the decision of a firm, but of this decision in conjunction with the decisions made by competitors. A marketing decision must be based on an estimate of what competitors are likely to do, even though their intentions may not be known in advance.

Table 6.   Estimated Annual Sales from the Assignment of Different Salesmen to Different Territories

Salesman	Territory			
	1	2	3	4
A	$90,000	$57,000	$82,000	$45,000
B	$73,000	$75,000	$40,000	$51,000
C	$60,000	$30,000	$51,000	$75,000
D	$92,000	$95,000	$75,000	$70,000

Game theory is the name given to the systematic investigation of rational decision making in the context of uncertainty concerning the moves of competitors. As an example, suppose Row and Column are the managers of two competing supermarkets. Every week, each of the managers chooses some item to promote as the "Special of the Week." Neither manager knows in advance what the other is going to feature. However, each can estimate the approximate profit that would result from every pair of possible choices. Suppose Row estimates the payoffs shown in Table 7.

Table 7. **Payoffs Resulting from Various Strategy Combinations**

		Column	
		Flour	Coffee
Row	Sugar	4	1
	Tea	6	−2

The table is interpreted as follows. If Row featured sugar and his competitor featured flour, Row would gain 4 (say in hundreds of dollars); that is, more of the marginal customers will "flow" to his store, and the profit derived from this extra trade is estimated as 4. And Column will lose 4.

If Row featured sugar and his competitor featured coffee, Row would gain only 1 on Column. If Row featured tea and his competitor featured flour, then Row would gain 6. However, if Row featured tea and Column featured coffee, Row would lose 2.

The problem is whether Row should adopt one item and feature it week after week (a *pure strategy*), or choose an item randomly each week according to a constant though not necessarily equal set of probabilities (a *mixed strategy*).

If Row is to use a pure strategy, should it be sugar or tea? According to one

doctrine, he should make the move which would minimize his maximum possible loss (the *minimax rule*). Tea would lead both to the largest possible gain and the largest possible loss, whereas sugar at least guarantees to Row a small but steady gain of 1.

Furthermore, Column can minimize his maximum loss by featuring coffee, and he undoubtedly will. This is a stalemated game where, so long as the same payoffs persist, Row will feature sugar and Column will feature coffee; and it would not be to either's advantage to make a surprise change. On the other hand, there are other payoff matrices which possess no such equilibrium solution, and where a mixed random strategy could be employed to advantage.

The Row-and-Column example illustrates one of the simplest types of games: *a 2-person, zero-sum game.* Only two players are involved, and they transfer a fixed sum of money between each other. The term "zero-sum" is used because in each play the sum of one player's gain (positive) and the other player's loss (negative) is zero.

More interesting, but at the same time more mathematically difficult, are the *3-or-more person, non-zero-sum games.* The 3-or-more-person feature allows the formation of coalitions where certain players can gain more by not acting independently. The non-zero-sum feature refers to the fact that competitive actions may expand the size of the market (that is, the total stakes) in addition to shifting market shares.

Game models have been designed for a variety of military and political situations, but some have interesting marketing possibilities. One is a game of timing involving two duelists (competitors) who at a signal are to begin approaching each other at some constant uniform rate. Each has only one available bullet (a new product) and is free to fire it whenever he wishes, with the knowledge that his chance of hitting the opponent improves as the distance narrows. When should the duelist fire?

Another game involves distributing an army over several battlefields, with the knowledge that each battlefield is "won" by the side which has disposed more troops in that battlefield. How should an army distribute its troops (or a company distribute its salesmen) in this situation?

Another game, "gambler's ruin," involves two competitors with different initial endowments of capital. A coin is tossed repeatedly with a probability p that competitor A will win and a probability $1-p$ that competitor B will win. The game ends when the capital of one competitor is exhausted. Given specific data, it is possible to estimate such things as the probability of "ruin" for each gambler, and the likely duration of the game.

Although to date game models do not seem to have much predictive power, they do suggest a useful analytical approach to such competitive problems as pricing, sales-force allocation, and advertising outlays. They may help to clarify the strategic implications of such moves as surprise, threat, and coalition.[3]

Finally, game theory should be distinguished from *operational gaming*. The latter term describes the modeling of a game around a realistic situation, where the participants actually make decisions (often in teams), and where the results of their interacting decisions are reported and become the data inputs for the next round of decisions. A large number of management and marketing games have been developed and used both in formal

[3] R. Duncan Luce and Howard Raiffa, *Games and Decisions* (New York: John Wiley & Sons, Inc., 1957); Martin Shubik, *Strategy and Market Structure* (New York: John Wiley & Sons, 1959).

management-training programs and in research settings.[4]

3. Brand-Switching Models

Marketing executives must watch their *market share* just as much as their profits. Present customers can never be taken for granted.

The attitude of marketing executives toward brand switching is quite simple: the switching-out rate must be slowed down, and the switching-in rate must be increased. The factors affecting brand choice must be analyzed, and this knowledge applied where possible in order to alter existing brand-switching rates.

Switching rates can be estimated from data showing the individual brand choices made over time by a representative panel of consumers. Suppose three brands are involved, A, B, and C. We can ask what proportion of those who bought A in the last period purchased A again, and what proportions switched to B and C. These proportions for each product can be conveniently exhibited in matrix form. Table 8 is a hypothetical example.

Table 8. Hypothetical Brand-Switching Matrix

		To		
		A	B	C
From	A	.70	.20	.10
	B	.17	.33	.50
	C	.00	.50	.50

Note that each row adds up to 1.00. The first row reads: Of those who purchased brand A in the last period, 70% bought A again, 20% bought B, and 10% bought C. Thus, A retained 70% of its

[4] J. F. McRaith and Charles R. Goeldner, "A Survey of Marketing Games, *Journal of Marketing*, Vol. 26 (July, 1962), pp. 69–72.

previous customers and lost 30%, with twice as many of its previous customers going to B as C. This means that B poses a more competitive threat to A than does C. The other two rows are interpreted similarly.

We have seen where A's ex-customers go. Where do new customers come from? This is revealed by column A, rather than row A. Note that A picks up 17% of the customers lost by B, and none lost by C. This is further evidence that A and B are in close competition.

The brand-switching matrix provides information about:

1. The *repeat-purchase rate* for each brand, indicated by the principal diagonal numbers. Under certain assumptions, the repeat purchase rate can be interpreted as a measure of brand loyalty.
2. The *switching-in and switching-out rate* for each brand, represented by the off-diagonal numbers.

But this is not all. If the switching rates are likely to remain constant, at least for the short run, the matrix becomes a useful tool in forecasting both the magnitude and speed of change in future market shares on the basis of the present market shares. Even where the switching rates change, if they change in a predictable way, a forecast of market shares is possible.

In this connection, important research has taken place to determine how switching rates are affected by price and promotion changes. Some of the products which have been studied in terms of brand switching rates are margarine, frozen orange juice concentrate, and instant and regular coffee.[5]

[5] Lester G. Telser, "The Demand for Branded Goods as Estimated from Consumer Panel Data," *Review of Economics and Statistics*, Vol. 44 (August, 1962), pp. 300–324; Alfred A. Kuehn, "A Model for Budgeting Advertising," in reference 2.

4. Waiting-Line Models

Waiting appears in many marketing situations—customers wait for service, and companies wait for both customers and deliveries. Waiting is of interest because it imposes a cost. The customer who waits in a supermarket line bears a cost in terms of more desirable alternative uses of her time. If she regards the waiting time as excessive, she may leave and buy elsewhere, and the cost of her waiting would be shifted to the supermarket.

While waiting time imposes a cost, so does the effort to reduce waiting time. The supermarket might reduce waiting time by adding more counters or personnel, or both. The decision problem is one of balancing the cost of lost sales against the cost of additional facilities. In marginal terms, the supermarket should increase its servicing facilities up to the point where the cost of an additional facility would just overtake the profits lost due to customer impatience.

The decision problem is illustrated graphically in Figure 2. The higher the average waiting time in the system, the greater the cost of lost sales (2), but the lower the cost of facilities and personnel (1). The two cost curves are added vertically to derive a combined cost curve (3). The lowest point on this combined cost curve indicates the average waiting time, W_1, which will minimize combined costs. The implied investment in service facilities is F_1. The lowest point on (3) can be found graphically, or through differential calculus if appropriate cost equations can be found.

The cost of additional facilities is not difficult to measure; but it is very difficult to measure the value of lost sales which take place due to customer impatience. People vary considerably in their attitudes toward waiting; and customer impatience is also a function of the difference between anticipated and actual waiting time, and anticipated waiting varies by situations. Also, customers who feel impatient may decide not to "abandon" the store if they think that alternative stores are no better.

Waiting line theory, also called *queuing theory*, is not designed to answer how much waiting time should be built into a system. This is primarily an economic question as shown in Figure 2.

The theory is designed instead to handle two preliminary questions: What amount of waiting time may be expected in a particular system? How can this waiting time be altered?

The waiting time depends on four dimensions of the system:

1. *The inter-arrival time.* The time between arrivals into the system has a probability distribution which can be estimated from frequency data. The mean, standard deviation, and other characteristics of inter-arrival time can then be derived from the probability distribution.
2. *The service time.* The time between the initiating of a service and its completion can also be viewed as having a probability distribution.

3. *The number of service facilities.* The number affects the amount of waiting time.
4. *The service method.* Usually customers are serviced in the order in which they arrive (called first-in, first-out). But other methods are to give service to the most "important" customers first; to service the shortest orders first; and to service at random.

When these four dimensions are specified for a particular system, it is possible to estimate queuing characteristics, such as expected waiting time, expected queue length, and the variability of waiting time and queue length. For certain simple queuing situations, it is possible to derive these answers mathematically; but for more complicated systems, estimates can be derived through *simulation*.

If the system breeds long queues, the decision maker can simulate the effects of different hypothetical changes. In the case of a supermarket with a serious queuing problem on Saturday, four possible attacks are indicated by the dimensions. The supermarket can try to influence its customers to do their shopping on other days—this would have the

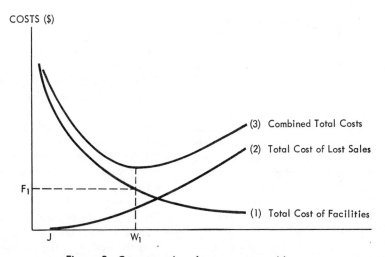

Figure 2. Costs as related to average waiting.

effect of increasing the time between arrivals on Saturdays. Or the supermarket can decrease the service times, as by employing baggers to aid the cashiers. Or more service channels can be added. Or some of the channels can be specialized to handle smaller orders.

Most of the literature about queuing deals with facility planning for telephone exchanges, highways and toll roads, docks, and airline terminals. Yet retailing institutions such as supermarkets, filling stations, and airline ticket offices also face critical queuing problems; and marketing executives of such organizations can be expected to show increased interest in waiting line models.

5. Critical-Path Scheduling Models

A technique called PERT (*Program Evaluation and Review Technique*) deals with the tactical questions of managing a complex project. As an example, consider new-product development.

Suppose that management has just finished reviewing and approving ideas for a new product. Some important tactical questions are: (1) What is the one best way to sequence the various activities which must be performed? (2) With normal departmental resources, how long will it be before the product is ready for sale? (3) What extra resources would be necessary to complete the project x weeks earlier?

Each new product will require the starting and completion of hundreds of different activities. The completion of an *activity* is called an *event*. As a simplified illustration, suppose the following six events must take place:

A. Corporate approval granted
B. Engineering and styling completed
C. Marketing analysis completed
D. Advertising campaign plans completed

E. Manufacturing preparation completed
F. Market testing completed

After these events are identified, a PERT analysis consists of three steps:

1. *Preparing a Program Network.* In what order should the above events take place? Certain events will be in a *priority* relationship, and others in a *concurrent* relationship.

   The best way to see this distinction is to work backward from the terminal event. Before a market test can be started, let alone completed, two prior events must take place. The advertising campaign plans must be completed and the product must be manufactured.

   But these two prior events are themselves in a concurrent relationship—the activities leading to the completion of each can be carried on concurrently. The next step would be to examine each of these events separately, to determine what events must precede each. When there are hundreds of events, the task of preparing a "network" for these events is neither easy nor free from ambiguity. But for the six events listed above, the most efficient network is fairly straightforward. By representing the events as circles and the activities as arrows connecting the circles, we would prepare the network shown in Figure 3.

2. *Estimating Activity Times.* The department responsible for each activity is asked to estimate the *most likely time* to complete that activity, given the department's normal resources. This estimate is supplemented by both an optimistic and pessimistic estimate, again assuming normal departmental resources. For convenience, the three estimates are connected by commas and placed alongside the activity arrows. (See Figure 3.) As an example, the department

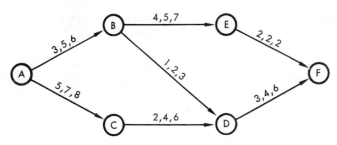

Figure 3. A PERT network.

responsible for event B estimates that it will take between 3 and 6 weeks, with the most likely time being 5 weeks.

3. *Finding the Critical Path.* What is the earliest time the market test could be completed? It is necessary to trace back through all the paths which must be traveled, and the total time each will take.

There are three paths leading to the market test: ABEF, ABDF, and ACDF. On a *most likely time basis* (a different measure is used in practice), path ABEF will take 5 + 5 + 2 = 12 weeks; path ABDF will take 5 + 2 + 4 = 11 weeks; and path ACDF will take 7 + 4 + 4 = 15 weeks. This last path is, therefore, considered the *critical path;* since it must be traversed and it consumes the greatest sum of time, it sets the earliest most likely time for completion.

What is equally interesting is that events along a noncritical path, such as ABEF, can take place later than estimated without necessarily delaying the 15-week estimate for the project as a whole. In other words, activities along noncritical paths have some "slack" in their required completion time.

In actual applications, the network will be extremely complicated, and its characteristics would be very time-con-suming to discern through manual calculations. However, a computer can be used to estimate the likely completion date and the slack times associated with the noncritical activities. Every few weeks a new computation is made, to reflect new information affecting the completion date. Alternative decisions about shifting resources can be simulated to see what effect they would have on completion time.[6]

PERT offers a number of benefits. It forces the various participants in the planning process to make careful estimates of activity completion time; it affixes responsibility; it highlights subtle interdependencies in the planning process; it suggests where resources may be shifted to shorten completion times; and it quantifies an estimate of meeting scheduled dates.

PERT will undoubtedly play an increasing role as a scheduling-and-control technique in the development of new products. It will also aid in the planning of other complex marketing projects such as advertising campaigns, special promotions, new-store development, and salesmen-training programs.

[6] Robert W. Miller, "How to Plan and Control with PERT," *Harvard Business Review*, Vol. 40 (March–April, 1962), pp. 93–104. For an alternative model to PERT, see Borge M. Christensen and J. R. Greene, "Planning, Scheduling, and Controlling the Launching of a New Product Via CPM," in reference 1.

Implications

Operations researchers have developed a number of other models to analyze special situations—such as replacement models and sequencing models—but the ones described here have the most relevance for marketers. The major purpose served by these models is to "organize our ignorance."

Yet model-building is only half the task. The other half is to find the necessary data. Sophistication in model building must be matched by further refinement in marketing research procedures.

A more quantitative approach is needed for adequate decision making in marketing. Nonetheless, there are clear limitations. Many of the known variables cannot be handled mathematically, and all the variables are never known. Intuition and experience and judgment can not be transplanted into a machine.

There is the danger also that mathematics might be used by some to lend authority to some essentially ill-conceived decisions.

Marketing men will be subject to further mathematical name-dropping in written reports and at their conventions —cybernetics, information theory, econometrics, distributed lags, Bayesian decision theory, and so forth. Although these terms stand for perfectly good ideas, they should be viewed as part of a larger plan to advance knowledge, and not just represent verbal glibness.

70

The Promise of Simulation in Marketing

Harold Weitz

One of the most promising techniques in the field of management science is simulation. This article presents some of the results of a survey to determine the role of this tool in marketing. The author discusses how simulation is being applied to marketing, its strengths and weaknesses, and its promise as a technique for future analysis. Although the future for simulation appears to be almost limitless, the reader is cautioned to remember that new developments in marketing have a tendency to stabilize over time at a certain level of use. This does not mean that simulation is a "passing fad," but that one must be careful about becoming overly enthusiastic about the value of a new tool.

Reprinted from the *Journal of Marketing*, national quarterly publication of the American Marketing Association, Vol. 31, No. 3, July 1967, pp. 28–33.

Simulation, as a technique, is one of the most talked-about methods in the field of management science today in spite of a rather negating definition from Webster's dictionary which states: "Simulation is the act or process of simulating; to assume an appearance which is feigned or not true; to counterfeit; to imitate; the act of willful deception; and misrepresentation." The results of a recent survey[1] show how simulation is being applied to marketing problems; its strengths and weaknesses; the different forms, structure, and purposes of simulation models; and its promise as a technique for future marketing analysts.

Range of Applications

During the past decade, simulation has been increasingly applied to a wide spectrum of marketing problems, both theoretical and practical. The range of applications includes: management information systems design and evaluation, industrial demand analysis,. investment analysis, pricing, pre-testing field interviewing plans, staffing of a service organization, physical distribution (including warehouse location), predicting media exposure, evaluating advertising-message effectiveness, marketing-games for training, and models for evaluating alternative market strategies.[2]

In spite of the clear and growing use of simulation in marketing, the full potential of this technique remains largely unexploited, at least insofar as can be ascertained from the applications described in the literature. (Clearly,

many applications of simulation are not reported in the literature. Some successful applications may be of a proprietary nature; other unsuccessful applications may remain unpublicized.) The reasons for this are numerous. Market phenomena are complex processes and not clearly understood. Sufficient knowledge of the effects of market-mix variables has not been generally available and such relationships are necessary to the construction of viable and meaningful models.

Another reason lies perhaps in the kinds of skills traditionally brought to bear on marketing problems. Not only is knowledge of management science techniques (including simulation) necessary, but increasingly it is becoming clear that the skills of the behavioral scientist (psychologist, sociologist) and the economist are also needed to attack what is basically a socio-economic problem. Much of the emphasis in early management science was placed upon analytical techniques which yielded optimum solutions. Unfortunately, the solutions offered required a simplification of reality that often made the results grossly inadequate. Because of decreases in the cost of computation and in the cost of obtaining information, the utilization of management and behavioral-science personnel and, because of increasing pressures by management to make more effective utilization of marketing resources, the use of simulation should grow manyfold.

Classifying Simulation Models

The lack of a precise and universally accepted definition of simulation makes difficult any classification of the different kinds of simulation models. No widely accepted terminology is available, but many terms frequently used to describe certain characteristics of simulation

---

[1] Harold Weitz, "*Simulation Models in Marketing,*" IBM Technical Report 17–192, IBM Advanced Systems Development Division, Yorktown Heights, N.Y. (1966).

[2] A description of the structure of each of these models, their characteristics, strengths, and weaknesses is included in footnote 1.

models are included in a three-level classification which may be useful as a starting framework for looking at simulation. This classification is by:

1. *Purpose*
   a. Prognostic models
   b. Process or behavioral models
2. *Degree of System Definition*
   a. Tactical models
   b. Strategic models
3. *Structural Characteristics*
   a. Static/dynamic models
   b. Deterministic/stochastic models
   c. Aggregate/disaggregate models

Purpose of Simulation Model

Almost all simulation models constructed have as their ultimate aim a predictive capability. *Prognostic* models are primarily intended to simulate the results of a system, whereas *process* models seek to simulate the dynamics of the system itself as well as future results. The two types might be distinguished by considering the classic "black box." In one case (prognostic) the interest is simply in the outputs of the black box; in the second (process), primary interest lies in exploring the phenomena occurring within the "black box"and in constructing theories to describe that behavior.

Degree of System Definition

In a *tactical* model, one is generally interested in exploring the impact of alternate decision rules or parameter values within well-defined and well-understood structures. Questions raised by such a model may be:

a. What is the impact upon either the waiting time or the size of the queue if the service time is decreased?

b. What is the effect on a production system of alternative priority rules for assigning shop orders?

In both these cases, the mechanisms or elements within the system are well-defined, such as the distribution of time required to service individual customers, or the time required to machine parts. The *strategic* model applies when there is an interest in exploring the behavioral properties of ill-defined problems involving elements and relationships which are largely unknown or which are poorly understood, for example, consumer behavior. A model in which certain behavioral relationships are assumed is constructed and then tested against reality. The emphasis, as with process models, is on understanding the dynamics of a system so that a theory can be constructed. Once the theory has been sufficiently validated, the model can be used to simulate the outcomes of the system under a wide variety of conditions.

Structural Characteristics of Models

A *static* model would seek to describe or predict the total response of a system as if it occurred at a single instant of time; a *dynamic* model would seek to explore the changes occurring within the system over some period of time. A *deterministic* model would contain no probabilistic elements; a *stochastic* model would contain one or more elements, or mechanisms, involving random or probabilistic characteristics. An *aggregate* model is so structured that it can only answer questions of an aggregate nature, for example, the total response to an advertisement; a *disaggregate* model (there are various levels of aggregation or disaggregation) is so constructed as to yield information of a more detailed nature such as the number of men between the ages X and Y, having incomes beyond R and S who respond to an advertisement. Unlike the aggregate model, the disaggregate model can respond not only to a variety of detailed questions, but is by nature a more microscopic representation or model of the phenomena under study. An example of a disaggregate model would be one in which the behavior of each member of a hypothetical data bank of persons is individually simulated. Other terms could be added to further distinguish the structure of simulation models such as discrete or continuous, fixed or variable time intervals. The above characterization will suffice for our purpose.

This classification is intended more to clarify the nature and uses of simulation than it is to serve as a universal classification scheme. It is somewhat arbitrary and the categories are not completely unique; a single model may be classified as: process, strategic, dynamic, stochastic, and disaggregate.

The Advantages and Disadvantages of Simulation

Marketing generally involves a complex environment about which relatively little is known with respect to predicting the *impact* of a marketing decision. Analytical optimization techniques, such as linear programing, frequently employ unrealistic simplifications as with a linear objective function (which is often not linear) that maximizes media exposure (which often is not the central problem). Another tool frequently employed is regression analysis which treats covariance; it does not treat cause and effect nor get at the dynamic characteristics underlying market behavior. Although valuable, Markov and other kinds of probabilistic models which have been proposed for predicting consumer buy-

ing behavior (for example, brand loyalty) similarly employ simplifications which detract from their utility.

Frequently in developing an analytical approach, simplifications are made in order to arrive at a feasible and reasonable solution. These simplifications may augment the utility of a model but not if they permit too significant deviation from reality so that the results become of questionable value.

Some important advantages of simulation are:

1. Solutions to complex problems can often be obtained more readily through simulation than by analytical solutions. Simulation overcomes the deficiencies of other methods for dealing with complex, interacting, dynamic processes which marketing generally entails. This technique utilizes a set of mathematical and logical relationships which represent the essential features of the process being studied, however complex these relationships may be. Simplifications and assumptions are not required for simulation to the extent that they are demanded by analytical solutions.

2. Simulation offers an opportunity for relatively inexpensive experimentation, even where precise data is lacking. A simulation permits one to conduct a series of experiments on a computer or by hand computation, using the model developed to describe some process without recourse to actual field studies. It permits the use of data which may be known only imprecisely which after simulation studies is revealed to be relatively insensitive over a wide range of values.

3. Analytical models which can yield optimum solutions can frequently be developed as a result of simulation studies. Without reservation, a model

which immediately and directly leads to an optimum solution is preferable to simulation. It is the difficulty which complex processes present that makes analytical solutions arduous and often questionable. Frequently, however, in developing and using a simulation model, insights are gained which, in turn, permit meaningful analytical solutions.

4. Simulation languages are available which offer further stimulation to the use of simulation because of lowered programming costs, and the relative ease of learning and applying simulation models to a wide diversity of problems. Just as FORTRAN is both easy to learn and less costly to program than machine languages, specially designed simulation languages are available which offer similar advantages. (The simulation languages most frequently used in the U.S.A. are: the General Purpose System Simulator (GPSS), and SIMSCRIPT.) Additionally, these languages offer a conceptual view of a system, or process which facilitates the construction and programming of simulation models.

5. The non-technical manager can comprehend simulation easier than a complex mathematical analytical model, and, in fact, less sophistication may be required to develop it. In general, a simulation model is simpler to understand and explain, for it is in essence only a description of the behavior of some processes or phenomena.

Simulation does, however, have basic problems which should be recognized by the marketing analyst. It does not easily produce optimum solutions. Each simulation run is, in effect, a single experiment conducted under a given set of conditions as defined by a set of values for the input variables. To determine an optimum, or close to optimum condition, a number of simulation runs will be required sufficient for a response curve to be established.

Simulation may be time consuming. This follows from the necessity to conduct a number of different types or successive simulation runs as previously described. As the number of input variables increase, the difficulty in finding the optimum values for a set of strategic variables increases manyfold and requires careful design of experimental runs and optimum search methods; otherwise, there may be excessive and needless cost. When the question relates to finding an optimum value for a single input variable, for example, the advertising expenditure for media X, several runs will be required using various values of this variable. As additional input variables (that is, strategies) are examined, the number of possible combinations requiring exploration increase in factorial fashion.

Simulation may become a convenient or easy alternative to applying appropriate effort toward the development of an efficient analytical solution, ideally, required. As the ability to employ simulation increases, there may be a tendency to rely on this technique because of its relative ease of application. Simulation should be used where appropriate; it should not be substituted for the use of analytical techniques which may be more efficient.

The Potential of Simulation

Previously cited were areas of marketing in which simulation has already been applied. More sophisticated, viable, and valid models will continue to be developed in these and other areas. Promising work is currently in progress. Furthermore, other aspects of marketing appear to be appropriate for the application of simulation.

Predicting Consumer Reaction to New Products

One area in which simulation should have significant impact in the future is that relating to the prediction of consumer reaction to new products. The capability of predicting a latent demand for a product not now on the market, without costly surveys, is certainly a desirable one. Such a capability would be based on the planned characteristics of consumers. It would answer questions relating to market potential: who would buy? What is the reaction of potential customers to the color, design, etc.? Knowledge, now unavailable, is required; research, now going on, offers some promise toward satisfying this "latent demand" objective. Volney Stefflre reported on techniques of product development which are based on the notion that "an individual behaves towards a new thing in a manner similar to the way he behaves towards other things he sees the new thing as similar to."[3]

Recently Abelson and Bernstein published a description of a model for the simulation of a referendum on the question of fluoride in the water supply.[4] The referendum simulation suggests techniques for simulating the test marketing of new products, as it would be for simulating an advertising campaign to answer the questions: what message? what media? and what frequency? The referendum model exposes some 500 hypothetical individuals having certain characteristics to a set of communication channels, each of which carries a particular message. The model specifies

two processes by which each individual may change his attitudes:

a. by exposure to public assertions appearing in the communication channels, and

b. via conversations with others who have some stand on the issue and who may also make assertions.

Each simulated week an individual is subjected, with varying probabilities of exposure, to several communication channels and to particular assertions made in these channels. Rules determine if an assertion is accepted, depending on the individual's attitudes towards the communication source, previous acquaintance with the assertion, the congeniality of the assertion, and his previous position on the referendum issue. As a result of the model's exposure process, assertions may be accepted, resulting in changes in attitudes towards the communication sources, the probability of exposure to the various channels, and interest in the issue as well as one's position on the issue.

The model's conversational phase considers the level of interest of the individuals in the issue, their compatibility, their respective positions on the issue, their acquaintance with the assertion, and the social network of each. The model is indeed complex, incorporating reasonable hypotheses regarding human behavior. At a recent presentation, Bernstein outlined how this model could be adapted to test marketing.[5] He asserted that for the exposure process, this would require knowledge on what assertions people make about a particular class of products. Instead of assertions reflecting peoples' attitudes toward

---

[3] Volney Stefflre, "Simulation of People's Behavior Towards New Objectives and Events." *The American Behavioral Scientist,* Vol. 8 (May, 1965).

[4] Robert P. Abelson and Alex Bernstein, "A Computer Simulation Model of Community Referendum Controversies." *Public Opinion Quarterly,* Vol. 27 (Spring, 1963).

[5] Alex Bernstein, "An Application of Simulation to Test Marketing." Paper presented at *First Annual Conference on Simulation in Business and Public Health.* American Statistical Association, New York Hilton Hotel, New York (March 2, 1966).

fluorides, for example, concern with the impact of fluorides on health, age, etc., the model would reflect attitudes toward the characteristics of a particular product class, for instance its taste, mildness, or color. Changes would also be required to indicate the locus of stores visited by a particular person, presumably to reflect upon product availability as well as in-store promotion. The effects of competitive efforts would also have to be considered. Although the appproach presented was not sufficiently detailed to permit evaluation, it was, nevertheless, intriguing in its possibilities.

Predicting Market Share

Numerous consumer flow models have been designed to predict the expected product market share. These are commonly referred to as brand-shifting, or brand-loyalty models. They basically take the form of Markov, learning, or other kinds of probabilistic models. These models suffer numerous deficiencies, largely because their use requires assumptions which are unrealistic. They further exclude such relevant factors as sales promotion, advertising, and competition. The promise of simulation lies in its capability to consider complex but realistic conditions which minimize the need to make unwarranted simplifying assumptions.

Samuel G. Barton pointed to a conceptual model for short term sales prediction which deserves atttention.[6] It encompasses many of the salient variables affecting a sale, such as advertising, pricing, and promotion. Although conceptual, it may offer a basis for a useful operational model for predicting short term sales, appraising the effective-

ness of alternative test-market programs, and guiding the allocation of promotional efforts.

The short term prediction model views a consumer as being influenced at two different times: prior to the point of sale, and at the point of sale. The factors governing these influences are termed consumer momentum, customer intention to change, share of space, and consumer-deal offerings. The weight of these factors, a function of a complex of other factors, varies among the different classes of buyers, that is, new, new repeat, and old customers. To illustrate, the principal factors affecting intention to change include:

1. Share of new product announcement
2. Share of general advertising
3. Share of consumer deal advertising
4. Share of shelf and display stocks

Sufficient data with adequate understanding of market processes to implement such a model probably do not exist, but they may serve as a framework for development.

Competitive Gaming Models

The value of market games, one of the forms which simulation may take, lies in their ability to introduce competitive forces explicitly into consideration. Here lies the potential of games as a vehicle for determining market strategy. Philip Kotler objects to most games because they treat consumers in a superficial way, as an aggregate which responds in some lagged and linear way to market decisions.[7] He outlined a competitive-market simulation which not only has a decision-rich marketing function but also has an environmentally rich market

---

[6] Samuel G. Barton, "A Marketing Model for Short Term Prediction of Consumer Sales," *Journal of Marketing* (July, 1965), pp. 19–29.

[7] Philip Kotler, "The Competitive Marketing Simulator—A New Management Tool." *California Management Review* (Spring, 1965).

of individuals. His prime interest is in observing whether such a tool could be useful for company predictions.

Typically, the model would have a representative sample of 200 households, differentiated by socio-economic characteristics, through which the computer will cycle each week to determine a buyer's choice as a function of:

1. Socio-economic factors
2. Previous brand choices
3. Interim experience
4. In-store experience

The last two factors are a function of management's decisions; the former are attributes of the consumer. Such a model could be used as a game either with player-managers or without players when an input-decision rule defines a strategy. The latter condition removes the need for player roles.

Input-Output Analysis

Input-Output analysis has until recently been largely regarded as an economic tool. Its power rests on a table of coefficients (see Table 1) which relates the inputs and outputs of 81 industry sectors of the National economy to each other and to final demand. Using this table, one can determine, for example, the direct dollar value of iron and steel required by the automobile and other industries as well as the iron and steel purchased directly by the consumer. The table also shows the intermediate inputs required to make the iron and steel.

From this basic table, a table of inverse coefficients can be derived representing the amount of input from industry i necessary to produce one unit of final demand (the ultimate demand by consumers) for products of industry j.

Input-Output analysis has been used in a variety of ways to determine the effect on an industry of an increase in the gross national product, the effect upon an industry if sales of some major sector of the economy experiences a significant change, the impact of the Federal highways program upon the U.S. economy, the contribution of the tobacco industry, and the effects of proposed changes to the industrial structure of the Appalachia region. Variations of the input-output model have also been used to forecast total demand for the iron and steel industry.

Some large companies are reported to have individual input-output models (describing the relationships between the various components of the organiza-

Table 1.   Inter-Industry Input-Output for the National Economy

	Industry Sectors	A	B	C	D	•	j
I	A	X_{AA}	X_{AB}	•	•	•	•
	B	X_{AB}	X_{BB}	X_{BC}	•	•	•
N	C	X_{CA}	•	•	•	•	•
P	D	•	•	•	•	•	•
U	•	•	•	•	•	•	•
T	i	•	•	•	•	•	•
	Total Output	A_T	B_T	C_T	D_T	•	•

Where $X_{BC} = \dfrac{\text{input from industry B to industry C}}{\text{total output of industry C, } (C_T)}$

tion) which are coupled to a national input-output model.[8] Such company models are intended to provide greater control and predictive capabilities. Still other applications have been reported; these extend to such areas as evaluating poverty programs for the Office of Economic Opportunity and to evaluating proposed transportation systems.

Efforts by the U.S. Department of Commerce to develop input-output data are currently under way which would be frequently updated for a larger number of industry sectors. With such data the market analyst would have a potentially powerful tool at his fingertips. In addition to those uses mentioned, the following would be permitted.

1. Evaluating more precisely the effects of technological change, for example, as changes occur in the materials used in the manufacture of some product, they would be reflected in the entries to the input-output matrix.
2. Measuring the full impact of a major new government program, such as a major increase in education, a new poverty program, or an economic development project for an economically poor community.
3. Estimating more precisely the future demand for products and services for each industry.[9]

Several companies offering computer service, including IBM, have announced the use of input-output models to simulate the potential market for a wide range of industries. These services process proprietary data as required, and at the same time, permit referencing it automatically, if desired to data banks of information gathered and maintained for management use.

The Future

Simulation has already been used in many diverse areas of marketing. It would be difficult to discuss all the areas in which this technique can fruitfully be applied. New applications are being developed continually. Other areas having potential are: strategic long-range planning,[10] the selection of distribution channels, and the location of merchandise and displays in the supermarkets.[11]

The major advantage and stimulant to the use of simulation in marketing lies in its ability to deal with complex, dynamic, and interacting phenomena which are characteristics of marketing. If the processes or phenomena permit adequate description, they can be modeled and experiments can be simulated. Unlike analytical optimization solutions, simulation models, by avoiding oversimplification, tend to be better descriptions of reality.

Simulation will play an increasing role in the future marketing function. Before long, many companies will have a number of market simulators available. These will take diverse forms including that of the strategic, or competitive, gaming simulator. Such models will invariably be complex, representing the channels of distribution, the competition, the environment, the customer, and the firm.

There are those who say that such simulation will form the nucleus of a "war

---

[8] Wassily W. Lenotief, "The Structure of the U.S. Economy." *Scientific American* (April, 1965).

[9] Typical Brochure: *IBM Industry Information Service*, (Form No. 520–1373) IBM, Data Processing Division, White Plains, New York.

[10] Robert Weinberg, "Simulation Models for Planning Management Strategy." Paper presented at the *First Annual Conference on Simulation in Business and Public Health*, American Statistical Association, New York Hilton Hotel, New York (3/2/66).

[11] Alfred A. Kuehn, "Simulation of Consumer Behavior." Same reference as footnote 10.

gaming center," typical of that of the Armed Services. Such a capability would readily permit one to investigate new strategies, to rapidly measure the impact of new marketing intelligence, and generally, to improve the operations of the firm. Such a center could be embedded within a larger framework—an Information System for Marketing Managers.

The availability of more powerful and less costly computing systems, larger and more accessible storage devices, and more convenient input-output devices, which can be used with relative ease by the non-programmer, will hasten the development of the "war gaming center" concept. The "conversational" terminal and time-shared systems are further indications of trends narrowing the gap between the computer and the user.

71

Computers Begin to Solve the Marketing Puzzle

Business Week

Increasingly, management science techniques are being used in marketing. With this has come the need to handle efficiently and quickly the great amounts of information that are being generated or that can be generated to help decision makers. The answer to this is the computer, or more generally, electronic data processing (EDP). This article takes a close look at some of the ways in which computers are being used in marketing at the present time (both for daily operations and broad decision making) and what the potential is for the future. One conclusion reached is that simulation models represent the ultimate contribution that EDP can make to marketing. This conclusion is questionable on many counts. For example, it implies that simulation itself is the ultimate in applying management science to marketing. There are many who would disagree with such a conclusion.

Routinely, every evening at J. C. Penney stores across the country, a chain of events begins that reflects the changing nature not only of retailing but of every other marketing practice.

Reprinted from the April 17, 1965 issue of *Business Week* by special permission. Copyright © 1965 by McGraw-Hill, Inc.

The small, punched tickets that have been taken off merchandise sold during the day are dispatched to either New York City or Los Angeles. There the tickets, coded to describe the merchandise to which they were attached until it was sold, are fed into machines that transfer the information to punched cards. From cards, the data can be put on magnetic tape or fed directly into electronic digital computers.

The computers have been programmed to know what each store should stock of so-called "staples"—men's shirts, socks, ladies' hose, lingerie, and similar goods.

Every two weeks, a computer will match a store's planned stock level against merchandise sold in that store; and, when a store needs merchandise, the computer will send out an order to buy, along with shipping instructions.

Theory into Fact. A retail store doesn't have to be as large as Penney— 1,700 stores and $2-billion annual sales —to use computers in this way to control its stock level and ordering procedures. A score or so of stores around the country are using some variant of the system. In fact, some local chains, such as Woodward & Lothrop in Washington and Goldblatt Bros. in Chicago, use more complex and sophisticated systems to give them daily reports of stocks and sales.

In theory, it has always been true that a store's buyers could give management a daily report of stock conditions and what was sold the preceding day— just as in theory someone in almost any business gets the pertinent marketing figures every day. But as a matter of hard, cruel fact—as opposed to theory —this just hasn't been so.

The importance of what Penney and other companies are doing is simply this: They are turning the computer with its fantastic computational speed into a new marketing tool. It may be just a big adding machine, as is often said, but it adds at a speed that hardly gives a man a chance to have a second thought.

Legerdemain. A customer of Owens-Illinois Glass Co. had that brought home to him recently. He had ordered some

containers from O-I's Libbey Products Div., changed his mind, and called to cancel the order. He couldn't cancel; the shipment was already at his plant.

This disconcerting legerdemain was possible because Owens-Illinois is one of the hundreds of U.S. companies that are managing production, finished inventory, and distribution with a mathematical system controlled by computers.

O-I's data processing headquarters in Toledo (10 computers and 100 people) is connected by wire to 100 different sales and manufacturing locations. An order comes in, the computer determines whether the product ordered is in stock, indicates where it is, and sends a release and shipping order to the warehouse, or orders to a plant to make it.

What the customer who couldn't cancel was relying on is an order-shipping-billing procedure that is passing from the industrial scene. Normally, weeks elapsed between the time a salesman took your order and you got the shipment and the invoice. At Owens-Illinois, says Thomas H. Browning, manager of data processing, electronic data processing cuts the time to no more than 35 hours.

Over the Wire. Helping to reduce the order-shipping-billing time is a system tying the computer that manages inventory to a data transmission network employing any one of a group of devices known as a Data-Phone. It is an adaptation of a normal telephone, and is used with what the trade calls a "terminal" (the exact designation varies according to who makes it).

Together they transmit voice and numeric signals. Instead of a salesman dropping around to fill out an order pad, orders are filed by punched card or tape over wires direct to the supplier's receiving equipment, where they are put into form to go into the computer.

At Beals, McCarthy & Rogers, Inc., a large Buffalo industrial distributor, the combination of computer-managed inventory and Data-Phone ordering in the past four years has meant a reduction of inventory of $200,000 and a sales increase of more that $2-million, according to Frederick L. Davis, the company's marketing manager. When you can know faster, and fill quicker, what your customers are ordering, you can carry a smaller stock.

It works if you're the customer, too. Davis reports it is common now for his customers to do without general stores and tool cribs entirely. Normally, placing an order cost $15 and up; a BM&R customer has reduced this by 17%. . . .

I. The Data Collectors Go to Work

The potential of EDP in marketing is great simply because of a pervading belief that there are not enough good, hard numbers in marketing to make a fair-sized computer work up a mild sweat. . . .

Bridging the Gap. Yet, it simply isn't true that data do not exist in marketing; they exist in probably greater quantities than in any other business function. Until now there has never been a means to collect the information or to analyze it fast enough for it to be useful.

With the "peripheral" equipment associated with the computer—input-output devices such as the Data-Phone, tape, ticket and card readers, and high-speed printers, for feeding information to the computer and getting it out—the vast gap between collection of information and its analysis has been bridged. . . .

There are computers whirring and blinking throughout U.S. business—for the accounting department. Now, with the input and output devices, the marketing department also is finding ways to get information for the computer to work on.

The Machine Knows What's in Stock

While the retailer is by no means in the van in the use of EDP, what's being done in stores around the country is exciting because it shows how much can be done.

You can see the future best, perhaps at Woodward & Lothrop Inc., in Washington, D.C. There, C. Robert McBrier, vice-president, finance, has installed what many authorities think is the most advanced EDP system in the country. Soon, Woodward & Lothrop executives every morning will get an 81-page report that, for each of the company's nine stores, will give the previous day's sales by store, by department, by dollar amounts, and a comparison with the previous year-to-date and the trend of sales. A record of sales for selected items will also be available.

The key to this astonishing flood of figures is a special cash register, for which McBrier designed the keyboard. There are eight keys across and nine from top to bottom, in addition to 13 control keys. The sales-person can punch in everything store management needs to know; every detail of every transaction is recorded on optical tape.

Each evening the information on the tape is read by an optical scanner and "exploded" into separate pieces for accounts receivable, accounts payable, inventory management, reordering and other store functions.

More and More. When additional equipment is received later this year and next, Woodward & Lothrop's system will include a direct connection from cash register to computer, a voice response from the computer when a clerk checks the credit standing of a customer, and even a daily report on the sales performance of each person on the selling floor. . . .

Buyers' New Role. Management's daily report of stock condition is already changing one hallowed role in department stores: the preeminence of the buyer. Since retailing began, buyers have been the leading figures, responsible for keeping their stores stocked with salable merchandise. But because of the enormous increase in the number of items a store now carries, the buyer has become too busy with a physical count of stock to try to know what the customer wants and when.

At EDP-equipped stores, management knows before the buyer does what's moving and what isn't. Some buyers find this disconcerting indeed. In the words of Jack Jacobson, Goldblatt's director of electronic processing, they "don't trust computers and are not analytically inclined."

But others use the freedom EDP has given them to get out on the floor once more to see what customers are like. Jack Hanson, senior vice-president of Macy's New York, says buyers now have a chance to "get back into the market where they were 30 years ago, to get better prices and better merchandise."

Penny's merchandise planning and control manager, Emerson Tolle, sees another advantage to the end of physical stock-taking (Penny's counts stock only every quarter): "Instead of being under the counter counting stock, the sales clerk can be standing up taking care of customers."

Precise Weapon. Putting accounts receivable—customer's charge account records—on the computer might seem to be only another accounting procedure. But it can be a merchandising weapon

of profitable precision. Macy's has more than 1.3-million charge accounts on magnetic tape. Depending on what it is told to do, the computer will break up those accounts any way the store wants them—by alphabet, by house number, by size of average charge.

Not long ago Macy's had its computer print out a list of all charge customers of the Herald Square store who lived in four counties, and invite them to a special after-hours sale of furniture and furnishings.

The results can't be measured precisely because nothing like it had been done before; but compared with other special sales using radio and direct mail, the computer-based effort cost less and sold more.

Smaller Stock, but More Stores

In food retailing, the problems are different from those in a department store, and EDP has scarcely penetrated the retail end of food distribution.

For one thing, food retailing is about the most hidebound of all businesses dealing with the consumer. For another, a food store's after-tax profit is normally less than 2% on sales—so operators look at the cost of EDP and blanch. Yet, their low rate of return is in itself a reason to get involved with EDP; it offers opportunities for cutting costs and raising profits. . . .

In food processing and warehousing, though, EDP has cut deep, mostly by use of an IBM-developed system known as Impact (Inventory Management Program and Control Technique). All major food manufacturers, as well as other companies that sell through supermarkets—Scott Paper Co. and Procter & Gamble Co., for example—have data links between sales offices, plants, distribution and shipping points, and are managing production, warehousing, and shipping by computer-programmed economics.

Latest Link. The newest trend is a data link between a manufacturer and a distributor for the automatic ordering of staple items.

This has barely started. Kellogg Co. warehouses are linked with warehouses of Safeway Stores, Inc., on the West Coast and of Wakefern Food Corp., a distributor for a group of New Jersey supermarkets. Pillsbury Co. has a similar hookup with Spartan Stores, Inc., a small chain in the Grand Rapids (Mich.) area —after having proved the procedure in experiments with Kroger Co. and Super Valu Stores, Inc.

Savings with this sort of system can be sensational; James Rude, Pillsbury director of information services and systems, quotes a Spartan official as saying the chain can save enough in lead time and storage to build another store.

There is no longer any question about the marketing power of a data link between supplier and customer. The clincher is what has happened in industrial selling.

Save Customers and Prepare for Systems

The data link between supplier and customer originated on the West Coast with Ducommun, Inc., an industrial distributor, about three years ago. . . . It is now in use all over the country, but has reached perhaps its most influential and precedent-setting level in the Houston area.

"Ordermation"—a very well-suited term coined by Industrial Distribution, a McGraw-Hill magazine—was just beginning to be known in Houston when J. K. Bevel, purchasing agent at Hughes Tool Co., took a worry to Jack P. Cunningham, whose Cunningham Bearing Co.

does an annual volume of about $1.5-million. Bevel wanted to cut down on the time his buyers were spending in placing repetitive orders, and thought an automatic ordering system would do it.

But he was aware of one danger: When you have a number of distributors in an area, each may use a different system; so a customer dealing with more than one distributor could wind up with a roomful of incompatible systems. Bevel warned Cunningham that, as a customer, he would use one data transmission system and expect his suppliers to conform. But that way, he pointed out, a single distributor could wind up with as many as 18 different systems.

Taking Off. From this came the Houston Industrial Distributors Assn. With an IBM salesman coordinating the efforts—the IBM 1001 in conjunction with the Data-Phone is the common transmission device—the association now has 30 distributors "on line" to 10 customers. It will take 40 to 50 customers for the system to remain economically feasible. Cunningham hopes the idea "will really take off once the results begin coming in from the customers already participating."

Although the Houston operation is being studied by groups of industrial distributors in other parts of the country —and is bound to be a pattern—ordermation has not aroused universal enthusiasm. Distributors' reservations come mainly from unfamiliarity with EDP; some fear the system will make them lose contact with customers.

That fear is not shared by Owens-Illinois Glass Co.'s Thomas Browning. He asks: "How much does it mean, for example, if we can cut delivery time for a good customer from six days to one day? It may not mean much in one case; in another, it may mean that we have retained business that might have gone elsewhere. How do you measure that?"

Goal. The data link alone, of course, cannot make a radical cut in delivery time. It is an essential input, though, to a procedure that goes a long way toward the goal of building a "total information system." And that is the goal at Owens-Illinois, at General Mills, Scott Paper, Procter & Gamble, Hotpoint Div. of General Electric, and other long-time EDP users. Westinghouse Electric Corp. is one of the very few companies that already has a total system.

To such companies, inventory management, sales analysis, a rapid order-shipping-billing cycle, though rewarding in themselves, eventually become as routine as the coffee break. But they are a necessary preliminary to more complicated and challenging EDP work—getting the information to use in making the decisions that bring higher profits.

The Ultimate Question. There's an example of where this is heading in the Carborundum Co., which has been using computers for about 10 years and, says Group Vice-President Robert W. Lear, is "still experimenting." Carborundum, with more than 1,000 programs on computers, is ready for the next plateau, which is defined best by a series of questions Lear asked in a recent speech:

"Which of our districts, salesmen, distributors, customers, markets, and products are the real profit producers? How much does it cost to make a sales call? What does it cost to process an order item? If it's four bucks, can we afford to continue accepting five-buck or even twenty-five-buck orders without some kind of surcharge or premium?

"What was the return on investment from our last promotion? Did we even try to calculate it? Which is more profitable—a direct sale, or one through a distributor? Did our last price adjust-

ment take into consideration the distribution cost for each item, or did we just study our factory gross margins and assume an arbitrary average for everything below the line?"

Those questions get to the heart of the reason for using computers in marketing, for you can't answer them without getting data. Then, for the first time in marketing, management can ask the question: "What if . . .?"

II. Marketing by Mathematics

Dr. Wendell R. Smith, president of the Marketing Science Institute, tells of a former business associate who constantly used computers to ask the question: "What if . . .?" He explained to Smith: "I can ask the computer without starting a rumor. If I went to the controller and asked him what would happen to our profits if we dropped a certain product line, it would be all over the plant before lunch that we were getting ready to go out of that particular business."

Storage in a computer of mathematical models that simulate a market or that duplicate a marketing situation is perhaps the ultimate contribution EDP can make to marketing.

C. A. Swanson, manager of P&G's Data Processing Systems Dept., lists four things his company expects from EDP: savings of money, accuracy, speed, and "doing things not otherwise possible."

There is wide agreement that model-building and simulation is perhaps the most significant of those things not otherwise possible without a computer. As of now, an electronic digital computer is the only device that can handle variable on top of variable and give management a choice of alternatives while there's still time to make a decision. . . .

The biggest change that model-building is bringing about in marketing management is almost defamatory to mention: It is forcing management to plan, and to define its goals. To John Stolle, of Booz, Allen & Hamilton, one of the things that has slowed down the use of EDP and model-building in marketing is simply the fact that "it exposes the non-planners." . . .

But already models are regulating some marketing programs.

It's Better Than a Crystal Ball

Just about a year ago, Chrysler Corp.'s top management asked its planners the sort of question with which all marketing efforts must begin, for it was about the future.

"Can you tell us what the market for heavy trucks will be in 1970?"

The market analysts broke out the significant components of the heavy truck market for every year back to World War II. They determined the relationship of truck sales, by weight class, to population, national income, industrial production, and so on.

In about a month, they had a mathematical model—a simulation—of the heavy truck market. They found that of 36 variables in the model only about a dozen had substantial significance. Applying these variables in different combinations, they plotted the range for heavy truck sales in 1970.

What's New? There was nothing new in the Chrysler people's approach to the problem. Examination of past relationships—multiple regression analysis —is a standard statistical technique— and mathematical models are ancient.

The new thing was the speed with which the analysts were able to process an enormous amount of data and in only a month or so give management the information needed for a decision. That speed was due to the electronic computer.

Light on Lamps. General Electric Co. (one of its divisions was the very first to put the computer to work on business problems, in 1954) has at least two models routinely assisting marketing management. One is in the Photo Lamp Dept. This division has 2,000 distributors, who customarily order in September (Christmas is the peak selling time for photo lamps) and pay in January.

The model is constructed on the assumption that each distributor has an interest problem; it takes into account 25 different types of distributors and interest rates and arrangements. It is designed to give answers to the question: What will happen if we let distributors delay payment—will they order more lamps?

At one of GE's heavy apparatus operations, a model is producing results that you'd expect only from a ouija board. This division sells on a bid basis, and the computer model is programmed to propose bids on the likelihood of what competitive bids will be. Says a GE man: "They have been amazingly accurate."

Routine. Simulation with computer models also is routine at all of the big package goods companies such as P&G, Pillsbury, General Foods, Libby, McNeill & Libby, and General Mills. Usually, companies such as these test in models the presumed results of price changes and promotions and what the probabilities are of competitive responses. . . .

Surprised Admen. Models were at the root of all the hoopla in advertising agency circles a year or so ago about using computers to select media. The intention was to simulate a market area, then test the exposure gained by differing combinations of media buys. The problem, to a large extent, was proper data. The agencies didn't have it. Now they are collecting it—and are finding some strange byproducts.

At Leo Burnett Co., Inc., accumulation of demographic and economic data for one account showed a wide open area for a new product. At another agency, the collection of data showed that the agency's principal client should have been very high on its magazine schedule, one of the "confession" books. The magazine has never made a presentation to the agency—and the client is not yet ready to concede that his customers have such reading tastes.

The agencies are still far from satisfied with the data that can be obtained. The biggest hole is pointed out by Seymour Banks, a vice-president at Burnett: "What happens when people are exposed to an ad?" The agencies, meanwhile, are doing the best they can with what they have. . . .

Bringing Marketing into Management

Advertising practitioners have always presumed that what they do is more art than science. So it may seem strange that all of the larger agencies now have people practicing operations research, which is presumed to be a science— the science of management. In reality it is not strange at all, for part of operations research deals with the weighing of alternatives—and the advertising man may have more numeric alternatives to deal with than anybody.

A media man with one ad and 30 media where he can spot it can be confronted with more than one billion combinations. The computer—that big adding machine—is the only way to run quickly through those combinations and weed out the obviously worthless.

What combinations remain are subject to management decision. The example used is in advertising, but it could just as well be in other marketing functions. Throughout marketing these days you are finding the computer used to weed out the obviously worthless things to do, leaving management with only a few alternatives to consider—sometimes, even, alternatives leading to a go or no-go decision:

What would be the returns now, compared to 60 days from now, on a cents-off promotion? Would it be more efficient to ship to Point A from Plant 1, or build a new distribution location to serve Point A and a potential future Point B? Would it be more economic to double our order for fast-moving baby food and receive shipments every other week rather than every week, even though it ties up more capital? Would it be more profitable to kill immediately Old Product, the life cycle of which is ending, and use the resources to push New Product harder?

Total. Decisions such as these involve determining the proper allocation of a company's total resources—in other words, operations research. Only now are the numbers so necessary for operations research being assembled for the marketing function, for only now is there a way to work with them: the computer. The more EDP sophistication pervades marketing, the closer a company moves toward a total management information system, toward true operations research. Says John Stolle, the OR man at Booz, Allen & Hamilton: "When we add marketing to our collection of trophies, we will be able to build models of total business systems."

It will still be some years before marketing's scalp hangs from the belt of the OR man, but the way marketing data already are being used indicates some changes the future may bring.

III. Big Brother Will Always Watch

What's ahead for marketing because of EDP is summed up pithily by Michael H. Halbert, technical director of the Marketing Science Institute. "A man can no longer get away with the excuse 'We've thought about it, but we don't know how to get it.'"

Today, if "it" exists in numbers, or can be assigned numerical values, "it" can be used in an EDP system. What this means, explains Robert G. Dee, vice-president, marketing, at RCA Electronic Data Processing Div., is that in the future "marketing staffs are going to get a greater amount of direction, and get a better hit value for the money spent."

One of the first groups to feel the effects of this will be the salesmen—no matter what they sell.

Bobbie Brooks, Inc., Cleveland-based manufacturer of ladies' sportswear, presents a fairly common example of what is on the way. Each week, the salesman gets a report showing the current orders and past activity of the stores in his area. This tells him where he should be spending his time.

Bobbie Brooks also prints out a report of each salesman's results by style, color, and frequency of order. "By looking at the report," says Burton L. Kamberg, vice-president, "our supervisors can tell if a man has perhaps prejudged a garment and left it in his car rather than taking it into the stores." If he's taking Thursday off, or avoiding certain stores, that shows up, too.

"The salesman gets used to living in a goldfish bowl," Kamberg says, "and we don't stress the Big Brother side of the computer, but the helpful side. It gives the salesman an excellent selling tool. He can, for example, tell his customers what styles are going best across the country, and help them in their purchasing."

Death of a Salesman, Birth of a Consultant

The computer not only is changing the selling function; it is going to change the salesman. He will have to know far more about merchandising than he does now; he will have to know far more about his customer's business and how it fits into an EDP system—already, some food companies report that their salesmen have had to show distributors how to fit new products into the IBM Impact system, which began with food distributors. In short, the salesman will have to be more of a consultant than ever....

Eyes and Ears. Data transmission devices cast a long shadow, blotting out the routine calls that salesmen have been accustomed to make. So in the future the salesman who now spends a good part of his time writing orders is going to have to spend more time digging out new accounts, and ideas for new products.

He will have one other, potentially enormously valuable function. He will be his company's eyes and ears, its intelligence agent, in his territory, compiling information on market growth and development, competitive efforts, and everything his company needs to know.

Lots of Products and Plans for Retailers

In perhaps no other area of marketing is EDP going to make as many changes as in retailing—which lags not only in use of EDP, but frequently in modern business thinking.

In a study of department store control systems, Douglas J. Dalrymple, assistant professor of business administration at the University of California at Los Angeles, found "that a small minority of the merchandising executives . . . believed that stock turnover was an important control factor, but to most executives it was only a vague concept of secondary importance." Yet, fast stock turnover was the weapon the discounters turned loose on department stores 15 years ago. The higher the turnover, the higher the profit on a constant amount of money used in the business.

But the computer is forcing retailers to become aware of the importance of stock turnover.

The EDP Way. Stock turnover is usually about four times a year for general merchandise and about twenty times for dry groceries. There's a traditional way to turn it faster: Simply sell more without carrying a higher inventory. But it's a rare merchant who can do that.

The EDP way to get a higher turnover is by keeping such fresh data on sales that you know what's moving fast and what isn't, and by having a data hookup that will give you automatic replenishment of the fast-moving or high-profit items. In food retailing, one estimate is that a 24-hour replenishment cycle will reduce inventory by 30%, without creating out-of-stock situations that hurt sales.

In general merchandising, Seymour Helfant, head of the Small Stores Div. of the National Retail Merchants Assn., says he has reports of stores using EDP that lower their inventory by 25% and increase profits by 25%. And a specialty store that formerly turned its stock six times a year has added one full turn.

Analysis of information handled by a store's EDP system can also guide store executives in when, what, and how to promote.

Big and Small. The benefits of EDP are not reserved for the big stores and chains.

An example of what a data processing center can do for small retailers is found at Santoro Management Consultants, Inc., in Houston. Santoro has 60 clients—whose volumes range from $50,000 to $500,000—for whom it provides a full package: budgets, advertising, merchandising, sales analysis and projection, inventory records. Says Mrs. Daisy Strother, of Forth Worth: "The service took the butterflies out of my stomach. We know which department is making money . . . our buying is controlled, dead merchandise eliminated and we have reorder money." . . .

A few months ago, B. S. Durant, president of RCA Sales Corp., did a little dreaming for a group of marketing executives. RCA, in common with other consumer electronics producers, is always in doubt as to how much of its product is in distributors' warehouses and how much is moving out of retailer's doors.

Durant began by conceding that a small retailer will probably never be able to afford a computer, "but he could afford a low-cost transactor of some type. . . . Before the dealer goes home at night, he would put the transactor device on standby. Somewhere along about a quarter after two, a central computer would interrogate the transactor and take from it the data covering the dealer's daily business transactions." Durant offered a new, and provocative thought: The independent distributor might have that central computer and be the retailer's data processing center.

If the distributor's computer could interrogate the retailer's transactor, then each night the manufacturer's computer could interrogate the distributor's computer. The next morning, the manufacturer's executives would have—for the first time in their experience—actual records of their product sales at retail the day before.

Gleaming Vistas. This opens vistas that gleam so brightly that any marketing man has to shield his eyes to avoid snow blindness. New product performance could be gauged day-by-day and promotion money deployed for maximum effectiveness. A product that isn't going to make it could be withdrawn from the market before it hurt either profits or reputation significantly. When you know precisely what is selling where, and when, you can identify your customers, plan future promotions intelligently, simulate all sorts of situations.

You would even know enough to advertise in Indianapolis.

IX

Postscript

72

The Changing Face of Marketing

John D. Louth

One of the most universal characteristics of business is change. This is particularly true in marketing. Thus, one of the most important management skills is the ability to exploit change. Certainly not all the changes in marketing are of equal importance. Accordingly, the author of this article discusses what he considers to be the six trends that will affect almost every company. Although one may not agree that these are the six most important trends, they certainly are significant.

Change is the dominant fact of life in every business today. Thus, the ability to master and exploit change has become the most sought-after of management skills. This is particularly true in marketing, where the very tempo of change is constantly quickening.

Today's marketing executive faces a baffling dilemma. Change gets costlier every day; yet to not change can be costlier still. So the trick is to know to what degree, and how and when, to change. And this is best determined against a master plan so that a company's marketing effort will have a constancy of purpose internally and a consistency of image externally.

Not all the changes in marketing have equal significance. For example, the growth of discount houses in selling small appliances or service distribution centers in the steel industry are peculiar to an industry; while other changes, such

Reprinted from *Dun's Review,* April, 1966. Copyright, 1968, Dun & Bradstreet Publications Corporation.

as the trend away from straight commission selling or the increasing use of marketing research, are more functional in nature. But out of the many trends in the changing face of marketing, there are six whose effects, I believe, will be felt by almost every business.

First, there is the continuing and growing dominance of the consumer as the motivating force in sales and marketing planning. Much has been written and said about the fact that the needs and wants of the consumer are the critical issues today in developing new products and services and the accompanying plans to merchandise them at a profit. But I would be remiss if I did not emphasize this point, and then add that the need to understand and anticipate future customers will become even more essential than in the past. This is because one of the aspects of the changing face of marketing is that the end users of a company's products are shifting in makeup, location and numbers—and at an ever-increasing rate.

The significance of this to the head marketing executive is twofold: 1) He cannot, indeed he must not, assume that yesterday's customers will be available to him tomorrow. 2) He had better be certain that he has adequate sources of information about his markets; for unless he can keep up with what is happening to his markets, the selling effort can end up being directed at the wrong people with the wrong products and at the wrong time.

Consider these examples of changes in the nature of consumers and markets:

- Sociologists and marketers agree that people are becoming more interested in use than in ownership. We may be approaching a point in the development of the economy where the time of usage may become more important than possession. You can rent or lease everything from garden tools to machine tools, from a secretary to a car. Excluding automotive vehicles, annual rental income is close to the $750-million mark, and the value of equipment being leased is about $1 billion. And that may double in five years. The significance of this trend is that it could affect the channels of selling, pricing arrangements, sales appeals, or even the characteristics of the product line (such as the increasing sale of disposable items).
- There has been a disproportionate growth in the market for personal services, including recreation, education and travel. Depending on whose statistics you choose to believe, consumer services now account for as much as 40% to 50% of all consumer purchases.
- There is a whole series of demographic changes that are of significance to the producer of consumer goods, in particular, the explosion of the teenage and young-adult market, the shift of the blue collar worker to the suburbs, the increasing per capita income and the ever-growing mobility of our population. To the consumer goods manufacturer, the wholesaler and the retailer, this means there is no such thing as stability of customers.
- People's tastes are becoming more varied, flexible and demanding. As just one example, look at the demand for wood products. The traditional lumber manufacturer now produces and sells a multitude of products virtually unknown twenty years ago— and all because product research teamed up with marketing to develop products that people wanted and were willing to buy.

Another important result of this growing consumer dominance is that today nearly all sales potentials are segmented. A total market should be thought of as a series of submarkets, each with its own characteristics and each requiring a different sales approach. In most companies it is a gross error to develop a marketing program aimed at the average customer, because today such a person, or such a company, no longer exists.

To sum up: The company that is not alert to the consumers' needs and the changing complexities of the marketplace is inviting disaster.

Step-up in Marketing Research

The second major trend in marketing is the increased use of marketing research, both in terms of the amount carried out and the variety of problems involved. This trend, of course, is related to the first; for if knowledge about future customers is essential, and if the quality of the marketing output is materially affected by the caliber of the informational input, then surely marketing research will increase in use and contribution as part of an overall interest in more scientific marketing.

The bulk of company marketing research today is devoted to such activities as development of market potentials (for both existing and new products), analyses of customer buying habits and requirements, share-of-market studies, determination of market characteristics, sales analysis, establishment of sales quotas and development of sales territories. However, I see a trend toward increased use of marketing research on such problem areas in marketing management as pricing, test marketing, alternative channels of distribution, methods of compensating salesmen, personnel requirements and product-line profit analysis. This broadening of the scope of marketing research cannot help but increase the efficiency of the total marketing function.

Furthermore, in some companies today the head of marketing research is a member of the product planning committee, a marketing strategy committee, or even a company-wide long-range planning committee. The primary reason for this is the growing recognition by top management of the contribution that marketing research people can make to planning decisions.

Trend Number Three is the growing use of electronic equipment as a major scientific marketing tool, for planning and directing as well as for reporting.

As a general rule, marketing managements have dragged their collective feet in recognizing and using electronic data-processing analyses, on-line communications, information retrieval systems, and even closed-circuit TV as tools to help make marketing more efficient. But, to coin a word, I believe the face of marketing will become considerably more "electronicized." Although this is a vast subject, here are a few examples of how these techniques are being used today:

■ A major insurance company with a total system of seventeen computers analyzes sales performances daily, weekly, monthly and yearly—compared with last year and this year's goals. The input information is fed into fifteen satellite computers at fifteen regional headquarters, which not only perform the multitude of routine details related to the insurance industry but feed back to two master computers the essential sales information. This information is then summarized, and printouts are made on Friday night. Monday morning, the reports are on the manager's desk.

■ A West Coast apparel manufacturer adjusts the initial merchandising forecasts in light of salesmen's bookings and then daily develops the cutting orders for three plants in relation to inventories on hand. Salesmen and management are kept abreast of trends daily during the key selling periods, and weekly thereafter; and major merchandising decisions are made on the basis of current information not previously available.

■ One of the largest industrial distributors in the West has set up an on-line EDP system with its key customers so that they can place purchase orders for major products by the use of prepunched cards that hold the price and quantity information. This purchase order is transmitted automatically to the distribution center for processing, billing and shipping. This frees the salesman from much of the routine order-taking and permits him to spend more time in helping to solve customer problems.

These are but a few examples of the use of electronic equipment as an aid to the marketing function. There are, of course, others. And in the years to come, the use of electronic equipment by marketing management will certainly increase.

Narrowing the Odds

Trend Number Four: the expanded use of test marketing. In my opinion, there will be increased controlled experimentation to narrow the odds of an error in making marketing changes.

Two major influences emphasize the need for further expansion of test marketing. The first is the rising costs of making marketing changes; for example, in introducing new products and packaging that make obsolete previous products, in developing new advertising and promotional programs and in retraining salesmen. The second is the mounting investment in product research and development. About half of corporate research and development activity in the United States today is for creation of new commercial products. As a result of this outpouring of new products, the product life cycle may be measurably shortened and the payout time correspondingly reduced. This is one reason why so many innovations in consumer goods are test marketed before being placed in national distribution, even though the new product may have been carefully checked out in the laboratory and the sales potential assessed through marketing research.

What kind of projects should be considered for test marketing? Here are a few examples: (1) evaluating new products or new product features in relation to market potentials; (2) assessing the advantages and disadvantages of new packaging; (3) measuring variations in demand at different levels of price; (4) evaluating the impact of a new sales incentive plan; (5) determining the advantages, if any, of new delivery and service practices; and (6) evaluating the effectiveness of alternative advertising media and approaches.

The availability and capacity of computers can help test some marketing projects quickly and relatively inexpensively through simulation. But irrespective of whether computers are utilized, I believe that increased use of test marketing under controlled conditions will be one of the characteristics of the future face of marketing.

The fifth trend is the changing nature of the field selling job toward a more integrated marketing effort.

The typical salesman today represents a major investment of company funds. According to a 1964 survey by the Sales Executives Club of New York, training costs were $8,731 per salesman excluding salary. And that is only to get him ready to sell. To keep him on the road requires, on the average, about $15,000 to $17,000 of direct costs per year, including his compensation.

To achieve a satisfactory return on this investment, the salesman must increasingly emphasize profits. And to do this, his role is materially changing from just the presentation of his company's product line toward the marketing of integrated systems.

For example, an apparel salesman now works with retailers in activities such as: selecting the products for the upcoming selling season and establishing inventory standards; maintaining stocks at proper levels and reordering as necessary (frequently using EDP); helping to train retail clerks; establishing advertising schedules and assuring proper in-store tie-ins; executing in-store promotions; counseling on style trends and helping to move or shift slow-moving merchandise. In other words, the salesman is carrying out a field marketing effort that involves products, market analysis, advertising, promotion and inventory control.

In another case, a salesman for chemical fertilizers helps his distributors sell to their customers (the dealers), including financing services and marketing research assistance. He may even have to set up merchandising programs to help select and train salesmen for his distributors.

Another important aspect of the changing nature of the field sales job is the increasing necessity for key-account, or selective selling. In most industries, there is a growing profit importance to a limited number of customers. This is true in industrial manufacturing, where 10% to 20% of the customers may account for as much as 80% of the output. As a consequence, key-account selling must become an important feature of the field sales job.

The point, of course, is that tomorrow's salesman is going to be different from yesterday's breed. He is going to be more highly trained and better paid; he is going to be planning oriented, service oriented, technically oriented, and in many industries knowledgeable about the use of EDP and other technical sales equipment. Truly a major change in the face of marketing.

The sixth and final trend is an ever-broadening application of the marketing concept to worldwide markets. Over the past decade, the marketing concept has become widely accepted in the U.S. In fact, I believe it has been too enthusiastically accepted and applied in situations where it has little chance for success.

But that does not invalidate the concept of a completely integrated marketing effort, and I believe it will be increasingly accepted, and become worldwide in many companies.

For example, expenditures by U.S. companies in plant and equipment abroad was $5.1 billion in 1963, about $6 billion in 1964, and was projected to be up another 14% in 1965. Perhaps of greater significance is the fact that for manufacturing operations alone (excluding petroleum refining), expenditures abroad in 1964 increased 26%, while domestic plant and equipment expenditures advanced about 16%.

Mergers, licensing agreements and formations of joint ventures and wholly owned foreign subsidiaries by U.S. companies overseas are continually on the rise. For the smaller company, this trend may emphasize the need to establish or strengthen export relationships in order to also market on a worldwide basis. And although I fully realize that overseas marketing is beyond the scope of many U.S. businesses, I also believe that in many companies the day will come when the U.S. will merely be a domestic division within the worldwide enterprise. And the face of the marketing function will have to change to match this development.

73

Marketing Snags and Fallacies

Leo Burnett

This article is a complement to the previous one. The editors believe this article to be a fitting one for concluding the book. The author, head of one of the largest advertising agencies in the country, feels that marketing men are handicapped by five major fallacies that guide the conduct of their operations. In addition to being alarmed at this situation in which the marketing man has placed himself, Mr. Burnett also points with pride to some of the things to be admired about marketing people.

By 1970 the United States can have an $800-billion economy; and by 1975 our economy can rise to one trillion dollars! This figure is so large and unprecedented in any economy that it cannot readily be grasped.

But in order to achieve this incredible rise in the economy, there will need to be at least one-third to one-half increase in consumer expenditures.[1] This means thousands of new products.

Our ability to produce the goods for this exploding economy is not the problem. What is really of concern is our capacity to ensure the consumption of them.

Our technology has been accelerating with a seemingly irrepressible momentum:

Reprinted from the *Journal of Marketing*, national quarterly publication of the American Marketing Association, Vol. 30, No. 3, July, 1966, pp. 1–5.

[1] Alvin Hansen, *Postwar American Economy* (New York: W. W. Norton & Co., Inc., 1964), pp. 34–35.

- Hundreds of millions of dollars are being spent today in a great variety of businesses on Research and Development, compared with a mere trickle of funds before 1950.
- In a single year du Pont scientists file as many as 800 patent applications.[2]
- The interval between discovery and application has been narrowing rapidly: It took 65 years from the time it was invented for the electric motor to be applied . . . 33 years for the vacuum tube . . . and 18 years for the x-ray tube. But it took only 10 years for the nuclear reactor . . . only 5 years for radar . . . and less than 3 years for the transistor and the solar battery.
- The cost of atomic energy has been slashed—contrary to all forecasts—from 60 mills per kilowatt-hour in 1957 to less than 4 mills today. With energy soon to be available almost

[2] *The Industry of Discovery* (Wilmington, Delaware: E. I. du Pont de Nemours & Company, 1965), p. 21.

everywhere, the distinction between the haves and havenots could rapidly vanish, expanding the market to the optimum.[3]

The basic issue is whether we have the ability to develop the marketing power necessary to discover, shape, and particularly to *move* the goods that will best fulfill the consumer's needs within the framework of desirable social and moral goals.

For far too long have we continued to venerate mere productivity as a goal. Yet high productivity is meaningless if it outstrips consumption and is not matched by marketing power.

In this generation of accelerated marketing power, is our marketing perspective adequate? Are we plagued by "diseases of the marketing eye," tending to limit our vision of the future?

Here are two of the symptoms of this:

1. *Fear of the inexact*—the fear of playing the odds, and the rejection of imprecise data.
2. *Lack of real consumer orientation*—too much research on consumer *preferences* as compared with consumer *satisfactions*.[4]

Five Fallacies in Marketing

To be even more specific, we are suffering from at least five fallacies in the field of marketing.

Fallacy as to Marketing Foresight

The first fallacy is that the people already in the marketing field are the ones who understand it best and know what the potential customer wants.

Yet in actuality the only person who really knows what he wants is the customer himself. For example, if television producers *really* knew what the public wanted in entertainment, the mortality rate in programs would not be so wastefully high each new season.

In this connection, consider how many developments in any field of knowledge so often originate *outside* the ken of those specialists supposedly with the greatest insights:

- Three of the greatest discoveries of surgery, without which modern surgery would be impossible, are anesthesia, asepsis, and X-rays—and none of them was discovered by a surgeon!
- Of four important railroad devices, not one was invented by a railroad man. These were the air-brake, automatic coupling, the refrigerator car, and the streamlined train.
- It was not a physicist, but an anatomist, Galvani, who discovered current electricity.
- The development of tetraethyl lead came from outside the petroleum industry.
- The most successful innovation in inn-keeping, the motel, was not devised or developed by the traditional hotel-keepers, who looked with scorn upon this interloper until the success of motels forced the hotel corporations to enter the field.[5]
- The great movie-chains did not pioneer in that singular success, the drive-in movie, until long after newcomers had proved its viability. Everyone in the movie business "knew" that automobiles were to drive around in, not to watch a movie in.
- The break with traditional art and the rise of modern art forms was not

[3] Mario G. Salvadori, "The Environment of Change" (Time, Inc., 1964), p. 18.

[4] Theodore Levitt, "Marketing Myopia," *Harvard Business Review*, Vol. 38 (July–August, 1960), pp. 45–46.

[5] John W. Gardner, *Self-Renewal* (New York: Harper and Row, 1963), p. 46.

encouraged by the museums and curators.

- Jazz was not developed within the halls of classical music.
- And the paperback books—one of the most successful revolutions in selling in our time—were not initiated by the giants of the book publishing business, who entered the field later and only when it was already thriving.

We continue to see some new products succeed and others fall by the wayside for the obvious reason that, although there seemed to be great need and promise for them and although they were heavily promoted, the consumer was less than enchanted. After all, the American purchaser is a "tough little baby" and does not have to be wrapped in cotton.

Given access to honest information, the consumer himself is the best judge of what he needs and wants, the form and the package it comes in, and the price he will pay. Moreover, he is most likely to get what he wants under a system in which thousands of business enterprises are competing fiercely but fairly for his favor.

Often he does not even know he wants a purple cow until he sees one.

David Belasco said that the secret of good showmanship is giving people what they want just before they know what they want. This also is one of the major challenges of marketing, whether achieved through better research, or more open-mindedness to fresh ideas from any source, or a combination of both.

Fallacy as to New Markets

The second fallacy is a limited definition of "competition," under which the chief marketing strategy is to attain the largest possible share of the existing market, rather than to create new markets and add to total consumption.

A few years ago the Brookings Institution completed a comprehensive study of successful and unsuccessful industries. The difference between success and failure hinged on a really simple thing— product leadership. Industries that failed to innovate and that failed to keep ahead of the market also failed to grow with the economy, and perished or were absorbed.

In the area of recent new product categories, consider the new "convenience" foods, which have had ten times the growth of foods in general over the last decade. Consider in this connection the "hi-fi" market of the last dozen years, bringing superbly recorded music to new and broader audiences. Consider also the record clubs by direct mail, which revitalized the whole record field—and which also flew in the face of conventional wisdom that "a person will not buy a record before he listens to it in a store."

We have had the recent boom in modified sports cars, with Ford's "Mustang" a tremendous success. And industry leaders invested some $200 million in developing color television without being sure whether people really wanted it or would demand it in large enough numbers to justify the investment.

It is true, of course, that many great companies are indeed bringing about innovation; and the overriding marketing strategy is to proliferate and diversify. Obviously, however, there is a tremendous need to *organize for change*—after all, the mere fact of corporate organization tends to conspire against it.

One way to lose money is to try to sell everyone on a given product. Many companies have learned this lesson just in time, and are now proliferating their marketing efforts to give the consumer what he wants rather than what the manufacturer thinks he ought to have.

Fallacy as to Competition

> *The third fallacy in the marketing world is that competition is a closed system, and that our competitors are those making substantially the same products, or offering the same services, that we are.*

In studying Nielsen share-of-market reports, do we sometimes know *too much* about our competitors? By putting such high priority on "me-too" products and competitive counter-moves, are there not serious dangers of standardization of products rather than market expansion?

Many an entrepreneur has made almost "seat-of-the-pants" decisions, then has plunged adventurously ahead— sometimes with failure, but often with brilliant success.

By no means does this imply any minimization of the value of the information available today. It does imply anxiety about our interpretations of it, and often our dogmatic reliance upon it.

It is a mistake to feel that the competition for a Cadillac is either a medium-priced car or another quality car such as a Lincoln or Imperial. The Cadillac is a prestige item. The true competitor of the luxury car is the swimming pool, or the summer place, or the private plane, or the winter vacation, and all the other prestige items dangled before people with large discretionary incomes.[6]

Likewise, the makers of bowling or billiard equipment are not competing so much with other makers of similar equipment as they are with other providers of "leisure-time" satisfactions—whether skiing, or photography, or record-players,

or ping-pong tables, or even adult-education courses.

All are competing for "disposable time" as much as for disposable income.

Fallacy as to Income Brackets

> *A fourth fallacy is the marketing theory of appealing mainly to present income brackets.*

In the past, it was commonly believed, and it was generally true, that people bought "according to income." But today people increasingly are buying according to *expectations of future income*. Individual purchases have come to be more and more like company purchases— based on a projection into the next few years, and not necessarily on current income alone.[7]

The vast increase in credit purchases during the last dozen or so years, therefore, should not be viewed as mass imprudence (although undoubtedly in some cases families *are* imprudent), but as an expression of self-confidence and as a projection of a continuing upward curve in income.

People no longer buy solely what they "need," or even what they "want" for the present. They are anticipating new and future needs; and the industries that have grown most have been the ones catering to this sense of expectation.

Take, for example, the present booming "knowledge market." One of the important things about the expansion in knowledge is that its main appeal is not to the *affluent and educated*, but to the *aspiring and under-educated*. The encyclopedia field is a classic example: many families which buy encyclopedias perhaps cannot really "afford" them, in a practical dollars-and-sense way. Yet the growth of sales has been enormous

---

[6] Peter F. Drucker, *Managing for Results* (New York: Harper & Row, 1964), p. 95.

[7] Peter F. Drucker, *Managing for Results* (New York: Harper & Row, 1964), p. 95.

precisely in this economic bracket, *because* these families have higher expectations for themselves, and most of all for their children.

All the demographic facts add up to a tremendous new market that is not based on the traditional concepts of "income" and "status" and "education" that have been our benchmarks in the past.

In addition, our cultural habits have changed enormously and are continuing to do so, and at a rapid rate. This also should make for a radical revision of our marketing concepts.

As one obvious example in the area of recreation alone, the game of golf used to be restricted very much to the so-called upper classes. Today it is an immensely popular recreation for all groups except the lowest economic fifth. Again, not so many years ago, skiing was considered a "class" sport. Each year, however, there are tens of thousands of new skiers drawn from a segment of the population which never would have been in the market a dozen years ago. They are taking up skiing as a part of their expectations, and not on the basis of present income.

In all this we have a dramatic example of *upward mobility*. The more prosperous we become, the higher do our expectations grow, and the more do new people become potential customers for markets that once seemed restricted.

Perhaps the most important marketing challenge of the decade ahead is properly to assess and satisfy the expectations and aspirations of this large group, rather than mapping out strategies on the basis of current income.

Fallacy as to Decision-making

The fifth fallacy is that because we are living in the age of the specialist, only qualified experts with specialized skills will be competent in the future to make basic decisions.

Actually, quite the reverse is happening. Our greatest need today is for the synthesizer, much more than for the specialist. He is not necessarily a computer programer; but he understands how computers work, and what they can do and cannot do.

In the field of advertising, he is not necessarily an accomplished copywriter or artist; but he has gone out of his way to understand what writing and artistry are about, as such acts are experienced by writers and artists.

He is not necessarily a laboratory technician; but he has absorbed enough science to understand and appreciate the scientific method.

After all the facts are in from the computers, research, and elsewhere, the "gut" decision finally must be made by a man, or by a very small group of men. And these men cannot afford not to know how their field relates to other fields, and how all of them interlock. The basic decisions in today's economy have much broader and deeper ramifications than ever before.

Information keeps on spewing from the computers; but there comes a time when somebody has to put his own value system on the block and to say go or no go. Computers merely print out numbers and letters on paper when fed an appropriate signal. This is not a decision.

In the search for a new breed of synthesizer or "generalist," business and industrial leaders are beginning to call for a different kind of graduate from the nation's schools of business; and the schools are responding rapidly.

The wheel has almost turned full circle. The industrialization that made men specialize has now given us automation as its final flower. And automation is going to drive many specialists into other fields.

What we need most in the immediate future are more truly educated men and women, that is, people who know one thing well, but many related things fairly well. And to be educated, in any useful sense of the word, means that you can differentiate between what you know and what you do not know, that you know where to go to find out what you need to know, and that you know how to use the information once you get it.[8]

So What?

What does all this mean to us as marketing men?

It means that change and the rate of change have been so rapid, and that the need for new marketing power is so great, that many a marketing man has been caught with his rusty calculus showing. He has not yet learned how to use the amazing new tools of cybernetics, electronic-data processing, and game theory, and is in fact scared silly by them, as he is by taking any kind of calculated risk.

Too many of us, I fear, who talk about "marketing" and the "Total Marketing Concept" still see it as a scientific, objective, statistical thing, which will be perfected as a mechanism, once we get sufficient information and data of a quantitative sort. Rather than regarding it as a *social* science, we are still trying desperately to emulate the physical sciences in precision, in calibration, in subtlety of analysis.[9]

We have research which describes the consumer in embarrassing detail—where she lives, what she wears, how many children she has borne, how much her

husband earns, and how much education she has had. She stands before us, seemingly stripped of her every secret, clothed only in the mantle of our statistics; but in a majority of cases we still do not know exactly what gives her the urge to buy or to prefer one product over another.

New research insights now tell us clearly that people are not all of a piece. They are rational and cautious in some areas and at some times, but enjoy adventures in buying in other areas and at other times. Also there are some products which are best defined psychologically rather than demographically, such as jewelry, alcoholic beverages, small appliances, and automobiles.

The successful marketing man has developed strong points of view (as he should) about the ingredients of success in the marketplace. These points of view have evolved from his pragmatic interpretations of experience. He has done something, and it has seemed to work. Frequently he has worked with a mix—a marketing mix—that has produced desired results. He has not always known which factors in the mix were working and which were not, but nonetheless he has had to adopt points of view. Parts of these points of view undoubtedly are valid, and others possibly are pure mythology.

We are becoming more perceptive about marketing and the various factors that together make up marketing. But also we are now beginning to witness *the clash of the new insights and the old mythologies.*

Yes, it is healthy for a marketing man to demand that research establish the legitimacy of its new insights. But it is vital that he be receptive to these insights and seek to understand them, even those phenomena known as "inspiration" and "intuition."

The man who can assimilate the new,

[8] Alfred N. Whitehead, *The Aims of Education* (New York: Mentor Books, 1956), pp. 16–17.

[9] John Madge, *Tools of Social Science* (New York: Anchor Books, Doubleday & Co., Inc., 1965), pp. 4–5.

who can refurbish his arsenal of marketing weapons, and who can put them to use is the one most likely to "survive" and to contribute most to the new marketing power so urgently needed.

The real fight now is to preserve, foster, and encourage a climate wherein marketing creativity can soar and leap and grow. The marketing process is a fascinating adventure. But we shall have failed the future if we have not set up within our own business firms a climate where individual imagination can flower.

Nestled in the bosom of every person in the whole marketing chain are one or more great marketing ideas. Yet many of these will never see the light of day because nobody has had the sense or the patience to listen.

Obviously the things to be admired most in a marketing man are:

- An unwillingness to settle for the tried and true;
- A desire to seek the inherent promise in every product or service;
- A constant effort to put himself realistically into the shoes of the consumer;
- A belief that quality and thoroughness are significant in every detail of every job;
- A conviction that what is worth doing is worth doing as creatively as possible; and
- A dedication to providing the right climate for individual growth as the best climate for meeting the new challenges confidently.